AW 2016

W9-DET-030

The History of Television, 1942 to 2000

The History of Television, 1942 to 2000

ALBERT ABRAMSON

FOREWORD BY Christopher H. Sterling

A companion volume to the author's
The History of Television, 1880 to 1941
(McFarland, 1987)

McFarland & Company, Inc., Publishers
Jefferson, North Carolina, and London

Frontispiece: First Ampex Arcuate head assembly with tape and gear drive. (Charles P. Ginsburg/Ampex.)

Library of Congress Cataloguing-in-Publication Data

Abramson, Albert.
The history of television, 1942 to 2000 / Albert Abramson :
foreword by Christopher H. Sterling.
p.   cm.
Includes bibliographical references and index.
ISBN 0-7864-1220-8 (library binding : 50# alkaline paper) ∞
1. Television — History.   I. Title.
TK6637.A27   2003   621.388'009 — dc21   2002000326

British Library cataloguing data are available

Manufactured in the United States of America

*McFarland & Company, Inc., Publishers
Box 611, Jefferson, North Carolina 28640
www.mcfarlandpub.com*

This volume is gratefully dedicated to Kathryn,
who made the whole thing possible.
Without her there would be no book.

Acknowledgments

First of all, I wish to thank the marvelous technical staff at the Ampex Corporation, Redwood City: Charles Paulus Ginsburg, Ray Milton Dolby, Charles E. Anderson, Alex A. Maxey, Charles Coleman, Walter Selsted, Ray Ravissa, Don McLeod, Fred Pfost, Myron Stollaroff, and Philip Gundy. Also George Morton, William Barnhart, D.C. Birkenshaw, Tony Bridgewater, Marvin Camras, Dr. V.K. Zworykin, Peter Hammar, Bill Henderson, Ray Herbert, Edward W. Herold, Dick Hill, Harley Iams, Phyliss Smith and Al Pinski (RCA), Ray D. Kell, Harold B. Law, Joseph Zenel, George Long, Arch Luther, Kurt Machein, Cecil Madden, Donald McLean, John T. Mullin, Ross Murray, Fred Remley, Albert Rose, Kenjiro Takayanagi, Prof. Manfred von Ardenne, Paul Weimer, Alda Bedford, George Sheirs, Gerhart Goebels, Norikazu D. Sawazaki, and Fujio Takashi and Gene Weisskopf (Hanford, Washington).

The following corporations and companies who contributed material and pictures of equipment, including the Ampex Corporation (Redwood City), RCA Labs (Princeton), Sony Corp. (Japan), JVC (Victor Company of Japan), Matsushita Electric (Japan), Westinghouse Electric (Pittsburgh), General Electric Co. (Schenectady), EMI Research Laboratory (Hayes Middlesex, England), BBC (London), BBC Archives (London), Norman Collins (High Definition Films (London), Du Mont Labs, Paramount Pictures, NASA, CBS, NBC, ABC and the US Airforce.

I wish to thank the various sources including the various books, newspapers, journals and societies for use of copyrighted material. Where it is not possible to find the original copyright owner, I offer my apologies for the non inclusion of their names.

Finally I wish to thank my dear wife Arlene who never lost faith in me during those trying times including a long illness when it looked like it would never get finished.

Albert Abramson
March 19, 2002

Table of Contents

Foreword:
Watching Television Grow

In the following pages, retired network television engineer Albert Abramson relates the full story behind the expanding cornucopia of television technology since 1941. This is the second volume of what now clearly stands as the definitive narrative about television's technical development.

As you read these chapters, Al Abramson's own television history is worth recalling, for he first wrote about the early part of this fascinating tale in a pioneering book published nearly a half century ago—*Electronic Motion Pictures: A History of the Television Camera* (University of California Press, 1955). I arranged to have the work reprinted two decades later as it was then still the only serious history available (Arno Press, 1974). There in text, diagrams, and photos, he related the rise of electronic television including early attempts to effectively record what was being installed at theaters here and abroad. The present volume is in many ways an expansion and continuation of that landmark book, as well as of his *History of Television, 1880 to 1941* (McFarland, 1987).

Over the years Abramson followed television's story with seminal articles on the development and improvement of TV recording methods, as well as biographical papers on mechanical TV pioneer C. Francis Jenkins and electronic TV pioneers Philo Farnsworth and Vladimir Zworykin, all of these appearing in the respected *SMPTE Journal*. The first volume of the present history—taking the story through 1941—appeared in 1987. The Zworykin paper was expanded into the definitive book-length *Zworykin: Pioneer of Television* (University of Illinois Press, 1995). In each of these studies, Abramson has maintained a careful balance in considering and comparing conflicting claims of "firsts" from a variety of individuals and companies. He has become widely recognized (and cited) as *the* technical chronicler of the medium so important in American and worldwide households.

Abramson's new volume completes the complex tale. Taking up where the first *History of Television* left off—the commercial inception of television on the eve of American entry into World War II—Abramson relates the many subsequent twists and turns in television's expansion to the rainbow of offerings and technologies available today. As he makes clear, it has rarely been a simple or direct path.

Along with millions of others, I grew up with television, and though then ignorant of what was developing behind the scenes, I remember several "landmarks" over the years. The first television screen I saw must have been in 1948 when I was all of five. My grandmother lived just outside of New York City and owned one of the first RCA post-war table models (see chapter 2). The wooden cabinet enclosed a seven- or eight-inch screen enlarged by use of a round magnifying glass placed in front of it. Though of course I didn't know it then, I was witnessing network television's first season of programming.

Back home in Madison, Wisconsin, we couldn't even watch television thanks to the Federal Communications Commission's long freeze on authorizing new stations (1948–1952—see chapters 2 and 3). The nearest television transmitter, indeed the only one in the state, was in Milwaukee, some 90 miles east. After the freeze ended in 1953, when the first two UHF stations aired locally, I had to rely on various neighbors' good graces, as we must have been about the last household to purchase our own TV set. I remember adults glued to their sets during the spring 1954 Army-McCarthy hearings that droned on for weeks— not that I understood what they were all about. I paid closer attention to the five-minute animated *Crusader Rabbit* episodes telecast after school.

We finally got our first receiver at home in October 1956, soon after Madison's only VHF outlet took to the air. Madison was now one of many "intermixed" markets with VHF and UHF broadcasting. The sole VHF channel quickly claimed most of the audience and advertising revenue, since the struggling UHF stations were often difficult to tune in. Our first set was a small RCA portable housed in a black metal case with a handle on top and a 12- or 14-inch black-and-white screen. An indoor "rabbit ear" antenna was essential for any kind of reception. The first week we owned the television I watched anything from ads to soaps to comedy. My parents paid more attention to coverage of the 1956 Hungarian uprising, the Suez crisis, and the U.S. presidential campaign.

By the time I began graduate study in this field a decade later, we still owned only one small black-and-white receiver. With other grad students, I made *audio*tape recordings of television's extensive news coverage of the pioneering 1969 moon landings, including the first television transmission from the lunar surface (see chapter 8). I no longer recall when I first saw color television, which had been available since the mid–1950s (see chapter 3), but my wife and I borrowed a color receiver in 1970 and finally bought our first color set a few years later (even commercials looked better in color!). With young daughters eager for television, we subscribed to cable television in the late 1970s, and were amazed at the improved reception and growing choice among cable services. Our first VCR was purchased only in 1986, more than a decade after the first Sony Betamax devices pioneered that market (see chapter 9).

As a part of an audience of FCC officials, I was fortunate to be a Washington witness at the very first American demonstration of high-definition television early in 1981. All of us were amazed at the picture definition pro-

vided by a huge array of Japanese equipment shrouded behind curtains. At that point the new service seemed almost around the corner. Little did we know how long it would really take to arrive (see chapter 13). Years later we bought our first camcorder (see chapter 11). Television's technical story continues into the new century with new consumer devices to make program selection and recording across over 100 channels easier (see chapter 14).

Reading Abramson's chapters takes the reader behind the scenes of what we watched over the past six decades, reconstructing how television developed technically. He makes clear how this developmental process was the result of many competing inventors and companies, such as the high-stakes battle over color television standards (fought largely between CBS and RCA and reviewed in chapters one through three). Much of Abramson's focus is on the steadily improving technology of cameras and recording methods (especially the Ampex development of video tape as discussed in chapter 4). He rescues the memory of a host of engineers and other key figures and companies who worked to perfect television equipment. And he details the increasing variety and capability of both television broadcasting equipment (cameras, recorders, and related devices) and improving consumer electronics options.

Abramson's focus extends beyond the United States. He notes the important developmental work done in Britain, France, Germany, and Japan, for example, as well as the failure to achieve a single global color standard (see chapter 5), largely for political and economic reasons. He reviews the world-wide trend towards digital systems and assesses their likely future in a video world converging with computers and information processing.

This is an important book as well as a vital record of a medium that is central in our daily lives. We can be grateful to Al Abramson for the prodigious research over many years that underlies the volume you now hold. The story it tells is well worth reading.

Christopher H. Sterling
Washington, D.C.

Introduction

This book is a sequel to my earlier book, *The History of Television, 1880 to 1941,* which was published in 1987. Most of my research into television history as a whole was done in the period 1952 to 1987. By that latter date, I had accumulated much of the information contained in this book. However, I decided my first book on the subject would stop at 1941, when America's entry into World War II changed everyone's priorities and television was sent back to the laboratory.

This was no arbitrary dividing line, for television after the war was more mature and ready to serve the world. Thanks to the efforts of many American radio companies, especially RCA, television emerged from the war years full-blown and ready for use. The rise of the American television industry in both manufacturing and programming was phenomenal. American industry dominated the postwar world. This picture, however, was soon to change. The invention of the Ampex video recorder gave the Japanese a chance to build competing machines, and build them with great skill. It wasn't long before the Japanese were dominating the global television market. Helped by the Japanese government, Japanese products were the envy of the world. This led to the demise of the American television manufacturing industry, and today there are very few American companies to give the Japanese competition.

All of this history is chronicled in the pages of this book. Luckily, I was able to use the resources of the Los Angeles Public Library and the UCLA Library before most of their material on the evolution of television was taken off the shelves and put into cold storage. I was also lucky to visit many archives and laboratories for information and pictures. One great source was my cherished friendship with Charles Ginsburg of Ampex; my yearly visit with him was manna from heaven. Seeing this modest gentleman, who always had time to discuss the future of the industry with me, was one of the highlights of my life.

During my research, I amassed a large quantity of photocopies for future reference. It never occurred to me (at the time) that most of the pictures I got would not be available anywhere else, as most of the companies went out of business When the time came to prepare this book, there was no longer any way to get fresh photographic prints. Even the existing companies had very little to offer me.

Hence the quality of many of the pictures in this book, for which I apologize. I felt, however, that even a bad picture was better than no picture of some extinct but important machine. Luckily my publisher agreed on this point.

I have done my best to tell the story in pictures and words for future historians who otherwise might not be aware of where and how television evolved. I have taken great pains to insure the accuracy of both text and pictures. Also, every effort was made to find and to credit owners of pictures and text — owners who, in most cases, disappeared long ago. As in my first book I assume full responsibility for all statements made and for any errors or omissions that may have occurred. Any additional information and comments (sent to me in care of the publisher) will be greatly appreciated.

Albert Abramson

Chapter 1
Television and World War II
(1942–1945)

The attack on Pearl Harbor by the Japanese on December 7, 1941, quickly put a halt to most television programming in the United States. Many American television stations reduced their schedules to about four hours a week or simply went off the air. A minimum number of civil defense programs were transmitted in order to keep their studios active and not upset the few thousand viewers who had purchased receivers.

The American electrical industry slowly converted to total war production. This included Western Electric and the Bell Labs, General Electric, Westinghouse, Eastman Kodak, DuPont and of course the Radio Corporation of America. Television research returned to the laboratory where it was to become a tool for guided missiles, long-range reconnaissance and two instruments of mass destruction. David Sarnoff of RCA had immediately telegraphed President Franklin Roosevelt: "All our facilities and personnel are ready and at your instant service. We await your commands." RCA's scientists and engineers would play a major role in the development of radar and sonar and of the electronic navigation systems known as LORAN and SHORAN. When it came to the use of television for war purposes, Sarnoff stated, "The potentialities of television-directed weapons seem to be of the greatest importance." He pointed out that RCA was the most qualified producer and "the only presently qualified supplier and the only one able to solve the remaining problems."[1]

In the United States this statement by Sarnoff was correct. RCA had been engaged in research in airborne television since 1935. In that year, work on guided missiles in the United States had been started at RCA under Ray Kell. This was based on a design of a flying torpedo by Dr. Vladimir Kosma Zworykin in 1934. In fact, most of the wartime advances in television weaponry were spearheaded by RCA in collaboration with the Office of Scientific Research and Development (OSRD) of the armed forces. Guided missiles were discussed in the early planning of division (A), at its second meeting, by the National Defense Research Council (NDRC) itself.[2] However, similar advanced research on television was also being undertaken in Europe by Germany and in occupied France.

On April 25, 1934, Zworykin had submitted a secret proposal to Sarnoff for a "flying torpedo with an electric eye." Basically, it outlined a program for the control of guided missiles by means of television. Sarnoff was so impressed with the scheme that he immediately set up a meeting with the Navy and War departments in Washington at which the inventor explained his radical concept to skeptical members of the armed forces. Zworykin met with admirals Ernest King and Harold R. Stark and generals Westover and Tschappat. Out of this meeting came a pledge of technical and financial support for Zworykin's ideas.[3]

In 1935, under the able direction of Ray Kell, who was later joined by Waldemar Poch and Henry Kozanowski, RCA began work on a lightweight airborne reconnaissance television system that was successfully demonstrated in 1937. Equipment was built using a model 1850 iconoscope camera that was installed in a Ford Trimotor airplane. Two years later, work was commenced on smaller and lighter equipment. By 1940 Zworykin's flying bomb design, incorporating radio control, won Washington's authorization to proceed with advanced aeronautical development. The new equipment was flight-tested in 1940-41.

On March 6, 1940, some of this experimental reconnaissance equipment was demonstrated to the public by RCA and NBC. A twin engine Boeing Mainliner owned by American Airlines took off from La Guardia Field on Long Island, N.Y., and circled the World's Fair Grounds, the Empire State Building, and the Statue of Liberty at an altitude of 2000 feet for about 45 minutes. The pictures from the plane were so clear that experimenters felt there "were possibilities of adapting such a tele-airplane in wartime, especially for reconnaissance flights, bombing operations and map making." The March 17 report in the *New York Times* mentioned that army and navy officials at Radio City and other outposts watched the demonstration with keen interest. This was the only indication that this exercise was part of the guided missile program begun by Zworykin in 1935.[4]

The consolidation of RCA's research laboratories into one facility (now called the David Sarnoff Research Center) in Princeton, New Jersey started in August 1941 and was finished in September 1942. It was the world's largest radio laboratory. Otto S. Schairer was named vice president of the RCA Laboratories. Other officers were Ralph R. Beal, director, who would have general direction of all research and development; Dr. C. B. Jolliffe, in charge of the RCA frequency bureau as chief engineer; and Elmer W. Engstrom, director, with both Dr. Vladimir K. Zworykin and Browder J. Thompson as assistant directors. Zworykin moved his staff and research facilities there. He had rented a home at 91 Battle Road in Princeton in anticipation of such a move, and kept this in addition to the summer home he maintained in Taunton Lakes.[5]

During the war, Zworykin would serve as a member of the Ordnance Advisory Committee on Guided Missiles, three important subcommittees of the National Defense Research Committee (NDRC), and later on the scientific advisory board to the commanding General of the United States Army Air Forces. His main research involved aircraft television fire control and infrared image tubes for the sniperscope (a carbine mounted aiming device) and the snooperscope (a portable telescope using infrared light for illumination). His work also included effective improvements in radar systems and storage tubes and several projects involving the use of television for reconnaissance and in guided missiles.[6]

In August 1940, RCA discussed with Richard C. Tolman its idea of a television-equipped radio-controlled aerial torpedo. RCA felt competent to undertake the television development but was not equipped to investigate the aerodynamic aspects. NDRC agreed that the proposal

was sound and in January 1941 work was started under Section A-E on both segments of the work. RCA agreed to develop suitable television equipment, and Hugh L. Dryden of the Bureau of Standards was appointed consultant on the aerodynamics. In 1927, Dryden had published the fundamental report on the subject: *Aerodynamics of Aircraft Bombs.*[7]

As was the case with much of the NDRC work before Pearl Harbor, this project was operated at first on a small scale with only a few workers. Progress was correspondingly slow. RCA studied the improvement of the sensitivity of the small lightweight television set they had already developed as suitable for remotely controlled planes, gliders, and missiles. They succeeded in producing a smaller iconoscope that used electron multiplication. This gave about eight times the sensitivity previously available, which was good, but still less than the goal RCA had set for itself.

In the meantime, an aircraft corporation had been granted a subcontract by RCA to develop the bomb carrier and had built a model which was aerodynamically unsatisfactory. The vehicle project was therefore taken over by the Bureau of Standards group under Dryden. Vidal Research Corporation contracted to do the actual building of the air frames.

The television-guided glide bomb, designated ROBIN, that was ultimately was built and operated, was unsuccessful and soon abandoned.[8]

Three basic television systems were developed for the military during World War II. These were known as BLOCK, RING, and MIMO. The BLOCK system consisted of several designs built to operate on different frequencies. This equipment was used by both the army and the navy: By the army in the GB-4-radio-controlled glide bomb and in old "war weary" B17s, and by the navy in TDR Drones and the GLOMB radio-controlled glide bomb.

BLOCK equipment employing the iconoscope or the new image orthicon was lightweight and compact. It operated at 350 lines, 40 frames/second, sequential scanning.[9] The camera unit weighed but 33 pounds and the transmitter unit 26 pounds. The camera was in the nose of the plane and was aimed by the pilot. It was designed to operate unattended and was in the main expendable.[10]

The RING equipment provided a more elaborate, high-resolution airborne television system for reconnaissance. It was designed for attended operation with two or more cameras, one installed in the nose of the plane and another in the waist position. It was not considered expendable. It worked within an 8MHz bandwidth, a frequency of 567 lines interlaced two to one at 20 frames/sec.[11] This system used both the C7543C 4½ multiplier orthicon and the newer 2P21 image orthicon camera tube.[12]

The MIMO system was similar to the BLOCK. It was, however, lighter and more compact and used a new developmental MIMO (miniature image orthicon). (Remington Rand's Vericon tube turned out to be unsatisfactory for this missile.) The entire system was to be mounted in the army ROC high angle radio-controlled bomb made by the Douglas Aircraft Company for which it was designed specifically and weighed but 50 pounds. A 325-line, 40-frames/sec sequential television transmitter sent a picture of the target to the bomb aimer. The pickup tube used in the transmitter had stabilized supplies, and the iris of the lens system was controlled by the video signal to give a constant average signal intensity. The first model of what was became known as BLOCK I television was flight-tested in April 1941 from an army B18 bomber at Wright Field, Ohio.

In November 1941, with a grant from the National Defense Research Council, three RCA-built television-guided missiles were tested successfully at Muroc Dry Lake in California. Work was intensified in the design of both aircraft and guided missiles in Project Ring, initiated in November 1942. Actual flight tests using television equipment were made at the Naval Air Station, Banana River, Florida, with a PBY-4 Flying Boat.[13]

RCA wasn't the only company working with television as a weapon of war. There was also much television activity in Germany during this period. The Germans claimed to have continued to run their Berlin television station at Witzelben for many years during the war. It has been claimed that the German television transmitter at Witzelben was operated daily for six hours until it was destroyed by bombing in 1943. One and a half hours of "live" programming was produced for entertainment of troops in hospitals. A total of 25 cameras including one super Ikonoscope were available. They also had two vans for outside broadcasts. They admitted having only 600 receivers since production of them was stopped in 1940. (It was claimed that the manufacturers had another 1,000 earlier sets on hand.)

In order to get a larger audience there were three cinema centers in Berlin which were connected by coaxial cables. One center had 800 seats and used Fernseh equipment built in 1938. There were also two smaller centers with 300 seats each. In spite of the claims that the Germans were on the air daily, it made no sense that they would use their transmitter in the heart of Berlin when it would act as an electrical beacon for enemy bombers. So it is presumed that most of the transmissions were done either at low power or by closed circuit.[14]

Since 1935, the Nazis had also been working on other means of mass destruction. They had secretly been working on long-range rockets to be used against England in the coming war. They had constructed an enormous secret underground factory at Peenemünde near the Baltic Sea which was manned by a mass of slave labor from concentration camps under the most horrible conditions. The German scientists there had been working on two secret weapons, to be called the V1 and V2 rockets, from sometime in 1935. Led by Werner von Braun, they had made great progress in building large rockets. Author Gerhardt Goebel mentions the use of television viewing concerning the rocket experiment work at Peenemünde.[15]

According to Walter Bruch, who was there, the experiments on the A4 rockets were monitored by two television cameras. When the war began, Bruch found himself working on military tasks but still made time to continue developing television. His knowledge

The RCA Laboratories, David Sarnoff Research Center, Princeton, NJ. (RCA.)

and skills in this sphere were soon in demand. The German Air Ministry became interested in his moonlighting and he was summoned to Peenemünde where the V1 and V2 rockets were being tested.

In 1941 he led a team at Peenemünde in developing and installing a closed-circuit television system to give low-risk monitoring of the rocket launches. A two-camera system was installed at the launch pad to relay live pictures along a cable to a control room 2.5km away. One of the compact cameras had a telephoto lens and the other a wide-angle lens, and one of them had to be replaced after being destroyed when the first V2 rocket blew up.[16] It seems that the television equipment had been built for the 1940 Olympic Games that were to be held in Tokyo and which had been canceled due to the start of World War II.

Bruch said that one camera was on the roof of a 2 kilometer distant assembly factory with three top Nazis. The second camera delivered a picture up to the moment at the employment of the ignition, and was then into a rank-storm dying out of the flames. Bruch was proud of the fact that it was in his words "Strictly Confidential" and that the first large rocket in the world was built in Peenemünde in 1942. It started as the A4-Rakete, but later became known as V2, he confesses, from a concrete bunker, built into the spectator embankment of a type of sport stadium, called Prüfstand VII. Werner von Braun, General Dornberger, Colonel Stegmaier and three technical assistants, were placed on the roof of an assembly factory beside it, the so-called Mebhaus, beside Prüfstand VII. The GenerAle and influential politicians with arranged of the start-place, of the neighboring driving mechanism "Triebwerkprüfstand using two pick ups, the different shot of immediate near the rocket. The second camera delivered a picture up to the employment of the ignition and was then into a rank-storm shrinking? that the fire-ray drove high.[17]

According to Gerhart Goebel, there was much activity starting in 1940 in research into flying bombs with television equipment. In spite of this research, it was claimed that these bombs never saw action. The Germans started a project called "Tonne" by Fernseh that was a flying bomb guided by a television camera. By 1943 they were experimenting with this bomb. It used both the Superikonoskope and the Farnsworth image dissector.

One source claimed that "Tonne" was built around a small image iconoscope (IS9) camera tube. The transmitter had 19 tubes with an f 2.8 35mm lens. It could pick up pictures with a density of 50 lux. About 400 were built, although some used a simplified iconscope. For reception, a universal receiver with an 8cm by 9cm picture tube with 6kV of power, or a high power receiver with a 11cm by 12cm tube at 12kV, was used. The author claims that

nothing is known of its use. There is also mention of using the image iconoscope in the trials of both the V1 and V2 flying bombs.[18]

It was also related that in 1940, development began of television-guided missiles, torpedoes, unmanned surveillance planes and related technologies such as radar and heat-seeking missiles, all under military directive. There were close parallels between RCA and Telefunken research into these areas (even after the blackout from America began).[19]

Goebel also stated that the Nazis had decided after June 1941 on a more peaceful and friendly use for television, and were intending to create an international European television network including France, Italy and Germany. This would use the German 441 line standard.[20]

In June 1943 in the USA, work was begun on the development of the GB-4 glide bomb for the air force. The GB-4 was an ordinary 2,000 pound bomb with an air frame attached. It consisted of a Signal Corps— developed radio transmitter and TV receiver operating at 300MHz. It operated at 625 lines, 20 frames, 40 fields interlaced scan. It used either an 1848 or 1846 iconoscope tube. It was claimed that many different types of camera tubes including image dissectors and orthicons having low-velocity scanning had been tested. However, these had little advantage over the iconoscope and for military reasons were found inferior.

It became apparent that photographic records had to be made of the field test, so a special photorecorder was built to take pictures from the receiver screen. The first glide bombs were completed in July 1943 and five GB-4 bombs were dropped in August 1943, at Eglin Field, Florida. Final tests were made at Tonopah, Nevada. A glide bomb group was ordered to England in June 1944. A "Castor" group which used the same equipment and which was made up of war-weary B17s, was also operating out of the same location.[21]

Under various contracts with RCA, a large number of engineers had been put to work on all aspects of the television problem. The main features covered improvement of picture quality, sensitivity, reliability, and selectivity, design of antenna, and reduction of size and weight.

By the fall of 1943 there were available proposed television systems from three different manufacturers, each having its own peculiar advantages. Hazeltine, using RCA equipment; Farnsworth developing its image dissector camera, and Remington-Rand developing a new two-inch orthicon called the Vericon. The Vericon was placed in five television units and tested. It was planned to use a 325-line, 40-frames/sec television transmitter in a remotely controlled bomb that sent its picture of the target to the bomb aimer. The "Vericon" tube used in the transmitter had stabilized supplies, and the iris of the lens system was controlled by the video signal to give a constant average signal intensity.[22]

The launching of the V2 rocket from Peenemünde in 1942 is monitored by television cameras. (G. Goebel/Walter Bruch.)

extremes of battle conditions, differ widely from civilian needs. Demonstrations of the relative merits of the different cameras were observed by a large number of army, navy, and NDRC representatives.[24]

RCA had developed several kinds of tubes to this time. First, was a 4½ multiplier orthicon type C7543C with five stages of electron multiplication for project RING. Second, was an improved 1840 Orthicon to be used in the BLOCK system. Third, there were experiments with a developmental two-inch orthicon that was made by both RCA and Remington-Rand.

Fourth, was the image orthicon developed by Dr. Albert Rose, Paul K. Weimer and Harold B. Law of the RCA Laboratories Division. Dr Rose of the Research laboratories of the RCA Manufacturing Company at Harrison had been working on a solution to improve the orthicon. It was based on the achievement of a near perfect two-sided target consisting of an extremely thin piece of *semiconducting glass* (Corning G-8). The light from the scene would strike the front of the glass that would be coated with a suitable photoelectric layer. With the proper parameters, it allowed the electrons to go through the glass where they would be discharged by the electron beam from the rear. This created the picture signal. While still a laboratory experiment, it paved the way for future improvements in television camera tubes.

On September 20, 1940, Dr. Albert Rose had filed for a patent disclosing the new two-sided glass target. However, the U.S. War Department decided that Rose's patent was a military secret and withheld it until the end of the war. This application was continued on November 28, 1945. Under an Office of Scientific Research and Development contract, Dr. Rose, working with Dr. Weimer and Dr. Law, started a top secret project to incorporate this target into a new orthicon camera tube for military purposes.

By early 1944, the basic orthicon tube had been tremendously improved with the addition of an "image section" (similar to that of the image iconoscope) and an "electron

While this tube seemed satisfactory, they decided to build an image orthicon (similar to RCA's) and requested help from RCA. This request failed; it seemed that they had assumed that RCA had promised assistance with this tube, but RCA did not give it. RCA was not about to give away their "expertise" on camera tubes to anyone. (After the war, Remington-Rand sued the government over this point and lost.)[23]

It was necessary to decide which of these features merited adoption, and no amount of separate observation was capable of solving the problem. A contract with the Columbia Broadcasting System Engineering Research Laboratory was therefore arranged under which competing equipment was given comparative tests under controlled conditions. These requirements, it might be mentioned, involving simplicity and reliability under

1944. Two airborne television cameras. *Above:* RCA orthicon mounted under the plane. *Below:* Remington Rand RC-3 two-inch orthicon mounted in the nose. (USAF.)

multiplier" based on earlier work of Zworykin, Farnsworth and others. Its sensitivity was about 100 times that of the regular orthicon. In addition, it was completely electrically stable at either medium or high light levels. The result was the development of the new highly sensitive tube called the image orthicon in 1944. It was a large tube, 15½ inches long with a three-inch round image section and a two-inch diameter scanning and multiplier section, and was quite complicated to build. The photocathode consisted of a semitransparent layer of cesium–silver oxide type. However, it was quite successful and showed great promise. The earliest model was the RCA/LM15 (C-7557-A) built in Lancaster, Pennsylvania.[25]

RCA was also working on a smaller version of the image orthicon. The resulting tube was developed by Dr. Weimer, Dr. Law and Stanley V. Forgue. It was designed on the same principles but scaled down to about nine inches long and 1½ inches in diameter. RCA promised to have a few models of the Miniature image orthicon (MIMO) ready for testing by the end of 1944, and reasonable quantity production a year or so there after. MIMO was, therefore, adopted as the sensing unit for the ROC missile. As a result of these tests, it was finally agreed that the RCA 2P21 image orthicon and the Miniature image orthicon (MIMO) (2P22) (C-73009) seemed best suited to military requirements.[26]

In June 1944, the air force started using "war-weary" B17s, (code named "Castor") that were television-equipped and radio-controlled to destroy targets in Helgoland. At the same time, GB-4 glide bombs with television were

1945. An early image orthicon with (from left) developers Dr. Albert Rose, Paul Weimer and Harold Law. (RCA.)

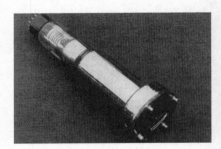

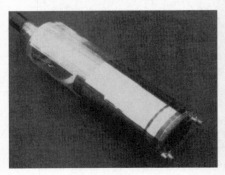

1945. Two experimental tubes. *Above:* multiplier orthicon. *Below:* early orthicon. (RCA.)

1945. *Above:* Image orthicon with smaller MIMO tube for guided missiles. *Below:* MIMO tube. (RCA.)

sent against V1 and V2 launching areas sites on the French coast around Calais. They were also used against the submarine pens at Le Havre and La Pallice, France. In 1944, navy television TDR-1 drones were used against Japanese shipping in the northern Solomons. In August a navy guided missile also destroyed a radar-equipped lighthouse at Rabaul Harbor. BLOCK equipment installed in reconnaissance planes after the capture of the Philippines was used for patrol work and battle damage survey. In addition to television-guided missiles, there were other glide bombs developed that used radar guidance which included the BAT, PELICAN and MOTH, and there was the radio-controlled AZON bomb.[27]

The army was planning extensive tests of the ROC at Wendover Field, Utah when the end of the war caused termination of the project. A few successful drops had been made of MIMO-equipped ROCs. Thus a well-conceived and well-executed program produced an expensive missile that failed to see combat. By the end of the war RCA had delivered more than 4,400 cameras and associated transmitting equipment including 500 BLOCK television cameras, to the armed forces for reconnaissance purposes and to guide pilotless bombs. In fact, this undertaking had actually produced results that were to change the face of warfare forever.[28]

Another new art came into being during this period — that of television recording of airborne television transmissions. Although commercial television started in the United States in 1939, there was little development in television film recording until the middle of World War II. With the development of BLOCK and RING equipment, it became necessary to make permanent records of the transmissions of this apparatus. Motion-picture film cameras were used to record the television images sent by these developments from aircraft and guided missiles. Film cameras were installed on television receivers on the ground and in other aircraft. One of these early motion picture cameras was a standard air force camera with a speed control to adjust the shutter to about 8 frames/sec.

An image of Ray Kell created by the image orthicon in full moonlight (the moon is reflected in Kell's eyeglasses). (Al Rose/RCA.)

Speeds as low as 4 frames/sec were available. The recorded pictures were very poor due to the different standards of the transmissions, the low light intensities of the recording monitors, and the many steps involved in the photographic processes. Shutter banding was noticeable in the film but did not destroy its value as a record. Further work was done with a Kodak Cine Special camera at 15 frames/sec with a 170' open shutter. During the immediate postwar period there would be a new interest in the recording of television images.[29]

Another new use for television viewing came into being with the development of the atomic bomb in the Manhattan Project. It had become known quite early, about 1942, that the handling of hazardous radio-active material would require some kind of remote viewing of the processes involved. The use of mirrors for instance was quite clumsy and inadequate.[30]

In a report dated November 1943, "three employees of RCA were brought to the Clinton Engineering Laboratories [Oak Ridge] to install some equipment." Finally, the report said that someone whose name had been blanked out stated that, "he recalled while taking a course at the Metallurgical Laboratory, University of Chicago in the

Above: RCA iconoscope gun camera.
Below: RCA orthicon guided-missile camera. 1944. (USAF.)

Summer of 1943, various lectures were made as to how television could be used in connection with work of the project. He believed that the talks on television were given by a representative of the RCA Laboratories." It has been learned that two of the employees were Ray Kell and Dr George Morton, both top scientists on television at RCA.[31]

This was confirmed in 1958 in *Television in Science and Industry* by V. K. Zworykin, E.G. Ramberg, and L. E. Flory. In the chapter entitled "Field of Application of Closed-Circuit Television, they stated, "There are countless ways in which television can protect personnel from physical damage. Thus it permits close visual control of the remote handling of high explosives and radioactive materials without the complex and duct-

work required by mirror systems and periscopes for direct viewing. In atomic energy installations, ordnance plants, and plants employing hazardous chemical processes, it makes it possible to increase the distance between the operations and the control personnel, since the brightness and sharpness of the picture can be made independent of the length of cable coupling it to the camera. Furthermore, corrective measures can be taken more quickly in reaction to happenings observed on a large, bright screen image than in response to observations made through a viewing port or periscope eyepiece." In discussing the chemical separating plants at Hanford, Washington, they stated, "that a unique system of periscopes and the very first use of American television sets were installed in the process area in order to allow operation by remote control. This system was implemented because the process areas became too radio-active for repair crews to enter."[32]

A late report (1945) noted that there was use of television at the Hanford complex.[33] "The crane cab in the Canyon Building is separated from the canyon by a concrete partition to protect the operator from radiation hazards. For this reason since the operator cannot directly watch the operation of the crane, recourse must be made to optical aids." Each Queen Mary canyon (so named for its size) was more than 800 feet long, 65 feet wide and 80 feet high. It contained 40 cells and each cell's lid could be removed by an overhead crane. (Each overhead crane that rolled the length of the building's long canyon weighed 35 tons.) The operators had been trained at DuPont in Delaware, at Oak Ridge, and on mockups at Hanford. Over 100 men were involved. Construction started late in 1944.[34]

"Two large periscopes, one on either side of the crane bridge permit the operator to view the crane hooks, impact wrenches and cell equipment with clarity," the report said. Although the field of vision is rather limited (to gain magnification), scanning may be obtained at the operator's discretion by electric motors which "telescope" the periscope across the canyon and rotate it on its axis. The eyepieces are automatically synchronized with the viewing direction of the objective ends of the periscope so that the operator is always looking in the true direction.

"Large negative lenses have been installed on the outboard side of each periscope's objective so that when the objective is rotated in this direction, a tremendously increased field of view is obtained. This allows the operator in one glance to get a general view of the canyon to see whether or not all cover blocks are in place and to see if anyone is on the deck.

"A television camera is also installed under the near, right hand corner of the crane bridge.

1944. US Air Force television recording camera for airborne TV. (USAF.)

The viewing angle of this instrument is varied by electric motors under the operator's control which rotate the camera on horizontal and vertical axes. The 'picture' picked up by the camera is transmitted by wire to the crane cab where it appears on the screen of a cathode ray tube. Although the television lacks the definition of the periscope, it has a broader field of view, is not as tiring to the eye, permits quicker scanning of the situation, and affords an additional view from another angle."[35]

From the heavily shielded cab behind a concrete parapet above the gallery, operators could look into the canyon with specially designed periscopes and television sets. They could see the 70-ton hook to lift off the cell covers and lighter equipment to work within the cell. With special tools and impact wrenches, they could remove connecting piping, lift out the damaged piece of equipment and place it in a storage cell. To perform such an operation successfully at 60 feet or more without direct vision requires extreme accuracy.[36]

More information about the TV installation at Hanford finally appeared. The optical sighting devices were made by the Kollmorgen optical company, which was the principal manufacturer of navy periscopes. As early as October 1942 DuPont prepared to use both visual (periscopes) and television viewing. Du Pont got a release from the Navy Department to manufacture the optical units. For security reasons, the first units were made in the Wilmington shops of DuPont. The company also received releases from both the navy and RCA for TV units. They found that RCA had made several wired units for the navy (BLOCK units) that had a five-inch screen with about 300 by 250 line scanning. After installation at the plant site, tests proved that the units did not give as clear a picture as had been anticipated. An engineer from RCA found that the iconoscopes used were of low sensitivity and required reprocessing at the factory. A substitute iconoscope of greater sensitivity was installed and tests for 72 hours indicated satisfactory operation of the unit. RCA decided that further tests on a typical installation were necessary and returned to them. All reports indicated that the TV units did not give good results. The pictures were not as bright or as accurate as those from the periscope, and obviously the intense radiation may have harmed the delicate photoelectric surfaces. So the novel idea seemed to come to nothing.[37]

Some early work on 1,029-line systems was started in Germany during the war, but as it had no direct military application, it was discontinued. However, the bulk of this experimental work took place in France during the occupation. The Nazis would not permit French companies to pursue work of industrial importance but would allow them to improve the French television system under their guidance. They contracted out television work with the laboratories of the Compagnie des Compteurs de Montrouge, under the direction of René Barthélemy. In a September 1945 article in *Electronic Engineering*, Pierre Hemardinquer claimed "that he had no choice in this decision. All Frenchmen were supposed to perform an effort for the occupying German government."[38]

Of course this would be considered collaboration with the enemy during wartime. Nonetheless, for René Barthélemy, this was a chance to continue on with his work, in spite of the circumstances. For certain Nazis, keeping this project going was a perfect way for them to remain in Paris and avoid any dangerous war duty.

At any rate, Barthelemy did much work on improving the iconoscope and some unsuccessful experiments with the low-velocity orthicon. In 1941 work was started on a high definition 1,015-line system by the Compagnie des Compteurs de Montrouge. An intense race began to find if it were possible to transmit a 1,000-line image. Much experimentation was done with a specially constructed "monoscope" to produce a standard image. Experiments were carried out with a small camera using an iconoscope that was self-contained. All of the circuits for the iconoscope, preamplifier, scanning circuits and time base generator were inside the camera. It also included an electronic viewfinder mounted on the right side of the camera which was modulated by a central amplifier.

A description of development work by the company showed a theoretical and practical examination of the requirements for a television system with detail limited only by visual acuity. The work eventually realized a complete system, including the radio link, on 145 Mc/s. The development included apparatus permitting a wide range of scanning, both in lines and degree of interlacing. The final selection of interlaced scanning with 1015 lines was based on tests over a wide range of values.[39] All in all, it was a quite novel experiment that later proved its excellence.[40]

There was also much work done on a tube using low-velocity beam scanning similar to the orthicon called the Isoscope. It was not a success. In spite of much research, it was finally admitted that, "All the difficulties have not been resolved, but the first applications of the Isoscope with high frequency modulation are full of promise."[41]

The Germans had allowed the French Broadcasting Service to resume experimental transmissions under German control in July 1940. When the Germans occupied Paris, they took over the Eiffel Tower television station and transmitter, and in 1943, they began a television service from the tower. The Vichy government arranged for the Nazis, under the auspices of the Luftwaffe, to undertake television transmissions in Paris on the German standard of 441 lines, 25 frames interlaced. They set up a broadcasting center called Magic City to entertain wounded German airman in French hospitals. This new television studio, Magic City, was built at 180 Rue de l'Université in Paris. The Nazis also planned to set up French, Italian, and German television networks.

Magic City had seats for 250 people and a large control room at the back with facilities for mixing up to six live cameras. There was also an elaborate telecine projector that was equipped with orthicon tubes. The technical equipment was furnished by both German and French companies. The cameras and receivers were made by Telefunken-Allgemeine Elektricitäts-Ges (A. E. G.), and Fernseh A. G. German television engineers were joined by the Compagnie des Compteurs under the direction of René Barthélemy on this project under a contract with the German Post Office (DRP). It seems that the television cameras had been built by Telefunken for the 1940 Olympics (originally scheduled for Tokyo, but canceled because of the start of World War II) and shipped to Helsinki where the Nazis planned to use them anyway. They never did.[42]

It was reported that the results in France were not good, transmission was poor and the synchronizing varied considerably during transmission. Later on it was claimed "that the French public, both on moral and material grounds, did not take much interest in Programmes under enemy control, but nevertheless this did allow certain manufacturers to develop receivers and undertake useful research."

However, the lack of success was dictated more by the fact that it was not a peaceful situation. A tragedy occurred in Occupied France. Professor Fernand Holweck of the Edouard Belin and Madame Curie Radium laboratories (whom Zworykin had met in Paris in 1928 and again in 1939) had joined the French underground and was imprisoned by the Nazis in December 1941. He was shot and killed while in custody, the Nazis claiming he had committed suicide.[43]

Magic City remained on the air until August 16, 1944, at which time the Nazis abandoned Paris. They took with them all of the studio equipment but left the telecine (motion picture) transmitters. There was general destruction of the Eiffel Tower transmitter itself, with fragile apparatus smashed and the oil-filled transformer hit by bullets. The aerial and feeder apparatus were supposed to have been blown up but were saved due to the haste with which the Nazis left Paris.[44]

On March 10, 1944, Colonel David Sarnoff had been called to active duty, to participate in the coming Allied invasion of France. He was scheduled for overseas service with the Signal Corps in London. He took a leave from the presidency of RCA and was made a special assistant on communications to General Dwight D. Eisenhower.

Above: German Super-Ikonoskop camera for "Tonne" glide-bomb. *Below:* German camera/transmitter for guided missile. 1944. (Goebel/Fernseh.)

Colonel Sarnoff did a superb job of organizing the radio coverage of the landings for the Allies. He then covered France, North Africa, Italy, saw the liberation of Paris, and finally ended his Signal Corps duty with an assignment in Germany. Sarnoff sailed for the United States on October 21, 1944, and arrived back in New York City on October 28, still on active duty. On December 7 he received his long-awaited promotion to brigadier general.

Five days later, on December 12, 1944, Sarnoff and Zworykin were honored at a meeting of the Television Broadcasters Association (TBA) at the Hotel Commodore in New York City. Sarnoff was the guest of honor that evening. As a special award he received the title "The Father of American Television" and a medal, "For his vision of television as a social force, and the steadfastness of his leadership in the face of natural and human obstacles in bringing television to its present state of perfection." The award was given by Paul Raiburn of Paramount Pictures.[45]

On December 13, Sarnoff was quoted by the *New York Times* as saying, "The nation which established television first will undoubtedly have the first great advantage in establishing its designs, its patterns, and its standards in the rest of the world and will thus gain a great advantage in the export markets."[46]

Zworykin was given the first award in engineering in recognition of his development of the iconoscope and the storage principle of picture pickup, resulting in the first practical television pickup equipment. Several other significant figures in the development of television were honored that evening, among them Philo T. Farnsworth, Dr. Peter C. Goldmark, Frank J. Bingley, Dr. Allan B. DuMont, Dr. W. R. G. Baker, and Dr. Alfred N. Goldsmith.[47]

Television research was mostly dormant in England during the war years. The great electrical laboratories such as Metropolitan Vickers, the British General Electric Co,

1945. French Iconoscope camera with electronic viewfinder. (Paul Mandel. *L'Onde Électrique.*)

John L. Baird and his high-definition two-color TV system. November 1942. (RTS.)

A. C. Cossor, Ferranti Electric, British Thomson Houston Co. and EMI were all engaged in work on perfecting radar systems. Airborne and seaborne radar systems had the highest priority. The chain of radar stations on the English coast had helped save England during the Battle of Britain.

An unhappy occurrence of the war was the untimely deaths of Alan D. Blumlein, C. O. Browne and A. Blythen, all of EMI, who were killed while testing the latest H_2S airborne radar system. On June 7, 1942, while experimenting with the new system, their Halifax bomber developed engine trouble and all were killed in the resulting crash. This was such a tragic loss that the news of their deaths was postponed until after the war.[48]

Another similar tragedy occurred in America. Directing one of the many research groups at the new RCA Laboratories in Princeton was Zworykin's associate and codirector, Browder J. Thompson. They had become very good friends; in fact, they even shared Zworykin's house for a while. Thompson was engaged in research in the use of radar and went overseas (although he was not required to do so) to evaluate its performance. When he arrived in Italy, Thompson insisted on going on actual bombing missions to truly evaluate the system's performance. On one of these flights, on the night of July 4-5, 1944, his plane was shot down by an enemy aircraft and both he and his pilot were killed. This was quite a blow to Zworykin and the entire staff of the RCA Laboratories.[49]

In England, John Logie Baird, who had been turned down for any kind of war service, was hard at work on new ideas. He was in exile at his home in Sydenham where he had a small laboratory and the help of two assistants (one being Ray Herbert).[50] On December 18, 1941, it was reported that Baird had perfected a working system of television in color and stereoscopic relief. The system consisted of a monochrome cathode ray tube and a three color rotating disc with a revolving shutter which was split by a mirror at the transmitter. At the receiver, the image from the cathode ray tube was sent through a similar two-color disc and a revolving shutter to prevent the eyes from seeing the wrong picture. The apparatus had a frame frequency of 150/sec. The scanning was altered to a field of 100 lines interlaced five times to give a 500-line picture — green, red and blue successively. There is no description of the quality of the picture.[51]

In November 1942, Baird gave a demonstration of a color TV system without the use of rotating color filters. It divided the picture into two colors that were combined by means of a lens system. The two colored frames were reproduced one above the other (or side by side). Lenses projected each of the images onto a second large lens equal to its focal length to the matte receiving screen. The images overlapped on the screen and by careful adjustment of the optical system exact superimposition became possible.[52]

Baird continued to work on color television. On July 25, 1942, he applied for a British patent on an electronic color vacuum tube. He described two versions: two colors or three. In the two-color version, two electron beams on opposite sides of the tube struck both sides of a thin mica sheet. In the three-color version, the back side was ridged so that the blue beam and the green beam came from opposite directions. The red beam was projected on the back side.

On August 16, 1944, Baird demonstrated the two-sided version of this color tube. Called the Telechrome, it received a picture from a 600-line flying-spot system. It appeared that he also built the three-sided version too. It

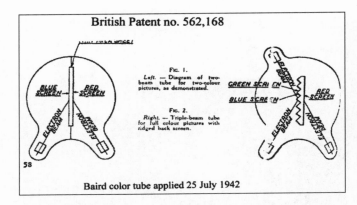

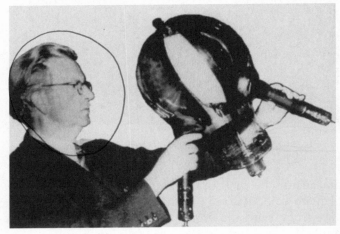

Above: British Patent no. 562,168, of July 25, 1942, for the Baird color tube. *Below:* John L. Baird and his tricolor tube of 1944. (RTS.)

David Sarnoff receiving his general's star (from an unidentified general) on December 7, 1944. (RCA.)

was the first all electronic color tube in the history of television. This was Baird's greatest achievement. It was ironic that the man who made his reputation based on mechanical television had invented, built, operated and demonstrated the world's first color television tube.[53]

In February 1944, a new large-screen projector was described by the Institute of Applied Physics, Zurich, under the direction of Dr Fritz Fisher. It was quite a large device standing some six feet tall. It used a film of oil on a rotating glass plate that was actually modulated by an electron beam. The light from an arc lamp passing through the liquid film was deflected by means of a pencil of light rays proportional in intensity to the degree of deformation and corresponding to each deformation point on the surface made visible by projection.

"A modulated cathode ray beam charges the surface of the liquid with electricity which gives rise to the charges needed to effect the deformation. The liquid film in the absence of electrostatic forces is 0.1mm thick. The glass plate underneath which is a system of lenses serves to focus the light passing through the slits between the lower slits exactly onto the upper bars. All the light rays, passing between the lower to the upper bars are subse-

quently interrupted by the upper lens as long as the surface is smooth and undistorted. Therefore, no light appears on the screen.

"The conditions are considerably altered when the surface of the liquid is deformed by the beam. All the rays of light which pass through the oblique side of the indentation are deflected in proportion to the depths of this indentation and are able to pass between the upper bars and thus form a bright spot in the television image."[54]

The CBS research labs were not heavily involved in war work. However, it did seem that the network's chief scientist, Peter Goldmark, was used by the government in some highly secret work that involved him going overseas.[55]

Also, in the summer of 1943, Bill Paley, the President of CBS, had accepted a commission as a colonel and joined the Psychological-Warfare Branch of the Office of War Information. His first assignment was in Algiers, headquarters for Eisenhower's proposed invasion of Italy. Overall, most of his work was peripheral. In January 1944, he got a transfer to London to join the psychological war-fare group preparing for Overlord, the invasion of France. He was to supervise broadcasts to Germany and occupied countries and to prepare radio messages to accompany the Allied invasion of France on D-Day. He was involved in both "black" and "white" propaganda. He was stationed at the elegant Claridges Hotel in London, but his stay was marred by the Little Blitz of March 1944 when the German V1 rockets were fired at the city. He went to France in mid–June after D-Day to secure loudspeakers to get the Germans to surrender. He stayed at the Hotel George V. He returned to London in August 1944 and was given a real colonel's commission, in order to better get things done. After V-E Day, Paley was in a small hotel in Heidelberg on May 9, 1945. At that time, he first saw the Dachau concentration camp and it had an overwhelming impression on him. The psychological warfare unit settled down in Bad Homburg near Frankfurt where he waited out the war. On August 23, 1945, he flew to London and from there to New York City. His wartime service was over, and he returned home in September 1945.[56]

In October 1944, CBS revealed the work it had done on Goldmark's mechanical color system. At this time, CBS was using this project as a delaying tactic. They really did not want to get into television yet as their CBS Radio network was doing very well. By keeping the color option open, they hoped to delay the black-and-white TV system from expanding. They proposed that postwar television go to color on the VHF spectrum.[57]

In England in March 1945, it was decided by the Television Advisory Committee (set up in 1944 under Lord Hankey) to stay with the old 405-line standard in six provincial centers at a capital cost of 1½ million pounds. The commission did recommend that an improved system of 1,000 lines or so be introduced as soon as possible, and that for some time the two should run side by side.[58]

At the time, this seemed a prudent move. First, the Alexandra Palace had come through the war unscathed and would be ready to return to service without much alteration. Second, the EMI cameras and equipment needed very little work to make them operate. Third, there was a ready-made audience (small though it was— 20,000 receivers) in London with receivers that could be turned on and used immediately. Finally, British pride was against using the American standards although there was no doubt of their superiority. To have changed to American standards at this time would have meant using RCA know-how and equipment. This would have included a change of line standards, the use of single-side band transmission, and the use of FM sound. This would have held up British television for a long period of time. As it turned out,

1946. Dr. Peter G. Goldmark with live orthicon color camera. (CBS.)

the 405 standard really was quite good and lasted for almost 50 years. Thus the stage was being set for the return of commercial broadcasting both in the United States and Great Britain in 1946.[59]

In the United States, RCA wasted no time in putting their new image orthicon tube into a studio camera. It appears that it was first privately demonstrated in January 1945. On a transatlantic visit, Professor J. D. Cockcroft of British Air Defense Research met with Dr. Zworykin and was given a demonstration of "a camera tube of such sensitivity that studio technique would be completely changed." Zworykin

1946. Live image orthicon camera. (CBS.)

considered that it would take from four to five years to make real progress, and this would include progress in color.

RCA had come out of the war with a tube, the 2P23, so sensitive that it could be used in normal room light. This new tube developed for military use was first revealed publicly in New York City on the night of October 25, 1945, at the Waldorf-Astoria Hotel. There was a demonstration of its ability to pick up scenes with dimly lit interiors and closeups lighted only by a single candle. The demonstration was given by Elmer Engstrom, research director of the RCA Labs, who explained the tube's complicated construction and operation. It was promised that the RCA Victor Products Division would have cameras containing these new tubes ready for delivery in about six months.[60]

On the same day, this tube was also used in Madison Square Garden where a rodeo was transmitted to their studios at NBC. This was followed by its use at the Army-Navy Football game at Philadelphia on December 1, 1945. This event was carried by NBC in New York and by coaxial cable to Philadelphia and by microwave to Schenectady.[61] It was as important to the development of television as Zworykin's iconoscope had been some 14 years earlier.

It did have problems at first. Its pictures were "noisy" (grainy), it had pronounced "halos" (or black edges) around bright objects and its tone of scales (tonal rendition) made faces look a bit unreal. This was typical of the earliest 2P23 camera tubes used in military functions. However, these faults were slowly overcome and for the next 19 years, it became the standard pickup tube in television cameras all over the world. The original image orthicon camera was equipped with a single lens, but soon

1944. Swiss television large-screen projector. (*Electrical Engineering.*)

it was furnished with a four-lens turret and an electronic viewfinder. This tube assured global supremacy for RCA in the development of postwar television.

On December 13, 1945, RCA gave a "live" demonstration of mechanical color television from its Princeton labs. It used an image orthicon tube and a rotating filter similar to that of the CBS color system. It operated at 120 fields/sec interlaced 525 lines, and 40 single-color fields or 20 interlaced full-color pictures per second. At the time, most of the CBS color demonstrations were from film or slides. There was also a demonstration of black-and-white television from New York to Princeton (47 miles). It was pointed out that black-and-white television was ready now but that color television was "five years away." This was the beginning of the "Color War" between RCA and CBS that would last for seven years. The demonstrations were directly viewed on new receivers (no mirrors) with picture tubes developed in wartime. This was another result of the television lab work done during the war by RCA.[62]

Also on December 13, 1945, it was reported that a 16mm television film recorder was developed by Du-Mont station WABD. It was to be used to record programs for distribution throughout the country.[63]

Jasmine Bligh and D. R. Campbell getting ready at Alexandra Palace, February 1946. (RTS.)

1944. CBS Orthicon color camera. (CBS.)

The end of the war in Europe found most of the continent in ruins. Even England, victorious, was austere and exhausted. Both Japan and Germany were devastated. Nonetheless, there were efforts made to return to peacetime activities. It was reported that the Moscow television studio was reopened, and that there were plans to make television sets in both Moscow and Leningrad. No further details were given.[64]

Late in 1945, at Champ-de-Mars or at Montrouge in France, the Compagnie des Compteurs under René Barthélemy demonstrated some of the equipment they had designed and built under the Nazi occupation. They had produced a modern iconoscope tube and showed an orthicon tube called the Isoscope that was not working. They also revealed a quite modern-looking camera with an electronic viewfinder. There was even a demonstration of a 1,050-line system on a 15-inch tube with a 15mH bandwidth that gave pictures of extremely good definition and contrast. It was claimed that "quality was comparable with that of an ordinary cinema." There were plans to go back on the air on a new French standard of 450 lines interlaced at 50 frames per second. A test transmission from the Eiffel Tower was given on October 1, 1945. When a program service was to actually start was not discussed at the time. However, it was ultimately started in March 1949.[65]

Chapter 2

The Postwar Era
(1946–1949)

With World War II over, some 15 television stations in the United States went back on the air in 1946. Most of these had operated under limited schedules during the war. They were still using their old orthicon "live" and iconoscope film cameras. It was estimated that there were no more than a few thousand receivers in the United States in 1946.[1] However, Sarnoff was determined to expand the service that had started on July 1, 1941. But this time, RCA had the new cameras, receivers, circuitry, and picture tubes that they had developed during the war. The problem was to convince the public that television had value. The war had dimmed the memory of summer 1941.

At this time the movie industry was operating at full capacity. During the war people were going to movies three or four times a week. Network and local radio were very profitable. Only RCA was ready to push television, as it had the most to gain. The rest of the radio industry was dragging its feet. CBS was the major force in radio broadcasting, Philco had the lead in radio receiver sales, and Westinghouse and General Electric were prime manufacturers of radio transmission equipment. Sarnoff was determined to change all of this.

The price of the new sets was high. For instance, RCA marketed a ten-inch table model set called the 630 TS for $375 ($2,566 in 2000 dollars), but others were even more expensive. Starting in September, about 10,000 sets were sold in 1946,[2] all made by RCA Victor.[3] Production of image orthicon cameras started in the second quarter of 1946, and RCA would sell them as quickly as they could be produced. As expensive as they were ($50,000) in 1946, the first image orthicon cameras were sold mostly to NBC

stations. RCA was also selling the tube to DuMont, General Electric, and CBS for use in their new cameras. The introduction of the image orthicon camera was the biggest boost to "live" production ever made. They were transportable and could go anywhere, and lighting conditions were no problem. The introduction of this camera really made television practical. The image orthicon cameras had an electronic viewfinder, a four-lens turret, with lenses of the photographic type, and "on air" and "off air" lights. This was a design that set the standards for TV cameras from then on.

Television in 1946 was primarily a "live" medium just like radio. Programming consisted mainly of "live" programs of minor character, mainly sporting events (wrestling, boxing, etc.), second-rate motion pictures (usually old Westerns), some newscasts, and demonstrations and discussion programs. While these were not very good, it was the novelty of the experience that made television grow. With a few exceptions, all programs originated within the studios. However the American public was enchanted with the new medium. Just seeing a picture in a store window was a new, exciting experience. Crowds would gather in bars and restaurants to watch sporting events and the new variety shows that were springing up. The American public was ready to accept the new medium without question.

Interest in the recording of television images continued after the war. The United States Navy started a series of experiments with its airborne television equipment. The first postwar black-and-white television film recordings were made on March 21, 1946, at the Naval Air Station at Anacostia, D.C. These were secured during a

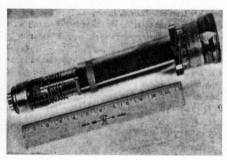

Developmental image orthicon with first commercial tube LM15. 1945/1946. (RCA.)

public demonstration of the navy BLOCK and RING airborne television equipment.[4] The recordings were part of a mock attack on Baltimore, MD, by airborne television.[5]

In this demonstration a JM-4 (B26) Marauder trained its RING cameras on a mock combat area below. It cruised over Baltimore and Annapolis.

Two smaller planes equipped with BLOCK equipment relayed their pictures to a bank of TV receivers at the Anacostia Naval Air Station. Thus they were seeing events far

1946. RCA table model 630TS with a ten-inch screen. (RCA.)

beyond the horizon while they actually happened. Certainly a look into the future.[6]

On March 26, 1946, the navy exhibited its new Gorgon jet propelled aerial bomb with television eye and receiver. So far there had been no confirmation of the missile.[7]

An event of supreme importance that seemingly did not concern television occurred early in 1946. The regular meeting of the San Francisco chapter of the Institute of Radio Engineers was scheduled for May 16, 1946, at the NBC studios. The featured speaker was John T. Mullin, who would talk about and demonstrate a new tape recorder brought back from Europe, a German Magnetophone. Their attention had been called to the machine itself, which had already been described in November 1945.[8]

He told how he found the machines he was demonstrating. In the fall of 1945, Mullin was in occupied Germany, part of a team looking for things of electronic interest left behind by the defeated German Army. One day, he met a British officer on a similar mission. The officer asked if he had heard the tape recorder they had down at Radio Frankfurt. Mullin had heard German tape

1946. Dr. Zworykin with two types of direct viewing receivers. (RCA.)

1946. Side view of early RCA Victor image orthicon camera.

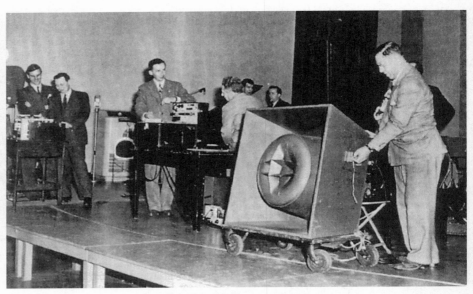

1946. Front view of early RCA Victor image orthicon camera with G. L. Beers (right) of RCA Victor. (RCA.)

recorders before, lots of them, abandoned in the field by retreating troops and correspondents. He had been unimpressed by their sound quality. However, he set off for Bad Nauheim, where Radio Frankfurt was being operated by the American Armed Forces Radio Service, but the technicians were predominantly German. When the officer in charge learned what he wanted, Mullin recalls that he summoned an assistant, who ran into another room, came out with a roll of tape, and put it on the machine. Mullin stated, "That's where I really flipped, because I had never heard anything like that. To my knowledge, there had never been anything like that in recording before. You couldn't tell whether it was live or playback; there was no background noise. I was thrilled."

Mullin was so thrilled that after he had rounded up the two working R22 Magnetphones required by the Signal Corps, he managed to find two more for himself. He photographed all the manuals and schematics and then disassembled the two machines into parts small enough to be shipped home to his mother. His biggest problem was getting the case into a mailbag. Nonetheless, he did send two complete machines home, including about 50 rolls of recording tape.[9] Reassembly with the help of William Palmer, a business associate, early in 1946 took three or four months, including the electronics which were wired anew with American parts. He demonstrated one of the two machines brought back that evening in San Francisco.[10] The meeting ended with demonstrations of sound from several reels of tape. An astounded audience heard the first wideband audio system played through high fidelity speakers. They were wildly enthusiastic in their applause for the sound quality heard.[11]

Among those jammed into the studio audience was Harold Lindsay, who would later join a small company

Above: May 16, 1946: John Mullin demonstrates the Magnetophone for the first time. *Below:* Magnetophone used by Mullin in the first demonstration.

John Mullin and Murdo MacKenzie at the first taping of the *Crosby Show* in August. (Photographs by John Mullin.)

called the Ampex — short for Alexander M. Poniatoff Excellence — Electric Co. of San Carlos. It had been founded by Alexander Poniatoff during the war to produce precision motors and other mechanical devices for the navy. With the war over, the small Ampex Company was looking for products to manufacture. Lindsay told Poniatoff what he had seen. At Ampex, Lindsay took careful measurements of Mullin's Magnetophone, and Ampex engineers were soon busy designing their own recorder, based on Lindsay's specifications.[12]

At the end of the demonstration, Bing Crosby's technical director, Murdo MacKenzie, asked Mullin to bring his machines back two months later to record and edit the first show of the season, a kind of dry run. At this time Bing Crosby preferred to record his show in advance, using 16-inch transcription discs for the purpose of editing out fluffs and cutting programs (which frequently ran overtime) down to size. This was an arduous and time-consuming task, which often did not turn out well. So Mullin started using the tape for broadcasts. It went so well that the network (ABC) had Mullin take over the job of taping shows for the rest of the season. Mullin's machines stayed in use on the "Bing Crosby Show" until program 27, when the first Ampex tape recorders (Ampex Model 200) showed up (April 1948) and 3M's Scotch recording tapes arrived to replace Mullin's original German-made machines and tapes.[13]

In England the BBC readied the Alexandra Palace for the renewal of telecasting. In February 1946, the press was invited to Alexandra Palace to see preparations for the resumption of television service. They were shown the old 405 line Emitron cameras and other operating equipment that had been so carefully stored during the war. The staff included Maurice Gorham, director of television, and old-timers such as D. C. Birkenshaw, superintendent engineer; Cecil Madden, program organizer; and Tony Bridgewater, engineer in charge, outside broadcasts.

On June 7, 1946, the BBC London television station reopened with some light entertainment including music by Mantovani. One of the programs on that opening day was the same Mickey Mouse cartoon that had been the last televised item in 1939. The rest of the program was devoted to speeches given by the Postmaster General and the Chairman of the Governors of the BBC.[14] However, the first major event televised was the Victory Parade the next day. This meant reviving a television cable that had not been used since 1939, linking the West End with the Alexandra Palace. This event came off quite well. The Emitron cameras picked up the arrival of the Royal family, a closeup of Winston Churchill, and a Royal Air Force flyby. It was claimed that a few thousand people at home or in their local pubs saw the telecast. An outstanding inauguration for an excellent (although outmoded) service.

The next outside broadcast (O.B.) of importance was the Lord Mayor's Show on November 8, 1946. It was covered by the O.B. van with one camera on the roof of the vehicle.[15]

It was announced a few days later that John Logie Baird had died in Bexhill-on-Sea on June 14, 1946, at the age of 58. The world had lost a true television pioneer. Unfit for military service and denied a chance to serve among the "boffins" in secret research work, he died tired but undefeated. Since 1941 he had been the consulting technical advisor to Cable & Wireless, free to do whatever he liked, and was paid £1,000 a year until 1944. They then paid him £500 a year until his death in 1946.[16]

On June 14, 1946, the Louis-Conn fight was held in Madison Square Garden. It used three new image orthicon cameras and two prewar cameras. The program was sent to the NBC studio at Radio City, the Statler Hotel in Washington, D.C., WPTZ, WRGB, and W3XWT (DuMont). It was presented on a 22-by-16-foot screen at the RCA Labs in Princeton.[17]

RCA was also going ahead with simultaneous experiments on color television. Until this time, RCA had been experimenting with a color television system using a rotating (sequential) color wheel, similar to that developed by Peter Goldmark at CBS, and the new image orthicon tube.[18] While the results were satisfactory, it had been decided by David Sarnoff that neither he nor his engineers cared much for a system based on a whirling drum.[19]

CBS had different ideas; however, Dr. Peter Goldmark had supreme faith in his system. In 1946, when RCA was preparing mass production of monochrome equipment at the Camden and Lancaster plants, CBS renewed its color initiative. It requested permission from the FCC to demonstrate what it described as an improved color system on December 17, 1946, and it added a persuasive postscript to its plea for immediate commercial authorization. David Sarnoff immediately objected. However, in the press and in government circles, a growing support for the CBS situation began to emerge, and Sarnoff realized he could no longer temporize through press conferences, speeches, and participation in industry forums.

At last he began a public assault on the CBS system, which he contended was flawed by insurmountable technical limitations, small screen size, color fringing and degradation, and lack of capacity for effective mobile coverage. Sarnoff insisted that true color — electronic color — was at least five years away, and that its logical precursor was monochrome TV, which the public was already accepting with boundless enthusiasm.[20]

Apart from the CBS technical limitations, Sarnoff maintained that the system was fatally flawed for economic reasons. Since the spinning disc transmissions required different broadcast standards from those approved for NTSC monochrome, sets already in American homes would go blank if CBS color were broadcast. Thus the public would be short-changed the millions of dollars already invested in monochrome sets. In Sarnoff's phrase, which soon became part of the American lexicon, CBS color was "incompatible," meaning that it was incapable of reception on existing sets in either color or monochrome unless the owner purchased a converter or an adapter to attach to their set.

On the other hand, RCA electronic color, when it was ready, would be compatible because its color transmissions would be on the same broadcast standards as those already approved and could therefore be received in monochrome. Thus the sets already sold would retain their value until that time in the future when they were replaced with color sets. The virtues of compatibility and the snares of incompatibility became a familiar Sarnoff theme as he sought to educate America on the technical semantics of the unfolding conflict.

CBS recognized its vulnerability on the incompatibility aspect of its system. It therefore became of paramount importance for Paley to obtain quick FCC approval of their color system so that manufacturers could switch to color production before a growing monochrome population engulfed them. In this race against time, the network's management was urged by Goldmark and fortified by his assurance that the RCA color system would never achieve technical perfection.[21] Goldmark was convinced that his system of color television would prevail over the VHF frequencies.

Finally, during the middle of the color controversy, the FCC announced it would meet on January 30, 1947, and make its decision as to whether it would open up commercial television to UHF and at the same time include color. In anticipating FCC support, CBS was getting ready to apply for UHF channel licenses in a number of cities where they already had radio licenses. To show good faith about UHF color, CBS agreed, before the FCC decision was made, to withdraw applications for VHF licenses in four major cities, keeping only the license they had at the time in New York City. This was to show the industry that CBS had so much faith in color and in UHF that it was willing to give up something potentially worth millions of dollars. CBS had also advised its affiliates against applying for monochrome licenses. On March 18, 1947, the FCC turned down CBS's UHF applications.

The ramifications of CBS's doomed color venture were many. After the FCC rejection, CBS had to reorder four VHF licenses that it was entitled to by FCC allocation. The purchase of stations in four major markets later in the 1950s cost CBS $30 million. It clearly had to pay exorbitant prices for TV stations that it could originally have had for very little.[22] The owners of these stations, smelling a nice gain, boosted the price and it cost CBS tens of millions of dollars. They paid $6 million for one station in Chicago alone, which they might have had earlier for "peanuts." As TV took off, CBS President Frank Stanton even offered to buy the ABC Network for $28 million in order to obtain three important TV outlets. CBS applied for VHF stations in San Francisco, Boston, and Chicago. (WBBM, Chicago, cost them $6 million in 1953; KMOX in St Louis, $4 million in 1958; WCAU, $4 million in 1958; and KNXT, Los Angeles, $334,000 in 1950.)[23]

Early in 1948 Frank Stanton expanded CBS black-and-white programs from 20 hours over five days a week to 38 hours over seven days a week, all virtually "live."[24] This was an effort to catch up with NBC Television, which had about 48 TV stations across the country and had nine out of the top ten television programs. Paley cut back on CBS color research but did not abandon it. Collectively, it added up to one of the biggest business mistakes of William Paley's career. Paley later stated, "Our efforts to develop a color system pushed RCA into developing their system in a crash program, which brought color television to the consumer long before it otherwise would have been on the market."[25]

Simultaneous color television was first privately demonstrated at the RCA Princeton Research Labs on October 30, 1946. The system used a flying-spot method for film and slides (no live camera existed) to create three registered images that were displayed simultaneously. In early experiments, a kinescope three-gun single neck tube, called the trinoscope, was used. It produced three rasters on separate parts of the face of the tube which were filtered to produce the three colors. This was not successful and was replaced with a projection type of receiver with a 15- by 20-inch screen using three small cathode-ray tubes simultaneously projected on the viewing screen. This same equipment was then demonstrated on January 29, 1947, over a radio-frequency circuit.

Even though England had won the war, it came out of it impoverished. Austerity prevailed. The winter of 1946-47 was extremely hard and grim even by wartime standards. There was a fuel and power crisis in Great Britain. There were shortages of materials and products such as bread and potatoes that had not been rationed during the war. It was claimed simply that "we have not got enough resources to do all that we want to do," and that "we have barely enough to do all that we must do."[26] One result was that the BBC Television Service was closed down from February 10, 1947, to March 11, 1947, and even then it was restricted to evening hours only. It wasn't until April 18, 1947, that full service began again.[27]

In March 1947, David Sarnoff made Vladimir Zworykin a vice president and technical consultant at the RCA laboratories. One of the first things Zworykin did after his promotion was to preside over the first public demonstration of a simultaneous large-screen color television. Zworykin hosted the demonstration on April 30, 1947, at the Franklin Institute in Philadelphia, using a 7½-by-10-foot screen. For the occasion, he gave an address entitled "All-Electronic Color Television."

This demonstration used a projection type of receiver capable of a brightness of 10 footlamberts. This was done by means of three cathode-ray tubes with colored phosphors in a cluster that were projected onto the large screen using color slides and 16mm motion picture film. The Franklin Institute demonstration was the beginning of RCA's efforts to provide a color system that would later fit into the 4mH bandwidth.[28]

Preceding this meeting, a preview of the demonstration was put on for a group of about 50 radio editors and technical writers, which Engstrom, vice president in charge of research at RCA Laboratories, described as a progress report on RCA's color experimentation. He reminded the group that last fall they had seen the first demonstration of the all-electronic system, when colored slides and movies were televised and reproduced on projection-type home receivers with screens 15 by 20 inches, and that in January RCA had transmitted live action scenes in color.

The next major step, Mr. Engstrom said, would be to show outdoor pickups in full color. He hinted that this might occur as early as that fall. Cameras and other necessary equipment were under development in the laboratories, he reported, and propagation field tests would be made that summer in the New York area.

These field tests, he said, would not be pictures, but radio frequencies at both ends of the experimental video band and broadcasted from the Empire State Building, the location of NBC's New York video and FM transmitters. The system they would utilize in this demonstration would be the same as that shown in Philadelphia, comprised of a mirror system at the transmitting end that would divide the image of the televised subject into three color signals, which would be broadcasted as three individual electrical signals, received individually, transformed back into three color images, and simultaneously projected on the viewing screen where they are combined into a single full-color image. What would be new would be the size of the received pictures, 36 times those shown previously.[29]

The subject matter comprised Kodachrome subject slides and 16mm color motion pictures, not broadcast but sent by coaxial cable from the transmitting equipment to the receiving unit in the same room. Pictures were clear and in excellent register, but the reds and blues were accentuated and in pictures where much of the area was red there was a shimmering or graininess.

Dr. Zworykin explained that the images were subject to the aspects of the original pictures and also said that more work was needed on the phosphor of the red receiving tube, which at the time had to be reinforced with a red filter. This was not true of the blue and green phosphors, it was explained, as they were developed more fully in research on black and white television, in which the red phosphors were not used; the development of these red phosphors was still going on in the laboratory.

Dr. Zworykin expressed confidence that this problem would be solved without undue difficulty. Credit for the demonstrated technology was given to Ray D. Kell, television section head, and his associates G. C. Sziklai, A. C. Schroeder, and K. R. Wendt.[30]

On April 7, 1947, the Allen B. DuMont Labs announced they had developed a method of recording television programs off the screen. It called its process "teletranscriptions." It was claimed that with the coming of network television by cable or radio relay, the need for broadcast photographic transcriptions of television programs had emerged. It was also stated that recording had already proved useful in providing delayed-broadcast network service beyond the limits of coaxial cable and radio-relay circuits. Sixteen millimeter was chosen because of the lower cost of the film stock and the cost of maintenance of the camera equipment.

While not a new idea, this was the first organized effort to make the recording of television programs possible since the war. In 1938 the first attempts had been made by RCA in the United States to record or film the screen of a cathode-ray picture tube. These early efforts used standard silent, 16 mm spring-wound cameras operating at 16 frames per second. With the low light intensity of the monitor screen, it was necessary to use the fastest film emulsion available at that time. Since the cameras were nonsynchronous with the 30-frame rate of the television screen, the film recordings were marred by the appearance of banding or horizontal lines (shutter bars) of over and under exposure caused by the uneven matching of the odd and even fields recorded on each frame of film. The film was then recorded at 15 frames per second, which succeeded in eliminating banding but was successful in recording only every other frame of the television 30-frame picture. This film was not suitable for reproduction at the conventional sound speed of 24 frames per second.

It was obvious that if commercial use was to be made of television recordings, the 30-frame television picture would have to be recorded on film at 24 frames per second to conform with the speed of standard 16 mm sound film, thereby permitting projection of the film either in a conventional sound projector for direct viewing or by a standard projector for rebroadcasting by television.

1947. *Left:* DuMont film recording equipment. (DuMont Labs.) *Above:* Eastman 16mm recording camera. (Eastman Kodak.)

DuMont Labs decided to build a camera that would record directly at 24 frames per second from the 30-frame TV images. This process is essentially the inverse of the projection system used in televising standard 24-frame film. A prototype camera was constructed and NBC took it to Eastman Kodak Company, which produced a commercial version of the camera.

Eastman Kodak announced its new 16 mm motion picture camera for recording television programs on film on October 23, 1947. This camera featured a 1,200-foot magazine for continuous recording of a half-hour program, separate synchronous-motor drives for the shutter and film transport mechanism, an f/1.6 two-inch coated lens, and a 72-degree shutter. The pull-down time was 57 degrees. Other features included a "bloop" light to provide registration with a sound-film recorder, a film loop-loss indicator, and appropriate footage indicators.[31]

It was claimed that at first, the 16mm film recorder had a separate sound track. A single system was only good for documentary purposes. It used a very fine grain, wide latitude DuPont film, type 602A. The same film was used for the soundtrack. The image on the tube had a highlight brightness of 100 footlamberts.[32]

A new improved Image Orthicon 5655 was introduced in 1947. It replaced the 2P23 with its high infrared sensitivity. It had a photosurface of silver-antimony sensitized with cesium. It needed only one tenth of the light necessary for the iconoscope cameras of the day. It was slightly larger than the portable image orthicon field camera, and was designed for use on either a dolly or a pedestal.[33] The 5655 was replaced by the 5769 in 1948 with the same target structure as the 2P23, but with the photo surface of the 5665.[34]

In June 1947, RCA planned to give the first demonstration of American television in Europe. They had sent Dr. Zworykin over to represent the National Academies of Sciences, the Institute of Physics, and of course RCA. He delivered papers in Rome and in Liège.[35] It was claimed that demonstrations were also given in Spain and Italy.[36] At that time, television was as new as can be in Europe. Few had even seen a television set, let alone bought one. In contrast, there were some 160,000 TV sets sold in 1947 in the United States.[37]

In July 1947, La Radio Industrie in France introduced a new small television camera to be used for 819-line high-definition pictures. The camera was called the Eriscope and it used a small iconoscope tube with an image

1947. New RCA Victor studio image orthicon camera. (RCA.)

area of only one square centimeter. It was claimed that it had a four lens turret and used 16mm movie lenses that could be used in light down to 500 lumens. The French also stated that the Eiffel Tower transmitter had resumed experimental daily broadcasting with the prewar 450 line picture.[38]

In Britain, progress was also made during 1947 on getting a workable commercial system of television film recording ready. With only one television station in operation immediately after the war, the need was different from that in the United States. The British realized that many topical events occur when the majority of viewers are unable to see the direct transmission. When recording topical or news events, the British considered it a waste of equipment and manpower to have both newsreel cameramen and television cameras cover them. This was especially true when the televised event could be recorded and readied

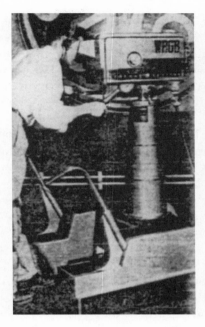

1947. Two television cameras. *Left:* General Electric image orthicon. (G.E.) *Right:* Radio Industrie Iconoscope camera for 819 lines. (*Electronics.*)

for broadcasting in such a short time compared with the regular filmed version. The British had developed the practice of repeating dramatic programs a few days after the original performance. The use of television film recording allowed them to repeat a performance immediately.

The early (1947) British efforts to record television programs were along the same lines as the Americans. The BBC tried to use intermittent cameras with quick pull-down times. Here the problem was in having to record a 25 frame television picture at 24 frames per second. The amount of pull-down time was about 12 degrees. So they compromised by recording only 50 percent of the picture, using the other 50 percent for pull-down time. These recordings were made on 35mm film but recorded only 188½ of the British 405 lines picture.

Later in 1947 they used another method of intermittent recording. A special shutter was open for 240 degrees and was closed for 120 degrees. This produced a film recording that was nonstandard, being recorded at 16⅔ frames per second. This was soon abandoned for a new mechanism that used no intermittent mechanism at all.[39]

Experiments in Britain culminated in the first public transmission of recorded television on November 20, 1947, when the BBC television service televised the Cenotaph Ceremony in the morning and televised a recorded version the same night. This film recording was later transmitted in America by NBC.[40]

It was in the same month of November 1947, that the BBC televised the marriage of H.R.H. Princess Eliza-beth with Lieutenant Philip Mountbatten, R.N. Cameras placed outside Buckingham Palace enabled viewers to see the departure of the Queen, and then the King with his daughter. Another camera position in Broad Sanctuary brought viewers the scenes outside Westminster Abbey, with John Snagge as commentator, but the wedding service itself was broadcast on sound only. Television programmes were interrupted later in the day to show the royal couple leaving for their honeymoon and a film of the wedding scenes was repeated later in the evening. This was another outstanding success for BBC television.[41]

In November 1947, a new viewing tube for color television was revealed. This new tube, called the "Chromoscope," was the invention of Arthur Bronwell of Northwestern University, Evanston, Illinois. The idea was to have a single viewing tube using a single electron gun, a single composite color screen, and inexpensive associated circuits. It was basically a sequential color system. Each screen was to be activated separately. The image screen was composed of four parallel, semitransparent screens (red, blue, and green, with a fourth screen serving as a constant potential screen). Each separate screen was to be activated by placing a high potential on it and a low potential on the others. The three color screens were optically superimposed to form a single three-color picture. It was claimed that experimental versions of these tube were being developed by the DuMont Labs.[42] No further information was found regarding this tube, and no more was heard of Mr. Bronwell."[43]

In February 1948 a new model of the CPS (Cathode

Potential Stabilized) Emitron Camera was described.[43] This tube, no match for the new RCA image orthicon, it was an English product and was to be used in most of the BBC cameras.[44] It was claimed that it had been used at the royal wedding, on an "ITMA" ("It's That Man Again") program, and the relay of "Cinderella" from the Edmonton Theatre.

It was basically an orthicon using low velocity beam scanning.[45] Its main feature was a new kind of mesh for preparing the mosaic. It was claimed that it was better than the original (RCA) orthicon, but had two disadvantages: (1) instability if too much light fell on the target and (2) blurring due to exposure time of one twenty-fifth of a second, which required a shutter operating at frame frequencies if light was sufficient.[46]

This new CPS Emitron was the work of Dr J. D. McGee and the EMI Research Laboratory. Since there had been no television research during the war years, the service reopened with the old Emitron and Super Emitrons. Starting in 1946, EMI began at once to build a new tube. Of course there had already been work on cathode ray tubes, for radar and for image tubes for infrared viewing.[47]

This work was confirmed in September 1947 by T. H. Pratt of the Royal Naval Scientific Service who stated that EMI was to undertake the development of an infrared converter tube based on a Philips design. After development, this tube was produced in quantity by the Gramophone Company and later by Lines Brothers. This was

1948. *Above:* The CPS Emitron tube. (EMI.) *Middle:* RCA 5820 Image Orthicon tube. (RCA.) *Below:* Pye Photicon (Image Iconoscope). (Pye Ltd.)

the basis of many thousands of infrared receivers that were manufactured between 1942 and 1945.[48]

Experiments with television recording were continued by the BBC in London. Early in 1948 a series of experiments was started using a continuous film recorder. There were many advantages in the use of continuous moving film. There were no high rates of pull-down time. There was no need to register the film accurately, although nonuniform film motion was a problem. And in a continuous film recorder, none of the video information was lost.

A 35 mm continuous motion picture projector, the Mechau made by A.E.G. in Germany, was converted to a camera for continuous recording. It had a rotating mirror drum, which for all practical purposes produced a stationary film frame. It used a form of optical compensation where, as the drum rotated in sync with the film, the varying tilt of the mirrors made the reflected images of the television picture follow the film on its downward course. Thus the image was stationary in relation to the film. In this way a succession of images was formed on the film as it passed through the gate, the brilliance of each image rising from zero at the top of the gate, then increasing to a constant intensity over the central part of the gate, and finally falling to zero at the bottom of the gate. This method eliminated any frame-rate difference. This machine also eliminated the high rate of pulldown and the problem of the picture splice in the center of the frame. No lines of the television picture were lost in the recording process. It was claimed that this method could be used in the United States by blacking out a part of the mirrors to avoid more than two fields being recorded on a single frame.

Experiments with this equipment showed that the mirror drum was fully capable of providing correct optical compensation. However, the film transport mechanism did not attain the same high standard. Therefore the equipment was to be redesigned completely, and three machines of this new type were to be installed by 1950.[49] It was operational by November 1949.

By this time the new art of kinescope recording, as it was now called, was becoming a major part of the television industry in the United States. An article by Robert M. Fraser of NBC in June 1948 stated "that a method of permanently recording the otherwise transient video signal was desirable in the advancement of the television art." With the rapid growth of television in the USA in the late 1940s, the need for program material to fill expanding schedules was tremendous. As in radio, the big production centers were in New York, Chicago, and Los Angeles. Since the United States was divided into four different time zones, showing the same program at the same time across the country presented a major problem. In radio, this was done, especially during daylight-saving time, by means of transcriptions on 16-inch acetate discs. This was quite an expensive process.

In the spring of 1948, the ABC Radio Network set up an ABC tape recording central in Chicago and installed ten magnetic audio recorders. Four were Stancil Hoffmans and six were Ampex Electric. This was the start of magnetic recording for delay and other uses. It was claimed that more network stations were fed from the delayed net than the regular net during the limited use of daylight-saving time.[50] It wasn't long before the other major networks followed suit.

By this time it was abundantly clear that even though television was basically a "live" medium, there were many reasons to preserve the pictures in a manner similar to sound recordings. A memory was essential.

The introduction of the image orthicon tube by RCA in 1946 had changed the look of the television image. The viewing public was seeing a new "different" kind of image from anything they had seen before. Its image was *striking*, with many features that "indicated" that what viewers were seeing was being done at the moment. This gave rise to a theory of "immediacy." (Immediacy is defined as "an immediate presence of an object or knowledge to the mind without any distortions, inferences or interpretation, and without involvement of any intermediate agencies." *Random House Dictionary*, p. 956.) It was associated with the image and sound of the event that was being presented on the screen.[51]

This was especially true in news reporting and sporting events. The grainy background, the halos around objects, the edge enhancement that produced a "sharpness of image," and the steadiness of the raster and the detail contrast ratio (that passes the fine detail right up to the bandwidth cutoff point) compared well to 35mm film. Television, with its superior resolving power that presented the high-frequency details at a low contrast ratio, thus giving a greater proportion of detail at high-contrast than 35mm motion picture film, and with its accompanying live high-fidelity FM sound, gave clues that this was not a filmed presentation.[52]

This was in contrast to the film offerings that were mainly 16 mm with their inherent jump and weave projected onto an iconoscope film camera that was lower in both contrast and detail and replete with shading problems. Also the poor quality of the 16mm sound track left much to be desired.

According to one authority (Goldsmith), "Essentially, television offered an extension of the human senses beyond the normal limitation of horizon, opaque obstacles, and materials which absorb or deflect sound. In doing so, it provides four important factors of information: (1) sound; (2) sight, at present in monochrome, later in color; (3) motion; and (4) immediacy. Thus, any sound

may be heard at a distance; the source of that sound and the surroundings may be viewed; the motion of persons or objects in the viewed scene may be observed; and all of the preceding may be [perceived] by the recipient at the very instant of occurrence."[53]

"It is unnecessary to stress the importance of sight and sound since it is well known that the major portion of available information reaches men through these senses; but it is worth observing that the combination of the two adds more than proportionately to total effective addition. Motion is an interesting and commanding factor in any viewed scene. And the sense of simultaneity (immediacy) experienced in viewing television presentations serves psychologically to bind the members of the audience to the program source in certain events. In horse racing for instance, the element of instantaneous presentation is obviously of outstanding importance."[54]

However, what happened when the program was kinescoped? What happened to the sense of immediacy? Was it still there? The answer is both yes and no. Yes, in that the viewer was watching the later replay of a spontaneous event. Only time had been shifted. No, in the fact that now an intermediate agency was between the scene and the viewer. Also the image was being altered by the same iconoscope film cameras used for regular film and much of the "live" look had been dissipated.

As a result, the first 16mm "kines" (short for kinescope recording) were no match for the live presentation. The replaying of a horse race, for example, had lost something. Now there was a layer between the viewer and the event. It was similar to motion picture film. No one ever saw a live film event. The film had to be processed first. Nonetheless, even with intermediate film systems, such as Paramount was promoting, viewers still enjoyed the production of events on a large screen. This, of course, was true with electronic large-screen projections which were done on the spot instantaneously.

There were several reasons for the choice of 16mm film for Kinescope recording rather than 35mm. The main reason was that the cost of 35mm was somewhat more than three times that of 16mm for the same period of recording. The quality of television images in 1948, which experts knew would undergo gradual refinement, was considered to be roughly equivalent to 16mm home movies, although actually somewhat better with reference to contrast and detail. No marked improvement, however, was to be had by recording on 35mm rather than 16mm at that time. With the use of fine grain high resolution 16mm film emulsions, no loss of resolution in recording the television image was noticeable.

In addition, fire regulations covering the use of 35mm film, which applied regardless of whether the film had the acetate safety base or the combustible nitrate base,

1947. Television recording camera with 12,000-foot magazine used by Paramount Pictures Corp. (Paramount Pictures.)

35mm film was installed, so in order to forestall trouble, all equipment had to be single-purpose 16mm equipment rather than dual purpose 35mm/16mm equipment.

Another factor in the choice of 16mm film at the time was the high cost of 35mm projection equipment. Most television stations were providing projection facilities only for 16mm film for this reason. In order to service these stations with syndicated programs photographed from the kinescope, 16mm prints would be needed.[55] This did not remain true for long, however.

In the spring of 1948 the ongoing battle between CBS and RCA entered a new arena. CBS announced the introduction of a new phonograph recording process. This was the long-playing record developed by Dr. Peter Goldmark. Until this time the standard 78 rpm record was used by millions of listeners. There had been several attempts in the past to produce a record running at 33⅓, but none had succeeded. While CBS had lost to RCA in the opening round of the color contest (on March 18, 1947, the FCC had turned down CBS's application for its color system), it did have an outstanding victory over RCA with the long-playing record.

In this period all manufacturers turned out records that played at 78 revolutions per minute, which allowed approximately eight minutes per side on a 12-inch disc. While this served adequately for popular music, it meant that an opera might require as many as half a dozen discs, with the listener subjected to pauses while changes were being made.

In the 1930s, RCA Victor had experimented with other speeds, most significantly 33⅓ rpm, and from 1933 to 1937 actually produced several discs for sale on adapted phonographs, but the line was discontinued because of public apathy. Next the firm experimented with another speed, 45 rpm, the idea being to record a single popular tune on each side of a seven-inch disc, and work on this system continued sporadically during and immediately after the war.

By 1948, RCA Victor had developed a 45 rpm record and player, known within the company as "Madame X," that could have been introduced at almost any time. The 45s were considered an addition to the line, and not a replacement for the 78s. Ever the one to milk a product and hold back replacements for as long as possible to extract the last drop of profits, Sarnoff saw no reason to go any further than the research and development stage. In 1938, CBS had purchased the Columbia Phonograph Company. Paley had visions of emulating the RCA organization by entering production. Just as Sarnoff had turned the trick by acquiring Victor, so Paley would do the same with a smaller, albeit respected operation. But Victor Red Seal remained the leading and most prestigious label, especially in classical music.

were rigorous. The cost of providing space that met these regulations for the use of 35mm was extremely high, and the changes needed in existing space were difficult to accomplish. Sixteen-millimeter films were available only with the acetate safety base that was classified by the Underwriter Laboratories as having a safety factor slightly higher than that of newsprint. The uses of 16mm films, therefore, was not restricted by fire regulations. It should be noted that in New York City these restrictions applied to space in which equipment capable of operating with

Now CBS had developed its own version of the 33⅓, known as the "long-playing" (LP) record, under the guidance of Goldmark, which Paley felt would revolutionize the industry. Not only might one record over half an hour on a single side, but CBS had perfected a new plastic, vinylite, which, unlike the standard shellac, was unbreakable and offered better tonal fidelity. Paley worked out an arrangement with Philco in which that company would produce LP phonographs, some of which would be sold under the CBS label. There was also some consideration of a merger between the two firms.

He then approached Sarnoff, demonstrated the new records to him and offered a license, which was rejected. Since RCA was a much bigger company than CBS (1948 revenues of $357 million versus $70 million), Sarnoff must have felt capable of crushing the LP with his own version. He told his staff to ready Madame X for the market. In order to make it appear novel, Sarnoff had them retool the 45 so as to have a larger hole for the spindle, which would require it to be played on a special phonograph, and the phonographs were rushed to the stores to compete with the Philco and CBS machines.

It was a case of too little, too late. Almost overnight Columbia won over devotees of classical music who had no trouble recognizing the advantages of the LPs. Within months the powerful National Association of Music Dealers voted to support the LP system, while Decca, London, and Mercury records went over to that speed, leaving RCA with a sole ally, Capitol, that had always emphasized popular recordings. Attempting to salvage something out of this debacle, RCA countered with a rebate scheme tied to a $2 million advertising campaign, but to no avail. It seemed nothing could stop the 33⅓, or help the 45s.

By 1949, phonograph companies were putting out new models that could play all three speeds. (The plastic disc that one had to insert in the larger 45 rpm hole complicated the matter.) Columbia record sales soared, while RCA's languished. Realizing that unless drastic action were taken he might lose the classical market altogether, Sarnoff hinted that RCA might abandon the 45 rpm field. But he would not turn out 33⅓s of his own. RCA still controlled most of the major classical artists. If the public wanted to hear them, they would have to purchase 78s or 45s. This was Sarnoff's last desperate gamble in the struggle with CBS.

He could not hold out indefinitely. Many RCA artists were unhappy with the 45s, especially when their CBS counterparts were outselling them. According to one source, Toscanini convinced Sarnoff that he would have to go over to the 33⅓s after hearing a Bruno Walter CBS recording. Reluctantly the general gave in. While the company remained wedded to the 45s for some of its popular songs, it soon after started recording in the 33⅓ mode, conceding to Columbia a major victory.[56] Goldmark was elated.[57]

On July 1, 1948, the *New York Times* reported that the Bell Telephone Labs had invented an electronic device to replace the vacuum tube. They reported that Walter Brattain and John Bardeen working with Dr William Shockley had built the first practical transistor in December 1947.[58]

The new device, operating on an entirely new principle and capable of many of the functions of the electronic vacuum tube, but having neither an evacuated envelope nor a hot cathode, was announced early in July. Known as a transistor — TRANS(fer-re)SISTOR — the device was essentially a triode form of the well-known germanium crystal diode. In its then experimental form, the transistor was a metal cylinder, $\frac{3}{16}$ of an inch in diameter and $\frac{5}{8}$ of an inch long. Inside the cylinder was a block of germanium soldered to a metal disc, the disc made a low-resistance contact with the germanium and grounded it to the cylinder. Two 2mm tungsten wires make contact with the upper face of the germanium at points about 0.002 inch apart.

An input signal, in series with a small positive bias voltage, was applied between the grounded face and the input cat whisker (emitter). A large negative bias voltage was applied between the ground and the output (collector) point contact. The output signal appeared across a load resistor in series with the negative bias. In this manner a power gain of 100 (20 db) was obtained between the input and output of a transistor. The early unit had a gain of about 15 db. This of course was the world-shaking invention that would change the face of electronics forever.[59]

On June 13, 1948, the navy revealed a highly secret shark-shaped jet-propelled flying bomb, known as the "Gorgon," capable of seeking out targets with unerring accuracy with television eyes. It was developed by the navy and RCA. It had a speed of 550 miles per hour and could carry from 100 to several thousand pounds of explosives. A television camera of the BLOCK airborne system was packed in its plastic nose and reproduced the pictures on a monitor screen of the same type carried in a plane by the bombardier who directed the flying bombs to the target. The bomb was produced in quantity during the war by RCA Victor, Camden, New Jersey.[60] At the present time, however, I can't find any evidence of its use.

It was reported that in June 1948, a novel motion picture camera called the "Cyclops" was in use in the Denham Studios in London. This was the first film camera in history that had a built-in electronic viewfinder. It was an ordinary 35mm film camera in conjunction with an electrical viewfinder in which a split optical system enabled the director to view the scene being shot through the lens of the camera while the camera carried out its

—Experimental Cyclop camera.

1948. The first tv/film camera combination. Experimental Cyclops camera used at Denham Studios. It used CINTEL experimental equipment of 600 lines at 50 pictures sequential scanning and incorporated a three-inch image orthicon camera tube adapted to both higher line and frame frequencies. (IEE, London.)

recording function in the usual way. This was the first application of direct television—"electronic viewing" in which the cameraman saw the same image that the film was recording.

This camera was essentially an ordinary 35mm film camera. It had a special optical system with a beam splitter for both the film and the television pickup tube. It used a three-inch image orthicon camera tube. The only electrical circuits in the camera proper were the essential deflecting and focusing coils and head amplifier. Everything else was removed to a "camera feed box" at the foot of the camera and connected between the camera and the camera control. The electronic picture was instantly visible at the rear of the camera on a small monitor screen. Next to it was an ordinary optical viewfinder. The actual performance of this novel camera was not discussed at the time.[61] It was claimed that the camera was actually used in the Denham studios in London in June 1948. This original combination of film and television was the forefather of all future film cameras using an electronic viewfinder, or as it is now called *video assist*.[62]

Yet some 11 years later (in October 1957) it was revealed for the first time by a foremost authority that the camera was actually used at closed-circuit film studio experiments using CINTEL experimental equipment of 600

lines at 50 pictures sequential scanning. It used a three-inch image orthicon camera tube adapted to both higher line and frame frequencies. Video bandwidth was up to 5 mc/s. The recorder used an experimental medium-fast pulldown 35mm camera constructed from a "mitcheldean" process projector with 90° shutter at 25 pictures per second, 450 lines recorded sequentially. Trials were made of various emulsions.[63]

In October 1948, an international congress on the relations between television and the cinema was held in Paris. The chief subject was television; a new frontier that lent itself to discussion more readily than the moving picture art (cinema) in which everything was already standardized. The advantages of the television camera over the film camera were discussed: (1) the high sensitivity), (2) an electronic viewfinder, (3) control over the image electrically, and (4) the use of multiple cameras. These qualities of television, it was said, had given rise to the belief that in the future the television camera would be substituted for the standard motion picture camera then being used.[64]

Surprising as it seems, this was by then an old idea. For instance, as I pointed out in my 1955 book *Electronic Motion Pictures* (University of California Press, Berkeley), as far back as 1946, "with the end of World War II and the start of commercial television film recording, it is small wonder that some far-sighted men envisioned the possibilities of combining the flexibility of the electronic camera with the permanency of motion picture film, not just for making records or transcriptions of a television program but for the primary purpose of making a motion picture."[65]

In September 1946, Allen B. DuMont wrote one of the first articles that mentioned the possibility of making motion pictures by means of electronic cameras. The DuMont Laboratories had been experimenting for a long time with television film recorders, among other devices. DuMont said, "Movies are the permanent record. Television is the more advanced way of getting the picture. As time goes on, the pictorial quality of televised images will steadily improve until it is on a par with motion picture film. Television-film recording will then be fully feasible, with television cameras transferring their images to a central control room where the director and his technicians will select the choicest scenes and actions for recording."[66]

By the middle of 1947, the British had also seen the advantages of this new method for making motion pictures. An article by Marcus Cooper predicted that the television camera would be used to make motion picture films, "On the floor our present cameras may be replaced by television cameras which transmit the picture to a monitor room where the director can see and hear the action on a screen while rehearsing or taking, and to a picture recording room where the television image is photographed by special motion picture cameras."[67]

The idea caught on slowly and in May 1948, another British article stated that when a suitable high-definition system was perfected, the director "can sit in the control room and direct not only the camera operation but also the cuts, dissolves, wipes, and fades that separate and link his shots and sequences."

It also stated that the picture could have retakes if necessary, which meant taking advantage of editing. This was an important point since many people at that time were under the impression that the ordinary film recording was "a continuous motion picture completely cut and edited." Although there was a certain amount of cutting (in its elemental sense) from one camera to another, full advantage of the editing principle was not and could not be realized in a "straight" film recording.

From a filmic viewpoint, a straight (unedited, exactly as photographed from the monitor screen) film recording leaves much to be desired. It possesses the physical characteristics of motion picture film but lacks the inherent capabilities of the true motion picture because it is restricted by the limitations of live television technique. Other articles were soon to appear regarding this revolutionary idea.[68]

In July/August 1948, the Olympic Games were held in London, the first since the 1936 games in Berlin. England had suffered severely after the war and was still enduring tremendously hard times in recovering. It was hoped that by having the Olympic Games in London it would help the economy. The Olympic Games of 1948 (only the second to be held in Britain, 40 years after the first, and in this case postponed from before the war) certainly made a great advance in outside broadcasting. Technically it was far superior to the 1936 Olympic Games held 12 years earlier in Berlin. Everything from the live coverage to the use of multiple facilities was done in modern style. There were 80,000 receivers in use in addition to the receiving equipment installed in the centers, camps, embassies and legations.[69]

Norman Collins, originally head of the light programmes, had succeeded Maurice Gorham early in 1948 as controller of the BBC. His first year proved to be one of special significance for it included the televising of the Olympic Games. The coverage of the 1948 Olympic Games, the fourteenth Olympiad, planned and executed by Orr-Ewing, Dorte, and Dimmock (who had joined the Corporation in May 1946), in cooperation with T. C. MacNamara, head of the planning and installation department, and Birkinshaw, captured public interest in television and that of the press to a hitherto unprecedented extent.

Sir Arthur Elvin, the managing director of Wembley Stadium, where the games were held, lent the BBC the old Palace of Arts, constructed for the British Empire Exhibition of 1924, to serve as a broadcasting center with eight radio studios and 32 channels. There were 15 commentary boxes and 16 open positions in the stadium and 16 commentary points at the Empire Pool.

There were also multiple television facilities and a coaxial cable was installed between Wembley and Broadcasting House. It was recognized long before the facilities were made ready that there would be ample scope for special programming. They prepared to break into afternoon programs where possible for peak events adding "that all the main events were to be scheduled and that there were to be trailers."

To make such large-scale broadcasting possible, both staff and equipment from the regions were mobilized earlier in London. The title of the daily program was "Olympic Sports-Reel 4" and a fourth camera was used overlooking "Olympic Way" to catch pictures of the crowds as well as that of the contestants. There were two mobile units controlled from a radio center in the Palace of Arts: one unit in Wembley Stadium itself, the other at the Pool. Each commanded three cameras, with producers watching events on monitoring screens and drawing on the stories of a dozen commentators. As many as 70 hours of television programs were prepared in 15 days— on one particular day, seven hours 35 minutes.

BBC television broke all records during the Olympic Games in the greatest fortnight in its history. From 2:45 P.M. on July 29, 1948, when the Emitron cameras first opened up on Wembley Stadium, until the evening of August 14, the total time expended on television outside broadcasts was 68 hours 29 minutes, or an average of nearly five hours a day. This was in addition to regular transmissions.[70] Outside broadcasting output was twice that originally intended. Norman Collins was inspired to cable New York to ask whether it was a world record as well as a BBC record. He was notified that NBC and CBS had only exceeded this daily average at the American political conventions.

The games were covered by the latest CPS Emitron cameras that could operate successfully even at sunset and were developed at EMI between 1946 and 1948. These new cameras made it possible at last to cover events at comparatively short notice. They now had a three-lens turret and an electronic viewfinder. It was claimed that the quality was excellent. It was also claimed that the cameras gave a much better picture, richer, clearer, devoid of smears, and, perhaps most importantly of all, had for the first time a useful degree of depth and focus— a quality which enables the viewer to see both the foreground and the background equally clearly. Previously the foreground had been clearly defined but the background was

1948. CPS Emitron cameras at the Olympic Games. (RTVS.)

a mere blur. This work was stimulated in the BBC by T. C. MacNamara, in charge of television engineering planning.[71]

The games had England overflowing with overseas visitors. Here was a wonderful opportunity of proving to the world that Great Britain still led in television development. The radio industry was not slow in seizing the opportunity as well.

It was claimed that the number of receivers in the London area had increased from 14,550 in 1946 to 66,000 by December 1948.[72] Technically it was a triumph of old and new. One mobile unit used for outdoor track events at the stadium had not been used since 1936; the other was entirely new. The presentation of these games was an artistic as well as a technical triumph and was much in keeping with the original spirit of the BBC television service.

In Zurich, a demonstration of the new Eidophor projector of the Swiss Institute of Zurich was given, September 5–10, 1948. It was claimed that the pictures, on 723 lines, were excellent.[73]

On October 3, 1948, the FCC announced a freeze on new television stations. The freeze, or temporary halt, only applied to pending applications, about 302 in all. It did not affect the 37 stations then on the air, or the 86 in various stages of construction. Two issues to be resolved were (1) interfer-

ence between stations and (2) the total number of stations that could be fitted in the then existing channels.[74]

CBS announced that a new television recording plant was being placed in operation during the week of November 18, 1948, in New York City. CBS was using the double system with a separate soundtrack in order to get better sound quality. A similar plant was to be opened later in Hollywood, California.[75] Thus CBS was finally to be the last of the major networks (NBC and DuMont) to install a permanent TV, or kinescope, recording process. In December 1948, DuMont introduced a new DuMont TA-124 image orthicon chain.

At the end of 1948 the three major networks in the United States, CBS, DuMont, and NBC, were making television film recordings of a great many of their programs. Ralph Little, supervisor of theatre TV engineering at RCA Victor, claimed in May 1949, "that over a quarter million feet of film are being used each week in New York City alone to record programs."[76] Thus a new kinescope film network rose to supplement the existing coaxial cable and the microwave networks. It lasted until the completion of a radio-relay link in September 1951.[77]

In January 1949, General Electric announced a new 16mm TV pulsed light projector. With a pulldown time of less than 7 milliseconds, the projector was synchronized with the vertical pulse from the sync generator

1949. Television film recording. NBC installation in New York.

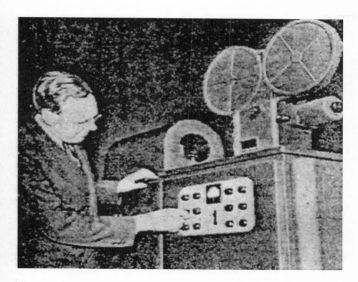

1949. Television film recording. Ralph Little with the RCA Kinephoto system. (RCA.)

and no special intermittent, as required for 35mm projectors. Later (April 1949) another article about this projector claimed that 16mm pictures had become the backbone of most TV station layouts. Sixteen millimeter film consisting of features, newsreels and commercials accounted for a large part of the program time, and for those stations without direct network facilities, video transcriptions on 16mm film had become one of the major program sources. It stated "that in a recent survey, about 50 percent of the program time was accounted for by film transmissions."[78]

In March 1949, it was announced that the Eiffel Tower television transmitter was on the air some 12 hours per week with programming composed mainly of movies. It was estimated that fewer than 5,000 receivers were in use at that moment. The video frequencies came from the Alfred Lelluch Center (named after a brilliant radio engi-

neer) who distinguished himself in the Resistance and was killed by the Germans. The standard was 455 lines at 25 frames/sec. It was anticipated that a new standard of 819 lines would be adopted in early 1950. However, the then standard was to continue until at least January 1958.[79]

In May 1949, Marconi's Wireless Telegraph Co. introduced their first image orthicon camera. With a 5655 image orthicon tube, it seemed to be an exact copy of the RCA image orthicon camera with a four-lens turret and an electronic viewfinder. This was to be expected because of the close ties between RCA and Marconi.

Tremendous progress was made in all branches of BBC television in 1949. In February, on the technical side, a new outside broadcast unit with Pye Photicons was brought into commission at the Albert Hall. The zoom lens was also introduced. In March, the London County Council, the city's governing body, agreed to the BBC developing the White City site as a television center. The Oxford and Cambridge Boat Race was televised for the first time from a launch, and telerecording began. In March 1949, the BBC introduced a new mobile control truck designed by Pye Ltd. The camera was called the Photicon and was an image iconoscope also made by Pye Ltd.[80] The new cameras made it possible at last to cover events at comparatively short notice.

In October 1949, the color situation in the United States was somewhat obscured by a prehearing confusion that produced garbled reports of the various systems, and rendered difficult, or impossible, the task of providing an accurate assessment of them. At that time, the following organizations had been asked by the FCC for information concerning their investigations: CBS, GE, DuMont, Philco, Westinghouse, Color Television Inc., Thomascolor Corp., RCA, and Dr. Charles Willard Geer of the University of Southern California who had applied for a patent on a color TV tube.[81]

1949. *Left:* Marconi image orthicon camera. (Marconi.) *Middle:* Pye Photicon Camera. (Pye Ltd.) *Right:* DuMont Type TA-124 image orthicon camera. (DuMont Labs.)

CBS, of course the top contender, described its standard mechanical color system. It was still displaying the best color pictures seen at the time. However, on August 25, 1949, the earliest release about a new RCA color development had been made by Dr. C. B. Jolliffe, executive vice president of RCA Laboratories Division. He described what was said to be a completely compatible all-electronic color system and called it a dot-sequential method with line and picture dot interlace. Time multiplex transmission was used with bandwidth of 4mH for full modulation. The color camera at the transmitting end produced three signals—green, red and blue. These signals were sampled electronically in rapid sequence, combined, and broadcast as a single signal.

At the receiver, separation was performed so that the signal representing each color went to an electron tube which produced a picture in that particular color. The green, red and blue signals were applied to their individual kinescopes. The three colors were then projected simultaneously and produced the complete full-color picture.

The RCA color television system was perfected in the laboratories in Princeton under the direction of Ray Kell. He was developing this system with the aid of such outstanding television engineers as G. C. Sziklai, K. R. Wendt, G. L. Fredendall, Randall Ballard, A. C. Schroeder, Alda Bedford and others. It was claimed that this new system would fit into the existing 525 line, 60 field, black-and-white scanning standards. It was a breakthrough of immense proportions.

It was called a "dot-sequential" system because a series of dots in primary colors appeared along each scanning line. Three sets of dots were interspersed in sequence along each line so that the color sequence rate was three times 3.8mc, or 11,400,000 cps. This did two things: it permitted more information to be sent by time-multiplex pulse transmission, and it permitted the use of a second form of interlace ("dot-interlace") which permitted the effective picture rate to be halved without incurring the flicker problem. Dot interlace added to line interlace, permitted the field rate of 60 to be retained, while the color picture rate was lowered to 15 per second. The low picture rate allowed a high degree of resolution to be retained in the color images, while the field rate of 60 insured that the large-area flicker performance was the same as that on the black-and-white system.

The three color images from the camera contained video frequencies up to 4mc. The components above 2mc of all three outputs were combined at once in an adder and the bandpass filter following it. This combined signal represented the fine detail in tones of gray in the manner of the mixed-highs technique developed for the simultaneous system. The components below 2mc retained separate identities and provided the color information. These latter components were commutated sequentially in a sampler circuit which was essentially a three-pole electronic switch rotating at 3.8mc. The electronic switch produced a succession of narrow pulses (color pulses), which were passed through a 4mc low pass filter. This converted the color pulses into 3.8mc sine waves whose amplitudes followed the changes in the respective color signals as the scanning proceeded. The three sine waves were in a three-phase relationship and could be combined vectorally into a single 3.8mc sine wave, and this carried the information on the signals of the three colors in separable form. The combined 3.8mc signal, the "mixed highs" signal and the sync pulses became the composite video signal. It was similar to a black-and-white signal except it had a strong 3.8mc component that carried the color information, including the dc components and video components up to 2mc. This signal was sent to the transmitter.

At the receiver, the information of each color was separated in time sequence from the composite 3.8mc sine wave. The "mixed highs" signal passed by the sampler switch that did not contribute to the color information, but did reproduce the fine detail. The separated color pulses were passed by the switch to three separate video amplifiers, which passed all components up to 4mc but cut off sharply at 7.6mc (the second harmonic of the 3.8mc signal). The positive half-cycles of each sinewave produce colored dots on the screen and the negative signals produced dark spots. Every scanning line was rescanned 30 times a second so the line was filled up with the two sets of dots at a rate half as great, and this rate applied equally to all three images. All points were scanned in red, blue and green at a color picture rate of 15 per second. These might be displayed on any device which presented the three colors in registration.[82]

Another system was proposed by Color Television Inc. of San Francisco. It was described before the FCC in September 1948, by its chief engineer, G. E. Sleeper, Jr. The main features of the system were the use of stationary filters in conjunction with a three lens optical system at the camera and receiver. Standard black-and-white equipment was modified in one major aspect—the horizontal scanning frequency was only one third of normal frequency, since each scanning line traversed three edge-to-edge fields in succession. Such a change was a simple one. Three equally spaced synchronizing pulses applied during the interval of one horizontal scan, were arranged to lock into operation so that each color was flashed at the correct time. At the receiver, superposing lenses were used to register three images, each through a different primary color in a single cathode ray projection tube, on a projection screen. The pictures showed up as black-and-white

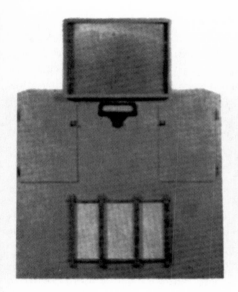

1950. Three RCA experimental color receivers. *Left:* projection with 15- by 20-inch picture. *Middle:* reflective optics and magnifying glass and direct view. *Right:* Direct view with digest chroic mirrors. (RCA.)

on an ordinary receiver, without difficulties. Horizontal linearity had to be precisely attained, however.

The camera system consisted of a standard black-and-white image orthicon camera with a multiple image lens and filter system. It had three 16mm motion picture types of lenses side by side with centers spaced approximately a half inch apart. A light-splitting lens using dichroic mirrors could be used as well. The three optical images were focused side by side and scanned as though they were a single image. The video signals generated were transmitted in the normal manner to a standard black-and-white amplifier and mixing equipment. At the receiver it was claimed that a single projection tube would combine the three images with a minimum of registration problems.

Another system somewhat similar to that of Color Television Inc., was the one based on the well-known ThomasColor method of making color films. A special optical unit designed by Richard Thomas utilized prisms to split the light from the scene into three rays. Each ray passed through its own lens and red, green or blue color filters. The three rays then fell upon one frame of standard motion picture negative film, recording upon it three discrete images. Two of these were placed side by side within the 35mm frame and the third occupied a position below them. The density of each image, when developed, depended upon the intensity of the light passing through the color filter associated with that image. Positive prints from such a negative would be made on ordinary black-and-white stock. There was no color associated with the film itself.

Upon projection, three images per frame were available and each of these, after passing through its correct color filter, entered the Thomas projection lens. The lens not only projected the images on the screen in the usual manner, but provided the mechanical adjustment to allow the three projected images to be superimposed accurately, giving motion pictures in natural color.

For television, Thomascolor, Inc., suggested using the special lens system placed in front of the camera tube in a simultaneous TV system and in front of a single (not a 3-unit) projection tube at the receiver. This meant, of course, that the tubes just mentioned, instead of carrying a single large picture, had three smaller pictures, each of which bore less than one third of the picture information contained in a single normal picture.

Dr. Willard Geer of the Department of Physics at the University of Southern California claimed patents for a system utilizing a special receiving tube for direct viewing. The screen was serrated in such a manner that while all three facets were visible to the viewer, only one was exposed to each of the three guns. One gun was used for each color — red, blue and green. The appropriate color signal was fed to each gun and excited its associated screen at the proper time. The colors blended and formed a picture in full color which could be viewed on a direct vision screen. It was claimed that this was very similar to the tube Baird exhibited in 1944 during the war. Baird's tube, however, was never demonstrated.[83]

At that moment there had been no new information given to the FCC by either GE, DuMont, Westinghouse, or Philco.

In September 1949, the A. B. DuMont labs introduced a new flying slide scanner. It used a ten-inch short persistence cathode ray tube. It had provision for 25 2 × 2 slides, automatic fade to black, gamma corrector and polarity inverter. "It was for slides only."[84]

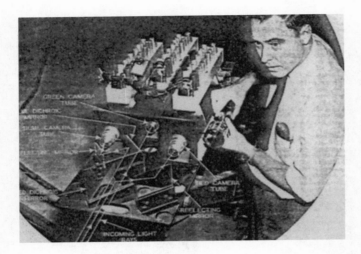

1949. *Above:* Three-tube RCA color camera. *Below:* Three-quarter shot of RCA three-tube color camera. (RCA.)

RCA introduced the 5820 image orthicon on September 26, 1949.[85] It used a new photocathode, or oxygen-treated silver-bismuth-cesium, surface. This had the response most similar to that of the human eye.[86] This tube devised for studio use became the most popular image orthicon tube yet introduced. It was used in about 90 percent of the studio installations throughout the United States as it was well-suited for outdoor remotes as well. It had a better gray scale and more "snap." Halos were almost gone, flesh tones were better and even though it had better resolution, it presented a milder, less harsh picture.[87]

In September 1949, RCA announced a new type of image orthicon. It was called the Image Isocon. It was basically the same as the image orthicon except that the return beam was treated differently. The beam was intercepted by an electrode so as to cause the electron beam to be out of focus. As the element became more positively charged, the larger became the current reaching the multiplier. It had excellent response at low levels, but under high lighting levels, the signal to noise ratio was so low that the picture was undesirable for entertainment purposes. It could have had applications where high picture quality was not a requirement.[88]

The next step in the FCC color hearings, after the completion of direct testimony, was two-day comparative demonstrations held November 21–22, 1949, in Washington, D.C. The color systems of CBS and RCA were shown beside black-and-white pictures produced on Du-Mont equipment. The purpose was to allow the commissioners to make a side-by-side comparison, under home conditions, of these systems. Color Television Inc. of San Francisco was not there, but would have their apparatus ready for demonstration in February 1950.

Chapter 3

The Second NTSC and Color
(1950–1953)

January 1950 started out with quite a prophetic article by Howard Chinn, chief engineer of CBS, who stated his objections to the then current method of kinescope recording. Chinn, who was in charge of the technical installations at CBS stations, was especially concerned with the mounting costs of the new kinescope recordings. The amount of film used every week was enormous. He was quoted as stating, "The television film transcription is a very complicated device for storing a video signal. It involves transferring the signal to a phosphor image, to a negative film image, to a positive film image, to a mosaic image, and back to the video waveform. There are too many electrical, chemical and optical processes involved, too many potential sources of distortion. And the TV transcriptions of the day show it." So, asked Chinn, "why not store the video signal on magnetic tape? Suppose you divide the video band of 4mc up into eight adjacent 0.5 mc bands. Suppose you work up the tape speed so signals could be accommodated and record parallel tracks on an extra-wide tape. The modulating, recording and demodulating equipment is not beyond attainment. Such a scheme would use up a lot of tape, but it might well be worth it, especially since the tape could be erased and reused almost indefinitely." Chinn, for his own part, admitted that "no originality is claimed."[1] It wasn't long before several companies started work on projects involving these principles.

Plans for the formation of a new NTSC (National Television System Committee)[2] to deal with the problems attaining industrywide agreement on technical developments which would bring color television to reality were announced on January 21, 1950.[3] These plans were confirmed in the March 1950 issue of *Radio and TV News* (p. 18).[4] Dr. W. G. R. Baker was named chairman. Assisting him would be Donald Fink, editor of *Electronics*, and David B. Smith of the Philco Corp. The second NTSC committee met formally on November 20, 1950. An ad hoc committee with E. W. Engstrom (RCA) as chairman, D. B. Smith (Philco), T. T. Goldsmith Jr. (DuMont), A. V. Loughren (Hazeltine) and R. M. Bowie (Sylvania) was set up to study compatible systems and to draw up broad standards on which field tests might be based.[5]

A very complete report of a February 8, 1950, demonstration revealed the following information. At the studio, NBC's Wardman Park Hotel station, WNBW, was opened to competitors and three cameras were set up (CBS, RCA and DuMont) to view each scene. RCA's color signals were transmitted on channel 4 from WNBW; CBS's signal was relayed to WOIC and radiated on channel 9; a relay link transmitted the signals from the DuMont camera to WTTG, operating on channel 5.[6] The latter station also broadcasted the sound accompanying the pictures. Duplicate prints of the same motion picture were used for film portions of the test.

At the receiving location on the roof of the government building in which the receivers were located, standard TV receiving antennas were erected connected to the respective receivers. The signals on all three channels were of good strength, well above the noise level. Receivers, three to a room, were placed in three medium-sized rooms into which about 45 persons, some seated, some standing, could be crowded.

Three separate rooms were provided for the demonstrations. In room 1, CBS pictures were magnified to appear as a 16-inch direct view RCA direct view (dichroic mirror type); DuMont 15" picture receiver. In room 2, RCA was the same as above, and a CBS 12" receiver; DuMont 12½ inch set. In room 3, was a CBS color converter attached to a ten-inch standard black-and-white receiver; and an RCA standard black-and-white picture 12" size to show the compatibility of the RCA color system with the then existing present standard.

The FCC commissioners, and other observers, were divided into groups and spent some time in each of the three rooms. Through the facilities of AT&T it was possible to switch either the CBS or RCA color signals through either the coaxial cable passing frequencies up to 2.8mc or through a radio relay passing 4.0mc. The effect of using the latter was not noticeable on either system but the coaxial cable removed all of the color from RCA's signal because it suppressed the 3.8mc "commutator" sync signal. The only effect of the 2.8mc cutoff on the CBS picture was a slight reduction in resolution.

The program material to be used was discussed in preliminary meetings of a committee composed of representatives of the principals in the hearing. The advice of the majority, however, was overruled by the representative of the FCC, who was chairman. The result was a long-drawn-out program. Instead of being of a type that could be observed and accurately recorded by technical observers, it was made up of average broadcast subjects. From this, only subjective impressions, difficult to record and easily forgotten, resulted.

The following illustrates the subject material presented: commercial objects such as canned goods, acts in a variety show, puppets, short play, film, slides, women's program. Each of the three companies engaged in these tests supplied portions of the material used.

In the comparison of monochrome and color, the DuMont equipment produced unusually sharp pictures, which in the case of the majority, gave the viewer as much, and often more, information than either of the color pictures. It appears in TV, as in the movies, that color is not necessary as a steady diet for entertainment. However, some scenes are meaningless without color; for instance, a flower garden.

On the other hand, many scenes that had but little contrast in monochrome were clearly and beautifully reproduced in color. However, it did not follow that color made up for the loss of definition if the information that the TV picture was to convey was contained in the moderately fine detail of the original picture; nor that contrast due to colors in the picture made up for a lack of brightness of the reproduced image.

Concerning definition, it was understood that the RCA equipment had made refinements at both the studio and receiving ends after the October demonstrations.

Projected pictures were not shown at the comparative demonstration so registration problems were reduced. The definition had been increased so that 325 lines from the resolution chart could be read. This was about the same as that obtainable from the standard monochrome system. The CBS resolution remained at 180–190 lines.

Finally as to color fidelity, in comparison with that shown by RCA, the color fidelity of the CBS system was rated "excellent." There was still something to be desired along this line, however, for the faces of the Negro choir shown on the CBS receiver appeared yellow.

In the case of RCA, the color fidelity was very poor. A purplish tint covered the entire picture for long periods of time. There were no good reds and browns were missing. The RCA engineers constantly tried to adjust the colors but the trouble, which was never explained, went deeper than this. Pure whites were a difficult test that could not be met. Large background areas of one color were often contaminated. RCA said they needed several more months to make desirable improvements, so it was hoped for a better color fidelity at the next comparative demonstration scheduled for February 23, 24, 1950.[7] RCA's demonstration showed that while its system had tremendous possibilities, it was not quite ready to come out of the laboratory.

In February 1950, the BBC acquired the film studios at Lime Grove, Shepherds Bush, which opened in November 1950.[8] Then on December 17, BBC television opened the installation at Sutton Coldfield.[9]

On February 12, 1950, the European Broadcast Union (EBU) was formed. Twenty-three broadcasting organizations around Europe and the Mediterranean put their signatures on a document ending the prewar (1925) International Broadcast Union, which had fallen into disarray following the postwar problems and the changes in Europe's political structure. Its aim was to promote cooperation between organizations of the entire world and to represent member's interests in the program, legal, technical and other fields.[10]

A year later, for all the successes, it was a rare O.B. when as many as eight cameras (including lightweight cameras produced by Pye Ltd.) could be used to televise the Boat Race, supplemented by an independent crew installed on a moving launch to provide closeup pictures. For the first time viewers could see the whole race, Bridge to Mortlake. The televising of the 1950 race by outside broadcast in the country was an enlargement of that of 1949. This program was "telerecorded" and was shown in the evening as well as the afternoon.[11]

In the midst of the color race between CBS and RCA, RCA introduced another of its engineering achievements at the March 7, 1950, IRE Convention.[12] This was the radical new Vidicon photo-conductive camera tube. This new tube was only one inch in diameter and six inches long. Up till now all camera tubes used photo emissive layers to produce their signal. In addition to its small size, it had neither an image section nor an electron multiplier. Yet it was sensitive enough that it could be used at normal lighting levels. Its resolution was claimed to be up to 500 lines. It was a low velocity orthicon type tube that used a special photoconducting surface to produce the video signal.[13]

According to Weimer, et al., work done during the war on infrared detectors focused attention on the basic advantages of photoconductivity. It was well known that the light sensitivity of photoconductive cells greatly exceeded that of photoemissive cells, which may have 50 micro-amperes per lumen while photoconductive cells have tens of thousands of micro-amperes per lumen. The earliest goal was to design a tube that (1) operated at lower light levels, (2) eliminated both the image section and the electron multiplier, and (3) scaled down all tube dimensions. Work had progressed during the prior several years. High-sensitivity materials for targets were found and many experimental photoconductive tubes had been tested.

The earliest photoconductive targets were those having *blocking* contact to the signal plate, amorphous selenium, and those having *ohmic* contact such as antimony tri-sulfides (Sb_2S_3).[14] The one shown at the IRE was in an advanced stage of experimental development.[15]

The Vidicon photoconductive pickup tube more closely resembled the orthicon (or iconoscope) in its operation, except that charge was transported away from the target surface by photoconductivity instead of photoemission. Like with the first-mentioned photoconductive pickup tube, the photoconductive material was formed as a thin layer on a conducting semitransparent plate. In this instance, material with a very high specific resistivity in darkness was employed. Normally, where the target was one or two microns thick, the resistance back to front needed to be at least 10^7 or 10^8 ohms per square centimeter. For an orthicontype of operation, the conducting plate

was made slightly positive with respect to the gun cathode. In darkness the scanning beam drove the surface to cathode potential. As soon as the beam left an element, the dark current

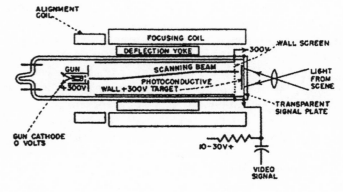

1950. *Above:* RCA experimental Vidicon camera and monitor. *Below:* Diagram of Vidicon tube. (RCA.)

flowing from the conducting plate to the surface charged it slightly. However, owing to the high dark resistance, the amount of charge accumulated during a frame period was small. Where illumination fell upon an element, the photocurrent flowing from the conducting plate to the surface was greater so that the charge accumulated was greater. The amount of current taken from the beam (i.e., not returned to the collector or multiplier) is therefore greater for the illuminated area than for the dark regions. Since the accumulated charge was proportional to the photoconductive current, which was, in turn, proportional to the illumination, the video signal had a one-to-one correspondence with the light image on the target.

The Vidicon owed its high sensitivity to the fact that photoconductive films can be given quantum efficiencies (ratios of numbers of electrons transferred to number of light quanta or photons incident on the target) close to unity, whereas photoemissive targets rarely attain quantum efficiencies exceeding one fifth.[16] Many materials may be used for photoconducting targets of the second type: amorphous selenium, Sb_2S_3, Cd_2S_3, Cd_2Se_3, and composite layers of these materials are examples. The factors which govern the selection are photoconductive efficiency, spectral response, time lag, and stability, assuming that the dark resistance of the material is suitable. It might be noted that many of these materials require a rather elaborate activation treatment.

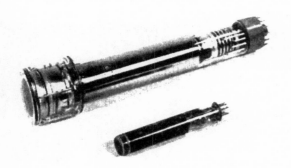

1950. Experimental one-inch Vidicon with standard image orthicon. (RCA.)

There are many more desirable features of photo-conductive pickup tubes. It is possible to build into the material a gain mechanism which gives a multiplication of ten or 100 or even 1,000 times. This plays the same role as image multiplication. The targets take full advantage of the storage principle. Operated as an orthicon target, they lend themselves to the use of a secondary-emission multiplier. Finally, the construction of a photoconductive pickup tube is very simple and rugged.[17]

"In practical photoconductive pickup tubes it has been possible to achieve sensitivities approaching that of the image orthicon. Such tubes perform satisfactorily in a wide range of applications. The Vidicon is a photoconductive pickup tube that approaches the ultimate in simplicity. It consists only of a photoconductive target on the glass end of the tube and an electron gun at the other. It is only 1 inch in diameter and ¼ inches long. In spite of its small size and simplicity, it has sufficient sensitivity to give an excellent picture in a normally lighted room. For a small compact unit, such as is needed for industrial television, the tube is almost ideal. A slight lag at low levels of illumination has been the major obstacle to its use as a general-purpose tube for broadcasting at this time [1950]."[18]

With the introduction of the image orthicon tube in new Marconi Company cameras, it was announced in May 1950 that the image orthicon tube was being manufactured by the English Electric Valve Company at Chelmsford.[19] Pye Ltd. was still building image Iconoscopes and EMI, the CPS Emitron.

Meanwhile in the color race, RCA now had another new innovation in store for the industry. It appears that according to Brown[20] the FCC got its first private look at the new tricolor tube on March 23, 1950. On March 29, 1950, at a press showing in Washington, the culmination of many months of research, experimentation and development was seen in the form of color pictures on the first RCA tricolor picture tubes. In previous demonstrations of the dot interlace color system, RCA had used huge receivers containing three individual cathode ray tubes having screens emitting red, green and blue light respectively. The three images were combined and superimposed by means of dichroic mirrors to secure a picture in color. Such a bulky layout, with its inherent registration problems, had been rendered obsolete by the new tricolor tube.[21]

For years the need for such a tube — for a simplified color TV receiver — had been evident. At least three TV tube laboratories other than RCA had been working on this difficult problem. Philco spent years in pursuit of what they called an "Apple" tube. While others also occupied themselves with versions of a proposal by E. O. Lawrence, (E. O. Lawrence; USA Pat no. 2,711,493; applied

1950. Harold B. Law, E. W. Herold and Russell Law with the first RCA tri-color tube. (RCA.)

29 June 1951; issued 11 June 1955) and another by Willard Geer. Leslie Jesty at Marconi Laboratories in England was trying to make a tube work with colored lines.

Credit for this RCA development goes to the scientists comprising the teams cooperating in the work at Lancaster and Princeton under the leadership of Dr. Engstrom.

It seems that the RCA laboratory group under Ray Kell had been thinking about a single-color reproducer for several years. Al Schroeder filed for a patent on this idea on February 24, 1947. However, it wasn't until September 19, 1949, that Engstrom explained to Edward W. Herold the need for such a device if the RCA color system was to be successful. Herold was promised as much manpower as available and no restriction on funds, as well as wide authority. The next day a confidential report "A Survey of Proposals for Single Tubes for Colored Television" by Dr. Albert Rose was circulated and discussed. As a result, five separate and different approaches were decided upon and the teams began 16-hour days to solve the problem.

Schroeder's shadow mask approach seemed the most promising. It was made practical when Harold Law invented the so-called "lighthouse" to permit the use of photographic and lithographic processes to locate the dots in correct position behind the mask. A small seven-inch tube was built and in three months a large staff working seven days a

1950. Early 15-inch color kinescope. (RCA.)

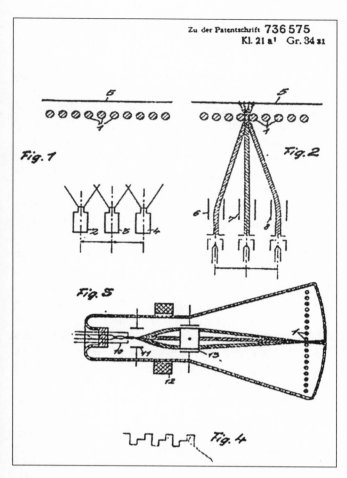

Zu der Patentschrift **736 575**
Kl. 21 a¹   Gr. 34 ₃₁

Fig. 1

Fig. 2

Fig. 3

Fig. 4

Original patent of Dr. Werner Flechig/Fernseh for tri-color tube. Files July 12, 1938, issued May 13, 1943. (US Patent Office.)

week produced a dozen or so 12-inch tubes. Two different shadow mask picture tubes were constructed: one with three electron beams and another with a single switched beam.[22]

These were the two tubes demonstrated to Commissioners Coy,[23] Hennock and Hyde who came that same evening to view RCA's latest electronic marvel. On the next day, a demonstration was given for over 50 patent licensees of RCA. The press had a field day. The official demonstration for the FCC record took place the following Thursday, April 6, 1950, at which time RCA introduced the new tricolor tube in Washington.[24] RCA also demonstrated their method of transmitting the RCA color signal over the narrow-band coaxial cable. (Another similar demonstration was given to the press and FCC on April 26).[25]

Before an audience of about 100 engineers, assembled in one of the unused studios of station WRC, were placed a monochrome table model TV receiver, a single-gun tricolor tube set and a three-gun tricolor tube receiver. A color program staged and broadcast from WNBW about two-miles away was received on those sets on Channel 4.

The crisp black-and-white picture showed that the RCA color system was 100 percent compatible and that black-and-white receivers in the hands of the public would continue to give good pictures with no alteration, when this system of color was being broadcast.

The picture in color on the receiver having the single-gun tube was very good, better than previous RCA color pictures seen in the several demonstrations that had punctuated the FCC color hearings. The colors were judged true to life, and there was no flicker, color breakup, or fringing. Although close viewing was not possible, from a distance of 25 feet the detail appeared adequate.

In the case of the receiver with the three-gun tube, the picture had all the attributes just described except it was noticeably brighter (18 kV as against 10 kV on the second anode of the tube) and color contamination was absent.

In terms of illumination, a loss of about 40 percent occurred in the red filter, caused by the low efficiency red phosphor then available. Thus the light measured was about 7 footlamberts for the three-gun and 4 footlamberts for the one-gun tube. Standard black-and-white sets had a brilliancy of around 30 footlamberts. Thus, the system suffered from low light output and very faint reds.

The direct-view color screen was composed of an orderly array of small, closely spaced phosphor dots arranged in triangular groups, each group comprising a green-emitting dot, a red-emitting dot and a blue-emitting dot. In the laboratory sample tubes used in the demonstrations there were 351,000 such dots, 117,000 of each color. The screen was viewed in the same manner as for a conventional black-and-white kinescope.

The manner in which the screen produced a color picture was best understood by considering first the operation of the three-gun tricolor kinescope. An apertured mask was interposed between the three guns and the dot phosphor screens in such a manner that the electrons from any one gun could strike only a single color phosphor no matter which part of the raster was scanned. The mask consisted of a sheet of metal spaced from the phosphor screen and containing 117,000 holes, or one hole for each of the tricolor-dot groups. The hole was so registered with its associated dot group that the difference in the approach angle of the three beams determined the color. The three color signals applied to the three guns produced independent pictures in the three primary colors, the pictures appearing to be superimposed because of the close spacing of the phosphor dots.

In so far as the color aspect is concerned, this three-gun tricolor kinescope could have been utilized in a receiver in much the same manner as three single-color kinescopes, except, of course, that no optical superposing or registration means needed to be provided and deflection power must only be provided for one deflection yoke.

One of the research types of receivers demonstrated employed the three-gun tricolor kinescope and high leveling sampling. This receiver utilized 46 tubes and consisted essentially of a 27 tube black-and-white receiver to which had been added 19 tubes for color synchronization, sampling and additional power supplies. Only minor refinements now were required to render the tube commercially available.[26]

The development of a successful color kinescope in a six-month period was a triumph seldom equaled in industrial research. Sarnoff set forth his plan of counterattack. He received the board of director's endorsement, as he knew he would. In prior actions, the board had approved more than $20 million for color development and field-testing expenditures. They could hardly turn their back on an investment of that magnitude now, any more than Sarnoff could. That would have been tantamount to confessing a massive error in business judgment, perhaps opening the door to shareholder suits charging waste of corporate assets.

As a first counterattack step, Sarnoff mobilized the Princeton laboratories for a crash color development program. Shifts would be increased to 16 hours daily, continuing through the weekends. No expense would be spared for personnel and equipment, and projects unrelated to color would be temporarily shelved. Bonuses in the thousands of dollars would be paid for significant technological breakthroughs. He was determined to get color of perfect fidelity, and not years hence, for now he was battling time as much as CBS. He designated Elmer W. Engstrom, then the corporation's vice-president in charge of research, to conduct the program. Engstrom, who had guided the RCA television program since 1932, possessed the unruffled type of scientific temperament that effectively interposed between the fiery importuning of General Sarnoff and the sensitivities of the research staff. Later he would describe the crash color program as the most intense, and exhilarating, experience of his career.[27]

To inspire his technical team, Sarnoff circulated an extract of testimony by Goldmark before the FCC in which he argued against further field tests of the RCA system because "I don't think the field tests will improve [the] system fundamentally." In the CBS scientist's view, "nothing" could be done to alter that fact. Asked by a commissioner if he advocated that RCA drop the system now, Goldmark responded: "I certainly do."[28]

The RCA team's ultimate success was the result of having an outstanding mix of research people of many disciplines: electrical and mechanical engineers, chemists, physicists, mathematicians, metallurgists, all who were used to working together on impossible tasks, free of red tape and budget worries. Ed Herold had not only organized the work program at RCA Laboratories but had called on the resources of engineering laboratories of RCA in Camden, Harrison and Lancaster as well as those of other companies with special skills.

There has been much heated discussion as to how Sarnoff achieved this magnificent task. It was all his doing, some say: he ordered, challenged, cajoled and offred huge monetary rewards as incentives. While this is true, actually the engineers of RCA were challenged by what seemed to be a formidable task and by the fact that so many experts said it couldn't be done. CBS statements alternated between saying that the shadow mask tricolor kinescope could not really be made to work satisfactorily, and that when it was perfected it would be useful for the CBS system.

The color kinescope developed was still far from satisfactory. In this developmental tube, a planar shadow mask and a flat phosphor-plate assembly were mounted in the bulb interior as a unit, yielding a picture nine by 12 inches a few inches behind the bulb face plate. In addition, it suffered from low light output and very faint reds. This planar or flat-mask type of construction had major disadvantages with respect to size, cost and shape. While great strides were made in the next few years to reduce the cost and improve the performance, the bottleneck was not broken until 1953.

RCA's success in achieving a tricolor kinescope spurred others to search for a better solution. Philco spent years in pursuit of what they called an "Apple" tube, while others occupied themselves with versions of a proposal by E. O. Lawrence and another by Willard Geer. Leslie Jesty at Marconi Laboratories and later at Thorn in England gave years of his life trying to make a tube work with lines of color phosphors. William Paley later stated (in 1953), "that our efforts to develop a color system pushed RCA into developing their system in a crash program, which brought color television to the consumer long before it otherwise would have been on the market."[29]

On March 28, 1950, New York's Paramount Theatre was host to European executives and technicians for a showing of a television program on the theatre screen.[30] On April 29, in England a large-screen demonstration of the Football Association Cup final was made to members of the CCIR (International Radio Consultative Committee) at the Odeon Theatre, Penge.[31]

An interesting effort at large-screen television was made in October 1950 in Paris. This was described by Paul Mandel on August 24, 1951, at the fifth session of the 1951 Radio Convention at the Cavendish Laboratory, Cambridge. His paper described a system of presenting large-screen television pictures for large audiences. Basically it was an intermediate film system based on the French standard of 819 lines. The source (35mm film) was scanned by a flying-spot scanner. The video signal was carried from the scanner by a UHF broadband relay system, and the picture was displayed by a high-voltage cathode ray tube. Here it was photographed by a synchronously driven camera with no loss of frames. Low-grain, highly sensitive 16mm film was used for recording. The exposed film ran continuously through the developing, fixing and drying apparatus, and after a 65 second delay, fed a motion-picture projector with a high-powered arc lamp.

It was claimed that the complete apparatus was first tested during the second "Salon de Cinéma" in Paris from October 5th to 20th, 1950. It was used for about two hours in connection with outdoor pickup TV equipment during the exposition. In December it was installed at the Cinéma Madeleine in Paris. Pickups were made from the Gaumont Palace where a mobile TV pickup unit was installed, and the signal was transmitted by microwave relay. It was also used in the studios of La Radiofusion Française, and the picture radiated from the Eiffel Tower transmitter. There were plans to guide further development of this work.[32]

This was really a complicated method of getting large-screen pictures in a theater. Paramount Pictures had been using similar intermediate-film apparatus in New York City for several years. The costs of the film and the processing were quite high. The use of a pure electronic system using cathode ray tubes and the new Eidophor machine had more promise. While an interesting experiment, however, no more was heard of the French system.

It seems that the introduction of television in theaters was not going well. It had been expected that this alliance between television and the movies would be of some benefit to the motion-picture industry. In brutal fact, television was devastating the motion-picture industry. Attendance at the local movie houses had fallen off precipitously, down some 11 million by 1952.[33] Employment in the industry was down 25 percent. Since 1946, box office revenue had dropped from $1.7 billion to $1.3 billion in 1950. Several thousand marginal theaters closed and entire studios shut down. The whole industry boiled in ferment of uncertainty and doubt.[34] The industry was already reeling from the effect of the 1948 Paramount Studios antitrust ruling that separated the studios from their wholly owned theater chains. The instantaneous feature of television was also fatal to the newsreels. An era had ended. The old studio system was dead and would never be revived.

The motion-picture industry tried new innovations such as Cinerama and "3-D" to revive flagging interest. Wide-screen 2–1 ratios and multiple soundtracks were introduced. But it was found out that a good film would survive without all these gimmicks. One result was the rise in so-called adult films dealing with the realities of human experience. They included films with "shocking" language, perverse violence and frankly sexual themes.[35] Strangely enough the salvation for the old studios was to start turning out programs for the little screen. In addition, at this time, the studios opened their vaults and found they had a gold mine in old, discarded movies.[36]

In July 1950, a new Vidicam system was announced by Television Features and was a direct application of the RCA Vidicon tube. It used a new and unique camera chain unit control, with the monitoring done off the set in the directors' booth. The TV cameras were synchronized with specially designed 35mm or 16mm film cameras, with the three cameras acting simultaneously in perfect unity.[37]

In July 1950, an experimental tricolor picture tube was described by the Rauland Corp. of Chicago. It claimed that it was using the French Patent no. 866,065 issued June 16, 1943, (the convention date was July 11, 1938). This, of course, was actually the patent of Dr. Werner Fleschig's invention for Fernseh. GmbH.[38]

An article appeared in *Tele Tech* in August 1950 in which the recording of both CBS and RCA color was described. This was "Video Recording in Color" by W. R. Fraser and G. J. Badgley. It stated that CBS field sequential color was first recorded by using a Berndt Maurer with a 25mm f1.4 Cine Ektar lens and daylight type Kodachrome. Later a Mitchell "16" with an f0.7 lens and then a Special Navy Type C 16mm with a Cine Ektar f1.4 lens were used. The first recording of the RCA "dot sequential" color system was made on March 10, 1950. A new Badgley camera with an f0.7 lens permitted this to be made at 24 f/sec.[39]

In August 1950, Hazeltine stated that they had made a great improvement in the dot sequential system. They were using a new sampling technique involving a constant luminance treatment. Brown reported that Hazeltine had been rephrasing the mixed-highs principle. The Hazeltine engineers had extended it to time changes and found it to be equally effective. In the RCA signal, they had formed the brightness signal by using equal electrical signals from each of the three camera tubes to yield a white signal. The Hazeltine proposal was to proportion the brightness signal in relation to the luminosity properties of the phosphors used in the display device of the receiver, so that interfering signals from external sources or from internally generated interference might produce effects on the display device of varying hues, but all stay of equal brightness or luminance. Thus the final picture was greatly improved over the arrangement RCA had been using. This principle was achieved by proportioning the brightness signal in a manner different from the way RCA had been doing. When the final standards were adopted

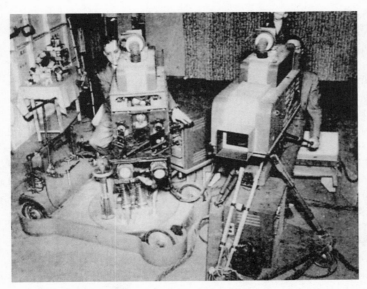

1950. Two experimental RCA color cameras in use in Washington, D.C. (RCA.)

by the FCC, the white signal was so proportioned that the green signal was 59 percent of the total signal, red was 30 percent and blue 11 percent.

The Hazeltine effort was under the supervision of Arthur V. Loughren, vice president of the company, and Charles J. Hirsch, chief engineer of the research division. They credited Bernard D. Loughlin with the ideas behind bypassed brightness and constant luminance, but it was obvious that there was also a very able assemblage of engineers in support positions.[40]

The Washington test before the FCC in September 1950 was a disaster for RCA.[41] It was reported that their color was approximately equal to the resolution of black-and-white. However, it was the uneven color balance that seemed to upset the fidelity somewhat.[42] It was reported that "RCA's electronic device acted like a crazed 'Van Gough,' [sic] it took the color of the wrestlers and spread it across the bodies and the gymnasium wall. *The monkeys were green, the bananas were blue and everybody had a good laugh.*"[43] A bowl of fresh fruit contained "green cherries and blue bananas."[44] It suffered from low light output and very faint reds. Daily Variety stated that "RCA Lays Colored Egg."[45] As usual, the CBS color system behaved beautifully and never looked so good.

It was reported that on March 13, 1950, the FCC Chairman Edwin Johnson had witnessed a successful demonstration of the Color Television , Inc (CTI) system. He stated that the system had improved remarkably since its previous showings.[46] However, a demonstration on May 17, 1950, in San Francisco of the CTI system was quite disappointing. In August 1950, CTI announced the abandonment of this system and was dismissed from the running.[47]

The FCC issued a document on September 1, 1950, stating that the CBS system would be selected because neither the line sequential system (CTI) nor the dot sequential system of RCA met the FCC criteria.[48] Chairman Wayne Coy admitted that the CBS system was not compatible. Some changes must be made in existing receivers in order to enable them to receive a black-and-white picture from CBS color broadcasts.

However, the Commission unanimously found that the CTI and RCA color systems were not suitable for adoption. "I am not going to attempt to restate in detail at this time all of the reasons we set forth in the report for arriving at this determination. However, I shall mention two of the fundamental defects. In the first place, the Commission found that the quality of the color picture produced by the two systems was not at all satisfactory. In the case of the CTI system there is a serious line crawl or jitter, and in the case of the RCA system, there is a prominent dot structure and a marked loss of contrast. Moreover, the colors are not true in either system. This is particularly true of flesh tones. At none of the demonstrations did CTI or RCA correctly reproduce flesh tones. Since the purpose of the hearing was to pick a color television system, it is obvious that no serious consideration could be given to a system that failed to present true colors.

"In the second place, the equipment required for the CTI or RCA system appears too complex for normal use. This is true both for receivers in the home and studio equipment at the station. At the outset of its conclusions the Commission stated that a color system adopted to produce a satisfactory color picture must be an apparatus that is simple to operate in the home, and is cheap enough to be purchased by the great mass of the American people.

"Third, at all of the demonstrations CTI and RCA trained operators who worked before each demonstration to make sure that the equipment was adjusted and in tip-top shape hovered over the equipment during each demonstration continuously making adjustments to obtain optimum performance. Despite all of their efforts, neither RCA nor CTI were unable to maintain accurate registration and color control at the demonstrations."

The commission was forced to conclude that no successful compatible color system had been demonstrated. Since existing receivers could be adapted to receive black-and-white pictures from CBS color transmissions at a reasonable price, the Commission felt that it was not fair to deprive 40,000,000 American families of the opportunity to have color simply because the owners of 7,000,000 or 8,000,000 sets might have to spend some money in adapting their present receivers.

"If adequate assurances are forthcoming from the

1951. CBS color receiver using CBS color system, (CBS.)

1951. Experimental RCA color cameras used at Radio City, Studio SH. (RCA.)

manufacturers that 'bracket standards' will be incorporated in receivers," the commission concluded, "we will postpone a color decision and look into the developments I have already referred to. If we do not receive such assurances, we will adopt a final decision and designate the CBS system as the standard color system."[49]

This report was greeted with widespread and great resentment, and it was immediately rejected by most of the radio manufacturers.[50] One important issue was "bracket standards" whereby each set could receive both television systems. The industry objected to having a receiver with a switch (one for color and the other for black-and-white). While the industry was not too fond of RCA, it was felt that the dot sequential system would produce better performance than the field sequential system which the FCC itself had described as incompatible.[51]

When the industry turned down the FCC findings, the commission adopted the CBS color system on October 18, 1950, but stated that it would have preferred a compatible system. The FCC authorized CBS to start color broadcasts on Nov 20, 1950.[52] On December 6, 1950, RCA demonstrated its improved color system,[53] but this was too late to change the FCC decision.

On October 17, 1950, RCA took the FCC to court in Chicago and lost. Later it took the commission to the U.S. Supreme Court, which ruled on May 28, 1951, that the FCC order was valid. Therefore, the FCC order became effective and after several delays, on June 25, 1951, regular color broadcasts were initiated in New York by CBS.[54]

The first CBS colorcast was a half-hour show featuring many of CBS's radio stars. It was planned to present two shows a day: one at 10:30 and another at 4:30. But they did not have sufficient studio equipment, nor were there any receivers in the hands of the public. (Even CBS executives and Peter Goldmark had no way of seeing the telecast.) So it was an exercise in futility. A Pyrrhic

victory for Peter Goldmark and an embarrassment to William Paley.

CBS got out of this predicament because of the war in Korea. On October 19, 1950, Charles E. Wilson of the

1951. RCA monochrome camera converted for CBS color with turret removed and added color disk in place. (CBS.)

1951 (June 25). First CBS color program from New York, featuring Robert Alda (right) and an unidentified actress. (CBS.)

Office of Defense Mobilization requested that all manufacture of color receivers be stopped to assist in the war effort. CBS stated that on October 19, 1951, in view of the insufficient numbers of receivers, all color telecasting would be discontinued.[55] However, Dr. Stanton stated that CBS Columbia Inc. would continue the manufacture of black-and-white television sets.[56] CBS also continued using the field sequential system for industrial uses and later space satellite color transmissions.

At this time, Paley had decided to go into the business of making television sets. Late in 1950, he started looking for a likely purchase. He decided on the Hytron Radio and Electronics Corporation of Salem, Massachusetts. Hytron was one of the oldest manufacturers of radio and TV sets and the fourth-largest in sales. On June 15, 1951, it was purchased for about $18 million in stock. It included the subsidiary Air King Products of Brooklyn, New York. For the first time in its history, CBS was manufacturing hardware.[57]

This purchase gave one more victory for CBS in the color television race. In 1953, two research scientists, Norman Fyler and W. E. Rowe, employed by (now) CBS-Hytron, in Newburyport, Massachusetts, announced the development of a method of applying the phosphor dots directly on the curved internal faceplate of the tube together with a curved shadow mask mounted directly on the faceplate.

The resulting picture was very pleasing, large tubes with large pictures became possible, and the manufacturing cost was sharply reduced. Within the year, the new tube was announced, on October 5, 1953.[58] On November 30, 1953, RCA negotiated with CBS to obtain a license

for the technology under the appropriate CBS patents for a sum somewhat less than $1 million dollars. This development by CBS immediately made possible the application of the phosphors by means of a photosensitive binder, an invention made by Dr. Harold Law at RCA Laboratories in 1948. Not needed until the CBS breakthrough, it was quickly put into use and a wholly different series of mass-produced color kinescopes appeared on the scene.

On Thursday March 22, 1951, RCA introduced a new eight-pound portable camera and a 53-pound backpack-transmitter, all battery operated. The combination was introduced by Dr. Zworykin who declared that, "'greatly refined' represents what the future may be like for rapid-fire newspaper photographic recording."[59] This was the first portable camera in television history.

On June 19, 1951, Dr. Engstrom, vice president in charge of research for RCA Laboratories, displayed a 21-inch tricolor tube. There was no demonstration of this tube, but Engstrom stated that samples of the 16-inch picture tubes and all technical information on it and the 21-inch would be distributed to all RCA licensees at no cost.[60]

1952. *Above:* Portable Vidicon camera. *Below:* Vidicon camera with lens and viewfinder. (RCA.)

1953. *Above:* Backpack transmitter using detached viewfinder. *Below:* Vidicon camera and detached viewfinder. (RCA.)

In July 1951, an article by E. A. Hungerford, Jr. appeared called, "Techniques for the Production of Electronic Motion Pictures." This was the first time the concept of making motion pictures electronically had appeared in an American technical journal. Hungerford of General Precision Laboratories related the many advantages of shooting "films" more quickly and economically using high-quality television techniques. He envisaged the major studios using these techniques for theater television first, and then the major networks also using them. He claimed the techniques created a new and tremendous market.[61]

In August 1951, it was reported that the NTSC had released an "ad hoc" committee report announcing that

it had reorganized nine new panels.[62] The ad hoc report outlined a broad new framework of a new composite system of color television. Dr. Engstrom of RCA had been appointed as an additional vice-chairman by Dr. Baker. There were to be a series of color tests on August 6 through August 10 at various laboratories.[63]

1951. Elmer Engstrom with 16-inch tricolor tube. (RCA.)

The result was that after a series of demonstrations at laboratories of G.E. at Syracuse on August 6, Hazeltine on August 7, RCA at Princeton on August 9, and Philco Philadelphia on August 10, the panels reached an agreement on signal specifications to be tested in the field and released their findings on November 26, 1951.[64]

On September 4, 1951, the transcontinental television radio relay link was completed. It was now possible to transmit "live" pictures from New York City to San Francisco. It was used initially for the transmission of scenes from the Japanese Peace Treaty Conference in San Francisco. Officially opened on September 28, 1951, it comprised 107 radio-relay stations. The overall length was 2,992 miles, with the distance between stations from 19 to 50 miles.[65]

In September 1951, the General Precision Laboratories, Inc. of Pleasantville, NY, introduced their new image orthicon camera. It was claimed that it could be used on both 525 lines at 60 cycles, or on 625 lines at 50 cycles (for future European use), or both. It did not use regular 35mm lenses, but specially designed lenses for TV containing built in iris diaphragms on each lens mounting.[66]

The first specialized television exhibition in the world was held in Paris at the Musée des Travaux Publiques from September 28th to October 1, 1951, under the name "Premier Salon de la Télévision." It met with great success and on the weekends, the crowds of visitors were such that the organizers had to limit the number of admissions. The possibility of prolonging the exhibition for a few days was considered, but other arrangements had been made and it proved impossible.

The organizers were the Télévision Française authorities and the Syndicat National de la Construction Radioélectrique. Excluding the press, there were 23 exhibitors. Three of them were aerial makers, two were valve and c.r.t. manufacturers, and the remaining 18 were television set makers. The Télévision Française had made a big effort and put up a complete studio comprising a semicircular stage, about 21 yards in diameter, surrounded by 800 seats for the public. Four dual-standard cameras (441/819 lines) were in use and the scene was lit by projectors with a total power consumption of 300kw. The "live" cameras were supplemented by films run from a film-scanner, which could be seen by the visitors through a 'glass panel. Program material, either direct or from films, was available to the exhibitors continuously from opening till closing time.

The VHF signals originating in the salon were sent by coaxial cable to outside-broadcasting vans packed in the street and thence by a 30cm microwave link to the studios of the Télévision Française. There they were demodulated, controlled and amplified, then sent to the Eiffel Tower transmitters through the usual coaxial cable. Depending on the standard in use, they went either to the old 441-line transmitter at the foot of the tower and by coaxial cable to the aerials on top (46 mc/s vision), or to the new 819-line transmitter on the fourth floor of the tower and by a very short coaxial link to the four-bay turnstile aerial (185.25 mc/s vision). The accompanying sound was radiated on 42 mc/s for the 414 lines and on 174.l mc/s for the 819 lines.

Thus in both cases the programs were received at the salon in the usual way through the standard transmitters, and the televisors were shown under actual working conditions. The three aerial makers exhibiting had supplied and installed on the roof of the building the necessary banks of aerials for both of the standards, and the signal was distributed to theater stands by ordinary coaxial feeders, altogether 81 different receivers were shown. They were made by Sonora, Ducreter-Thomson, Ariane, Philips and Radiola.[67]

A demonstration of a new version of the tricolor picture tube of Professor E. O. Lawrence of the University of California was given to the press on September 21, 1951, at the laboratories of Paramount Television Productions. It was stated that the cellular structure of the older Lawrence tube had been replaced by a linear arrangement of phosphor strips and wires. It was noted that the vertical line structure was prominent. However, the color values were not equal to either the CBS or RCA systems. It was planned to continue the development at the Chromatic Television Laboratories in Stamford, Conn.[68] It was claimed that the tube was handbuilt in Lawrence's garage and made from the parts of other tubes.[69]

On October 2, 1951, television broadcasting in Holland began. Transmission was a remote on a 625 standard to the transmitter at Lopik. There were transmissions twice a week, on Tuesday and Friday evenings. The transmissions were also relayed by a second unit to the

1951. *Above:* Prof. Ernest O. Lawrence and home-built tricolor tube. (*Tele-Tech.*) *Right:* Proposed model of Lawrence's new tube. (*Electronics.*)

Philips transmitter in Eindhoven. There were four types of receivers in use: three built by Philips— a nine inch, a 12 inch and a projection type of 17 inches— and another by Erres with a 12-inch screen. Due to high costs, most viewing was done in restaurants and cafés.[70]

At this time in 1951 it was reported that some *550 million feet of film* would be required each year for television recording in the USA. NBC was shipping some 44 hours of kinescope each week and CBS some 42 hours. Each of these networks rushed out about 1,000 separate film prints each week.[71] Most of this was being done in New York by NBC, CBS, ABC and DuMont. Even though the bulk of this was 16mm, the costs of film processing and machinery was enormous and the method wasteful. While it solved the problems of television delay for a variety of purposes, it was a cumbersome, time-consuming, expensive system. It was evident that a more efficient, less costly system of television recording was needed.

Oddly enough, the completion of the transcontinental relay system in September 1951 had not lessened the need for kinescope recording. In fact, it had increased it. The big problem in the United States was that the country spanned four major time zones. All three networks (DuMont was lagging in this process) desired to maintain a uniform program schedule. While the networks were willing to allow for the difference of one hour between New York and Chicago, the three-hour difference between New York and Los Angeles was formidable. NBC, CBS and DuMont (DuMont had only four stations) had their main recording facilities in New York. ABC had decided to use Chicago. Soon both NBC and CBS were also recording their delayed broadcasts in Hollywood.

Thus began what was to be called the "Hot Kine Era." Started in 1952, this "hot kine" system was continuously improved. The biggest change was the use of 35mm film to get better quality. As a result, only the East Coast ever saw all major "live" shows, and the Midwest and, especially, the West Coast always saw an inferior kine recording.[72]

About this time, "live" production was slowly moving to the West Coast. Both NBC and CBS had set up elaborate kinescope recording operations in Hollywood. Both were recording their main shows in 35mm to get the best quality. But this was not good enough. Even though this was done under almost laboratory conditions, there were too many factors involved in the kine process. The image orthicon cameras at the time were still marginal; while quite sensitive, they had several major faults. They were "noisy," had an exaggerated gray scale and suffered from bad halo effects. These were exaggerated in the film-recording process and the end result left much to be desired. Yet they were the only way at the time to preserve a television program for future use.

Both NBC and CBS-Hollywood were making the finest 35mm kine recordings at the time. So when a new CBS show starring Lucille Ball and Desi Arnaz was proposed, it was planned to use the "live" facilities of CBS on Sunset Boulevard to do their show. CBS was already involved in such three-camera shows as "The Frank Sinatra Show," "The Al Pierce Show," and "The Alan Young Show." These of course were done live at 5:00 and seen "live" in New York. Three hours later the kine was shown in Los Angeles and on the West Coast. Other included a "Jack Benny Show" special and "Life with Father."

It was planned to do the new "Lucille Ball Show" the same way, "live," in the same studio. A trial program was shot at Studio A at Columbia Square on Sunset Boulevard using a regular CBS three-camera crew. This episode was called "Pepito the Clown." A 35mm kine was made of it, and it is alleged that when Desi saw the result, he was unhappy with the quality. The episode was shot on March 2, 1951, and was claimed to have gone out "live."[73]

1952. NBC, Hollywood Acme 35mm TV recorer. (NBC.)

1952. CBS Hollywood television recording room. (CBS.)

Furthermore, Arnaz saw no reason to do the show "live" as it went on the air. He wanted to film it in the CBS Studios, but due to union requirements, this could not be done. (CBS was using IBEW (International Brotherhood of Electrical Workers) personnel and only a rival union, IATSE (International Alliance of Theatrical Stage Employees), could shoot film, but not on CBS property.) This was the beginning of a long battle by CBS to be able to shoot anything they wanted (film or live television) on their property. Arnaz convinced CBS Television that he could do the show outside CBS Studios (which gave him more control over it) and even made a deal to get the rerun rights for nothing. CBS acquiesced.

Desi Arnaz teamed up with cameraman Karl Freund and they worked out a system for using three conventional film cameras "emulating television technique" that gave them 35mm film quality. So even though the production time and overall costs were much higher, the end result was that the show made a fortune in its many reruns. With its success, the three-camera film process became more popular. It is interesting to speculate how things would have been different if better cameras and the video recording process had been available at the time. We shall never know. At any rate, the first "Lucy Show" premiered "live, even though later episodes were recorded."[74]

Audio magnetic tape had by now taken over the radio industry. Almost all network programs were being taped in advance, saving time and money. The stations were pleased with it as they could redo sections if mistakes were made. The actual physical cutting of magnetic tape made it easy to rearrange or update audio programs. NBC, CBS and ABC had set up elaborate tape rooms in their three main cities, New York, Chicago, and Los Angeles to facilitate this. The days of "live" radio were largely over.

Among the companies making tape recorders was the new Ampex Electric Corp. of Redwood City, California.

By 1950 Ampex had surpassed the older companies such as Studer, RCA, and Fairchild, and dominated the market. Ampex had now become the number-one producer of audio tape recorders for the industry. Their machines were reliable, easy to maintain and achieved excellent audio quality.

While many television researchers turned their attention to magnetic tape, the problems in using it for video were enormous. With a range of 15 to 15,000 cycles, any professional recorder could record and playback audio with a minimum of hiss, noise and distortion. The need for a videotape recorder was a must. But how to do it. The obvious alternative was to record the picture on magnetic tape as was done with audio. However, simply speeding up the machine four or five times only extended the range to about 50,000 or 60,000 cycles—far cry from the necessary 3- to 4-megacycle bandwidth needed to record and play back a video signal. However, the challenge was there and many laboratories started projects to solve this problem.

There were four possible ways to accomplish such a task: (1) the high speed longitudinal (single or multitrack) approach; (2) the longitudinal track, multiplex method whereby the signal was divided among a number of recording heads (Chinn's idea); (3) the use of a rotating head in either an arcuate, transverse or helical manner; and (4) an electronic approach using a cathode ray tube in such a way that as the beam swept across the moving tape, the signal was recorded transversely across it.

The first effort to try to solve this problem was made by John T. Mullin and television project engineer Wayne Johnson who had been associated with Bing Crosby Enterprises in Los Angeles since 1948–49. Working with magnetic sound recording equipment, they altered a standard audio recorder (the Ampex 200) and gave the first demonstration of video signals recorded on magnetic tape on November 11, 1951.

Ampex was well aware of the Mullin (Bing Crosby) project. It has even been claimed that Ampex altered the machine *for* Mullin. The relations between John Mullin and Ampex were quite warm.

In order to get this wide band signal onto magnetic tape, they ran the recorder at high velocity past specially built *stationary* heads. The results were barely visible. According to the *New York Times*, "the equipment was bulky and the audience saw a series of images (with sound) on ordinary plastic sound recording tape. Recorded from a television show, the images were blurred and indistinct, but Mullin stated that they were far enough along to straighten out the snarls. Mullin stated that the tape costs one-tenth of the price of movie film and that both picture and sound can be recorded on the same tape." It was a longitudinal, single-track, high-speed approach.[75]

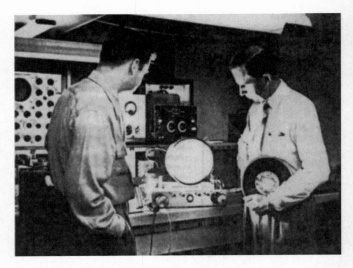

1951. John Mullin (right) and Wayne Johnson with mockup of the first magnetic tape recorder and playback machine. (John Mullin.)

Similar high-speed projects were soon being undertaken by RCA, Webster-Chicago, General Electric, BBC Research Laboratories, Magnecord, Freed Radio; some were under contract from the air force, Signal Corps, and navy to build a wide-band magnetic recorder. Only the Alan Shoup Laboratory in Chicago took a rotating head approach.[76]

Later Mullin used a multitrack, multiplex, high-speed approach that still consumed an enormous amount of tape but gave better results. This was reported by Mullin in a paper presented on Thursday, April 30, 1953.[77]

Some time in October 1951, after several disputes on the question of how television recording could be done on magnetic tape, Poniatoff with Walter Selsted and Myron Stolaroff, his two top technical aides, agreed that a small

1951. DuMont image orthicon camera. DuMont labs.

sum of money be appropriated for the purpose of investigating a rotating-head approach. This was to be used rather than high-speed techniques and time division multiplexing schemes. This had been decided after consulting with Dr. Marvin Camras, the noted audio inventor and pioneer of the Armour Research Foundation of the Illinois Institute of Technology in Chicago, who agreed that a rotary head approach had the most merit to solve the video recording problem. Ampex was a licensee of the Armour Research Foundation.

Early in 1949, Dr. Camras had also turned his attention to the building of such a device. He was among the first to realize that means other than longitudinal recording was necessary to build a practical device. It is claimed that late in 1949, he had put together a mockup of a rotating-head device, arcuate in principle, to see if the idea was feasible. According to Myron Stolaroff, "Camras had decided that the device was impractical and he decided to abandon the idea." But not before Walter Selsted, head engineer of Ampex Corp., visited him in Chicago and heard his ideas about such a device. Being a mechanical

Dr. Marvin Camras and his 1951 mockup of the first rotating head video recorder. (Author's private collection, taken June 12, 1980, Chicago, Ill.

engineer, he realized that the solution had to be solved mechanically with a rotating head. It seems that Selsted had been shown a mockup of a rotary-head device. This would allow them to run two-inch magnetic tape at a normal speed of 15 (30) inches per second. In spite of rumors, it is quite clear that no demonstration was ever actually given by Dr. Camras.[78]

Selsted came back from Chicago and after a meeting with Poniatoff, Stolaroff and other members of the board, decided to see how the concept would work. Stolaroff was so impressed with the idea that he sent a note to product engineering to go ahead with it. His letter was amazing, as he foretold a machine using two-inch tape running at 15 inches per second. He highly recommended the hiring of one Charles Ginsburg who he felt would be a valuable asset to Ampex. In November 1951, the project was started after the letter from Myron Stollarof approved it.[79]

Ginsburg, who at the time was working as a technician at KCBS in San Francisco had become friends with Selsted and when the Ampex project was approved, he hired Ginsburg to head it. Selsted wanted someone who had fresh ideas and was not a "by the book engineer." Ginsburg filled the bill admirably. (Or, as TV historian Wolpin put it, Ginsburg was "an engineer naive enough not to know the impossibility of the job ahead.")[80]

Ginsburg was hired in December 1951 and given a small budget ($14,500) to start the project. The machine was to have three heads mounted on the flat surface of the drum, scanning in arcuate fashion across the surface of two-inch tape. The head to tape speed was to be approximately 2,500 inches/second to allow recording of a 2½ megacycle signal with the tape moving at 30 inches per second.[81]

The first thing that the Ampex patent department did was to research the field. As usual there were a multitude of prior patents for magnetic recording for both audio and video dating back to 1922. There were various methods of rotating the heads to impart the information, such as by helical or transverse means. Now rotating heads were old in the patent process. They had been proposed several times before, including fax machines by Wildhaber in 1929, de Forest in 1931, and Hickman in 1949, to name a few. Of particular interest was one by Luigi Marzocchi (USA no 2,245,286; filed May 26, 1936; issued June 10, 1941), and one by Eduard Schüller of Hamburg (DRP 660,377, filed December 24, 1933; issued May 21, 1938.)[82]

The project had low priority, low funding and low security. In May 1952, work was suspended for three months for Ginsburg to work on a one-of-a kind instrumentation recorder. On this project, he became acquainted with one Ray Milton Dolby, who had no formal engineering training, but whose technical understanding and ingenuity

1952. *Left:* Early three-head arcuate disk. *Right:* Scanning pattern. (Charles P. Ginsburg/Ampex.)

made him a key figure in the program from his first contact with it. Dolby, who was a friend of Poniatoff, started to work in his engineering laboratory while still a senior at high school. He began as a technician and tester in the summer of 1949 on audio projects at the Ampex factory, five hours a day. He graduated high school in the summer of 1951. Dolby was just finishing his first year at San Jose State College when he met Ginsburg in April 1952. Dolby stated that he soon became aware of Ginsburg's work (even though it was supposed to be a secret) by just walking into the lab and asking him, "I understand you are trying to develop a television recorder. What approach are you taking?" With this Ginsburg told him about the project. They worked together on the special audio product and became great friends. When it was over, Dolby officially joined the video project in August 1952.[83]

Dolby was bright, able and cooperative, and he and Ginsburg got along fabulously. Together they built a crude machine and gave a demonstration on November 19, 1952.[84] Another machine was built using four heads, an AM signal system and optical control track, that was demonstrated in March 1953. They had the able assistance of Shelby Henderson who built the mechanical parts, Fred Streib who wired the new tape transport, and Duane McQueen who wound the head cores and assembled the heads themselves. The use of four heads running in arcuate fashion across the moving tape left much to be desired. Even though it had been redesigned, it was not much of a success.

Ginsburg relates this demonstration with a little mirth. He had recorded part of a Western from a local TV station to replay. After calling in Poniatoff and Paul Flehr, the head of the legal firm that did Ampex's patent work, he played this part of the tape. When it was over, Poniatoff clapped his hands, walked over to Ginsburg and with his deep Russian accent said, "Wonderful! Is that the horse or the cowboy?" (Another version told to me was, "Tell me Charles, which is the cowboy and which is the horse?")[85]

Soon after, on March 31, 1953, Dolby was drafted and left the project to the disappointment of coworkers like Ginsburg. Shelby Henderson, George Long, Fred Pfost, Gene West, Fred Streib, Alex Poniatoff, and Walt Selsted.

Remarkably, the project was stopped totally in June[86] as Ginsburg was assigned to other "high priority" programs.[87] It is likely that some in management held very little hope for the VTR project and opted for some more lucrative audio projects.[88] This hiatus lasted until August 1954! Nonetheless, on May 3, 1954, Ampex applied for their first patent on Ginsburg's and Dolby's work. (This was USA no. 2,916,546, filed 3 May 1954; issued May 5, 1955.)

However, Ginsburg told me another story of why the project was actually stopped. It concerned a newly hired supervisor (or consultant) who was assigned to his project. Someone in management decided that the project needed the assistance of an experienced inventor of rotating heads. This appeared to be one Eduard Schüller of Hamburg, Germany. Somehow, he was sent to assist the Ampex program; they were looking for a "German" scientist as Germans supposedly knew everything about magnetic tape recording. Schüller, a German engineer, had invented the enclosed ring head for magnetic recording. In 1938, he had also patented a spinning head audio recorder capable of expanding or compressing sound playback. (E. Schüller, USA Patent no. 2,352,023; filed in Germany August 26, 1938; in the USA August 23, 1939; granted June 20, 1944.) He was soon gotten rid of, however, as he was of no use to the project. To put it bluntly, Ginsburg "couldn't stand him."[89]

Schüller was put in charge of head design of the six-channel Todd-AO magnetic sound project. In addition Ampex decided that he was such a "fine" engineer that he was put in charge of the videotape project. Ginsburg was his only employee! According to Ginsburg, "He was a real turkey!" He complained to Selsted who tried to tell him to hang on for a few more months. But it was more than he could stand. Ginsburg also told me that Schüller insisted on using the helical scan principal rather than the arcuate system that they were already committed to. So he couldn't wait to get rid of him.[90]

So after six weeks of this, in June of 1953, Ginsburg just upped and quit the videotape project and went to work on another assignment. Ampex then got a look at Schüller's head work on the Todd-AO job and fired him on the spot. But the videotape project was now moribund, and Ampex had found more lucrative projects to work on for the next year.[91] This unwanted advisor had resulted in the VTR project being shelved for almost 14 months.[92]

After Schüller left Ampex, he applied for a German patent on a helical scan television magnetic recorder in July 1953. He suggested using 35mm perforated tape running at 0.46 m/sec, and using either one or two heads. With a single head and unperforated tape, sync would be achieved by using a control track.[93]

It seems that in spite of the enormous need for such a machine as the VTR, the Ampex project had a low budget and low priority, as well as low security. Everyone in the plant seemed to know of the project. Even John Mullin knew of it, but he felt that it would never succeed.[94]

Meanwhile, Dr. Camras seemed to have had second thoughts about his idea of a rotating-head magnetic recorder. On January 12, 1953, he applied for a U.S. patent covering a three-head arcuate video recorder similar to that which Ginsburg and Dolby were actually working on.[95]

Starting in June 1953, the Allan Shoup Laboratory in Chicago designed and built a monstrous videotape machine that had a 17.2-inch rotor rotating at 90 revolutions/second. It had six heads and the tape speed was 40 inches/sec, which gave a head to tape speed of 5,000 inches per second. It was claimed that it was capable of recording up to 5mc of information. It was an arcuate machine with the recording paths in "Swaths" similar to the earliest Ampex machines. It had provision to lay down sync pulses on the tape to synchronize the rotor movement, one pulse per turn of the rotor.

In dimensions, it was amazingly similar to the specification of the Masterson patent. Only Masterson's was a helical scan device using 12-inch tape running at 30 inches per second with a 17-inch disc with four heads. It had a control track impressed on the bottom of the tape. It is hard to believe that such a huge machine was even considered, and why the Signal Corps was willing to finance such a monstrosity is anyone's guess. Ampex never considered anything but two-inch tape from the beginning.[96]

While I have no proof of this, it is very conceivable that Shoup in Chicago consulted with Dr Camras and decided that this was a good way to approach the wide-band video problem.

Another air force wide-band magnetic recording system project was undertaken by General Electric at its electronic division in Syracuse, New York, and started on June 8, 1951. A report dated February 11, 1955, showed the lack of progress by General Electric. Basically their machine, the Model III Transport, was a multitrack (as many as 20 tracks) of eight channels, or three channels using five-eights inch tape running at 100 inches/sec. Its only novel feature was that the reels were to be stacked in order to save space. This of course presented many problems in running the tape at high speed. G.E. promised to start a

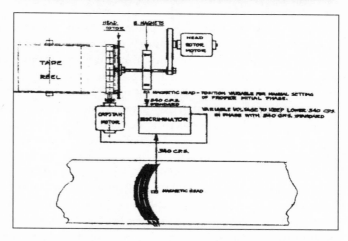

1954. *Above:* Front view of Shoup broadband arcuate video recorder. *Middle:* Rear view of Shoup video recorder. *Below:* Diagram showing arcuate sweeps. (Shoup "Final Report," December 1954.)

new six-channel, 2mc system using a new Model IV transport as their next project.[97]

A magnetic videotape project was started at RCA on September 27, 1951.[98] In that same month, David Sarnoff was celebrating 45 years of his association with radio. On this occasion, the Princeton Labs were renamed the "David Sarnoff Research Center." During the celebration Sarnoff asked for three gifts to be delivered within five years. They were (1) a true light amplifier, (2) a "videograph" recording both black-and-white and color on magnetic tape, and (3) an electronic air conditioner for the home.[99]

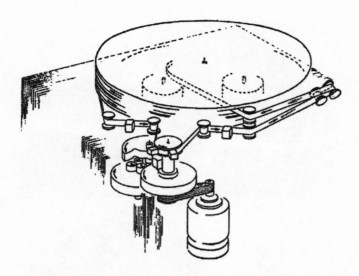

1955. Proposed General Electric wide-band recorder TV transport. (From "General Electric Interim Report," Feb. 11, 1955.)

As a result, a magnetic videotape recording project was initiated. The project was under the direction of Dr. Harry F. Olson, the director of the acoustical laboratory at RCA, and he gathered together a group of top-notch audio engineers. It appears that all the major RCA video engineers were tied up in the color television project. While RCA had the most to gain from such a project, Olson never even considered anything but a straight forward high-speed (longitudinal) approach. This seemed, to him, like the likeliest and easiest path to follow.[100]

Strangely enough, an RCA engineer named Earl Masterson saw the advantage of a rotating head and applied for a patent on it on November 30, 1950. This is before the Olson project began. But RCA totally ignored it. Masterson claims that he approached the RCA patent department with the idea and they of course applied for a patent for it. It never seems to have gotten the attention of Dr. Olson, though. At any rate, the device described in Masterson's patent was monstrous! It was a helical scan device using 12-inch tape running at 30 inches per second with a 17-inch disc with four heads. It had a control track impressed on the bottom of the tape. In other words all the necessary ingredients for a successful machine if scaled down properly.[101]

Thus the Olson project proceeded to follow the high-speed longitudinal approach. According to author George H. Brown, RCA made the error of failing to instigate a thorough search of the literature and patents in order to be familiar with prior art. This is hard to believe as it is almost axiomatic to make such a search before undertaking a major project. (Also, the RCA patent department was one of the best in the electrical world.) Besides, a look at the references cited in the Masterson patent contradicts this. It had a complete list of patents from Wildhaber in 1929 to Hickman in 1953.[102]

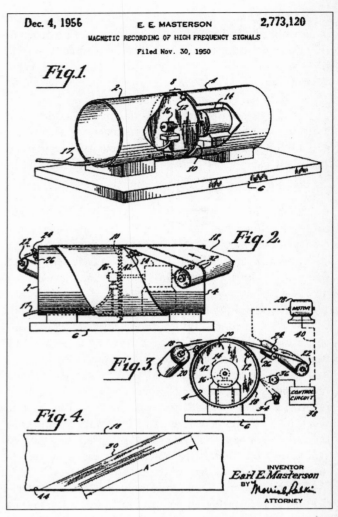

1956. First helical recording patent. Earl Masterson, USA no. 2,773,120, filed Nov. 30, 1950; issued Dec. 4, 1956. (RCA.)

The truth is that Dr. Olson was an excellent electrical engineer, but treated this project as simply a high-speed audio project and was not willing to take new paths. At any rate, their project was doomed to failure.[103]

On February 20, 1952, Norman Collins, formerly of the BBC, gave a paper to the film production division in London relating to a new process of making motion pictures. He had founded a new organization called High-Definition Films, Ltd. The purpose of this company was to produce standard motion pictures using "electronic photography." Collins had teamed up with T. C. Macnamara who was his chief engineer. Collins pointed out the limitations of the optical camera, claiming that it was essentially the same instrument as in the days of Lumière and Friese-Green. The purpose of the project was to reduce production costs without spoiling the product due to the limitations imposed by the optical camera.

Collins mentioned six faults of regular film shooting. (1) No one except the camera operator would have a

1954. High-Definition Films, Ltd. *Above:* Pye television camera. *Below left:* control unit. *Below right:* Moy film recorder. (Norman Collins.)

true picture of what was being shot. (2) In order to get good results, there was a repetition of takes until the director was satisfied that they had what they wanted. (3) The use of multiple cameras was unwieldy due to the lighting factors. (4) The amount of shooting time was defined by the amount of film in the camera. (5) The usual day's work was unavoidably confined to some two or three minutes of film a day. (6) All work was assessed later (usually the next day). (7) Only at the end was the finished product assembled piece by piece in a cutting room.

The authors, therefore, advocated the use of the full electronic process which they described as possessing the following advantages. (1) It involved small, light and entirely silent cameras of high sensitivity which required no reloading and could be operated in any position with remote focusing if necessary. (2) It completely enabled the director and his assistants to see every shot in its entirety, with the certain knowledge that what appeared on the master screen had been faithfully recorded on the final

film. (3) It offered unlimited length of take and the ability to make as many master negatives or positives as may be desired, with the additional facility of quick development of a positive for immediate playback, either on the master screen or in a projection theatre.

It was accepted by the authors that the technical quality of the pictures produced by the electronic method must in no way be inferior to the normal theatrical release standard, in order that the product may be acceptable. They were confident that, using high-definition electronic cameras of the recently developed type, the requisite quality could be obtained. They decided that a picture built up from 1,000 to 1,300 lines at 24 frames per second would permit detail of the normal 35mm motion picture. Being closed circuit, a band width of some 15 to 20 megacycles could be used. It was claimed that cameras capable of this definition had been developed. Also monitors of some 2,000-line resolution recording on fine grain film stock would be used. It was stated that the system would soon be presented.[104] They later made several short films: "LaBoutique," "The Door," The Merchant of Venice," and "The Baby" from the play by Chekhov.[105]

On March 3, 1952, at the IRE convention in New York City, CBS demonstrated their color television system using an all-electronic tube of RCA manufacture. CBS made the demonstration to show the flexibility of its system with any kind of color tube. However, Dr. C. B. Joliffe stated that "even with a tri-color tube, the CBS Color system remains incompatible."[106]

On April 13, 1952, the FCC lifted the 3½ year old "freeze." It provided for the opening of 2,635 new stations (only 105 stations were then in use), and opened 70 new channels in the VHF (470 to 890MHz) spectrum.[107]

On June 23, 1952, the House of Commons gave the BBC ten more years to operate. They were to introduce color television and VHF frequency sound broadcasts.[108]

On August 9, 1952, regular television broadcasting started in Tokyo, Japan. It was revealed that there were only two studios and only four cameras available, and all equipment had to come from the USA, which made the operation quite expensive. It was hoped that the industry there would soon manufacture its own studio equipment at moderate prices.[109]

Also in August 1952, the CCIR study group no. XI, with delegates from Belgium, Denmark, Italy, the Netherlands, Switzerland and Sweden, expressed its preference for a 625-line television system.[110]

In September 1952, it was reported that an Eidophor color TV system for theater use had recently been demonstrated by 20th Century–Fox in New York City.[111] It was indicated that demonstrations of the Eidophor-CBS system had been done in Zurich, Switzerland, earlier that year.[112]

This demonstration in Fox's New York preview theater filled a 15 feet screen with a color picture so bright and detailed that some visitors thought they were seeing a Technicolor movie. It employed the field sequential process of CBS and used synchronous color wheels at the camera and the projector. Spyro Skouras, President of 20th-Century Fox, stated that an order for 500 Eidophor installations was in the process of negotiations between Fox and General Electric.[113]

Around August 1952, both the Democratic and Republican political conventions in Chicago and San Francisco were covered by television. Also for the first time, the new RCA portable Vidicon camera was used by NBC on both occasions. Named the "Walkie-Lookie," it used a C73162 Vidicon tube. It had a four lens turret and an electronic viewfinder. It was claimed that pictures and sound were transmitted to a control point within a mile from the camera.[114]

1952. John Mullin with his developmental videotape recorder. (John Mullin.)

On October 2, 1952, Mullin gave a demonstration of his machine to prove that his process merited attention. The picture had certain good features, the gray scale was outstandingly good and the picture was sharp and clear. However, it also had a diagonal pattern that was always prominent, considerable flicker was present, and under certain conditions a series of ghosts was noticeable.[115]

Later, on December 30, 1952, Mullin gave another demonstration of his machine in Hollywood. Mullin was accompanied by representatives of the Ampex Electrical Corporation that had assisted in the building of the recording machine. Mullin agreed that a way had been found to eliminate the "grainy quality." A future demonstration was planned for May 1953 and commercial production of

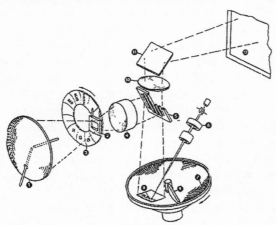

1952. *Above:* Color Eidophor projector. *Below:* Diagram of Eidophor. (*Radio/Electronics.*)

1952. Mullin videotape recorder and amplifiers. Wayne Johnson is at the console. (John Mullin.)

1952. *Left to right:* John Mullin, Frank Healy, Wayne Johnson and Bing Crosby with first videotape machine. (John Mullin.)

the recording machine was scheduled to get under way in January 1954.[116] This demonstration may explain why Ampex at this time was loath to continue the Ginsburg magnetic tape project. Obviously, if the Crosby machine was a success, Ampex would build the machines for them. An article in Electronics showed a picture of Bing Crosby with the Mullin recorder. The article stated that the tape cost was estimated at $80 a half-hour against $150 for kinescope film. The article announced that ½-inch tape would be used in the next prototype models which were promised in November or December 1953, at about $60,000 each.[117]

Publicity about the Crosby project was brought to General Sarnoff's attention, as it seemed to be the only project having some degree of success. According to Daily Variety, Sarnoff and members of the board of directors asked for and were invited to view the Crosby recorder in Hollywood. This they did on a visit on March 13, 1953.[118] This is highly reminiscent of Sarnoff's visit to the Farnsworth Laboratories in May 1931.[119]

On March 26, 1953, Dr. Zworykin introduced a lightweight camera, some two by five by ten inches in size except for the lens. It was to be used in the home and plugged into the receiver. It had only three tubes and took its power from the receiver. It was demonstrated at the convention of the IRE on March 26.[120]

On June 2, 1953, the BBC televised the coronation of Queen Elizabeth II. It was covered by 15 cameras. One camera was over the west door of the Abbey. Another looked out from the Annexe, two were on the Colonial Office site, and another was on the roof of Abbey House.

Three cameras were at Victoria Memorial, with another camera mounted on the roof of the Palace and yet another at ground level inside the forecourt. Three more cameras were located on a stand near Grosvenor Gate, Hyde Park with a BBC mobile television control room located nearby. All the cameras were phased and locked (synched) together from the central control room. Finally on the Thames Embankment were three cameras, televising the outgoing procession and later in the day, the fireworks display. All cameras were using image orthicon tubes, and zoom lenses were used on several cameras.[121]

In addition, it was reported that the coronation had also been received in Great Britain in color by 300 children in a hospital. This was according to Richard Hodgson, President of Chromatic Television Labs, who described the complete success of this historic telecast. All color pictures were viewed on receivers using the Paramount-developed Lawrence color tube.[122] No details were given of whose cameras were used, with what color system and, finally, how the signal got to the hospital.

It was also reported that the coronation was seen in Berlin on the first international TV program.[123] No details were given as to how this was done. If "live" it had to be done with a standards converter since the BBC was on 405 lines and Europe on 625. According to a report on April 28, 1953, the BBC had beamed a TV program simultaneously to four European countries.[124]

CBS televised its first color show under the new NTSC standards on Thursday, October 8, 1953. According to critic Jack Gould, "both the color and show were

1953. Ernest Lawrence and the Chromatron tricolor tube. (Chromatic TV Labs.)

not very good." CBS was using its converted single tube General Electric Chromacoder cameras with a spinning disc. The registration and stability of the CBS color images were disappointing. CBS installed three of its own color receivers using the new CBS-Hytron tubes at the Waldorf-Astoria Hotel in New York City for invited guests.[125]

The first NTSC demonstration took place on October 15, 1953, also at the Waldorf-Astoria. Thus the NTSC demonstrations for the FCC were completed. The FCC approved the standards on December 17, 1953. The second NTSC continued on until February 3, 1954, when it was officially disbanded.[126] The best coverage of the second NTSC is contained in the book by Donald Fink.[127]

RCA gave a coast-to-coast demonstration of its color videotape recording on November 3, 1953. The telecast originated at the Colonial Theatre in New York City, and was received in the NBC Studios in Burbank, Calif. It was claimed that the reception was technically perfect. In fact, the color, in definition and consistency, was deemed the equal of anything that movie theaters had to offer.[128]

Then on December 1, 1953, RCA gave its first formal demonstration of its color recorder at the David Sarnoff Research Center in Princeton to a group of top television and motion picture executives. The results were "remarkably effective and the system possessed great potential advantages in television and more remotely, the motion picture screen."[129]

The tests were conducted under the direction of Dr. Elmer Engstrom. The large machine used ¼-inch tape for black-and-white recordings, with video on one channel and sound on the other. For color, five channels using ½-inch tape were used. In either case the tape traveled at 30 ft/sec. The five channels were for red, blue and green, and for sync and sound. The video bandwidth was 3mc per channel. The color was demodulated and applied separately to each of the color channels. There was no NTSC subcarrier transmitted. The equipment used reels 17 inches in diameter and could record a four-minute program. A 19-inch reel permitted a 15-minute program. It was stated that new high-frequency video heads and a "servo-type" transport for almost constant tape speed had been developed. It was claimed that the playback of the tape for black-and-white was about 90–95 percent as good as the original quality, while for color a figure of 85–90 percent was ascribed. Finally, it was stated that the commercial versions of this prototype were not to be available for about another two years and then only for broadcast and commercial recording installations.[130]

Jack Gould, the New York Times television reporter, stated that while the pictures were superior in quality to kinescope and somewhat below the level of "live" telecast, ultimately the quality would be the same as "live" broadcast. He also stated that others in the race to produce a tape machine now included Minnesota Mining and Manufacturing Co. and General Precision, with both Eastman Kodak and DuPont reported doing some research into the problem.[131]

On December 17, 1953, Brown of RCA reported that "we also leaped into the air when we heard that the FCC had adopted the NTSC specifications as the law of the land with commercial broadcasting authorized to begin on January 22, 1954. Webster, Sterling and Lee had not only concurred but wrote separate statements in support of the decision. Commissioner Hennock was present at the December 17 meeting but for some unstated reason did not vote."[132]

Brown continued, "The work of the National Television System Committee was an outstanding example of cooperation on the part of a large number of engineers joined in an effort to bring about the best solution of a major technical problem of common concern. While the various panels weighed a multitude of factors, the major contributions were those of RCA and Hazeltine. For instance, the burst to synchronize the colors was a Bedford invention which prevailed in a lengthy patent interference. The use of a subcarrier where hue was determined by phase variation and saturation was measured in amplitude, as described

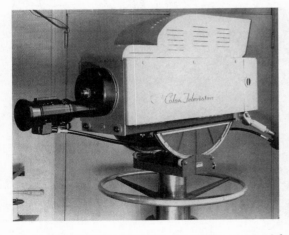

Above left: 1952.RCA TK40, the first RCA commercial color camera. (RCA.) *Above right:* 1953. RCA TK11A monochrome camera. (RCA.)

in RCA Exhibits 207 and 209. The NTSC choice of 455 times one half of the horizontal line frequency was the same value which I had proposed at the FCC hearing and which was confirmed by our field testing in 1952. The orange-cyan wideband proposal came from RCA Laboratories and an appreciation of the principal of mixed highs made possible the success of the compatible system. The constant-luminance principle came from Hazeltine Laboratories as well as much advice in regard to the composition of the color subcarrier. While not a part of the signal specifications or the standards, the Hazeltine concept of by-passed brightness apparatus contributed heavily to practical success in both studio equipment and receivers.

Without the RCA shadow-mask color kinescope, the NTSC signal specifications would have been meaningless.

"Without the contributions of RCA, which Philco tried hard to deny us, there would have been no NTSC solution. On the other hand, RCA unquestionably could not have received FCC approval on a system proposed by only one company for the FCC's collective fingers had been burned as a result of the FCC approval of the CBS incompatible color system."[133] In any case, the system started by RCA in 1949 led to the superb compatible system of color that has been used worldwide since (with meaningful changes of course). A new era in television had begun.

Chapter 4

The Ampex Revolution
(1954–1956)

On January 1, 1954, in a discussion over the row concerning color tv, *New York Times* critic Jack Gould stated, "The leadership provided over the years by Mr. Sarnoff during the color row is too clearly a matter of record to be debated seriously. He is entitled to a bow. By the same token, the NTSC contribution is too real to be minimized. Many an anonymous engineer helped enormously. The irony is that CBS took its licking with good grace and sportsmanship. And the FCC swallowed its pride without undue whimpering."[1]

In January 1954, RCA announced a new RCA-6326 Vidicon to be used for the televising of motion picture films. Until this time most of the film scanners were using the old, large, bulky iconoscopes. It was claimed that this new tube made it possible for simpler, lower-cost TV film scanners and associated equipment.[2] It was to be installed in the TK12 film pickup technology.[3]

French television pioneer René Barthélemy died in February 1954, age 65. René Barthélemy was a French physicist who made many advances to early French television. All of his work was done for the French Compagnie des Compteurs de Montrouge. It is claimed he gave his first television demonstration on April 14, 1931. Barthélemy did much work on improving the iconoscope and some unsuccessful experiments with the low-velocity orthicon. In 1941–42 work was started on a high definition 1,015 line system by the Compagnie des Compteurs. Later, Barthélemy was elected to the Academy of Sciences with the grade of Commandeur de la Légion d'Honneur.[4]

In March 1954, a Marconi color fast pulldown flying-spot film scanner type BD 678 was described. The film was scanned by a spot of light from a special cathode ray tube with very short afterglow. The colored light passed through a special optical system that separated it into its red, green and blue components, each of which was directed to a separate photomultiplier cell. After preamplification, these simultaneous outputs could be viewed on a high-quality color picture monitor and after bandwidth compression, fed to a transmitter for broadcasting. The machine could also be used for colored slides, so that either films or slides could be transmitted by the same device.[5]

Also in March 1954, at the 1954 IRE convention, John Mullin gave technical details of his improved 12-channel video recorder. Mullin claimed that the new sampling technique, with its sharp edges, resulted in a crispening effect since there could be no smear in this type of recording. There was less flicker, jitter was nonexistent, and the screen pattern had been rendered far more viewworthy, with ghosts being virtually suppressed. Mullin mentioned that since both picture and sound were on the same tape, that editing could be made with a single cut using the familiar pressure sensitive adhesive tape.[6]

On June 1, 1954, an article describing the redesigned and improved Crosby VTR was given. It claimed that the device was now ready to be put into production in limited quantities for military applications. It was said that ten video tracks were used, each capable of recording 339,000 bits of information. With ten heads, the machine was capable of recording 1.69mc. Vertical and horizontal sync were recorded on track no. 11 to be free of sampling errors. Sound was recorded on one track by means of a high quality FM system. The half-inch tape ran at 100 inches/second, so 16 minutes of recording was possible.[7] It was later reported (September 1954) that Westinghouse was going to buy one of the Crosby VTRs for planned airborne tests, with the USAF having eventual ownership.[8] In spite of all the contracts let out by the air force for a practical wide-band magnetic recorder, no one had produced or would ever produce a practical model.

On June 26, 1954, members of the British Kinematograph Society of London visited Highbury Studios and inspected the high-definition film installation.[9] A paper was given at a meeting of the film production division on October 20, 1954. The paper was read by T. C. Macnamara of High Definition Films Ltd.

He gave a progress report on what had happened in the two years since work began on the new equipment required for the installation described in his paper. Macnamara claimed that the studio, which was the only one of its kind in the world, was now in full production. Several half-hour plays had been televised, one "The Baby" by Chekhov, had been shown by the BBC. He describe the equipment as follows. "First, it was closed-circuit operating on either 834 or 625 lines 24 frames/second sequential scanning with a bandwidth of 12 mh. Up to 4 camera channels can be accommodated. [The Pye Photicon camera was to be used in England, while the 5820 image orthicon was to be used in the USA.] Recording comprises two channels for recording the programme on standard 35mm motion-picture film. The recording tube has a 9" flat face with anti-pincushion alignment and including spot wobble [to remove the line structure.] The system also incorporated two recording cameras specially built by Earnest F. Moy, Ltd." In the discussion that followed, there did not seem to be much enthusiasm for the project.[10]

This reaction by "film" people was to be repeated many times in the future. Any attempt to try to change the "tried and true method" of film production was to run into the same brick wall. (Some 46 years later, the same attitude prevails.) Simply stated, film people resented using television methods for production. As film was the senior member, the young interloper with all of its advantages was simply not going to replace the normal way of shooting film. This was especially true for the directors of photography and camera operators who felt threatened in that, for the first time, their exclusive domain — i.e., that only *they* could see what was going on — had been invaded.

In a report of this process in the *New York Times* on September 19, 1954, a Mr. Pack claimed that it took a sharp eye to distinguish these elec-tronically produced films from what he called the "old-fashioned" method.[11] High Definition Films was headed by Norman Collins, former controller and program chief for the BBC and a crusader for commercial television. Collins claimed that with careful planning and dry rehearsal, his studio could shoot one complete dramatic film plus a simple quarter hour musical in only one day's shooting. He claimed that costs would be considerably below those of conventional film production.[12]

In July 1954, in *Philips Technical Review*, a new experimental photoconductive tube for television was revealed. Work was being done at the Philips Research Laboratories in Eindhoven, Holland. The company claimed that the light-sensitive material used in the tube was a specially prepared lead oxide. It appeared that the tube was built primarily for x-ray purposes and that the lead could absorb x-rays to a considerable extent. Thus it was possible to convert an x-ray image directly into a television signal. It was hoped to rid the tube of the inertial effects in order to permit its use in broadcast television. A picture was shown of the new lead-oxide tube compared with an image iconoscope.[13]

Also it was reported that the first 4½-inch image orthicons had been made by the English Electric Valve Co. The BBC was supposed to have been the first to use the device in a camera in 1954.[14] The earliest 4½-inch image orthicon had been the work of Dr. Otto Schade of RCA in 1949-50. Basically he had scaled up the three-inch image orthicon and was using it for laboratory use only. As it used the larger photocathode area, regular lenses could not be incorporated into it. As a result, RCA produced a few 4½-inch tubes experimentally but only put out a commercial version later.[15]

In 1950, G. E. Partington of Marconi saw the possibilities of the 4½-image orthicon and the research on the tube was put into the hands of G. B. Banks of the English Electric Valve Co. about 1951. According to *International TV Tech Review*, Banks made two important changes in the tube. The photocathode image size was retained at 1.6 inches (40mm), the same as in the three-inch tubes, so

1954. *Above left:* Philips TV camera with lead oxide photoconductive tube. *Above right:* (1) New lead tube for the image iconoscope; (2) the image iconoscope. (Philips Labs.)

that the same lenses could be used. First, he separated the field mesh from the focusing electrode and operated it at a potential to suppress secondary emission at the mesh by the scanning beam. By 1955 the electric valve pickup tube was so far advanced that it was introduced in the Marconi Mark III camera channel. It was then superseded by the Mark IV and sold in quantity all over the world including the USA. In Britain the BBC adopted the 4½-inch image orthicon as its standard.[16] Not only was it a superb tube but it was an English achievement that went beyond both the American image orthicon and the British CPS Emitron. The 4½-inch Marconi Mark IV camera was introduced in the USA in 1959 by Ampex.

On July 5, 1954, CBS demonstrated a 19-inch color tube knows as the CBS-Colortron which offered 205 inches of picture screen area. CBS President Charles F. Stromeyer announced that several leading TV set manufacturers, including CBS-Columbia, Capehart-Farnsworth, Motorola and Westinghouse, intended to incorporate the CBS-Colortron 205 in their fall lines.[17] It was announced that RCA had taken a license for the use of CBS patents on color tubes on November 30, 1954. The patent involved was that of Fyler and Rowe (USA no. 2,690,518, filed June 1, 1953; issued September 28, 1954). RCA stated that it would not build the CBS 19-inch tube but would build its own version in a 21-inch size. The agreement was for five years.[18]

In July 1954, Dr. Vladimir K. Zworykin reached 65 years of age and due to RCA corporate policy was forced to retire on August 1. Shortly thereafter, the board of directors of RCA elected him an honorary vice president — the first such appointment in the history of the company. This was another way for David Sarnoff to thank him for his efforts on behalf of RCA.

In honor of his retirement, a seminar entitled "Thirty Years of Progress in Science and Technology" was held in McCosh Hall at Princeton University on September 18, 1954. The panelists included Dean Hugh Scott Taylor, who discussed synthetic materials; Dr. J. C. Hunsaker, who spoke on aeronautics; Dr. Isadore I. Rabi, who commented on high energy particles; and Dr. James Hillier, who examined electronics and vision in medicine.

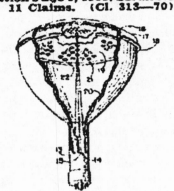

2,690,518
COLOR PICTURE TUBE
Herman F. Fyler and William E. Rowe, Newburyport, Mass., assignors to Columbia Broadcasting System, Inc., Danvers, Mass., a corporation of New York
Application June 1, 1953, Serial No. 358,712
11 Claims. (Cl. 313—70)

1. A picture tube for the presentation of television images in color comprising, an envelope having a curved surface, phosphors for emitting light of the three primary colors, red, blue, and green being symmetrically disposed in groups of three light-emitting types in discrete portions in a single layer over said surface within said envelope, three electron guns within said envelope, each of said guns generating an electron beam to excite separately phosphor portions of each light-emitting type, a mask having a contour substantially matching that of said curved surface disposed within said envelope between said electron guns and said curved surface, but closer to said curved surface, said mask having a plurality of apertures formed therein, said apertures being so disposed relative to said curved surface and said electron guns that the beam from each gun can trace a straight line from the deflection plane thereof to only phosphor portions of a given light-emitting type, and support means free of lateral tension projecting inwardly of the inner wall of said envelope around at least a portion thereof for retaining said mask in substantially fixed spaced relationship to said curved surface.

1953. USA Patent no. 2,690,518. (US Patent Office.)

Theodore von Kármán had been invited to speak on aviation but declined on the grounds that he would be in Europe on that date. All of this was of course quite a compliment to Zworykin.

After the seminar, Dr. Elmer W. Engstrom, who was now executive vice president of RCA laboratories, introduced the main speaker of the evening, Brigadier General David Sarnoff, chairman of the board of RCA. Sarnoff gave a speech lauding Zworykin's achievements. He received a great laugh when he repeated the story of how Zworykin had convinced him many years before that he could produce a new, revolutionary cathode-ray tube for some $100,000. Sarnoff stated, "Look at Zworykin, how he deceived me. Before we got a dollar back from television, we spent fifty million dollars!" It was obvious from the speech how much Sarnoff respected his longtime colleague. Certainly his faith in Zworykin had never been betrayed.

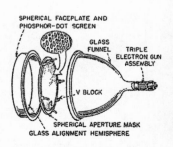

SPHERICAL FACEPLATE AND
PHOSPHOR-DOT SCREEN
GLASS FUNNEL
TRIPLE ELECTRON GUN ASSEMBLY
V BLOCK
SPHERICAL APERTURE MASK
GLASS ALIGNMENT HEMISPHERE

1953. CBS spherical faceplate color tube. (CBS.)

Above: **Dr. Vladimir K. Zworykin on his retirement from RCA, August 1, 1954. (RCA.)** *Right:* **1953. David Sarnoff shows off magnetic tape demonstrated on Dec. 1. (RCA.)**

There is no question that most of the great RCA achievements in television had come out of Zworykin's television laboratory. Together with Elmer Engstrom, he had been the focus of all the activity that had taken place at RCA since 1930.[19]

In August 1954, Walter Selsted and Ross Snyder of Ampex presented a paper which was a review of the available magnetic recording methods. Among those mentioned were (1) pulse width modulation, (2) direct recording, (3) direct pulse recording, and finally (4) FM recording. According to the article, FM had many advantages. (1) Phase, amplitude and frequency may all be faithfully recorded and played back; (2) there was little deterioration due to the age of tape; (3) it permitted the recording of frequencies down to 0 cycles; (4) amplitude effects caused by tape conditions had little or no effect on the accuracy; (5) print-through did not occur; (6) there was an absence of "modulation noise" behind the signal. The disadvantageous aspects were mainly those of cost, complicated circuitry, stability of the transport, and poor tape economy, making the requirements imposed upon the mechanical and electronic components severe. Finally the prevailing FM theory stated the upper frequency limit for recording, as information could ordinarily not exceed 20 percent of the carrier frequency. However, since recording was possible, essentially down to 0 cycles, the number of octaves that might be recorded on FM systems approached infinity.[20]

It was almost certain that all of this news of the "successful" demonstrations by both RCA (on December 1, 1953) and Crosby (in June 1954) had an effect on the Ampex project. After almost 14 months of hiatus (June 1953 through August 1954) Ginsburg made an urgent request to management for an 80 man-hours authorization to modify and demonstrate the revamped machine, which was known to him as the Mark 1 machine.

As a result, the Ampex VTR project was restarted. Ginsburg now had assistance from one Charles Anderson who joined Ampex in April 1954. Anderson was assigned to work with Ginsburg on a miscellaneous audio project. Secretly, they both did bootleg work on the defunct VTR. Anderson had changed the control system and they gave a demonstration in August 1954 to a management committee. Several major technical changes were made. (1) There was the changeover from an arcuate to a four-head transverse head configuration. This was at the suggestion of Walter Selsted who told the management of the problems of arcuate scan and suggested that they go with "straight across" scan and see if the tape could handle the curvature necessary.[21] (2) There was development of an automatic gain control (AGC) system to compensate for the continuous, as well as the step-function, type of amplitude functions characteristic of the rotating head approach. (3) The tape speed was changed from 30 inches/sec to 17.5 inches/second. (4) The drum speed was reduced from 300 rps to 240 rps. The demonstration was a success, and on September 1, 1954, the VTR program commenced in earnest.

Later that September, Anderson and Henderson were joined by Fred Pfost in September, and in October by Alex Maxey. A now little-known-about experimental recorder was devised by Maxey in November 1954. He had proposed a magnetic recorder using four-inch tape with

1954. RCA shows first video recording machine. (RCA.)

a single head. The tape was to be curved around the single spinning head and then flattened out at the take-up reel. The idea was to cut down the number of heads, record preamps and amplifiers, playback preamps, and most of the playback switcher. This radical proposal was not met with enthusiasm even though Maxey did put together a breadboard to try it out.[22]

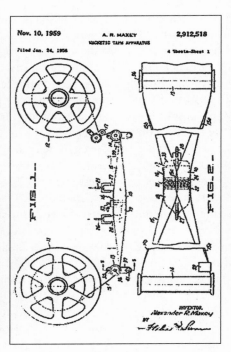

Above left: Alex Maxey and his four-inch "Tubular" single-head recorder in November 1954. *Above right:* USA patent 2,912,518 filed Jan. 24, 1956. (Charles P. Ginsburg/Ampex.)

In the meantime, after many minor improvements, they got their first pictures using the new transverse head drum. In December 1954, Ginsburg got his first picture using the new head geometry. The results were gratifying; however, the AGC system was not ready for use and it was apparent that the problems facing it were extremely difficult.

Because Anderson could not get the AGC system to work properly, he decided to investigate a vestigial side-band FM system.[23]So in late December, he proposed the use of a vestigial side-band FM system rather than the old amplitude modulation (AM) system. This was a bold step for which Anderson deserves great credit. According to Dolby, Ampex had much experience with multivibrator FM modulators. (See also Selsted and Snyder, August 1954.) Previous FM modulators operated at a maximum frequency of about 75kHz with a deviation of ± 40 percent. The problem was to design multivibrators that would operate in the multimegahertz region. According to Dolby no one had heard of such a thing.[24]

Anderson began work on the new system on January 2, 1955, and early in February they saw the first FM pictures off tape. Anderson built an FM system using fairly conventional reactance-tube techniques, heterodyning the side bands from the 50 megacycle region to frequencies suitable for reproduction from tape, and subsequently moving the information on playback up to 50 megacycles, for transmission through high-frequency amplifiers and limiter circuits.

Ray Dolby was released from the army on January 1, 1955, and rejoined the project. According to Dolby, "the timing was perfect." Now the VTR project was assured of success.[25]

Dolby had no doubt that Anderson's FM method would work, but he thought that he could develop a simpler and cheaper alternative to it based on pulse techniques. Then Dolby designed and built a multivibrator that could be modulated by applying the composites signal directly to the control grids.[26] By January 13, 1955, Dolby had a rudimentary FM system going on the bench. More work was done on the system and on February 1, 1955, the first successful tape FM runs were made. The pictures obtained with the multivibrator modulator on February 25, were even better than those with the reactance system earlier in the month. The audio track was added (on the other side of the tape from the control track) the first week in March.[27]

1955. Working on new transverse recorder (old arcuate machine in the left foreground) are (left to right) Fred Pfost, Alex Maxey, Charles Ginsburg, and Shelby Henderson. (Charles P. Ginsburg/ Ampex.)

On March 5, 1955, they gave a very convincing demonstration to the board of directors. Dr. Frederick R. Terman, dean of electrical engineering at Stanford University, was also there and Ginsburg was concerned that he would ask questions about the unusual FM system they were using. He did not.[28] The resolution was extremely low as the system was less than 1½ megacycles wide and the signal to noise ratio was about 20db. The monitor had to be operated with a short-time constant in the horizontal AFC because of velocity variations in the belt-driven head drum. The demonstration was a success and subsequently the board lifted the restrictions on budget. A result was that Philip Gundy moved the project to a closed area with five times as much room.[29]

In January 1955, the electronics division of Willy's Motors described a flat picture tube. It consisted of a phosphor screen mounted between two glass plates. The electron beams were injected and flowed in a field-free region along the horizontal edge of the tube, adjacent to a row of transverse deflection plates. By controlling the voltages on these plates, the electron beam was bent at any desired place along the edge of the tube. The beam then flowed vertically in a second field-free region between a series of transparent horizontal deflection plates and the electrically charged phosphor screen. By controlling the voltages on the horizontal deflection plates, the beam was deflected into the phosphor screen at any desired level. A raster was scanned by sequentially changing the voltages on the vertical and horizontal deflection plates simultaneously. All plates were kept at a high voltage except those

opposite the position at which it was desired to bend the beam. It was claimed that tubes with 14-inch screens were built as well as those of 24 inches. It was reported that the picture tube could be used for color as well, using multi-layered screens. Color modulation would be accomplished by changing the relative potential of the three phosphor layers.[30]

Meanwhile at RCA, according to author George H. Brown, pressure "from above" insisted that an installation of the RCA magnetic recorder be made at the NBC studios in New York for a field test beginning in April 1955. As one of Sarnoff's "birthday presents," all efforts were being made to produce a workable machine. The "improved" machine was still far from ready, but it could produce an NTSC type of signal. So a publicity stunt was cooked up. On May 12 and 13, 1955, a tape-recorded demonstration was given from RCA's new color recorder installed at the NBC studios in New York, and the pictures traveled by closed circuit to the new 3M Research Center in St. Paul, Minnesota, for viewing on six 21-inch receivers.[31]

A progress report by Dr. Olson stated that: (1) tape speed had been reduced to 20 feet per second, permitting storage of an entire 15-minute program on a 20-inch reel; (2) an improved servo system held tape speed variations down to less than one part in five million to minimize tape jitter; (3) multiple magnetic heads and amplifiers had improved to reproduce a bandwidth of over 3mc. Still further improvements were promised both in the machine and in tape resolution before the commercial version was brought out.[32]

Also present for the RCA color tape demonstration in St. Paul, Minnesota, was John Mullin. He stated that NBC's recording of "Desert Song" was nearly perfect in every detail. He stated that the first delivery of a Bing Crosby Enterprises radar recorder with color TV principles under government contract was scheduled for September. Frank Healy, executive director of Bing Crosby Enterprises, was also there. He estimated that the cost of commercial equipment would be between $50,000 and $75,000. He stated that progress was being made by Armour Research Foundation, Brush Development, the Ampex Corp., Magnecord, Inc., and that others were not too far behind either RCA or Bing Crosby Enterprises. This was the first time that any mention of the Ampex videotape project had been made publicly. Of course Mullin was in contact with Ampex who was either supplying parts and/or building his machines, and while he may not have known how far they had gone, he was aware of what they were doing.[33]

Also in August 1955, Ampex announced the series of 800 flight-test magnetic recorders available in models from two tracks up to 28 tracks, using two-inch tape. The recording methods were either by means of pulse width modulation data, wide-deviation FM, or wideband direct data.[34] Ampex also announced that a new research and development laboratory was to be established under Walter Selsted.[35]

In March 1955, Al Simon of Al Simon Productions described a "new" dual-purpose film/television camera. It was a combination 35mm film and video camera that used the picture from a single lens. The television camera was a Vidicon from RCA. Simon claimed all the advantages of being able to see the actual picture being shot, and that the scene could be recorded on color film. The only difference in the film was that the negative required adjustment of two printing lights. He envisioned the time when videotape was perfected, and it would be natural for such a combination camera to be used for the production of television films.[36]

The DuMont Electronicam system was described on October 6, 1955. It was claimed that this was a system for recording high quality pictures on motion picture film in either 35mm or 16mm, and in color or black-and-white. Multiple camera operation with simultaneous viewing on the several films was monitored and controlled by television viewfinders so that the director could shoot continuously and rapidly in the manner of television broadcasting, with the result being direct high-quality film recording.[37]

This was the last major attempt to combine television with film cameras. Starting in September 1955, the DuMont Electronicam system was used successfully on the Jackie Gleason "Honeymooners Show." This program, which was done as a live show in front of an audience, ended up as a 16mm kinescope recording. This was used as a work print to assemble the various pieces of film from the three cameras. The only stop was about half way through the program, when they had to change film magazines. Thirty-nine episodes were recorded with this system.

DuMont had such faith in this sophisticated system that he had a special truck built and shipped to Hollywood in hopes of getting Hollywood interested in it. DuMont had set up a mobile operation in which a pair of trailers could be moved from studio to studio and set to set. This reduced capital investment in permanent stage installations. The system could be leased to movie studios at from $1,500 to $3,000 a week depending on the facilities required. A DuMont field engineer would accompany each mobile system.

The first problem encountered was union-based. Although the DuMont engineers were IATSE, they did not want to be subservient to the film cameramen who were making five times as much as they were ($100 a day, rather then $20). Also another potential problem was a dispute between the Screen Actor's Guild (SAG) and the American Federation of Television and Radio Artists (AFTRA) for control of "electronicam" performers.[38] It was also announced in April 1955, that ABC had signed a contract with NABET which gave the IATSE the right to film shows on the ABC lot while NABET was now concerned only with live production.[39]

At that moment (October 1956) a unit had been leased to Paramount Sunset studios in Hollywood. DuMont expected 15 mobile units to be in use by the end of 1957. But this was not to be. Here DuMont ran into a stone wall, with the main opposition coming from the cameramen's union who were not quite ready to abandon all of their tried and true techniques developed over the past 50 or so years. So the system died an early death as did the DuMont network.[40]

During 1955 the American television industry had continued to improve the established kinescope recording or "kine" process. The three-hour East-West time differential required a rapid method of television recording since all three networks desired to maintain a uniform program schedule. Thus an era of "hot-kines" or "quick-kines" arose in which the recording and playback of a

Above left: 35mm DuMont Electronicam TV/film camera. *Above right:* 16mm DuMont Electronicam. (DuMont Labs.)

monochrome television program was made possible in three hours or less.

In a typical recording operation, the program was recorded on the West Coast on two machines simultaneously: one 35mm and one 16mm. The 16mm recording had an optical track, but the 35mm had no soundtrack, its sound being recorded on either magnetic film or magnetic tape. The program was recorded in 30-minute segments and was pulled out of the recorder tails and rushed to a developing laboratory where it was quickly developed, washed and dried.

On their return from the laboratory, these recordings were then projected as negatives with the 35mm as the "air copy" along with its accompanying soundtrack and the 16mm as "protection." This "hot-kine" process had begun with the completion of the transcontinental microwave system in September 1951.

With the adoption of the NTSC color system in December 1953, a color recording process became necessary. It was reported in 1954 that NBC was developing a color-kine system using a Triniscope (three separate ten-inch kinescopes) optically combined by means of mirrors and recorded on 35mm color negative film. The results were only "reasonable" so a color hot-kine process needed another solution.[41]

Early in 1955, Eastman Kodak announced that NBC would be using a lenticular color film process by the fall of 1956. Since lenticular film lent itself to the same quick processing methods as monochrome film it could prove to be a solution to the color time-zone problem.

On November 14, 1955, Bing Crosby Enterprises gave a demonstration of their first color tape. The test was made up of two segments, one of Judy Garland's "Ford Star Jubilee from TV City in Hollywood" (September 2), and the second "The Great Waltz" of Max Leibman (November 5). The recording machine consisted of two large reels (14,000 feet) of ½-inch-wide tape, which ran at 180 inches/second which was "relatively low" for 20 minutes of program time. The tape contained about 2.5mc of information of coaxial quality. The best quality was on the "Judy Garland Show," both in definition and color balance.

An article of the period said that other means of saving costs were being looked at by DuMont for its Electronicam system and another at McCadden Studios (whose system was Al Simon's). Healey stated that these devices were merely stopgaps until the day when the tape system was available. (How wrong he was!)[42]

Many attempts were made in England during 1955 to adopt the American NTSC color system to English standards. Marconi built a special two-tube color camera using two three-inch image orthicons. One camera tube received the high-definition image and the light was divided by a lens. The second tube had a low definition color grid. The signal from the second tube went through a suitable decoder which separated out the required color information in accordance with the prearranged pattern of the color elements of the grid. This appears to be the first use of the separate luminance channel in a color camera. The CBS Chromacoder system was also adopted by EMI for use in England. Finally there was mention of an early three–Vidicon camera by Philips in Eindhoven.

On February 6, 1956, George I. Long, president of Ampex, announced that "Ampex had completed a practical system for the recording and reproduction of TV pictures on magnetic tape." No details were given. This was the first public announcement of what Ampex had been working on for the past 18 months.[43]

Also early in 1956, Alex Maxey started to work on the first Ampex helical recorder. This was for a wide band magnetic tape recorder for the Rand Corporation. The project was started before February 1, 1956, as on that date, work began on a priority project for the air force: a 600-line, 8mc wide-band magnetic recorder with an s/n ratio of at least 30db.

The design of the new tape transport by Maxey was described in a report dated February 1–March 1, 1957. This machine, designated "Pan X," consisted of two reels stacked on top of each other (coaxial) with the head disc between reels. It used two-inch tape recording full frame/scan. The Stanford Research Institute was consulted on magnetic head design and improvements took place from March 20 to July 20, 1957. The head design had started in December 1956. Design of "Pan I" was completed between March 1 to July 20, 1957, with a disc diameter of 8½ inches rather than the 19 inches of Pan X. It used an end-butting arrangement rather than edge butting. The disc was driven at 60 rps to record 262.5 lines (one field) with a rim speed of 1,600 inches/sec. The signal dropout during head crossover was about 75–150 microseconds.

Due to labor troubles, work on Pan I was stopped around July 10, 1957, but I assume from my interview with Maxey (September 1981) that work was continued on the machine as soon as the strike was over. Thus a "working machine" (prototype) was in the Ampex laboratories in mid–1957.[44] A later article pictures a helical machine with the date of 1956 on it.[45]

This machine of course was not too successful. Even with the use of the new FM modulator, they had two inherent problems concerning tape stability. They were tape speed (longitudinal tape motion) and tape guiding (vertical movement). While the machine was simpler to operate and capable of certain tricks (such as still framing and slow motion) and potentially less costly (less electronic circuitry), Ampex did not want to tip their hand on this, especially in light of the success of their new

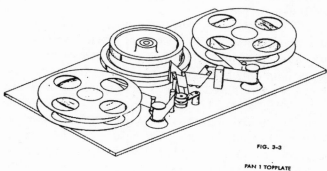

FIG. 3-3

PAN 1 TOPPLATE

1957. Above: Alex Maxey with 1957 Ampex helical-scan recorder. *Below:* Diagram of pan 1 top plate helical-scan recorder. From "Rand Report," July 1957. (Charles P. Ginsburg/Ampex.)

four-head transverse machines. So it was kept hush-hush for some four years.[46]

At the annual IRE meeting in New York City on March 20, 1956, RCA made several claims that its color tape recorder had been considerably improved. It could now record 15 minutes on a 20-inch reel of tape (mainly because of thinner tape). Speed had been reduced to 20 feet per second, and there were improved heads with response up to 1.5 mH plus a fifth channel for carrying the combined highs recording and reproducing the television signal. It included several servo systems and a movable head to improve tape stability. O. B. Hanson, RCA vice president of operations engineering, stated that NBC was now field-testing one such unit. A second unit may be turned over to the network by fall and Mr Hanson said that perhaps with experience, by late 1957 or 1958, they might have two units for actual broadcast use.[47]

At an opening meeting on March 5, 1956, top American color TV engineers described to a visiting group of Europeans the steps in the achievement of the U.S. color TV standards. Particular emphasis was laid on the need for compatibility, which had guided American developments.

This was the start of a five-month study tour of the world's color TV systems by the Europeans, which would ultimately determine the system adopted for all of Europe. The study tour began at the United Nations Building in New York in March 1956, as the American color TV industry played host to almost 100 radio and TV engineers from 21 European countries, including Poland and Czechoslovakia.

The meetings between the European and U.S. experts were held under the aegis of the International Radio Consultative Committee (CCIR) of the International Telecommunications Union, a U.N. agency. Hosts for the affair were the NTSC, under the chairmanship of Dr. W. R. G. Baker, and the U.S. State Department.

Following the meetings, the group witnessed numerous demonstrations of color TV. Sets shown were Admiral, Capehart, DuMont, Emerson, and Magnavox, using the shadow-mask tube; a Philco using the "apple" tube; a G.E. with postacceleration tube; and a Hazeltine, projection type color receiver. RCA was not participating; they held separate meetings with the CCIR group later.

At the conclusion of this American tour, the group was to proceed to England, France and the Netherlands, where they were to witness further demonstrations of color television. The final European color standards were scheduled to be drafted at the CCIR meeting in August in Warsaw, where it was to be decided whether Europe's color system would be compatible with existing monochrome standards, or whether color would be incompatible and operated in the UHF bands.[48]

In April 1956, live color was demonstrated with a low power transmitter at Alexander Palace, London by the BBC. At the demonstration the sets, operating on 405 lines, were alongside standard black-and-white units receiving the same signal and giving black-and-white pictures. The sets used were made by E. K. Cole, Cossor, Electric and Musical Industries, General Electric Company, Marconi, Murphy, and Pye.

Murphy Radio had supplied the BBC with eight of the 12 sets ordered by the Corporation for its series of tests. One further set had gone to the Post Office. These 21-inch receivers were bulkier than the 21-inch black-and-white units. They were British-made except for the tube and associated components which were of American origin. The tube was of the shadow mask type of 21-inch color tube made in America. A normal monochrome set usually had eight controls which the owner could adjust.

The Murphy color set had 11 in this category, plus a tone control for sound. The three extra controls were a "color killer" which turned the set into an ordinary black-and-white receiver, a "hue" control to line up the colors, and a "saturation" control which in effect was for color brightness. Sets of this type could be produced in quantity at a retail price of between $840 and $980.[49]

Reporting on the demonstration, Wireless World stated, "the pictures on the direct-viewing receivers were markedly superior to the others— particularly in colour rendering, brightness and definition. Indeed they were the best colour television pictures that … [we] have ever seen. That is not to say that they were perfect. There was quite a wide divergence of colour rendering between different receivers and in some cases the divergences appeared on the same set. On one screen for example, the flesh colour of a performer's hands was completely different from that of his face, although neither could be said to be unnatural. On another set, the hue of an actress' lemon yellow dress fluctuated from greenish yellow to almost orange in a matter of a few seconds.

"Some of the colour receivers were designed for operation on wide band colour information and some for narrow-band colour information, but one could see no difference between the respective pictures, except occasionally in areas of very small colour detail.

"The monochrome receivers, incidentally, gave a very good picture on the compatible colour transmissions and we had to examine the screens very closely in order to see the sub-carrier dot pattern. What was really remarkable, however, was the demonstration of reverse compatibility that is, the colour receivers showing black-and-white pictures from ordinary monochrome transmission (which the B.B.C put out after the colour transmissions). It was difficult to believe that the black-and-white pictures were actually being produced by red, green and blue cathode ray tube phosphors until one took a magnifying glass to the tube screens and saw the individual phosphor dots fluorescing in their respective colors." This was proof positive that the NTSC color system had reached its goal of both forward and reverse compatibility.[50]

During this period Ampex made many important improvements to its system. They went to the sandwich type of heads, the modulation system was extended to operate with a carrier frequency as high as six megacycles, and the switching unit, a two-mode device, was replaced by a four-way switcher that would only allow one channel at a time to conduct. The head drum was stabilized so it could be used with a standard monitor. Dolby states that they tried to use as many standard Ampex components and products as possible. These included mechanical parts for the tape transport; Model 359 audio electronic assemblies for the control track and an audio track; Model 375 power amplifiers for motor drive; and Model 391 speed control units, now used for serving both the rotary head and the longitudinal tape motion. Later, Anderson designed the elegant Mark IV console with its two sprawling racks.[51]

In February 1956, an in-house demonstration was given to a small Ampex management group. They recorded and played back part of the "Bob Crosby Show" from the local CBS affiliate. The results were sensational. Management were thinking of

1954. Four TV cameras. *Above left:* French TV camera. *Above right:* English Marconi Mark II TV camera. *Below left:* German Fernseh TV camera. *Below right:* RCA TK12 camera. (RCA.)

1955. First handbuilt video head assembly, with manual guide, carbon brushes, and solid-drum assembly. (Charles P. Ginsburg/Ampex.)

1955. The Mark III videotape machine. (Charles P. Ginsburg/Ampex.)

giving a surprise demonstration at the National Association of Radio and Television Broadcasters (NARTB) convention to be held in Chicago in April 1956.[52]

Then early in 1956, they had visitors: Bill Lodge, engineering vice president of CBS, accompanied by Howard Meighan; Blair Benson, an engineer in the CBS general engineering department; Frank Marx of ABC; Sir Harold Bishop, director of engineering of the BBC; Francis McLean, deputy director; and Norman Grover of the CBC. They were all sworn to absolute secrecy. Of course anyone from NBC and especially RCA was excluded.[53]

As a result of Lodge's visit, arrangements were made to use a demonstration model, the Mark IV (which had not yet been assembled), for a surprise showing to the

1955. Ampex Mark II machine. (Charles P. Ginsburg/Ampex.)

annual CBS affiliates meeting that was to occur the day before the formal opening of the 34th annual convention of NARTB at the Conrad Hilton Hotel, Chicago, on April 15, 1956. It had also been decided that the Mark III should be used for a press demonstration in Redwood City on the same day as the NARTB was to start. Ray Dolby was to take charge of the recorder during the Redwood City showing.[54]

The Mark IV was disassembled and shipped to Chicago. Despite some preliminary troubles, the machine was making the best pictures they had ever seen from tape. Nevertheless, CBS complained that the pictures were not good enough, the signal-to-noise ratio was too low, and the noise banding was intolerable. The situation was improved by the arrival of some new tape samples from 3M (two five-minute reels) that greatly exceeded in performance anything they had seen before. It seemed that Ampex had been using Reeves Soundcraft two-inch tape for their experiments.[55] Moreover, this first Ampex VTR had been developed without 3M ever having seen it before.[56] It appears that 3M's connection with both RCA and Crosby had kept Ampex from using any 3M tape until then. They were now ready for the Chicago demonstration.[57]

It started on April 14, at 10:30 A.M., at a special press conference simultaneously in Chicago and at the Ampex factory in Redwood City, California. In Chicago were Ampex president, George I. Long, and Philip Gundy, while in Redwood City, board chairman A. M. Poniatoff with instrumentation manager Robert Sackman gave the press its first glimpse of the new machine. The Chicago press conference was given at a meeting of more than 200 CBS Television network officials. According to one source, the demonstration began simply and quietly. The recorder was in another room. The speaker's remarks

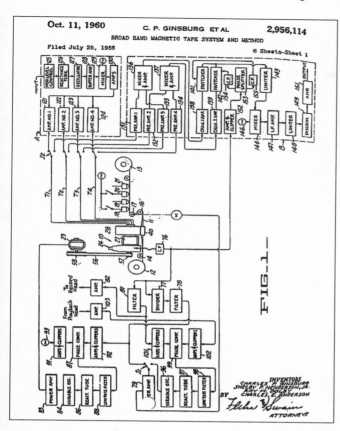

1955. The famous Ampex FM wideband patent, USA Patent no. 2,956,114, filed July 25, 1955; issued October 11, 1960. (US Patent Office.)

1956. The entire Ampex videotape recording staff. (*left to right*) Philip Gundy, Shelby Henderson, Alex Maxey, Fred Pfost, Ray Dolby, Charles Ginsburg, and Charles Anderson. (Charles P. Ginsburg/Ampex.)

were recorded on the tape as he delivered them. Then the tape was immediately played back on the recorder and the signal fed to a TV monitor. There was a moment or two of stunned silence as the astonished audience witnessed both picture and sound with no apparent difference in quality from the live program recorded moments earlier. Then an outburst of cheers, stamping feet, whistles and pandemonium broke loose.[58] Almost immediately Ampex was flooded with orders.[59]

In Redwood City, Ray Dolby was in charge of the technical aspects of the program. As in Chicago, the demonstration was a bombshell; the performance was sensational, exciting, and satisfying.[60] After the Redwood

City demonstration, Dolby took a plane to Chicago and joined the industry presentation that Ampex was making there.[61] Ginsburg gave a demonstration every 15 minutes throughout the five days of the convention at the Conrad Hilton Hotel.

Over a leased video circuit, from CBS station WBBM, TV shows were taped on the Ampex machine and played back instantly. Again, astonished audiences witnessed both picture and sound with no apparent difference in quality from live programs moments earlier. This was the first closed-circuit use of the new recorder.[62]

Predictably enough the reaction from the RCA camp was one of bewilderment and incredulity. George H. Brown found that as NBC and RCA continued to experiment, friends at NBC asked him many times to rescue them from the predicament they had found themselves in. But there was little that Brown could do as the technology was one of Sarnoff's "birthday presents."[63]

Brown was at the NARTB convention but had not witnessed the original Ampex presentation. (No one from RCA had been invited!) However, he was invited to a demonstration of what he called a "really novel device" before the day was over.[64] The next day he telephoned

1956. Four photos showing progress on Ampex machine. (Charles P. Gunsburg/Ampex.)

The Mark IV videotape machine, first shown in Chicago on April 14, 1956. (Charles P. Ginsburg/Ampex.)

Elmer Engstrom to tell him of the Ampex triumph and to send someone to confirm his observations. Robert Sarnoff, president of RCA, was obliged to tell his father by telephone that some people from California had stolen one of his birthday presents.

There was no choice but to use the Ampex method for video recording. NBC ordered three machines: two went to Burbank; the third was delivered to the commercial products division of RCA in Camden where a team of 25 engineers took it apart and worked to bring out a prototype machine of their own. There such experts as Ray Kell, Al Bedford, Wendell Morrison, Eric Leyton and Gordon Fredendall were ordered to *reverse* engineer the Ampex machine with the big difference that color was to be there from the start.[65]

Sarnoff still believed in his RCA machine; obviously he had no idea of what had really happened in Chicago. He even wanted a new team to augment the old one. He was used to pulling victory out of defeat. In October, many meetings were held to discuss the operational details. The NBC people declared that six machines would be required in Chicago to handle a one-hour show without interruption because of the small amount of program on a single reel of tape, and because of the time needed to bring them up to speed and to stop the reels and reload the machine. While Engstrom was present, no word of criticism or dissension was offered, but as soon as he left the room, the chief engineer of NBC, Oliver B. Hanson, immediately urged Brown to tell Engstrom how hopeless the situation really was held to be. When Brown suggested that they should tell Engstrom of their true feelings, they protested that it would be better if he did so.

By the beginning of November in 1956, Brown could not restrain himself further and he established Gordon Fredendall, Al Bedford and Eric Leyton to act as a study committee to evaluate the various methods of videotape recording. Brown, Ray Kell, and Wendell Morrison joined many of their discussions. Two weeks later, Brown wrote a very impertinent letter that stated very clearly: "Drop the project for Chicago. It is generally agreed that the present performance is not commercially acceptable and would not be used by NBC if they had the equipment in its present form." In addition, he proposed that they accelerate their efforts to record color signals on the Ampex machine.

Above: First public demonstration of Ampex recorder at Conrad Hilton Hotel in Chicago on April 14, 1956. Ginsburg is seen in the upper middle of the picture. (Charles P. Ginsburg/Ampex.) *Below:* 1956. Ray Dolby operating the VRX-1000 at the CBS suite at the Conrad Hilton Hotel in April. (Charles Ginsburg/Ampex.)

3M video tape introduced in 1956. (3M.)

Within a few days, Elmer Engstrom had broken the news to Sarnoff that one of his toys was broken beyond repair and Sarnoff agreed to stop the nonsense. Engstrom telephoned Brown from New York to give him the good news and told Brown to drop the RCA project for Chicago. When Brown reminded him that he was not the project leader, he replied that he would pass the word through other channels. (Note: I have never come across any mention of the term "Simplex" in relation to the high-speed RCA recorder while it was being designed and built. This term came much later.)

Common sense had finally prevailed and the RCA machine was dropped. No one wanted to head the new project (Olson wasn't even considered) and it seems that Brown's objections to the old machine made him a candidate to run it.[66]

On Monday, April 30, 1956, it was reported that Ampex had received orders for 82 commercial units at a price of $45,000 each. Ampex was shocked; they had thought earlier that perhaps as many as five prototype machines would be delivered to government agencies for evaluation, along with a program leading to gradual delivery of the machines for television in 1957.[67] Both CBS and NBC had ordered three units each at $75,000, with CBS having priority. ABC stated that it would stick with its kinescope film system. Meanwhile officials of Bing Crosby Enterprises stated that they were continuing research and development for a "fully compatible" color and monochrome machine for the industry. They added that they were working on slowing down the machine and making other advances.[68]

In July 1956, several new portable television cameras were described. On July 22, 1956, RCA announced a transistorized portable TV Pickup station for spot news and other TV field pickups. It had a four-pound camera and detachable electronic viewfinder. It used a tiny half-inch Vidicon. The backpack contained a synchronizing generator, battery power supply, and a 2,000mc transmitter.[69] CBS also announced a 28-pound portable camera based upon a French design. The camera was built by Intercontinental Electronics Corp. They also displayed a smaller version which weighed 1½ pounds and was developed by the Lockheed Engineering Research Labs.[70] ABC also announced a miniature TV camera made by Grundig Majestic in Germany.[71] It also used a lens a quarter inch in diameter.[72] ABC displayed a camera made by the Philco that weighed four pounds and measured 3½ by 6¼ inches. It too was linked by a cable.[73]

These were to be used at the August political conventions in Chicago and San Francisco. The CBS camera weighed four pounds (including lens and an electronic viewfinder). The camera measured 7 by 3¼ inches. The 32-pound back pack consisted of the video transmitter and power supplies. French scientist Raymond Cohen demonstrated the two-pound camera. The

How much should a Tape Recorder cost?

$45,000* The new Ampex Videotape Recorder at $45,000 achieves flawless reproduction of TV picture and sound. The system not only promises to revolutionize network telecasting but will actually reduce material costs by 99%. In hundreds of TV stations throughout the country Ampex Videotape Recording will repay its cost in less than a year.

$1,315* The Ampex Model 350 studio console recorder at $1,315, costs less per hour than any other similar recorder you can buy. Year after year it continues to perform within original specifications and inevitably requires fewer adjustments and parts replacements than machines of lesser quality.

$545* The Ampex Model 601 portable recorder at $545 gives superb performance inside and outside of the studio. This price buys both the finest portable performance available and the most hours of service per dollar.

YOU CAN PAY LESS FOR A TAPE RECORDER BUT FOR PROFESSIONAL USE YOU CAN'T AFFORD TO BUY LESS THAN THE BEST

*Net price as of August 1, 1956 and subject to change.
SIGNATURE OF PERFECTION IN MAGNETIC TAPE RECORDERS
934 Charter Street • Redwood City, California

ELECTRONIC INDUSTRIES & Tele-Tech • September 1956   For product information, use inquiry card on last page.

Left: 1956. First ad for the new Ampex video recorder. (*Electronic Industries & Tele-Tech*, Sept.)

Left and above: 1956. CBS portable camera made by Intercontinental Electronics Corp. (CBS.)

smaller 1½-pound camera developed by Lockheed Aircraft measured 5 by 1¾ by 2 inches.[74]

Ampex announced that it would ship three hand-made prototypes of its VR 1000 recorder to CBS and two to NBC by the week of September 24, 1956. Ampex was making only 13 prototypes: CBS was to get five and NBC three; the rest were going to government laboratories. According to Joe Roizen, the first 16 hand-built machines were called VRX 1000s.[75] Production orders now amounted to 84 units with two going to Associated Rediffusion, London, England.[76]

NBC-TV demonstrated its new lenticular color film process to the press and set dealers on Tuesday, September 11, 1956. The demonstration comprised a special 50-minute musical revue originating from NBC in Burbank

and distributed from San Diego to Seattle. Consolidated Film Industries was building a special plant in Burbank for processing the new film. Newsmen present were "not enthusiastic about the picture and color quality."[77] The *New York Times* reported that it did not show off its color to its best advantage. The blues were purplish and images tended to be fuzzy. Overlapping and bleeding of colors were frequently evident. It was claimed that inferior results were produced for color and black-and-white.[78]

The color process was made possible by the presence of many vertical lenticles or lenses which were embossed on the base of the film surface and acted as prisms to separate the color into color difference stripes. The special Eastman Type 5308 embossed kine-recording film had 25 lenticles/mm and approximately 390 across the width of a 35mm frame. The system used three kinescopes having P16 phosphor screens displaying negative polarity. A special prism was placed in the position of the color filter. Since the light from each kinescope could only reach that strip behind the lenticle reserved for one color, the recorded film could be considered a color separation negative. As in the monochrome kine process, the lenticular film was quickly processed and threaded on a special projector. This consisted of a three–Vidicon film chain with a mask in front of each camera tube designed to pass only the correct color information.[79]

NBC inaugurated the lenticular color kine process on a three-hour delay on 29 September 1956, with the Esther Williams "Aqua Spectacular of 1956." NBC had promised that most of the bugs would be worked out. In spite of all the time and money spent

1957. The entire Ampex engineering staff with two versions of the videotape machines: Mark IV and Mark III. (Charles P. Ginsburg/Ampex.)

1956. Four European cameras. *Above left:* Russian (Super Orthicon). **Right:** French (Vidicon). *Below left:* Emitron (Emitron tube). *Right:* English Pye (5820 Image Orthicon) type 2014. (*Radio und Fernsehen*, Nr 7/1956.)

on this process, it was a dismal failure. This process continued at NBC on a daily basis until February 19, 1958, when it was announced that all time-zone delays would be done by means of color videotape recording.[80]

On September 19, 1956, it was reported that production of the Chromatic (Lawrence) single-gun color tube and the color set using it would be undertaken by the Allen B. DuMont Labs.[81] It was expected that mass production of both the tube and the set would be completed within a year.[82]

On October 1, 1956, 3M announced that Francis Healy was to be general manager of a new 3M company called Mincom. It had taken over the research and development activities formerly conducted by Bing Crosby Enterprises.[83] The transaction involved the payment by 3M of $75,000 for the Crosby equipment and inventories including the video recording equipment. A number of Crosby patents to be transferred to 3M would be paid for from future sales. The main reason for the purchase by 3M was that it wanted to keep abreast of TV recording developments and to have improved magnetic tape products available in the market when needed. However, it was claimed that they were developing a color recorder based on the Bing Crosby Enterprises machine. Meanwhile Mincom was marketing a wide-band recorder for instrumen-

tation applications. It was claimed that units had been delivered to Westinghouse, Wright Field and Evans Signal Lab. In light of the Ampex disclosure, this project was to be short-lived.[84]

On Monday, October 3, 1956, RCA demonstrated three major developments that David Sarnoff had requested five years before. They included an electronic air conditioner, an electronic amplifier of light and a magnetic tape player that showed TV programs through standard receivers. The tape player was housed in a cabinet the size of a high-quality tape sound reproducer, and used quarter-inch tape traveling at 10 ft/sec. Three prerecorded tapes were shown: two off the air and one specially prepared. There was no description of the quality of picture or sound. The demonstration was given by Dr. Engstrom and Dr. Olson to General Sarnoff.[85]

On October 25, 1956, a new flat picture tube was described by its inventor Denis Gabor. This was supposed to be the first step toward being able to hang a television on a wall or stand it on a mantelpiece. Basically the flat tube had the electron beam folded behind the screen and bent upward to scan the picture horizontally. The tube completed a line scan automatically and the whole process repeated itself. Provisions were made for color through a basic shadow mask and three beams. Picture size was approximately 3½ inches for a 12-inch diagonal and 4½ inches for a 21-inch screen.[86]

On Friday, November 30, 1956, the first videotaped network broadcast was made by CBS TV with "Doug Edwards and the News" from Television City in Hollywood. It was a 15-minute news show. This was telecast to the Western affiliates of CBS. CBS was taking no chances; however, the broadcast was backed up by both 35mm and 16mm kines for protection in case something happened. This was the first use of the Ampex recorder in broadcast history. By February 1, 1957, two machines were in use every evening.[87] "Time shifting" of television material, which had begun with the kinescope recording process, had just gained its foremost ally. The Ampex Revolution was under way.[88]

In December 1956, a new miniature half-inch Vidicon tube was described. It was a half-inch in diameter and three inches long. A new photoconductor had been developed with more sensitivity to overcome the small size of the target. It was claimed that resolution and lag were adequate for many applications where small size was

First videotape network broadcast from TV City, Hollywood, November 30, 1956. Running the machine is John Radis; behind him is Jim Morrison. (CBS.)

attractive. It required only one fourth the heater power and one third the deflection power of the conventional one-inch Vidicon. The use of transistorized circuitry aided the development of a tube that small. It was designed to use an 8mm motion picture lens.[89]

In December 1956, a new transistorized television camera using the miniature Vidicon was described. It was made possible by recent transistor developments which allowed for the design of cameras that were extremely small and used low power. Two versions of the camera were described. One was a closed-circuit camera that weighed only three pounds and used three watts of power. It was connected to an antenna of any standard receiver. Another version was a completely portable pickup station capable of picking up a scene and relaying it on a 2,000 megacycle carrier to a base station about a half-mile away. It consisted of a camera, synchronizing generator, and monitor completely transistorized except for the transmitter. It weighed some 20 pounds including batteries for six hours of operation. It was used in covering the 1956 political conventions.[90]

On Thursday, December 13, 1956, Ampex delivered the first recorder to NBC in Burbank. It was claimed that NBC had privately tested the machine the previous week by showing segments of certain shows by closed circuit to New York.[91]

Then on December 20, 1956, CBS transmitted by closed circuit the "Art Linkletter Show" (which had been done the day before) from Hollywood to CBS at 485 Madison Avenue. It was claimed that the quality was impressive.[92]

Late in December 1956, it was reported that Ampex was expected to have a color tape recorder ready by the following April. This had low priority of course as Ampex could barely keep up with the demand for the basic black-and-white recorders. However, they hoped to present a prototype unit at the next NARTB Convention.[93] It seemed that Ampex had given a contract to the Stanford Research Institute in hopes of getting a method of recording color on videotape. This was unsuccessful.[94]

Chapter 5

Europe Turns Down NTSC
(1957–1960)

On January 1, 1957, as a result of George Brown's "rash" actions, he found himself as the newly appointed chief engineer of the commercial electronic products division of RCA in Camden with a dual mission: to make a commercially acceptable videotape recorder with color capability available for sale as soon as possible and to put into production a large transistorized data processor.[1]

The BBC changed over to vestigial side-band transmission when they moved from the Alexandra Palace to the Crystal Palace in January 1957.[2]

On January 30-31, 1957, the BBC transmitted a special color program for members of Parliament. The show originated at the Alexandra Palace but was radiated from the Crystal Palace. The system was basically the American color NTSC system but modified in details for 405 line transmission. While the reviewer was very impressed with the overall results, he had reservations about the economics of producing receivers at a price within the purse of common people. He recommended looking into alternative systems and even suggested that compatibility was not an essential in picking such a new system. This was not the first time that the NTSC color system was to come under attack in Europe and elsewhere.[3]

Broadcasting noted in January 1957, that of the three Ampex machines ordered by NBC, two went to NBC in Hollywood for immediate use, arriving on December 14, 1956. While RCA was using the Ampex machines for daily network repeats, it had not heralded this revolutionary event with its usual fanfare. This was the beginning of the RCA effort to downplay the magnificent role that Ampex had played in producing such a marvelous machine.[4]

Broadcasting reported that during the week of January 15, 1957, NBC quietly plunged into a full-scale "Ampex operation." Five NBC-TV Monday-Friday series—"Today," "Home," "Truth or Consequences," "News Caravan" and "Tonight"—were all taped off the line in the East and repeated three hours later for the West Coast.[5]

The third Ampex machine went to the Broadcast Studio Engineering Laboratories, Industrial Electronic Products at Camden, New Jersey. Here the machine was immediately taken apart and distributed among five different RCA engineering and research divisions to carry on the development work. The project went forward and as soon as the various parts of the "new" machine were completed, they were moved to the Broadcast Studio Engineering Laboratories where the complete engineering model of the recorder was being assembled. It was claimed that continued refinement of circuits, mechanisms and operating techniques resulted in pictures of excellent quality. During the months of August, September and October, a number of private demonstrations were presented.

In March 1957, Peto Scott Electrical Instruments in London reported that it had designed a small lightweight studio camera designed around the one-inch Vidicon (staticon) camera tube. It was to be tested under the exacting performance demanded by the BBC engineering department. It was felt that the equipment had been designed with light weight and small size in mind but not at the sacrifice of electrical performance.[6]

Also in March 1957, RCA introduced its first one-inch Vidicon camera for broadcast use. This was the TK-15 Vidicon. It provided high-quality pictures for commercials, "live" news and other scenes in which the light level was adequate for Vidicons. It was meant to be used as an adjunct to the other high TV cameras then being used for commercial broadcasting.[7]

It was revealed on April 1, 1957, that ABC was in the process of installing its three Ampex units. It was claimed that the use of tape was saving the networks close to $10,000 a week in film and film processing. CBS estimated that each hour of delays cost around $350 for film and processing, and tape would save $8,400 a week in film stock and processing alone. Finally it was stated that CBS now had enough confidence in the Ampex machine to stop using 35mm and 16mm kine backup. However, NBC was still using kine backup. The article commented that since the introduction of its machine at the 1956 NARTB, Ampex had managed to compress three years of progress into 12 months.[8]

Ampex also announced in 1957 that it would have a prototype of its color machine ready at the NARTB convention in Chicago, about 18 months away.[9]

In June 1957, RCA reported that the lenticular film process was producing inferior results. It was also mentioned that RCA was working on its compatible color tape recorder to solve this problem.[10]

In August 1957 *Electronics Magazine* congratulated Ampex, and especially Charles Ginsburg, for winning the 1957 Television Academy Emmy Award for its videotape recorder.[11] Ginsburg also won the David Sarnoff Gold Medal, from the Society of Motion Picture and Television Engineers (SMPTE) in 1957; the Vladimir K. Zworykin TV Prize from the Institute of Radio Engineers in March 1958; and the Valdemar Poulsen Gold Medal, Danish Academy of Technical Sciences on November 23, 1960, and was elected to the U.S. National Academy of Engineering. These honors were all very well deserved.[12] He was also awarded the Howard N. Potts Medal of the Franklin Institute on October 15, 1969, for his being the "key contributor to the development of an extended range magnetic recorder capable of recording and reproducing video signals, an innovation which has made a major impact on the television industry."[13]

In an article by Ross Snyder of Ampex in August 1, 1957, it was mentioned that Ampex had a method of splicing and editing videotape. It had a means of identifying the line on videotape that represented the vertical pulse. The tape was wiped by a harmless solution which rendered the magnetic recording visible. Since the vertical pulses had a characteristic appearance, they could be located with precision. A particular point could be cut and matched to a similar line, then spliced with precision.[14]

At this time, according to Ginsburg, an officer of Ampex was contacted by an RCA official who informed them that RCA had perfected a color TV recorder and

1958. 3M videotape splicer for the Ampex VTR. (Ampex.)

wished to demonstrate it to Ampex. This demonstration took place on August 15, 1957, at the RCA Camden Laboratories. Present were Walter Selsted, Charles Ginsburg, Harold Lindsey, Myron Stolaroff and Paul Flehr, the Ampex patent attorney. They were ushered into the room where the demonstration was to take place. The machine demonstrated was part of the third machine that had been shipped to Camden earlier. Ginsburg commented that "enough of the mechanism could be seen to determine that they [RCA] used much of the essential mechanism of the Ampex recorder." This included the rotating head assembly and the FM modulation system. The demonstration was excellent. The colors were vivid and there was no distortion of the images.[15]

At the same time, a representative of the RCA domestic licensing activity began negotiations with Ampex to secure rights to the pertinent Ampex patents. Brown's associates had achieved great success with the color adaptation and this knowledge was attractive to Ampex—so attractive, in fact that Ampex, out of fear that they may infringe on RCA color patents, agreed on anything that RCA proposed. Consequently, a cross-licensing agreement was signed on October 14, 1957, which gave each party royalty-free rights to domestic and foreign patents and applications of the other party as these inventions pertained to the videotape apparatus. For this, RCA paid Ampex $100,000, a ridiculously low figure considering what they got, and agreed to teach them the RCA method of achieving color recording on the Ampex machine. In exchange, Ampex gave RCA the details of the highly valuable FM system. This agreement was amicably terminated on October 10, 1968, but the termination created no hardship for either party since the licensing rights continued to the expiration date of any patent resulting from an application filed prior to the termination date.[16]

Unduly worried by the amount of color experience and patents held by RCA, it was decided to consider any proposition that RCA might offer in the way of an amicable agreement. After giving careful consideration of the situation, Ampex officials decided to ask RCA for a proposal. It was evident by that time that RCA was suggesting cross-licensing between Ampex and RCA with respect to all pertinent patents and patent applications. After some negotiations, the agreement was executed by both parties. This gave RCA the rights to use any of Ampex's future patents or applications without further payment. This was a disaster for Ampex as it was to come up with many innovative ideas that RCA was free to use, copy and sell.[17]

Later in September 1957, another new compatible color system was demonstrated by M. Henri de France of the Société Nouvelle RBV-La Radio Industrie. It was called SECAM (Séquential Couleur Avec Mémoire). It was basically a sequential system in which the main purpose of the sequential transmission was to simplify the receiver circuitry by eliminating the need for complicated expedients such as synchronous detection, which were necessary aspects of the NTSC system. A loss of vertical definition was expected, but as it was tried on the 819-line system, any such loss could not to be noticed. So it was necessary to transmit only one set of information at a time instead of both at once as in the NTSC system. While this simplified the system somewhat, the additional expense of the delay lines made the receiver as costly as the NTSC receiver. Results were very fair, with the color picture being quite good and not very noisy.[18]

In the SECAM system, the color signals were transmitted alternately on a single subcarrier and stored in a one-line memory at the receiver. One stored and one direct signal, thus provided the two-color difference signals. This way of handling the chrominance information cut the vertical definition for color in half. But it was claimed that even halved, the color definition was higher than the resolution of the human eye. Another disadvantage was that the frequency interlace principle did not work for an FM subcarrier. Also, use of a frequency modulated subcarrier, a change made in May 1962 to the SECAM system, decreased the signal-to-noise ratio by about 4 to 5db. The chief advantage of the SECAM system was its almost total immunity from differential gain and phase effects.[19]

The article also mentioned for the first time that for three color television, the photoconductive tube had the greatest possibilities. It said that the new type of tube used a layer of lead monoxide as described in a Philips paper.[20]

In late September 1957, Ray Dolby left Ampex. During his senior year at Stanford University he had applied for and had won a Marshall scholarship to study at Cambridge University; however, now he would soon be bound not for Cambridge, but for Southampton University. As he stated, "the VTR development had been an exhilarating and rewarding experience in my life, but I also wanted to do other things."[21]

In October 1957, Ampex announced the introduction of a new editing device. Its main feature was a simple visual process for locating exactly the place on the tape where the deletion was to be made and a splicing device that would do the job without losing the sync pulse that kept the picture and sound together. It was said that it would be ready by November.[22]

In October 1957, a second series of color tests were made by the BBC in London. These came from the BBC's Crystal Palace station. They were of a modified version of the American NTSC color system. The tests were (1) to provide a source of high-grade color signals, (2) to get further experience in operation of color studios and transmitting equipment, and (3) to obtain further knowledge of the comparability of the particular system being tested.[23]

Just two weeks after RCA and Ampex had reached their patent agreement, the RCA engineering prototype was introduced on October 21, 1957, with a presentation of a recorded color show from RCA's Camden Broadcasting engineering studio via network lines to both New York City and Burbank, California. Theodore Smith, executive vice president of RCA industrial electronic products, hailed the new system not only as practical but a major engineering achievement of incalculable benefit to the economy, efficiency and flexibility of color to broadcasting." He stated that in addition to the one used in the demonstration, several prototypes were under construction and hoped for the delivery of the first of these early in 1958.

The demonstration consisted of portions of several color shows carried by NBC over the weekend. Observers found the playback uniformly good and considerably superior to kinescopes. When asked about how the recently signed agreement between Ampex and RCA figured in the equipment being demonstrated, Mr. Smith replied that he "couldn't say about that." He added, however, that

1964. First Ampex Editec programmer. (Ampex.)

1957. RCA color videotape recorder-reproducer, October. (RCA.)

of the two systems, Ampex's was for black-and-white and RCA's was for color, but they were compatible. (This was another of RCA's efforts to minimize the fact that the machine had been built around Ampex's basic ideas using a rotating head and FM modulating system.) RCA's major cosmetic change was that its machine was rack mounted,

Dr. George H. Brown (*left*) and Theodore Smith with the RCA prototype video recorder at the Camden Broadcast Engineering Studio, October 1957. (RCA.)

similar to the Olson model, and not in an elegant console like the Ampex recorder. It was an ungainly device. Being rack mounted made it difficult to handle the two-inch tape for either threading or position control; editing would be a chore. One machine took up half of a wall with its nine racks of equipment.

Regarding costs, Smith stated that it could cost under $100,000, but much more than the cost of an Ampex at $46,000. Mr. Smith emphasized that the VTR could be used to tape in black-and-white also, but that color was the goal. Also present at the demonstration was Dr. George H. Brown, chief engineer of industrial electronics.[24]

At this demonstration, Robert Sarnoff announced NBC's order for six preproduction units. The first color machine, TRT-1AC, was priced at $63,000 and the TRT-1A for black-and-white at $49,000. It was revealed that the color VTR would be offered for sale and was to be called the RCA Videotape Recorder.[25]

On November 19, 1957, RCA announced that the delivery of the first production models of color and black-and-white tape recorders was to begin in December 1958. Price was $63,000 for color and $49,500 for black-and-white. RCA planned to send six prototypes to "Tape Central" in Burbank late in 1958.[26] This of course was to forestall the orders for Ampex machines until RCA had built its own operating machines.

In November 1957, the General Electric Company showed a new and smaller type of live color camera at the opening of the WGY-WRGB Broadcasting Center in Schenectady, NY. The camera weighed about 215 pounds, about 75 pounds lighter than most current color cameras. It was claimed that printed circuits and transistors were used to cut down its size. A new optical system eliminated the many glass surfaces resulting in improved color quality. It was to be priced competitively at around $50,000.[27]

In December 1957, it was reported that the BBC was undertaking a second series of color tests. The purpose was to demonstrate a modified version of the NTSC color system.[28]

On Thursday, January 9, 1958, a paper was read about a new French portable TV camera by one Joseph Polonksy (Compagnie Générale de T.S.F., Paris). The portable camera (CP 103) used a one-inch Vidicon. (The half-inch Vidicon was not quite ready to be used.) The camera consisted of an RCA Vidicon type RCA 6198, and had a standard 16mm cinema lens of 25 to 160 focal length or a zoom variable from 25 to 100 mm. It had an optical 16mm cinema viewfinder. All controls were automatic. The camera could be used on either 819 or 405 lines standards. It had a five-watt transmitter with a power pack of 18 pounds. The normal five-watt transmitter was capable of sending picture signals from 300 to 600 feet. This was the camera used by CBS at the August 1956 national conventions in the USA.[29]

On January 15, 1958, RCA showed its new color videotape machines to a group of 100 broadcasters and engineers at Camden, New Jersey. It announced firm prices of $63,000 for color and $49,500 for black-and-white and promised delivery at the end of the year. Performance of the machines was hailed by spectators. Mr. A. H. Lind of the RCA broadcasting equipment group at Camden told the audience that RCA and Ampex were holding discussions on standardization so that they could use VTR tape interchangeably on each other's machines. He expressed the opinion that standardization would soon be coming from either the SMPTE or the Electronic Industries Association. The equipment was the same as that shown in October 1957.[30]

In February/March 1958, RCA decided to tell its version of how the videotape recorder was developed. In an article by A. H. Lind, he attempted to relate how RCA had gone through a period of several years of research and tried out a number of methods of recording wide-band electrical signals on magnetic tape. This was not true. RCA had spent from 1951 on one approach only—the high-speed longitudinal approach of Dr. Olson. There is absolutely no proof that Olson ever tried anything *but* the high-speed longitudinal approach.

(In a personal interview with Arch Luther in Los Angeles on May 3, 1983, Lind stated that there was another project at the Camden laboratories. He said that it was a multitrack VTR project [similar to that of the defunct G.E. project?] It is possible that RCA also had a contract with the air force, separate from the Olson project, that they never publicized.)

Lind went on to say that the approach they finally adopted involved a series of closely spaced transverse tracks in two thirds of the total tape area being magnetized, with the recording still being reproduced coherently. This of course was the successful method that Ampex had invented, patented, developed, manufactured and brought to market. Yet in the entire article, the word Ampex never appears once.

Lind finally comes to the color processor that RCA was using. It was the only original part of the machine that had *not been* part of the five-track New York prototype. Basically it was a very clever way of canceling the "jitter" of the color signal by heterodyning it to a signal that had the same jitter. When combined electrically, the jitter was removed and the color picture stabilized.[31] This concept of course seemed valuable to Ampex at the time.

The color processing in the RCA Television Tape Recorder involved canceling phase drift in the chrominance signal by translating this signal to a higher fre-

quency spectrum and then heterodyning this translated signal with a signal that also contained the phase drift and was of such a frequency that the different signal frequencies fell back into the original frequency band. If this was derived from a signal recorded on the tape, it would contain the same phase-drift effects as those in the translated chrominance signal, but the different signal obtained by heterodyning would be free of phase drift because errors had been canceled by subtractions.[32]

Lind also came up with a new term to distinguish the newer RCA tape recorder from the original Ampex transverse magnetic recorder—he called it the "Quadruplex system." Here he was making a distinction that truly did not exist. It is strange that nowhere in the prior literature is there ever any mention of an RCA Simplex, Duplex, Triplex or Quintuplex recorder. So what did the term "Quadruplex" mean? Where did it come from? Did he mean the number of heads, the number of tracks, or perhaps something about the electronic headwheel delay lines that allowed the four heads to be electrically aligned to each other in quadrature relation? It was never made clear.[33] The first mention I can find of the word "quadrature" in any context is in an article by H. H. Klerx[34] in which he mentions the electronic quadrature relationship of the four heads but does not mention the word "quadruplex." Sadly the term stuck; it had a nice ring to it and the public was quick to adopt it as the name for the existing transverse recording system. (Ampex did start using the term Ampex VR1000 "Videotape Recorder" to describe its machines.)

Lind tries to give the impression that every obstacle such as signal timing stability, signal transfer linearity, wide-band signal spectrum, tape stretch and shrinkage, and the problems of magnetic heads had been solved by the great team of RCA engineers who had taken apart the third Ampex machine and copied it down to the last bolt and nut. What RCA had done, any good engineering laboratory with endless resources could have done.

How big a problem is there in taking an existing machine apart and reproducing the separate parts, especially when those taking it apart had been furnished the electrical diagrams and schematics? Just knowing that something works makes the problem easier. No foreign territory to pass through, no dead ends—the engineers just copy what they have. Lind concludes the article by patting himself on the back, stating that this was another example of RCA being able to concentrate a great wealth and diversity of talent on a difficult and complex problem. Where was all of this talent during the formative years while RCA was putting its money on the Olson project?

This article, to RCA's great dishonor, was certainly done deliberately with no intention of giving Ampex any credit at all. Just as RCA had tried to make a nonentity in the 1930s and 1940s of the work of Philo Farnsworth, now they were giving Ampex the same treatment. It wouldn't work, though; Ampex's brilliant research and development department kept on making improvements on the basic machine and RCA could never quite keep up with them.[35]

In March 1958, it was reported that over 100 tape machines were in use throughout the country.[36] In April 1958, the first Ampex video recorder was introduced into Japan.[37]

It was reported that NBC Tape Central went into operation on Monday, April 30, 1958. It consisted of eight black-and-white Ampex machines converted to color by RCA. There was also one RCA color and one black-and-white machine. Three more Ampex black-and-white machines were in use in a different area. A photo of a smiling Robert Sarnoff pointed to the lonely RCA color recorder.[38]

A similar article in *Broadcast News* was careful to show only the four RCA color recorders.[39] Color videotape recording that began at NBC on April 27, 1958, signaled the end of the hot-kine era, but did not mean the end of the television film recording process. On the contrary, much effort would be put into perfecting the process to take advantage of its potential cost savings and flexibility. The impetus was that film was the universal medium. Any 35mm or 16mm film could be shown on any 35mm or 16mm projector anywhere in the world. Tape was not so fortunately placed.

Ampex showed its new color process for the VR1000 for the first time at the April 1958 NAB Convention. It was described in *Broadcasting* on April 24, 1958. It was a coding-encoding system in which the encoded chrominance information was reduced back to the I and Q video components and then re-encoded with the luminance signal. Burst was added. The signal coming from the tape was divided by appropriated filter networks into a luminance channel of approximately 3mc in bandwidth and a chrominance channel of 2mc in bandwidth. The burst signal from the tape was used to drive the burst lock oscillator and the nominal 3mc signal thus generated was phase shifted and applied to a pair of diode clamp demodulators, providing quadrature demodulation of the color video information. Since the regenerated 3.58MHz signal was being corrected in phase at the start of each horizontal line, its relation to the encoded chrominance signal on each line remained constant and therefore the recovery of the color signal was reasonably precise.[40] It was quite different from the RCA color system that Ampex had received in its patent agreement with RCA. (Thus it turned out that Ampex never did use the RCA color method and gave away its FM patent for a pittance.)

In April 1958, at the NAB TV convention, Ampex showed its new videotape splicer. It was an accessory that made it possible to splice together two pieces of tape without causing a discontinuity in the picture. It was basically the same as an audio tape splicer except it handled two-inch tape. Ampex machines were laying down edit pulses within every field in the vertical blanking area on the lower edge of the control track. Ampex claimed that it was possible to "develop" the tape with a special iron carbonyl fluid called Edivue and use these pulses for editing and splicing the tape. While Ampex had earlier maintained that the machine was mainly for "time delay" purposes, they were preparing the machine for more advanced uses.[41]

Unknowingly, however, Ampex had opened up a can of worms. It was immediately brought up as a labor relations problem. ABC went on record as stating that videotape was never spliced. But both CBS and NBC were to have different opinions.[42]

Besides the splicer, the use of the videotape recorder on a daily round-the-clock basis introduced a host of new problems that the networks had not anticipated. The first question was whether VTR was "film" or "live"? With kinescope there was no question that it was film. Yet at all three networks, the recording of kinescope was done by electric technicians, and this had never been questioned. In its infancy, the television industry had allowed its electrical technicians to handle all operations of the presentation of film, from loading it to splicing it and projecting it.

Why wasn't this work done by members of the film union (IATSE)? There are several reasons. First of all, in the early days of television, it was not considered important enough to get jurisdiction over it. The amount of jobs were in the tens or twenties. While the film union considered the projection of film in the theaters a must, it had figured that television in its early days was barely worth fighting for. So they let it go by them.

When it came to electronics, the only electrical departments at the film studios were run by sound technicians. Sound was recorded on either film, disc or magnetic tape. The personnel here were highly trained in electrical amplifiers, mixers, microphones and the like. The sound departments at all the major studios had been made up of ex–RCA or –Western Electric graduates who had to have a greater education in electricity in order to fill their positions. Many of these people had come from radio. However, they were few in number compared with the overwhelming majority who were camera, props, grips, lighting people, so on, who made up the bulk of union personnel and who were all under the umbrella of IATSE.

The problem was that the television industry had to make up its mind which way to go. While none of the networks had any love of the labor unions, they had to get along with the electrical unions in radio to get proficient people: hams, ex-ship radio operators and other experts, most of whom had first-class FCC radio licenses which in many cases, they were in the midst of transferring to television. They also had to get along with the stage people who had charge of the physical sets, props and lighting.

Television at the time was a highly skilled technical job. Lining up an image orthicon camera sometimes took over half an hour. On the new tape machines, it took over an hour to get a good head alignment, correct FM modulation and picture and get sound levels correct. CBS temporarily solved the problem (after a two-week strike) by allowing its technicians to edit videotape physically. NBC at first did a double recording on a 16mm film system, using a 16mm kinescope, and cutting the film and then the tape to match. ABC was delaying any decision in hopes of someone else showing them the way. At any rate, the battle lines were drawn and this would be a jurisdictional fight to last for many years. The battle also involved the actors from SAG and AFTRA. In 1956, CBS had signed a pact with AFTRA covering actors in TV shows telecast on tape. SAG regarded video recording as just another form of prerecorded shows. So the battle was on.[43]

In May 1958, it was reported that the BBC had converted two 35mm film recorders at Lime Grove to a stored-field system. This gave full information in each frame. The older suppressed-frame method only gave half the information.[44]

On May 23, 1958, the BBC announced that its engineers had designed and built a three-track videotape recorder after two years of development in the BBC research department.[45] Started in 1952, the project had been under the control of Dr. Peter Axon. The machine was called VERA, for Vision Electronic Recording Apparatus. A 15-minute program could be accommodated by a 20½-inch spool. It was recorded at 200 inches/sec using standard half-inch tape. It could record a 3MHz bandwidth, high for a longitudinal recorder. It had heads with ferrite cores with a gap width of 0.5 microns and a closed-loop tape drive system, which held tape speed to 0.04 percent by locking to an external sync generator. There were two tracks for video and one for sound. On July 25, 1958, this new magnetic videotape recorder went on the air in London. It was stated that "there was no fundamental reason that the machine should not be developed to enable recordings of other systems such as C.C.I.R. or N.T.S.C."[46]

Just two weeks later, in August 1958, it was reported that the first Ampex videotape machine had been delivered to Associated Rediffusion in London and demonstrated to *Wireless World*. The machine had been converted to 405 lines by Rank Cintel Ltd. The demonstration was quite good, with only some small problems showing up. However, the performance of the machine could be

1958. VERA: Vision Electronic Recording Apparatus, introduced May 23 by the BBC Labs. (BBC.)

considered satisfactory, and the slight defects would not be noticeable under domestic conditions. The machine cost £20,000 and a roll of tape cost £100 for a 12½-inch reel, but it could be used at least 100 times. Three spare heads were furnished with the machine and there was a trade-in scheme operated by Rank-Cintel.[47] It was also reported in May 1958 that the first Ampex machine had been delivered to Germany. Siemans & Halske converted the first Ampex machine to CCIR. The results were poor; it did not meet the 625 line standard.[48] It was reported, too, that the new Ampex color process was used for the first time for Smith, Kline and French in a San Francisco Hospital.[49] It employed a color converter.

In July, Philips, at the 1958 Photokina Exhibition in Cologne, Germany, displayed a new storage device for still pictures in which single television frames could be displayed on a TV monitor. It consisted of a rotating magnetic wheel of 15.75 inches running at 3,000 rpm. It had a magnetic rim where the picture was stored and the signal was directly recorded. It was used to demonstrate flash photographs where the subject would see themselves on the monitor screen.

In 1959, a similar system was shown at the Radio and Television Show in Brussels by Philips. It was recorded by an FM modulation method. The company also showed stationary pictures on a monitor. Another use for the system was for display of x-ray photographs by Philips/ Müller. This seems to be the first single frame magnetic storage device ever to be used.[50]

Television was going through its "golden era" of live

1959. French TV camera. (*L'Onde Electrique*.)

1959. Magnetic wheel from Philips. (Philips Labs.)

tember 1956. The hour and a half show was done "live" from Hollywood and shown at first by 35mm kinescope to the West Coast, and then late in 1957 by repeat tape on the Ampex machines.[51]

In November 1958, John Frankenheimer decided to do the Ernest Hemingway story "The Old Man" on tape, but not "live" because of the logistics of the severely technical

dramatic television. Such shows as "Studio One," "Philco Playhouse," and "Climax" were putting on live dramas that would never be equaled again. The "live" medium was attracting the best producers, writers, actors, directors and technicians. CBS had been doing the superb live series "Playhouse 90" (every Thursday night) since Sep-

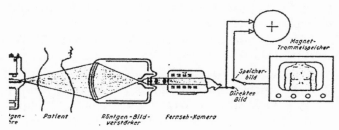

1959. First single-frame video device. (*Funkschau*.)

Ross Murray and John Frankenheimer (seated) editing "The Old Man" for *Playhouse 90*, November 20, 1958. (Art Garza/CBS.)

moves on the stages, including flooding the basement of TV City in Hollywood for the program.

Frankenheimer decided to pre-tape it first and then put the edited pieces together and present it as a "live" telecast. A superb technician, Ross Murray, volunteered to cut the show together even though such a job had never been done before and he had nothing but the Ampex edit block and a can of Editall to show where the edit points were. There were some eight hours of taped material that contained 61 edits and was finally edited down to a 90-minute program. Murray put it together flawlessly and got raves from the whole industry. The Old Man was pre-taped for four days and telecast on Thursday, November 20, 1958, to the entire CBS network. This set the standard for videotape editing for years to come. From then on, CBS was able to edit any tape in a film style without any noticeable changes. It was ironic that the best live dramatic shows had shown the way to use videotape in such a manner as to kill "live" TV. The rest of the industry was slow to follow.[52]

In November 1958, the *Journal of the SMPTE* printed five classic papers on the development of the Ampex Videotape Recorder. Three of those papers had been presented at the SMPTE convention held in Washington, D.C., on April 29, 1957.[53]

In December 1958, several demonstrations of the new large-screen Eidophore Swiss projector were given at the convention of the American Association for with Advancement of Science. The demonstration was given by CIBA Pharmaceutical Products. It used a color projector using the field-sequential color system. It produced pictures up to 32 by 24 feet in monochrome and 16 by 12 feet in color. The cost was still over $32,000 for color and $16,000 for black-and-white. CIBA said it was working with 20th Century-Fox Film Corp. for broad commercial use of the system.[54] The machine was later demonstrated in July 1959 with pictures transmitted from University College, London, and received at Mullard House.[55]

On December 17, 1958, a new three–Vidicon color camera was shown before the Royal Institution in London. It was meant for industrial uses (medical, primarily, but also for merchandising, process control and the like). It could be operated on any of three standards: 405, 525 and 625 lines. The literature did not specify which color system was being used in the machine.[56]

At the 1959 NAB convention, both RCA and Ampex announced that they had sold many units: RCA sold 25, and 25 more tentative; Ampex with 23 firm orders. Ampex claimed that they were now making two models a day. The important issue of standards was being taken up by the SMPTE, covering maintenance, adjustment and operation. Ross Snyder of Ampex lauded the cooperation among engineers, manufacturers and broadcasters in

achieving the standardization required to meet the interchangeability requirements.[57]

Also at the March 1959 NAB Convention, Ampex introduced its new Model VTR1000B Videotape Recorder. It was a two-tier model with the TV monitor, oscilloscope, switching panel and audio monitor mounted in a rack above the machine.[58] New features included guaranteed signal-to-noise ratio of 36db, faster (two-second) start-up time, and tape playback speed

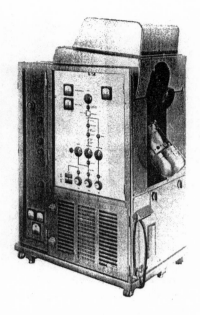

1959. CIBA Foundation Eidophor large-screen sequential color projector. (JRTS.)

control for lip synching with an external audio recorder. Deliveries were to start in June at $52,950.[59]

Ampex had gone international. In April 1959, at the CCIR conference in Los Angeles, the company announced a new feature for its recorders. It was an engineering modification called "Inter-Switch." This feature, added to the recorder, made it possible for the machine to record and playback either 525 lines, 60 fields (USA), 405 lines, 50 fields (England), 819 lines, 50 fields (the French standard), or 625 lines, 50 fields for the rest of Europe. With multistandard recording, it was possible to use the same machine to record and play back in one set of standards and then, by using the switch, to record and play back in a different set of standards. In any case, switchable cameras and monitors were needed. Ampex machines were now able to record and play back on any international standard. Ampex claimed that 25 percent of its later sales were to foreign markets. However, the Inter-Switch was not a standards converter.[60] Around the same time, in March 1959, it was reported that NHK had built the first copies of the Ampex Video recorder.[61]

On April 16, 1959, RCA announced that they would bring color TV to the American National Exhibition in Moscow that summer. A fully equipped color studio would originate eight hours of live and film programming daily, carried by closed-circuit receivers throughout Sokolinki Park fair grounds.[62]

In August 1959, General Electric revealed a new super sensitive electronic eye that helped the nuclear submarine Skate to probe a path under the Arctic ice. The was a new low-light-level image orthicon camera tube that

1959. Russian videotape recorder. (SMPTE.)

1957. Above: Dr. Norikazu Sawazaki (front row center) and his associate researchers, clockwise from top left: M. Iwasaki, M. Yagi, G. Inada, I. Sato and T. Tamaoki.

was said to be 100 times more sensitive than other tubes of its type. The key to the tube's sensitivity was a special film target. It was claimed that the tube was then being tested by the army and air force for military applications.[63]

Another important development took place in September 1959. A Toshiba VTR-1 prototype videotape recorder was demonstrated to the public at the Matsuda Research Laboratory, Kawasaki, Japan. This was the first Japanese helical-scan videotape machine. It had one video head and the tape was run in a helical loop around a cylinder containing the video head. It used two-inch tape running at 15-inches. An FM modulation system was used to conveniently record the signal on tape. The SNR was about 35db. Due to the single head, the video signal was interrupted for about 100–300 ms. A special inhibition gate was used. A processing amplifier was set up to reshape the synchronizing waveform, in which the horizontal sync pulses from this part of the tape were cleaned up

Above: 1959. Russian image orthicon camera. (*Funkschau.*) *Below:* 1960. Japanese color camera. (*Funkschau.*)

with new pulses being generated, reinserted and a standard television waveform reproduced. It was claimed that this new system could reproduce pictures at any speed, whether fast forward, slow forward, rewinding or even stopped. This was because each television field was recorded on one long track, so that as the head rotated at

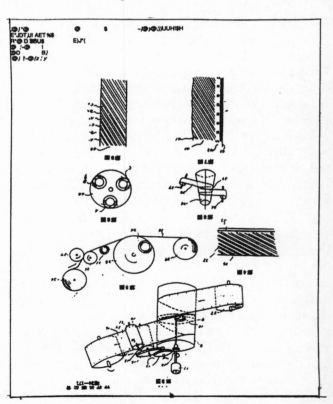

Japanese Patent 1955-8424 (Japanese no. 252,253) applied March 2, 1955, issued May 26, 1959, for a helical-scan recorder. (Toshiba Research and Development Center.)

60Hz, it would repeat one field even when in the stopped position.

This machine was the result of a project started in 1953 by Dr. Norikazu Sawazaki who claimed that work on the system had begun after reading about the RCA video-tape project. They realized how hopeless this project was and decided on a rotating head. This was quite a step for Toshiba as they didn't have any experience in audio magnetic recording or making heads with a 5MHz response. The first experimental machine was completed in 1956 and it could, to some degree, record and reproduce signals. On March 2, 1955, Dr. Sawazaki of the Matsuda Research Laboratory, Tokyo Shibaura Electric Co. (Toshiba), Tokyo, applied for a Japanese Patent 1955-8424 (Japanese no. 252,253) for a helical scan videotape recorder. This patent was issued on May 26, 1959. It was for a one-head (or three heads for color) machine with a 360 wrap. The patent indicated the use of sprocket holes to maintain sync with the rotation of the head drum. There was provision for an audio track at one end of the tape. The earliest machine had no control track and was using perforated two-inch magnetic tape. Dr. Sawazaki had assistance from the following associate researchers: M. Iwasaki, M. Yagi, G. Inada, I. Sato and T. Tamaoki.[64]

By 1958, the first practical machine was produced and it was shown publicly in 1959. At the end of 1961 one unit had been delivered to NHK for evaluation and testing. In addition to the one-head machine, Toshiba also described a two-headed helical-scan mechanism in which the tape was only half wrapped around the video head.[65]

What they did not know was that Ampex was also experimenting with helical recorders as early as 1956. Strong evidence indicates that Maxey did have a helical recorder working in the laboratory in 1956 (Ampex has pictures of it).[66] So Alex Maxey of Ampex in 1956–57 has precedence over Sawazaki of Toshiba who started in 1955 but did not have a working machine until late 1957.

Maxey had an extreme advantage over Sawazaki. In his research he had the use of the Ampex FM modulator, Ampex's experience in making video heads and, of course, in using video circuitry. By 1957, there was enough information out on the FM modulator for Toshiba to replicate it in its laboratory. The revelation of the Ampex machine in April 1956 must have given them clues as how to process the video. Obviously Toshiba later had access to the Ampex FM patent in order to get reasonable pictures. Nonetheless, Toshiba gets the credit for showing the first helical scan machines publicly.

In any event when it comes to patent priority in helical scan machines, Masterson is number one. The top five are as follows: (1) Earl Masterson, USA Patent no. 2,773,120; issued December 4, 1956 (2) Lee DeForest, USA no. 2,734,318, filed April 13, 1953; issued April 24, 1956 (3) Schüller on July 1, 1953 (4) Sawazaki on March 22, 1955 (5) the Ampex patent in 1958 (Maxey USA Patent no. 2,998,495, filed March 26, 1958; issued August 29, 1961.) However, according to Ampex, Maxey had a machine built and running in 1956. So Ampex gets the priority for the first helical recorder as well as the first transverse video recorder.

As promised in April, RCA brought a fully equipped color studio to Russia in July 1959 and proceeded to originate eight hours of live and film programming daily, carried by closed-circuit receivers. It consisted of two RCA color cameras, a color film projector and an Ampex color recorder. As far as can be ascertained, all recordings were to be shown by closed circuit; there was no provisions to convert the pictures for showing on Russian television.

Among the first RCA people to arrive for the exchange was Dr. Vladimir Zworykin who arrived in the Soviet Union on July 6. In Moscow, he was an honored guest at the first Cold War cultural and scientific exchange between the United States and the Soviet Union, organized by President Dwight D. Eisenhower and Soviet Premier Nikita Khrushchev. This was the occasion for an American national exhibition at Moscow's Sokolinki Park, part of which was a working demonstration of color television consisting of two RCA color cameras and an Ampex color videotape recorder. With Zworykin in Moscow were Waldemar Poch of RCA, Philip Gundy, vice president of the Ampex Corporation of Redwood City, California, and two of his top engineers, Joseph Roizen and William Barnhart. Roizen, an engineer with Ampex for many

1957. First Toshiba experimental helical-scan VTR (VTR-0). *Above left:* First experimental machine. *Above right:* The first image from the Toshiba VTR-0. (Toshiba Research and Development Center.)

years, was chosen for his engineering acumen as well as his ability to speak Russian; he was running the Ampex machine.

The world-famous "Kitchen Debate" between Vice President Richard Nixon and Khrushchev occurred on July 24, 1959. Sixteen and a half minutes of this rough and tumble debate was recorded live by Roizen. He turned the videotape over to Philip Gundy, who smuggled it out of the USSR that same night. It was immediately flown back to the United States, where it was broadcast the next day, first by NBC and then by ABC and CBS. The Soviets were furious at first, claiming that it was to be broadcast simultaneously in both the USSR and the U.S. (This was not possible as the machines were not equipped to record on Russian 625 line standards.) They threatened an international incident just short of World War III, but the affair was soon smoothed over with no lasting consequences.[67] Joe Roizen received an Emmy for his recording of this debate.[68]

In October 1959, the Ampex color system was again described for the field, this time in the *Journal of the SMPTE*.[69]

That same month it was reported that Ampex would market the British made Marconi TV camera in the USA. The Marconi camera used the 4½-inch image orthicon camera tube made by Marconi's Wireless Telegraph Co. Ltd., in Great Britain. It was to be offered with Ampex's Inter-Switch modifier which would make this system easily convertible from 525 lines (American) to 405 lines (British) or 625 lines (European Continental). Ampex was now stiffening its competition with RCA. RCA had still not produced a 4½-inch image orthicon camera.[70]

In December 1959, General Electric revealed that a new image orthicon tube, GL-7629, was being released for general broadcasting. It was claimed that it needed only 5 to 10 percent of the light required by the standard image

1960. Marconi Mk IV 4½-inch image orthicon camera. (Marconi's Wireless Telegraph Company, Ltd.)

orthicon. It would also permit color casting with no more than regular black-and-white lighting requirements. It was claimed that it had freedom from "burn-in" and stickiness with the supersensitivity. The extreme sensitivity, it was said, was due primarily to the high-gain, thin-film target of magnesium oxide about two-millionths of an inch thick. It used electron instead of ion conduction which eliminated "burn-in" and "stickiness."[71]

In December 1959, Westinghouse also had a new image orthicon camera tube on the market. It was guaranteed to last twice as long and cost only 20 percent more than existing types, which cost about $1,200. It was claimed that image retention had been completely eliminated.[72]

Japan adopted the NTSC color system at the end of 1959. Seven new stations began: four were part of the NHK government network and three were commercial stations. Licenses were granted to NTV (Nippon Television Co.) and NHK (Nippon Hoso Kyokai) to go ahead with color telecasts using the USA system. Japan was the only major country to adopt the NTSC color system. (Two conferences in May 1958 and August 1959 had failed to provide a single world standard.) The entire Japanese electronics industry signed licensing agreements with RCA, renewable every five years. Japan became the largest single foreign contributor to RCA income which was growing by leaps and bounds.[73]

On December 23, 1959, the General Electric Company announced its new TPR, or Thermoplastic VTR. It was the invention of one Dr. William E. Glenn. In the process, images were converted electronically to coded signals which were reduced to variations of a beam of electrons. The beam played back and forth across the film in a vacuum and deposited a pattern of negative charges, which were converted to a pattern of depressions and ridges which could be observed visually. Passing a beam of light through the film into an optical system converts the film into a visible image. It was claimed that the plastic film could be played back immediately. In a demonstration using an 8mm projector, the images were fairly good, it was said, although they were marred by surface imperfections and scratches on the film. It was expected

An image from the Ampex videotape that recorded the infamous "Kitchen Debate" between Soviet premier Nikita Khrushchev and U.S. vice-president Richard Nixon on July 25, 1959, in Moscow. (Ampex.)

that experimental recorders would be available by year's end. One tape manufacturer (Audio Devices) stated that, "it [TPR] will not replace most magnetic recording even in the future."[74] They were quite right; after about a year of intense publicity, the device and its principle were soon forgotten.[75]

In February 1960, Eastman Kodak finally announced that it was going into the production of videotape sometime in 1961. Eastman was of course the expert in making large reels of acetate film and laying down several layers of emulsion. Videotape would be a different kind of challenge for them.[76]

On March 24, 1960, the CBS Laboratories under Dr. Peter Goldmark demonstrated an audio long playing tape machine. It had a tiny, single reel cartridge (cassettes have two reels) that played an hour of high fidelity music at a speed of 1⅞ inches per second. The tape had three tracks on tape one-seventh of an inch wide. This was the first tape cartridge player. Ampex announced that it had also developed a means of recording at 1⅞ inches/sec and that if the industry would agree to a single standard they would cooperate with anybody on a royalty-free basis. Columbia Records provided the repertoire for the tape.

A year earlier, RCA had come out with a two-reel cassette with tape enclosed in a plastic shell that played at 3¾ inches/sec. It was large, about the size of a paperback book. It was to be used in a changer, but that was prone to jamming. (It was followed in 1962 by an advanced "drop-in" tape cartridge. It had four tracks and played up to two hours of monophonic or one hour of stereophonic music on each cartridge. At a speed of 3¾ inches per second, it claimed a range of 50 to 15,000 cycles/second.)[77]

The CBS device used a single-reel cartridge about 3½ inches square. The changer mechanism fished the tape from its cartridge, wound it onto a take-up reel within the changer, and, after playing was finished, rewound the tape back into the cartridge. Dr. Goldmark interested 3M in it and they funded a three-year project. The new cartridge player was released by 3M though its subsidiary, the Revere-Wollensak Company. It was claimed that Zenith would manufacture the equipment in the USA. In Germany, the Grundig Company had acquired a license for the machine, but the other major recording companies did not follow. This device was not too successful but was the first cartridge player and represented the beginning of the videocassette player. Another first for CBS Labs and Dr. Goldmark. In 1963, the Philips Company of Eindhoven negotiated with 3M to put the CBS machine on the European market.[78]

In 1963, Philips also came out with their mini cassette called the Pocket Recorder. The cassette was 2½ inches by four inches, played at 1⅞ inches/second and had enough one eighth tape for 90 minutes of playing time. Originally planned for voice dictation with low quality, it at first languished, then the addition of the Dolby Noise Reduction system soon transferred the audio cassette into a major recording and playback medium.[79]

At the 87th semiannual Convention of the SMPTE held in Los Angeles in April 1960, Ampex demonstrated several new innovations. The first was called AutoTec, an automatic time element compensator which made it possible to automatically eliminate geometric distortions in the tape playback system. It was the invention of Charles Coleman who had been an engineer at CBS in Chicago. CBS patented it and immediately sold the rights to Ampex who brought out a commercial version called Amtec. CBS and Ampex had had a close relationship ever since the first Ampex machines were delivered to Hollywood late in 1956.[80]

Amtec consisted basically of electrically controlled, continuously variable delay lines, the delay of which varied in sympathy with the time variations present in the input voltage. The correction voltage was obtained by comparing the signal going to the equipment with an internally generated train of flywheel pulses. Thus a positive or negative delay in each line brought its starting time to within 0.03 microseconds of a stable external reference. This device was first called Coltec. Its cost was $7,000.[81]

At the NAB convention in April 1960, Ampex also announced a new accessory called Intersync to be used with the Ampex videotape recorder. This was a device which enabled the capstan servo and head drum servo of the videotape machine to be brought into position, coincident with an external sync source. Thus the recorder could be locked line by line as well as vertically, field for field. With this development, it became possible to cut to or from a videotape machine without getting any rolls or discontinuity. Also, it made dissolves and special effects feasible. Until this time, all videotape recorders were running asynchronously with the studios' sync system. It was not possible to cut or dissolve to a tape while running. Now, for the first time, the tape machine could run in phase with studio sync, thus allowing cuts, dissolves and other effects to other tape machines or cameras. This included both line and frame sync. (RCA announced its version of Intersync called Pixlock in November 1962.)[82]

At this exhibition, Ampex also showed its new console recorder VR1000C. It could be equipped for color television and use many of the Ampex accessories such as intersync. Also shown was a Conrac picture freezer memory tube that had been on display at the prior NAB convention in Chicago.[83]

Ampex was concerned after the announcement of the Toshiba VTR-1 helical in September 1959 in Japan. It was presumed that Toshiba would send a model to the 1960 NAB Convention. In order to protect their priority in helicals, Ampex shipped a helical scan video recorder to Chicago, but it was only to be shown if Toshiba exhibited something similar. At any rate, Toshiba did not bring a machine, much to Ampex's relief. "Ampex did not want to do anything to disturb the ascending sales of its transverse scan machines." So they did not uncrate their helical and sent it back unopened to Redwood City.[84]

RCA also introduced its new 4½-inch TK-12 television camera in April 1960. The TK-12 was a monochrome studio camera, entirely new in every respect. One of its outstanding features was the use of the 4½-inch image orthicon camera tube, type 7389A, which was capable of producing pictures with measurably better resolution, lower noise and improved gray scale. It was claimed that the camera had only two operating controls. This simplification, together with inherent stability, made it possible for one video operator to handle as many as six camera chains.[85]

While similar to other image orthicons, the 4½-inch Type 7389A was larger in size. The significant difference between it and the three-inch tubes lay in the larger area of the glass target. This larger area accounted for the ability to get increased resolution, or more significantly increased contrast in fine detail, by a factor of almost 2 to 1. For example, measurements indicated that the signal output level of the 7389A at 400 TV lines (without aperture correction) was about 60 percent of the output at 100 TV lines. By comparison, the 400-line output of the three-inch tube was only 30 percent.

Though the target of the 7389A was large, the photocathode (i.e., the active diameter) was the same as that of the three-inch tube. Hence the same types of camera lenses may be used in either the 4½-inch or 3-inch tubes. Magnification of the electron image in the 4½ inch tube was brought about by suitable strengthening and shaping of the magnetic focusing field in the image section of the tube.

Another important feature built into the 7389A was relatively close spacing between the glass target and the mesh. This had several de-

This Ampex helical-scan recorder was taken to NAB in 1960 but not shown. (Charles P. Ginsburg/Ampex.)

sirable results. Signal-to-noise ratio was increased. The linear portion of the transfer characteristic was longer, permitting more accurate reproduction of the gray scale. Also, broad redistribution of secondary electrons was reduced. This characteristic minimized overshoots and halos, as usually seen in pictures from the 5820. All these characteristics — better detail and contrast, higher signal-to-noise ratio and reduced overshoots and halos — were important contributors to better picture quality.

To realize the full benefit of these improvements, it was imperative that the image orthicon have proper electrical adjustment and correct illumination or exposure. In the TK-12 camera, proper electrical adjustment (once initial adjustment was made) was assured by a high degree of inherent circuit stability. However, the requirement for proper exposure had to be satisfied by careful operation of studio lighting and of the remote iris control in the camera chain.[86]

On April 27, 1960, color television pictures using the new French sequential color system were relayed from Paris to London. The program consisted of a lecture of the new Henri de France system of television on 625 lines. A 500km television relay system was used from the P.T.T. establishment in Paris to the Post Office station at Tolsford Hill in England, where it was relayed to London. Outside of a loss of vertical definition, the pictures were considered satisfactory. What seemed important was that the French were using 625 lines instead of 819. It was hoped that this would help set up an international monochrome standard.[87] In June 1962, the French Broadcasting System announced that their new network schedule, to commence in 1963, would be on 625 lines. This was to agree with the other European countries of the 625 line, 50 cycle standard.[88]

It was reported in May 1960 in the *Journal of the SMPTE*, that the Russians had designed a video recorder for high-quality videotape recording and reproduction. A special tape of 70mm was used in this machine.[89]

On June 1, 1960, the findings of the Television Advisory Committee in London were published. The committee suggested that a 625-line standard with an 8mc bandwidth offered worthwhile improvements in quality. It concluded that an adapted NTSC system was the only one usable with 405 lines. All decisions should be postponed until a monochrome standard was approved, it stated.[90]

In September 1960, it was reported that Shiba Electric, Tokyo, had developed their version of the Ampex Intersync control. It was called the "Intersynchronizer" and was an exact copy of the Ampex device. It could be used with two videotape recorders or with one recorder and the studio camera.[91]

Ampex announced a new 4 megacycle instrumentation tape recording system in September 1960. It comprised their new AR-300 and FR-700. It was different from the regular Ampex transverse recorders in that it recorded 5 million binary bits per second. A reel lasted 60 minutes and held over 7 billion binary bits compared to PCM which was limited to less that one million per second even at higher tape speed. Tape speeds were 12½ ips and 25 ips with Mylar 1.0mm tape (using 10½-inch reels). The AR-300 mobile or airborne unit (that weighed 175 pounds) was for record only. The FR-700 was a single-rack laboratory record/playback unit that was 75 inches tall and weighed some 600 pounds.[92] It was shown at the National Telemetering Conference in Chicago in May 1961 and, according to reports, the color signals ran through with good quality.[93]

Later, in May 1961, Ampex actually revealed this new airborne reconnaissance tape system, the AR-300, which was being sold to the military under an air force contract. It was a wide-band 4mc system that was not compatible with commercial Ampex machines, but could record through regular machines. Because it weighed only 175 pounds, the AR-300 displaced only 3.5 cubic feet. It cost $60,000, and an auxiliary unit for power cost another $84,000.[94]

In October 1960, the development of a small (20 inches by 20 inches by 100 inches) transistorized videotape recorder was announced. It was a joint effort of RCA and the U.S. Navy. It was the recorder used in the submarine *Seadragon* that took pictures of the undersides of giant icebergs in the Arctic Circle. The tape, in 10½-inch reels, moved past a regular scanning head at 15 inches/second. These tapes could later be played on a RCA-TRT-1A for training purposes.[95]

Chapter 6

From Helicals to High Band
(1961–1964)

Nineteen sixty-one brought many changes in television technology. With the help of the Japanese government, through MITI (Ministry of International Trade and Industry), many companies had become involved in the manufacture of television cameras and recorders and studio equipment. Two Japanese companies, Toshiba and Japanese Victor (JVC), brought out commercial helical scan recorders. They were also making their own cameras and studio equipment. No longer did Ampex or RCA have a worldwide monopoly on the manufacture of VTRs and cameras.

In January 1961, the Victor Company of Japan announced a new two-head helical-scan color videotape recorder.[1] Actually two sets of magnetic heads were used: two wide-track heads for recording and two narrower heads for monitoring (while recording) and playback. The two recording heads were mounted 180 degrees apart at the edge of the rotating drum and produced one complete television picture for each 360 degrees of rotation. It was claimed that editing and splicing were made simple because this machine could reproduce a "single frame" while the tape was standing still. The picture could also be monitored while in reverse or fast forward. Tape speed was 15 inches/sec and the machine could record up to 90 minutes on 7,200 feet of tape. It had an FM modulation system and a special color processor (which frequency modulated the luminance signal and directly recorded the carrier chrominance signal) to produce standard NTSC color signals. This machine was to be marketed as the Telechrome JVC Model 770 in the USA.[2] Telechrome stated the recorder was a joint venture of Telechrome, Engineering Industries, Ltd. and the Victor Co. of Tokyo. It would be manufactured in the USA.[3]

In February 1961, Toshiba of Japan announced a new product that was a color television tape recorder using a single-head slant track monochrome unit. It was based on the monochrome version with added circuitry. They also announced that they were making an image orthicon camera.[4]

On March 14, 1961, at Redwood City, Ampex demonstrated its first helical scan recorder, the Model VR8000, for closed-circuit industrial, educational and military use. It did not meet the FCC technical standards in time-base stability. It was a single video head helical recorder, used two-inch tape running at 7½ inches per second, and could record two full hours on a standard 12½-inch reel of videotape. The price was to be $20,400, less than half that of the broadcast model. However, it did have as many as three different sound tracks. It was expected to be used for nothing but nonbroadcast closed-circuit recording.[5]

On March 20, 1961, the Sony Corporation of Japan introduced a 65-pound transistorized two-head helical scan recorder using two-inch tape. This was the Sony Model SV201. It was shown at the IRE convention in New York City. It was to cost about $10,000 but did not meet FCC specifications.[6] It featured single- or stop-frame capabilities.[7]

During this period, according to one source,[8] Sony and Ampex had developed friendly relations in which it appeared that Sony had agreed to build less expensive machines than Ampex's commercial transverse recorders. According to another source, George Gundy recognized Sony's expertise in transistor circuits. So a deal was made with Sony whereby they would design the transistor circuitry for the Ampex machines, and in exchange Sony would get the right to make VTRs for nonbroadcast customers. It was so friendly that on July 10, 1960, without benefit of counsel, Akio Morita, Masaru Ibuka and Phil Gundy, vice president of Ampex, signed a one-page memorandum indicating a royalty-free exchange of each firm's respective patents including Ampex's seminal Ginsburg patent. Again as in the RCA-Ampex patent agreements of 1957, Ampex had given away her priceless patents for what turned out to be empty promises.

Within months a team of engineers headed by Nobutoshi Kihara produced Sony's first two-head, open-reel model. This seems to be the very first product that introduced Sony into the field of videotape recording. Sony reneged on the deal with Ampex in 1961 when it put out a transistorized (transverse)[9] recorder known as the SV201. Ampex was livid by now. Japan had become a source of headaches for Ampex. In addition to filing patents that threatened Ampex's position, several Japanese companies made VTRs that resembled Ampex's without, of course, obtaining Ampex's permission. When Ampex complained to the MITI (Ministry of International Trade and Industry) they were told in no uncertain terms that they had better take on a Japanese partner if they wished to sell VTRs in Japan. Ampex then went into an alliance with Toshiba and set up a joint venture. In September 1964, the Ampex Corp., Redwood City and Toshiba/Tokyo-Shibura Electric Co. received approval from the Japanese government for the formation of Toamco, a joint venture to manufacture and market Ampex products in Japan. Toshiba would have a 51 percent interest in Toamco while Ampex owned the remaining 49 percent. It was capitalized at $1.1 million. Ampex now had operations in Reading, England; Nivelles, Belgium; Hong Kong; Calgary and Annecy, France. Ampex sales in 1963 were $140 million and Toshiba's was $700 million.[10] As soon as Ampex played by the "Japanese rules," the sales of VTRs in Japan increased. While the agreement, of course, insured that Ampex products could be sold in Japan, it also gave Toshiba a powerful ally in its struggle with Sony, which was still going on.

Other Japanese companies that had been infringing on Ampex patents were soon paying royalties. Sony, however, continued to refuse to pay royalties to Ampex, and soon after, the SV201 was followed by the PV100 transistorized helical scan machine. According to a Sony historian, their first machine was the PV100 — the first helical scan successfully implemented for commercial services. Later came the 1.5-head system. Then came the VR-1100, the first full-transistor QUAD/VTR machine.[11]

In 1966, Ampex realized what it had given away and new management asked Sony to pay an 8 percent royalty for the use of the Ginsburg patent. They also sued for patent infringement in the USA. Sony balked at this and

1961. Two views of Toshiba single-head color VTR and equipment. (Toshiba Research and Development Center.)

no mutual resolution could be found. Sony then countersued for breach of contract.[12]

While the discussion went on, Sony continued to introduce one new machine after another. Finally in November 1968,[13] Sony and Ampex made an amiable out-of-court settlement of their dispute, by which time Sony had become the number-one Japanese competitor of Ampex in the field of helical recorders.[14]

During this period, Ampex had also been improving its helical recorder and realized that with the introduction of the Japanese helicals (by Toshiba, JVC and Sony) that it was time for them do something with their own. As a result, Ampex now decided to concentrate on the development

1962. Ampex VR-1100. First two-inch transistorized Ampex recorder. (Ampex.)

1962. *Above:* Ampex model VR1500 two-inch all-transistorized portable helical-scan. *Right:* model VR-660 (1963). (Ampex.)

of a two-headed, 180 degree wrap machine that was quite successful. (This was the VR1500.)[15] Also it was claimed that Frank Marx of ABC had been given a private showing of the machine and was quite enthusiastic about it. Ampex believed secure in their sales of the transverse recorder and felt that the market could accommodate both types of machines.[16]

On April 20 and 21, 1961, a demonstration of the new French color system of Henri de France was given, now called SECAM (séquentiel à mémoire). It was claimed that changing the subcarrier from AM to FM resulted in a reduction of noise where it was only 4 to 5db worse than the NTSC system. A comparison of the two systems showed that they were close, depending on one's personal viewpoint. The pictures were generated by a flying-spot scanner at the Hirst Research Center of G.E.C. and transmitted over radio link and cable.[17]

In May 1961, Ampex demonstrated their new direct color recovery system called Colortec at the NAB convention in Washington. In operation it was said to accomplish line-by-line compensation of timing errors in the composite color signal by sampling burst phase of the signal at each horizontal interval, with respect to the external 3.58MHz signal. The instantaneous phase difference between the sampled and reference signals was converted

to a proportional voltage, which adjusted the delay time of a voltage controlled delay line in the video signal path. Thus the resultant signal was within the required stability limits for direct color playback. The machine's cost was $9,750.[18]

Also shown at the NAB was an RCA MR700 helical scan recorder that ran at 7½ inches/second. Priced at $18,500, it was for closed-circuit, military and space trade only. RCA also displayed a new TV electronic tape editing system.[19]

In May 1961, Ampex also announced a new "Electronic Editor" for use with any Ampex 1000 machine equipped with full track erase and "Intersync"[20] It was claimed that it could insert or add

1961. RCA MR-700 slant-track CCTV recorder.

new material to a previously recorded tape by pushing a button without any physical cutting or splicing. It enabled the assembly of any number of short items into a sequential program with no restriction as to time or location of the assembly process. The material could come from any video signal, "live," film, tape or slide. It was priced at $3,000. A completely new design philosophy had been adopted by Ampex in the new

1961. RCA color TV tape and helical-scan exhibit. (*Broadcast News.*)

1961. RCA TR-22 all-transistorized videotape recorder. (RCA.)

system in which no attempt was made to stop the tape or store individual frames. Rather, splices were made while the tape was running at normal speed. These splices did not involve physically cutting and joining the tape, but were accomplished by activating recording circuits while the tape was running so as to record a new scene onto an existing scene or program. Scenes in the original program could be transferred to other tapes or erased. The splices thus made were splices in the recorded information, but not in the recording medium.

The new electronic editing equipment was easily installed in any videotape television recorder. It allowed the recorder to be started and stopped between recordings, at will, without any loss of synchronization in the final tape. Thus, it became possible to assemble a first-generation, completely edited tape using motion picture shooting techniques with only one camera and one recorder. Scenery changes, costume changes and other effects not feasible with the continuous action usually employed in television recording, became easily achievable on tape. The recorder could also be used to insert new scenes into the middle of an existing program at some time after it was originally recorded. In this mode, commercials or announcements could be inserted into a program, or a scene containing a production "fluff" might be replaced by a new one.

In other words, the end of the last wanted frame on the tape must occur at exactly the same time as the beginning of the first frame of the pictures to be added to the tape. This video phasing was accomplished by equipping the recorder with an Intersync unit. This unit, a precision servo control mechanism, guaranteed that synchronizing information recovered from tape was in very close time relationship with synchronizing information reaching the recorder from an external source. In this way, any possibility of splicing in, for example, an extraneous quarter of a frame, was avoided.[21]

This of course was another of Ampex's revolutionary innovations introduced to change the

1961. Single-frame magnetic storage unit by Siemens & Halske. (Siemens & Halske.)

use of videotape. The concept of recording the new material after the old was ingenious. With the quality that Ampex had now achieved with its machines, the inserted material was first generation with no loss of quality. This concept was to forever change the ways of editing videotape and eventually motion picture film.

In May 1961, Siemens & Halske introduced their single-frame magnetic storage recorder. It could record a single field or a single frame, one or two tracks, onto a rotating storage foil. The distance between the foil and the video heads was stabilized by an adjustable air current. Frequencies up to 10 mc/sec could be recorded and FM was used in signal recording, incorporating the double heterodyne system.[22]

In August 1961, Loewe Opta in Germany announced its first helical-scan videotape recorder. It was the Opta-cord 500. It used two-inch (50.8mm) tape running at 7½ inches (19 cm/sec). It cost DM 30,000, and seems to have been for closed circuit only.[23]

In September 1961, it was reported that Eastman Kodak was experimenting with electron-beam recording of film in a vacuum. The company said that the new process involved electron-beam recording

1976. Ampex BCC-2 portable color camera. (Ampex.)

1961. Ampex VR-8000 helical-scan videotape machine. (Ampex.)

Above left and right: 1961 German helical-scan VTR by Loewe-Optacord 500. (*Funkschau.*)

directly onto silver-halide emulsion. It was claimed that this method offered several advantages over normal recording, particularly in speed, photographic resolution and absence of grain.[24]

At the German Television Society convention, September 25–29, 1961, two items of interest were reported. First was a report of an excellent demonstration of a Philips three-Vidicon color camera. The Vidicons were those using lead dioxide photocathodes. With a light level of 400 footlambert there was a remarkable absence of smear. However, it was claimed that Philips was still having troubles with the short life of the new photocathodes. Also the company demonstrated a new one-head videotape recorder with excellent picture quality.[25]

In November 1961, ABC announced the use of videotape for the playback of slow motion. ABC planned to use it for recaps of knockouts and a second look at crucial plays in football games. They called their system "VTX" (videotape expander). First use was on the NCAA football game between Texas and Texas A&M on Thursday, November 23, 1961.[26]

In November 1961, it was announced that the Outstanding Engineering Achievement Award had been made to the English Electric Valve Company for their work in developing the 4½-inch image orthicon.[27]

In March 1962, RCA announced an experimental color camera which produced four signals: three in color and one in black-and-white. This was the TK-42X. The M channel used a 4½-inch image orthicon tube, and three one-inch Vidicons for the red, green and blue channels. The Y, or monochrome signal, was derived directly from the image orthicon tube. The three Vidicon tubes were matrixed to form the NTSC color difference signals. The faces of the Vidicon tubes were specially cooled to reduce effects due to black current.[28] It was claimed that the camera produced color pictures of unprecedented richness and detail. A built-in zoom lens was incorporated for ease of operation.[29]

RCA also announced a new TV film recorder described as having a 50 percent increase in resolution (900 lines), compared to 600 lines in conventional kinescope recording. Coupled with Eastman's Viscomat processor, it was claimed that film was ready for use in less than two minutes.[30]

In March 1962, General Electric announced a new studio camera that could use either a regular three-inch image orthicon or the larger 4½-inch tube. The camera using a three-inch tube was the type PE-20-A, and the other, using their 4½-tube, was the type PE-20-B. It was all transistorized and had an improved eight-inch viewfinder with either preamp output or camera channel output.[31]

In May 1962, Ampex announced that it was setting up an advanced research laboratory. Its head would be Walter Selsted and its first members were Harold Lindsay, Alex Maxey and Alan Grace.[32]

In May 1962, Eastman Kodak gave a progress report on its new electron-beam recording system. A complete 16mm recorder had been built as a laboratory model. It was claimed that this system offered advantages in speed, photographic resolution and absence of phosphor grain over systems using conventional cathode ray tube photography. The only problem seemed to be in the time required to pump down the vacuum chamber.[33]

An important event of 1962 took place on July 10. For the first time, "live" images were transmitted over the Atlantic Ocean by means of the AT&T experimental Telstar

1962. First four-channel TK-42X color camera. (RCA.)

satellite. They were transmitted from Andover, Maryland, to Pleumer Bodou, France, and Goonhilly, England.[34] This was the start of a worldwide communications system that would eventually cover the entire planet.

An equally important event of 1962 was the introduction of the new closed-circuit portable videotape recorder, MVR-10, produced by Mach-Tronics Inc. of Mountain View, California. Announced in June, it was the first helical-scan recorder that used one-inch tape running at 7½ inches per second. Thus 96 minutes of programming could be recorded on a 10½-inch reel. The unit was self-contained, weighed less than 100 pounds and took up only 2.3 cubic feet, including its built-in eight-inch monitor with an integrated audio channel. It was all transistorized and represented a giant step forward in the evolution of helical-scan recorders.

Kurt Machein, Mach-Tronics' president, stated that this recorder was designed primarily for closed-circuit use and was not of broadcast quality. However, he stated that by redesign of certain circuitry, it could be raised to broadcast standards. The MVR-10 was priced at $10,300 with an eight-inch monitor, and $9,800 without it. This was compared to $40,000 for full-scale TV recorders then on the market.[35]

It turned out that Kurt R. Machein had been engineering manager of Ampex's international operations before his resignation in October 1961. On November 1, 1961, Machein and Henry W. Howard, a San Francisco lawyer, had persuaded several members of the Ampex staff to join them in their new venture. Those old Ampex hands were Alan Bygdnes, Michael Bradley Maryatt, Arie C. Van Doorn, Walter E. L. Davis, C. Thompson, Uwe Reese and Hans F. Hoyer.

Ampex immediately sued Mach-Tronics claiming that the defendants had conspired to use confidential information from Ampex employees in order to go into competition with Ampex by producing a portable video recorder similar to recorders constructed or designed by Ampex. Ampex asked the court to enjoin Mach-Tronics "from engaging in the manufacture and sale of portable video recorders embodying any of the characteristics or specifications of the portable video recorders constructed or developed by Ampex." Ampex asked for $2 million and the costs of the suit. Machein's reply was that the "Ampex Corporation does not now, nor has it ever, successfully produced a low cost, light weight, simply truly portable video recorder comparable in any sense

1962. *Above top:* Kurt Machein with his Mach-Tronics one-inch videotape recorder. *Above middle:* Back side. *Above bottom:* Bottom view. (Mach-Tronics, Inc.)

1962. *Above:* First Mach-Tronics one-inch portable videotape recorder with built-in monitor. *Below:* Late 1962 commercial version (without monitor). (Mach-Tronics, Inc.)

to the MVR-10 even though the need for such equipment has been apparent for many years."[36] This was true as Ampex was about to release a new series of two-inch portable helicals (the VR1500). Ampex did not release a one-inch portable, the VR7000 (the first of the Type A format VTRs) until 1965.[37]

At any rate, Machein was on safe ground in his design of a one-inch helical scan recorder except for the use of the Ampex FM patent. This of course was crucial and could not legally be used at that moment without a license from Ampex. As it was, this was the most advanced helical-scan videotape recorder in the world. First, it was all transistorized. Its components were modular. The use of one-inch tape running at 7½ inches/sec meant that the scanner using two heads was half the diameter of helicals using two-inch tape. This meant that the magnetic track covered less distance on the tape and was less prone to time base errors on playback. Oddly enough, even though this machine's superiority was so obvious, Ampex was committed to, and indeed released, a new series of two-inch portable helicals in the next year.

In August 1962, Mach-Tronics filed a countersuit against Ampex, charging that Ampex was in a conspiracy with RCA to restrain and monopolize the TV tape recorder field. Mach-Tronics claimed that potential customers had been frightened away while funds were being diverted to fight the Ampex action. Mach-Tronics asked for an award of $1,125,000 and for an injunction to halt the alleged Ampex-RCA conspiracy.[38]

In August 1962, Mach-Tronics filed a formal denial that it had pirated trade secrets from the Ampex Corp., and categorically states that former Ampex employees then working for Mach-Tronics were innocent of all plagiarism charges.[39]

In anticipation of the upcoming adoption of a new 625-lines standard, the BBC had placed an order in 1962 with the Ampex Research Laboratory in Reading, England, for two VR1000C recorders modified to accept a 625-line NTSC type of color signal with a color subcarrier of 4.43MHz. What started out as a small project finished as a major program. Advances in tape recording were made, the most important being the optimization of the signal system with significant reduction in moiré and delay distortion, and extension of the base band, all done with no increase in writing speed or video track width. (This was the start of the Ampex high-band system of 1964.)[40]

In October, RCA announced that the new TR-22 recorder was capable of recording in color with a single new module. It was claimed that the first two units were sent to ABC's Washington news facility. Another was delivered to the U.S. Navy Photographic Labs in Washington for use in producing training films.[41]

In November 1962, RCA introduced its newest 4½-inch image orthicon camera, the TK-60. It offered simplicity of operation, remained stable for long periods of time and produced the highest quality pictures. RCA claimed that it had built and shipped more than 2,000 cameras of the image orthicon type during the previous ten years.[42]

On Monday, November 5, 1962, the BBC started an experimental 625-line service on the UHF band (Channel 44). Both modified NTSC and French SECAM color standards were transmitted.[43] Studio H at Lime Grove had modified two Marconi color cameras for use on the experimental 625-line transmissions.[44]

In December 1962, Ampex introduced a portable TV tape recorder for nonbroadcast use in a showing in New York City. It was to be used for closed-circuit recording in education, industrial, military, medical science, sports and many other fields. The new VR1500 would be available after July 1963 at a price of $11,900. The suitcase-size recorder was about one twentieth the size of previous Ampex recorders.[45] The VR1500 weighed 130 pounds, ran at a tape speed of five inches per second and used standard two-inch television tape.

On January 25, 1963, Sir Isaac Shoenberg died. Very few people had ever heard of him and what he had accomplished. Nonetheless, he was one of television's great pioneers. After working for the Marconi Company, he became part of EMI. Here he was in charge of the development of the all-electronic system that was started in London in 1936 and adopted by the BBC in 1937. His belief in electronic television made this possible. He was knighted in June 1962.[46]

On Wednesday, January 9, 1963, a new tape-to-film system dubbed "Gemini" was revealed by MGM Telestudios. It consisted of an RCA TK-60 TV camera that shared

1963. Gemini combination RCA TK-60 television camera with 16mm motion picture camera. (Electronics ad.)

its lens with a 16mm motion picture camera mounted beside it. A beam splitter lodged between the lens split the light before it entered the camera, thus allowing simultaneous operation on videotape and 16mm film. The purpose was to eliminate the kinescope that was considered the last remaining obstacle to commercial production on tape.[47] The system was updated in November 1965 with an RCA TK-60 and a 16mm Auricon film camera.[48]

In April 1963, an overseas version of the Mach-Tronics MVR-10 was released as the Type PI-3V. The company also showed the new MVR-15 at the NAB in April.[49] It was marketed and manufactured by the Precision Instrument Company of Palo Alto, which held a license from Mach-Tronics, and was for closed-circuit system use only. It was available in either 405-, 525-, 625- or 819-line versions and was suitable for operation on either 50 or 60 cycles. On 50 cycle current, it used one-inch tape at a linear speed of 6.25 inches per second. Over 100 minutes of program could be accommodated on a 10½-inch reel. It was to be distributed in the United Kingdom by Carrion Television Systems Ltd. of Reading, Berks.[50]

On June 24, 1963, a new home TV recorder called Telcan by Telcan Ltd, Nottingham, England, was demonstrated. The public display gave very fair video quality on 17-inch and 21-inch domestic receivers.[51] It reportedly permitted home taping and replay of TV shows, and the playing of prerecorded tapes and tapes from video cameras. The machine weighed 15 pounds and was 17½ by nine by six inches. Sound and pictures were recorded simultaneously on standard quarter-inch double track tape. The tape speed was 120 inches/second (10 feet) and an 11-inch reel held a half hour of recording. The system band width was listed as 2mc and the resolution 300 lines. Signal-to-noise ratios were 28db on video and 40db on the soundtrack. The price was listed at about $175.[52] It was expected to reach the market before the end of 1963 in England and late 1964 in America.[53]

In July 1963, there was a report of a new color camera being developed by Philips of Eindhoven. It stated that Philips had developed a color camera that was smaller than the smallest black-and-white cameras then in use

and ten times more sensitive than the best U.S. cameras. Unfortunately, Philips had a problem — some of the prototypes did not work. They were trying to get the bugs out and the camera into production.[54]

In July 1963, it was reported that ABC-TV had been using the new Mach-Tronics MVR-15 portable TV recorder for many sports and news events. Everything from President Kennedy's European tour to the July 4 Daytona stock car championship races. The machine was also carried aloft in a small three-man helicopter and recorded the race from above. Emphasis was placed on the excellent quality of the machine for broadcast purposes. ABC claimed that they had helped in the development of the new machine. It was also announced that Storer Programs, Inc. of Miami would hold its first public demonstration of the Mach-Tronics MVR-15 on July 23–23, 1963, at WITI-TV Milwaukee.[55]

In July 1963, the BBC gave demonstrations of all three systems (NTSC, SECAM and PAL) to all 17 EBU countries. A series of demonstrations starting on July 8, 1963, ended with two days limited showings to the public on July 15 and 16. All three systems could employ the same transmitters and networking equipment used for the 625-line broadcasts. Great Britain was to start a 625-line service in April 1964.[56]

In September it was announced that Cinerama, Inc. had negotiated with Telcan Ltd. for the rights to develop and distribute the firm's proposed home television tape recorder in the USA and Western Hemisphere.[57]

Also in September 1963, Ampex announced that the VR660, which was a broadcast version of the VR1500, would be released. This was a two-head helical videotape recorder using two-inch tape. Weighing just under 100 pounds, it was designed for mobile and studio use. The price was $14,500. The machine was all-transistorized and could be used with no additional studio equipment. It was to be demonstrated during mid–September in New York and deliveries were to begin in early 1964.[58]

In September 1963, North American Philips Co. announced their entry into the television camera field with the introduction of the new lead-oxide Plumbicon tube developed by Philips in Holland. The tube was a variation of the Vidicon that was demonstrated the previous summer (1962) before the EBU in London. The CBS Engineering Labs were acting as consultants with Philips in adapting the new tube into a color camera about the size of a normal black-and-white camera. Philips stated that the Plumbicon's low noise level made it especially suited for

1963 Telcan home videotape recorder using quarter-inch tape. *Above left:* Tape deck. *Right:* Home recorder-receiver. Telcan Ltd.)

videotape recording, and that it provided high-quality reproduction of the gray scale with high sensitivity and low dark current. The company expected to have the camera on the market sometime in 1964.[59]

In September 1963, the BBC announced that its engineering department had developed a new electronic converter that changed television signals from one standard to another. It was then being used to convert the European standard of 625 lines to the British 405 lines. (The British were presuming that the 405-line system would be used for many years). The converter had almost 3,000 transistors and gave better definition, contrast and geometry. It was also cheaper to operate, as supervisory and manual control was eliminated.[60]

In October 1963, it was reported that the BBC had declared itself in favor of the U.S. NTSC color system. Color TV development had been carried out by the BBC for eight years. However, any decision on what method to use had been complicated by the arrival of two new methods, the French SECAM and a new German PAL (phase alternation by line) system. This seems to be the first publicity of the new PAL system which had been developed by Walter Bruch of Telefunken G.m.b.H and which was being considered by the EBU (European Broadcasting Union).

The PAL system was based on work done on the NTSC system by B. D. Loughlin of the Hazeltine Laboratories in November 1951. According to author George H. Brown, it was called color phase alternation. However, the PAL system made the color phase alternation line by line rather than by field, thus giving rise to the different name, "phase alternation by line." It also involved a delay line in the receiver just like SECAM. PAL was meant to correct for errors in the system, to alleviate the effects of ghosts in the picture and to correct for errors, including those in tape recording and microwave transmissions. The basic PAL technique reduced the vertical resolution by 50 percent, but this was justifiable because the human visual system cannot resolve this chrominance information anyway.[61] Loughlin stated that NTSC did not adopt line-rate PAL as it involved the use of a delay line, which probably made it impractical (at that time) for commercial receivers. Loughlin stated that many engineers today consider delay-line PAL to be more rugged than NTSC.[62]

The BBC wanted whatever system it adopted to be a standard, in order that it could facilitate frequency allocations, program exchanges and the export of TV sets.[63]

In January 1964, Ampex announced a new Editec Editor for use with its Editec system. It was now possible to assemble a program, in full color, scene by scene, frame by frame, in a manner heretofore possible only with motion picture film. Norman Bounsall, Ampex senior engineer stated that studios and production houses could now produce "on-the-spot" commercials and special programs in both black-and-white and color utilizing all the effects common to film production. Each scene was precisely located by means of tone bursts on the cue track of the tape. The markers gated the recording and monitoring circuits electronically so that splice time-base errors were reduced to less than one microsecond. The Editec system was priced at $9,500. The Ampex electronic editor used with it cost $3,850.[64]

At a meeting on February 25, 1964, in London, electronic experts from over 20 countries failed to agree on color TV standards for European telecasting and suggested that color standards be established the following year. The three major systems — NTSC, SECAM and the German PAL — were considered. Study Group 11 was scheduled to meet in Vienna in 1965. If it recommended a single standard for European color TV, it would submit it to the full CCIR in 1966.[65]

In March 1964, a new one-inch portable videotape recorder was announced by Dage, Inc. The recorder, priced at $12,450, had a bandwidth of 3mc. It used one-inch tape running at 6 inches per second and could record 63 minutes on a standard seven-inch reel of tape. A built-in monitor was included. It was claimed that the action could be slowed down or held stationary for up to an hour.[66] It was the same with the JVC DV220.

On April 2, 1964, David Sarnoff dedicated the RCA Official Color Television Communications Center at the 1964–65 New York World's Fair. He promised that television would soon be a global service and he noted that both Telstar and Relay communications satellites made it possible to give television a global character.[67]

In April 1964 the Fairchild Camera and Instrument Corp. of Syosset, NY demonstrated its new home television tape recorder. It could record from the input of a home television receiver and record from an additional camera. It was under development at the Winston Research Corp., Los Angeles. The Fairchild recorder used

David Sarnoff dedicating the RCA Color Television Center at the New York World's Fair on April 2, 1964. (RCA.)

1964. *Left:* Winston/Fairchild home videotape recorder. *Above:* Portable tape transport. (Winston/Fairchild, Inc.)

stationary heads and had a tape speed of 120 inches per second using quarter-inch tape. The company claimed it could be mass-produced for under $500. Only 15 minutes could be recorded in one direction using 9,000 feet of tape. However, it recorded four tracks on the tape and each pass was for 15 minutes. A mechanism played each track automatically. The picture showed a slight lack of sharpness on picture outlines and small objects, and because of the gradual roll-off, there was no ringing in the picture. Nonetheless, most viewers thought the picture excellent.[68]

In April 1964 the Ampex Corporation introduced its new "high band" VR2000 videotape recorder at the NAB convention in Chicago. Ampex stated that the new VR2000 was capable of producing higher quality recording than any previous machine. It incorporated normal "low band" standards, permitting tape interchangeability

1964. The magnificent Ampex VR2000 high band color recorder. (Ampex.)

with present day recorders. This machine introduced a revolutionary new "high-band" record-reproduce standard.[69] This new concept in videotape recording was developed primarily to serve the more stringent requirements of the BBC's new 625-line system on BBC 2, which went into operation on UHF with an 8mc bandwidth and FM sound from the Crystal Palace on channel 23.

The VR2000 included Intersync, cue channel and monitoring facilities. The Editec time element control system, electronic editor, Colortec and Amtec were available as options. The machine was shown at the 1964 NAB convention for three days only as it was en route to the BBC in London. The BBC immediately went into service. It was the first to use the new Ampex machine.[70]

It had long been realized that the original recording standards, while more than adequate for the U.S. 525-line and the BBC 405-line systems, were lacking in both frequency response and S/N ratio for the more demanding 625-line system. As early as 1958, when the first Ampex machines were delivered to the German television authority, it became apparent that much work remained to deliver the higher quality required. Negotiations were instituted under the auspices of the EBU to allow a higher carrier frequency to become standard for European broadcasters in order to permit a higher video bandwidth than 4.5MHz. The new British standard was designed to operate on the third-order shelf with a 7.8MHz carrier frequency; sync tip was 7.16MHz and peak white was 9.3MHz. A pre-emphasis boost of subcarrier was 8dB and the 3dB point for the bandwidth was 6.0MHz. The S/N ratio, unweighted, was 43dB. New video heads were developed so that frequencies in excess of 11MHz could be recovered from the tape. The differential gain was less than 5 percent, differential phase less than 5 percent, color phase error on 75 percent saturated bar @ 2c. It had better than 2 percent K factor. (The American standard was designed to operate on the fourth-order shelf with a 7.9MHz carrier frequency. Sync tip was 7.05MHz and peak white was 10MHz. Pre-emphasis boost of subcarrier was 8db and the minus 3db point was 4.5MHz . S/N ratio was 46db.)

Joe Roizen described the new Ampex VR2000 high-band color system. "The biggest changes were made in the FM modulator record amplifiers and the video head assembly. The VR2000 employs a dual heterodyne modulator, a pair of oscillators driven in opposite directions, one increasing in frequency, with the other decreasing. These oscillators operate in the 100mc region and utilize varactor capacity devices as the modulated device. Careful design of the mixer stage results in an extremely symmetrical FM output with very little AM components. It was necessary to move the modulating frequency to a higher level. It was to operate on the fourth-order shelf. Special heads were designed that recovered frequencies in excess of 11mc. Also, Nuvistor preamps extend the head resonances to the higher frequency region."[71]

During the development stage, Ampex delivered two modified VR1000C recorders to the BBC that had been specifically modified with the new high-band modulation/demodulation system and Nuvistor preamps to permit evaluation of this new recording technology. This new machine, first called the VR1000D, was built for the BBC.[72]

Then early in 1964 the BBC received the first VR-2000s delivered to anyone in the world. The new machines had such excellent quality that it was now possible to make up to fourth generation dubs in color with minimum loss of quality. The only drawback was that there were now three sets of video recording standards. Using the same heads and tape, the machine had (1) black-and-white, (2) low band color and (3) one high band module. The success of this machine led Ampex to transistorize the machine and bring it to market, both the foreign and the domestic. The company was still setting the standards for videotape recording worldwide. Another great success for Charles Ginsburg and the superb engineering staff at Ampex.[73]

There were many new devices shown at this convention. Ampex introduced two new versions of its all-solid-state VR1100: one a playback only unit and the other a two-part unit for either studio or remote use. Mach-Tronics showed its broadcast-quality, 83-pound machine that sold for $15,750. It could record nearly two hours on a 10½-inch reel of one-inch tape.

A TV signal stabilizer was shown by Sony for its PV-100 Videocorder. It was a 1½ inch–head design. It had a main scanning head and an auxiliary head for scanning during the vertical blanking interval. It had an effective servo system and a processing amplifier to cure inherent jitter, thus improving the time-base stability and making it compatible for broadcast use. Its cost was $14,400. It used rotary transformers that improved the signal to noise ratio and had slow and stop-motion controls.[74]

RCA showed the TR-22 and the TR-3, a playback only device, a TR-4 priced at $34,000 and finally a TR-5 in a mobile cabinet at $19,500.[75] RCA claims that it also showed a "high band" equipped TR-22 at the NAB con-

1964. Sony home video recorder (BV-100?). *Above:* Deck. *Below:* With built-in monitor, TVC-2010 (1966). (Sony Corp.)

vention. It also claimed that it had worked with the BBC to develop an international high-band standard.[76] (I have never come across a paper telling of RCA's development of the high-band standard. I am certain that the company took the work of the Ampex engineers and claimed it as their own. The patent agreement between RCA and Ampex allowed them to do this. So RCA came out with its own version of Intersync (Pixlock), Amtec (ATC automatic timing corrector), Colortec (Color ATC), Editec (Electronic splicer), by just changing the names.)[77]

RCA had not given up on television film recording. In April 1964 while the company was experimenting with electron-beam recording, they announced a completely new TV film recorder, the TFR-1. It was a completely new concept in that it had a new subscreen picture tube, a new camera, self-adjusting circuits and programmed control. It featured a new picture tube that had the screen on a substratum glass mounted a short distance behind the faceplate. This eliminated light dispersion while increasing resolution capability. The recording camera was clawless, with only one reciprocating component weighing less than eight ounces. A special shutter located in the optical path was made to fade in and fade out over some 40 video lines. Because of this feathering action of the picture splice, a bar did not develop. It also featured automatic exposure control which set both contrast and brightness. The TFR-1 was built to mate with the Eastman Viscomat processing machine. This processed film at a speed of 36 feet/minute with no mixing of solutions. The new recorder was to be used for film commercials or promotional films. Multiple film copies could be made when it was necessary to telecast simultaneously in several markets and immediacy of release was not critical.[78]

In May 1964, the General Electronics Corp. of Newark, NJ, announced that it was negotiating with Paramount Pictures to produce a small-screen color tube using the Paramount developed Chromatron principle. Paramount

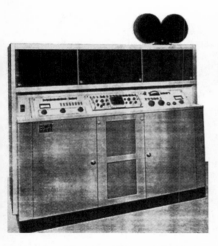

1964. RCA television film recorder, TFR-1. (RCA.)

had previously given a nonexclusive license to the Sony Corp. to manufacture and sell Chromatron tubes in the USA and Canada. However, the tube had not yet advanced beyond prototype production.[79]

On May 7, 1964, Telstar II went into orbit and before the week was over had been used for two TV programs. With its successful launch, it was expected that Europe could see "live" shots of astronaut L. Gordon Cooper's 22-orbit flight scheduled for May 14.[80]

In June 1964, CBS-TV revealed that it had acquired a Minicam Mark II wireless TV camera with studio quality features. The portable unit weighed less than 29 pounds including camera and transmitter pack, could be operated under normal lighting conditions and met the same standards as the standard studio image orthicon. The camera weighed only 6½ pounds and measured five by four inches including the lens. The camera pickup tube was the Plumbicon developed by Philips. This seems to be the first commercial use of the new Plumbicon tube.[81]

In July, the 1964 Olympics were held in Japan and televised to the rest of the world by means of the Syncom III satellite which hovered some 36,000 km above the Pacific Ocean. Signals were sent to the satellite from a ground station in Kashima, Japan, and received at Point Magu near Los Angeles. From Los Angeles the signals were sent across the USA and to Canada. At Montreal they were recorded on tape and flown by jet to Hamburg for distribution to Europe.[82]

On July 31, 1964, Ranger VII sent the first pictures by TV of the moon's surface, before it crashed there. The cameras were made by RCA for the National Aeronautics and Space Administration.[83] Also in July, two weather satellites were expected to be launched into orbit 575 miles above the earth. Nimbus A and Tiros had three special Vidicon cameras, a miniature television tape recorder and radio transmitter pointed towards the earth. RCA made the cameras for both Tiros and Nimbus.[84]

In July 1964 a television film recording system called Electronovision was used to record directly on 35mm film the play *Hamlet* starring Richard Burton at the Lunt-

Fontanne Theatre. The five RCA TK 60 cameras were used to feed two new RCA TFR television film recorders. The director monitored the output of the five cameras and selected the pictures to be recorded. The play was repeated three times and the directors had separate films of each performance to choose from. The finished picture was exhibited in over 1,000 theaters on September 23 and 24. Noting that the picture was shot with existing light, RCA was quick to point out that high-quality TV film recordings could be produced at low light levels. They agreed that their recording compared favorably with regular motion pictures.[85]

In July 1964, Philips Research Laboratories of Eindhoven announced their new "Plumbicon" camera tube. It was basically a Vidicon tube but with much better features. It was of small size, simple construction with a low dark current, high speed response and good resolution. Its glass face plate was coated with a thin transparent conducting layer of microcrystalline lead oxide. The photoconductor was in three layers: the middle layer was almost pure lead oxide, on the gun side layer the lead oxide became

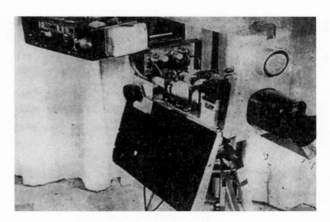

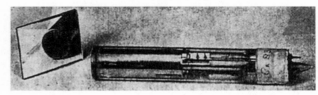

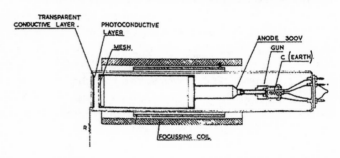

1964. *Above:* Experimental three–Plumbicon color camera with zoom lens. *Middle:* Philips Plumbicon tube. *Below:* Diagram of tube. (Philips Labs.)

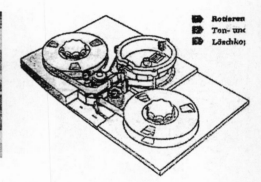

1964. *Above left:* Philips Video-Recorder 3400. *Middle:* Top view of scanner. *Right:* Schematic of tape path. (Philips Labs.)

a "P" type semiconductor due to doping, and the layer on the signal electrode was an "N" type semiconductor.

Philips claimed the that multilayer structure of the target led to a very small dark current and to a much higher sensitivity than was obtainable with a simple P-N junction. By choosing the individual layer parameters it was possible to produce a tube of excellent spectral sensitivity, a very good resolving power and a high speed of response. It did seem to have a limited red response at first. These were desirable qualities in medical applications, for radiological examinations in particular, or for making tubes combining high sensitivity with long service life and reasonable speed of response.[86]

In August 1964, Fairchild Camera and Instrumentation Corp. again demonstrated its home television recorder at the WESCON electronics show in Los Angeles. It was priced at $500. Fairchild was negotiating with several companies to build the machine.[87]

In September 1964, the Sony Corporation of Japan announced that a new Sony home recorder would be exported to the USA in 1965. The machine used half-inch tape running at 7.5 inches/sec, weighed about 18 pounds and measured 15 by 14 by 6½ inches. It ran 2,400 feet of tape for a maximum 63 minutes of recording time. This seems to be the first video recorder using half-inch tape.[88]

In September 1964, Philips announced their new helical-scan video recorder, the 3400. It was a single-head machine and the head was made of Ferroxcube which gave it a very long life. The one-inch tape was scanned at a rate of 23 meters per second while the tape ran at 7.5 inches per second. An eight-inch reel of tape ran for some 45 minutes. The machine was not for professional use.[89]

In September 1964, it was announced that the Sony Corp. would market a color television set built around a new 19-inch one-gun picture tube, first in Japan and then later in the USA. The picture tube was a Chromatron one-gun type that had vertical color stripes and a deflection grid. This would be the second Japanese set using a Chromatron type of tube. The Yaou Electric Co. of Japan had introduced an eight-inch tube and a line sequential system the previous spring. It was reported that research was under way at Sony on a three-gun Chromatron that was expected to be three times as bright.[90]

According to author Nick Lyons, Sony had secured a license under the Chromatron patent in 1962 and immediately started an intensive program to develop its own tube. By September 1964 they had sold 13,000 sets in Japan, but the more they sold, the more defects they found. Soon after, they determined that is was technically and financially not feasible, so it was quietly dropped.[91]

In October 1964, a new home television tape recorder by the Loewe-Opta A. G. of West Germany was announced. At a demonstration in late September, viewers were impressed by the reproduction fidelity of the recorder. The recorder had a tape speed of 7 inches/sec and an eight-inch reel gave about one hour of time on one-inch tape. It was fully transistorized. At a cost of $3,000, officials of Loewe said production would start in 1965 and that perhaps 3,000 units might be available.[92]

In December 1964, Sony announced a new half-inch home video recorder. It ran at 7.5 inches per second using a 2,400 reel of tape that ran for a maximum of 63 minutes. It weighed about 18 pounds and measured 15 by 14 by 6½ inches. Sony planned to export it to the USA in 1965.[93]

In December 1964, Ampex introduced the VR650 which met all broadcast standards. It featured stop motion for the first time. It weighed 96 pounds. With a low tape speed of 4.1 inches/second, it could record up to three hours on one reel of two-inch tape.[94]

Chapter 7

Solid-State Cameras
(1965–1967)

During the week of January 18, 1965, a portable unit of RCA was in Moscow giving demonstrations of the American NTSC color system. RCA was touring Europe with a mobile van at the request of the Department of Commerce. This van carried color cameras, several color receivers, film and slide scanners and a videotape recorder capable of recording and playing back color signals on 625 lines. In the spring of 1964, concerned by the loss of the NTSC system as a worldwide standard, the Department of Commerce had asked RCA to set up a mobile van with a color videotape recorder to present the NTSC color system using 625 lines at 50 cycles.

The van started by touring northern Europe. Cameras were installed in the Moscow studio and four 1½-hour programs were broadcast in color. During the programs, the NTSC signals were experimentally transmitted over 1,000 miles on the Russian microwave system and back to Moscow where they were broadcast with very little degradation as seen on the receivers. Earlier C.F.T. had demonstrate SECAM in Moscow and comparative tests had been arranged by engineers of the Russian State Committee between NTSC and SECAM with help from Britain and France. Later in February, the RCA mobile unit went to Paris where demonstrations were given at the laboratories of O.R.T.F. After Paris the RCA truck went to Frankfurt, Nuremberg, Zagreb, Milan and Vienna.[1]

In February 1965, the Ampex Corporation announced a new television tape recording system, the VR303, for the closed-circuit market. The VR303 was a 95-pound machine using quarter-inch tape that ran at a speed of 100 inches/sec. It could record 50 minutes on a 12½-inch reel. This unit was the first commercial Ampex recorder using a single stationary head that laid down a longitudinal track. It used 12,600 feet of quarter-inch tape which recorded some 25 minutes and then reversed its direction and recorded another 25 minutes on another track. It claimed a bandwidth of 250 to 1.5mc (at 3db). The VR303 was offered as part of the Ampex Videotrainer System with an Ampex camera and receiver, tripod and microphone in a complete mobile system.[2] Why Ampex decided to come out with a longitudinal recorder at this late date is hard to figure out. At $3,950 there were other helical machines that were cheaper and had better quality.[3]

Also in February it was announced that the new Plumbicon color camera would soon be marketed in the USA. The Norelco camera, to be shown at the NAB convention in Washington, used the Plumbicon color tubes that were developed in 1963.[4] Visual Electronics Corporation was marketing the new cameras in the USA and it was rumored that CBS would be the first to get delivery of them. The cameras were to cost about $65,000 each.[5]

On Tuesday, March 30, 1965, Electrovision planned to use its new four TV camera system and the RCA TFR-1 kine recorder for the production of the motion picture *Harlow*. It was to be shot on a five-day schedule. The picture was budgeted at $1,500,000 which, it was claimed, was a savings of between $3,000,000 and $3,500,000 on what it would have cost if normal motion picture techniques were used. Electronovision had filmed *Tami*, which was shot in only two days. For Harlow, 27 sets had been built and were ready for use, just as in a regular TV production. The savings in time was considered the system's greatest asset. The film was to be released on May 12 to 6,000 theaters.[6]

1965. Ikegami type TVR-301 helical-scan recorder. (Ikegami Ltd.)

Produced on 35mm film, for all intents and purposes it was a regular motion picture. Although aesthetically a poor picture, it was a milestone in motion picture production since it was the first electronic motion picture made for theater release.

1965. Loewe-Opta videotape recorder. (Loewe-Opta A. G.)

At the NAB convention held in Washington in March 1965, the new Norelco PC60 Plumbicon color cameras with a removable servo-controlled 10:1 zoom lens were shown. The servo-controlled zoom lens weighed about 41 pounds. Together, the camera and viewfinder weighed 120 pounds.

Also in March at NAB, the Ikegami Tsushinki Com-

1967. RCA TV four-tube camera, TK-42. New image orthicon tube used for the luminance channel. (RCA.)

pany of Japan introduced a new home video recorder. This was the Type TVR-301. It was a two-head helical using two thirds of an inch tape. It was capable of recording for 63 minutes maximum and was for closed circuit only.[7]

RCA showed a new color camera using the new Selenicon camera tube. It was reported that RCA was replacing their Vidicon tubes in their TK-42 four-tube camera with their new "Selenicon" tubes. It was claimed that this new tube used selenium in its photosensitive layer to multiply the sensitivity to light. The selenium alloy was deposited on the inner surface of the glass windows at the front of the tube. As used in the RCA TK42, three tubes were combined with a 4½-inch image orthicon for the luminance channel.[8] Later, in January 1966, it was reported that only one lone Selenicon camera had been on test at NAB, and that at an undisclosed station.[9] RCA was still promoting the four-tube approach. G.E. was also using a four-tube approach with its GE 4V (Vidicon) color film chain.[10]

EMI Electronics showed both Vidicon and Plumbicon cameras. Philips showed its Norleco PM-50 by Visual Electronics, a solid state black-and-white camera. Visual Electronics showed its Mark 10 black-and-white camera with 10:1 lens. Ampex showed its line of British Marconi cameras including the Mark V. Thomson-Houston showed a transistorized Vidicon camera, the TH-T 600, and a three-inch image orthicon camera, TH-T-679, that weighed 99 pounds and was for studio use. They also showed a combination TV and movie camera, the TH-T-605 which as a single unit used 16mm film and live TV.

Other cameras shown were a new portable three-inch image orthicon camera, PE-26, by G.E. The Sony Corp. showed its new three-inch image orthicon that was compact, lightweight and used a 5-inch viewfinder. It was priced at $10,900 without lens.[11]

1966. Philips Plumbicon color camera. (Philips Labs.)

1965. Black-and-white Philips Plumbicon camera for CCIR 625 lines. (Philips Labs.)

Shibaden Corp. of America displayed the Shiba two-tube color camera ($49,999) used by Japanese broadcasters to cover the 1964 Olympics. Two three-inch image orthicon tubes were used in the camera: one for chrominance and the other for signals sampled by a color stripe filter.[12]

A new entry in the major high-band color category was the Visual/Allen Continental recorder model V/A 100 G. It was developed by Allen Electronics Corp., which was now a division of Visual. It was specially designed to make color masters as well as multiple generation copies. (Allen had been making special electronics for videotape recorders for several years.) The machine cost $100,000.[13]

RCA presented its new TR-70 recorder ($82,500) as the "first fully integrated TV tape recording system for high band color recording and playback." It had a switch for the choice of the three recording standards and built-in facilities for equalizing headwheel performance. RCA also showed its new deluxe TV tape recorder, the 22HL. Fully solid state, it was priced at $72,000 and had high-band or low-band modules. Also shown were the TR22, which was also completely solid state, the TR3 for playback only, and the TR5.[14]

Sony showed its push-button operated BV-120 Video-Corder system which included a portable VTR at 145 pounds, waveform monitor, and signal stabilizer. The recorder used two-inch tape, running at 4½ inches per second; the machine could be single-framed for 15 minutes and incorporated slow motion from stop to one third normal.[15]

The new MVR-65 portable videotape machine was shown at the 1965 NAB convention. This was made by the MVR Corp. that had been licensed by Precision Instruments. It weighed 85 pounds and had a video response of ±3db from 10cps to 3.5 mc, and on S/N ratio better than 40db. Its horizontal stability was within FCC standards. The MVR 65 sold for $14,350 and a spare head disc cost $375.[16]

Also shown for the first time by Mach-Tronics at the MVR exhibit was a disk-type TV recorder housed in a solid-state unit. This device selling at $15,000 used an aluminum disc, coated with magnetic material, which was spun like a phonograph record. The top of the disk recorded 20 seconds of video for instantaneous reproduction; the bottom side recorded stills. The disk could be erased and used over again.[17]

In April 1965, Ampex demonstrated the first electronic editing accessory for their helical VR660 portable and announced that it would soon be available. This device, called the Edicon, was designed to permit push-button editing of tapes for broadcast without cutting or splicing.[18]

Up to this time it was not possible to physically edit helical recordings due to the length and angle of the recorded tracks. Ampex, that had introduced electronic editing for their transverse recorders in 1961, had now given this same ability to its helical machines. Ampex had great faith in the future of helical scan machines.[19] This seems to be the first time that helical scan machines could use the same techniques as their transverse brothers— another first from Ampex. Ampex claimed that the first domestic deliveries of their high-band VTR2000 were to begin within the month.

In April 1965, it was announced that the Mitchell Camera Corporation, the world's leading manufacturer of 35mm studio cameras, had produced a new "System 35" camera which combined the Mitchell Mark II Studio Reflex, mounted in a new Mark II sound blimp, and a Vidicon camera that scanned the reflex image. The output of this camera was displayed on an electronic viewfinder on the camera where it could be conveniently seen by the camera operator. The output could also be fed to any number of video monitors so that all concerned could see what the camera saw as it was being used. It was expected to revolutionize film production in the next few years.[20]

By this time this was an old idea. However, it was doomed to failure as the use of a geared head meant that the camera operator could not drive or steer the camera or focus it. This still had to be done by others. But its acceptance by the Mitchell camera company gave it some credence. However, Hollywood's response to it was lukewarm

1965. Mitchell "System 35" combination film and video camera. (Mitchell Camera Company.)

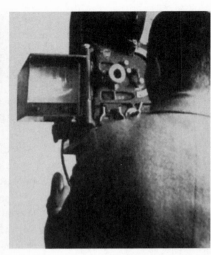

Above left: 35mm camera. *Right:* Rear of camera with electronic viewfinder. (Mitchell Camera Company.)

as usual. It smacked too much of a television system. It would be several years before the attachment of a television camera as a viewing device (video assist) would be standard equipment on all major 35mm cameras.

In May 1965, it was agreed that there would be no international color standard for all of Europe. In a vote by some 200 delegates of the CCIR from 45 countries, the majority vote went to SECAM with 22 votes, PAL was second with 11, and NTSC third with only six votes. In the UK, the Television Advisory Committee appeared to be favoring the PAL system. West Germany had announced that the PAL system would be put into effect in 1967 and the French were expected to adopt the SECAM system, regardless of the system recommended by the CCIR![21]

On May 5, 1965, at the Edison Electric Institute Convention, Westinghouse showed an electronic system that played TV pictures from a phonograph record. This was the PHONOVID system for recording and playing back still pictures and sound on a television screen from an ordinary home tape machine or phonograph. The pictures could be line drawings, charts, printed text or photographs. The system displayed the tape pictures on a conventional television receiver, or the taped pictures could be transferred to the grooves of the record and played back. Some 1,200 pictures and accompanying sound could be stored on a standard seven-inch (1,200 foot) reel of narrow slow-speed audio tape, or some 400 still pictures and sound could be put on the two-sides of a standard 33⅓ record called a VideoDisc. The system consisted of four components: (1) a slow-scan television camera, (2) an audio-tape recorder, (3) a scan converter to convert the taped signals to standard TV signals, and (4) a conventional TV receiver.[22]

In June 1965, Precision Instrument Co. announced

a new portable videotape recorder with variable speed control to display a picture at normal speed, at any degree of slow-motion or with the machine stopped. This was the Model PI-4V which featured Variscan playback speed control and two audio tracks. During playback, a single control knob was rotated to vary the TV image from a dead stop through any degree of slow motion to normal full speed, with the transition between any speeds free of flopovers or image distortions.[23]

In July 1965, it was announced that a new 16mm camera system using a solid-state imaging device had been developed by the Aerospace Division of Westinghouse Electric Corp. under a NASA contract. The imaging device was a mosaic made of 2,500 photo transistors. The mosaic was square with 50 light-sensitive semiconductor elements on a side. Each element was made of a three-layer photo transistor that controlled a current which ran through it. The current in turn was modulated by the light that hit each element. Output from each of the elements was stepped up by a video amplifier before transmission. All the circuitry was in microminiaturized wafers or chips and the power input was four watts or less. Instead of an electron beam to scan each row of elements, digital logic circuits scan the wafer at 60 frames/second.[24] This appears to be the first report of a solid-state imaging device.

There was a report of an early 256 × 256 RCA solid-state camera using thin film technology in 1967.[25]Weimer also stated that in 1969 and 1970 two important new devices were reported which made possible an entirely new type of solid-state scanning. These were the bucket-brigade circuits of Sangster of the Philips Company and the charge coupled device (CCD) of Boyle and Smith of the Bell laboratories.

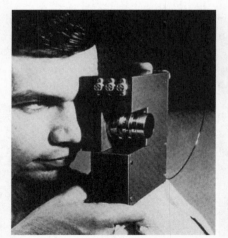
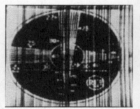

1967. Above left: RCA battery-operated solid-state camera using thin-film sensor of 256 × 256 elements. *Right:* Photographs taken with this camera. (RCA.)

Brother Dowd claims that the first demonstration of solid state sensors using thin film transistors was done by RCA in 1964.[26] Sadashige claims that a device was proposed in 1963 by Morrison of Honeywell, and in 1964 the "Scanistor — A solid-state image scanner" was put forward by Horton, Mazza and Dym of IBM Corp. Also Sadashige states that the first known demonstration of a working solid-state device was made at Wescon in Los Angeles in 1967. The device used an array of photo diodes such as the photon-electron transducer and a scanning system based on sequential X-Y addressing to enable each sensor element to transfer its photon-generated images.[27]

In July 1965, Westinghouse announced the availability of a more rugged and long lived three-inch image dissector tube which had a high resolution of 3,000 TV lines/inch. Designated the WL.23110 the new tube was reported ideal for microfilm readout, TV scanning, and high-speed flying-spot scanning.[28] It was stated that the image dissector despite its inherent low sensitivity surpassed all other camera tubes in resolution. No other camera tube using a cathode ray beam could be as sharp, as exact in its electronic imaging as the dissector or an image converter tube.[29]

Thus some 38 years after its conception by Farnsworth the dissector tube was still a useful and productive device while its main competitor, the iconoscope, had long since retired from the scene. As far as can be determined at this time, the last iconoscopes were made in the period of 1950-1951.

In July at the Fourth International Television Symposium and Equipment Exhibition at Montreux, Dr. Brown of RCA remarked wryly "that Europe seems to have devised very successfully a method by which no decision on a common standard could possibly be made." (How right he was!)[30]

RCA made the statement that the new method of tape recording (high band developed by Ampex) was well able to cope with the stringent requirements of wider bandwidth, smaller timing, differential gain and differential phase errors. In particular the Ampex VR2000 and RCA TR-4 were demonstrated and showed their ability to cope with these and other problems.[31]

In July 1965, it was reported that ABC was using the Ampex 660 for slow and stop motion for the "Baseball Game of The Week."[32] Using the isolated camera technique to replay key action of the game gave the director the option of taping from a live camera or a standby camera, and offered them a broader selection of shots to catch closeup action as it developed. The plays might be televised immediately or during the half-time break.[33]

On July 13, 1965, the MVR Corporation of Pala Alto, California, gave the first demonstration of its Videodisc recorder VDR-210 CF in San Francisco. It is claimed that

the first use of this device was by CBS for the Baltimore Colts football game on August 6, 1965. This was the first broadcast application. It was the first commercial device devised to allow both

1965. MVR videodisc recorder. (MVR Corp.)

freeze frames and 20 seconds of instant replay. The use of a spinning disc made it possible to return to the start of the recording, as the heads were mounted on a rotating screw. A tape machine could do the same thing, but was much slower. This was the first of new series of devices to free television from its straightjacket of real-time performance.[34]

MVR's videodisc was a portable magnetic disc recorder adapted for a wide variety of nonbroadcast applications. The recorder incorporated a spinning magnetic disc on which real-time video or other wide-band signal input was recorded in a continuous spiral, and sequential stop-action pictures or 33ms wideband signals were recorded as discrete closed loops. The unit was designed for push-button operation by nontechnical personnel.

In its broadcast configuration, the recorder stored up to 20 seconds of real-time signals from a live TV camera or other video source on the top surface of a 12-inch aluminum disc coated with a nickel cobalt recording medium. The recording could be immediately played back as a continuous real-time sequence, as a series of stop-action pictures or in any combination of action and stop action. The recorder was used in closed-circuit systems to monitor manufacturing processes, vehicular traffic flow, surgical operations and the like.

In one of the newly developed nonbroadcast configurations, the device was used as a sequential wide-band recorder, utilizing one or both sides of a 14-inch disc to store up to 1,600 stop-action pictures or other 33ms wideband signals, each separately recorded automatically at a predetermined time interval or by manual control at irregular intervals.[35]

In August 1965, CBS used its new Norelco Plumbicon color cameras for the first time on the "Ed Sullivan Show" and the "Red Skeleton Shows" from CBS-TV City in Hollywood. It was found that the Plumbicon cameras were much more sensitive than the image orthicon color cameras they were using. Lighting levels of 200 to 250fc could be used versus 400–500 for their regular three-tube color cameras. The only problem was the lack of edge enhancement and fine detail found in image orthicon cameras. In addition to their lighter weight (they were less than 200 pounds), setup and maintenance were found to be no problem. Tube life was expected to be over 1000 hours.[36]

In September 1965, it was announced that Eastman Kodak was trade testing videotape in New York City at CBS. Eastman had first marketed sound tape in March 1962 and this was part of a continuing video and computer tape development program. However, the company had made no plans to market the videotape at that time.[37]

In September 1965, Ampex announced an advanced version of the VR660 recorder called the VR600B. It was to replace both the VR660 and the VR1500.[38]

Also in September 1965, the suit between Ampex and Mach-Tronics ended with a federal jury award of $600,000 to both Mach-Tronics and the Precision Instrument Corporation which held a license from Mach-Tronics. The court had decided that Ampex had violated the antitrust laws.[39]

In September 1965, Sony placed its new home video recorder on the market. It was the Sony TVC-2010. It was a two-head helical scan that used half-inch tape running at 7½ inches per second. It had a built-in TV set which was used for recording and on playback. It ran for one hour on a seven-inch (2,370 feet) reel of tape. Head speed was only 30 revolutions per seconds, so each field was recorded twice, and the tape to head speed was about 433 inches per second. Resolution was approximately 180 lines. On playback, which had to be done on the built-in monitor, a servo was used to stabilize the video output.[40]

In October 1965, RCA's Dr. Brown stated that he had dim hopes for a single color standard in Europe. NTSC had been relegated to third place with France backing the French SECAM system and Germany the PAL system. Also Great Britain who had gone along with NTSC was now seriously considering the PAL system.[41]

In October, Ampex asked for a new trial charging patent infringement and piracy of trade secrets. It wanted $3 million in damages. The judge urged both sides to consider an out-of-court settlement.[42]

In October, Precision Instrument Co. of Palo Alto announced the model PI-7100 that incorporated Variscan which permitted observation at any selectable tape speed. It featured stacked coaxial reels and helical scan closed-loop drive recording on one-inch tape. The recorder allowed forward and reverse playback continuously at variable speeds from zero to 16 inches/sec.[43] In Germany, it was distributed by SABA as the 7100.[44]

In November 1965, the Minnesota Mining and Manufacturing Company (3M) described a laboratory model of an electron-beam recorder. It used 16mm film and had

an intermittent shuttle mechanism phase-locked to the television signal, together with a time-deflection gate of the electron beam to convert from the television 30 frames/sec to film 24 frames/sec. Exposure control was obtained with a beam-sampling servo system. A two-vacuum system, with the film providing its own seal, minimized startup time and prolonged the electron gun filament life. It was claimed that this recorder made possible 16mm television recording free from the fixed noise patterns of phosphor faceplates, a resolution in excess of 600 lines and pictures free from shutter bar.[45]

1965. *Above:* SABA 4V videotape recorder. (SABA Precision Instrument Co.) *Below:* Portable one-inch videotape recorder, PI-7100 (1966). (Precision Instrument Co. [USA].)

In December 1965, Ampex reached a final agreement with Precision Instrument: Ampex was to pay Precision $150,000 cash and give it royalty rights to certain contested patents. "MVR," the new name for Mach-Tronics, and Precision were awarded treble damages of $600,000 each on grounds that Ampex had conspired to control the world market for TV tape recorders. In the countersuit, Ampex was awarded $20,000 on charges that MVR had pirated trade secrets and infringed on Ampex patents. On March 7, 1966, Ampex announced that it would continue its suit against MVR for the remaining $2,980,000.[46]

In January 1966, Moscow television announced a new videotape recorder that was going into production. It was to replace an old machine that came into use in 1961. The new machine used 70mm wide tape that required a larger head assembly and ran at a higher tape speed. It used a heterodyne modulator operating between 6.5 and 10 megacycles. The designer claimed a bandwidth of 6.5mc with a 38–39db signal/noise ratio. The wider tape also permitted three audio tracks and a control track. The drum was slotted for mechanical quadrature adjustment, although delay lines were also used. There was no time-base correction accessory, it was reported that there were problems when using British tape, and the head life

1966. Soviet videotape recorder in Leningrad. This recorder used 70mm tape. (*Electronics.*)

1966. *Above:* The Westel Portable 20-pound camera and seven-pound self-powered TV recorder, battery contained. *Middle:* Camera and TV recorder, WRC-150. *Bottom:* WTR-100 "Studio Model" with WCM-200 color module. (Westel Co.)

was only 50–70 hours. With Russian made tape, this was reduced further to 40 hours.[47]

In January 1966, Photo-Sonics Inc. of Burbank introduced a new kine-recording camera for producing high-resolution motion pictures. It was available in three models: 16mm, 35mm and 16/35mm. The camera operated on the U.S. standard and used the two-field system. The shutter was a 288 degrees (open) type and the intermittent used registration pins. Film capacity was 3000 feet.

In February 1966, a report was given of the progress being made by RCA and Westinghouse in developing a tubeless television camera.[48] In November 1966, it was reported that RCA thin-film technology had yielded a tubeless TV camera. It functioned by means of 132,000 thin-film devices on four one-inch glass slides; some 32,400 of the devices were the photo conductors located at the intersection of a 180 line matrix of thin metal conductors. RCA under an air force contract chose the thin-film course, using sulfide photoconductors over a glass substrate.[49]

Also in February, Sony announced a new color home tape recorder. It came in two versions, one adapted for one-hour playback onto a single TV set with a Sony color converter and a second advanced type for all receivers.[50]

Again in February, Marconi announced their newest color camera using four Plumbicons. This was the Marconi Mark VII. They had joined the group that believed that the fourth camera tube (the luminance channel) was necessary to insure sharpness and fine detail.[51]

The NAB convention was held the last week in March 1966, in Chicago. At this show, The Westel Co. of Redwood City, California, introduced the first portable television camera and backpack recorder, the model WRC-150. It was called the most significant development of the show.[52] The video recorder held a 30-minute supply of one-inch magnetic tape. The recorder used the Coniscan

principle which directed the tape at 10 inches/sec around an inverted three-piece, flat-top cone. The whole center section, which housed the single recording head, rotated against the tape. This created an air cushion to reduce the tape friction. The recorder used special motors of the printed-circuit type, high torque and low inertia. It contained a full-scale internal sync generator to provide a clean and stable source for all timing functions of the camera and recorder.

The WRC-150 backpack recorder was a record-only module weighing some 23 pounds complete with tape and rechargeable nickel-cadmium batteries and the cable linked Vidicon camera head weighed rather less than seven pounds. Reels were coaxially mounted, with a 6½ inch reel giving some 14 minutes of recording and the eight-inch reel some 33 minutes. The camera head included a novel small CRT for viewfinding that could be switched to operate as an "A" scope. In the interest of low weight and power, rewind and fast forward functions were not included and there was only one audio channel. Westel claimed specifications of 10c/s to 4.2MHz ±2db bandwidth with a signal/noise ratio of 42db peak to peak.

The console model WTR.100 was a professional

videotape recorder weighing some 75 pounds. Electronic editing was available as a built-in option. The addition of a color module WCM-200 provided final electronic time-base correction on a line-by-line basis, synchronized to an external reference and allowing direct recovery of NTSC color signals. Video stability and time-base and sync structure met all FCC requirements The cost for the camera and recorder was $10,500. The console model was $15,000 for black-and-white and $25,000 with the color addition.

The Westel innovations involved two unique systems: one a highly compact 2½ cubic feet studio record and playback machine ($15,000) that could handle "wide-band" color when a plug-in color module ($10,000) was attached and the other a lightweight backpack recorder with tape camera ($10,500, less lens) that made spot news, sight-and-sound coverage, ready for the air immediately.

Westel's systems were 60 percent integrated circuits and featured a highly proprietary single head Coniscan recording device that eliminated many interferences and alignment problems inherent in four-head systems, as well as tape and head wear. Tape pressure of the head on the one-inch tape was said to be around three ounces. The systems also use servo controls and were both mechanically and electronically self-correcting after each scan line; the company claimed that the systems actually improved faulty tape recordings of other machines by making corrections in the rerecording.

The Westel TV and sound recording camera was transistorized and features cathode screen viewing so that the camera operator could see exactly what they were shooting. Being a "live" type TV camera, it was more sensitive than a film. It weighed seven pounds, and the backpack, containing video recording facilities of broadcast quality, weighed 11 pounds—the batteries added another 12 pounds. The system could shoot a full half-hour continuously with plenty of reserve time for preview and setups and it could work anywhere a person could go.[53]

It was reported that some 100 units were sold at the show, including to CBS-TV which had cooperated with Westel in suggesting design need and technical requirements. It was the most significant product development of the show. Among the engineers were Moghazi Barkoki who demonstrated the "Video Cruiser."[54] Others were Alfred W. Bolls Jr., Robert L. King, Alex R. Maxey, Allan G. Grace, John Streets, Theodore Pickett, David Castillo, M. F. Barkourt, Don J. Cochran, Guido Salcedo and W. H. Butler.[55] This was the first self-contained portable camera and video recorder ever made.

Sony also revealed two new TV disc recorders in March.[56] These were two machines using thin plastic discs to record and playback monochrome motion pictures and still pictures in color. The first machine was the Video-

mat which recorded black-and-white motion pictures for immediate playback. This machine contained a camera, lights, discs and a 19-inch television set. The disc had an aluminum rim with an "inside surface of material identified with videotape." The second machine, the Video Color Demonstrator, was reported to record up to 40 still pictures on the disc for playback over a standard television monitor. Showing of the pictures could be repeated or the pictures erased from the disc if desired. The Videomat was expected to cost around $3,000 for a complete unit and the Video Color Demonstrator about $1,700 to $1,800. This unit was demonstrated at the IEEE 1966 convention held in New York.[57]

Meanwhile it was announced that both ABC and NBC had signed up for orders of the MVR Videodisc recorders. This was due to the successful use of this machine by CBS on a Baltimore Colts August intrasquad football game.[58]

In April 1966, Ampex introduced a VR1100E primarily for mobile use. Ampex also announced three new accessories for their high band VR2000 recorder: (1) a low band switchable standard unit to facilitate switching between high band, low-band color and low-band monochrome; (2) a head alignment kit which allowed adjustment of head resonance without the use of a separate oscilloscope and sweep generator; and (3) most important of all, an automatic velocity compensator to eliminate color hue banding.[59]

This last accessory was designed to eliminate color hue banding due to differential velocity errors. The compensator was designed around the fact that mechanical conditions which produced these errors were generally fixed and cyclic, repeating themselves with each rotation of the head. A memory bank containing 64 individual capacitor stores was provided with a series of incremental error voltages that were derived from the combined geometric and color correcting delay line errors. The 64 stores when charged contained error information for each television line scanned by a full rotation of the head drum (four heads, 16 lines per head). Before any given line was repeated on subsequent rotations of the head assembly, the store representing that line was read out and its error signal was applied to a ramp-forming capacitor which generated a waveform whose slope was proportional to the velocity error component. This ramp was applied to the geometric correcting delay line as a modulation voltage which caused the Amtec delay line to change its delay over the active period of the television line from the preset level established at the start of the line to the level predicted by measurement of the incremental error of the previous rotation.[60]

In April 1966, Sony announced that they had developed a "chromatron" tube which used a wire grid color system as opposed to RCA's shadow mask tube. It was reported that complicated electrical makeup produced color images at a much greater brightness. They admitted that the chromatron was first developed as an engineering concept called the Lawrence chromatron color tube.[61]

In May, 3M's Revere-Mincom Division of St. Paul announced a new Wollensak VTR-150 home television recorder. It was a helical-scan machine designed for educational, industrial and military uses. It was all transistor, using sold-state circuitry with a two-motor drive. The machine ran at 7½ inches/sec and could record one hour of material on a seven-inch reel of half-inch tape. It had a 2Hz bandwidth, video SNR of 35db, audio SNR of 40db, and weighed some 50 pounds. It was priced around $1,495.[62]

In May 1966, the use of combination film and television cameras for producing direct film was being done in England. It was reported that A. P. B. Studios, Elstree had installed the ADD-A-Vision system by Livingston on a single camera basis for a TV color series. It was claimed that the picture on the electronic viewfinder was crisp enough to be used for range finding. In addition, the Electronicam system using Arriflex 16mm cameras was being used to a great extent in British Studios. As a three-camera system, it used about 350 to 400fc for color film as against 250fc for color TV, with Marconi Mark VII color cameras.[63]

Ampex revealed that its model VR-6000 home recorder would be available in June and would cost some $1,095 to $1,495. It used one-inch tape running at 9.6 inches/sec. Horizontal response was 2.5mc and resolution is 250 lines. It was also stated that the VR-7000 for industrial, educational, military and similar uses would be available and that some 900 had been delivered since production started in January.[64]

On June 13, 1966, it was announced that Ampex and MVR had settled all litigation between them. MVR now

acknowledged the validity of the contested Ampex patents (FM modulator?) and was forbidden from future production of videotape recorders using this patent. In return MVR acquired rights to various Ampex patents in its continuing production and sale of videodisc recorders.[65]

1965. Ampex videotape home recorder. (Ampex.)

In June 1966, a new company, Vidtronics, was formed by the Technicolor Corporation to concentrate on the research and development of improved techniques to transfer color videotape to film. The firm had previously developed a system to produce motion picture film prints from material photographed on videotape. The new division would concentrate on the transfer of color videotape to 35mm, 16 mm, 8mm and Super 8 film. Joseph E. Bluth was appointed vice president and general manager.[66]

In June 1966, NHK, Japan, announced a small-sized high performance color videotape recorder. The machine ran at seven inches/sec and used a high-band recording system with a frequency range of 7.03 to 10MHz.[67]

In June 1966, Sony announced a new more elaborate version of the Sony home recorder. This was the Model TCV 2020 that included a timing device to record a program.[68]

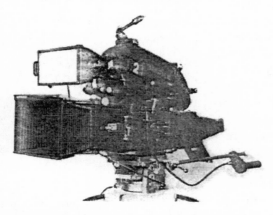

1967. Arriflex AF300 35mm electronic film camera with mirror shutter. Used one Plumbicon for viewfinder. (RTVS.)

1966. Sony video recorder PU-129UE. (Sony.)

In July 1966, the Illinois Institute of Technology Research Institute showed its color videotape recorder for the home, which it claimed could be marketed for less than $500. It was a fixed head, longitudinal unit using standard one-quarter-inch tape on a seven-inch reel. It operated at 120 inches/sec with video and audio recorded on three tracks. Weighing only 20 pounds it took 14 circuit connections to any color set or monitor. The inventor was Dr. Marvin Camras, IITRI scientific advisor.[69]

In July, North American Philips announced the "Norelco-Schoolmaster," a unit designed for education, training and documentation. It was a self-contained unit with a TV camera with viewfinder, a videotape recorder, and a 23-inch monitor. It was designed to have all the elements for production, storage, and playback of program material originating from educational stations, commercial stations or on-the-spot events.[70]

In July, G.E. announced that it would soon be in the home videotape recorder business. It was estimated that they would cost some $850 for black-and-white and $2,000 for a color model.[71]

In July, Sony announced that it had come up with a portable home videotape recorder that could be taken outdoors for amateur telecasting. The new recorder, expected to be on the market by July 1967, could not play back the 30-minute recording; that required another videotape recorder. The machine was a 21½-pound battery-operated outfit that could be strapped to both shoulders. One shoulder could take the 9½-pound recorder; the other, the five-pound rechargeable battery (up to 4 hours) and hand-held seven-pound TV camera. The camera had a tiny one-inch TV monitor. Once a recording was made, it could be played back on Sony's standard 66-pound $995 home videotape recorder. Sony also announced that it planned to sell $695 TV tape decks the following months, August 1966.[72]

It was finally reported that the CCIR meeting in Oslo which ended July 22, 1966, could not come to any conclusions about TV, leaving the adoption of standards to be decided by each country. Only ten countries had preferred NTSC; 17 chose the PAL system, and 35 the SECAM standard.[73] Author George H. Brown reported that nothing came out of the July CCIR Oslo meeting except for a statement by Great Britain that it would start colorcasting in 1967 using the PAL system. West Germany stated that it would begin color at the same time .The French and Russians were less definite on a starting time, but adhered to the SECAM system. At one point, France suggested a six-month moratorium before deciding on a single color TV system, but the other nations declined to continue the impasse any longer. The battle was over. The indecision was political, not technical.[74] The United States and NTSC had lost the battle for a world standard.

In August 1966, the Acme Film and Videotape Laboratories of Hollywood announced that after three years of experimentation, they had perfected a process of transferring color tape to color film of broadcast quality. The process would be made available to networks, stations and advertising agencies.[75] The introduction of the new Ampex high-band color machines made this possible for the first time.

In August 1966, the Precision Instrument Company of Palo Alto offered a portable TV recorder, with variable playback control to display a picture at normal speed, any degree of slow motion or with motion stopped completely. The machine P1-4V incorporated Variscan playback speed control.[76]

In September 1966, a new German high-band transverse color video recorder was shown by Fernseh GmbH, Darmstadt. Its frequency response on 625 lines was 8MHz ±2db. It looked very much like the latest RCA machines.[77] This was the first transverse recorder made in Germany or elsewhere in Europe. However, it was claimed that Fernseh had made a monochrome recorder model BM20 which was put into operation in 1963.[78]

In September 1966, a new electron-beam film recorder was announced by the Revere-Mincom Division of 3M. The new Electron Beam Recorder (EBR) used fine-grain film in a vacuum where it was hit by tiny electron beams; exposed film yielded a sharper picture fidelity. The machine used Revere-Mincom film made in Italy and is a 1,000-pound machine measuring 46 by 65 by 30 inches. It consisted of a console assembly, recording mechanism, two film cassettes (1,200 feet) and two filament replacement units. There were two chambers housing film on one side and an electron gun on the other. Separating them was a gate valve (collecting ring) with a device (Faraday cage) serving as a secondary electron-beam collector of charges that bounced off the film.[79] It was intended to produced motion picture film with improved resolution and reduced picture noise. Its values were supposed

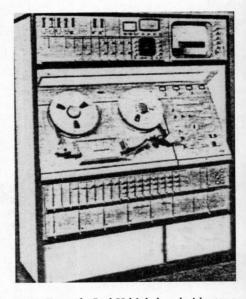

1966. Fernseh GmbH high-band videotape recorder type BC M 40A. (*Funkschau* 1966.)

1966. electron-beam recorder by Revere/Mincom. (3M Co.)

miniature camera from Westinghouse using the secondary electron conduction (SEC) tube.

The SEC camera tube consisted of three main sections: image section, SEC target assembly and hybrid gun. The scene was optically imaged on the photocathode causing electrons to be emitted by the photocathode material. These electrons were accelerated by the high potential between the photocathode and the SEC target. This target, the unique feature of the SEC camera tube, consisted of an aluminum oxide layer, a very thin layer of aluminum, and a low-density KCl film. When the accelerated electrons struck the target, they passed through the aluminum layer and impacted the KCl film. Secondary electrons released by the KCl film were collected by the signal plate and the wall screen, leaving a charge pattern in the KCl film. Since the persistence of the film was high, it held the charge pattern for long periods until it was discharged by the reading beam.

The reading beam was supplied by a Vidicon type of gun, a hybrid arrangement with electrostatic focus and magnetic deflection. (Electrostatic focusing permits simple external circuitry and has low power requirements.) As the reading beam scanned the target, the beam current discharged the KCl film back to cathode potential. This discharging action produced the video signal.

An important characteristic of the SEC target was that it was almost completely discharged by the beam, leaving negligible signal pattern for the next readout unless recharged by the scene. This eliminated the image-smear problems that occurred with Vidicons and Orthicons at low light levels. Of course, smear would occur if the image was moved within a frame period.

Electron gain of the SEC target provided target gains in excess of 100. With an S20 photocathode, the combined sensitivity of the image section and the SEC target was typically 10,000 AU/lumen. Since target gain was a

to lie in the entertainment field and in data storage. Initially, the process was in black-and-white only.[80]

NASA had two miniature cameras for its Apollo man-on-the-moon project. For the Apollo mission scheduled for mid–December, NASA had a function of the accelerating potential, target gain was controlled by adjusting the accelerating potential (-2 NTSC to -8 NTSC).[81]

The Westinghouse cameras operated at 10 frames/sec with 320 scan lines, 30 frames/sec. It weighed some 7¼ pounds. Four lenses were provided: wide angle, telephoto, a narrow aperture lens for lunar day, and wide aperture lens for lunar night conditions. It was anticipated that the pictures would be put through a scan converter to produce a standard 525-line picture. These would be furnished to the TV networks for transmission to the public. The pre–Apollo mission had cameras provided by RCA.[82]

Finally, the Teledyne System Co. of Los Angeles delivered two miniature TV cameras to NASA which weighed some 1½ pounds. These used a half-inch Vidicon tube. One of the cameras contained a low-powered transmitter that broadcast to about 100 feet.[83]

In October 1966, the MVR Corp. of Palo Alto announced a Videodisc recorder (Model VDR-210CF) that had been adapted for a wide variety of nonbroadcast applications. The recorder could be used as a sequential wide-band recorder, utilizing one or both sides of a 14-inch disc to store up to 1,600 stop-action pictures or other 33 milliseconds wide band signals, each separately recorded either automatically or at a predetermined time interval or by manual control at irregular intervals.[84]

In October 1966, RCA announced a new module — a velocity error corrector called CAVEC (Chroma Amplitude and Velocity Error Corrector). It was to improve a color program by compensating for tolerance defects inherent in the TV tape system. The module plugged into the RCA TR-70 high-band color machine.[85] (Another Ampex clone!)

In November 1966, it was reported that RCA thin-film technology yielded a tubeless TV camera. A lens focused an image on a pattern of sensors that were scanned in sequence by an electric current applied through a matrix of thin metal conductors. The resulting impulses were then combined into the form of a conventional TV signal and transmitted by microwaves.[86] (This was the second tubeless TV camera; Westinghouse had the first.)

In November 1966, NHK, Japan, began using a new color kinescoping system. It used three separate color kinescope tubes that had adequate luminance. Since each of the primary colors was independent of each other, it was possible to obtain perfect matching between tube and the high-sensitivity color reversal film used. Thus color pictures of excellent resolution were obtained.[87]

NHK was also using a Monocolor System featuring striped filters mounted on the aperture of the camera for pickup operation. The light that has passed through the striped filters produced vertical stripes of different spacing by means of red and blue. These were sensed by the film and recorded as color signals. A monochrome rapid processor was used. After developing, the signal was picked up by a Vidicon camera and converted into an electrical signal. This signal was frequency separated into red and blue signals by means of the monocolor attachment; and after separation into three primary colors, it was formed into the NTSC signals.[88]

In November 1966, there was the first mention of an IVC-500 videotape recorder by the International Video Corporation of Los Gatos, CA.[89] No information on this machine was given at the time.

1968. MVR/Visual VM 90 slow- and stop-motion video recorder. (MVR/Visual.)

1966. First IVC 500 one-inch videotape recorder. (International Video Corp.)

In December 1966, Data Disc of Palo Alto announced a TV disc recorder said to be capable of showing a still picture for thousands of hours. The model F stored up to 20 pictures on a concentric track, and each track was scanned by a separate head. The model M with a single movable head, used interchangeable discs that stored 262 pictures, 131 on a side. Model F was $5,193; model M, $4,953.[90]

In January 1967, MVR of Palo Alto announced the MVR Videodisc Slow Motion recorder. This was an advanced model to be used for sports events and featured a slow-motion instant replay which permitted transmitting an individual play at three different speeds: slow, medium or fast. The recorder also had the stop-action or freeze capability of the earlier model. The new machine, which weighed less than 75 pounds, could be recued in less than half a second.[91]

In January 1967, RCA introduced its new four-tube color camera, the TK-44. RCA claimed that it had a new three-inch image orthicon for the luminance channel. It was to be demonstrated at the NAB convention in April. The camera was in the $80,000 price range.[92]

In January 1967, a one-tube color camera was developed by the Tokyo Broadcast System and Nippon Columbia that used one three-inch image orthicon tube. It picked up frequency-separated color information by means of a color sampling method using a color sampling filter and a horizontally scanned electron beam in the

pickup tube, simultaneously with the picking up of the luminance information. (It was claimed this was the same system as used in the Monocolor film system.)[93] The optical system was composed of trimming filters, field lens sampling filters and relay lens. The color sampling filters comprised a transparent and red-reflecting dichroic striped filter (pitch was about 130 ÷) and a transparent and blue-reflecting dichroic filter (pitch about 175 ÷). These generated 3.4MHz and 4.7MHz carrier waves by means of the scanning beam. Since the optical system was mounted between the camera and the zoom lens it was easily removable. Nippon Columbia had also developed a single-tube compact color system by applying this method to the Vidicon camera. Its application in the medical and other fields was expected.[94]

In February 6, 1967, it was reported that CBS Labs had developed an electronic system capable of transmitting color film at costs equal to those for black-and-white. While no details were given, it said that the black-and-white prints were made from color film and transmitted in color by special gear.[95]

In February 1967, the RCA high-band TR-70 was described. It was designed to rerecord taped programs into the fourth generation with little loss of picture quality. It had instant selection by switching between three recording standards: low-band monochrome, low-band color, and high-band color or monochrome. It was priced as $82,500.[96]

In February 1967, the Technicolor Corp. of America announced a new color videotape to film transfer process to be offered by its Vidtronics Division.[97] Basically it was a method of separation of the red, green and blue signals from the videotape. The signal was completely decoded: the red, green and blue information was taken out as black-and-white images which represented the information in the red, green and blue signals. These were displayed on a monitor and photographed separately. The color video-tape was played three times to produce the three separation signals. These signals were electronically enhanced and then recorded on film. The three separation elements in monochrome were recombined by normal Technicolor laboratory process to give a final color print in either 35mm or 16mm. The process required about five to seven days from the time the tape arrived until the prints were ready.[98] The process could also be used with 8mm and Super 8mm color film, both of which were for application with Technicolor's own cartridge-loading portable motion picture processors, sold as educational and sales aids.[99]

In Feb 1967, the Shibaden Company of America introduced a solid-state portable videotape recorder model SV-700. This machine employed two rotary magnetic heads in a helical-scan system to provide a response of 3MHz or more with 300 lines of horizontal resolution and a signal to noise ratio of 36db. Use of half-inch tape permitted 60 minutes of recording at 7.5 inches/sec.[100]

In March 1967, the General Electric Company announced a new "long-life" camera tube with a second generation electron conducting target which showed no deterioration after 8,760 hours of operation. It had a normal resolution of 650 to 700 lines in the 8.5mc band and 1,000 lines in a 12.5mc band. It was developed after some six years of research.[101]

In March 1967, the General Electrodynamics Corp. of Garland, Texas, announced a new tube, the Oxycon, which was their version of the lead oxide Vidicon.[102]

In March 1967, the Palmer Television Film Recorder was made available in two new models for recording on either 8mm or Super 8mm film The regular 8mm recorder used prestriped double 8mm film stock and featured a special tape delay which directly permitted recording with the 28-frame soundtrack used in the Fairchild Mark IV projector. A similar tape-delay unit was used in the Super 8 film recorder which produced Super 8 film with optical sound for playback in Technicolor 1000 projectors. The Super 8 recorder was also available for recording on magnetic tracks. Price for the regular 8mm recorder with magnetic sound was $12,000 and the Super 8mm recorder with optical sound was $13,400.[103]

In March it was announced that ABC was using a new Ampex color-replay system labeled the HS-100. It had been first used on March 18, 1967, during ABC's "Wide World of Sports" skiing events. The new device was a high-band color system and could provide 30-second replays of slow motion frame by frame, stop action, and reverse action. The machine, that cost some $110,000, was to be exhibited at the NAB convention to be held in Chicago. Any portion of a 30-second recording could be cued for on-the-air use within four seconds. (It was stated

that the MVR machine used by CBS could not produce slow-motion effects and that these were achieved by using film, i.e., using a quick kine process to shoot the action, processing it and then showing it on a slow-motion film projector as soon as fixed.)[104]

Ampex announced that at the NAB held in Chicago in March 1967 they would show a portable battery-powered camera and recorder combination weighing less than 50 pounds. This was the Ampex VR-3000. It was claimed to be the smallest standard broadcast recorder ever built. It was capable of taping in high-band color from studio cameras without modification and production of either high-band or low-band monochrome tape for instant replay on any standard transverse recorder. The recorder weighed some 35 pounds and could record some 20 minutes of picture and sound on an eight-inch reel of two-inch videotape. The battery permitted some 20 minutes of continuous recording and an additional 20 minutes of preview operations of the camera only or "live" telecasting. The accompanying monochrome camera that weighed some 13 pounds used a Plumbicon tube. The system was priced at $65,000.[105]

In March 1967 Sony showed two of its newest color videotape recorders: the CV-5100 at $1,500 and an EV 200 professional unit at $3,550 not including a $2,000 color adapter. Sony also showed two monitors: one a shadow mask tube and a 19-inch three-gun Chromatron that observers noted was distinctly sharper.[106]

According to author Nick Lyons, Sony had finally turned down the GE in-line tube concept and Senri Miyaoka was running some experiments on their new picture tube. By accident, using a single gun with three cathodes, he made a mistake that became a different concept. It did produce a blurred picture at first, but led the way to the successful Chromatron. By February 1967, they had eliminated the blur and produced a decent picture with the new gun. They decided on the aperture grid instead of the shadow mask. After much work to solve the problems of the aperture grid, it was first demonstrated on October 16, 1967. The first public demonstrations of its new color television tube, to be called the Trinitron, were April 15, 1968, in Tokyo, and May 21 in New York. RCA's response is worth citing. With no opportunity to evaluate the new tube, they said that "many color television tubes had been announced over the years, but only one has stood the test of time. That is the three gun shadow mask tube developed by RCA."[107]

One of the early descriptions of how the Trinitron worked was given in July 1968. The Triniton came from the old Chromatron color picture tube. It was a one-gun tube that used color-switching grids to move the beam among red, green and blue color stripes on its screen. The associated troublesome, expensive switching, was later eliminated by a three-gun adaptation called the Chromagnetron. Neither version really caught on even though some Chromatron color sets had been sold in Japan.[108]

Electronics World said: "Now, Sony designers after much experimentation have taken advantage[s] from both and built a color picture they call a Trinitron. It has only one electron gun structure, but it produces three beams from three cathodes. Color phosphors are still applied to the screen in vertical stripes. The three beams—from the red, green and blue cathodes—go through three holes in the first two grids (the modulating grids). Then all three go through a succession of cylindrical grids that shape and focus them. In front of the gun are four flat plates that converge the three beams electrostatically. The Trinitron has an aperture grille between gun and screen. It is similar to the shadow mask of conventional color CRT's except that instead of holes it has vertical slits that match up with the color-phosphor stripes on the CRT face. Image brightness is said to be as good and crisp as that in the Chromatron, which is pretty good."[109]

The April issue of *Broadcasting* reported the demise of the Westel camera and recorder system that had been the hit of the 1966 NAB. It was revealed by the chief engineer, William Seaman, that Westel had run into problems which had made it impossible to deliver any equipment and a new approach had to be taken. New engineering models were in the works and it was anticipated that production would start before the end of the year. This never happened. But they did bring out a different machine in April 1969. This was the Westel WRR-350 for high-band operation. The unit used one-inch tape and would record up to 96 minutes on a 14-inch reel. Full electronic editing was an optional feature. The unit sold for $3,500.[110]

The same issue of *Broadcasting* showed a new backpack camera VTR that weighed 50 to 111 pounds. It included the new Ampex model VR3000 portable recorder that was said to be the smallest standard broadcast recorder ever built. It was capable of recording in high-band color from studio color cameras and producing either high-band or low band monochrome tape for instant replay on any standard four-head recorder. The equipment was priced at $65,000 with delivery to start in early 1968.[111]

Other video recorders shown at the NAB were an RCA new TR-70 high-band recorder, RCA's new

1968. Ampex VR3000 portable color video recorder. (Ampex.)

economy high-band model TR-4HB, and an updated version of its compact TR-4C.[112] Ampex showed its new high-band color recording system, the HS-100, the first to give instant replays in slow motion and stop-action color. It was reported that ABC had ordered the first three built.[113]

In May 1967, Newell Associates of Sunnyvale, announced a home color TV recorder that recorded 16 channels on quarter-inch tape and sold for less than $500. It was the product of Chester W. Newell, formally associated with Ampex. It claimed to have a simplified tape transport that had only three rotating parts. It was a high-speed device in which the tape was held as solid mass thus allowing it to travel at speeds of several thousand inches per second. It could record 100 tracks per inch of tape.[114]

Color television made its debut in Great Britain on July 1, 1967. But it was claimed that only some 1,000 to 2,000 TV sets had been installed. It used the German PAL system. Germany was to start color broadcasting on August 25.[115] The rest of Europe followed: France on October 1, 1967, with SECAM, the Netherlands officially on January 1, 1968, with PAL, and the USSR would start on the SECAM in October; the rest of Europe would come later.[116]

In July 1967, CBS asked the FCC for a permit for the use of tone transmissions on remote pickup channels about 25mc wide. This proposal would provide more efficient use of small portable wireless TV cameras, particularly color cameras.[117] CBS wanted to use a cableless portable color camera at the 1968 presidential convention. In August, the company claimed that it had developed a one-man TV station.[118] Also in August 1967, CBS showed a picture of their one-man portable camera with a transmitter and camera. It weighed 54 pounds.

RCA had also developed a mini TV camera weighing some two pounds for space use. It was conjectured that it could be used by the network in the future.[119]

At the Montreux Television Symposium and Exhibition in July, Philips had gone on record as favoring the three-tube principle. They gave as their main reason that once the cameras had been adjusted on a monochrome chart, perfect color matching was assured when switching from one camera to another, and that due to the low scattering losses of the triprismatic system, the three-camera tube system could work at illumination down to 250 lux.[120] They were correct of course, but the three tube versus four tube battle was to continue for another year or so.

There was an ad on August 2l for the new RCA TK-44 Isocon camera. It was to use a new RCA three-inch Isocon camera tube in the luminance channel and three lead-oxide tubes in the chrominance channels. It claimed that the three-inch isocon tube combined the inherently low noise characteristic with the known advantage of the image orthicon (the "knee" in handling the contrast range). "The best of both worlds" it was claimed.[121]

The RCA TK-44 camera had finally eliminated the costly 4½ image orthicon camera tube for the luminance channel and the company would soon drop it completely. There was also a three-inch P880 image Isocon made by English Electric Valve Company designed to operate at low light levels. This seems to be the first commercial use of the image Isocon. Somehow, English Electric or RCA or both had overcome the shortcomings of the image Isocon. It was claimed that its electron optical system reduced noise in the output signal and eliminated the dynode effect. It had (1) a scanning beam that was smaller and better focused; (2) most of the scattered electronics were eliminated from the system; and (3) the dynode background was eliminated.[122] At any rate, its use in a TV camera was short-lived. It was also announced that English Electric Valve was then making the lead-oxide tube which it called the Leddicon.[123]

On August 28, 1967, the Columbia Broadcasting System Laboratories introduced a revolutionary new system called EVR (Electronic Video Recording). Essentially this was a device to playback on conventional television receivers prerecorded programming from motion picture film and videotape. The program was contained in a seven-inch cartridge (a cartridge is a single-ended device, as opposed to a cassette which is self-contained) which was simply inserted in the player. There were three main stages in the system. (1) Prerecording — a sophisticated electronic process transferred film or videotape programming to a special 8.75mm unperforated thin film. (2) Cartridge — the film was then stored in a cartridge seven inches in diameter and about a quarter inch thick. (3) Reproduction — the cartridge was inserted into a player attached to the antenna terminals of the TV receiver and automatically "played" on the TV screen. Applications of the device were expected to include home entertainment as well as education because of ease of operation and low cost. Since EVR was a playback system only, there were no facilities for recording off the air or at home.

Dr. Peter Goldmark who had developed the idea of an LP record for playback only, wanted to do the same thing for television. Goldmark thought of it as the "video long-playing record of the future."[124] His video machine seems to have been based on the earlier 1960 CBS/3M Wollensak Revere audio tape machine which was also fed by a cartridge. The miniature cartridges were capable of carrying up to one hour of high fidelity music at a speed of 1⅞ inches per second.[125]

Goldmark's original idea was for it to be used in education. He envisioned its use in everyone's home in which great libraries would be available to everyone, just like library books. After CBS had initially turned down his idea he went to several educational institutions and book publishers all of whom also turned him down. Finally he went to the air force (which ran one of the world's largest correspondence schools) who liked the idea and gave him a small amount of money ($37,000) to get started. This did not last long and the project was abandoned, as Government funds had stopped and Bill Paley had turned the project down as he believed that it would never work in the home. The EVR program was stopped several more times for various reasons. Finally, CBS had a change of heart and with the blessings of both Paley and Frank Stanton, the project was launched. EVR made its debut in December 1968 at the New York Hilton.[126]

The EVR cartridges were capable of carrying up to one hour of black-and-white programming or one half-hour of color programming. An unusual aspect of the technology was that color programming was recorded as monochrome and yet reproduced as color on a color set. The film moved at a speed of 6 inches/sec. A major advantage of the EVR system was that the film could be stopped anywhere and a still frame displayed as long as desired. No further technical details were released at this time.[127]

The machine was to be marketed first in England in the spring of 1969. CBS had entered into a partnership with Imperial Chemical Industries Ltd. of England and CIBA, while Thorne Electrical Industries Ltd. would manufacture the "prototype production" models of the EVR players.[128] Motorola was to manufacture the players in the USA.

Also in August it was announced that Ampex had received an Emmy for its development of high-band color videotape.[129]

In October 1967, the Electronic Engineering Co. of Santa Ana, CA, announced the new EECO "On Time" System. This was a timing system for rapid editing of television videotapes and for controlling the starting and stopping times of television recorders and allied equipment. The heart of the system was a special time code that was recorded on the cue track of two-inch videotape. A control panel mounted on the videotape recorder allowed the operator to read the time from the tape at any speed, in playback or rewind, and in either direction. The code was an AM modulated code using 60 bits with a carrier frequency of 600Hz. The time code, rather than the older system of cue tones recorded on the cue track, was used for editing. The basic time code generator cost $3,000 and the control elements $7,500.[130]

EECO was a tremendous advance over the older cue-tone system as well as the cumbersome Japanese method of time code, in that it allowed the editor to pick their edit points to the exact frame and allowed for the starting and

1968. Norelco PCP-70 portable color camera. (Philips Labs.)

weighed 23 pounds including the camera head and zoom lens. With an electronic viewfinder and harness, it weighed 44 pounds. The price was to be $41,450. The camera was to be introduced in November at the exposition of the National Association of Educational Broadcasters and the Armed Forces Television Conference in Denver.[132]

In November 1967, the International Video Corp. of Mountain View, CA, introduced a new portable color

1967. The 44-pound Philips Plumbicon mini color camera, PCP-70, with camera head viewfinder and zoom lens. (Philips Labs.)

operation of auxiliary machines. Previewing of the edit was possible and it pointed the way for all future edit systems. The concept was that of Dick Hill, a former CBS engineer in Hollywood.[131]

In October 1967, Philips announced its color minicamera using Plumbicon tubes. It was the Norelco PCP-70 and it

1968. Philips 6½-pound, three-plumbicon color camera. (Philips Labs.)

television recorder, the IVC Model 800. The machine was a full 4.2MHz NTSC color videotape recorder weighing some 52 pounds. Features included remote control and a timer reading in minutes and tenths. Sixty minutes of recorder time required only 2,150 feet of one-inch videotape on an eight-inch NAB reel. The machine ran at a speed of 6.9inches/sec and was a one-head

helical-scan recorder using a 360 degree alpha wrap. The modulation was pulse interval modulation, not FM, and this was the first commercial machine ever to use it rather than Ampex's patented FM system. The recorder was priced at less than $4,500.[133] Ampex's monopoly on the modulation system had finally been broken.

In November, it was reported that ABC-TV was to use a new Ampex hand-held color camera. It was developed specifically for ABC and weighed some 35 pounds, operated with cable, or a total of 50 pounds with its battery-powered unit. Its details were revealed later.[134] Called the BC-100, it was an 18-pound camera using two Plumbicon camera tubes. The red and blue channels were utilized to achieve high performance in such a small camera. The Y channel tube was on full time and the red and blue channels were used in a time-sequential sharing of the second tube. (It used a spinning disc à la old CBS system to separate the colors.) The output was a nonstandard color signal that was converted to NTSC color in the camera control unit.[135]

The color system was reminiscent of the old Goldmark/CBS color system. The color wheel separated the red and blue fields going to the straight line Plumbicon tube. The wheel was locked to vertical sync and the resulting signal was red-blue in field sequential form. The

1968. *Above:* Ampex BC-100 two-tube color camera. *Below:* Diagram of BC-100. (Ampex.)

other Plumbicon tube provided the luminance signal, which after processing also yielded the green signal. The missing fields were replaced by a 262-line delay

1968. Institut für Rundfunk slow- and stop-motion PAL recorder. (*Funkschau.*)

in conjunction with field frequency switching. Since the delay line output had red and blue fields in reverse sequence to the input, the field switch outputs could be two fully simultaneous outputs of red and blue. Each color field was thus used twice: once as the original signal, and once as delayed signal, displaced in vertical position by one line. The three color signals were then fed into a matrix in which green was obtained by subtracting appropriate proportions of red and blue from the luminance signal. A 30-cycle flicker was removed by the 262-line delay which was produced in a miniature videodisc recorder. The camera had a one-inch air force green phosphor tube. A microwave option with battery pack upped the weight somewhat.[136] The Ampex studio camera, the BC-210, was essentially the same camera. It weighed 50 pounds including viewfinder and was 20½ by 13½ by 8½ inches and cost $50,000. The camera cable was the smallest ever used on a studio broadcast camera — it measured 0.485 inches, ran for 2,000 feet and weighed only 300 pounds.[137]

1969. Ampex BC-210 two-tube Plumbicon color camera. (Ampex.)

At the NAEB (National Association of Educational Broadcasters) conference held in November in Denver, Ampex showed two new high-band color recorders, the VR2000-B and the VR1200-B. Ampex also introduced two new compact portable recorders for closed-circuit use: the VR5000 was priced at under $1,000 and the other, the VR7500, was priced between $10,000 and $16,500. According to the company, each met FCC requirements for monochrome broadcasting. Both were helicals that used one-inch tape and had color capability.

RCA introduced its new TR-50 color recorder for broadcast use, Norelco demonstrated its new portable PCP-70, Ampex showed its VR3000 backpack recorder, and Sony displayed a very tiny tape recorder camera useful for remote nonbroad-

1968. Thomson (C.S.F.) four-tube Plumbicon color camera. (Thomson C.S.F. [France].)

cast applications ($1,200). IVC unveiled a new low-cost color camera for closed-circuit use. This was the IVC-100 that used three Vidicon tubes. It was priced at some $12,600.[138]

In November, Dr. Goldmark hinted that it would be possible that a camera could be developed within a year for use with the CBS EVR system.[139] In December, CBS Labs gave a presentation on BEVR (Broadcast Electronic Video Recording). It was to be different from EVR in that the master was made on 16mm sprocket hole film rather special thin film on a reel. It was to be played back through a special attachment to the camera. It was hoped to present 35mm quality on 16mm film at costs far below those of conventional film or tape.[140]

In November, ABC was scheduled to make use of what it claimed to be the first truly hand-held color camera. It was made for them by Ampex. It used miniature cable or could be used as a battery operated unit via a built in microwave.[141]

In November 1967, at the National Association of Educational Broadcasters in Denver, the International Video Corp. introduced a new video recorder. It was solid state and boasted NTSC color but was not for broadcast use. It cost $4,200. IVC also announced a new low cost live studio camera with three Vidicons. The IVC-100 sold for $12,600.

Around this time in Germany, it was claimed that Fernseh GmbH had developed a transistorized color video recorder using both the low- and new high-band standards. This was the first European recorder ever made for transverse recording in color. (There was an earlier monochrome recorder made by Fernseh.)[142]

Chapter 8

Television's Finest Hour: Apollo 11 (1968–1971)

In February 1968, Arvin Industries' electronic system division introduced the first videotape cartridge color VTR. The machine dubbed the CVRXXI could record in both black-and-white and color. It was a recorder using the longitudinal fixed head recording technique. The transport was the high-speed indexing tape transport devised by Newell Associates. With this principle the machine recorded both audio and video on the same tape track and compressed ten tracks on a half-inch-wide tape packaged in a self-threading cartridge. The first track was recorded from left to right, and when the tape approached the end of the reel it stopped and reversed direction in less than a second. Eighteen hundred feet of tape that ran at 160 inches/sec gave six minutes per track. So ten tracks gave an hour of recording. The system was easy to operate with only stop, start and tape-direction buttons. The recorder's frequency response was flat from d-c to 2 megacycles. Color response was from d-c to 20kHz. Horizontal resolution was 200 lines. It cost between $1,000 and $1,500 and was not expected to be in production until the following year (1969).[1]

It was also reported in February 1968 that RCA was going to market the IVC-800 helical VTR. This unit had a 360 degree wrap around the head drum. Color reproduction on the IVC-800 was demonstrably excellent with a 4.2MHz video bandwidth and one-inch tape.[2]

The NAB Convention was held in Chicago during the last week in March 1968. Philips unveiled an experimental color TV camera using ⅝-inch Plumbicon tubes. The unit weighed some 6½ pounds and was about the size of a 16mm movie camera. Philips was reportedly working on a wireless version that would eliminate the cables.[3]

In March 1968, the D. B. Miliken Co. of Arcadia, CA, announced a new quality 16mm kine-recording system called the DBM-RI. the heart of the system was the DBM-64A camera that eliminated the shutter bar problem. The camera used compressed air to transport and stabilize the film in less than the vertical blanking period. The camera had a magazine for 2,400 feet of film.[4]

In March 1968, RCA announced a new Tape Editing Programmer for use with any RCA high-band television tape recorder. Working in conjunction with an electronic splicer, the device automatically activated the splice mode at the preprogrammed point. Thus the editor could preview the splice before actual editing began. Timing of the editing operation was controlled from a master cue placed on the tape 14 seconds or more before the point where the edit began. It was priced at $7,000.[5]

In March 1968, the Ampex Corp. announced a high-band color disc recording and editing system called the HS-200. The system consisted of a computer-controlled disc that recorded frame-by-frame color animation and permitted the operator access to any recorded frame from a push-button editing console. The HS-200 was self-contained in a console that contained the disc system, electronics controls, special effects switches, programmer and equipment for operation of the system. It was priced at about $130,000. It was a total production tool or it could be used in conjunction with a high-band recorder. It was to be available that fall.[6]

More details as to how the HS-200 worked were given in September 1968, at the International Broadcasting Convention held in London where Ampex displayed the machine. The signal was recorded on concentric tracks

1968 Ampex HS-200 color disk recording and computer editing system. (Ampex.)

NBC mini camera at 1968 convention. (RCA.)

of a magnetic disc. The record replay jumped from track to track for continuous recording. If the recorder replayed one track, it produced a still frame. Slow motion was accomplished by programming the head movement to include a recap action so that scanning speed was maintained but the ground covered was less. The machine was to cost £400,000.[7] At this convention, AMPEX devoted a separate exhibit for helical-scan recorders. It included the VR7800 (up to $16,500) that would give good NTSC color for as little as $12,000.[8]

In March 1968, the Sony Corp. of America announced a videotape recorder model EV-210. Used with the Sony CLP-LA Color Adapter, the recorder was capable of NTSC color recording as well as monochrome. The EV-210 featured slow- and stop-motion capability in both color and monochrome. It cost $3,750 and the CLP-IA was priced at $1,000.[9]

In March it was announced that the three major networks had new portable cameras for the 1968 political conventions to be held in Miami by the Republicans and Chicago by the Democrats. RCA announced that it would use four of its new Man-Pack color cameras. CBS stated that it had a new three-tube color camera capable of transmitting more than a mile without wires. It weighed 18 pounds complete with zoom lens and three-inch viewfinder, while its associated backpack weighed 30 pounds. The camera used one-inch hybrid Plumbicon tubes.

The CBS camera developed by the CBS Labs was called the Minicam VI. It used three one-inch Plumbicon tubes (made by G.E), and could be linked to its base station by a single-conductor coaxial cable or could be operated with microwave control signals on either 150, 450, or 950 MgH. The microwave transmitter operated at either 2, 7, or 14Ghz with different modules. The camera with zoom lens, and three-inch viewfinder weighed 18 pounds. The backpack weighed 32 pounds with battery or 12 pounds without it.

ABC stated that it would use the Ampex portable camera. It was claimed that it was the first such hand-held color camera to be used commercially. The head weighed less than 20 pounds and was fully equipped for microwave operation. An improved model now used all solid-state delay lines to replace the videodisc recorder formerly used.[10]

At the same time, Philips Research Labs in Eindhoven announced the development of a color-TV camera no larger than a 16mm movie camera, with a cigar-sized color camera tube. The ultraportable color camera weighed some 6½ pounds with associated electronics and zoom lens. Philips claimed that its performance was surprisingly good. The experimental color tube was five eighths of an inch in diameter and employed electrostatic focus and magnetic deflection, and the photoconductive surface was a variant of the new extended red sensitive Plumbicon. Philips announced that they had developed a processing technique whereby the lead monoxide layer was capable of picking up the deep reds. The cutoff of the conventional Plumbicon had been extended from 640 millimicrons to beyond 800 millimicrons which is beyond visible red.[11]

In March, CBS announced that it had developed an image enhancer combined with a "crispener" that increased the sharpness and detail of color television images. Called image enhancement, it was said to be particularly effective in sports. It was developed by Renville H. McMann, CBS Labs vice president and director of engineering, and was being patented by CBS Inc. The technique used a small sold-state device weighing less than 20 pounds. It automatically adjusted vertical and horizontal picture details as needed to eliminate color softness. The devise took a single line of video and compared it element by element, with the line preceding it and following it. Any differences were added to the original signal in the proper phase to reinforce the difference between the line compared, thereby enhancing the picture outlines and contrast. Another feature was crispening to sharpen the details without increasing the picture noise. While the Plumbicon tube was as "sharp" (in terms of resolution 600–800 lines) as the image orthicon, being a Vidicon type of tube it lacked the inherent image enhancement (edging) of the image orthicons that made their pictures seem sharper. The image enhancer was most effective. It made the Plumbicon camera seem as sharp as any image orthicon camera tube including the 4½-inch model.[12]

For the first time, most of color cameras used the Plumbicon camera tube. Even RCA introduced its new TK-44A three-Plumbicon color camera then, although they stated that their older four-tube TK-42 would still be available. This marked the beginning of the end for the 4½-inch image orthicon tube and the four-tube separate luminance camera. It would soon mark the end of the image orthicon altogether, the tube that had been so successful since its introduction in 1945. The RCA TK-44A was priced at $74,800 and was to be available in January 1969. It weighed some 98 pounds exclusive of the 10:1 zoom lens, and featured simplified optics. It was claimed that more than 400 of the older TK-42s were in use. G.E. commented on the current controversy over three-tube versus four-tube cameras and said that it had built one-tube (the CBS Chromacoder), two-tube, and three-tube cameras and found none equal to "our separate luminance four tube camera."[13]

G.E. showed its new PE-350 color TV camera using four lead-oxide tubes. It weighed some 160 pounds with viewfinder and 10:1 zoom lens. Norelco showed the latest of its new PC-70 color cameras. The newest models were to feature the extended red response Plumbicon that had just been developed.

In May 1968, Visual Electronics Labs of Sunnyvale, CA, described their new slow-motion videodisc recorder, model VM-90. A joint effort of MVR and Visual Electronics, the recorder used a single aluminum disc which was first coated with nickel-cobalt and then given a rhodium flash coating. The disc was addressed by two record-playback heads, one on top of the disc and the second on the bottom. They were driven by reversible stepping motors and recorded odd fields on top and even fields underneath. Recording and playback started at the inside edge of the disc. It would record 30 seconds of video using a stepper mode of operation. It could be played in either forward or reverse and had a unique cuing system of 30 tally lamps. Any point on the disc could be located in about three seconds. In the slow or stop-motion mode, one field was used many times over. Reconstructing the signal, the system provided monochrome interlace or chroma dot interlace in color.[14]

In May 1968, Nippon Columbia released details of a new single-tube color camera.[15] A description of it was given in June. By setting up a modified filter response, it was possible to extract properly modulated color information in overlapping red and green; green and blue passed through entirely, while the red component modulated the carrier. The final striping arrangement alternated stripes that passed red+green+blue with stripes that passed green+blue. The same arrangement was made in overlapping the green and blue channels. The final filter sandwich was placed in the cameras single optical path. The output was nonstandard and was converted to NTSC color through a matrixing and filtering system carried in the operator's backpack. According to Nippon Columbia, the camera had been undergoing field testing at NHK since December 1966.[16] It claimed that it had applied for a patent in Japan in 1962.[17]

In May 1968, it was reported that the rivalry between the PAL and SECAM color systems had been resolved with an agreement between Compagnie Française de Télévision, which held patents on SECAM, and AEG Telefunken, which owned the PAL patents. By the CFT-AEG agreement, the French set manufacturers were given a license to make and sell PAL receivers and the German set manufactures were given a license to make and sell SECAM receivers. A patent dispute between them had been settled in which it was claimed that CFT owned a patent that somehow pertained to the PAL system.[18]

In July 1968 at the National CATV convention held in Boston, IVC showed its three–Vidicon color camera, the IVC-100, that weighed only 65 pounds. With broadcast color standards it was priced at $18,500.[19] It also showed its IVC-800 using one-inch tape running at 6.9 inches/sec. It used the pulse interval modulation system that provided 4.2mc bandwidth. It sold for $4,700. IVC mentioned that it was only two years old and was building a 150,000 square-foot building in Sunnyvale, CA.[20] In September it was stated that IVC was already number two in the industry in the field of video recording.[21]

In November 1968, at the NAEB convention in Washington, RCA announced a new single-tube color camera (PK-730) for closed-circuit use. The basic one-tube camera without lens or viewfinder was sold at $6,500, or fully equipped at $9,850. A slide film version was available at $ 9,850. A demonstration showed quite good color except for the fact that its resolution was low (250 lines) and its noise level visible.[22]

The resolution of the camera was about 200 lines, adequate for most educational purposes, but far short of the 525-line broadcast quality. RCA claimed that they had used a principle they had developed in 1950 (Kell-SRI?) but discarded. They devised a basic design whereby dichroic optical filters in a sandwich configuration identified

1968. IVC-800 one-inch color VCR from International Video Corp., Mountain View, CA. (International Video Corp.)

an ordinary one-inch Vidicon (8507A) that cost $130. RCA admitted that it knew that the Japanese had also been experimenting with single-tube color cameras and they decided to announce theirs first.[23]

Other color cameras shown included Ampex's two-tube selling for $50,000 and IVC's three-tube priced at $19,000 to $25,000. Also shown was Visual Electronics' three-tube camera selling in the $65,000 to $75,000 price range. CBS showed its "starlight" miniature camera especially developed for the medical field. It could operate in the dark and transmit live pictures by a special fiber-optics tube to operating-room monitors for the reference of doctors and students.

IVC showed a black-and-white videotape recorder said to be capable of recording 2½ hours on a 12½-inch reel. It cost $9,000, Later, a color version could be had for $12,000. Sony's image buffer that permitted broadcasting of video

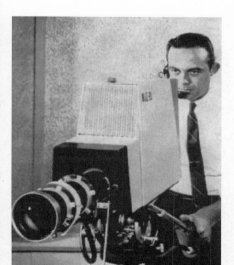

1968. RCA one-tube color camera (RCA.)

the red and blue color before the light reached the Vidicon. The red-blue-green image was then carried whole to the tube where it was converted into electrical signals. It was basically a black-and-white system, so there were no registration problems. The studio camera with viewfinder cost $9,850. It was 10 inches high, 11 inches across and about 25 inches long, and weighed about 45 pounds. It used

recordings by stabilizing the sync (pulses through an optical scan converter device) to cost $5,000. G.E. showed its new line of one-inch lead oxide Vidicons. Philips showed its new one-inch Plumbicon (6¼ inches long) in monochrome and also one-inch tubes suitable for color.

Visual Electronics showed three-inch and 4½-inch Isocon tubes, developed by English Electric Valve Co., which were said to have extremely low light capabilities. Visual Electronics claimed that the Image Isocon had the inherent advantage of using only one of the tube's return beams. This resulted in a noise-free tube in the black areas. It also had a dynamic range ten times greater than that of the image orthicon.[24]

In November 1968, the Mincom Division of 3M announced a new 16mm electron-beam recorder. It was claimed to have 1,000 line resolution. The EBR-100 recorded for 33 minutes on each 1,200 ft reel of low-cost fine-grain 16mm film at 1,000 line resolution. The film could be processed like any 16mm film. The unit weighed about 1,000 pounds and cost about $55,000.[25]

CBS gave its first public demonstration of its EVR system on Tuesday, December 10, 1968. It was announced that it would be some three to five years before EVR would move into the home entertainment business. The demonstration was in black-and-white only. Motorola experts

1968. Mincom 3M electron-beam recorder. (Mincom 3M.)

expected that a color EVR would be in production in the last part of 1971. The pictures were sharp and clean and showed the machine's ability to display stop, slow scan, fast forward and reverse, all at the punch of a button. A similar demonstration was given the next day in London.[26]

In December

1969. CBS EVR player.

1969. Watching the first demonstration of EVR are (l. to r.) Felix Kalinski, president CBS/Comtec; Elmer Wavering, president Motorola, Inc., Dr. Peter Goldmark, president CBS Labs; Frank Stanton, president CBS; Arthur Ochs Sulzberger, president *New York Times*; and Arthur Brockway, president EVR Division. (CBS.)

1968, RCA announced that its TK-44A was the best of the three-tube cameras using lead-oxide tubes (Plumbicons). It stated that with its many engineering innovations, it produced pictures that were sharper and more detailed that any other three-tube color camera.[27] This camera was a milestone. It was the first RCA studio color camera that did not use any form of image orthicon. It also had a

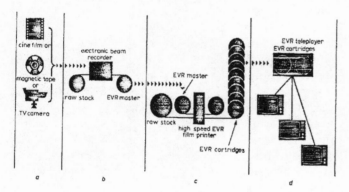

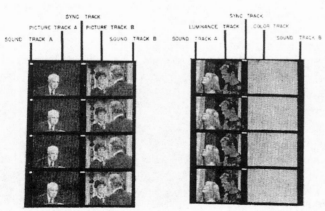

1969. CBS EVR cartridge player. *Above:* Steps in process. *Below left:* Side-by-side images from the player. *Right:* EVR color process. (CBS.)

three-camera tube, thus ending the three-tube versus four-tube controversy. Finally its use of the Plumbicon tube was proof that no RCA tube could compare with it. As with the Trinitron picture tube from Japan, RCA had lost the race for the best color tube to Philips in Holland.

In December 1968, IVC announced that it had 50-cycle versions of its machines available for operation on the PAL, SECAM and NTSC systems. The IVC-811 was designed for PAL, the IVC-801 record and playback machine for SECAM, and the IVC-810 for NTSC. Optional slow motion was available for an additional $350.[28]

In February 1969, IVC announced that its IVC 600 Series helical-scan video recorders would to be marketed through RCA, Bell and Howell, and the GPL division of the Singer Co.[29]

Also in February, RCA began marketing its new three-tube color camera, the RCA TK-44A. It was claimed that it could operate at the level of only 15 foot-candles! It had a device called Chromacomp which allowed the operator to color match the RCA TK-44A without unbalancing the gray scale. It also included a new "contours-with-a-comb" device (similar to the CBS image enhancer device) that made color pictures sharp and as well defined as desired.[30]

Again in February, it was reported that MVR had been acquired by Data Memory Corp. This was the first step in producing and marketing a full line of video magnetic disc recording systems. Kurt Machein was vice president of DMC.[31]

Once more in February, a report was given of the progress being made by RCA and Westinghouse in developing a tubeless television camera. Westinghouse had begun a process using less complicated silicon photoconductors in a mosaic sensor array. The company had delivered a 220 by 256 element array for NASA and expected to complete

1969. RCA TK44A three-tube color camera. (RCA.)

a 400 by 512 element array in November 1969. The Westinghouse process used aluminum interconnections for its arrays. Paul Weimer of RCA stated that the major problems were those of uniformity of video lines, cost and sensitivity.[32]

In March 1969, Matsushita Electronics Ltd. announced a new high-speed duplication process for black-and-white and color tape. It claimed that it could duplicate a one-hour tape in two minutes. It used what was called the "bifilar winding" around a tape reel. Both a master tape and the duplicate tape were wound together on a take-up reel after passing through a pressure roller that squeezed out any air that might be trapped between them. When the reel was full, a 50- or 60-cycle transfer field was applied for a few seconds. The signal was thus transferred to the duplicate tape. After the transfer the tapes were unwound on their respective reels. The audio track, due to its lower frequencies, tended to print through, so it was rerecorded later on.[33]

In March, it was revealed that G.E. had stopped selling helical VTRs. They had purchased some 2,400 from the Sony Corp. and were using the G.E. label. In the beginning, G.E. had stated that its VTR program was a mainstay of company production and was part of a package to sell their color cameras. The remaining recorders were sold to GBC Closed Circuit TV Corp. These were being sold for $397.50. GBC said that when these were gone, there would be no more.[34]

In March 1969, Data Memory showed their VDR/222C Color Videodisc. It was a magnetic-disc system that recorded, played back and stored up to 25 seconds of color or monochrome signals. It stored the signals on a 14-inch disc for stop-motion or slow motion. Price was around $39,500.

International Video Corp. showed its IVC-825 preview color tape recorder. The $5900 helical-scan, fully solid-state instrument contained a capstan servo that provided fast lockup, fast forward and rewind. IVC also showed its IVC-600 series helical-scan recorder that played one hour on an eight-inch reel containing 2,150 feet of tape. The machine was all solid state with 60-second replacement of recording heads, servo controls and a single motor design for fast lockup and stabilization.[35]

1969. Sony model EV-310 video tape recorder. (Sony.)

In the spring of 1969, it was announced that the Vidtronics division of Technicolor had given a number of impressive demonstrations of their new tape-to-film transfer process. They used an Ampex 2000 machine and the composite output signal was decoded into separate red, blue and green signals, each of which was enhanced and subjected to other signal processing. During three separate runs, three color separations were obtained which could then be combined by the Technicolor process into a single film negative that is suitable for making contact prints. Technicolor had invested £250,000 in their Harmondsworth plant.[36]

Technicolor in Hollywood in November 1969, stated that they were spending $2 million to develop a closed-circuit system called Technivison with 2,000 scan lines for theatrical projection. Claiming that shooting direct on tape had the advantages of speed, postproduction flexibility and the elimination of lab work and instant viewing, Technicolor mentioned that directors Ralph Nelson and Jerry Lewis had been using tape as an aid in shooting film for several years. Technicolor's new system would have at least 1,000 lines.[37]

In April 1969, the Sony Corp. came out with its first cassette TV recorder. With the success of the new Philips audio cassette, Sony decided to do the same with video. Sony was also hoping to head off the new EVR system of CBS by developing a VCR cassette system. It was also hoping to line up allies. The machine could record as well as playback. The cassette measured about 6 by 10 by 3¾ inches, and used one-inch tape with two tracks. The two reels were mounted coaxially. Tape came off one reel, passed around a hub that was slightly larger than the head drum, and then wound onto the second reel. When the cassette was inserted into the VTR, the hub slipped over the drum locking the cassette in place. This rotated the hub so that a window in it let the tape contact the drum. Tape speed was 3¾ inches per second and color recording was a modification of the NTSC signal. The luminance signal was recorded by the FM modulation of a subcarrier. Its frequency was about 3MHz and the modulation swing was from 3MHz to 4.5MHz. This left room on the same track for the NTSC color signal which was shifted to a center frequency of 900kHz and recorded with a bandwidth of ±700kHz around the center frequency. The second track was for audio. For playback. the color signal was both amplified and phase modulated like a regular NTSC color signal and only needed to be shifted back to its rightful space in the signal spectrum. Sony claimed that it could produce a VTR with playback only for about $370. Prerecorded tape would cost about $28 a piece.[38]

It was just at this time, April 1969, that Matsushita Electronics announced that it had developed a new method for rapid duplication of color and monochrome tapes.

1969. The first Sony cassette color tape recorder. It used two reels mounted coaxially. (Sony Corp.)

They could duplicate an hour tape in two minutes, they claimed.[39]

In May 1969, a portable VTR by Westel Co. was shown at the NAB convention. It was claimed that Westel, which had first created a false stir at NAB in 1965, was back with a professional quality high-band color portable recorder and a companion studio recorder. Westel said that it was in the whole market to stay this time (they had been selling to the military). The portable recorder weighed only 37 pounds and recorded 26 minutes on an eight-inch diameter reel (tape width was one inch). The studio unit, which fit in a 19-inch rack, would play back at full broadcast standards. High-resolution ferrite heads provided an S/N ratio of 56dB, better than other recorders, the company claimed. Price of the studio recorder playback unit was $60,000; of the portable recorder, $19,500.[40]

In June 1969, the IVC introduced two new helical-scan color recorders, models 825 and 860. They both featured improved time-base stability and higher signal to nose ratios. Model 825 contained a capstan servo which compensated for changes in tape tension and signal timing by varying the capstan speed. The model 860 featured refinements in the color process, higher signal to noise ratio, and was equipped with color editing and slow-motion facilities.[41]

In June 1969, the Victor Company of Japan decided to market a video cartridge recorder. The Victor cartridge was 5.51 by 5.51 by 0.91 inches and contained one half-hour of half-inch tape played at 7.5 inches per second. The recorder, that measured 18 by 16 by 8 inches, weighed nearly eight pounds. It used the direct FM combined recording system that permitted it to record the 4.5MHz NTSC color signal at the slow tape speed. The recorder had a built-in modulator so that color or black-and-white programs could be played by connecting the recorder to the TV antenna terminals. Audio was on two tracks. The machine was to sell for $550. Unrecorded cartridges would be priced at $27.[42]

The Apollo 11 moon shot was a tremendous success. On July 20, 1969, U.S. astronaut, Neil Armstrong, set foot on the moon. Live television pictures showed him getting out of the spacecraft and stepping on the gray surface. Every move was transmitted back to Earth and the whole world saw him as he took his first cautious steps. It later showed Edwin Aldrin as he walked on the moon's surface. The camera was built by Westinghouse and used a secondary electron conduction (SEC) Vidicon low-light camera tube.

It was proper that these cameras had been built by Westinghouse. Westinghouse had a

Neil Armstrong on the moon, July 21, 1969. (NASA.)

long, proud history of television starting with the kinescope of Dr. Zworykin in 1929. (The kinescope was the most important invention in television history.) Their SEC tube was a direct descendant of the Iconoscope that had made television possible. This tube was built to operate at a range of 0.007 to 12,600 footlamberts of illumination. It was also able to withstand temperatures of 250 degrees (daylight) to 300 degrees below zero at night. It had four fixed-focus lenses, a wide-angle, and a 100mm telephoto. The camera also had two general purpose lenses. The camera was limited to a 500kc bandwidth operating at 10 frames/sec to produce a resolution of 250 lines.[43] This $453,000 Westinghouse camera was left on the moon.

The color camera in the command module used a two-color wheel (à la old CBS system) comprising two sets of blue and green filters. The wheel span at 600 revolutions per minute. The camera, which had a zoom lens, also used the Westinghouse SEC camera tube. The sequential color signals were transmitted back to the NASA Goldstone earth station in California where they were sent to Houston for conversion into NTSC signals for broadcast all over the world.[44] Television pioneers such as Farnsworth, Zworykin, Takayanagi and von Ardenne, among others who were still alive, must have beamed to see what television could do for mankind.

Baird, Barthélemy and the rest who were dead, would have done the same. This was what television was all about.

The utility of television aboard spacecraft and in manned planetary landings had been proven beyond all doubt. In the case of Apollo 10 and 11, the amount of public interest in space television was shown to be significantly greater than anticipated when NASA televised the crew, indicating their condition, and a multitude of other applications, mostly in the area of remote viewing of inaccessible locations and hostile environments.

NASA was planning extensive use of closed-circuit television on future missions. In the larger space craft television would be used for onboard monitoring. Many activities would be undertaken by one man, and the other crew members could monitor his movements on television for routine observation and safety. Closed-circuit color television with higher resolution than commercial television was planned for much of the monitoring.[45]

In August 1969, Sony introduced its model EV-320. It featured capstan-servo electronic editing in color and black-and-white. Noted for its electronic editing, the recorder allowed sequences from a variety of effects to be inserted into the master tape. It cost $4,000.[46]

In September 1969, the Ampex Corp. showed a model VP4900C color videotape recorder that handled one-inch color or black-and-white tape in a helical mode. Video bandwidth was 4.2MHz, black-and-white horizontal resolution 350 lines, and video S/N ratio 43db. Maximum playing time was one hour.[47]

In September 1969, Philips announced a new light-weight videotape recorder, the LDL-1000 that measured 16½ x 13⅜ x 7⅝ inches and weighed 25 pounds. It was a two-head helical recorder that was said to provide 220 lines of resolution. It used a special half-inch tape formula called Crolyn, for chromium dioxide, made in the USA by Memorex. It was priced under $650.[48]

On Tuesday, September 30, 1969, RCA announced a new system called Selectavision that would be a color-TV tape player for home entertainment. Its new technology was quite radical, involving holograms and lasers. The tape player would be attached to the standard home color TV set. It was a playback only unit similar to EVR and was to cost under $400.

1969. Philips LDL-1000 half-inch tape recorder using chromium dioxide tape. (Philips Labs.)

Tape cartridges were to cost from $10 for a half-hour show to $20 for a full hour.

RCA stated that it was not in competition with EVR which at the moment was concentrating on the educational-industrial field. RCA did state that they had chosen this new system as they did not want another (EVR) to be the only system on the market. This seemed to be a repeat of the old CBS/RCA color battle, or the 33⅓ versus 45 rpm recordings. Again it was CBS and Dr. Peter Goldmark who were RCA's nemesis. EVR had started a new trend in TV home entertainment. The use of a cartridge or cassette made the device easy to use. Reel to reel was "messy," it involved threading the machine, as in film projectors, which made it unpopular with the public. The success of the Philips audio cassette was a sure sign that this approach would be acceptable to both the public and industry. RCA could not stand the thought of conceding this new market to CBS. So the battle was on.[49]

RCA had never pioneered advances in videotape recording. It had lagged badly behind Ampex and was content to copy all of their new advances. This was also true of their Japanese competition. At this time, there were already at least three major manufacturers showing home video recorders with cassettes. They included Sony, Japanese Victor, and Matsushita in Japan. There were also the home recorders of companies such as Telcan and Winston/Fairchild using reel to reel.

So they, RCA, looked afield for something from the future. They chose holograms and lasers. This was the basis of Selectavision. RCA emphasized that it would be a low cost color tape player only (no facilities for recording, which made it the same as EVR). At the time, George Brown of RCA did not consider the technology was ready for disclosure, in regard to its potential performance; he also did not think it yet warranted patent protection. However, it captured the imagination of Robert Sarnoff, then president of RCA, and Chase Morsey, vice president for marketing. After picking a proper name for the new recorder, research and development was begun.[50]

Technical details were given by Dr. James Hilliard, executive vice president RCA research and engineering, and Dr. William Webster, vice president RCA laboratories. They stated that they saw no conflict between EVR, which at the time was aimed at the industrial-educational market, and Selectavision which was aimed at home use.

A description of the process was given. The master was made from photographic film or magnetic video recording. The program was lasered frame by frame onto a plastic tape coated with clear photoresist in the form of a phase hologram. After development, the exposed photoresist was washed away leaving hills and valleys on the tape which were then nickel plated. The tape with its irregularities was sandwiched between two rollers with the

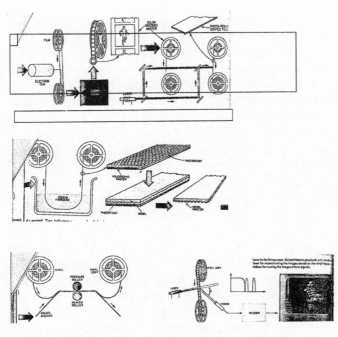

1969. RCA Selectavision hologram-laser process. (RCA.)

clear vinyl film that was to be the copy. Roller pressure embossed the bump pattern into the vinyl. Color was electronically encoded on bands in the hologram's upper-frequency spectrum. For playback, the clear tape packed into a cartridge ran smoothly through light from a 2 milliwatt helium-neon laser. The images produced were recovered by an inexpensive Vidicon camera. The adapter included laser and Vidicon circuitry to decode color bands and soundtrack. The adapter fed the signal directly into the TV set.[51]

A demonstration given at the time was rather poor. The black-and-white was good considering that the recording technique was new, but there was a slight speckling and moiré effect. The color demonstration flickered a bit, faded out every few seconds, and did not look natural. A rather dismal beginning.[52]

A demonstration given in November 1969 showed a very poor playback. The NBC Peacock was red-blue with varying shades of both. There was noticeable poor detail and motion blurring. It had granular interference patterns and rather poor resolution. Not very encouraging. According to reports, the demonstration pictures were far from broadcast quality and the system did not have a sound track.[53] Even George Brown of RCA stated that the quality of "the picture ranged between poor and lousy."[54]

On September 30, 1969, RCA gave a technical presentation of its new single–Vidicon color camera. It used a set of dichroic filters (at angles to each other) that separated the colors. Other details were given about the electrical processing which provided three color outputs.[55]

In November 1969, the new Matsushita (Panasonic)

cassette videotape recorder used an oversized Philips cassette. It was about 11 by 6.4 by 0.9 inches. It contained two reels that could be removed for operation in reel-to-reel machines. The tape was wound coated side in, rather than out as in the Philips cassette. The magazine had four slots which fit over two capstans and two movable tape guides which were moved outward during record and playback to force the tape against the drum. The recorder used direct recording of NTSC without pre-processing or pilot signal. Improved heads made it possible to record frequencies up to 10 megacycles. Using half-inch tape operating at 7½ inches per second, the machine could play back a half-hour of color or black-and-white material. Matsushita had developed a double heterodyne automatic phase control system that removed the jitter for the playback signal.[56]

In November 1969, Sony announced that its old cassette recorder was already dead. In its place Sony was introducing a machine with a far smaller tape cassette. It had reached agreement with Philips and Grundig on the tape format and cassette design, and was aiming at establishing the system as a worldwide standard. The new cassette measured eight by five by 1¼ inches and weighed one pound. Inside was enough ¾-inch tape operating at 3½ inches/sec for 1½ hours' playing time. The Sony cassette was designed so that the magnetic

1969. Matsushita cassette color videotape recorder. Reels could be removed. (Matsushita.)

coat was inside and the tape was pulled out of the cassette and over the recording drum. Tape wind on the drum was equivalent to the omega wind; because of the geometry, it was actually a U wind because it didn't double back. For compactness, reels were omitted as in the Philips audio cassette. The recorded signal was processed NTSC, rather than pure NTSC as recorded by Matsushita.[57]

On November 18, 1969, this new Sony

1969. Sony ¾-inch cassette video recorder, later called the U-Matic. (Sony Corp.)

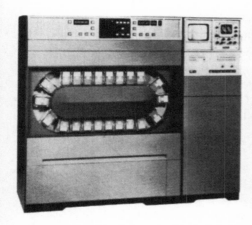

1972. RCA TCR-100 automatic cartridge playback machine. (RCA.)

1969. RCA video cartridge tape system. (RCA.)

1970. Panasonic (Matsushita) magazine loading VTR. (Matsushita.)

videoplayer was demonstrated in New York by Akio Morita, founder of Sony. It was expected to cost around $340 and could be connected to any color set. It was noted that the tape could be stopped anywhere and taken out without rewinding. An adapter that permitted direct recording in color or black-and-white cost $100. It was to be introduced in the USA in late 1971.[58]

In December 1969, RCA revealed the first video cartridge color or black-and-white tape system for television stations. It recorded and automatically put on the air taped commercials and programs housed in small preloaded cassettes. Each cassette could handle up to three minutes of tape. It had the capacity for 18 cassettes. It used standard two-inch tape with high-band standards. Each machine used a special tape transport and automatic threading mechanism. The machine pulled out the tape and put it into position, then the mechanism was retracted so it did not interfere with the playback or record operation.[59] This was one of RCA's few original concepts.

In January 1970, it was reported that two Japanese firms, Sony and Panasonic (Matsushita), had unveiled cassette recorders that were incompatible. Panasonic had shown its half-inch tape cassette during NAEB in Washington in November 1969. It was a helical scan with a head drum inclined at an angle of three degrees and 11 inches. Tape speed was 7½ inches/sec and the format was fully compatible with Panasonic's half-inch reel-to-reel recorder. In fact the reels could be removed and the tape played or edited on a standard machine. The output was NTSC color and rendering on an 11-inch monitor was quite good.[60]

Sony also showed its new cassette VTR using ¾-inch tape running at 8 cm/sec (3.15 inches) that played for 90 minutes and produced a 250-line color picture with two channels of audio. It was about the size of a standard home stereo tape deck. A demonstration on a Sony Trinitron receiver showed crisp, well-defined pictures with ex-

cellent color. Initially it would be for playback only and sell for about $350. Sony's Akio Morita indicated that the company planned to incorporate a counter mechanism to see how many times the tape had been played. Its standard was incompatible with all other VTRs, both reel to reel and cassette. It was indicated that if Sony was successful in its European negotiations, the "era of the home VTR may at last be upon us."[61]

On January 31, 1970, the Ampex Corp. announced its new high-speed color tape duplicating process. It was said to duplicate an hour show in about six minutes. It was felt by Ampex that this new concept was almost as important as the high-band television recorder itself. A statement by Charles Ginsburg, who spoke of the process, claimed that quality was indistinguishable from the original recordings.[62] Ginsburg stated that it was possible to print as many as five slave tapes simultaneously from the same master. The master tape was high coercivity (800–100 oersteds) while the slave was conventional. The master tape must be modified to give a mirror image. Audio recording was done later by separate heads. Even though tape loss was 3db, a demonstration tape showed color and resolution to appear identical.[63]

In January 1970, a new low-light camera, GTNV-1, was introduced by STC in London. It used a special Vidicon tube with a three-stage image intensifier having a very high overall gain. Typical brightness magnification was 35,000. Minimum scene brightness was $2 \times 10½$ foot candles so that it could respond to scenes that were invisible to the human eye.[64]

In February 1970, it was announced that David Sarnoff, after 63 years of service, was retiring as chairman of the board of RCA. The new chairman was Robert Sarnoff who was named president in 1966 and chief executive officer in 1968. David Sarnoff had been hospitalized for more than a year.[65] It was noted that with his retirement, an era of problems and promises that he largely conquered and fulfilled, had ended. Certainly RCA would never be the same again, nor would the world of electronics. Whatever he may have been, said or done, his dream of a working television system was his eternal reward.[66]

In February 1970, CBS Labs announced that they developed a "color corrector" permitting engineers to adjust color variations after the color had been encoded. This made it possible to make a final match for various signal sources at a central location. The machine would be available in April at below $3,000.[67] This unit and the Mark II CBS image enhancer were demonstrated in August 1970.[68]

In March 1970, it was announced that the Vladimir K. Zworykin Television prize had gone to Charles H. Coleman, senior staff engineer for video engineering at Ampex. This was for technical achievements in the field of videotape recording. Coleman had invented AMTEC, which straightened out the geometry of early TV images, and played a part in the development of high-band recording. He was scheduled to receive his award at the National Electronic Conference in Chicago on December 7, 1970.[69]

Also in March 1970, Sony announced that a new series of AV VTRs helicals using half-inch tape, had been established by the Japan EIA (Electric Industries Association). The Sony AV series format was similar to that of the CV series. There were to be two video heads and a single audio head. Tape speed would be 7½ inches/sec, 60 minutes of play time, and the machine would use seven-inch reels. It would also have video bandwidth of 2.5MHz, and a video signal to noise ratio of more than 40db.[70]

On March 30, 1970, it was reported that the Sony Corp. had suggested that a single standard for videotape players be established. Sony stated that this would make possible to use videocassettes in any recorder. Seven companies had agreed to a single standard: AEG -Telefunken; Grundig, Weko GmbH, West Germany; Industria A. Zanutti, S.P.A., Italy; Matsushita and the Victor Company, Japan; North American Philips, USA and NV Philips, the Netherlands.[71]

According to several reports, early in 1970, Sony showed its videocassette and videocassette cartridge along with technical specifications and test results to representatives of Matsushita and JVC. After weeks of contemplation, they responded favorably. However, they suggested a few modifications to the Sony format. They wanted the color recording technique of JVC, an increase in the size of the head drum to make manufacturing simpler, and an increase in the space between the tracks to reduce the tracking error. Sony, according to Kihara, "answered decisively that we would compromise." But they did not. All they succeeded in doing was antagonizing their competitors.[72]

On Tuesday, March 24, 1970, CBS and Motorola gave

the first public demonstration of EVR at the Pierre Hotel in New York. Guests were impressed with the sharpness and fidelity of the EVR's colors and the apparent ease with which the system was operated. It was becoming apparent that EVR was heading for the mass medium of the home market. Fox Films stated that some of the company's feature films would be made available to EVR five years after their theatrical release. This of course was a surprise as the movie industry was adamant about releasing any of their pictures on any kind of home recorder.[73]

In March 1970, the International Video Corp. announced their new model IVC model 900 broadcast color helical recorder.[74] It used one-inch helical-scan tape that permitted a continuous playing time of 3¼ hours on one 12½-inch reel. The machine was said to permit stable picture lock in four seconds or less for color from a standby position. The price was $12,000 to $18,000 depending on optional attachments.[75]

In April 1970, Commercial Electronics Inc. of Mountain View, CA, introduced their new CEI 270 color camera incorporating three Westinghouse WL-31683 SEC low-light Vidicon tubes. It made a full-color scene at 10 foot-candles with the lens at f/5.6. It had a limiting resolution of 700 lines and a response of 35 percent at 400 lines that compared favorably with the performance of 30mm lead oxide tubes. It had a broader spectral response than other Vidicons. A single base plate attached to the three tubes included a f/4 relay lens that provides carriage focus. The camera was to cost around $35,000 and the company said it should save money for the studio with its lower lighting requirements.[76]

At the NAB convention held March 28–30, 1970, Ampex announced its new color videotape recorder, the AVR-1. This was a third-generation recorder; the VR1000 was first, and then the high-band VR2000. The AVR-1

1970. IVC model 900 color helical VTR. (IVC.)

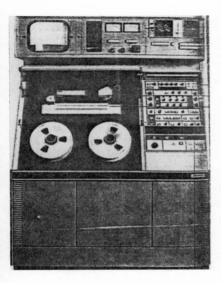

1970. Ampex AVR-1 video cassette recorder. (Ampex.)

was adaptable to station automation, through the use of digital control circuits. It had improved reliability and simplified maintenance. The AVR-1 started instantaneously. Reel takeup and feed could lag because the tape transport consisting of a capstan tape loop and a vacuum column required only the capstan to be up to speed. Light sensing elements in the tape vacuum columns adjusted the servo-controlled reels to maintain uniform tape feed to the columns. The AVR-1 could record nonsynchronous picture-signal source material. Its output was continuously synchronized and automatically adjusted for maximum picture quality. High or low band modes were picked by the machine automatically; threading was automatic too. Air guides were used in the tape path to reduce tape wear. Single-frame editing was possible. A truly magnificent machine. Worthy of Ampex at its best.[77]

Ampex also showed its new BC-230 color studio camera. It was a versatile three-tube Plumbicon camera with fewer controls and faster setup with 1,000 hour stability. The company had finally dropped the two-tube format. The camera weighed only 60 pounds.

Ampex showed a new videocassette recorder (cart machine) that used six-minute refillable cassettes. This was the model ACR-25 which was capable of automatically playing up to 25 units, each ranging from ten seconds to six minutes. It had two tape transports: one loaded and cued a cassette while the other was playing a cassette. Rewind and cue-up was less than ten seconds. The system operated at either 7½ or 15 ips. The cassettes were sucked up into the transport device through a vacuum system. The machine could be programmed to deliver any of the 25 cassettes in predetermined sequence; it had random access capability. The ACR-25 was priced at $165,000 with deliveries promised by mid–1971.[78]

Ampex had also gone into the studio switcher business. It had the VS-600 production video switcher in which the control panel could be located up to 1,500 feet away. Ampex also showed a new prototype high-speed contact printer. Finally, to make the line complete, the company showed a complete line of VHF and UHF mod-

ular TV transmitters with solid-state circuits. It had set out to truly become a maker and distributor of all video equipment.[79]

In cameras, Philips showed a new PC70S-2, and working models of a digitally controlled PC-100 and the Minicam PCP90. From Germany, a newly imported three-tube color camera made by Fernseh, also digitally controlled, was displayed.[80]

In May 1970, Dr. Goldmark disclosed that EVR would soon switch to a diazo type of film that had no silver content, no grain, and was almost half the cost of silver prints. He stated that there was no difference between it and the silver type of film then being used. The system's target date was still 1972.[81]

Also in May 1970, the Sony Corp. showed some new models of their videocassette player that were different from the machines displayed at the previous fall's NAEB convention. The new player handled two new cartridge sizes: 100 minutes and 30 minutes. Sony was still claiming that it had an agreement with other manufacturers to use this new standard. They were Matsushita and Nippon Victor Company (Japan); Telefunken and Grundig (Germany); Zanuzzi (Italy); Philips (Netherlands); and North American Philips (USA); Sony's machine was self threading and showed good color. It used ¾-inch tape running at 3.18 inches per second; therefore it was incompatible with all other VTRs.[82]

In June 1970 at the Consumer Electronics Show in New York, another new entry into the home video recorder market was announced. The AVCO Corp. and its subsidiary Cartridge Television, Inc. unveiled their Cartrivision CTV system, which was said to be the hit of the show. The new system was demonstrated for the first time from June 28 to July 1. Its principal component was a

1970. Sony U-Matic color video player. (Sony Corp.)

Cartrivision player shown in June 1970. (Cartrivision Inc.)

solid-state combination receiver-recorder playback unit consisting of a cartridge videotape deck and a full-sized TV color receiver built into a single self-contained unit. It used half-inch tape running at 3.8 inches/sec. Video was recorded using only every third field and playing back three times. (Sony had tried a similar approach by recording every other field and playing back twice; but it was soon abandoned because of many serious problems.)[83] Price was to be in the $800–$900 range. It stated that hundreds of prerecorded full-length movies would be made available for rental. Units were scheduled for sale in early 1971.[84]

In June 1970, the first annual Alexander M. Poniatoff award was given to Charles E. Anderson of the video engineering section of Ampex Corp., products division. Anderson was credited with developing the FM system which had led to the development of the first practical video recorder by Ampex. He received a gold medal and a cash award.[85]

On June 24, 1970, the first Teldec videodisc, another contender for home video players, was demonstrated in Berlin. Teldec was a research organization jointly owned by AEG-Telefunken and Decca. The playback disc was either 12 minutes on a 12-inch disc or five minutes on a nine-inch disc. The disc was rotated at 1,500 rev/min (for 50 cycle systems) and had from 120–140 grooves per millimeter. Resolution of the replayed picture was claimed to be 250 lines (3MHz bandwidth) with signal to noise ratio better than 40db. The demonstration showed good entertainment quality pictures though some dropouts could be observed on the prototype discs. Estimates of the cost of the playback unit were in the order of £100. Color capability was predicted.[86]

During playback the disc rode on an air cushion. A new pickup principle had been developed whereby a spe-cial sled-shaped needle and a piezoelectric transducer responded to variations of pressure exerted by the groove elevations, rather than to needle motion as in the conventional LP record. AEG Telefunken said that the videodisc had a big future not only in home entertainment, but also in the educational sector.[87]

In July 1970, Philips showed their latest half-inch videocassette home recorder. It was demonstrated at the Film Industry Organization at Brighton, in the south of England. Each cassette contained enough tape for an hour's play. Two soundtracks were available. A player only cost about £120 and £140 for a color machine. A second version that recorded in black-and-white and in color also was to cost £230. The film industry was involved, as the machine was intended for playing their programs.[88] It was claimed that a number of other manufacturers had agreed to use this system. They were Blaupunkt, Grundig, AEG Telefunken, Loewe Opta, and Zanussi.[89]

On July 14, 1970, it was reported that a new process had been invented by Video Recorders Inc.— it was a refinement of the Electronovision process. With this process and Norleco cameras, it was feasible for work on location in natural light. Use of this new tape-to-film process made it possible to bring in a film for $250,000 — 25 to 30 percent less than the cost of shooting it directly on film. A picture, Subject to Change Without Notice, was to have a three-week shooting schedule consisting of three days a week. Pre-edited tape was delivered to Technicolor for processing. The movie was to be previewed in a Los Angeles theater on July 27, 1970.[90]

At this time, in July 1970, the use of film for television was an object of discussion for the SMPTE. Film was lauded for its mobility and greater flexibility in single-camera photography. In addition, when it came to editing, film with its superior postproduction capability, had the advantage. As far as the recording of news events was concerned, the CBS engineering department reported

1970. Philips VCR cassette video recorder. (Philips Labs.)

that, "As of now,… it is simply not possible nor [sic] economically feasible to compete with 16mm film for this application. In this case, electronic photography must simply plead — no contest." It wasn't long before CBS would eat its words.[91]

However, on the other hand, it was reported that the CBS engineering department thought it was time for a new approach to TV production. While it approved the use of 16mm film for news purposes, it suggested that perhaps for drama or situation comedies, it was time to replace 35mm film with videotape. It was indicated that as far as quality was concerned, there was at present little to choose between good film and videotape as seen over a broadcasting system. It was claimed that film had become fast and highly efficient, which had reduced the time and cost advantages of traditional electronic production. While tape had generally been used for multiple camera work, it was considered that tape's advantages of instant replay and reusability made it the ideal stock for all types of production, especially in a single-camera approach. The main snag for electronic photography expanding its production role seemed to be the editing process.[92] Of course, CBS was working secretly to solve this problem.

In September 1970, the Ampex Corp. announced a new line of home tape recorders and playback machines for closed-circuit TV and home recording. Ampex stated that its new Instavision system would be available in mid–1971. The recorder-player used standard half-inch wide videotape enclosed in a small circular plastic cartridge 4.6 inches in diameter and 0.7 inches thick. It was said to be compatible with all other conventional reel-type recorders using the new type-1 standard that had been adopted by manufacturers of half-inch recorders. The recorder-player weighed less than 16 pounds complete with rechargeable batteries and measured 11 inches by 13 inches by 4½ inches. A unit to both record and play back color would cost about $1,000. The units would be made in Japan by Toamco, and that company would also market them in Japan. Ampex would have the rights to the rest of the world.[93] In October 1971, it was reported that it had not met FCC specifications and pre-production problems had to be worked out. Introduction was delayed to the spring of 1972.[94]

It is interesting that Ampex chose to use a cartridge as in the EVR system rather than a cassette as used by Sony. In the New York demonstration, it had good color (no smear) and no rolls but had a few dropouts and line jitter. Features of the player included autosearch, slow motion, stop action, elementary editing and a second audio track. Video resolution was 300 lines in black-and-white with a signal to noise ratio of 42db.[95] In March 1971, the system was renamed Instavideo as it was found that the original name had been previously used by a firm in Minneapolis.[96]

On September 22, 1970, the EVR plant in Basildon, England, was officially opened. It was planned to produce a wide range of programs there by April 1971. The Basildon plant included three Ampex VR2000 machines, a helical scanner, a Marconi telecine and a number of RCA sound tape units. It also included the CBS electron-beam recorder. The teleplayer to be produced there was to cost £360 and would be suitable for monochrome or PAL color.[97]

In October 1970, at the AES convention, the 12-inch videodisc from Telefunken was demonstrated October 19–21 by London Records that was owned by Decca. Although it was only in black-and-white, the developers said that color should be available in 18 months. Work was begun on the project in 1965 by four German scientists headed by Horst Redlich in conjunction with Arthur Haddy, chief engineer for Decca Records Ltd.[98] Tentative prices were $150 for a player with manual play and $250–300 for an automatic record changer. Discs were to cost the same as the LP records.[99]

In November 1970, it was reported that EVR Partnership, London had reached agreement with Hitachi, Ltd. Tokyo for the manufacture by Hitachi of EVR players in Japan and elsewhere.[100]

In March 1971, a preview of Sony's prototype color camera was shown. It used a single Vidicon tube with an intregal optical grating and electronic filter system to separate the colors. Signal was standard NTSC; signal to noise ratio appeared high as did resolution. Color rendition on a Trinitron monitor was impressive with some lag in evidence, but light levels were nominal, indicating efficient optics.[101] The color camera with attached electronic viewfinder weighed 16½ pounds and operated on solid-state circuits. First of the new cameras were expected to sell for around $1,000, but it was anticipated that the price would ultimately decrease toward the $500 mark.[102]

1970. Ampex portable color cartridge video recorder, Instavideo. *Left:* Complete system. *Right:* Player. (Ampex.)

1971. Sony single-vidicon color tube camera. (Sony Corp.)

In March 1971, the IVC Corp. announced that they had developed a new helical-scan video recorder. It was available in either black-and-white or color. A maximum of 3½ hours' recording time was possible. They had also developed a new color time-base corrector that corrected the time-base error of an IVC 900 to ±7 nanoseconds. Jitter was removed in two steps: with the monochrome corrector (IVC4100) to ± 75 microseconds, and with an add-on color corrector (IVC-4102) down to the nanosecond figure. It was claimed that stability was so good that it permitted intermixing of both helical and transverse programming. The studio console version sold for $14,000 and the color time-base corrector for $9,000. Ampex promised that the new Ampex line 7800–7900 would equal or exceed the IVC specs.[103]

Also at NAB in March 1971, a new tape-editing system, the CMX-600, was first displayed by Memorex. Developed in the United States by CBS and Memorex, it was designed to permit editing from a random sequence to a single frame. The CMX unit would also later automatically assemble the final program. The system included disc packs as an intermediate transfer storage medium. Program material was transferred automatically into the direct-access disc system that simultaneously stored the picture-audio and frame-code information. Each disc stored five minutes of material, and up to 12 could be incorporated to store 60 minutes. The edit console had dual monitors for viewing entry and exit points which could be selected and reviewed by pointing a light pen at the CRT display of the frame number. In practice, the light pen was the only tool used by the editor, thus dispensing with push buttons or lever controls. A variable speed system made it possible to do precision audio cutting. High-speed minicomputers performed every tedious chore, remembering editing decisions and accomplishing the assembly. The system was to cost some $250,000.[104]

It was hoped by CBS that this new editing system would result in film producers switching their prime-time shows and commercials from film to tape. Because of its production capability, single-camera techniques and out-of-sequence shooting were possible. It was immodestly billed as the "most important development in television production since the advent of videotape itself."[105]

There would be many problems in its introduction. Until now, most videotape editing was done by technicians belonging to the electrical unions (IBEW and NABET). It was quite foreign to the film studios. As videotape was introduced into the television studios, it was only natural that their electrical technicians were the ones best qualified to set up, operate and play the recordings. All editing techniques had been developed by these technicians starting with two-inch tape, cut with a razor blade, to the latest sophisticated electronic editing devices made by Ampex and others. Unfortunately most editing was done "on line" on the same machines that tape had been recorded on. This of course tied these machines up for hours. After a while, certain machines were designated for editing purposes only. While this was a step forward, there remained the problems that all editing was linear and searching for new material was quite time-consuming. Random-access editing was not possible with tape machines, until the CMX600.

However, CBS was determined that these new machines would not be used by the electrical union (IBEW). They proposed to set up a new system of shooting single-camera film style with film people using videotape and then sending this tape to be processed by the CMX600 by a film editor. After they had edited the program, it was

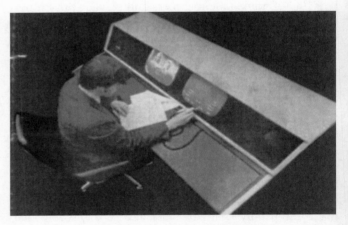

1971. CMX600. *Above:* The editing table with light pen. *Below:* Table with memory banks. (CBS/Memorex.)

then to be automatically assembled on videotape at the recording rooms of the studio. This was a blunt effort to take away the tape jurisdiction from the electrical union and turn it over to the film union (IATSE).

CBS had long complained that they were not allowed to use film in their television studios due to union contracts. This went back as far as the "Lucy Show" in 1951 when CBS allowed Desi Arnaz to shoot his show on the outside. In 1966, CBS bought the Republic Studios in North Hollywood for some $9,500,000. CBS planned to make its own major motion pictures there. While the moviemaking project was a failure (a loss of $30 million) the property itself became quite valuable and was developed into a studio for television film production called "Studio Center." In Hollywood, Television City was solely for "live" (on tape) production and Studio Center was strictly for film production.

However, certain CBS management people thought that it was time to change that situation. According to Edward L. Saxe of the CBS services division, the program had started some five years before. CBS had the concept and Memorex had the computer-storage technology and could manufacture the product. The project had been cohesive some 3½ years before.[106] A paper entitled "Why Use Film?" proposed this new single electronic camera technique.[107] The CBS-Memorex project was the opening gun in CBS's effort to turn videotape over to the film industry. Proof was that it was reported that the first CMX600 was scheduled for delivery to CBS-TV Studio Center (a film facility) in April 1971.[108]

On March 11, 1971, the noted American television pioneer Philo T. Farnsworth died. Farnsworth had been ill for many years and plagued with economic and family problems. He had long ago severed any relationship with the television industry he helped found. In 1949, the assets of Farnsworth Television and Radio Corporation were taken over by International Telephone & Telegraph Co. (ITT) and he had left the field. There was no mention of his dying in the press or elsewhere. His wife Elma and family did their best to restore his name and reputation. He was posthumously inducted into the National Inventors Hall of Fame in 1984, and there was also a statue to him placed in the nation's capital on May 2, 1990.[109]

In April 1971, it was rumored that RCA was having trouble with its Selectavision process. One published account reported early the month before that Selectavision was being shelved and that RCA officials were talking with Avco and Sony about a deal involving one of these systems. Of course, RCA stoutly denied the reports.[110] However, in October RCA's Robert Bitting stated that if Selectavision failed, there would be a magnetic tape unit to fall back on.[111]

In April 1971, AKAI America Ltd. announced a new $1,295 VT-100 audio-video recording system. It included a 20-pound camera, optical viewfinder, and built-in mike. A battery operated quarter-inch VTR with twin rotating heads, gave 20 minutes on a five-inch reel. A video monitor with a three-inch screen and an AC/DC adapter-battery charger was available for the 6 volt system.[112]

In May 1971, the nomenclature sub-committee of the SMPTE video recording committee agreed that the preferred term for transverse recording was "Quadruplex recording."[113]

Also in May 1971, it was announced that Charles Coleman of Ampex was to get the Alexander M. Poniatoff Award. This award was traditionally made to an Ampex scientist who had accomplished a significant scientific breakthrough or developed a process which made for technical excellence at Ampex. In addition to his invention of the original Ampex time-base corrector, Coleman had taken part in the development of high-band recording, and lately, in new time-base techniques for the Ampex AVR-1 "third-generation" recorder.[114]

At the Berlin Home and Video Show in August 1971, the Teldec color videodisc was demonstrated for the first time. In order to get color on the disc, the red, blue and green colors were recorded in sequence. On playback, delay elements were used so that all three signals were available at the same time. The mixing process was used only for low frequency information, less than 1MHz so sharpness was not lost.[115]

Another television triumph came in August 1971, with the Apollo 15 moonshot of Colonels David R. Scott and James B. Irwin. Again the whole mission was transmitted to earth by means of television cameras from the mother ship Endeavor. Westinghouse furnished the cameras for the shots in space, RCA's astroelectronics division furnished the camera for the lunar rover. They worked even better than had been expected. Both cameras used the field sequential color system of Dr. Goldmark. The RCA camera used the silicon intensifier target that was burn proof. The scanning for both cameras was 30 fields/ sec providing 425 lines of resolution on 4.5MHz bandwidth.[116]

In October 1971, the first color full-length feature made by a video-to-film process was released. This was *200 Motels* directed and starring Frank Zappa. It was called a "stunning achievement" by critic Robert Hilburn. He stated that Zappa "had created a minor classic." Hilburn was obviously not aware that there had been several prior attempts to make a movie by means of television recording. However, *200 Motels* enjoyed a wide run in theaters all over the country and the public was not aware (or cared) that this was a tape-to-film production.[117] It was shot in England and processed by Vidtronics for United Artists in the 625-line British color standard using fine-grain film.[118]

In October 1971, a cross-licensing patent agreement was made between Sony and 3M. This agreement would permit Sony to make and sell 3M's High Energy tape and allow 3M to manufacture and sell Sony's ¾-inch U-matic videocassette equipment. The recording system would be manufactured and sold by 3M through its Mincom division under the Wollensak brand name.[119]

In October 1971, the Victor Company of Japan announced a reel-to-reel half-inch videotape recorder. It had a rotary two-head system with horizontal resolution of 230 lines and used seven-inch reels. It was also available with electronic editing.[120]

In October 1971, the Eastman Kodak Company demonstrated a feasibility model of a cartridge-loading video player for Super 8 film at the SMPTE convention in Montreal. It was known as the Kodak film/television system and featured both color and sound. It had controls that permitted forward projection, stop motion, instant playback as well as automatic rewind of the film into the Super 8 cartridge. Kodak claimed that they had spent ten years of research and millions of dollars in developing the system. Cartridges varied in capacity from ten feet to 440 feet or 42 minutes at 18 frames/sec. It was priced at $900. While Kodak felt that it had a limited market at the moment, with a substantial market the video player would cost considerably less. However, they stated that it would be two more years before the unit was commercially produced.[121]

Japan's Fuji Film was supposed to be in pilot production of a Super 8 player for television. It used a continuous pull-down system, eliminating intermittent motion and shutter noise with a 16-face revolving prism. Like the Kodak machine, it used a flying-spot system. It too was to be priced around $750–800 in Japan.[122]

In October 1971, IVC introduced a low-cost color camera, the IVC-150, which combined Plumbicon tubes with a new silicon diode tube for extended red response. It was claimed to produce excellent pictures below 10 foot candles. Adding an external encoder brought it up to full FCC and EIA broadcast specifications. The price was from $14,800.[123]

In November 1971, the IVC Corp. announced the manufacturing of its 5,000th video recorder. It was an 820 model.[124]

David Sarnoff died on December 12, 1971, at the age of 80. He had been ill and undergone a series of mastoid operations since September 1968. New York Governor Nelson A. Rockefeller delivered the eulogy and stated "that General Sarnoff had given America a voice through radio" and "was the father of television in this country."[125]

Elmer W. Engstrom, who had worked for him for a generation, said, "For more than 35 years I had the honor of serving under David Sarnoff, first in his role as President and later when he became Chairman of the Board and Chief Executive Officer of RCA. During those years, it was my privilege to bear witness to an era of unparalleled progress sparked by the vision of a truly remarkable personality. More than any other man in his time, David Sarnoff was the driving spirit who must be credited with transforming electronic technology from its research beginnings into a vital force that now permeates all phases of our lives.

"With unbounded faith in scientists and engineers— at times more faith in them than they were willing to express themselves— David Sarnoff committed himself without qualification to the principles of industrial research. He has, therefore, left us with a legacy of inspiration to guide the further progress of electronics for generations to come.

"For those of us who served with him, for those who follow in his footsteps, the story of David Sarnoff's dedicated life encompasses all of the opportunities America holds forth for the achievement of greatness. He was not content merely to dream impossible dreams. He fulfilled them. And by doing so, he has made it possible for all who continue to labor in this field to fulfill their own lives— if they have the will. Thus, there is only one way to properly conclude a tribute to the life of David Sarnoff. Neither nostalgia nor memories will suffice — only challenges."[126]

On December 13, 1971, the first commercial installation of the new CBS–Memorex 600 edit and assembly unit was made at Consolidated Film Industries in Hollywood, California. Another installation was to be made at Teletronics Corp., New York City.[127]

On December 22, 1971, CBS announced that it was closing down its EVR project. Beset by technical problems and with videocassettes and videodiscs on the horizon, Bill Paley called it quits.[128] All cassette processing operations were terminated. Property was converted to loans in its equity in the EVR Partnership, Imperial Chemical Industries, Ltd. and CIBA-Geigy, Ltd. CBS stated that its future role would be that of a program producer and licenser of the EVR system. Ralph Briscoe, president of the CBS/Comtec Group, stated that the videocassette market had not progressed at the pace that had been expected. CBS hoped that the Japanese would spur EVR development in world markets. The losses from the EVR experiment were close to $25 million.[129]

So Dr. Goldmark's dream of the long playing video recorder had come to naught. Goldmark sadly remarked that "We had created our own Frankensteinian competition."[130] It had been the very first video cartridge for home and educational use and had spawned the whole industry of video home recorders including both tape and disc. While he was offered an opportunity to stay on as CBS's chief scientist, he decided to retire on his 65th birthday. William Paley was only too glad to see him go. He stated that he "began to look upon Peter Goldmark, whose fame as an inventor for CBS had spread far and wide, as a thorn in my side."[131] (A rather sad commentary from the once benevolent head of CBS.)

However, in a tribute to Goldmark, CBS President Frank Stanton said that "his devotion to science and to the application of science to products that bring enjoyment and enrichment of life has left an indelible impression on our times. The LP record, field-sequential color television and the videocassette are only three of his many extraordinary contributions."[132]

However, EVR was not quite dead in Europe. At the Videocassette Exhibition in Cannes in March 1972, four different kinds of players were on display. One by the Bosch Company made in Germany, a third by Rank made in Britain, one by Thomson which appeared to be a Motorola player with the Thomson name on it and the fourth by Mitsubishi and made in Japan. Pictures reproduced on the players were better than those shown in the USA, even on large-screen monitors.[133]

Chapter 9

The Rise of Electronic Journalism (1972–1976)

In January 1972, it was announced that the JVC Nivico (Victor Company of Japan) had joined the cassette battle royal by introducing the recording and playback system of Sony's U-matic machine. This was supposed to reach the American market in mid–1972. It was also announced that Panasonic had recently demonstrated a similar machine.[1]

In January 1972, Editel Productions of New York and Montreal announced a new portable color camera. Called the Mark III, it weighed less than 20 pounds (the backpack weighed an additional 17 pounds) and gave studio-quality color pictures. It could be operated from 12 volt car batteries. It was designed primarily for videotaping of remotes. Editel claimed that it had first been used during the Sugar Bowl game on January 1, 1972, on ABC. It was priced around $75,000 to $80,000. Editel said that it had been developed by a production house.[2]

A new important camera tube was developed around this time by the Bell labs for their Picturephone. It was basically a target of reverse-biased silicon photodiodes that were accessed by a low-energy scanning beam similar to that in conventional Vidicons. The planar array was made up of 840,000 reversed biased silicon photodiodes, 750,000 of which were portioned for use on the half-inch-square wafer. Diode failure was the biggest problem. According to an article in *BM/E*, such a tube was developed by Bell Labs in November 1968 and a successor in May or June 1969.[3]

It seems that the Bell labs also made the first silicon target Vidicons for their Picturephone. The tube had a special target made up of a mosaic a few thousands of an inch thick, by photo etching holes through a silicon dioxide layer on n-type bulk silicon. P-type silicon was then diffused through to form the diodes. A charge pattern was formed by the light scanned by the scanning beam generating the video signal.[4]

The target was made by depositing an array of 1,000 by 750 diodes on a wafer of n-type single crystal silicon, which was scanned in the usual ½- by ⅜-inch raster. The diodes were formed on a ⅞-inch wafer of n-type single crystal silicon. Boron or other p-type dopant was diffused throughout the array of holes which cut through a previous grown layer of SiO by a photolith process. Some manufacturers applied an insulating layer to prevent the SiO from accumulating a charge. This was called a resistive sea. Another way called for was deposition of metal islands over the diodes reducing the area of SiO, thus preventing an excessive charge buildup. After the diodes were formed, the wafer was etched to the proper final thickness of approximately one mil and a metal contact ring was provided around the wafer for contact to the target substrate. A silicon target had all the advantages of the Plumbicon and the broadest spectral response ever obtained in an image tube. Ranges were from 350 to 1,200 nanometers, well into the infrared region.[5]

RCA had a silicon intensifier tube known as the SIT tube with an image matrix and a light amplifier.[6] Norelco had developed a new Vidicon with a target composed of discrete, reverse-biased silicon diodes but with a faceplate consisting of fiber optics. The photocathode was deposited as a coating on the inner surface of the fiber optics and emitted electrons in proportion to the light. The rest of the operation was very similar to that of the normal SEC tube. This version was called the Electron Bombardment Induced Conductivity (EBIC).[7]

1972. Tubeless camera from RCA Laboratories. (RCA.)

On March 15, 1972, RCA demonstrated a research model of a black-and-white camera that had a solid-state sensor about the size of an electric razor. The camera's image sensor was a silicon integrated circuit with no vacuum tubes. The camera measured 2 by 2¼ by 3¾ inches and weighed less than a pound. It employed a 32 by 44 element charge-transfer bucket-brigade sensor. It was claimed that at low resolution it produced pictures at levels of 5–20 foot candles with a dynamic range between 10:1 to 60:1.[8] A demonstration model was diffused with small white spots and RCA stated that much research was required before this type of camera would be ready for news coverage.[9]

Westinghouse had an imaging surface of 200,000 photo transistors and a hybrid scanning control panel. Together they formed a novel camera which was completely self-contained.[10]

In March 1972, Philips Broadcast announced their new Norelco PC-100A. It was a three-tube camera using one-inch "anti-comet tail" (ACT) Plumbicons. It was digitally controlled with light weight triaxial cable that weighed one tenth as much as conventional camera cable.[11]

By March 1972, a new color videocassette system that used conventional 8 mm film had been developed by Vidicord Ltd. of Britain. The first prototype was shown in Cannes, France at the VIDCA videocassette show. It used an EMI-improved phosphor flying-spot CRT with a 0.1 microsecond decay time and a 1.5 square inch raster. It was claimed that the system's main advantage was the wide availability and low price of compatible software. It would sell for about $1,000 and hit the teaching and training market early in 1973.[12]

In April 1972, IVC announced a new IVC-500 color camera that used two Plumbicons for the green and blue channels and a special red channel tube of the silicon diode type. It was claimed that the new silicon diode tube had the broadest spectral response of any image tube. From 350 to 1,200 nanometers, well into the infrared region. It was claimed that the red color rendition was remarkable. It was made by Texas Instrument Company and called the Tivicon. The cost of the camera was in the $30,000 area.[13]

In April 1972, it was reported that the Ampex Corporation was on the way out as a viable company. It seems that since the previous November, Ampex had taken many steps to change this situation. It had lost $12 million in 1971 and was facing a $90 million loss in 1972. It seems that Ampex's ventures into consumer products had been the cause of its downfall. This included prerecorded tapes, consumer audio equipment and Ampex records. As a result, it was discontinuing operations of its consumer equipment division. Its only consumer product to remain would be the semiprofessional AX300 recorder that listed for $695.

It also removed itself from the switching and transmitter business. It would stay with areas which it knew best — namely videotape recording, discs, cameras and their ancillary equipment. Plant operations were to be concentrated in Colorado Springs as the primary manufacturing site; Sunnyvale would be where systems were built and Redwood City would be the heart of the engineering and management operation of the new overall audio-video equipment division under Charles Steinberg, who would report to new president Arthur H. Hausman.[14] Ampex's ambitious plans to be another RCA or Westinghouse had gone astray. By venturing outside its specialized field, it had almost destroyed itself. But the company was still dominant in the video recording field and would remain so for many years.

At the NAB convention held in Chicago in April 1972, Philips Broadcast gave a demonstration of the Norelco VCR videocassette record-playback system. It was highly compact and both sound and picture were carried on half-inch tape which is contained in a cassette about the size of a paperback. One cassette played 50 minutes of color or black-and-white programming. Norelco said that the early market was for educational, industrial and governmental, not the consumer, market.[15]

However, in May it was announced that Norelco would begin producing its new recorder and that an initial delivery of 23,000 Norelco VCR units would be put on the market by the following January. The price was around $1,425. It was said that this action was being taken after a study showed it to be the most effective measure for making the Norelco VCR available quickly for an

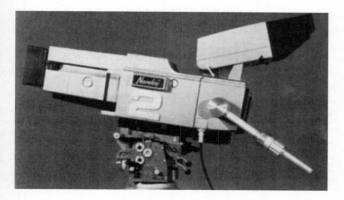

1972. Norelco (PHILIPS) PC-100A color camera. (Philips Labs.)

1972. Philips model N video cassette recorder. (Philips Labs.)

extraordinarily wide variety of applications.[16] At this time the Sony U-matic machine was becoming the unofficial American standard.

Also at NAB, an all-new, all-digital time-base corrector was shown for the Ampex 7900 and the IVC 960. It was made by a new company, Television Microtime Inc., a subsidiary of Anderson Labs. Called the Delta-44 it would correct instabilities of ± 2.2 microseconds or less, giving it a larger correction range than any other TBC. It would stabilize the VTR down to ±3 nanoseconds, permitting it to be used as a transverse machine. It was priced at $10,500.

Ampex showed for the first time a half-inch helical-scan recorder, the VR420. It was a reel-to-reel machine first announced in January. Ampex claimed that it had sold over 150 AVR-1s since its introduction. Also at NAB for the first time, both the Philips half-inch cassette player and the Sony U-matic cassette machine were on display.[17]

Also shown at the NBA convention was the new RCA TK-630 with three lead-oxide tubes and a built in image enhancer. It had a simple one-piece optical system. It featured a plug-in viewfinder and carrying handle. Price was below $40,000. Philips showed its new PC-72 three-tube Plumbicon camera — price, $75,000. Fernseh showed its new KCR hand-held camera using three one inch Plumbicons. It weighed 15 pounds with viewfinder and zoom lens — price, $50,000 to $75,000. G.E. showed its "high resolution" PE-403A at $65,000. It weighed 90 pounds, less viewfinder and lens. The Shibaden Corp. showed its FP12-00 camera featuring automatic and remote iris setting. It had individual red, blue and green outputs and a five-inch viewfinder — cost, $16,165. Commercial Electronics showed its CEI-280 color camera. Setup and operating controls were remote — cost, $20,000. The new Editel Mark III hand-held camera was shown.

The camera was being sold as part of a package that would be leased to broadcasters for $20,000 down and $7,500 a month.

For television titling, CBS showed its Vidifont X, a third-generation unit that included random-access memory and use of changeable font styles. Preset messages could be retrieved on command. The price was $35,000. Chiron Telesystems presented its Chiron II titling system. It had the ability to transfer to vidiloop cartridges and all kinds of artwork fonts. It had off-line editing ability and disc-pack storage of up to 10,000 titles, as well as instant access. Datatron exhibited its Vidicue videotape editing system. It had remote control for three VTRs and could be interfaced with a digital computer for automatic editing. Its cost was $10,000.[18]

In May 1972, a miniature tubeless camera built by the RCA Laboratories, USA was again described. This research model measuring $2 \times 2\frac{1}{4} \times 3\frac{1}{4}$ inches used a solid-state image sensing panel consisting of a 0.2 inch square metal oxide semiconductor (MOS) integrated circuit with 1,408 photo-sensitive elements. The scanning was based on "bucket brigade" charge transfer method.[19]

RCA's research into solid-state image sensors followed two main courses: standard silicon integrated circuitry technology with charge-transfer scanning and thin film deposition of elements with scanning by x–y addressing. In the early seventies, the thin film method allowed much larger numbers of photosensitive elements to be fabricated on a panel. By 1972, a 512 by 512 element panel had been made by RCA. Paul K. Weimer stated that wire-grill masking facilities would allow fabrication of integrated sensors having up to 1,000 by 1,000 elements on one-mil centers.[20]

In May 1972, it was announced that the new 80,000-seat Superdome Arena in New Orleans would have a huge large-screen display, with six full-color 40-foot screens suspended from the ceiling. The projectors were the latest version of the Eidophor manufactured by Gretag, Ltd. of Switzerland. It was to be used to present instant replays, and key action closeups. Eidophor was sold in the United States by TNT Communications.[21]

In May 1972, it was announced that the EVR Partnership reached an agreement between Imperial Chemical Ltd., Ciba-Geigy, Switzerland, and a Japanese consortium, to exploit EVR on a worldwide basis. The Japanese companies were Teijin, Hitachi, Mitsubishi Electric and Mainichi Broadcasting System.[22] It was planned to start building EVR players on European standards. Customers for the players were expected to be mainly professional organizations, Motorola saw very little possibility of a domestic EVR market in the immediate future.[23]

In May 1972, the National Academy of Arts and Sciences honored the EECO company (Electronic Engineering

Co. of California) with a special commendation. The achievement was EECO's development of serial time-code editing equipment. The first editor had been installed at CBS Studios in Hollywood in 1967[24] and it was soon adapted as the SMPTE edit code.[25]

In June 1972, International Video Corp. announced that it would introduce a new series of high-performance compact video cartridge recorders later that year. It offered "ease of operation and broadcast quality color pictures far superior to [those at] any available VTR." The new VCR-100 series would be much smaller and lighter than the Sony ¾-inch recorder. First showing was to be in October.[26]

On Tuesday, June 13, 1972, RCA at the Chicago Spring conference of the Institute of Electrical and Electronics Engineers announced the first major change in its color picture tubes since 1954. It had abandoned the tricolor shadow-mask concept and was using slits in the masks instead of holes and had the phosphors arranged in parallel lines. Electron guns were aligned side by side and utilized a simpler design that resulted in a shorter electron gun structure. (This was similar to an earlier G.E. concept.) RCA would make color tubes of the new design in 15-, 17- and 19-inch V screen sizes. The 15-inch V tube would be produced first at RCA's Marion Ind. plant in late 1972, followed by the 17-inch V and 19-inch V the following year. In the 19-inch size, it would be produced in a black-matrix, negative-guard band format. The tube was designed for operation with a solid-state chassis. RCA was also working on a 13-inch V version of the tube.

RCA had come up with a newer version of an old design that it hoped would become the industry standard for all screen sizes of 19 inches and less, and perhaps later the larger sizes as well. The major improvement in the new tube, according to RCA, was that it would never require any dynamic convergence adjustments—in the TV set factory, in the service shop, or in the consumer's home. The new development, said RCA, made picture tube installation as easy in a color set as in a black-and-white receiver.

The new tube combined a number of principles already adopted by tube manufacturers in the United States and Japan, plus a new yoke that was permanently cemented to the neck of the tube and preadjusted in the picture tube factory. The tube was of the slotted-mask variety; instead of the conventional round holes in the shadow mask, there were vertical oblong slots.[27] The screen contained vertical phosphor stripes of alternating red, blue and green in place of the conventional phosphor dots. The gun structure was one "unitized" piece containing red, blue and green guns side by side on a horizontal plane instead of in a triangular (delta) configuration. This in-line-gun technique had been used by Gen-

eral Electric in its Porta Color tubes since 1965. This made for lower deflection power requirements, as well as improved convergence and registration. The tube had a narrow neck (29mm as opposed to the conventional 36 mm). The new yoke was of the toroidal type; it was said to be extremely simple to produce, and to use only 20 percent as much copper as the conventional saddle yoke. Many other neck components were eliminated, including the 12 convergence adjustments. The yokes could be salvaged and reused in tube rebuilding operations. The tube itself, with standard 90 degree deflection, was 1.8 inches shorter than a comparable old type of tube, and the tube and neck components removed 2½ pounds from the total weight of a color set. The new tube (excluding cost of the yoke) would be made available to set manufacturers at the same price as a conventional color tube of the same size and type, resulting in a factory cost saving said to be in the neighborhood of $5; plus, there were obvious savings to the consumer in convergence costs. Since the set required no convergence, technicians working on a set with this type of tube need not bring along their convergence equipment. It appeared to be RCA's answer to Sony's Trinitron.[28]

If the new RCA tube system met the acceptance of set manufacturers, other tube makers were expected to manufacture similar devices. Meanwhile, though, some other new designs were being demonstrated. Sylvania had a more conventional tube, with standard wide neck diameter, but with an in-line gun structure and toroidal yoke that reduced the convergence adjustments from the standard 12 to four. G.E. said that its new 10- and 16-inch Porta Color tubes required no convergence adjustments and the company was also planning a slotted-mask version. Zenith had introduced "Super-Chromacolor," which was said to have a much brighter, sharper picture than its predecessor, resulting from a new gun system, new phosphors and larger holes in the center portion of the shadow mask.[29]

John B. Farese, executive vice president of RCA Electronic Components, cited these advantages of the new tube system: elimination of dynamic convergence components and corresponding setup costs, making possible important savings; reduction in overall length of the color tube by 1.8 inches from the existing 90 degree color tube; and finally, reduction of weight by 2.5 pounds.[30] Like the RCA image orthicon, the shadow-mask tube had lasted for some 18 years and of course sparked the revolution in color picture tubes.

On July 1, 1972, station KDUB of Dubuque, Iowa, went into operation using Super 8 color film for the first time. It was reported that its use could save the station about 65 percent in film costs alone. It also claimed that the Super 8 cameras cost about one fourth the price of a normal 16mm film camera. Also all six newspeople had their own cameras and did not use a camera pool. It was claimed that the average viewer could see no difference between 16mm and the new Super 8 film. It was noted that Super 8 color was softer than 16mm, but this problem had been overcome by using an image enhancer at the projection unit. It was said that NBC-TV was using 24 million feet of film annually which cost $1.7 million; Super 8 would cost about one half or even one quarter of that.[31]

In July, Ampex announced that their new ACR-25 broadcast videotape cassette recorder (cart machine) had been delivered to KTEW (TV) Tulsa, Ok. Ampex claimed that it had a $10 million backlog of orders for the machine from TV stations in the USA and Europe.[32]

In July 1972, RCA finally gave up on its holographic Selectavision recorder. It revealed details of its upcoming home color cartridge videotape recorder which it called Mag-Tape Selectavision. The company said that this new machine would be offered in the summer of 1973. It had already had some success with the technology, having licensed Bell & Howell to market a unit for the professional market and Magnavox one for the home market. RCA said its Mag-Tape Selectavision record and playback system would be offered on the consumer market in late 1973 as a deck with VHF and UHF tuners for recording off the air, and a digital clock-timer for unattended recording. "Target price" of the complete deck was $700.

The major innovation in the RCA system was "in-cartridge scanning." All other videocassette systems announced to that date removed the tape from the cartridge to wrap it around the revolving head drum. In the RCA system, a hinged lid at the forward end of the completely enclosed two-reel cartridge was automatically lifted when the cartridge was inserted in the slot in the deck and the

one-piece headwheel entered the cartridge. The headwheel contained four record-playback video heads to scan the ¾-inch-wide tape, which moved at three inches per second. The deck was designed to play through any television receiver when attached to the antenna terminals. Excellent color and picture quality were observed at a recent demonstration of the new VTR. RCA estimated that a blank cartridge containing enough chromium-dioxide tape to play for one hour would cost about $30. The system used two narrow sound tracks, similar to those employed in audio cassette systems, to provide an option of stereophonic sound for prerecorded musical videotapes when a home stereo system was used along with the television receiver.[33]

In July 1972, CMX announced a new CMX Edipro-300. The company acknowledged the high costs of investment with and impracticality of the old CMX-600 machine. The costs of using the CMX-600 were sky high. Edit houses were charging $330 to $400 an hour or $1,200 to $2,000 a day to use it. At $300,000, only busy studios or large production companies could afford it. CMX made several changes in the new machine. First, the laborious disc transfer was gone; editing was to be done directly at the studio's VTR facility. Second, the light pen was gone; it had a keyboard patterned after the familiar teletype machine that controlled the CRT display. Three VTRs could be controlled so that dissolves, as well a A/V cuts, A only edits and V only edits could be made. A minicomputer was part of the system, and a preview mode that allowed the editor to see their decision. When the editor was satisfied with their decision, they pressed the record button and the playback VTRs (up to three) made the recording. Alternatively, he machine could be used with the CMX assembler, meaning the final tape would be made up automatically after all editing was done. The so-called simplicity of the original CMX-600 was gone.[34]

Also in July 1972, Central Dynamics Ltd. announced the PEC-102 editor. It was a simple device using the SMPTE time code to identify each tape's position. It employed a low-cost minicomputer and had a CRT that did not display the picture but did show graphically the positions and edit command status. It was designed to interface with a video production switcher. It was planned to use helical-scan machines for the editing process and superimpose the time code over the picture. By selecting the edit points, a schedule of edits could be built up on a teletype reader and the final assembly made automatically.[35]

In July 1972, it was reported that Sony had won its first battle to sell cartridge television to the military in the USA. It seems that the U.S. Army was dissatisfied with the Ampex one-inch machines that it had previously used. They had ordered 500 more Sony machines that would be

1971. Ampex ACR-25 video recorder. (Ampex.)

added to the number the army was then using. The main reason the army chose the Sony machine was that it was the only commercially feasible unit available. Both the army and navy had been using Ampex one-inch machines, but the navy was reluctant to follow the army's lead in not buying "American."[36]

According to one authority, Ampex's one-inch machine was heavier than Sony's and its tape-guide system was erratic, so that programs recorded on one machine could not be played back on another. Users felt that although Sony's machine did not have all the "bells and whistles" it was more reliable. So the army gradually replaced their Ampex machines. It was claimed that if the one-inch machine would not work, Ampex would take it back, fix it then resell it, and finally take it back again. They would sell the same machine two or three times. Ginsburg agreed that Ampex had made a lot of bad machines during this period which did little to add to the company's stature in the industry.[37] In the TV stations, the maintenance people could fix them and keep them going, but in business, commerce and schools it was a cantankerous machine.[38]

Later (in October) it was reported that after the trial run of 600 U-matics by the army's audiovisual division, the army had decided to standardize with Sony's system and would buy 6,000 to 10,000 more units the following year. It was also reported that it was being adopted by such corporations as Coca-Cola, Prudential, Merrill Lynch, Maytag and the Ford Motor Co. Sony's plan to corner the market with the machine as a training tool for business, industry and large organizations was coming to fruition.[39] In March 1973, it was reported that Sony was about to increase production of its U-matic recorder in excess of 10,000 machines that year.[40]

In August 1972, the Bell Laboratories announced that they had built the first all-solid-state color camera. It used arrays of charged-coupled devices (CCDs) that the Bell Labs had developed and announced in March 1972. The color camera had three CCD arrays, fabricated with tungsten metal electrodes deposited on silicon dioxide substrate. Each contained 128 by 106 elements. The camera was announced by Michael F. Tomsett who had helped develop the original CCD chips. Also important was that it made up the interlaced scans needed in a standard TV picture. Doubling was needed because the CCD array was divided into two halves; an image section and a storage section. To achieve a 525-line picture, 263 elements would be required in each section. It was claimed that CCDs would have a striking advantage over traditional Vidicons, in addition to small size and low power consumption, their fabrication and readout mechanism were far less complicated than those of the other thin-film and silicon solid-state cameras.[41]

1975. Experimental solid-state device by the Bell Labs. (Bell Labs.)

In September 1972, it was announced that Echo Science Corp., formed 18 months before by the merger of Westel Corp. and Kinelogic Corp., was going to start producing a full line of helical-scan videotape recorders for broadcast use and allied applications. The new equipment would be shown at the NAB the following March in Washington.[42]

In September 1972, AMPEX advertised that its new VPR7950 was the world's highest-performance one-inch color/monochrome recorder. It featured the very high carrier mode (7–10MHz), had two independent audio tracks and used high-efficiency ferrite video heads with 500 hour warranty. Capstan-controlled high-speed tape cycling modes, velocity loop tension servo, direct coupled drum servo, and a new digital time base corrector were also features.[43]

In October 1972, Ampex decided to scrap its Instavideo project. In the reorganization of Ampex, Instavideo was the last home market machine to be closed down. It was decided that an adequate return was not possible in the current market place. This was the most recent act of a company that was desperately trying to recover from a self-acknowledged "catastrophic" financial period.[44] Another contender for the home recorder race had withdrawn. This group now included CBS with its EVR, RCA with its Selectavision and now Ampex with its Instavideo.

1972. CBS shooting *Sandcastles*. (CBS.)

In October, the first single-camera production produced for CBS, "Sandcastles," was presented on Tuesday, October 17, 1972. The show had been taped on location at Malibu Beach and CBS Studio Center. A single hand-held Norelco color camera was used for all but one scene. The equipment was included in a special vehicle built by Compact Video Trucks, Inc. for Metromedia Productions. Equipment included a Norelco PCP-70 camera and a high-band Ampex VR3000 recorder at a cost of some $400,000. Editing was to be done with a CMX-600 off-line editor interfaced with a VR2000.

The CMX-600 had been developed by CMX Systems as a joint effort of CBS Inc. and Memorex Corporation. It was specially devised by the CBS-TV network engineering and development department under William Connolly. It had reportedly cost some $5 million and taken five years of development.[45] The result was an electronic editor that was supposed to replace the technical part of videotape editing . The trained film editor was meant to sit down and start their edits. It had no keyboard — only two monitors and a "light pen." It was to be used like the old-fashioned "moviola." All good takes were to be transferred to a bank of disc drives and be ready for instant use. They could be called up in any order; in other words, in a random-access manner. By pointing the light pen at the right-hand monitor, the editor could do everything necessary to edit the various takes into a finished program. The results of their decisions were sent to a computer memory tape, so that with an automatic VTR assembler, the show could be done complete with cuts, dissolves and so on.

It didn't work that way, though. It seems that the new machine had many faults. First was the high cost, around $500,000. Second, there was the high cost of maintenance. Then third, there was a limit of 27 minutes of disc time. The disc drives had poor video response — some 150 lines in black-and-white. The audio was also very limited.[46] The amount of time that it took to transfer the tape to the various drives was enormous and nothing over 5 minutes could be transferred to a disc. A whole list of time-code numbers had to be entered into the computers along with the audio portion. Then anywhere from three to six studio VTRs would have to be used for final assembly. None of this was mentioned in reference to the machine's ability to do instant edits once all this prior work had been done. The machine was only capable of straight cuts, although it was claimed that it could do fade-ins, fade-outs and dissolves.

It was known that the CMX-600 had been moved to CBS Studio Center where it would be used to edit the picture. Of course this was all done in defiance of a union contract that prohibited any electronic shooting, taping and editing from being done at Studio Center. While the union (IBEW) complained bitterly, CBS went ahead anyway. Things progressed so badly with the new machine that it was claimed that CBS wanted to station it at TV City in return for TV City doing the videotape assembly. This of course was unacceptable to the union.[47]

However, CBS really didn't care about the machine. The important thing was that videotape had been shot and edited at Studio Center and nothing would change that fact. A new era of labor relations had started. CBS, which once was the jewel of the television industry for its employees, was now showing a grim side that had never been seen before.

The program took 32 days to finish and deliver, with a 12-day shooting schedule. The program was very poor, it got bad notices, and soon disappeared. According to the *Los Angeles Times*, "it was only an experiment, but by working within the limitations of using a single camera, we ended up making the picture at about the same cost and length of shooting schedule as if we had used film." As a result, Metromedia abandoned plans to shoot its next theatrical feature "Catch My Soul" using the CBS system and used only film cameras. Part of their problems was the crew: "[CBS] spent half their time educating them in use of the electronic equipment." So much for film people using video equipment.[48]

Daily Variety was quoted as saying, "The first use of single camera video-production techniques edited by the CMX-600 for a TV movie hit an unfortunate snag. What was going on in front of the camera? Tape method came off with appearance of a live performance, [and] what was being taped was lifeless."[49]

The only rave review given to the process was by Delmer Daves, an old-time cinematographer, who watched the shooting and was so amazed at the wonders of electronic production (instant playback, color correction, shooting at low light levels, and so on) that he was overwhelmed. As he put it, "Oh baby, you HAVE come a long way!"[50]

1967. Ampex battery-operated VR3000 with monochrome camera. (Ampex.)

In October 1972, a new videodisc player was introduced by Philips of Holland. Color television programs of 30 to 45 minutes' duration could be recorded on one side of a new kind of disc, resembling a gramophone record of normal LP size. For playback of these video records, a player had been developed, based on an optical pickup principle, for connecting directly to a television set. The system was flexible in use, providing stills, slow-motion or reverse-motion pictures from the recorded scenes.

Information was stored on the disc along a spiral-track. The disc rotated at a speed of 25 revolutions per second (European standard) and each 360 degree revolution of the spiral track contained the information needed to reproduce one complete television picture (two fields). The track consisted of a series of microscopically small oblong pits. All pits were of equal depth and width, and it was their variation in length, and distance from one another, that contained all the information required. For example, the luminance information was carried by the

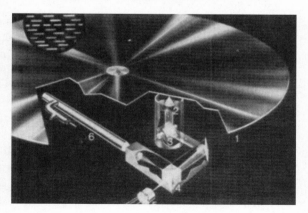

1972. N. V. Philips video long-play disk system. *Above:* Video player with disk. *Middle:* Closeup of grooves for signal. *Bottom:* disk and player mechanism. (Philips Labs.)

varying distance between corresponding points in successive pits, and the chrominance information by the varying length of the pits. When the pits were transformed by playback from a spatial pattern into a temporal sequence the resulting electrical signal was a train of pulses constituting a carrier. Luminance information was therefore conveyed by frequency modulation of this pulse carrier and chrominance information by pulse duration modulation.

In the player, an extremely small, high-intensity spot of light produced by a helium neon laser was used for information pickup. This spot was automatically centered on the track by an optoelectronic control system, allowing an extremely small track pitch. Light reflected by the record, and modulated by the moving pits, impinged on a photodiode; this delivered an electrical signal which, after processing, provided a signal to be fed to a television set. Since information was picked up without mechanical contact, neither the record nor the pick-up system wore out.

In manufacture of the discs, a compound similar to gramophone record material was pressed between molds. After pressing, the records were coated with a thin, reflecting metallic layer. "Cutting" the master record took as long as the duration of the program, so the output from normal cameras, videotape recorders on telecine, was comparable with the production process. Philips stated that the cost of the player would be about the same as a 26-inch color set.[51]

Late in October 1972, at the 48th annual convention of the Educational Broadcasters in Las Vegas, IVC introduced its first new cartridge video recorder called the VCR-100. It was specially designed for the top end of the closed-circuit television market as well as for industrial, educational, medical and government use. It was stressed that the new cartridge recorder was completely interchangeable with all of IVC's recorders. Three VCR-100 models were available: a color playback unit at $1,900; a monochrome recorder-player for $2,300; and a color recorder-player for $2,700. Deliveries were to start in March 1973.[52]

At this convention, Sony announced that it was going to produce at least 100,000 U-matic players during 1973. According to a Sony spokesman, the main buyers were industry and government. They were not pushing the entertainment industry at the moment but he did not preclude it. Also shown were Magnavox's single-tube color camera and Shibaden's one-tube unit, both to be available the following year.[53]

In November 1972, a new helical scan recorder was announced by Robert Bosch Fernsehanlagen GmbH and the Electroacoustic Division of Philips. They had taken the basic one-head Philips machine of 1961 and had turned it

1972. *Above:* International Video Corporation's (IVC's) new one-inch cartridge recorder/player. *Below:* Closeup of player. (IVC.)

into a professional color recorder. It followed the recommendations of the EBU. Using chromium dioxide tape, it had a signal to noise ratio of 44db over a bandwidth of 5.5MHz.; the moiré value was greater than −35dB; and differential amplification and phase errors were less than 5 percent and 5 degrees respectively. The K-factor (2T and 20T) was less than 2 percent. The time error between playback signal and studio sync was less than ± 2.5 nanoseconds. Either PAL or SECAM could be recorded. In addition to a time-base error corrector, it had a velocity error compensator. Finally, a built-in dropout compensator was included.[54]

In November 1972, a new development in the video player field by RCA had the television industry wondering and there were some predictions that it could be as revolutionary as color TV. At press time RCA was making no comment except to concede that the development did indeed exist and that the following description in *Radio Electronics* was substantially correct.

"RCA has quietly begun demonstrating to a few select television set manufacturers and others in the TV industry a long-playing color videodisc system that is said to use an inexpensive player and low cost conventional-appearing records. The device has not been seen by the writer or any representative of the press. But we have talked with enough qualified engineers (none from RCA) who have witnessed a demonstration to feel that it is of major significance as a potential new home product.

"What RCA was demonstrating to a select few was a device that resembles a conventional phonograph, plays 12-inch discs, but is attached to a color TV set and is capable of playing 20 minutes of color picture plus stereo sound from each side of the disc—a total of 40 minutes for both sides. It is a playback-only device and can not make recordings. It spins at 400 to 500 rpm and apparently uses the traditional needle … [and] grove pickup system. Those who witnessed RCA's demonstration were impressed with picture, color and sound." The eventual price for the player was to be under $400.[55]

On December 12, 1972, MCA unveiled its Disco-Vision videodisc system. In poor demonstration, the pictures were soft and deficient in the red area and there were innumerable dropouts. It was admitted that the showing was "premature" but they didn't wish to have RCA's system become the industry standard. The pickup was a low-powered helium-neon laser. The 12-inch disc was made of .010 inch-thick Mylar and was far more pliable that LP records. The disc was inserted into the player inside its plastic container. It was single-faced and played on the bottom side. Pitch was 80 microinches per revolution with 12,500 tracks per radial inch and speed was 1,800 rpm. It was claimed that in addition to random access, it allowed high-speed, slow-motion, reverse-play and picture-by-picture replay.[56]

In January 1973, it was reported that film still dominated the news. Sixteen millimeter film cameras were less expensive and far more accessible and it was stated that "one doesn't send a $90,000 camera to the scene of a riot." Most stations were set up to process and edit their own 16mm film. As far as video was concerned, the most popular equipment was the versatile Norelco PCP-90 portable color camera and the Ampex VR3000 portable high-band color recorder. It was claimed that videotape footage of Henry Kissinger's speech in October 1972 went on the air on CBS while the news film was still in the processing tanks.

However, the major deterrent to the use of video gear for news work was convenience. While the portable camera could be used directly, by microwave link, editing was another problem. It would have to be edited at the station for use on broadcast machines that were usually being used to record or air programs. Editing facilities for videotape similar to those for 16mm news just didn't exist at that moment. Unless TV cameras were self-contained, and VTRs lighter and more fool-proof, stations that might like to switch were not sure that they should. In addition, the editing problem still had to be resolved.[57]

However, in January 1973, NBC began regular news coverage with a PCP-90 color camera at its Washington station WRC-TV. It then installed another one at WNBC in New York in February and would soon install a third one at KNBC in Los Angeles. The PCP-90 camera was the same camera used by CBS News. In fact it was the camera that was developed by CBS Laboratories as the Minicam and now licensed for manufacture by Philips Broadcast Equipment Corp. It was described as "the smallest thing that does regular, broadcast quality, live and tape, electronic picture taking," by NBC News president, Richard Wald. Wald became a believer when CBS News, on a couple of occasions, scooped the NBC News people thanks to the use of this camera. At an affiliates meeting in Los Angeles in May 1973, the PCP-90 camera was on sale for between $180,000 and $200,000. None were sold to the affiliates, though. No word was mentioned about the recorder that CBS News was using, but it is presumed that it was the AMPEX-3000.[58]

In March 1973, Echo Science Corp. showed a new one-inch VTR, the WR201C. Total weight was 38 pounds with rechargeable battery. The recording format was the two-head helical system that had a scan angle of 13 degrees and a track length of 3.7 inches. It had a tape speed of 15 ips, writing speed 1,460 ips, and a record time of one half-hour on an eight-inch reel. Electronics was high-band, NTSC color direct. Echo also showed the WRR411C, a studio model using the same format. It was a table model weighing 140 pounds with an overhead bridge-holding picture, waveform, and audio monitors. Playing time was one half-hour on a 12½-inch reel. Both systems met broadcast specifications.[59]

In March 1973, it was reported that the Avco Cartrivision recorder had hit the consumer market. In order to accommodate two hours of playing time, a new type of rotating drum was used. It had three heads that permitted recording every third field and then three scannings to reproduce the video. Since this system was nonstandard, it came complete with a color TV as a total package. It was to be sold by Sears, Montgomery Ward, Teledyne Packard Bell, and Admiral.[60]

At the NAB convention in March 1973, the time-base corrector (CVS-500) of Consolidated Video Systems was first shown. It was the hit of the show, even though it had to be seen at suite K708 in the Shoreham's Ambassador Room, as Consolidated had applied too late to get a regular booth. It was called "revolutionary" and the "biggest thing since the introduction of the VTR itself." It was described as a time-base corrector with an exceedingly wide window, one about 30 times greater than that of other TBCs. Thus it would work with a wide variety of VTRs. The only connection between the recorder and the CVS-500 TBC was through the video output of the recorder. The composite video signal was converted to digital pulses and stored. It was then processed *in time* against "house" sync (or the built in EIA sync generator) and *in quality* by stripping and reinserting burst information. It locked up in milliseconds. Remarkably, it did this entire analog to digital conversion and the signal processing, and still only $8,750.[61]

When it was plugged into a helical VTR unit, such as those available from Ampex or IVC (selling as low as $2,500), it would produce a color picture comparable to that previously available only from significantly more costly transverse VTR units. The savings to the financially limited broadcaster or CATV operator were in excess of $75,000 according to CVS officials.[62]

At this same time, the people at Television Microtime Inc. down in Shoreham were displaying a similar unit — the Delta 44 time-base corrector, which was the end-product of four years of evolutionary systems. Delta 44 had a price range of $5,500 (for a monochrome-only unit working with half-inch VTR machines) to the top of the line at $20,000. A midline unit selling for $9,300 was compatible with all four standard tape configurations — two, one, three quarters and one half inch. Unlike the CVS representatives, who emphasized the use of their unit with helical machines, Television Microtime's engineers felt that the Delta 44 would be most attractive to possessors of older transverse units equipped only for black-and-white, who could utilize the product in lieu of purchasing a new color-equipped transverse machine.[63]

At a conference of the National Association of Broadcasters in March 1973, Ray Schneider of CBS-TV stated that for news gathering, videotape was faster, cheaper and potentially less obtrusive. Schneider told the engineers that CBS News Washington had been divided 50-50 between film and videotape crews. He said that in all instances "videotape gets to the editor faster and on the air faster than film."[64]

In May 1973, at the first International Television Symposium held in Montreux, Philips showed their new prototype, the LDK15 portable color camera. It was fitted with a combined one-inch Plumbicon tube and image intensifier.[65]

Also shown in May for the first time was the new IVC 9000. This revolutionary machine was a segmented scan machine using two-inch tape. (Segmented scan was the invention of Alex Maxey of Ampex who had applied for a patent on it on June 24, 1959, and received USA Patent no. 3,159,501 on December 1, 1964.) Segmented scan was

1972. BCR GmbH 60 broadcast color recorder. (*Fernsehen.*)

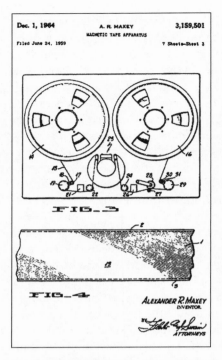
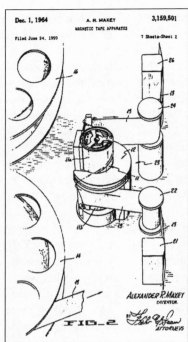

FIG_3

FIG_4

1959. First segmented helical-scan patent. Alex Maxey, USA Pat. no. 3,159,501 filed June 24, 1959; issued Dec. 1, 1964. Assigned to Ampex. (U.S. Patent Office.)

chosen for a variety of reasons. First, the EBU wanted something better than the two-inch transverse machine then in universal use throughout the world. The two-inch transverse recorder was some 16 years old, and seemed to have reached its peak of perfection. Based on experiments on the BCR 60 (Bosch), the IVC 9000 (IVC) and the Ampex 7900 (which failed due to audio problems), they wanted a new standard for helical recorders. The machine had to have 90 minutes' playing time, two high-quality audio tracks plus a control and cue track, video signal-to-noise ratio at least 44db, differential gain of less than 5 percent (weighted), differential phase of less than 5 degrees, and moiré less than −35db.

As a result of cooperation between two European partners, Rank in England and Thomson CSF in France, the new standard was expected to replace the old transverse standard worldwide. Segmented scan was chosen for a variety of reasons. First of all, ferrite heads could be used that gave a flat response to 18MHz. (Ferrite heads were so brittle that they could not stand up under the pressures of the transverse recorders.) Second, it allowed the

use of high-energy tape. Third, a longer head life of 3,000 hours could be achieved, as could a play time of two hours on two-inch tape running at a tape speed of 8 inches/sec. The machine used two heads. IVC went to super-high-band 9.9–12.3MHz that reduced moiré characteristics in both PAL and SECAM. In addition, there were two high-fidelity sound tracks, a cue and control track and a SMPTE address track. The company claimed that the machine had low operating costs, especially in tape usage. The price was to be under $100,000.[66]

What was surprising was that both Ampex and RCA were considering new standards for their transverse machines due to the EBU request: RCA, a so-called QUAD II, and Ampex, a new proposal in general. The RCA QUAD II expected to use a tape speed of 15cm/sec (6 inches/sec) on two-inch tape, two high-fidelity audio tracks and video that met EBU objectives. Signal-to-noise ratio would be improved and segmentation errors lowered. The machine would be able to use high-energy tape for improved signal-to-moiré ratios. RCA expected to be able to use narrower video tracks and to reduce guard bands to get room for a second audio track. According to RCA's Arch Luther, this was possible as the head had servo capability. Video performance was upheld by use of a super-high-band modulator and a time-base compensator, plus a chroma compensator which used a continuous inner pilot tone in the recording signal. RCA said the QUAD II machine would be switchable to play standard transverse, and therefore called it a compatible new standard.[67]

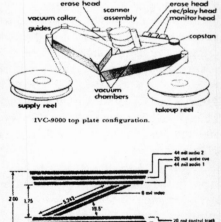

IVC-9000 top plate configuration.

IVC-9000 PHYSICAL PARAMETERS

1973. Above left: IVC 9000 segmented helical color recorder. *Top right:* IVC top plate. *Bottom:* Physical parameters. (IVC.)

Charles Anderson of Ampex contemplated the following changes "as a small adjustment of several parameters." Ampex was running experiments to: (1) reduce the headwheel radius by about 1.5mm; (2) reduce the vacuum guide radius by a slightly smaller amount from 26.24mm to about 24.8mm. This reduced the head-to-tape pressure and allowed the use of ferrite heads and thus longer life; (3) Modify the entrance geometry of the vacuum guide to minimize disturbances caused by the contact of the video head with the tape; (4) reduce the longitudinal tape speed to at least 19 cm/sec (7½ inches/sec) and possibly to 12.5 cm/sec (5 inches/sec); this would require an improved capstan and servo to achieve the necessary tracking stability; (5) consider the addition of a pilot tone to achieve improved correction of velocity errors and cheaper time-base stabilization; because the headwheel and vacuum guide radius had been reduced, room was now available for the addition of a second, good-quality audio track; (6) see whether noise-reduction schemes may be used; (7) to check if high-energy tape in the 450–500 Oerstad range allowed for narrow tracks and lower writing speed and thus less tape usage, even though the cost of high-energy tape was greater. Anderson said the new format could reduce tape costs by two thirds and head costs could be halved. Because Ampex would change headwheel dimensions, the machine could not play conventional transverse unless the headwheel systems were interchangeable, an approach Ampex was considering.

Anderson and Luther looked at various parameters that could be changed — tape, writing speed, tape speed, heads, track widths and format — and the outcome was a case against helicals. One of the great difficulties with a segmented helical was that stop motion, slow motion and other special effects feasible with them were not possible at that moment. (Later on, means were made to achieve such special effects). Neither helical nor segmented could be spliced physically. Luther claimed that RCA had an experimental model of the super-high-band machine operating in their laboratory in Camden.[68] Ampex knew that what it had proposed was not compatible with existing transverse machines without some kind of machine alteration, and that many of RCA's proposals had merit. The truth is that both these proposals were too late; they were obsolete without the companies knowing it. A new series of helical-scan machines would soon take over their duties.

In July 1973, RCA announced a new portable videotape recorder, the TPR-10. It was claimed that the tape, speed, format and high-band signal were fully compatible with such RCA machines as the TR-60 and TR-70. It provided 20 minutes of recording time and was designed for both news and special events coverage. It was housed in two packages: the transport, weighing 45 pounds, and the electronics, weighing 65 pounds. No price was given. It was quite similar to the portable Ampex VR3000.[69]

In July 1973, it was reported that, for the first time, a time-base corrector, a Delta 44-328 made by Television Microtime, Inc. had been used with a Sony U-matic cassette machine. It seems that Sterling-Manhattan Cable TV was looking for another high-end color helical recorder. Instead, they bought a Delta 44 and connected it to the U-matic recorder. They found that they could take the output of the ¾-inch recorder and stabilize it so that it was indistinguishable from play back on transverse machines, even on home TV sets with trigger-happy horizontal locking circuits. They stated that while it may seem absurd to put a $9,300 TBC behind a $2,000 recorder, it had paid off. They were able to dub from the U-matic to a professional machine for editing and other purposes. The output was NTSC phased color even though the input was heterodyne color.[70]

In October 1973, it was reported in London that a new system for sending written material for on-screen display (teletext) was being developed by the BBC called Ceefax. The Independent Broadcast Authority was showing Oracle. Both Ceefax and Oracle were thought to be the simple first steps towards a home data terminal. In each case, the consumer used a telephone type of push-button array to select the material they wished to view. The material was sent in "pages" and included news, stock market reports, weather updates, and police and traffic information. Generally the material would be presented in black-and-white. It could also be used for deaf or foreign language viewers.[71]

In October 1973, an all-solid-state television camera was demonstrated by the space and defense systems division of Fairchild Camera and Instrument Corp. It was the size of a cigarette package, measuring 3½ by 1½ by 2¼ inches, weighted six ounces, and had a power consumption of one watt. The resolution of the camera was about 100 lines. The unit displayed had 10,000 discrete CCD photosensors. The CCD sensors were basically bulk silicon that released charge carriers in proportion to the amount of light received. The charges were transferred by a clock system and transmitted to a TV receiver. The camera was developed for the U.S. Navy as a low light level imaging device. It was a commercial product and Fairchild said that it would be on sale later that year.[72]

On November 1, 1973, Eastman Kodak Company showed for the first time two new products for use with Super 8 film. There was a new Super 8 single-system sound camera loadable with either 50 or 200 foot magazines. There was also a new ultra fast processor called the Supermatic 8 that took the film in the cartridges and processed it with a dry-to-dry time of about 8½ minutes. Pictures shown at the conference seemed in the top

1973 Fairchild MV-100 all-solid-state TV camera. (Fairchild Corp.)

bracket. Acceptability for news gathering would remain an open question until a substantial tryout had been completed. Eastman said that the products would be available around June 1974.[73]

In November, a four-year patent controversy between the Ampex Corp. and International Video Corp. (IVC) was started again as IVC filed a $25 million antitrust suit against Ampex in Chicago. It was a countersuit against an Ampex patent infringement suit filed the previous month. IVC claimed that Ampex had engaged in monopolistic practices in the late 1950s and that Ampex refused to grant to IVC the same licensing privileges that it granted competitors before. IVC claimed that it had to design equipment around Ampex patents, resulting in higher costs to it. The Ampex suit against IVC alleged that IVC had infringed on Ampex's patents, particularly in the use of an FM broadband magnetic tape system. The suit was a continuance of a 1969 suit by IVC asking the court to determine that it was not infringing on Ampex patents. The lawsuit was later withdrawn by IVC.[74]

In November 1973, it was reported that CBS News was using a new three-tube Ikegami Tsushinki color camera weighing 12 pounds that had been developed by Ikegami in cooperation with NHK's engineering department. It seems that NHK in Japan was looking for a smaller color camera than the large American color cameras. A CBS engineering delegation visited NHK in Japan to discuss technologies. At NHK they were told about the new Ikegami (HL-33) lightweight camera. CBS was so impressed with it, that it bought it in order to start an all electronic news station at KMOX in St Louis. Other networks such as ABC soon followed CBS's lead.[75]

The videotape recorders used with the Ikegami camera were VCR-100s by IVC, Sunnyvale, CA, and the time-base corrector were CVS-500s from Consolidated Video Systems of Santa Clara. Marshall Davidson, vice president of CBS News, pointed out that the entire system cost about $30,000 for the camera: time-base corrector, $8,750; two VCRs at $3,000 each; and camera at about $15,250. He

pointed out that CBS's use of the system was the first time that a network had combined a small portable color camera with a helical-scan videotape machine. He said he hoped to have three more systems in use by 1974, and that by 1976, 50 percent of CBS's news operations would be so equipped. Other CBS news units were using the Norelco PCP-90 portable color camera and the Ampex VR3000 portable high-band color recorder.

The principal problem with the system was in editing one-inch tape. Davidson complained that there was no up-to-date small editing devices to be had. Even though CBS/Memorex had developed a helical-scan editing device for $100,000, it was "too sophisticated. We are looking for an inexpensive, desk top unit." Nevertheless, the new system was limitless and would be invaluable in covering fast-breaking stories by eliminating the problems encountered in film coverage. Dan Crossland of CBS News in Los Angeles and Al Pierce of WBBM Chicago, both concurred. Davidson concluded that it was not the be-all and end-all he was looking for, which was a complete system weighing 25 pounds that could use half-inch or quarter-inch tape.[76] Nonetheless, the change over from film to tape for news had begun.

In November 1973, Ampex announced a miniature video recording machine weighing only eight pounds using one-inch tape in a helical-scan wrap. Called the MS-1 it had a 20-minute recording time, a bandwidth of 3.5MHz, a dynamic range of 35db, and took only 40 watts supplied by a nicad battery pack. It was intended to be used in the instrumentation of analog or digital devices, as well as in television.[77] The recorder cost $39,000 and the playback unit, MX-1, $120,000: both would be available early in 1974.[78]

It was reported that as of January 1, 1974, that there were 118,500 cartridge and cassette recorders in use in the USA. More than half of the devices were the Sony U-matic machines, with 65,000, and second was the Philips half-inch helical scan with 27,500.[79]

In January 1974, Broadcast Management/Engineering did a survey of the battle between tape and film. They concluded that tape had certain inherent advantages that would allow it to take over more and more of film's territory, but a takeover by tape was not for right now. *Broadcast Management/Engineering* found that film had its strongest supporters among a body of directors and producers (plus the majority of directors of photography) who had lifetime experience in film; when asked why they did not change to tape, they answered that film had become a "habit" for them.

Because of the widespread use of the Sony U-matic, many producers had set up networks for distribution and other tape usage. Thus certain large postproduction shops such as Reeves, Teletronics, and Screen Gems had a massive business in tape duplication. This taste of tape had many producers wanting to use tape all the way. For the broadcaster, the video camera was looking more and more like the dominant visual recording instrument of the future.

When it came to editing, it was here that tape had made its major inroads. Professionals agreed that editing a program on videotape was now 50 percent cheaper (mainly in the cost of time) than editing the same program on film.

In distribution at that moment in 1973, it was 55 percent film, 45 percent tape. Everyone agreed that tape was moving forward at the expense of film. When it came to news gathering, 16mm film was still the dominant medium in television. However, the number of crews using TV cameras was increasing considerably in spite of the tremendous costs of converting from film to tape ($50,000 for film to tape as against $17,000 for tape to film).[80] In May 1974, it was estimated that some 700 staff crews and 3,000 freelance film crews consumed some 260 million feet of film annually at a cost of more than $55 million.[81]

Sony had created a defacto standard with its U-matic. It had made the exchange of information as easy as putting a cassette in a machine. In the audiovisual world there would be no more clumsy 16mm film projectors to thread up, focus and run. The dominance of 16mm sound film for information, education and communication was finally being challenged. The audiovisual world eagerly took the U-matic to its bosom. Television as an educational medium was about to show its power. Industry and government found it a superb means of communicating with its facilities wherever they may be. The low cost of mass duplication made it a very attractive medium. The high cost of the machines at first, well over $1,000, didn't seem to be a barrier. Finally, shipping costs of the cassettes were reasonable.

As one author stated, the U-matic aroused surprisingly strong interest from educational, industrial and even professional customers and Sony quickly proceeded to modify the machine and supply accessories, such as an editor/player with those markets in mind.[82] The Sony U-matic was the right machine at the right time and in the right place. It was well designed, quite reliable, well-built and needed few repairs, and it didn't need a technician to run it. Unlike EVR, Selectavision or any videodisc, an added feature was that the machine could also record programs either off the air or from a camera if needed.

In February 1974, Consolidated Video Systems announced a new CVS 504 signal digital video corrector to bring nearly all helical-scan color signals up to broadcast color standards. It would work on any nonsegmented he-

lical using from half-inch to two-inch tape. The unit had a built-in EIA sync generator, processing amplifier and velocity compensation. It was priced at $9,850.[83]

In February 1974, IVC announced new models of the IVC-500A broadcast color cameras. They now used two Plumbicons and a silicon diode tube for the red channel. Over 300 of the IVC-500-As had been sold in the last two years, according to IVC.[84]

On March 19, 1974, at the meeting of the Association for Education Communications and Technology, Sony introduced a new U-matic videocassette recorder-player about the size of a portable typewriter and weighing less than 31 pounds. It operated on rechargeable batteries and on AC or DC, and was the world's first such portable unit. A demonstration showed quality comparable to broadcast quality. The videocassette recorder was expected to be priced at about $3,000 and a portable camera at $3,500 to $5,000 when the equipment became available at the end of that year.[85]

In March 1974, it was reported that Cinemobile Systems (a Taft Broadcasting subsidiary) and Consolidated Film Industries in Los Angles had built a $500,000 portable TV facility. They had a complete studio with two Fernseh KCR-40 color cameras and a RCA TPR-10 portable color recorder. This merger of TV and film was the first effort of the film industry to take advantage of tape's flexibility in both shooting and costs. Consolidated was one of Hollywood's largest film processors, thus it had a foot in each camp. Also the work was done by the film union which insured them some jurisdiction over electronic cinematography.[86]

In March 1974, RCA's electro-products division announced that it had achieved full TV resolution in a solid-state device for the first time. It used a CCD that had four times the resolution of any disclosed CCD imager. The device had a bandwidth of 3MHz and date rate of 6MHz. It was claimed that the pictures, for all practical purposes, were indistinguishable from those produced by a commercial Vidicon. The 512 by 320 element area array built by RCA's three phase imaging technology was contained on a 500 by 750mm superchip. It was laid out in the standard three-section format: a 256 by 320 element image area; a 256 by 320 element storage area; and a 320-stage output register which shifted the video signals out at the 6MHz rate. The image seen was interlaced on an alternative field to generate the required 512 by 320 picture elements per frame. In actual use, only 486 lines (243 per field) were displayed, leaving the extra elements for varying the system's blanking and timing to avoid nonuniformaties at the picture's edges.[87]

In March 1974, at the NAB convention in Houston, both Ampex and RCA were there with new machines. It was Ampex and RCA's answer to the introduction of IVC's

VR-9000 the previous year. Both American machines were supposed to have many new features.[88] RCA announced its new technology TR-600 transverse tape recorder; Ampex brought its new AVR-2 which was a modular machine that could be built in many configurations.

RCA's TR-600, company officials said, featured simplified operation, was sharply reduced in size and weight, making it suitable for either studio or mobile-van use, and had been designed with built-in automatic systems formerly available only as options. It was said to provide one-second machine lockup for stabilized color pictures and, among other advantages, to offer substantial savings in electrical power consumption, using 1.5kw as against 3–5kw for comparable recorders. The new unit weighted but 700 pounds. It could be run at either 15 ips or 7½ ips. To further combat IVC's thrust, RCA talked tentatively about how it might offer two audio tracks on the machine. The TR-600 would be available in 1975. Its specs were fine: video (highband) S/N ratio 46db (43db); K factor 1 percent (1 percent); low-frequency linearity 1 percent (2 percent); differential gain 3 percent (3 percent); differential phase 3 degrees (3 degrees); Moiré 43db (32db); audio S/N ratio 55 degrees (55 degrees); wow/flutter 0.1 percent (0.05 percent); and brackets for 625 lines/50 standard.[89]

The Ampex Corp. which was responsible for videotape recording in the first place, displayed several models of its latest generation VTRs at the NAB. Headlining its exhibit was the AVR-2, a modular transverse recorder Ampex described as the world's first. As the name suggests, the new hardware built up from simple to complex configurations, all offering performance Ampex considered competitive with far more elaborate units. The basic unit was in two parts, with deck and associated time-base corrector unit, each capable of being carted by two people together. They could assemble either in a studio or in a mobile van.

1975. RCA TR-600 transverse color recorder. (RCA.)

More ambitious operators could add a low-boy console with a monitor bridge that would operate at either 7½ ips or 15 ips. The VTR listed from $69,000 to $92,000 depending on the number of bells and whistles one wished to add.[90]

It was reported that Ampex had scored something of a coup. Without advance publicity, the company had unveiled a modular-design studio transverse unit. The two-piece system — three pieces if one included a monitor bridge — was designed as a studio unit which could be reassembled to fit portable or mobile requirements. It was stripped of some of the automatic features found in the AVR-1.

Operationally the unit was designed to run at 7½ ips and 15 ips and to deliver two audio tracks. Implying that the AVR-2 achieved much of what the IVC-9000 boasted, Ampex said, "the AVR-2 studio console is designed to work side by side with standard transverse recorders/reproducers in the Ampex tradition. We believe the AVR-2 fits the right needs at the right time." To get the two audio tracks, Ampex did resort to a compromise: it split the existing audio track. This meant signal-to-noise dropped to 46db (from peak operating level) on the dual mode but this could be restored to 50db if Ampex 176 tape (a new formulation) was used (specs applied to both 15 ips and 7½ ips). For single-track operation, S/N ratio was 53db, both speeds.

The total system, electronics, tape transport, a monitor bridge, weighed approximately 630 pounds. The transport was 150 pounds and the electronics module was less than 200 pounds. Any of the modules could be lifted easily by two people. Power drain was very low — 1.5 kilowatts. Fast lockup time (one second in NTSC) was a feature, as a result of an extremely wide time-base corrector. The AVR-2 was *ready* to meet NTSC, PAL, SECAM and PAL-M standards, the company said.[91]

It was stated that by Ampex coming out with the AVR-2, they had leap-frogged RCA which announced that the TR-600 would be out for 1975 but that the Quad-II concept was not quite ready. Ampex came out with a position paper on quad arguing against certain RCA proposals. However, many of the RCA proposals had merit, but no more was heard of the Quad-II concept.[92] Ampex sold over $2 million worth of AVR-2s two weeks after the convention.[93] It was claimed that by December 1975, RCA had shipped more than 240 machines.[94]

RCA also showed its TR-70C. An RCA source called the TR-70C "our answer to helical-scan." Officials said that most transverse VTRs had switchable 7.5 and 15 ips speeds but that 15 ips was usually used because it produced better results. Now, though, they said, technological advances had made it possible to achieve high performance levels at the lower speed, as in the modified

1975. RCA miniature transverse recorder, TPR-10. (RCA.)

TR-70C. Half-speed operation was one factor in the Quad II format that RCA planned to propose to the industry when it completed the formal development.[95] RCA also showed its new miniature transverse recorder, the TPR-10. It was a portable unit using two-inch tape in high-band color. It was RCA's answer to the Ampex VR3000 which was then going out of vogue. It was meant for use in electronic journalism (EJ) or in small vans.[96]

However, while the AVR-2 was Ampex's brightest feature at the NAB, it was not alone as a new VTR development. Behind was the VPR7950A, a helical machine that featured a time-base corrector and had a base price of $31,480. It had unusually good stability by virtue of the built-in digital time corrector (the TBC-800) that featured a wide correction window (± 1H). The machine could lock up in four seconds and the stability was equal to that of transverse.[97]

As far as the new IVC 9000 was concerned, it was reported that six machines had been installed in Europe and that 44 more were back-ordered. U.S. orders were to be filled in July.[98]

Also shown at the NAB was a plethora of time-base correctors. In addition to the first original Television Microtime and Consolidated Video Systems, TBCs were those from: (1) Ampex, which had a TBC digital unit with a $10,000 to 15,000 range due in 60–90 days; (2) 3M, which had another digital corrector with a similar price; (3) IVC-Quantel had the TEC-2000 which they promised would have a 60-day delivery and be priced at $14,000; (4) CBS Labs, whose model CLD-1500 was due for fall delivery; (5) Lenco, whose machine would cost $3,500, but could not yet be delivered; (6) Kansas State Network, whose analog unit called the Signal Master, priced at $2,950, was aimed at CCTV; and (7) Dynasciences, with the model 5000 priced at $6,000 and due in 90 days.[99]

There were also many portable cameras on display. These were from Fernseh, Philips, RCA, Marconi, Asaca, Commercial Electronics, Editel, Hitachi Shibaden, Ikegami and TeleAlpha.

RCA's new TKP-45, a 20-pound shoulder mounted unit with a 6x zoom lens, had many automated performance features. Thus the cameraman could concentrate on composing pictures rather than making adjustments. For example, the TKP-45 included Chromacomp color balance, automatic lens iris, scene contrast compression and bias light. It could operate up to 1,500 feet from the CCU. It was part of the new TK-45A (successor to the TK-44A) color camera family.[100]

Fernseh's answer for electronic journalism was its KCR unit which was part of the family of KCR cameras. One of Fernseh's cameras was put to use covering President Nixon's visit to Houston. The backpack contained an automatic processing amplifier and batteries. Fernseh offered several options for getting the video signal into the broadcast system: via microwave link, with a second person carrying the microwave transmitter; via cable (triax); or via recording, on a portable recorder (carried by a second person).

Marconi's unit unveiled at the show was part of a family. It was dubbed the Mark VIII-X. One of the very smallest (three tubes) electronic camera systems on display was Asacas's ACC-5000 which had made a hit the previous year. Its self adjust and auto-control features made it easy to operate and it had a genlock capability which permitted it to be used as part of a system.

Also back again was Editel. This year the company had, in addition to the previous years, Mark III, a hand-held camera designed specifically for one-person electronic journalism. Called the ENC-1, the unit included three broadcast Plumbicons. It was a complete system in that it could be battery-operated. (A triax cable would permit up to 500 ft extensions.) A complete complement of lenses was available.

An extremely light three-tube Plumbicon TV camera was the Ikegami. It included a microwave system in its backpack. This unit had seen use by CBS News on the West Coast. Called the Handy-Looky, it could operate on a single coax up to 1,500 meters (5,000 ft) from the base station.

A rugged unit that was designed for use by NHK Broadcasting, Japan, was shown by

1974. *Above left:* Two RCA commercial solid-state cameras using the RCA 512 × 320 element CCD sensor. *Right:* Actual image sent by the camera above. (RCA.)

Hitachi Shibaden. The unit incorporated a special single-tube camera and was being used with a portable cassette VTR (Philips VCR) as a complete news gathering system. Through the use of a CVS TBC, the recorder output could be brought up to broadcast standards.

Something of a real surprise was a full broadcast-quality portable backpack unit unveiled by Commercial-Electronics, Inc. It used three Plumbicons or, optionally, a silicon diode red tube. The camera was very small by virtue of all tubes being located in a single plane. It was equipped with a 10:1 zoom.

One of the most interesting systems, though it was not working, was the TeleAlpha, Inc. with an Akai camera, half-inch cassette and cartridge playback-editor deck which they called a NewsTape Processor. One could play back the tape through a TBC. The Sanyo tapes played for 20 minutes and were not much bigger than an 8 track cassette. Most of the above systems were in the $35,000 to $40,000 range.[101]

In May 1974, it was reported that Joseph Roizen, President of Telegen and a video consultant, had been awarded the EMI Premium by the Royal Television Society of Great Britain for a paper on the Rank Cintel 9000 Broadcast Video Recorder. He had been consultant to this project from its inception until November 1973. He was invited to receive his prize at the Royal Television Society Flemming Memorial Lecture held in London in April 1974.[102]

In June 1974, it was reported that more than 7,000 Ampex and RCA transverse machines were in use, 4,000 in the USA alone. When it came to helicals, IVC claimed that they had sold over 12,000 of their one-inch machines for closed-circuit operations. This was in addition to several thousand Ampex, Sony and Panasonic closed-circuit machines.[103]

In June 1974, it was reported that Engineers at the BBC Research Department had built an experimental machine for recording color television signals in digital form. It used a standard instrumentation tape transport, and the information describing the eight-bit digital signal was divided amongst 42 parallel tracks along the one-inch tape. It was a longitudinal recorder running at 120 ips.

Most of the signal processing was carried out on 42 identical printed circuit boards. The machine could be locked to an external clock, timing and skew correction being carried out automatically. A system which detected and concealed most of the disturbances resulting from tape dropouts had been designed with the particular characteristics of digital magnetic recording in mind. Results were very good.

The recorder was intended for use as a research tool in the development of improved methods of error detection and correction and to ascertain whether a number of possible techniques for reducing television bit rate might be safely applied several times in succession during the history of a signal. Earlier work by the BBC team in this field had produced, among other things, a digital stereo sound recorder.[104]

1974. BBC digital VTR using 42-channel longitudinal recorder with one-inch tape at 120 ips. (BBC Labs.)

In July 1974, it was announced that Consolidated Video Systems had been awarded the 1974 Emmy Award for "The application of digital video techniques to the 'Time Base Corrector.'"[105]

In September 1974, NBC News announced that it had purchased 29 hand-held Bosch-Fernseh color cameras. The 40-pound Fernseh compared favorably with NBC's Ikegami cameras, which would stay in use. Fernseh promised a steady delivery schedule and won the contract over competion from Ikegami. NBC News stated that it cost $200,000 to equip each news crew, but estimated that with the Fernseh equipment they would save $4,000 per crew on the costs of film and processing.[106]

In October 1974, CMX introduced their latest CMX System/50 stand-alone computer-assisted videotape editing system. For the first time, the machine was using Sony U-matic cassettes instead of the disc drives. The system had a keyboard so that the editor could actually create accurate cuts, wipes and keys. Previews of edits and re-edits were visible, and the edit decisions could be auto-assembled on any on-line System 300.[107]

In November 1974, Amperex (the new name for Philips in the USA) introduced a new ¾-inch Plumbicon color tube. It was claimed to have higher resolution than any other comparable sized pickup tube. Aimed at the EJ market, it could be used in poor light and had high stability over a wide range of temperatures. Picture smear was near zero.[108]

In December 1974, the Ampex Corp. announced a heterodyne accessory to its new TBC time base corrector that permitted either direct color or heterodyne color recovery from helical scan video recorders. The kit was priced at $1,995. It was stated that ABC had ordered five of the units for electronic journalism.[109]

Late in January 1975, RCA showed a series of CCD TV cameras that were supposed to operate on the 525-line standard. The sensor was a silicon imaging device with an array of 5,123 by 320 elements, for a total of more than 1,630,000. It was the largest such device yet offered and had the highest resolution. RCA said its resolution was comparable to that of ⅔-inch Vidicon tubes. It had high reliability, low power, low size, long life, and highly stable and precise picture geometry.[110]

In January 1975, CBS News director Marshall "Casey" Davidson spoke of the progress that CBS News had made in the field of electronic journalism. He stated that for some years they had been unhappy at the 1.5 million feet of film shot every year covering the news. Davidson was disturbed that Super 8 was being considered as a substitute for 16mm film, so he thought it would be wise to go directly electronic. He claimed that the hardest part of this conversion was to "convince our engineering people that this was indeed a straight replacement for 16mm; as it turned out, the quality was much better than film."[111] Starting in 1971, they had equipped a few crews with PCP90s and the Ampex 3000 to get a feel for electronic gathering of the news. A series of outstanding newsbeats in 1971 and early 1972 gave the impetus for electronic journalism, but obviously lighter, more flexible cameras and recorders were a necessity. This effort was aided by the CBS engineering department. The result was that CBS News settled on the Ikegami camera with the Sony portable U-matic model 3800.

A two-person crew handled the two units easily, with all the benefits of EJ. First, they could take this equipment abroad (where there were no film processing facilities) such as the Near East and Moscow. Using Sony editing units they were able to get edited material on the satellites within a very short time of shooting it. No standards conversion was needed as the signals were NTSC and excellent pictures were received. As far as the future was concerned, Davidson expected digital cameras, smaller more efficient recorders and microwave units. "In ten years," he said, "the way we handle the news now will look very old-fashioned."[112]

NBC was working towards electronic journalism, but at a much slower pace than CBS. They also started using the Philips PCP90 and the Ampex 3000. NBC claimed that this combination gave excellent results but was too bulky and heavy to replace the 16mm film cameras. So they went to the Ikegami camera and Sony 3800s and Microwave Associates microwave transmission equipment. NBC was cautious and claimed that only 50 percent of their news coverage in three years or so would be fully electronic, and perhaps 85 percent by 1980. They claimed that EJ was just at its beginning.[113]

ABC also had a few crews equipped with Ikegami cameras, Sony 3800 U-matics and Microwave Associates microwave equipment. However, ABC complained that the slowness of tape editing, compared to 16mm film editing, was holding them back.[114]

In January 1975 at a conference of the SMPTE held in San Francisco, Edmund DiGiulio, president of Cinema Products Corp. (the leading manufacturer of 16mm film cameras) had a few well-chosen words to defend 16mm film in its demise at the hands of electronic journalism. He resented being the "man in high button shoes" fighting the last ditch defense for news film, but he was doing just that. He questioned that the price of EJ could really be so reasonable and that it could really return its cost in some seven years. He stated that Eastman Kodak had never been known as a "shrinking violet" and expected that "we're going to develop new hardware, and new techniques and we're not going to go, 'Smiling into the sunset.'" He finished by stating that "we are going to enjoy the competition. We're going to welcome what has been done electronically."[115]

In February 1975, Fairchild Camera and Instrument Corp. announced a new all-solid-state camera, the MV101, incorporating charge-coupled device technology. The sensing device had 10,000 photosensors on a standard 24-pin dual in-line integrated circuit unit. The camera had a 100-line horizontal resolution and a bandwidth of 1MHz. It came with a five-inch TV monitor adapted to the 123 frames per second sweep rate.[116]

In February 1975, Sony announced a new two-inch helical-scan tape recorder for direct high-band NTSC recording. Its servo-controlled, dual-capstan transport minimized jitter. It had a full-field video head configuration that virtually eliminated switching transients, color banding and other problems associated with multihead systems. It was not intended for broadcast use, but rather for the industrial-educational sector.[117]

In March 1975, Asaca Corporation of America showed its portable one inch four head transverse color backpack recorder. It was a high-band portable using a six-inch reel, could record up to 30 minutes and was compact, weighing only 35 pounds. It used long-life ferrite heads and performed erase, fast forward and rewind. Instant on-the-air playback was possible with a time-base corrector.[118]

The unit was described as the AVS-3200. It served as the basic unit for the portable color video system. Compact size, light weight and high reliability were achieved through the use of integrated circuits. Together with a heterodyne system modulator and low-impedance driving video recording amplifier, the AVS-3200 had a built-in video preamplifier playback system. The portable VTR playback adapter APA300 enabled full demodulator output. Naturally, by adding the time-base corrector ATC-300

1975. Asaca one-inch transverse color backpack recorder. (Asaca.)

to the demodulator output, perfect color reproduction was obtained. Moreover, all the functions of the servo system were housed in the portable VTR. Using a 6½-inch reel made exclusively for the portable VTR, the device permitted 30-minute video recording. The reel hub conformed to NAB standard and it could therefore be mounted on a stationary VTR. Power was supplied to the AVS-3200 by the battery unit (ABU-300) or by the AC pack (APU-300).[119]

In March 1975, Ampex announced that it had delivered its 200th AVR-2 recorder. The historic machine went to the Canadian Broadcasting Company which then had 32 AVR-2s.[120]

In March 1975, Consolidated Video Systems claimed that they had received a basic patent covering the general technique of correcting certain video signal errors by means of a time-base corrector. (The patent issued January 14, 1975, was USA no. 3,860,592.) As described by Bill Henderson of CVS, it was an all-inclusive patent for digital time-base correction that might put them in a commanding position. Consolidated Video Systems also described a new CVS 600 synchronizer which could store a full frame of video, thus permitting full synchronous operation between any two video sources. It also had an option to compress the signal into one quarter size and position it anywhere in the picture.[121]

Consolidated Video Systems stated that by May 1975 they had an 80 percent share of the time-base corrector market. They claimed that with its wide window of over 90 microseconds and an impressive 57db signal-to-noise ratio, the 504A, plus optional improvements, totally corrected velocity errors from either heterodyne or direct color VTRs.[122]

Also its acceptance as an accessory to the new Sony U-matic recorders assured its supremacy. It seems that using the Consolidated Video Systems technology meant that the TBC gen-locked to the studio, which was convenient. Working with the Micro-Time System, the studio had to be gen-locked to their TBC. This was awkward at first, but later on the their TBC could be locked to studio sync also. Television Microtime Inc., which had started a year before Consolidated, was fighting a losing battle.[123]

In March 1975, Sony introduced a new line of U-matic machines: the VO3800, with two audio channels; the VO2850 editing VTR, using vertical interval insert switching; and the RM400 automatic editing control unit with slow speed search and freeze frame.[124]

On April 16, 1975, Akio Morita held a press conference in Japan announcing the company's new small portable videotape recorder, the Betamax SL-7300 deck. It was introduced in the USA as the console model SL-6300 which came with a 19-inch Trinitron included. At $2,295, its appeal was limited until the arrival of the Betamax deck LV-1901 which went on sale in February 1976 at $1,295.[125]

The LV-1901 was a recorder deck only and attached to any TV set. It could record a program being viewed, record a program on a different channel, record automatically with a digital timer and play prerecorded tape.[126] Blank tapes were selling at $15 or $16 a piece for a full hour. According to a noted authority, the new deck took off immediately. It seemed that many rich people wanted to be the first in the neighborhood to have it, and sales soared. The company claimed to have sold 25,000 decks and a quarter of a million tapes to support them.[127]

The story of the development of the Betamax is interesting.[128] With adoption of the U-matic as a de facto standard worldwide, it was decided by the middle of 1974 that Nobutoshi Kihara had built a prototype that fulfilled the requirements laid down by Masaru Ibuka. It was dubbed the Betamax. (Beta is a Japanese painting and calligraphy term for a brushstroke so rich that it completely covers the paper area beneath it, just as the video signal would now completely cover the tape.)

In some ways the Betamax was a scaled-down U-matic, but provided the same recording time in about one third of the tape surface needed by U-matics. The tape was a half-inch thinner and ran at 1.6 inches/sec. The two video heads were canted 7 degrees in opposite directions and provided for increased recording density by eliminating the guard bands between adjacent video tracks. Since the color signal was recorded at the low frequency of 688kHz, special processing was needed to eliminate cross-talk. A comb filter was used to lift out the desired signal and cancel cross-talk components.[129]

By coming up with a gentler and more exact tape transport and guide system and a new formula for the binder, which reduced the tendency of the tape to stick to the head, Kihara had managed to decrease the thickness of the tape by 25 percent. He had cut the track width from 85 microns to less than 60, largely by incorporating a smaller recording head and using tape with magnetic powder made from a cobalt alloy. These refinements, along with the key breakthrough of azimuth recording, had paved the way for an overall drop in the rate of tape consumption of about 75 percent, from 2.81 square inches to 0.78 square inches a second.

It was claimed that a patent for azimuth recording had been applied for in 1959 (Japanese Utility Patent no. 39-23924 filed June 20, 1959, issued August 18, 1964) by one Shiro Okamura, a professor at the Tokyo University School of Communications. It seems that Matsushita Electric had used it in a two-hour black-and-white recorder in 1968. In azimuth recording, the two heads are mounted at angles slightly off perpendicular to the tape — one slanted to the left and the other to the right. This results in an improvement in the ability of each head on playback to pick up only the track it meant to play, and a significant falloff in its tendency to pickup the adjacent track laid down by the other head. While it works well in black-and-white, it does not work so well in color because much lower frequencies are involved and a loss of response which varies with the frequencies. (The ¾-inch tape of the U-matic moved at a speed of 3.75 inches a second; the half-inch tape of the Betamax at 1.57 inches a second.) The Betamax cassette, with a recording capacity of one hour, was indeed the size of a paperback — scarcely more than a third the volume of a U-matic cassette — and it could be manufactured for half the price. The machine, when it went into production, would weigh 40 pounds compared with the U-matic's 60. Equally important from a cost standpoint, Kihara and his colleagues had integrated the circuitry into as few units as possible, drawing on a body of expertise that Sony had developed while making its well-regarded Trinitron televisions.

Everyone who counted at Sony now believed that the long-cherished goal of a VTR for the home had been realized. But for the Betamax to fulfill this high hope, Masaru Ibuka (Sony's founder) and Akio Morita (Sony's chairman) thought that it needed one attribute — compatibility. They wanted to make the Betamax, like the U-matic, an industry standard. So, on September 29, 1974, the two vice-presidents of Sony, Kazuo Iwama and Norio Ohga, took a one-page diagram and a sample cassette to Matsushita Electric's headquarters in Osaka and proposed that the two companies (along with Matsushita's affiliate, JVC) jointly adopt it. Matsushita was three times bigger than Sony. With Sony's technological skills and Matsushita's marketing clout, the Sony people reasoned, the Betamax would be an unbeatable contender against any home videocassette recorder (or the equivalent) that another company — American, European, or Japanese — could possibly develop. A week later Iwama made the same presentation to the top people at JVC. Sony intended to put its first Betamax models into production by the end of the year, but the company took the position that Matsushita and JVC would not suffer by coming along a few months later because history showed that the demand for a new product built slowly. All three companies, Sony argued, would be starting off on essentially the same footing.

More than a month passed, however, without any response from either Matsushita or JVC, and in the middle of November, impatient for a resolution, Morita went to Osaka to talk president to president with Masaharu Matsushita of Matsushita Electric. "I told Mr. Matsushita that the home videocassette recorder will be the biggest item, next to the color TV, in the whole next generation of home entertainment," Morita recalled. Word came back that the engineers at Matsushita Electric had been unable to comprehend the details of Sony's design merely from a diagram and a single cassette. The company would need to see an actual machine before it could decide.

On December 4, delegations from Matsushita and JVC were received at Sony headquarters in Tokyo and treated to a demonstration. Ibuka and Morita had been nervous about disclosing so much before they had a commitment, but they took solace in their faith that a Betamax in action would surely resolve whatever doubts the people at Matsushita and JVC were feeling. It didn't. The JVC people responded perfunctorily, as if they weren't really interested. The Matsushita people, at least, raised some questions. Hiroshi Sugaya, the general manager of Matsushita's planning and engineering division, brought up the one-hour recording capacity. Matsushita's market surveys, he said, suggested that a home video machine ought to be able to record a two-hour program, and he asked if Sony would consider altering its format to that end. He was told that Sony had examined the market and had determined that an hour would be enough — at least to begin with. Sony took the position that a small and inexpensive cassette was a higher priority than recording time. In any case, the company had already cast dies and made other preparations to be in production, so it was too late in the day for fundamental changes.

Once again Sony received no clear response to its offer — "We're still evaluating it," the Matsushita people kept saying — and the management began to get fidgety. If they delayed much longer, Ibuka and Morita were afraid the Betamax would lose its competitive edge. Sony prided itself on being ahead of other companies in product development, but what was the point, they had to ask themselves, if they didn't market a product when it was ready for the market? Sony was lucky that none of the other attempts at a consumer VTR had caught on, but there would be more to come.

After six months of waiting, Sony's patience ran out. On April 16, 1975, Morita held a press conference to announce the introduction of the first Betamax — the SL-7300 deck. Kihara was on hand to demonstrate what a Betamax could do, and an observant American reporter asked if he was, in fact, the inventor of the product. Morita gave the reporter a lecture in reply. "It would be bad for company morale," he said, "to single out an individual engineer's part.

The SL-7300 cost 229,800 yen (when U-matics were selling for nearly 400,000 yen), and Japanese consumers found it much more pleasing than any of the previous "home" VTRs that had come their way. The Betamax might not be for everybody—not yet—but railroad engineers, airline pilots, and other high-salaried types with odd working hours took a strong interest in the ability to turn any time into prime time.

In the United States, the marketing began with the console model SL-6300, which came with a 19-inch Trinitron included. At $2,295 the SL-6300's appeal was limited. The real test, Sony knew, would come with the arrival of the Betamax deck, and when it went on sale in February 1976 at $1,295—a price that, with the severe inflation of the early seventies, was comparable to what black-and-white and color TVs had cost in their infancy—interest increased dramatically. "It was fantastic, really," Harvey Schein of Sonam said later. "When you have a new product that is as jazzy as a videotape recorder, you really skim off the cream of the consuming public. The Betamax was selling for over a thousand dollars, and the blank tapes were fifteen or sixteen dollars each. But there were so many wealthy people who wanted to be the first in the neighborhood that it just went whoof like a vacuum. It flew off the shelf, and then the tapes flew off the shelf as well, and there was a tremendous shortage of tape. At one point, I remember, we were amazed that we had sold something like twenty-five thousand videotape decks, and we had about a quarter of a million tapes to support that. We had expected people to buy six or eight blank tapes with each machine. Instead, they were buying twelve or fifteen or more. And lo and behold, all the tapes were gone!"[130]

In March 1975, RCA announced an experimental "tubeless" color camera. It used three postage stamp size charge-coupled devices, one for each of the three colors. The image size on the CCD was 7.3 by 9.75mm or close to that of $2/3$-inch camera tubes. The CCDs were 512 by 320 element devices. Known as a SID (silicon imaging device), each sensor had the ability to resolve more than 163,000 picture elements which could be read out at 525-line rates.[131]

In April 1975, it was announced that the CBS Laboratories might be close to closing. CBS president Arthur Taylor said that the labs' professional products division was being acquired by Thomson-CSF, a leading French electronics company, effective May 1, 1975. However, Mr. Taylor said that the CBS Labs in Stamford, Connecticut, would continue to be the focal point of CBS's remaining research activities under the overall responsibility of Harry E. Smith, CBS vice president, technology. Renville H. McMann, Jr. would leave his post to become president of Thomson-Laboratories, Inc., as the new Thomson subsidiary would be known. Low profits were regarded as the main cause for the closing down.[132]

In June 1975, RCA took off the wraps of its capacitance disc system. The RCA disc was a plastic-metal-plastic sandwich with grooves like a phonograph record. The grooves, in the form of transverse slots, were read by a sapphire stylus containing a metal electrode. The electrode detected the changes in the capacitance of its tip and the distance between it and the disc's metallic layer. RCA planned a 12-inch disc for 30 minutes of playing time.[133]

It was reported in June 1975 that Cartivision—which produced the half-inch skip field system—had filed for bankruptcy. Even though the system had great support from many manufacturers, mechanical problems plus late deliveries of hardware and software sealed its doom. An investment of over $100 million had been wiped out, and the customers who had bought the machine were left without support.[134]

In June 1975, the first home VTR V-Cord system was introduced by Toshiba and Sanyo. It had a unique half-inch one-reel cartridge that conformed to EIA Japan type-one format. It could play at regular speed or half-speed in which the picture quality was good enough for home use. It was to be marketed in Japan at about $1,000. An advantage of the machine was the vast library of tapes now available for the EIA Japan standard and to be made available to consumers for rentals. To help this recorder along, Matsushita announced a tape duplicator that could turn out a 60-minute copy in three minutes.[135]

In June 1975, ABC announced that it had entered a $250,000 agreement with Consolidated Video Systems for four CVS 600 series electronic video synchronizers with video compression option. The synchronizer allowed signals transmitted by remote to be put on the air without time-base correction compensation. Compression allowed remote signals to be compressed to one quarter normal size and positioned on the screen in corners or overlap.[136]

In June 1975, Television Research International introduced a new $5,000 editor that was as easy to operate as a moviola and quite precise for nontime-code editing. It was claimed that the majority of film editors had put the video editing medium down and forced producers to use film or wait in line at a tape production house. The problem was not only in getting the film editors to learn electronic editing, but to even consider editing on line. Television Research claimed that they had broken this last barrier. Editors could now afford the luxury of rocking videotape reels back and forth when they were on low priced helical scan machines. Anything that resembled television technique was beneath them, though. They considered film as the only way to go, and old habits are hard to break. They didn't want anything with knobs and buttons in their way. So the industry was forced to make the editing of tape so similar to that of film that they would at least use it.[137]

In July 1975, RCA introduced its new TK-76 portable video camera. RCA stated that it had been patterned after 16mm film units. Self-contained with no backpack, it was priced under $35,000.[138] The three-tube portable featured a shock mounted optical system with a prism efficiency four times that of a standard field system. It weighed only 17 pounds including camera head, 10:1 zoom lens and electronic viewfinder. A separate power pack weighed ten pounds including batteries.[139]

Also in July 1975, RCA announced the TR-1000, a U-matic type of portable tape recorder. It used the KCS-20 U-matic tape cartridge and provided NTSC-type color signals. It was priced at $3,500.[140]

On November 5, 1975, Robert W. Sarnoff resigned as chairman of the board of directors of RCA. It seems that several years after David Sarnoff's death, the RCA Corporation, as it had been legally renamed, was experiencing management turmoil and internal stress to a degree unprecedented in corporate annals. The resulting turmoil at the top started in November 1975, when RCA's board voted unanimously not to renew the expiring five-year

contract of Robert Sarnoff, then 57, as chairman and chief executive officer.

Among the 15 outside and inside members, only one was a holdover from the last David Sarnoff board, but not one came to the defense of his son — even though he had personally selected, or approved the election of, each board member. They professed disenchantment with a lackluster earnings record and with internal executive conflicts. To the stunned second-generation Sarnoff, who had guided RCA for nearly a decade, the charges were unfair and without foundation. But he was unable to rally any support and his family's 44-year rule of RCA came to a headline-making end.[141]

As his successor, the board chose Anthony "Andy" L. Conrad, a career RCA employee who had risen through the ranks to the company's presidency in 1971, and who was one of the leaders of what the New York Times described as a "palace revolt" against the younger Sarnoff. Andy Conrad, a genial, low-key manager, lasted only ten months and 11 days. In the most bizarre episode in the company's history, Conrad, under pressure from the Internal Revenue Service, revealed that he had failed to file income tax returns for the preceding five years, even though he had paid most of his taxes through payroll deductions. On the advice of his attorney, he refused to explain why and the board summarily fired him.[142] He was succeeded by Edgar H. Griffiths.

In November 1975, it was reported that the Sony 1.3cm Betamax cassette system was being prepared for marketing in the USA for $2,295. The outstanding feature of the Betamax system was the low tape consumption. This was made possible by reversing the color phase polarity between adjacent tracks, thus eliminating the guard band. A comb filter technique was used to deal with the remaining cross-talk.[143]

In December 1975, CBS spoke of the remarkable growth of electronic journalism. All of the CBS-owned-and-operated stations were using it. Nonetheless, CBS was still a big user of film and would continue to use it. They didn't know what the final mix of film and tape would be. Capital costs of EJ were higher: $220,400 per news crew compared to only $87,000 for film. However, film stock costs $83,000 per crew per year against $5,982 for tape. Film cost $285.90 per hour versus $28.76 for tape. According to NBC, the competitive advantage of live pictures made conversion of TV news to all-electronic systems "only a matter of time."[144]

In 1975 in New York, General Electric demonstrated a new projection-TV system. It transmitted wide-screen pictures with standard equipment. The color TV camera was equipped with a cinemascope type (anamorphic) of lens to compress an 8 × 3 view into the standard 4 × 3 television format, which was then handled as an ordinary

AT LAST, A PORTABLE TV CAMERA WITH FILM CAMERA FREEDOM. RCA TK-76.

A way through the maze.
Today, portable TV cameras come in so many degrees of convenience, performance and price that a wise choice is hard to make.
A way through the maze is to ask these questions about any portable camera:
1—Can it be ready for instant use in fast-moving situations?
2—Does it handle like your film cameras?
3—Will it work with as few controls and with the same ease as a film camera?
4—Will its weight, size, automatic features and freedom allow your newsperson to concentrate on getting the best news pictures?
5—Does it have the quality for sports, documentaries, and some local spot news action?

or a comfortable, waist-worn 6-pound rechargeable battery belt.

Under $35,000.
Cost is a feature that makes the TK-76 downright revolutionary.
If you are going for two high quality

1976. RCA TK-76 portable color camera. (RCA ad.)

TV signal. At the receiving end, another anamorphic lens broadened the picture out again into the wide-screen 8 × 3. The process of compression and re-expansion was optical rather than electronic. Pictures could be up to 20 feet wide, which might make network wide-screen theater television practical. (This was some 25 years in the future, however!)

To get the light necessary for large-screen projection, G.E.'s single-gun light valve system was used. Illumination from a 650-watt sealed-beam xenon tube was modulated by passing it through a deformable membrane composed of an oily substance. The membrane was scanned by three electron beams that passed through three diffraction gratings, each of which transmitted one of the color television signals. Deformation of the membrane in accordance with the electrical signal caused it to transmit more or less light from the xenon tube. The optical image thus produced was focused on the projection lens which spread it out in the large-screen ratio.

The single-gun light valve was already being used in a number of industrial applications. Its single gun needed no convergence adjustments, and it was free of the problem of adjusting the image for picture and color registration that was practically insurmountable in the wide screen format for any system using three optical paths. It was thought that these advantages might hasten the day of the wide-screen "teevie" house.[145]

1975: RCA announced that its Magtape Selectavision home VTR deck using ¾-inch tape was behind schedule again. It was now planned for 1977 or later. RCA stated that the old deck was noisy and the controls were too hard to use. A new redesigned VTR was being worked on.[146]

In January 1976, Fairchild Camera and Instrument Corp. announced its new solid-state MV-201 which had 244-line resolution and a bandwidth of 1.86MHz. Its sensor contained more than 46,000 photoresistive elements. Designed for military and industrial use, it was priced at $4,000.[147]

In January 1976, an article discussed why tape was taking over in the electronic journalism field. At the station involved, WOR-TV, it seems that costs were the main reason. They reported that the conversion from film to tape would save them an estimated $50,000 to $65,000 a year. Raw stock (16mm) was costing about $65,000 a year alone. It was estimated that even with the high cost of tape equipment, the savings on film alone paid for all three Minicam systems, plus the time-base corrector, in less than one year. Labor costs were also less — it was now possible to send a two-person team, the camera operator and the reporter. Here the key person was the "universal" engineer who was responsible for every phase of the non-reporting operation. They ran the camera, brought the tape in from the field and worked with the reporter to edit the story onto the final two-inch tape. The engineer was not just a technician: their knowledge of every phase of creating the end product made them something of an artist as well. Furthermore, the engineer did not require special training in the operation of the Minicam — only familiarity with the equipment.

However, choosing the engineer produced some union problems. The people chosen were mostly studio camera operators who had covered news with large cameras and had the most experience with baseball, football, and other sporting events. Their knowledge of electronics also enabled them to make proper adjustments (and certain repairs) in the field, thereby saving stories that may otherwise have been lost.

WOR had to solve the union problem even though all employees were IATSE. Some employees objected to the *engineers* being assigned the news-gathering work. The dispute was solved by the NLRB which, in August 1975, stated that engineers could perform the news-gathering work assigned to them. The company then laid off the film crews, film processors and film editing operations staff, and reduced the crew to two people (plus the reporter of course). Finally, when the engineer was not in the field, they could work in the studio doing camera, sound, maintenance or similar duties. This gave the company full use of that person's time. This attitude was quite different from that in some of the major networks which claimed that their technicians were not creative and did their best to take their jobs away from them.[148]

CBS News chose a different approach to the union problem. CBS TV had a wide pool of excellent live camera operators, videotape editors and maintenance personnel to choose from. These technicians had been doing remote news (from trucks, busses and vans) for years using both recorders and live microwave transmissions. They were used to sports, remotes, field production, conventions, anything away from the studios. There was no problem in giving this new electronic journalism equipment to these people. The electrical union had jurisdiction over this equipment and the company did not argue this. However, according to Casey Davidson, over 50 percent of the camera operators were ex-film people and *all* his ENG videotape editors were film editors. Over 80 percent of his tape technicians were not in the news division before EJ. There were several minor attempts to give the editing jobs to reporters, but this was not pursued. It turned out that most reporters at the time would rather sit back and let an accomplished technician put their news together without having to worry about the techniques involved.[149]

In January 1976, the Ampex Corp. reported that profits for fiscal year 1975 were $10.3 million. Total revenues were $244.9 million, down 1 percent over 1974. It had recovered nicely from the depression period of 1972.[150]

In January 1976, Cinema Products camera company announced the new Cinevid-16 video assist system. They claimed that it was easy to attach to a CP-16R camera. It picked up the image directly from the reflex ground glass screen and transmitted it to any number of remote monitors or videotape recorders (for instant dailies). This was done by means of a ⅔-inch silicon matrix tube camera. The company claimed that there was virtually no loss of visible light in the reflex viewing system. The system included a video control console (with three monitors, plus wipe and dissolve controls) and a crystal controlled sync generator. This use of video for instant viewing was an old device. No longer was the camera operator shooting blindly; with this system, what was being shot could be seen instantly and played back if recorded. It was designed to give the film camera operator the same advantage that the electronic camera operator had had for years; namely, instant viewing. Cinema Products knew that the electronic camera was cutting into film's use steadily. They knew that by using an electronic viewfinder, it would speed up shooting, which it did. Of course, this was one more step to the "electronic cinema" where film would be eliminated completely and all shooting done on videotape.[151]

In February 1976, Ikegami claimed that over 300 of their cameras were in service, which was more than the total for all other manufacturers combined.[152] Also it was reported that the Transcendental Meditation Movement had ordered ten IVC-9000 recorders.[153]

Also in February 1976, Thomson-CSF Labs introduced the "Microcam" which they claimed was the lightest portable color camera out. It weighed eight pounds including lenses and viewfinder. (This was lighter than both the popular Cinema Products CP-16 and Frezzolini 16mm film cameras when fully equipped.) The camera used three ⅔-inch tubes and had a motorized zoom and a 1½-inch viewfinder. The camera unit included a two-line image enhancer, a comb filter,

1975. M-1 CP-16 reflex camera with Cinevid-16 video-assist camera. (Cinema Products Corp.)

full I and Q encoding and a three-position sensitivity switch that would make it possible to shoot video down to as little as five foot candles at a f1.4 lens opening. Resolution was 500 lines at the center of the picture and the signal-to-noise ratio was 52db at 4.2MHz. The total price of the unit was around $30,000.[154]

In February 1976, the Ampex Corp. and the International Video Corp. settled out of court an eight-year-old fight involving patent infringement. The settlement allowed each company access to each other's patents involved in the suit. The case was settled when it became evident, to IVC's attorney, that the case could not come before the district court for some time.[155]

In February 1976, a new Ampex digital recording system was unveiled on election night by the CBS-TV network. It was called ESS (electronic still store) and was a joint effort of CBS and the Ampex Corporation. ESS electronically converted the analog TV signal into digital form and stored the information on magnetic disc packs. Slides and stills could be randomly selected from bulk memory with access time of less than 100 milliseconds. It could store up to 1,500 frames on line. Access to the system was through keyboard controls located on an electronic rack or from remote-access stations. In addition to the recording and reproducing modes of operation, ESS could rearrange preselected stills in any sequence for inclusion in a program and independent outputs permitted previews, dissolves and mixed and special effects to be performed in the normal way at the studio.[156]

In March 1976, the 54th annual NAB Convention was held in Chicago. It was the biggest and most exciting show ever held. It was claimed that the highlight of the convention was the celebration of videotape's 20th birthday. On hand to celebrate this event were five of Ampex's

1976. Electronic still store (ESS) with Ampex DM331 disk drives. (Ampex.)

pioneers. They were Charles Ginsburg, Alex Maxey, Ray Dolby, Charles Anderson and Fred Pfost. (Missing was Shelby Henderson.) Ginsburg was still with Ampex as vice president of advanced research in video. Anderson was also with Ampex in charge of long-range video product planning. Maxey had left in the mid sixties to join Westel to promote his segmented helical-scan recorder for military applications. He had remained as vice president of Echo Sciences (formerly Westel) which had become Arvin Industries. Dr. Ray Dolby, of course, was becoming the biggest name in audio with his Dolby noise reduction systems. Fred Pfost left Ampex in the mid fifties and went into private consulting work. He made significant contributions to the first slow-stop motion disc by MVR and DMI. He was now associated with Videomax Corp. which refurbished video heads.[157]

There was also a luncheon on March 22nd featuring Douglas Edwards who narrated a series of archival videotape segments. There was a chronology of important events from the Nixon-Khrushchev kitchen debate to the Apollo moon landings. For this event, CBS took one of its original VTR1000s out of service and had it on display, with suitable graphics, on the NAB exhibit floor. Twenty-four individuals were honored for their pioneering efforts to get video recording developed.[158]

After 20 years, Ampex had shown that it was still the leader in videotape technology. It proved this by introducing a brand-new one-inch helical-scan recorder, the Ampex VPR-1, that provided still frame and slow motion. The most important feature of the recorder was a revolutionary device called "auto scan tracking" (AST). This completely eliminated tracking and interchange problems with helical-scan machines. It was so effective that there was absolutely no noise bar crossing the monitor during slow motion or frame stopping.

The VPR-1's automatic scan track system employed a special head system that moved in two planes. This technique allowed the head to be electronically deflected over the actual video path during playback to automatically follow any deviation from the "ideal" path.

The sensitive AST system instantly adjusted to a tracking error or interchange problem during playback without causing any picture disturbance. The customary guard band "noise bar" which showed up as the head shifted to a new track when the tape was slowed down, was entirely eliminated on the Ampex unit. (Any change in track was done during the vertical interval and was invisible.) It was quite remarkable to see a perfect picture maintained on the VPR-1 even during slow speed and still-framing with no jitter and a perfect still frame. This feature meant that AST could also play back many tapes which may have been improperly recorded and would be otherwise unrecoverable because of severe tracking errors. The AST system included a video head for conformity proof. It was to cost $9,000 extra. This feature allowed the user to see a simultaneous reproduction of a recording as it was being made. Prices started at under $20,000. Versions of the VPR-1 were to be available for NTSC, PAL and SECAM.[159]

To handle the special demands im-

1980. Block diagram of Ampex AST (auto scan tracking) servo system. (Ampex.)

1976. NAB convention — 20th anniversary of Ampex pioneers (l. to r.) Charles P. Ginsburg, Alex Maxey, Ray Dolby and Charles Anderson. (Ampex.)

1976. Ampex VPR-1. *Below:* Details of VPR-1 automatic scan tracking (AST) system. (Ampex.)

posed by the slow-motion and still capability of the AST system, a special digital time-base corrector accessory was offered. The TBC included a dropout compensator which replaced missing video information with material from the previously cophased line, and a velocity compensator, which insured high-quality, multiple-generation dubs. A burst-lock color recovery system was also available. In addition, the VPR-1 recorded all of the VIT and VIR signals. Only the first ten lines of sync were missing and were reconstituted on playback.[160]

The history of automatic scan tracking was told in April 1980. Ampex was looking for a way to correct tracking errors in helical recorders. Two parallel programs were started in 1968, and by 1973 the first AST-like device was built. A piezo-electric approach seemed practical. It used a bimorphic strip. By dithering the head up and down at a high rate (450Hz), both error amplitude and phase error could be determined. Next, the AST deflector was split lengthwise — the main portion of the element could be used to deflect the head and the smaller portion to send a signal to the positioning servo. Both sides of the bimorphic strip used separate deflection voltages. Three servos were used: (1) a static (DC) which took care of elevation difference between record and reproduce heads; (2) dynamic (AC) which followed the video track; and (3) was a scheme in which logic decided when it was time to leave one track and jump to the other (always in the vertical interval). The result was a no-compromise slow-motion recorder providing truly continuous slow motion. Credit for developing this system was given to Dick Hathaway and Ray Ravizza under direction of Don McLeod. It was officially introduced in 1976 with the Ampex VPR-1 type C helical recorder. It was called the most significant break through in recording technology since high-band recording was introduced in 1964.[161]

Ampex's biggest competitor, Sony, also came out with a new one-inch helical-scan machine. It seems that Sony at last was going to enter the studio broadcast industry that was dominated by transverse machines. Theirs was the compact full-broadcast-quality one-inch helical VTR, the BVH-1000. It was a 1½-head design. One video head was followed by a second head to pick up the vertical interval pulses between fields which was a unique (though old) design feature. It also could display still frame and slow motion with no tracking problems.

Both the VPR-1 and the BVH-1000 offered good tracking, still frame, slow motion and frame-by-frame editing. The Sony achieved good tracking by virtue of four servo systems: a drum servo, a dual capstan servo system and reel-take-up servos. (It was not, however, the equal of the Ampex AST system.) The dual capstan feature metered tape onto and off the drum with even tension. So that the servos never lost control, a second sync pulse head picked up where the video head left off. This was a unique feature of the Sony design.

Both Sony and Ampex offered two full bandwidth audio tracks plus a cue channel. Both had built-in SMPTE time code generators and reader for easy editing. Sony's price was $32,000 without the TBC, or approximately $45,000 with. The Ampex cost about $20,000 but without the AST feature.[162]

While Ampex didn't realize it at that moment, the introduction of automatic scan tracking made sure that the one-inch helical scan would soon make obsolete the two-inch transverse recorder that it had invented and put so much effort into. AST made it possible to do all kinds of slow- or fast-motion effects with absolutely no chance of head mistracking. A comparison of the two designs showed that basically they were very close to the same. In writing speed, Sony was 1,000 ips while Ampex was 1,010 ips. Also track geometry was different (one head versus one and a half). It was suggested that slight changes in Sony's (not Ampex's) format would make it possible to have a single one-inch standard. It was the latest and probably the most important of all of Ampex's great achievements.

Soon after the announcement of the BVH-1000, Sony was already making deliveries of the machine. The first three went to CBS-TV, Hollywood. Other customers were WXLT-TV, Sarasota, FL, and the Transcendental Meditation Group (which had recently bought 10 IVC 9000s). The Ampex VPR-1 became available late that summer. The first customer was Sask-Media, Regina, Saskatchewan.[163]

There were other new video recorders as well. Bosch Fernseh introduced its BCN line which was supposed to take the place of transverse recorders. This became known as the Type B standard. The company had worked out an agreement with IVC, Philips and RCA to make and sell the BCN segmented scan system.

The BCN design was fundamentally different. To circumvent the tracking problems heretofore encountered in helical machines, the BCN system used two heads and a segmented-scan approach. The length of any field was thus half that of a one-head machine — only 80mm. The field was divided into a number of segments. Each segment consisted of a package of 52 lines (the precise number of segments per field depended on whether the system was PAL or NTSC). The BCN system boasted absolutely no interchangeability problems. Two heads meant that there was the possibility of banding occurring, but this was automatically adjusted for by the BCN. In terms of comparison with early transverse machines, the system occupied about one third the space and consumed one third of the power. Tape consumption was also one third.

Three units were available that were designed to

meet all applications. The BCN-20 portable battery powered unit (44 pounds) offered one hour of recording time and featured an assembly edit capability. The BCN 40 was designed for use in OB vans. The BCN 50 was a full studio machine including processing and time-base correction functions, a monitor, an oscilloscope and a vectorscope.

The same standard scanner was employed in all three system versions. Its weight was one third that of conventional transverse machines. The scanner (a self-contained, independent unit which also incorporated the driving motor) could be replaced easily. Automatic "air lubrication" between headwheel and tape was a special feature of the headwheel. A better than 300-hour life of the video heads (made of hot-pressed ferrite) was expected. Two rotating erase heads on the headwheel permitted electronic editing with single-frame accuracy. There was a fast forward and reverse mode (30 x) to find edit points quickly.

The BCN format had four additional tracks: two broadcast studio audio tracks suitable for stereo recording with the Dolby "A" noise reduction system, another for cue recording (e.g., time code), and a control track for the servo system. Bosch Fernseh demonstrated excellent pictures at NAB (including a demonstration of 11th-generation dubs).

In the way of a comparison, all of the new one-inch systems offered lower initial costs, lower tape costs and quality equal to or better than that offered by transverse machines. Bosch guaranteed 300 hours on headwheels which it said could be replaced in minutes (the scanner came out in seconds). Sony said it guaranteed 500 hours from its heads and that a replacement of its single crystal ferrite head was only $300. Changing a head was a 20-minute job. There were no figures from Ampex. The Ampex machine did have a second verification head. Presumably this added to cost and to tape wear since there were two heads riding the tape. Operating and replacement costs of heads were bound to be a factor which broadcasters would look at closely.[164]

However, Ampex was still relying on the transverse machine that it built so well. The company showed an improved version of its AVR-3, which was a dual band VTR compatible with existing broadcast equipment. It featured a new development called "Super High Band Pilot" (SHBP) which enabled it to provide incomparable picture quality. SHBP virtually eliminated "banding" due to velocity and internal errors.

Equipped with an optional edit controller, the AVR-3 could be programmed to handle a wide range of editing functions then possible only with computer-editing systems.

The AVR-3 also offered automatic switching between

1976. Ampex AVR-3. (Ampex ad.)

bands and tape speeds. It could be configured with one of several pairs of bands for NTSC, PAL and SECAM — SHBP/high-band; high-band/low-band color; or low-band color/low-band monochrome — and for 15 ips and 7.5 ips operation. Standard on the AVR-3 were a digital time-base corrector, editor, a new digital auto tracking system, fully servoed reels, constant-tension tape servo, video-head optimizer and vacuum capstan. It wasn't inexpensive; prices ranged from $105,000 to $137,000. It was the ultimate two-inch transverse recorder.[165]

Since super high band and pilot had been a subject of some controversy in the past between RCA and Ampex, Ampex issued a position paper setting forth its strong views on the matter.

IVC was still counting on the IVC-9000. There was also a new half-speed version of the IVC-9000 called the IVC-9000-4. At 4 ips, a single reel ran four hours. S/N ratio was 47dB (as good as most transverse machines). Its prime application was archival storage and it offered big savings in tape. A standard 9000 could be converted to play at 4 ips in about 15 minutes. It was priced around $95,000.[166]

In the video enhancement area, a new "Crisp-Matic" by Yves C. Faroudja, Inc. not only increased the S/N signal but improved it. A newcomer to the field, it reduced noise and chroma/luminance cross-talk. Improvement was stated to be 3db for an input S/N of 40db or better.

Details were not available because of a pending patent, but apparently the rise time of signals was improved. The Crisp-Matic did use a special horizontal enhancement process which depended on the generation of new frequencies in the luminance path which were above 2MHz and gave the subjective impression of a full bandwidth. The residual subcarrier and other interfering modulation products were combed out of the composite signal and noise coring was used to improve the S/N ratio. Price of the unit was $29,500.[167] It was claimed that the device had been sold to the U.S. Army, Sony, CBS and the AFRTS. A PAL/SECAM version manufactured by YFI was introduced at the IBC convention, it had been assigned to a British firm for European distribution.[168]

When it came to portable cameras, Thomson-CSF showed its new eight-pound Minicam camera. (CBS was to take the first 50.) The RCA-76, one by NEC, the Ampex BCC-4, a new Ikegami HL-77 weighing only 13.2 pounds, Hitachi with its new SK-80—all were there at IBC. The Asaca 2000 prototype was there too. It was an 18-pound camera using three ⅔-inch Plumbicons in parallel arrangement. It had a resolution of over 550 lines and a signal to noise ratio of 50db. It featured two-line image enhancement. Sony introduced its BVP-100 portable.[169] Akai unveiled its VTS-150 system incorporating a 5¾-pound camera using two Vidicon tubes: one for green and the other for red and blue. Horizontal resolution was more than 300 lines with a signal to noise ratio of 40db. The recorder used quarter-inch tape running at 10 inches per second giving 26 minutes of recording time. It was a two-head helical with crystal-ferrite heads. To use the recorder, a TBC such as the CVS 504A was needed.[170]

1968. CBS Minicam VI with three Plumbicon tubes. (CBS.)

In full-size cameras, there was the Ikegami HL 37. Harris showed its TC-3 portable which was actually the Asaca ACC-3000 with a Harris nameplate. JVC unveiled the 4800 and Panasonic its WV-2000. Finally, Philips was showing the Magnavox camera. Sony displayed its full-size BVP-200.[171]

There were new developments in disc recorders at NAB—at two ends of the price spectrum. At the lower end, using flexible discs, were Arvin Systems and Eigen Video. Arvin Systems' unit was intended primarily for still storage. Eigen's units were intended for slow-motion (sports, editing, freeze frame, animation). Three Eigen units were offered: a ten-second player at $12,500, a 20-second at $27,500, and a 30-second at $40,000.

Ampex introduced an updated HS-100, the HS-100C. The new unit included a built-in TBC, an integral clean-air system, and automatic circuitry. To avoid damage to the disc or heads, automatic lifters raised the heads free of the disc until rotation stopped. To avoid damage during freeze-framing, a flashing light alerted the operator when it was time to move the head to the next location. Prices started at $95,540.[172]

The previous year, Data Disc had created a stir by showing a unit smaller in size than the HS 100 and lower in price. Data Disc claimed unusual reliability for its machine since it had had experience designing such units for NASA. The company had not promoted this product to broadcasters in 1975, but it was back at NAB again, saying it was ready to go. The unit featured continuously variable slow motion, both forward and backward.[173]

Another area of improvement was time-base correction. Time-base correctors had made it possible to play inexpensive helical machines on the air while still meeting FCC sync and frequency requirements. Since the signal from the VTR had to pass through the TBC it was natural to try to improve that signal if possible. Dropout compensators, proc amps, and the like were common additions. In 1976 at NAB, Microtime showed a device that dramatically improved the signal out of a U-matic cassette. Not only did it correct timing deviation but it increased the signal to noise level and sharpened picture softness. Further, picture breakup caused by tape deck movement during recording was solved. All of these features were incorporated in the Microtime 2020 electronic signal processor. Video noise off tape was reduced by several decibels, resulting in a playback S/N ratio approaching 50db. Picture "crispening" was provided by the built-in Image-Ex, with front-panel control of image, which compensated for the softness exhibited by ¾-inch U-matics.

The 2020 also eliminated another U-matic characteristic—that of the shifting of chroma relative to luminance as head wear progressed. A control was provided which moved chroma over a range of 400 nanoseconds. The correction range of the 2020 was ± 2H lines— approximately 30 percent greater than in prior units. To eliminate picture breakup caused by a moving deck, an Auto-Track feature was incorporated.

A new digital "universal" signal processor capable of producing broadcasting quality signals from all color videotape recorders was introduced at NAB by IVC. The new TBC-2200 worked with direct and heterodyne helical machines, noncapstan-servoed VTRs and segmented field VTRs. The TBC-2200 had a 3¾-line correction window and a five-line store. This wide correction range permitted correction of extremely difficult to handle color signals. A "look-ahead" velocity compensator measured errors line by line and corrected on that basis. A dropout compensator reinserted correctly timed luminance and chrominance of the proper hue and saturation as long as the dropout lasted.

When used in conjunction with an ENG system, the TBC-2200 accepted nonstandard synchronization sometimes inherent in hand-held cameras and introduced a standard output. Noncapstan servoed VTRs required the use of the MDA-150 power amplifier to play back synchronized, standard NTSC signals. It was produced by Quantel Ltd. for IVC. The TBC-2200 was priced at $18,000.

Consolidated Video systems surprised broadcasters by introducing a nine-bit, four-times subcarrier sampling technique in its new CVS model 520. The higher sampling rate meant improved bandwidth capability, K-factor specs, and signal to noise ratio (60db p-p signal to rms noise). The 520 was designed to handle transverse machines; the IVC-9000, helicals and U-matic machines. The 520 could stabilize noncapstan servo (line-locked) VTRs (although maybe not to broadcast standards).

In line-lock, the internal sync generator could also supply drives to auxiliary equipment, allowing inexpensive VTRs to be used for live production sources. By engaging the color interlace switch, time-base corrected tapes could be dubbed to any master recorder, including a transverse. When played back, these tapes contained color interlaced signals. By locking the output signal from the 520 with other sources through a special effects generator, fades, wipes, and so on were possible from inexpensive VTRs. The window was 1.5 lines. With a capstan-servoed VTR, the lock-up time was in milliseconds. The unit included a built-in DOC, VELCOMP, and PROC AMP.

CVS also introduced a $5,500 TBC, the CVS 510. This unit employed a six-bit, four-times subcarrier sampling circuit. The window was one horizontal line of correction. The unit included a built-in EIA sync generator plus a PROC AMP, DOC and color interlace.

One of Sony's new broadcast products was a TBC,

the BVT-1000. Among its features were a large window (±2H) for its price range ($12,000), a superior S/N ratio, extremely fast lock-up time, a built-in DOC, VELCOMP (line by line), and EIA composite advance sync.[174] Sony also introduced an new portable U-matic machine, the BVU broadcast editing recorder, the BVU-200, and the BVU-100 portable broadcast editing (field EJ) recorder with greatly improved picture quality and SMPTE capability. It was claimed that out of some 400 stations, 85 percent were using the U-matic format.[175]

There were a multitude of other products: switchers, graphic generators, editors, synchronizers, video enhancers, chroma correctors, electronic still stores, film projectors and even new film from Kodak.[176] Something for everyone.

In April 1976, it was reported that in the USSR they were using a combination 35mm film camera while observing the picture on a TV monitor, and recording both picture and sound together. The Soyuz TV film complex was designed for the purpose of using this equipment. The TV optical viewfinder used a rotating reflex-mirror shutter and therefore had no parallax. It could be used for conventional or wide-screen photography in black-and-white or in color.[177]

In July 1976, Hitachi introduced a new Saticon model H8397 ⅔-inch camera tube. It was characterized by a heterojunction target between tin-oxide and selenium doped with arsenic and tellurium on its photo conductive layer. It claimed nominal amplitude response of 45 percent at 400 TV lines.[178]

In August 1976, it was reported that producer George Schlatter had just completed a picture for MGM called *Norman Is That You?* which was to be released on September 24, 1976. This picture was shot on videotape and edited on both tape and for film for release on film.[179]

In 1976, the Sony Corp. developed a long-playing color videocassette recorder capable of continuous color recording and playback for nine hours. In the fields of recording, analysis and control of increasingly diverse information,

1976. USSR combination film-video camera. (*Journal of SMPTE.*)

there had recently been a growing need for a long-playing color video recorder. This recorder was developed with considerations of picture quality, reliability and operability. It was believed to be the first long-playing video recorder of the color cassette type to attain a recording-playback time as long as nine hours.

The incorporation of a specially developed cylinder mechanism afforded a constantly stable, noiseless picture, even when an image recorded in any of the modes is played back in normal. It could also provide still pictures and step-back (reversed playback), so that the searching and checking of tapes became easier yet.

A wide range of uses was anticipated for this recorder, including analysis in research where color photography was required. It would be suitable, for example, in hospitals and laboratories on movement or growth of organisms or chemical changes and the like; in video fields; and on special safety monitoring, including traffic monitoring.[180]

In 1976, Sony introduced the one-touch video Betamax with simplified operation. The new Betamax operated with half-inch tape in a cassette measuring 156 × 96 × 25mm. Designed for home use, it had a rotating two-head helical-scanning system capable of 60 minutes of recording and playback. The development of high-density tape and the use of the azimuth recording system achieved high-density recording on a narrow track of 60 microns. In addition, the simplification of circuitry using the entirely new short wave length recording system and integrated circuits and development of a color system of azimuth recording, enabled commercialization of a recording-playback video deck, which was compact and had high resolution and reliability. Like the earlier Betamaxes, this model could be connected to any color TV receiver and the built-in TV tuner enabled a program to be recorded from a channel other than that being viewed.[181]

Also in 1976, the Victor Company of Japan, Ltd., developed a compact, lightweight half-inch cassette VTR for home use, with a two-hour recording capability. The recorder employed a high-density color recording system known as VHS, which enabled efficient tape use by re-

cording at extremely high density (more signals per unit of tape length). Moreover, long-playing recording for two hours, which had been regarded as difficult with a cassette recorder, had been achieved without any loss of picture clarity.

The use of a new parallel loading system for the loading mechanism (which had previously accounted for a large part of the VTR weight) and the extensive use of integrated circuits enabled the realization of a compact, lightweight recorder — its main unit weighed 13.5kg (30 pounds). This VTR had a built-in RF converter and could be connected to any television receiver, while the built-in tuner allowed recording of a program on a channel other than that being viewed.[182]

JVC's entry into the home videocassette recorder race at this time went back many years. In 1945, American bombs nearly destroyed JVC's factory. Eight years later JVC was at bankruptcy's door and would have gone right on through except for Konosuke Matsushita, who bought a majority of the stock and placed the company under the Matsushita umbrella. Characteristically, though, he agreed to let JVC maintain a high degree of autonomy, and that became a point of almost obsessive pride with the company. Matsushita people would routinely refer to JVC as a subsidiary, but anyone who used that term with a JVC person was asking for trouble. "The only relationship we maintain with Matsushita is capital involvement — that's it," JVC executives would say.[183]

After the war in 1946, Professor Kenjiro Takayangi, the founder of the Japanese television industry, joined JVC as the head of the television research department. By 1950 he was director and chief engineer of the company, and in 1953, became managing director. So Matsushita was buying into the great wealth of experience in television that Professor Takayanagi had supplied.[184]

In 1959, JVC developed a two-head video recorder and by 1960 a color version for professional broadcasting. In January 1961, the Victor Company of Japan had announced a new two-head helical-scan color videotape recorder.[185] The first of its kind. In 1964, JVC put out the DV220. In January 1972, it put out its version of the Sony U-matic under license.

Almost as soon as the U-matic format was adopted, JVC began preparing to develop a true home VTR and if possible overtake Sony. In their efforts they had developed a large VTR with a two-hour capacity, but with poor quality. Then, in December 1974, Sony demonstrated the experimental Betamax for Matsushita and JVC.

Sony was hoping that they would accept it as the standard similar to the ¾-inch U-matic. But JVC was not impressed. They had determined that Sony's Betamax was nothing but a miniature version of the U-matic. JVC believed that "Our instrument is not finished yet, but it's

1976. Sony half-inch Betamax videocassette system with adjacent Trinitron receiver. (Sony Corp.)

better. In six months we can really make it into some-thing." Their machine's recording time had been in-creased to two hours.

If the Betamax itself did not make a profound impres-sion on JVC, Sony's attitude toward it did. "They didn't ask if we had any questions [or] if we had any opinions," one JVC engineer recalled. "They just asked if we would like to go with this. They were very confident. The overall im-pression that we got after attending the meeting was that we had no choice." The U-matic had been a "genuine joint development," he added. "Betamax, on the other hand, was really a finished product, with all the design and the size and everything, so there was no room for compro-mise. And then we heard from some component manu-facturers that Sony had already tooled up. They had al-ready prepared the molds to make the equipment." The JVC people read this to mean that Sony intended to go into production before anyone else and take a high mar-ket share—just as it had done with the U-matic. JVC's management concluded that "the 'sharing' of technology would obviously work in only one direction."

At Matsushita, some people formed a similar im-pression. After the demonstration, Matsushita's technical people met with their Sony counterparts and reported that they liked everything about the machine except the one-hour recording capacity. One of the Sony represen-tatives replied, "It may be a problem, but we've already started tooling up, so it cannot be changed."

"Our executives knew that Sony had already com-pleted its molds and dies—and Sony wanted to sell the product the following year, 1975," the general manager in charge of video engineering at Matsushita, said later. "So it was almost like an ultimatum. There was no room for negotiation, no room for exchange of ideas. They were saying, 'This is it. We've completed this one. If you're in-terested, follow us.' With three-quarter-inch U-matic, the three companies—JVC, Matsushita, and Sony—got together and came to a single standard in a friendly way. This would not be the case with Betamax. Of course, we proposed a modification to expand Beta to two hours, but Sony didn't listen because their marketing schedule was already set."

By the summer of 1975, JVC's project, although still a secret from many of the company's own officials, was shown to Matsushita. They found the JVC prototype in-teresting enough to make a few modifications. At the time, JVC was working with a half-flanged cassette, in which the two reels of tape overlapped. In order that the JVC cassette could be comparable to Sony's Betamax, they changed it to a full-size flange.

In January 1976, Akio Morita assumed the post of chairman of Sony, and Masaru Ibuka, at the age of 67, be-come honorary chairman. Morita announced, "This year will be the first of the video age." He might equally have said, "The Beta-max will be the first product of the Morita age." He

1978. Sanyo V-Cord II model VTC 8200. (Sanyo Electronics.)

had great confidence in it technically and he was con-fident of its appeal to consumers once they had become accustomed to it. However, the prospects for standard-ization seemed to be getting cloudier.

Toshiba and Sanyo were still promoting their skip-field system, the V-Cord. The V-Cord Two was a rotary two-head helical with a tape speed of 2.91 ips for one-hour operation. Color resolution was 250 lines. It had a two-hour mode in which it ran as a single-head system for skip-field recording.

Matsushita's Kotobuki had come up with a new ver-sion of the VX-100, the VX-2000. This was a one-head machine using half-inch tape running at a tape speed of 2 ips. Video resolution was 220 lines, with a signal to noise ratio better than 42db. The small cassette could run for two hours. This machine was called the "Great Time Machine." Finally there were rumors that JVC might have yet another incompatible format in the works. Sooner or later, Morita knew, Matsushita Electric (which was three times bigger than Sony) would enter the home VCR mar-ket in a serious way. If it went with Betamax, the rest of the industry would almost surely follow suit. If it decided on some other system, there was no telling what would happen.

Kokichi Matsuno and Hirobumi Tokumitsu invited Morita, Iwama and Ohga to see the prototype. What they saw was a considerably smaller machine than the Betamax (although it was hard to judge the significance of that since prototypes are often smaller than production mod-els). Mechani-cally, too, VHS had a notable distinction: the use of a loading system called M loading, in which two small posts in-stead of one big one pulled the tape front

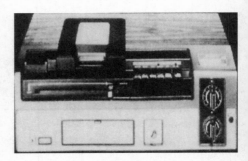

1978. Quasar's (Matsushita's) Great Time Machine. (Matsushita.)

into the cassette and moved it directly to the drum, rather than taking the circuitous, back-door route of the U-load-ing system of Betamax (and the U-matic). M-loading was not unfamiliar to the Sony contingent — it had been tried in some of the early U-matic prototypes, and the company had filed a patent on it in 1969. In other respects, JVC's and Sony's machines were strikingly similar. Both were two-head, helical-scanning machines using half-inch tape in a U-matic type of cassette. Both, unlike the V-Cord, the VX, and indeed all the color video recorders to date, used azimuth recording and countered the problem of cross-talk by juggling the phase of the color signal. So the Betamax and the VHS were in a class by themselves as far as tape efficiency went. The real difference between them lay in how the two companies had chosen to exploit that advantage: Sony to make the cassette paperback size and JVC to achieve a two-hour recording capacity (with a cassette that was about a third larger).

Eventually one of them suggested that the two machines were basically the same except for the larger cassette size of VHS, and he asked: "Isn't the VHS changed only to record two hours?" Now it was Matsuno's and Hirobumi Tokumitsu's turn to get testy. They agreed that two-hour recording was important — indeed, vital — but so, they said, were the other differences, notably M-loading and a JVC-developed recording process known as dual-limit frequency modulation, or DL FM.

At last Morita said what all of the Sony representatives were thinking: "It's a copy of Betamax." Iwama and Ohga — with fists clenched, according to one account — added words to the same effect.

The JVC people had prepared a kind of script for this meeting. Matsuno and Tokumitsu were to conclude by urging Sony to adopt VHS, in the interests of uniformity, and Konosuke Matsushita was to lend his endorsement. But the script, and all pretense of diplomacy, went out the window as soon as the word copy had been spoken. Tokumitsu, Morita's old naval superior, responded vehemently. He said, "VHS was the product of an R&D program that went back to a time well before anyone at JVC had seen the Betamax. Two hours will be the mainstream for home video, so there is a basic inadequacy to the Betamax," he said. "Technology is moving forward by leaps and bounds, so it is natural that the product coming out later is better." This was the end of negotiations between Sony and JVC. The end result was that even in spite of the fact that the Betamax had a slightly better picture, the two-hour recording time was the thing that finally defeated it. Morita was wrong and Sony was to suffer its first defeat in the marketplace.[186]

It was in September 1976 that the image enhancer called the "Crisp-Matic" made by Yves Faroudja, Inc. of Los Altos was licensed to Television Microtime for ex-

The author (right) with Vladimir K. Zworykin at RCA, Princeton, NJ, August 1976.

clusive manufacture and sale. It operated by applying comb filtering, noise reduction, and frequency synthesis to sharpen luminance transitions, remove color cross-talk and reduced noise. It was called the Image-EX image processor.[187] The Microtime 2020 which featured the Crisp-Matic had a beneficial effect on U-matic cassette recordings.

In September 1976, NBC marked it 50th anniversary. It had started out in 1926 with nine radio stations; had 230 radio stations and 217 TV stations by 1976. In 50 years, NBC and its competing networks had formed the chief connective tissue by which the nation received its information and entertainment.[188]

In September 1976, RCA announced its new TR-600A with integral time-code editing. It also included the Super Highland/Pilot Tone (that Ampex had introduced earlier) that automatically corrected banding and other errors with high levels of accuracy. It had manual editing built in with $20,000 in accessories included.[189]

In September 1976, JVC announced its new CR-4400U color portable capstan-servo ¾-inch U-VCR. It weighed only 24½ pounds complete with battery and standard 20-minute cassette inside. It had a signal to noise ratio of better than 45db. It had a full-function keyboard.[190]

Late in 1976, Hitachi also introduced a four-head two-inch transverse VTR for broadcast use. It had many digital functions such as the servo circuit and TBC. It had an auto tracking function, full sync process circuit, and electronic editing functions.[191]

In October 1976, Ed DiGiulio again spoke out on behalf of news gathering by film. He stated, "Why price 'immediacy' when there is rarely an event newsworthy enough to interrupt scheduled programming. When 99 times out of a 100, ENG equipment is used merely to

1975. Hitachi J-19 portable four-head videotape recorder. (Hitachi Denshi America, Ltd.)

record events on tape." He finished by stating the "16mm newsfilm is still the mainstay of a balanced rational news gathering operation."[192]

In November 1976, the International Broadcasting Convention held in London was covered by *Broadcast Management/Engineering* magazine. Its writers reported that they had been shown the new portable Ampex VPR-10. It was a co-axial reel machine that had color video verification capability, automatic-assemble editing as it recorded and a full hour of material on one reel of tape. They also had a private demonstration of the new Sony BVH-1000 one-inch, 1½-head, helical-scan recorder. RCA was not there, but the British firms of Rank, Marconi, Thomson-CSF, Link, EMI and Pye TVT were. During an electronic journalism panel, there was criticism of the poor quality of the U.S. clips available from Eurovision. The quality of the U.S.-made pictures was worse because conversion from 525/60 to 625/50 showed up limited bandwidth and the 50 cycle power frequency meant the picture played slower.

It was stated that CBS and NBC news bureaus were switching to all-electronic news (NBC by '77; CBS by '78). Barnathon of ABC stressed the need for reliable equipment (more important than quality) and equipment that was simple to operate and use (by film camera operators for example). Comparison of costs of going from transverse to segmented helical recorders gave a slight edge after five years. But the benefits of adopting a new standard for small companies were doubtful. The report did not cover the new one-inch machines.[193]

In December 1976, CBS Broadcast Group president John A. Schneider spoke of the revolution in EJ. He stated that CBS was now in its third generation of ENG equipment, but he was quite unhappy over the weight of the equipment, the power to run it, and the lack of sensitivity of the cameras, and hoped that resolutions to these

1976. Philips LDK-II portable color camera. (Philips Labs.)

problems were on the way. When it came to the broadcasting operation, he said that it was "competitive and we want to do it the most effective and economic way." His solution was to use more videotape. "Film is more flexible but its twice as expensive to use. So if we are successful in working out satisfactory labor agreements, we plan to start using tape at our Studio Center film stages in Hollywood where many of our situation comedies are made before live audiences." However, he stated, "We will need an electronic editing device; something to handle the 300 to 400 edits presently made in each hour-long program by a Movieola." Obviously he was not told of the CMX-600 editing device already in place (since April 1971) and gathering dust at Studio Center, and for good reason.

A later (1977) appraisal of the CMX-600 suggested that it only be used when the choice of takes was large and the sequence of scenes was subject to experimentation. The 25 minutes of capacity was a limiting factor, although it was possible to use additional disc packs. The random-access aspect was still its only positive point even though the audio quality was poor and the video an inferior black-and-white only.[194]

If CBS was really serious about doing situation comedies on tape at Studio Center, they could have allowed IBEW personnel (with dual membership in the IATSE) to work at both TV City and at Studio Center; that would have been the answer and satisfactory to all concerned. Actually dual unionism was very common in network television in Hollywood. NBC for instance had NABET personnel run the cameras and all technical equipment, while the IATSE had charge of lighting, props and grips.[195] CBS, however, had other plans in mind.

Chapter 10

Television Enters the Studios
(1977–1979)

In January 1977, *Broadcast Management/Engineering* magazine conducted a survey of the progress made in electronic journalism. It stated that at a meeting of 80 news directors of NBC affiliate stations, 75 percent were into EJ. In addition, it was found that Minicam and ¾-inch tape were producing commercials. For the first time, moving into a store did not mean tearing up the store to bring in lights and other heavy equipment. In addition, electronic equipment was used to revive documentary production. The use of tape rather than film meant enormous savings where sometimes the ratio of shooting was 30 to 1. They could shoot for hours, then "dub off" the good takes and re-use the tape. In addition, there was no substitute for the "live" minidocumentary on the spot. Only in dramatic production was there any doubt that ¾-inch tape was not up to industry standards. However, it was planned to use a system whereby each camera was tied to its own broadcast recorder, just like film, and then the good takes could be edited. Some of the new video editing machines were more comfortable to the average film editor. The article concluded that "the last barrier to all of this production was solved (late last month) when a labor contract was signed by the IATSE/film industry which will facilitate tape production in film studios."

It was strange that the film industry was to take over videotape production. It had never really wanted it. I had never heard of or talked to a film editor or film camera operator who wanted to get into videotape production. They were content to use the machinery they had become accustomed to. Only when their jobs were threatened did they show any interest at all in the new electronic techniques. Actually it was pushed on the film industry by

one of the TV networks who thought that by doing so, the studios would immediately start turning out cheaper productions on tape for television. As we shall see, this never happened. CBS's engineering department's predictions as to the use of film versus tape in the future was completely wrong. It did succeed, however, in taking away electronic production from the people most qualified to use it and give it to a reluctant industry.[1]

In March 1977, Matsushita announced that its subsidiary Panasonic would soon offer a videotape recorder of its own that could carry four hours of programming. RCA had become a licensee of Matsushita while its rival Zenith Television had become a licensee of Sony. In late August, 1977, RCA announced that they had entered the home VCR market. The new RCA model would record for 4 hours and sell for $1,000, less than competitive models from Sony, Zenith and Toshiba.[2] This soon started a war between RCA and Sony that saw RCA become the leading power in videocassettes. The VHS recorder went on sale $300 cheaper than the Betamax. The "battle of the speeds" VCR war was on.

How RCA became involved in the Beta versus VHS conflict is quite interesting. Sony was still trying to get other Japanese companies to agree to its format, and by the beginning of 1977, had succeeded in getting Hitachi, Mitsubishi and Sharp to adopt the Betamax format. They had also gotten support from Toshiba, Sanyo and Zenith in the United States. JVC was still holding out and in September 1977 announced that it was going into production of its own VHS format. On January 10, 1977, Matsushita stated that it too would produce a VHS model in the spring. At this time, Matsushita thought of making a deal with RCA.

RCA, as has been chronicled in these pages, had never been able to put out a satisfactory VCR at a reasonable price. Besides, they were fully committed to the development of a home videodisc system that was obviously years off. RCA certainly did not want to give Zenith a clear path in the home VCR field, so Matsushita sent a delegation to visit RCA and persuaded them to join the VHS group. Edgar Griffths, who was then RCA's president, was characterized as a man not afraid of putting RCA's name on other products. RCA's real power was in its marketing ability to sell almost anything with the RCA name on it. RCA had been approached by Sony, but thought their price too high, and by JVC whose delivery schedule was too long.

So Matsushita's proposal was that the two-hour VHS was a vital necessity. However, when their delegation got to the USA, Sony announced a two-hour version of the Betamax. This meant that the VHS had no real advantage over the Sony. However, after seeing the VHS machine demonstrated, RCA suggested that a four-hour format would fill the bill, and they would sign a contract with Matsushita. Matsushita was horrified at this idea and said that it couldn't be done. Nonetheless, they turned the idea over to the JVC engineers who, by some miracle, in six weeks made a machine that could record for four hours with reasonable quality.

By March 1977, the four-hour prototype was finished and Toshihiko Yamashita, president of Matsushita, met with Roy Pollack, vice president for consumer electronics of RCA, in Osaka to have Matsushita make and RCA buy some 55,000 machines that year and between 500,000 and a million in the next three years. Matsushita had scored a stunning victory. RCA was one of the USA's most experienced and successful forces in the home marketing area and before long it was the leading power in the videocassette field.[3]

In April 1977, it was reported that CBS-TV had ordered 15 production models of the new Sony BVH-1000 videotape recorder. (Five were to go into a new editing system, five for dramatic productions, and five to replace old tired-out recorders.) NBC had ordered two with options for five more. Bosch Fernseh said that they had sold over 140 BCN units, primarily in Europe and Australia.

CBS went on record as not appearing to favor Sony which of course it was doing. The CBS engineering department was very influential in the broadcast industry. When it came to buying equipment, most of the industry followed CBS's lead. So this move to buy Sony equipment would certainly influence the whole broadcast industry, and Sony knew this quite well. Their purchase flew in the face of the fact that the Ampex VPR-1 (with

Full broadcast quality color VTR no bigger than a breadbox.

FERNSEH means television.

1977. New RCA home VCR with four-hour record time. (RCA.)

1976. Fernseh BCN 20 segmented helical-scan color recorder. (Fernseh ad.)

AST) was demonstrably superior to the Sony BVH-1000. It was claimed that over 30,000 recorders using the Ampex format were in use worldwide.

CBS also claimed that Sony's Omega machine with its extra head was the ideal storage medium for a super editor such as the original light-pen CMX-600. It was admitted that one of the limiting features of the CMX-600 was the tedious task of loading program material into the computer discs. It was a tiresome task and the storage time was limited. If a decision called for selecting something from a disc pack that was not on the machine, unacceptable delays were encountered. It was expected that use of the Sony machine would solve these difficulties.[4]

Ampex announced that Marconi was licensed to build the VPR-1 and that Thompson-CSF had showed the Sony BVH 1000 playing in PAL and SECAM. Electronic journalism was there with exhibits by Thomson-CSF and its Microcam, Philips with its Video 80 system, and RCA with its TK-76 camera. Consolidated Video Systems showed its time-base corrector model 517 which could cope with PAL and SECAM. Character generators by Chryon were shown by Ampex and those by Vidifont by Thomson-CSF. Digital video recording was also prominent in the technology of J. L. E. Baldwin of the Independent Broadcast Authority of the U.K. His machine showed some remarkably clear pictures. There was a complete discussion on different means of digital video recording.[5]

Also at Montreux it was revealed that CBS had built a tape production facility at its Studio Center film complex. It was built into a trailer that could be moved from studio to studio. It had five Sony BVH-1000s one-inch Omega helical-scan VTRs, four Thomson-CSF 1515 color cameras, a Thomson-CSF Microcam, associated time-base correctors, plus a post production switcher and other gear.

It is interesting to note that the lack of a production switcher was the justification that CBS used to claim this was "film style" camera production, not multicamera as used in regular TV production. There was no need for a production switcher as each camera was connected to its own recorder. This of course was CBS's *explanation* that this was not regular television production but single-camera shooting which they considered was permissible at this facility. CBS claimed that one inch videotape compared favorably with 35mm film and of course was much cheaper. It was hoped that this development would somehow change the amount of single-camera production that was long the domain of 35mm film.[6]

In operation, the four cameras each fed their pictures to their own videotape recorder. It was claimed that no changes were made in the film stage and that the "creative people" (all former film people) could continue in precisely the same way as in film production. Of course

1977. Videotape equipment at Studio Center. *Above:* Trailer. *Middle:* Interior of trailer with Sony recorders. *Bottom:* Control console at rear of trailer. (CBS.)

this was not true. As there was no director (he was out on the floor watching the scene) to tell each camera operator what shot they should be taking at what time, there was chaos on the studio floor. All instructions came from an assistant director (live TV style) who was telling the camera operators what their next shots were to be. Without tally lights or another indication that they were on the air (an indication that *this* was the correct shot to be used), each camera would really just take up a position to cover a certain part of the action. Hopefully the right shot was in one of the recordings. Then of course, after the taping, the four tapes were synched up and fed to the postproduction switcher where 70 to 80 percent of the edits were made and recorded. Another step of post production was necessary to insert music, sound effects, and other extras. It was claimed that editing took only four hours and the final postproduction six to eight hours. How this could be called "single-camera production" is beyond comprehension, and, of course, the vaunted CMX-600 was not part of this technique. It showed how little the CBS engineering department really knew of film techniques. It was an exercise in futility.[7]

In June 1977, RCA described a new silicon intensifier target tube which had a silicon diode array as a photocathode. By introducing an energy absorbing "buffer layer" in front of the target, the useful gain was above 300 volts. An SIT tube with a gain of 1,600 and a photocathode sensitivity of 140 microamps would be approximately 50 times more sensitive to tungsten light than a silicon target with a published sensitivity of 4,350 microamps. Used in low-level television cameras, the tube had many applications for the military such as night flying, and for law enforcement such as parking lot surveillance.[8]

In July 1977, Sony announced a BVH-500 one-inch high-band portable videotape recorder. It was small in size (360mm wide, 177mm high and 440mm deep) and weighed less than 37 pounds. It permitted recording of up to 60 minutes on Sony high-density videotape. It was priced at $30,000.[9]

Sony also announced that they had developed a compact color television camera using a Trinicon, a single-tube color image pickup tube. It was small and lightweight and had applications in the medical and other industrial fields. It weighed 4.9kg with viewfinder and zoom lens.[10]

On July 11, 1977, Sir Charles Curran, director general of the BBC, gave a presentation of the competition between videotape and film. His conclusions are worth including here. "I return then to the general balance between film and videotape and what it will be in the eighties. The basic question is whether electronic picture making will take over. Eventually it may do so, but, I now think, not for a very long time. It is not only a question of how programs are recorded: there has to be an operator to show the pictures to the audience. The simplicity of film compared with the present stage of electronic picture presentation gives it an important advantage. The great flexibility of film

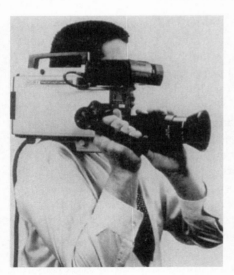

1977. Sony portable single-tube color camera. (Sony.)

for showing by different means and without standards, conversion is important. The ease of making multiple copies is an advantage. But electronic picture making offers a more direct communication between the originator and the user. The influence lingers on the fact that, at one time, all television, other than filmed sequences, had to be broadcast live. Program production by television is quicker, although perhaps less polished, than film, and the delay with film between the action and seeing the picture seems to create something of a barrier. Often the time lag does not matter from the program point of view, but free interchangeability between the two recording media would eliminate most of the difficulties associated with either. In the end, I suspect, it will not be a question of whether electronic origination takes over from film. The two processes will merge imperceptibly until they lose their separate identities to become a single versatile tool of the program maker."[11]

In August 1977, it was reported that a new standard format had been agreed between Sony and Ampex. The SMPTE working group had come to agreements as to audio head placement and video head drum structure. The drum structure and writing speed was that of Ampex; the audio format was that of Sony. Both agreed that the 1½-head feature of Sony to record VIT and VIR signals on lines 17 to 21 was necessary. Ampex was allowed to keep its AST (automatic scan tracking) feature and there was room to get audio record verification as done by Ampex. Ampex stated that customers of old VPR-1 equipment would be able to retrofit their equipment if they wished. Sony stated that modifications on its BVH-1000 would be made for $1,000.[12]

In August 1977, it was announced that Dr. Vladimir Kosma Zworykin, aged 87, had been elected to the National Inventors Hall of Fame. Zworykin was involved in many television developments including the Iconoscope and the Kinescope. He was elected an honorary vice president of RCA after retirement in 1954 and had an office at the David Sarnoff Research Center where he engaged in independent research in medical electronics and related fields. Others also elected were Edwin H. Land (Polaroid), Lee de Forest (electronic tubes), George Eastman (Kodak), and George Steinmetz (electric power).[13]

In October 1977, RCA reported on a new color television tube, the Saticon. This tube was made with a Selenium-Arsenic-Tellurium photoconductor. Started by RCA, the tube was realized by NHK and the Central Research Laboratory of Hitachi. It was claimed that this new tube was an improvement over the existing lead oxide photoconductors.[14]

In October 1977, it was reported that the Hollywood Editors' Guild had set up a training program to acquaint film editors with videotape techniques and other modern technology. It was a six-week training program of three hours' duration. Each student was given a certificate of completion.[15]

In October 1977, there was a report on the success of the new technology station at WBBM-TV in Chicago. Much was made of a new media room which contained most of the stations' record and playback services. All commercials, promos, public-service spots, and other short material were recorded off line onto cassettes. All news was done electronically, making news film an endangered species. Finally CBS stated that there had been an increase in the use of tape for situation comedies and talk shows by means of the new production techniques known as film-style shooting. Two shows mentioned as examples were "Betty White" and "We've Got Each Other." "One result of all this is the number of syndicated shows on tape is on the increase." (Both of these shows were quickly canceled.)[16]

In November 1977, further details on the one-inch video format were released following the announcement of July 7 that the SMPTE working group had reached general agreement on a new standard. Specific details of the agreement were ready shortly thereafter.

The SMPTE group working on one-inch nonsegmented helical video recording would identify the proposed practices and standards for "One Inch Type C Helical Videotape Recordings for 525-line, 60-field NTSC Television Systems."

Some of the details for the 525/60 format are as follows. The recording of each field was divided into two parts: the video track and the sync track. The video track contained all active picture lines and the interval starting with line 16 and ending with line 5: thus VITS and VIRS were retained. The video track had a ten-line vertical-interval signal gap. The sync track contained the ten lines of the vertical-interval not recorded on the video track plus an adequate overlap. For users who did not require the information contained in the sync track, the format allowed for omission of this track but no other information could be recorded in the allotted area.

The rotating scanner drum had six head tip locations. The design provided for separate record and erase heads for both video and sync tracks. Optional features such as video and sync confidence heads and an automatic tracking head could be retained. When a particular head was not used, a dummy head tip would be put in its place.

The linear tape speed was nominally 244 millimeters/sec (9.61 ips). Three program-quality longitudinal audio tracks of equal width were provided. Two adjacent audio tracks, near the top edge of the tape, could be used as separate audio tracks or for stereo signals. The third track can be used for time code, cuing purposes or as an additional audio track. A separate control track had been provided that identified the odd and even fields and alternate frames. All longitudinal tracks were recorded at the same position perpendicular to the edge of the tape and downstream on the tape path.

The video signal was recorded using the high-band FM technique. The audio signals were recorded using conventional bias recording techniques, and the control track was recorded using saturation recording techniques.

The SMPTE working group that was studying the type B segmented helical one-inch video recording format also has completed its initial assignment. It drafted five specifications that describe the type B format, which was based essentially on the Bosch-Fernseh "BCN" format. One-inch type A helical video recording was based on the original Ampex one-inch system introduced about two years before. Type C differed from type A and type B in that there were then no manufacturers of Type C equipment. Both Ampex and Sony had announced their intention to manufacture equipment which met the type C specifications, though other manufacturers might enter the race if type C became the preferred format for broadcasters. IVC, Philips, and RCA held licenses to manufacture the BCN format documented by the type B standards.[17] By the end of 1977, it was reported that more than 200 type C machines had gone into service and almost the same number of B types in Europe.[18]

In December 1977, Cinema Products announced that they would be carrying the new NEC MNC-71/CP ENG camera. The company claimed that it was now able to provide the perfect combination for the electronic side of a balanced TV news operation. It was obvious that Cinema Products felt that if you can't beat them, join them.[19]

In December 1977, an article in *Broadcast Management/Engineering* explained why film producers were loath to go to tape. All agreed that the reliance on film was based on its superior quality, its higher resolution, color saturation and contrast. They often talked about below-the-line cost savings of tape as myths. The "reality feel" of tape was a detriment. They all agreed that the craftsmanship traditional to film was not present in the videotape genre. "Creativity follows technology and … in time video will be as craft orientated as film." Film people took a great deal of pride in what they did. Film technicians loved their craft. Every person working was creative. They liked having three people running a camera in spite of the costs. While admittedly film was an expensive craft, the advantage was that every person on the set was an expert. They admitted that shooting on tape was less expensive because wages and other conditions were less onerous. There was no doubt that tape could be produced less expensively than film; but what did one have with the savings? They all agreed that quality was worth the extra cost.

Someday, they claimed, there would be a "dry process" that would work as well for dramas as for comedy, but that someday was maybe five years down the road.[20] They were right, of course; the tradition of film making was not about to undergo any changes.

What the article failed to mention was the fact that the three-person crew was operating blindly. It made no difference how skilled they were, the final result on film was unknown to them. In spite of the fact that with much experience the results were often satisfactory, there was still the doubt as to what was actually recorded on film. So the same scene was taken over and over for their own protection. This was the reason for the elaborate (and costly) system of "dailies" or "rushes" that prevailed throughout the industry. Only when seen on a large screen did they know what they had achieved.

This of course was quite the opposite experience of the video camera operator. With their electronic viewfinder, they knew exactly what was being recorded. In addition, of course, they were able to do this all by themselves — no dolly pusher, no focus puller — they were in complete control of the camera at all times. The video camera operator was just as dedicated and skillful as any film camera operator.

Another look to the future of film making took place in April 1978. Cinema Products announced their new "Steadicam" (Universal Model A) camera stabilizing system that allowed the camera to be mounted on a special harness that could be operated by one person. It gave the camera a floating action. It included an Arri 35 BL 35mm film camera connected to a Cinevid video assist unit for picking off the reflex image so that it could be seen on the Steadicam viewing monitor. This unit became quite popular with producers as it allowed one operator to do a great variety of shots and movements that up to then had to be done with a three- or four-person dolly crew.

The most important part of the unit was the electronic viewfinder so that the camera operator could see what they were shooting. During the experimental stages, in vain they tried everything from fiber optics to wire finders with no success. Without the electronic viewfinder of course, there was no system. This was the first camera unit with video assist to become popular at the major movie studios. Electronic viewfinding was now to become part of major motion picture production.[21] In 1978, it won a class 1 scientific/technical Oscar from the Academy of Motion Picture Arts and Sciences.[22]

In February 1978, RCA announced that it would market Sony's one-inch type C helical-scan recorder. It would come out under the RCA label as the RCA model TH-100 high-performance type C helical scan recorder. It consisted of five modular sections that could be mounted in any fashion. It was priced at $37,000. They also an-

nounced a portable version, the TH-50, at $35,000. The RCA service organization would give complete technical support including spare parts and training. RCA had never made a commercial helical-scan recorder before, preferring to put their name on other manufacturers' equipment (such as IVC's). Thus RCA was aligning itself with Sony against Ampex. With the emergence of the new one-inch recorder, this was RCA's temporary withdrawal from competing in the broadcast recorder race.[23]

By March 1978, Americans were buying more RCA Selectavision VHSs than Betamaxes. To that point in 1978, RCA had 27.5 percent of the market while Sony had 27.5 percent. For 1978 as a whole, RCA's share was 36 percent and Sony's 19.1 percent. The four-hour speed and sleeker styling of the RCA machine made the difference. Before long Matsushita was turning out two thirds of the world's home VCRs. JVC and Hitachi were also exporting VHS machines to the USA. The VHS home system of Victor Company of Japan had been adopted by Sharp, Hitachi, Mitsubishi, Matsushita, and Akai Electric. Equipment for use on PAL and SECAM standards had also been developed.[24]

In May 1978, it was announced that the Beta format of Sony had been adopted by Toshiba and Sanyo. In the middle of 1979, VHSs were outselling Beta by two to one. Even when Sony went to longer play and dropped Beta's price, nothing could stop its demise.[25] As one authority stated, "no matter how long a Sony Betamax could record, Sony went on paying for its 'original sin.'"[26] A failing giant (RCA) had destroyed Sony's plans for worldwide domination of the home videotape market for all time, and somehow, no one had any sympathy for Sony.

In May 1978, CBS was still complaining that no one was using its Studio Center facilities. Two shows ("The Betty White Show" and "We've Got Each Other") had been canceled and no other producers were interested in using this system. (Both of these programs could have been done better, faster and cheaper at CBS-Television City.) Word had gotten around about the problems of shooting in this fashion, but CBS blamed the problem on two factors. (1) Union restrictions that prevented them from shooting their own shows on the one-inch system. This, of course, was not true — CBS was free to shoot all of its own programs on tape as long as it was done at TV City. (2) The lack of an appropriate editing system. This was strange as CBS had long since acquired the CMX-600, its expensive answer to the editing problem. It was stated that CBS was continuing efforts to get a different editing machine designed.[27]

Interestingly enough, CBS had installed a new CMX system 340X that fulfilled all of these requirements at TV City using new one-inch helical-scan recorders. The system had been in use since August 1977, and it was claimed that it had sufficient flexibility to be easily adapted to meet future needs as they were recognized.[28]

On December 7, 1977, Dr. Peter Goldmark was killed in an automobile accident in Westchester County, New York. Only two weeks before, he had been awarded the National Medal of Honor at the White House. One of television's greatest pioneers had died. His accomplishments have been documented in this history.[29]

In May 1978, there was a report of a new portable van in England that was equipped with four film cameras with electronic viewfinders. There were occasions when, on location, a director would like to be able to combine the versatility of film with the degree of remote control possible with electronic cameras. A useful step in this direction had been taken by equipping this van to control up to four film cameras fitted with electronic viewfinders. The equipment in the van included communications equipment, a small helical-scan video recorder, a simple video switcher, and four television monitors which displayed the pictures received from the electronic viewfinders All of the equipment could be quickly removed from the van and used elsewhere, for example, inside a building.

The recorder could record from any one of the viewfinders or from the output of the switcher, thus allowing cutting from one camera to another and the making of an intercut recording where a number of cameras were used on continuous action. Program sound was also recorded. The videotape recording could be replayed immediately in the vehicle or studied later.

The cameras were usually connected to the vehicle by a cable which could be up to about 100m (330 ft) in length. One camera could also be operated over a radio link that carried viewfinder output and intercom, so that completely isolated and distant operation was possible. Except when the radio link camera was in operation, all the electronic viewfinders were synchronized, giving stable operation and clean vision cuts and videotape recording. Cuts to and from the radio camera were possible but there could be some picture disturbance.

All of the equipment in the vehicle was powered from a heavy-duty battery which had sufficient capacity for a normal day's filming. The battery could be continuously recharged from a charger in the vehicle if a mains supply was available at the location.[30]Here was the best of all worlds—quality film and the instant viewing of the picture by an electronic viewfinder. A look into the future of film making.

In May 1978, it was reported that Consolidated Film Industries Videotape in Hollywood had expanded and relocated it postproduction facilities. A third transverse editing system had been put in operation, comprising four AVR3 recorders. This edit facility controlled six VTRs and there was provision for two more machines. Telecine had been moved, to relocate the tape-to-film transfer to a new area, and expanded to included separate control rooms for each telecine chain. Hollywood was starting to take television seriously.[31]

In May 1978, Rank Precision Industries announced their new Rank Cintel Mark III flying-spot color telecine. It had new techniques for the multiple scanning of film frames using digital video storage and provided excellent resolution with low signal to noise ratio without problems of flicker and minor picture instability. It used a large diameter CRT, with photoelectric cells and had a simple optical path. It was available as either 35mm or 16mm uniplex equipment. Price depending on makeup and accessories was around $100,000.[32]

In June 1978, the Sony Corp. announced that it had built a solid-state, experimental color camera using three large-scale charge-coupled devices. Each chip had 226 horizontal elements and 492 vertical elements giving a total of 111,192 picture elements. Even with a ⅔-inch optical system, the camera had 280-line horizontal resolution and 700 lumens illumination.[33]

In June 1978, the Ampex Corp. and N. V. Philips of Holland announced their cooperation in the field of one-inch helical broadcast recorders and ENG/EFP cameras. Philips would market the Ampex VPR-2 and VPR-20 videotape recorders worldwide, and Ampex would adopt the Philips ENG/EFP cameras as part of their broadcast-camera range. This gave Ampex a powerful ally in Europe and Asia.[34]

1978. Rank Cintel flying spot color telecine. (Rank Cintel.)

In September 1978, a paper on a digital television recorder with low tape consumption was given by J. L. E. Baldwin of the Independent Broadcast Authority, England. He described the problems with making a digital recorder and their solutions. His original work had taken place with a two-inch segmented format. He used a special IVC Rank Cintel 9000 because the head speed could be doubled. Then he went to a one-inch segmented recorder. This machine (BCN) was finished, and on November 31, 1977, it was decided to give a demonstration of it to the Institute of Electrical Engineers on January 26, 1978. It was not very successful as only half-pictures could be displayed. A half-minute of full pictures was shown but with an excessive error rate. Clearly, much work remained to be done.[35]

However, the work on digital video recording resulted, early in 1978, in the public demonstration of a system capable of producing full-width pictures on one-inch magnetic tape at a tape speed of under 10-inches/sec. These demonstrations utilized the BCN one-inch segmented recorder made by Bosch Fernseh, who carried out modifications to make it suitable for the IBA digital system; the system could also be used with static-head or with other one-inch helical machines. Preliminary investigations were also carried out with a one-inch Sony non-segmented helical machine.

An important factor of this digital system was that no bit-rate reduction of the picture information was necessary. Signal-sampling for the first PAL 625-line demonstrations was at 2 *fsc* representing a digital bit-rate of about 80Mb/s. However, there appeared to be no theoretical need for major changes to make it suitable for composite-coded NTSC 525-line pictures sampled at 3 *fsc* or for component-coded signals such as may be required in

1979. First IBA digital VTR built on an IVC/Rank Cintel 9000 frame. (IBA.)

countries using the SECAM system. Work on the system continued.[36]

In October 1978, Ampex announced its first type C format helical-scan recorder, the VPR-2. It retained all of the exclusive features of the VPR-1 including automatic scan tracking and broadcast quality slow-motion and still-frame playback. It was to cost from $29,950 to $40,850. They also announced the portable VPR-20 high-band color unit for electronic news gathering or other remote productions. Prices ranged from $34,950 to $39,950.[37]

In October 1978, it was announced that the 90-minute Hallmark Hall of Fame production of *Return Engagement* starring Elizabeth Taylor would be done on videotape. It was shot "film style" using three full size RCA TK-45 TV cameras and three two-inch videotape recorders. It was claimed that the real reason for doing it on tape was financial — 35mm film production was usually about one third more in cost than that of two-inch tape. Most of the production was done using two cameras with the director on the set. Much was made of being able to see precisely what the cameras were getting as each scene was rehearsed. It was claimed that the lighting director concentrated on a "film look." All editing was done in postproduction, which took about two weeks. It was edited at Metromedia using four ¾-inch machines and a CMX-340-X editing system. Unlike in film editing, all dissolves and fades were viewed as the work print was being built. Sound sweetening, music, dialogue, and sound effects were also done with the CMX-340-X system. The show was to be recorded on 35mm film for use in Europe. It was claimed that while there were still some advantages to film, it was obvious that tape now provided the industry with some very important production advantages.[38]

In October 1978, it was announced that the NHK Laboratories in Japan were experimenting with a high-definition color system employing 1,125 lines at 60 fields/sec. NHK displayed this image on a special 30-inch color screen with an aspect ratio of 5.3 which come closer to wide screens used in motion pictures. To provide the images, NHK had developed a 70mm telecine using three Vidicons and an RGB color camera with three return-beam Saticons as the pickup tube. The result was an exceptionally sharp image with a smooth structure which rivaled high-quality color printing.[39]

In November 1978, Ampex presented a paper outing the newly adopted SMPTE type C helical-scan format. Among the improvements was that the head drum had six heads. Actually, a compatible type C format tape could be recorded and played on a VTR with only one operational rotating video tip. Unfortunately, as the tip started and ended contact with the tape, it created longitudinal disturbances in the tape that traveled around the drum. These tip disturbances, in turn, created time-base errors which had a tendency not to cancel on playback if the record and playback machines had tips in the same location on the drum. Without this cancellation, it was difficult for a time-base corrector to eliminate the "velocity" effects and visible picture defects resulted. In order to reduce this problem, the type C format required that non-operational tips be placed in "unused" locations, with tolerances for minimizing velocity errors.

Four format features led to the logical conclusion that six heads were required. The four features were (1) recording of sync in addition to video; (2) inserting edits using flying erase; (3) confidence playback during recording; and (4) separate record and play heads to allow tip design optimization. Starting with one record-play video tip, a record-play sync tip plus two erase tips could be added for a subtotal of four. Video confidence playback during record was considered an extremely important feature for many users, so one more tip could be added. Finally, since there were now separate record and play tips for the video channel, performance improvements were possible if each tip design was optimized for its purpose. To utilize this advantage, it was necessary to rotate the drum phase by 120° on playback with respect to record. In order to play back the sync channel, it was necessary to add a playback (confidence) head in the sync channel, and this last one gave a total of six tips. It should he emphasized that any number of these tips, up to five, could be replaced by high-reliability, low-cost, nonoperational tips depending on the features desired in a fully compatible type C format VTR.[40]

In February 1979, it was reported that the French had discovered the advantages of single-camera videotape production. One electronic camera was used for recording, connected to a director's desk where the action was viewed. There was similar monitor setup for the sound engineer. All shooting was done with the director on the floor, and after each take, it was checked out on the floor monitor. The equipment used an IVC-7000 color camera and a portable VTR BCN 30, as well as one color monitor and one black-and-white monitor. When shooting, the director stayed on the stage with the actors. Two video engineers were used to control the VTR and make color corrections.

Everything went like film. It was claimed that this method was used on the French six-hour production of "Offenbach" and a 90-minute special "The Night Watch." It was also claimed this method gave the directors the advantages of video with the flexibility of film. Editing techniques were still being worked on.[41]

On February 2–3, 1979, the 13th annual winter conference of the SMPTE was held in San Francisco. Here

1979. First Ampex digital videotape recorder. (Ampex.)

the Ampex Corp. publicly introduced the first all-digital videotape recorder. They showed an engineering model of a digital VTR. The unit was designed around the Ampex AVR-3 and used an "octo-plex" (eight head) system that divided the data stream into two parallel streams.

The Ampex paper, authored by Joachim Diermann and Maurice Lemoine, stressed that the unit developed at Ampex's labs was only designed to be a "development tool" in Ampex's research and was not designed as a product or even a prototype product. Nevertheless, a demonstration tape played before the SMPTE audience and again at a private demonstration later in the evening showed

1979. Ampex engineers Maurice Lemoine (left) and Joachim Diermann demonstrating the first Ampex all-digital videotape recorder. (Ampex.)

convincing evidence that the digital recorder would one day find its place in the television broadcaster's equipment bank.

A full set of test signals on the demonstration tape included a remarkably even gray field and red color field, clearly defined color bars and multiburst, and extremely sharp images from a live camera feed which had been dubbed from a transverse master. With error concealment and error correction, the system delivered a signal to noise ratio greater than 65db.

Because the Ampex engineering team was designing an engineering milestone rather than a product, they decided to opt for a no-compromise system which could transmit a full eight-bit PCM signal in both 525-line (86 megabits/sec) and 625-line (106 megabits/sec) standards at $3 \times fsc$ sampling rate. To achieve a 43MHz bandwidth at the 83 Mb/sec the sampling rate would have required a 3,000 to 4,000 ips writing speed (impractical because of tape and energy consumption and machine strain), Ampex decided on an "Octoplex" system in which two parallel heads recorded the bit stream. Each channel therefore carried only 43Mb/sec at a writing speed of only approximately 1,600 inches on two parallel 5mm tracks with a guard band of 2.5mm. An eight-head record drum was used. The machine operated at 15 inches/sec using two-inch tape and was housed in an AVR-3 console.[42]

For the PAL system, there were major changes. The writing speed was approximately 2,100 ips. The digital video signal was recorded on two channels with a bit rate of 67.5Mb/sec. The composite PAL 625/50 signal was sampled at $4 \times fsc$ and each sample was digitized into an eight-bit word. Linear packing density was 33kb/inch. Track width was 2mm with a guard band of 6mm at a longitudinal speed of 6.6 inches/sec.[43]

Although shown without digital audio, it was indicated that as many as four 16-bit audio channels, sampled at 50kHz, could be accommodated by writing blocks of audio data with the video heads in the area now known as "overlap." Two of the eight heads were actively reading or writing at any given time. During the write cycle, they accepted their bit streams from a buffer memory which was fed by an input A/D converter. Identification signals and error detection bits were added before recording. During playback, the two parallel head-tape channels were recovered, equalized and decoded. Skew errors between the channels and time-base errors were removed by using the identification signals. Dropouts were restored by error detection and masking circuits, a key factor in the overall subjective acceptance of the digital picture. The detection and masking circuits worked by identifying the error detection bits added to each video word at the time of recording. Chrominance and luminance from lines preceding and following the dropout line were interpolated separately.

Ampex had also been tackling the field of digital audio recording in conjunction with its digital VTR experiments, although the demonstration at SMPTE used a conventional audio track to identify the test signals. It was assumed that any final digital VTR product would have at least two digital audio tracks with additional digital tracks for cuing and editing information (as were then found on one-inch helical VTRs). Ampex felt that the audio circuits should be able to make use of many of the same circuits as were used in the video portion of the recorder, providing that a common clock could be employed to sample both audio and video (a 50k samples/sec sampling rate). A space of 200mm at the end of each video head swipe provided enough space for recording four audio channels at a resolution up to 16 bits per sample. Samples were stored in memory until the video head reached the audio recording area. Each audio channel data stream was recorded twice to obtain immunity from dropout, and an error detection and correction circuit insured the validity of each sample. The only problem foreseen by Ampex for the audio portion of its VTR was that the 50kHz result of the sampling rate might be difficult to convert to the 32K samples/sec standard for European audio transmission.[44]

Playback of various test signals and program material was demonstrated, including a section in which record currents were varied over a two-to-one range to demonstrate its insensitivity to that parameter. Even though the receivers used in the hall were a limiting factor, the complete lack of banding of velocity effects and the extremely low chroma noise were readily apparent. The machine was made available for close viewing later.[45] Again the Ampex Corporation had shown its leadership in the field of videotape recording. Since 1956, Ampex had led the way to almost every major advance in videotape recording. (The only two exceptions would be the color-under system invented by JVC and the azimuth recording system that had been patented in 1958 by one Shiro Okamura.) Under the aegis of Charles Ginsburg, Ampex was still the world leader in its field.

In March 1979, a report on the 57th annual convention of the NAB in Dallas, Texas, was given. The big news here was that the Sony Corp. had demonstrated an engineering prototype of its digital VTR. It was pointed out that the digital VTR was not yet a practical alternative to current technologies.

The transport was a helical BVH-1000 C VTR. It was claimed that the tape and head speed were the same as type C. The quality of the Sony DVR recording was impeccable, providing 58db signal to noise ratio—the theoretical limit for eight-bit $3 fsc$ sampling system used. The scanning system was a two-track parallel format using block-coding techniques. The data rate was 115Mb/

1979. Sony's first digital video recorder using standard BVH transport. (Sony.)

sec. According to a Sony spokesman, their machine provided eight times the information-packing density of the experimental DVR shown by Ampex at the recent SMPTE winter conference. However, the electronics which governed the sampling, error concealment, and other data processing resided in several large rack-mounted enclosures measuring 19 inches by nearly 6 feet high.[46]

Sony also showed its BVH-1100 type C recorder with dynamic tracking, something that Ampex had introduced in 1976. It was claimed that a bimorph dynamic tracking head had been added to provide dynamic tracking. When tied to a new BVT 2000 digital time-base corrector, stable color playback at speeds up to ten times normal and stable black-and-white playback at speeds up to 50 times normal were possible in either direction. Sony was to start building the DTR-100 dynamic motion controller and the new BVE-1000 editor at the new Sony Technology Center in Palo Alto, CA. The BVT-2000 was a nine-bit, 4 *fsc* sampling system that could be expanded to provide a 12h window. It was reported that the new dynamic tracking unit could be installed in older Sony machines for $5,500. (At the present time, it is not known what arrangement Sony made to use the Ampex invention.[47]) The total price of the new machine was about $72,000.

At the time Ampex boasted that it had shipped over 250 VPR-2s to U.S. and overseas customers. It was noted that NBC had ordered 41 VPR-2 recorders, 41 TBCs, nine SMC-60 slow-motion recorders, six VPR-20 portable recorders, and 17 HPE helical editing systems— for a total cost of $4 million. This was for NBC's coverage of the 1980 Moscow Olympics.[48]

Also at this show, NEC introduced a new type C recorder, the TT-7000. It cost about $38,000, more with other added accessories. Hitachi also introduced two new type C entries. The HR-200 which used a new air tape-guide system. No part of the tape drive with the exception of the heads touched the tape. A portable version, the Hitachi VTR, HR-100, was substantially the same weight, about 42 pounds, and with its own battery could provide up to 90 minutes of operation. Other type C machines included the RCA TH-200 which was made by Sony. It also

could be ordered with the dynamic tracking unit. Marconi showed its unit which was made by Ampex.[49]

Bosch-Fernseh showed its line of BCN type B recorders including a long-heralded BCN-5 portable one-inch cassette recorder as a production model. This 26½-pound field recorder could provide 40 minutes on an internal battery. Also shown was a slow-motion controller for the BCN system. For the first time NEC and Cinema Products introduced a new IEC type "D" recorder. The TTR-7 was portable and the TR-5 used a compact cassette format. Priced at $35,000, the unit operated on either 110/115 v or external 12 v power supply. The recommended TBC for these machines was the NEC NTC-5000 which listed at $15,000.[50]

IVC was there even though it had been in much financial distress for the previous two years. They introduced a new IVC-1010 one-inch helical 10MHz recorder, meant for medical, security and military applications. According to a spokesman, IVC continued to enjoy considerable success in the overseas market. In the previous year, it had reported a profit of $1 million on $11.5 million of sales.[51]

Merlin Engineering showed a Betamax half-inch recorder modified for high-band performance. Dubbed "Jupiter" it achieved its performance by tripling the head and tape speed which shortened the play time. Merlin expected that machine to play an important role in the home VTR field. It was also likely that Merlin was going to change over from the Beta format to the VHS format to achieve longer playing times.[52]

Cameras included the RCA TK-47 which claimed to be the most automatic camera with 89 functions. Toshiba International said its new PK-40 went even further. Hitachi showed its new studio camera, the SK 100. Ikegami was using digital encoders with its HL-EFP. Toshiba showed its PK-40 with a built-in microprocessor. Harris exhibited its TC-880A using diode gun tubes, and IVC its 7005 camera with a seven-inch viewfinder.

Ampex announced a new ⅔-inch diode gun tube for electronic news-gathering applications. RCA announced a new one-inch high performance Saticon (BC4395) and a ⅔-inch Saticon (BC4390) that sold for $1,665. EEV announced a new EEV P-8160 Leddicon and a new high-resolution (1,600 lines) Vidicon.[53]

There were numerous editing systems: Mach One by Fernseh, Inc. which had a program that would instantly convert from standard 525 NTSC to 24 frames for transfer of audio to motion picture film and 25fps (625) for PAL tapes. CMX announced that the final version of its Videola would soon be available. It converted pulse and SMPTE time-code edit format to the CMX format and stored the material on floppy disk. Working as an off-line videocassette editor, complex transitions could be stored.

Convergence Corporations ECS-103 was shown as complete three-source machines by taking a modular approach. Dynasciences model 104 could perform A and B dissolves without the use of a microprocessors. In graphics, Chryon, TeleMation and Vidifont all had full blown digital graphic systems incorporating font composers, animation programs, and so on, and all incorporated large-scale outboard computers.

Teletext was shown by only one manufacturer, Sofratev, in a system called Antiope that was developed for use in France. CBS was conducting tests of two teletexts systems at its station in St Louis.[54]

Yves Faroudja Inc. showed a line of processing equipment that included the Record Booster and the YFI Comb Filter Separator. The Record Booster was used before recording any color-under videotape recorder. The Comb Filter separated the luminance and chrominance components from any standard NTSC encoded signal without ringing or high frequency luminance cross-talk.[55]

Both Cinema Products and Frezzolini concentrated on their growing line of video products. Cinema Products showed its new KM-16 low-cost telecine (film-to-tape transfer system) for the first time. They suggested bringing the unit into the field where only film images were accessible and microwaving the images via satellite or microwave. (Nothing was said about the film processing.) The film image was illuminated 60 times a second through a condenser system with one-to-one magnification. The image was further projected through a 45 degree mirror for reversal. Film movement was a pin registered pull-down of 50 degrees. Finally, Eastman Kodak revealed that over 85 percent of prime-time programming was still produced on film. However, the company added, U.S. stations that had had 1,500 newsfilm crews now had only 1,200 — and 1,200 EJ crews.[56]

In March 1979, it was reported that the Eidophor Projection System by Conrac had been used at the Miss America Pageant at Atlantic City's Convention Hall. The picture size astounded an audience of 23,000 as it was almost 50 feet wide and it was claimed to have up to 7,000 lumens of light output.[57]

On June 3–10, 1979, at the tenth International Television Symposium, the Bosch Company was the main exhibitor. Robert Bosch GmbH was celebrating 50 years of being in the television industry. Robert Bosch had joined with John Logie Baird, Zeiss Ikon and Loewe Radio on July 3, 1929, to form a new television company, Fernseh A.G.[58] Half a century later, they were promoting their new one-inch BCN segmented tape recorders. They showed freeze frame, jogging, still projection and special digital effects from this machine. This was done by means of new digital field store devices.[59]

They also showed the first working model of a BCN 5 portable cassette recorder. It was a one-inch studio-quality recorder weighing about 12kg. It had an optional color verification playback, was battery-powered, and had insert-assemble edit features. Reels could be extracted from the cassette in seconds for replay on any other BCN B format VTR.[60]

Also in June 1979, Bosch introduced the FDL 60 dual-format, digital telecine film scanner. It was a tubeless solid-state machine using charge-coupled devices (CCDs) which offered good color reproduction and high resolution. The digital frame store and the continuous capstan-driven film transport allowed slow motion, fast motion, jogging, and still and search modes, in forward or reverse.[61] Picture information underwent RGB separation in a prism system and was scanned line by line by CCD sensors before being written into a digital frame store. CCD sensors replaced pickup or scanning tubes and operated on low voltage dc. They offered long life, no burn in, afterglow or field lag. The machine had automatic color correction and shading, and fixed pattern noise and white and black level.[62]

On July 25, 1979, the Technical Research Laboratories of NHK (Japan Broadcasting Corp.) described an experimental digital videotape recorder which, they claimed, had been demonstrated on March 23 that year. The drive mechanism and heads were based on a modified Sony BVH-1000 using the SMPTE type C one-inch helical format. A three-track system was chosen. Tape speed was 9.606 inches/sec, and tape-to-head speed was 1,008 inches/sec. Modulation was interleaved NRZI (nonreturn to zero inverted) and scrambling. It had class IV partial response, no bias, and used normal tape.[63]

On September 7, 1979, just ten days before the type C Emmy was awarded by the National Academy of Television Arts and Sciences, Ampex won an Emmy for its development of automatic scan tracking (AST). On September 17, 1979, both Ampex and Sony shared the technology Emmy for their work in developing the type C videotape format. Both companies had introduced their machines at the 1976 NAB convention.[64]

In November 1979, work continued on the issue of teletext in the USA. CBS reported that the British Oracle, Europe's Ceefax and the French Antiope system would work in the NTSC domain. William Connolly stressed that the burden of a viable teletext system would be placed on TV receiver manufacturers. The report admitted that little was known of the commercial viability of teletext. As CBS Broadcast Group president Gene F. Jankowski asked: "as viewers use their sets to get teletext, will they also turn to teletext during commercial breaks?[65]

Julian Barnathan, president of ABC operations and engineering, also gave his objections to teletext by stating "that teletext should not conflict with the programs being aired" and that "the sponsor should have the right to ask that his program is not being interfered with. If the local sponsor wants it on his program, it is his business. But ABC as a national program supplier, does not want any interference with our programming from the FCC or anybody."[66]

In December 1979, CBS described an experimental editing system that used six Sony Betamax decks as its record and playback decks. It was simply an updated CMX-600, the system that had cost over $250,000 and failed miserably. This updated version was to cost about $50,000. There still were no operating controls—all commands were done by means of the light pen on the menu monitor. After all the years since the CMX-600 was introduced in 1971, nearly all editing devices had included a keyboard of some kind for the performance of functions.

However, the CBS engineering department was holding out. Two color monitors were used to review the edited material. Without the disc drives the machine had lost its random access ability, and still required tedious transfer of material to the tape. In this case, three copies of each good take were made from the one-inch master. The recorders were specially made Sony Betamax machines. There was one U-matic copy for viewing dailies, one serial Betamax copy, and one Betamax for separate good takes. Through a complicated process, whereby each scene was picked up from a different cassette, a so-called rough cut was put together.[67]

Again claiming that postediting with videotape had been too clumsy and inefficient, CBS said that with this new technology, a significant percentage of prime-time programming would be shifted to "electronic cinematography."[68] Of course, they had predicted the same thing about the CMX-600 in 1971 and the percentage of film programs had gone up. According to a poll taken of 17 edit controllers in June 1980, all used some kind of keyboard for their data input.[69] The only thing that CBS got right was that they "clearly recognize that producers, cinematographers, and others currently doing prime time programming will not instantly flock to a new electronic medium." They didn't. This was another futile attempt by CBS engineering to promote the CMX-600 concept at all costs.[70]

In 1979, it was announced that for the first time in 15 years, the BBC had bought no transverse video recorders. Instead they had bought 40 one-inch machines of the SMPTE/EBU format C type. However, they had reduced the head drum speed to 50 rev/sec from 60 rev/sec which resulted in a lowered writing speed. The EBU Group stated this was preferable to establishing a new one-inch format radically different from that adopted by the SMPTE.[71]

Chapter 11

Introduction of the Camcorder (1980–1984)

In February 1980, Philips and Grundig introduced the Video 2000 videocassette recorder system. It was one of the most advanced home recorders ever conceived. It boasted eight hours of playing time on one cassette at the price of only $5 a tape hour. The new tape cassette and VCR format was jointly developed by Philips in Holland and Grundig in Germany. Their VCR system was incompatible with the Japanese recorders that had cornered the market, but it was tops in tape economy and technical features.

Long play was achieved by a unique reversible, dual-track cassette that flipped over just like the familiar audio cassette Philips had pioneered. The cassette was about the size of a paperback book, and the two tracks on standard half-inch tape gave four hours of playing time in both directions, for a total of eight hours on one cassette.

Each ultranarrow video track was a quarter of the width used on the earlier Philips N1700 deck, which had only three hours' capacity and cost four times as much per tape hour. This development was made possible by a high-precision electronic-control system called dynamic track following (DTF), a professional concept applied for the first time to consumer equipment. The rotating video heads used for helical scanning were mounted on piezo-electric crystals. They were fed with a control signal from a servo to keep the heads in continuous alignment with the magnetic tracks. This was of course the first video-cassette to make use of the AST feature that Ampex had invented.

This self-correction technique made it possible to eliminate the extra track of synchronization pulses along the tape edge used by all other video systems. Thus there

was room for wider sound tracks for improved audio response or future stereo. Frequency range on stereo still extended to a medium fidelity of 12.5kHz, thanks to the wide audio tracks. There was also space for an additional "cuing" track to locate specific recordings anywhere on the tape. These were visually identified by a four-figure counter on the deck. A "search" button found them after the selection was made on a digital keyboard.

Tape speed was 2.44cm/sec (0.96 ips), slower than on earlier Philips models, which added playing time. Another benefit of dynamic track following was that tapes recorded on one machine were fully compatible for playback on other decks or on future machines based on the 2000 system.

The new VCR was equipped for automatic recording of TV programs through the use of a microprocessor circuit. The microprocessor memory could store instructions for 26 TV channels, and five programs on different stations could be preselected up to 16 days in advance. The machine automatically returned to the tape starting point once the recording had been made. Since the deck sensed which of four tape lengths was being used, the microprocessor could alert the operator if they had exceeded the recording time available for automatic operation.

The microprocessor also simplified mechanical operation of the deck. If one wanted to remove a cassette while the machine was playing, for example, one could press the eject button. The machine stopped automatically, rewound the tape, and ejected the cassette. Magnavox, an affiliate of Philips, would market the video deck in the USA.[1]

The 58th annual convention of NAB was held in Las

Vegas from April 13 through 16, 1980. The main theme of the convention was: "TV engineers want to do everything we do in film, faster and cheaper." It was implied that to do so would require electronic production and postproduction with the quality of 35mm film. This, of course, was suggested by the CBS engineering department.[2]

Among the new products shown was the latest RCA TR-800 type C VTR. It was emphasized that this new machine was of RCA's own design and manufacture. (The company had been selling the Sony type C machine under the RCA label.) It offered remarkable speed and tape-handling capabilities. A 90-minute tape reel could be rewound in less than 135 seconds. A 30 second recue could be made in less than four seconds. It featured fully servoed tape handling, two-hour reel capacity, fast locking, acceleration, and deceleration, and was all-microprocessor-controlled. A new feature, Supertrack (Ampex AST), had ⅕ to 2x play, broadcastable pictures, frame-by-frame jogging, and frame accurate control. A companion TBC-8000 was fully digital, had six-point surround DOC and digital chroma converter. A multirate video controller (MRVC) was incorporated for slow motion and instant replay. The AE-800 editing system featured full time-code editing and special effects editing.[3] the machine had a signal to noise ratio of 48db and two program audio channels with 57db S/N at 3 percent harmonic distortion.[4] It was called the first of the second generation type C machines.

The 3M Company announced the introduction of their new type C one-inch video recorder, the TT-7000. They claimed that it had all the standard features of other C machines plus full audio and video confidence heads, sync channel, and the like. It also featured auto track following (the Ampex ATS system) as an option. The machine was made for them in Japan by Nippon Electric Company. It cost about $11,000 and required the NEC TBC.[5]

Ampex announced its new VPR-2B, which among other things could provide reverse slow motion capability. It had improved audio performance, selectable muting, and a posterase capability. Its TBC-2B had a higher speed A/D converter, a 16-line window, and a one-line DOC. A new option was the STC-100 multipoint search-to-cue device which provided up to 99 searchable cue points for slow-motion control. It had a read-write memory so that once cue points were coded, the tape could be played back to its cued locations on any other STC-100 equipped VTR.[6]

In April 1980, Ampex also introduced the Ampex Video Art (AVA) system which gave the television graphic artist a way to create and store work. Using an electronic stylus and pallet, the artist had at their command a broad selection of colors, shapes, and hues, to create original art or modify existing pictures, charts or diagrams. It included a powerful DEC PDP-11/34 minicomputer with 256 of RAM, and a choice of disk drives. It was priced between $150,000 and $200,000.[7] Ampex announced that its third quarter and nine month figures for earnings, sales, orders and backlog were the highest in the company's history.[8]

IVC introduced its new high-band, one-inch, non SMPTE standard, color videotape player-recorder, the IVC 1-11. It used the high-band signal system of the IVC 9000, and had Dolby noise reduction on its two-quality audio tracks. Video signal to noise ratio was rated at 49db and audio S/N at 55db. Priced at between $30,000 and $35,000, it was intended as a low-cost mastering and multigeneration machine.[9]

Sony demonstrated an experimental DVR recorder. It was capable of recording data at 198.22 Mb/sec, had a tape speed of 122mm/sec (4.5 inches/sec), and a head-drum rotation of 60rps. It was capable of recording 16 channels of digital audio interlaced with the video. The audio sampling frequency was 50.4/1.001kHz quantisized. The newest version also used a 4 *f*sc sampling rate, rather than the 3 *f*sc shown before, and had slow motion and variable shuttle speed. Sony stated that later that month, they would demonstrate an experimental DVR using a U-type transport. This was to take place in England.[10]

At a special press conference, William Connolly of CBS outlined some concerns regarding DVR technology. Connolly and Sony's Morizano threw their support behind a component encoding scheme rather than a composite standard such as being considered in Europe. Connolly said, "Component digital coding offers the opportunity to remove the limitations of NTSC, SECAM and PAL

1980. NHK experimental digital videotape recorder. (NHK.)

standards and to obtain a universal standard that is impossible to attain with analog or composite digital standards." Both agreed that the answers were three to five years in the future.[11]

Ampex also unveiled a new portable production camera, the BCC-20 Digicam, which was made in Cupertino, CA. It was claimed to be the first to be set up by a computer. It had the extraordinary ability to achieve 0.05 percent registration in all three zones and to reduce shading error. With a microprocessor in its head, it could be set up automatically and remotely. It was capable of using an integrated fiber optic RGB transmission cable with power conductors built in.[12]

Thomson-CSF offered a new TTV-1525 camera using a one-inch lead oxide tube in the luminance channel and ⅔-inch diode gun tubes for red and blue. It could be operated either from a camera control panel or from a centralized location automatically.[13]

An unusual new TV camera was introduced by Ikegami. It was the Ikegami EC-35 electronic cinematography camera. It looked and felt like a 35mm film camera; indeed, it was designed as an electronic alternative to the 35mm. The EC-35 used ⅔-inch diode gun Plumbicon tubes with minimum 100 percent modulation depth at 400 lines. Special horizontal aperture compensation and detail correction circuits adjusted for out-band and in-band responses. Corner modulation was improved with dynamic-beam focus. Signal to noise ratio was 56db. To provide a wide dynamic range similar to film, a unique compensation circuit compressed signal levels from 400 percent of the rated signal level down to the 100 percent level. This avoided video saturation on highlights. A dynamic-beam stretch circuit effectively reduced comet tailing. It was possible to operate four stops in excess of normal peak video level.

1980. Ikegami electronic cinematography camera. (Ikegami brochure.)

Auto setup was another feature. No skilled video engineers were needed to set up or operate the camera. It came with a microprocessor setup system. When pointed at a special test pattern, the computer automatically set up the camera without any human help. One button established black-and-white balance, gamma tracking and registration. A special set of lenses had been developed by Canon for Ikegami so that the camera was equivalent to a 35mm film camera.[14]

Sony introduced its DVX-1800 camera which featured the newly developed Trinicon imaging tube that provided low lag and high sensitivity — never before possible in a single-gun camera. Its S/N was 48db and the horizontal resolution 300 lines.[15] Panasonic showed its new WV-3900 single-tube camera with a new high sensitivity Newvicon that boasted good colorimetry. Ten foot candles of illumination at f2 was the minimum lighting required.[16] RCA showed its new TK-47EP camera that used low-capacitance diode-gun Plumbicons. A narrow scan on the 30mm tube reduced geometric distortion and improved registration accuracy.

RCA also demonstrated for the first time a CCD (charge-coupled device) color camera. It was designed for educational and training, not broadcast. The CCD image sensor was a solid-state device that was an integrated circuit made from a silicon wafer. It comprised a matrix of 512 × 320 elements, the chip, therefore, contained more than 163,840 elements. It had a 12.2mm image diagonal, larger than that of a ⅔-inch Vidicon. The image was transformed into thousands of electrical charges which were then read out rapidly by charge transfer techniques. Integrated circuits processed the signals, combined them and fed them into the monitor. The resulting image was fully compatible with standard 525-line video displays.[17]

Harris Electronics stated that its TC-80 A camera would be available with full automatic setup later that year.

Each camera detailed above had its own microprocessor.

1954. New DuMont "Tel-EYE" TV camera mounted on 16mm movie camera. (DuMont Labs.)

The show had its usual new lines of editors, time-base correctors, switches, character generators, and other accessories. [18]

Faroudja Laboratories showed a new version of its Image System. It consisted of two units: (1) Record One, a small booster designed to be attached to a standard U type of portable recorder, and (2) Playback One, a playback processor. When used together, the color output was greatly improved with sharper edges, less ringing and a better signal to noise ratio, in both luminance and chrominance, of 6db. There was also automation. A "pilot training" signal was inserted in the nonpicture part of the playback unit and this automatically adjusted the degree of correction of the picture. The record unit was priced at $2,100 and the playback unit at $5,995. [19]

A special system for converting videotape to high-resolution film was shown by Compact Video Systems. Known as Image Vision, it was a new encoding-decoding system that provided high-definition television, overcoming the technical limitations of NTSC, PAL and SECAM. [20]

Finally, at the Antiope booth was a monitor displaying teletext messages from local CBS station KLAS. Closer to adoption was the Antiope closed-captioning system that was for the hard-of-hearing. It was developed in conjunction with CBS-TV engineering to be used on "60 Minutes." [21]

In May 1980, it was announced that the Signal Companies, a worldwide multiindustry company with sales of over $5 billion, and the Ampex Corp. had entered into an agreement for the purchase of Ampex by Signal through an exchange of stock. Forrest N. Shumway, Signal Chairman and CEO, stated that "Ampex is a well-managed company with a great future. We contemplate no changes in its operating philosophy or in its existing management. It principally designs, manufactures and markets worldwide professional audio and video systems, computer memories and data-handling products, magnetic tapes and accessories." The merger was expected to close in mid 1980, [22] but it was announced in August 1980 that the merger had been terminated due to economic conditions and depressed stock prices. [23] However, on January 15, 1981, the merger finally went through. Ampex became a wholly owned subsidiary of Signal Companies. [24]

On July 1, 1980, the Sony Corp. unveiled a new home movie camera that recorded on magnetic tape rather than film. The unit weighed only 4.4 pounds and was roughly $7.6 \times 6.8 \times 2.4$ inches. It was a two-head rotary model, with FM modulation, azimuth recording, 250 lines of resolution, a 45db signal to noise ratio, and recorded 20 minutes on $\frac{5}{16}$ metal cassette tape. It used a cassette 2¼ inches wide, 1½ inches high, and a ½-inch thick. It had a micro-sized solid-state CCD on a single chip as a sensor with 570 horizontal by 490 vertical elements, and had a through-the-lens viewfinder. Akio Morita, chairman and chief executive of Sony, said that it wasn't expected to be a commercial item until 1985. Sony expected to meet with other manufacturers to decide on a compatible format that would make the smallest video camera standardized worldwide. What was interesting to one editor was that Sony was showing a model that worked and showed quite good pictures. [25]

In July 1980, a survey of the gear used in electronic journalism was published by the School of Journalism at Southern Illinois University. Starting with cameras, the survey found that the most used camera was the RCA, with Sony next, followed by Hitachi and Ikegami. Field recorders found Sony in first place, with JVC second. Sony also dominated in editing recorders, with Panasonic and Convergence behind. In time-base correctors, CVS was first, followed by Microtime. When it came to reliability, the RCA-76B was first and Ikegami second. They were followed by JVC and Hitachi, and ending with Thomson-CSF. In field recorders, they found the Sony BVU-50 preeminent in reliability and Sony's BVU-100 was somewhat better than its VO-3800 and JVC's machine. In time-base correctors, Adda and Ampex had the highest ratings in reliability, with the much used CVS also doing well. When it came to EJ versus newsfilm, most (54 percent) stations said that EJ was more expensive. When it came to getting stories on the air, EJ got 78 percent of the vote; newsfilm only 22 percent. [26]

 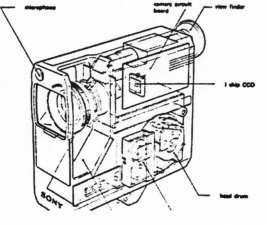

1980. *Above:* Sony CCD video movie camera. *Below:* Inside diagram of camera. (Sony.)

1980. Technicolor compact portable VCR used quarter-inch tape. (Technicolor.)

In September 1980, Technicolor Incorporated introduced its new portable color videocassette recorder which weighed seven pounds with batteries. It used quarter-inch tape that would record for 30 minutes. The tape was supposed to be of the VHS format for possible use in future recorders. The unit measures ten inches square and three inches deep. It was developed jointly with Funai Electric Trading Company of Japan who would make the recorder, camera and accessories. The machine had freeze-frame capability and slow and fast viewing speeds, sound dubbing and a video signal to noise ratio of 43db. It was claimed that the unit went on sale in August for $995.[27]

In September 1980, one of the best kept secrets of prerecorded programming to this time was revealed — pornographic films had given the industry its initial impetus. It was confirmed that the x-rated business until then had monopolized the sales of prerecorded tapes. Finally, it was claimed more activity was taking place in the area of general and family entertainment. Yet, according to one author, the two longest lines at the summer Consumer Electronics show in Chicago were to see the JVC videodisc — and the porn star Marilyn Chambers![28]

Another author claimed that "retailers who only a year ago expressed serious reservations about merchandising pre-recorded videocassettes have changed their minds. This attitude can be attributed to the increasing availability of 'family type' fare from major film studios which has caused a marked decline in the share of x-rated tapes *which previously accounted for the bulk of pre-recorded activity*. Many dealers were reluctant to sell tape programming at all, fearing [that] consumers' association of the category with porn would tarnish their image in the community."[29]

Even the British were pleased at porn's downfall. One editor stated that "as to video porn itself, it has already lost much of its relative dominance of the market and, although unlikely to vanish from this corrupt and mindless world, it will soon shrivel to the proportions of a tiny aberration in the electronic information society." Fortunately, like it or not, the so-called aberration helped to launch the infant videocassette industry.[30] In July 1981, "adult video" was still the second-largest sales category.[31]

At this show, RCA showed the final production model of its SST-100 CED player. The company planned to put this system on the market in the first quarter of 1981. RCA chairman, Edgar H. Griffiths, said that they would begin initial shipments to distributors for demonstrations in December 1980 and anticipated selling as many as 200,000 players in the first year. Also shown was the competing Japanese Victor VHD (video high density) disc player. It was announced that G.E., Matsushita, Panasonic and Quasar would all be selling this machine. It was claimed that this machine could play at many speeds of forward and reverse search, and had still-frame capability as well as stereo sound. Its biggest handicap was its lack of a software (programs) catalog, something which the competing RCA machine had. JVC planned for the player to reach the USA market by the end of 1981. RCA hoped by that time to have sold about 100,000 of *its* new players.[32]

In October 1980, Hitachi introduced a new developmental one piece camera/video recorder called the Mag Cam. It combined a solid-state color camera and a videocassette recorder-player in a 39.5 × 7.7 × 3 inch package. It weighted 5.7 pounds and used a new quarter-inch cassette that gave two hours of recording time. It had a simple chip, a metal oxide semiconductor (MOS) with a ⅔-inch image sensor surface, and a through-the-lens viewfinder. Hitachi stated that they hoped to release the recorder in only two years.[33]

1980. Alexander M. Poniatoff (left) and Charles P. Ginsburg. (Ampex.)

Alexander M. Poniatoff died on October 24, 1980. (Ampex.)

On October 24, 1980, Alexander M. Poniatoff died at age 88. He was the founder of the Ampex Corporation that gave the world the first practical videotape recorder. It was reported that at his death Ampex had sales of $500 million dollars. He died at Stanford Medical Center, which was using one of Ampex's medical products.[34]

1980. Charles P. Ginsburg (left) with Dr. Vladimir Zworykin at 122nd SMPTE conference. (Ampex.)

In October 1980, it was reported that CBS had petitioned the FCC to adopt a single teletext standard, namely its modification of the French Antiope system. Receiver manufacturers were not pleased with CBS plans, as the Antiope system, which was asynchronous, required more design changes in receivers than the Oracle/Ceefax system which was synchronous. CBS also called teletext the best means for transmitting close captions for hearing-impaired viewers.[35]

In November 1980, it was reported that Compact Video had installed a control room at Paramount Studios for the production of the ABC TV situation comedy, "Bosom Buddies." This, of course, was for a three camera show using regular television techniques. Paramount Pictures had long had an interest in television production, and had owned TV station KTLA in Los Angeles, one of LA's pioneer TV stations. It wasn't long before every studio in Hollywood was going into television production using the three-camera approach.[36] This was, naturally, in addition to the traditional major productions being filmed there.

In November 1980, the 122nd technical conference of the SMPTE was held in New York City. It was claimed that Monday afternoon was pure nostalgia. Dr. Vladimir Zworykin, "father of television" at the age of 91, was on hand to watch a taped interview with him made for the SMPTE. He made a brief speech and then met with another television pioneer, Charles Ginsburg of Ampex, and officers of the SMPTE. Zworykin was presented with the Fellowship Citation Plaque of the Royal Television Society of London.

BBC authors, Phil Sidey, Bob Longman and Tony Pilgrim, gave a presentation of the history of British television, including historical films and tapes dating back to

the early thirties. They also had with them an actual Emitron camera that was used in the coverage of King George VI's coronation in 1937. There was also a two-hour presentation by Joe Roizen on the history of television technology. A historical paper by George Shiers of Santa Barbara entitled "The Rise of Mechanical Television 1901–1930" was read by SMPTE archivist Steve Chamberlain. Finally, a film produced by the Bell Labs in 1926 to explain the new Vitaphone film sound system, was shown.

Richard Streeter of CBS described the design considerations that must go into TV cameras made for electronic cinematography. He pointed out that to get the "film look" and 35mm quality took special attention to features such as resolution, S/N ratio, transfer characteristics and enhancement.

First of all, his remarks about the various video camera manufacturers trying to capture the nebulous film look were not quite true. The image from a film camera and the image from a video camera by their very nature cannot look the same. At that moment, the various video camera producers were trying to placate the film people with the idea that perhaps they could emulate the so-called film look, but this is just not possible. What they were doing was to make a video camera look and feel like a film camera complete with matte boxes, follow-focus mechanisms, and changeable lenses so that they would not "alienate" any camera operators who were adverse to video. (I do believe that I even saw a video camera equipped with a video assist [through the lens] at one of the trade shows!)

Streeter did not describe the film look at all. The question then arose, just what was the *film look*? Basically, it was an advertising gimmick by a certain film manufacturer to convince their old customers that film provided the best image available and that it was somehow sacrosanct. The company implied that film had a certain set of characteristics that could somehow be defined. Yet it is well known that each film emulsion (and there were literally hundreds) "looked" different. Film varies from manufacturer to manufacturer, batch to batch, and from lab to lab processing it, whether it is in color or black-and-white. All that films have in common is that they consist of a multilayered emulsion on a cellulose base. So how does one define something with so many variables? The answer is that one *does not*.

The film look was simply *tradition*, something people had lived with for almost a hundred years. What Streeter was really discussing was a complicated admixture of psychological sensations, granular structure, picture jump and weave and a 24-frame rate that was barely compatible with human sensing abilities (60 cycles appears more in tune with our human visual perception of motion). It was a part of a mass experience (the theater environment) with all of its ramifications. What was called the film look was simply an old friend we'd seen for years and were used to.

In order to clarify this phenomenon of an unwillingness to break with tradition, let me provide two examples. In 1925, Western Electric came out with electric sound recording which was a vast improvement over the old mechanical recording system. Yet when the public first heard these records, they complained bitterly over strident and harsh sound and it took a while to overcome this reluctance. The famous Chinn/Eisenberg experiment with FM sound was another example. From behind a curtain, they tested the public's response to the new high-fidelity 15,000 cycle FM sound by comparing it with normal AM 5,000 cycle response. When the audience was asked which sound they preferred, the overwhelming choice was the old radio system. They rejected the new system even though they didn't know why.

The same type of event was taking place in the early eighties with the introduction of high-definition television. The pictures available from HDTV were vastly superior in tonal range, color response, contrast, and brightness to the normal motion picture we saw projected in a theater. It also had a complete lack of grain with absolute picture steadiness. Indeed, these pictures were different from the so-called film look and many people (especially professional camera operators and others unfamiliar with these new images) were reluctant to admit what their eyes were telling them. The truth was that these electronic pictures were closer to what the eye saw than the pictures projected from a film frame. This, of course, disturbed many in the industry as well as the status quo. It is easy to understand the position of the film manufacturing companies as they felt the heat of the competition to their tried and true product for recording pictures. At the end of the day, though, the tradition held back progress.[37]

Charles Ginsburg gave a paper (first read in 1957) and showed slides of the very first pictures obtained from an arcuate-scan predecessor to the transverse machine Ampex finally developed. It was mentioned that over 14,000 transverse recorders had been put into service since 1956 and that other format VTRs reached into the millions. Ginsburg was honored with a picture of him and Dr. Zworykin together. These two pioneers had done more to advance television technology than anyone else in the world.[38]

In January 1981, Ampex introduced a new "true-frame playback helical scan recorder." An option for the VPR-2B doubled the vertical resolution of the freeze frame, greatly enhancing the vertical resolution, which improved the quality of the picture in this mode.[39]

On February 6–7, 1981, the 15th annual SMPTE television conference was held in San Francisco. There were four sessions: digital video recording, new camera technology and digital techniques, future directions for television, and the all-digital studio. A series of demonstrations were given of digital video. One of the highlights of the program was the first demonstration in North America of 1,125-line color NHK high-definition television by Dr. Takashi Fujio. The broad-band camera used two-inch Saticon pickup tubes, and there was also a direct-view picture tube with a high-definition faceplate. The picture quality was judged to be excellent.[40] Also present was Francis Ford Coppola who told of his experience using TV equipment as an aid to film making.

From April 12 to 15, 1981, the 59th NAB annual convention was held in Las Vegas. In 1981, Ampex was celebrating its VTR silver jubilee — 25 years of growth of an industry. Ampex claimed that it had sold over half of the broadcast VTRs used all over the world, that it had delivered its 2,000th VPR-2B recorder to Datacommunications in Paris, and that in March 1981 its 3,000th VPR-2B was sold to Donald Douglas. This represented for a total of 5,000 machines. The Ampex VPR-2B was the world's most widely used studio videotape recorder.[41]

3M was also celebrating the 25th anniversary of the introduction of commercial videotape recording. It was mentioned that over 14,000 transverse machines had been sold during that time and they used great amounts of two-inch tape, much of it from 3M. In conjunction with Ampex, a tape was shown of memorable events that had been recorded on videotape. The Nixon/Khrushchev kitchen debate, the Kennedy inaugural and tragic aftermath of the assassination, the Apollo moon landing, and the U.S. hockey team winning the Olympics.[42]

This NAB convention was also important for the fact that several of the major camera manufacturers displayed their first new portable video camera-recorders for EJ or EFP use. The most publicized machine was the RCA revolutionary unit named "Hawkeye." While the cassette was the same size as that of VHS, its recording format was new. Recording for 20 minutes, it was claimed to give better quality than the high-band U-matic. It used a single half-inch Saticon or diode-gun Plumbicon. No price or when it would be available was mentioned.[43] This was the most revolutionary camera yet introduced by RCA. While Sony had shown a smaller, developmental camera-recorder in May 1980, it was only a laboratory model that the company expected would not be ready for the consumer until at least 1985.

The camera was designed and manufactured by RCA Broadcast Systems and the recording units manufactured by Matsushita to RCA specifications. While the Hawkeye uses the same size cassette as VHS, it incorporated new circuit technology, head design, and recording approach. It was called the "M" format or later Chromatrak.[44]

A component signal was recorded on two different tracks, thus avoiding noise and phase errors of continual encoding and decoding as in ¾-inch machines. Luminance was recorded on one track, and chroma on the other. The chroma components were on separate FM carriers— amplitude modulation was not used. By recording components, RCA eliminated the crosstalk and moiré problems of earlier systems in which chrominance and luminance shared a common track. Because the color signal was recorded without the use of a color subcarrier, color editing was made as simple as monochrome editing, and in the PAL system the need to identify the eight field PAL sequence to avoid a "jump left'" or "'jump right'" had been eliminated.

Chromatrak employed the helical scan of only ½-inch tape. The wrap had at times been referred to as "M" wrap. It was the head drum in the Chromatrak format that enabled the separate recording of luminance and chrominance on completely independent tracks. The chroma head lagged the luminance head and staggered vertically from it about 0.13mm. In addition, there were two flying erase heads mounted on the upper drum to provide the opportunity to cleanly insert new video. The two pairs of video heads on the drum were spaced 180 degrees from each other: field one was always recorded by one pair and field two by the other pair. Since the tape was wrapped just over 180 degrees around the drum, two successive passes of the head were needed to record an entire frame in 360 degrees of drum rotation. Both drum rotation, which was at a speed of 1,800 rpm, and tape motion were in the same direction, in direct conflict with type C practice. By choosing tape direction and drum rotation to be the same, the Chromatrak designers were able to improve frequency response related to head-to-tape contact. Chromatrak recorded a chrominance bandwidth of 1.0MHz and a luminance of 3.8MHz, and did this at a head-to-tape speed of only 4.7 meters per second. The signals were recorded employing an FM carrier. These signals were directly derived from a Hawkeye camera, but when the recorder was fed from an external coded or composite source, a combtype of decoder derived the base band signal. The component signals were converted to FM signals: R-Y deviation from 5.5 to 6.5MHz and B-Y from 0.95 to 1.55MHz. Four stationary heads recorded audio at 8 inches/sec on a high-quality soundtrack, using track three for time code.[45]

RCA's Hawkeye camera weighed in at 23 pounds including batteries. It used a half-inch Saticon or diode-gun Plumbicon. The Saticon was the first broadcast quality half-inch Saticon tube made. It was claimed to have a response at 400 TV lines of 40 percent, with lag performance less than 2 percent.[46]

By coincidence, and introduced privately at NAB, was the new Sony BVW-1 portable camera-recorder. It was called the Betacam (Sony was not about to give up that name). It had a camera using a single-tube high band SMF Trinicon tube. It used a Beta half-inch cassette which gave 20 minutes of recording time on L-500 tape, but had a new high performance format that was compatible with current worldwide analog and digital standards. It had a 20 percent faster writing speed for greater resolution and higher signal to noise ratio. It would also be available in a three-mixed-field-tube version. (This was the three-tube BVP-3.) It weighed 13 pounds with batteries and lens.[47]

Panasonic Video Systems also showed their entry in the one-piece camera-VTR sweepstakes. The 22-pound unit included a camera, the Panasonic AUAK-100, and used three ⅔-inch tubes and prism optics with a luminance signal to noise ratio of 48db. The nonstandard VCR used a unique component signal recording reprocess (the same format used in the RCA "Hawkeye.") The unit incorporated a new editing system, the Panasonic NV-A790 with SMPTE time code.[48] Panasonic's new compact recorder weighed about 22 pounds with lens and mic.

1982 RCA Hawkeye camera-recorder. (RCA.)

1983. Sony Betacam BVW-3 ⅔-inch camera/recorder. (Sony.)

Its cassette also ran for 20 minutes. As the recorder was not compatible with VHS machines,[49] it was presumed, at the time, that it would use the same tape standard as the RCA Hawkeye Other camera-recorders were the Ikegami HL-83 which featured three ⅔-inch Saticon or Plumbicon tubes. The camera was adaptable to an attachable recorder in addition to a remote studio control unit and standard EJ recorders.[50]

In April 1981, Matsushita Electric Industrial Co. Ltd. of Japan introduced its new camcorder called the Micro Video System. It used a micro videocassette that was 94mm (h) by 63mm (w) by 14mm (d) in size. It contained a metal evaporated tape with flux density ten times greater than that of regular tape. It ran for two hours at a speed of 14.3mm tape/sec. The camera tube was the 12.5mm Cosvicon, the smallest in the world.[51]

Also in April 1981, Matsushita announced that it had recently produced its two millionth VHS recorder since April 1977. Although it took more than two years to make the first million recorders, the second million was produced in one year.[52]

In May 1981, RCA claimed to have sold 43,000 SelectaVision disc players to distributors during its first month on the market — 22,000 to customers alone. In early 1982, RCA announced that a stereo version of the player would be introduced. Over 130,000 players were sold in 1982 (compared to two million videocassette players). By the end of 1983, over 500,000 players had been sold. RCA was predicting that by the 1990s business would be $7.5 billion a year for videodiscs.[53]

1981. First Matsushita portable color camera-recorder. (Matsushita.)

At an SMPTE panel discussion on high-definition TV held in New York City on September 9, 1981, Francis Ford Coppola of the Zoetrope Studios told of his experiences with TV system techniques to edit his picture *Apocalypse Now*. The edit decisions were made on half-inch Beta machines to produce an edited cassette, the equivalent of a film "work print." This tape served as the film editor's guide to assembling and editing the film takes. Coppola complained that the lack of random access slowed down the edit process.[54]

The story of Coppola's shooting of the movie *One*

1982. Panasonic Recam portable camera-recorder. (Panasonic.)

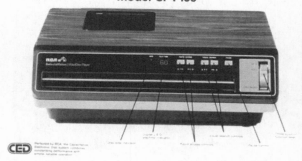

1980. RCA Selectavision disk player model SFT100. (RCA.)

From the Heart was related in October 1981. It was Coppola's first (and last) attempt to combine movie making with television equipment. His aim was to prepare for the "time when movies will not be made on film, but on high-definition video which will ultimately surpass film in both image quality and image manipulation capabilities." However, Coppola was not shooting in high definition and was using video only as a crutch. He was a true genius who made superb motion pictures, such as the *Godfather* films and *Apocalypse Now*, but somehow his vision about how to use the new medium was muddled and he probably put electronic film making back several years.

Instead of shooting movie style using video cameras and recorders, he complicated the system from storyboard to actual shooting. The most successful part seemed to be the use of video assist whereby everybody seemed to have their own monitor and headphones (lighting people, sound designer, sound recorder, dialogue coach, script supervisor, and so on — pure television!) After each take, the tape was immediately played back for instant approval or rejection by the DP or director. After complicated editing, the picture was completed. However, Coppola was not satisfied with the video editing technology. Unfortunately, the picture ran out of money and 400 members of the cast agreed to postpone payment of their salaries to keep the cameras rolling. Sadly for all this effort, it was a rather poor picture and did not last long. Even geniuses like Coppola have their bad days! But this picture would have been just as bad if it had been shot with a 70mm Cinerama camera, 8mm, 16mm, plain old 35mm, or videotape. It is not the medium that makes the difference; it is the people.[55]

At the RTNDA convention in New Orleans September 10–12, 1981, the combination Hawkeye camera-VTR was displayed. It caused much concern as many news directors were under the impression that the Hawkeye system was not compatible with U-matic and one-inch formats. (It was not.) However, interfaces with the Sony BVE-500 A were demonstrated. Shortly after NAB, CMX/Orrix, Datatron and Convergence made commitments to build interfaces for their controllers and the Hawkeye playback unit. Unaware of this *compatibility*, some CBS affiliates complained about the apparent push to change EJ formats. They finally accepted the sentiment that the new camera/VTR was not an engineering problem, it was a communication problem.[56] Actually this was to be a repeat of the VHS versus Beta war, and the opponents were the same; i.e., Hawkeye was from Matsushita and Betacam from Sony.

Specifications on the HC-1 Hawkeye showed a weight of 22 pounds, including lens and batteries, the use of three half-inch diode-gun Plumbicons, a signal to noise ratio of 52db, resolution of 400 lines, and sensitivity of 700 lux

with Saticons and 460 with Plumbicons. It was priced at $38,500 for the camera only and $53,500 including the recorder. It was available in NTSC, PAL-B, PAL-M or SECAM IIIB standards.[57]

In September 1981, the CCIR agreed on international standards for digital video. The decision heralded the standardization of digital equipment on a worldwide basis. The primary standard agreed on was that compatibility be maintained for programming made in one country and distributed to others. No longer would producers have to worry about standards conversions for programs made in NTSC that were to be played in countries that used PAL or SECAM. The agreement did not, however, indicate what standards countries would use within their own borders, but it was assumed that most countries would conform to the worldwide parameters.

In the USA, the SMPTE had had considerable input into the discussions on digital standards through extensive and in-depth international cooperation and liaison. William G. Connolly of CBS presented a paper on the significance of the agreement to the SMPTE in October.[58]

On October 12, 1981, Hitachi introduced their new trielectrode pickup tube. It used a Se-As-Te Amorphous Photoconductor. It was claimed that a trielectrode tube had higher resolution than a color filter striped tube. The resolution was over 500 lines, the highest value possible in a single-tube color camera. The 353 triplets of color filter stripes were constructed on a 29mm glass plate, thus a special lens was needed to use this tube. It had high resolution, low lag, and good color reproducibility.[59]

In December 1981, Hitachi announced a new FP-10 one-tube camera with three-tube resolution. It included the new electrode one-inch Saticon tube. The company claimed the camera had 450 lines of resolution and no registration problems. It had a built-in image enhancer, (ABO) automatic beam optimization, an extended dynamic range, and guaranteed easy highlight handling. It could be used as a studio camera with an optional five-inch viewfinder and remote operation unit (ROU).[60]

In December 1981, Sony introduced a similar tube. It was called the HBST (High Band Saticon Trinicon) tube. It too used 27m striped filters of RGB aligned on the faceplate, a selenium-based photoconductive layer. Transferring the luminance signal direct to the encoder produced a superior signal to noise ratio of 52db (4.2MHz unweighted) and chrominance bandwidth of 1.0kHz or 45db.

The Sony tube was to be installed in the company's BVP-110 camera. It had a built in sync generator, encoder, ABO, two-line image enhancement and auto white balance with digital memory. It had only one connection to a VTR, such as the BVU-50. It was claimed that it could compete with modern ⅔-inch three-tube cameras.[61]

In February 1982, Ampex announced its new BCC-20/21 Digicam camera. Starting with an EFP configuration, it could be upgraded with a built-in computer. It could be made into a studio camera by simply adding studio frame and electronics.[62]

In March 1982, it was reported that the noted French television pioneer, Joseph Polonsky, had died. Polonsky had pioneered in the use of very short (CM) waves for the first monochrome EJ units using the Vidicon camera and portable backpack transmitter. These camera units were used by CBS in 1956 to cover the major political conventions in the USA, forerunners of today's widespread EJ operations. Polonsky was a member of the French Resistance during World War II. He was affiliated with various French firms such as Thomson-CSF where he was technical director of the broadcasting division. He was equally fluent in French, English, Russian, and his native Polish language.[63]

On April 1, 1982, Harry F. Olson died at the age of 81 years. He had retired in 1967 as staff vice president, acoustical and electromechanical research for RCA Laboratories. He had over 100 patents on devices and systems in the acoustical field. He developed several types of microphones, underwater sound equipment, and sound motion picture systems. He guided the development of the ill-fated high-speed RCA video recorder. He had been a member of the National Academy of Sciences since 1959.[64]

On April 4–7, 1982, at the NAB convention held in Dallas, Sony showed its new prototype Betacam camera-recorder. It was claimed to be 30 percent lighter than its competitor and more than 40 percent smaller. The device used a high-band SMF Trinicon single-tube pickup system. It recorded for 20 minutes on a Beta L-500 cassette and ran for a full hour on the batteries contained in the unit. A separate playback unit interfaced with existing equipment.[65]

The higher head-to-tape speed allowed the recording of the newly developed compressed time-division multiplex component format. Luminance was recorded on one track while R-Y and B-Y color difference signals were compressed 2:1 in time and alternately recorded on a second track. In the playback process, R-Y and B-Y signals were restored to their original form and delayed 2H. The time difference was compensated for by digital retiming built into the BVW-10 player unit.[66]

RCA was again showing its Hawkeye portable camcorder. They had 21 units on display and for sale. Ikegami simply added a recorder on the side of its HL-83. It also used the M format. Bosch showed its KBF-1 which with lens, viewfinder, and battery weighed only 15 pounds. The camera incorporated three half-inch Plumbicons. It used a quarter-inch cassette similar to that of Funai, but had

chosen the color-under approach that gave two-track luminance and chrominance of bandwidth of 3MHz and 1MHz respectively. The VTR portion could only record for 12 minutes. The Bosch format used the quarter-inch Lineplex system. Taking advantage of the fact that the density of the chrominance recorded signals in NTSC is three times less than that of luminance, Bosch elected to use signal expansion and compression techniques to record equal densities by expanding luminance by a factor of 1.5 and compressing chrominance by two. Two tracks were to record odd and even tracks of multiplexed luminance and chrominance. By displacing heads, two horizontal line intervals were located in parallel in correspondence with appropriate picture elements.[67]

There were many EJ cameras on display. Harris showed its TC-90 which weighed only seven pounds. It was a three-tube camera with over 600 lines of resolution and an S/N of 57dB. Sharp showed its full featured XC-800 using three Saticon II tubes. It was to be sold for under $13,000. Ikegami came out with its ITC-730, also with 600-line resolution and lots of features. JVC showed its KY-2700A and claimed 600 lines of resolution for it. Panasonic also had a moderately price camera, the WV-777. It too had most of the convenience features of small cameras. Finally, Ikegami showed upgraded versions of its electronic cinematography cameras, which included a follow-focus mechanism and the popular J-4 zoom control.

In VTRs, Ampex showed its new VPR-80. It had a built-in editor with microprocessor communications and variable play. It interfaced with the TBC-2B time-base corrector for slow motion and still frames. It was to cost about $34,900. Sony's new BVH-2000 was half the size of the BVH-1100 but handled two-hour reels. It offered high-speed dynamic tracking (AST), a plug in TBC, and versatile system interface. It was to cost about $39,900 without the time-base corrector. 3M introduced its 3M/NEC TT 8000 recorder. It featured color playback without a TBC. It also met a new FCC Part 15, EMA spec which was mandatory after October 1982.

There were two solid-state cameras shown. The first was the NEC Model NC-2000. It used two CCD image sensors. Resolution was only fair, some 240 lines. The other was the Hitachi SK-1 which used three MOS image sensors. It had a higher resolution, some 450, but lower sensitivity. Picture quality was quite close to that of tubed cameras. It was priced around $20,000.

Bosch-Fernseh brought two new one-inch type B VTRs: the BCN 21 portable and the BCN-51 studio version. The portable weighed 20 pounds and was half the size of the BVN-20. Delivery was promised for the following year. IVC, which had been having financial troubles during the past year, had been taken over by Cezar International. They showed a new IVC-1. It used the tape

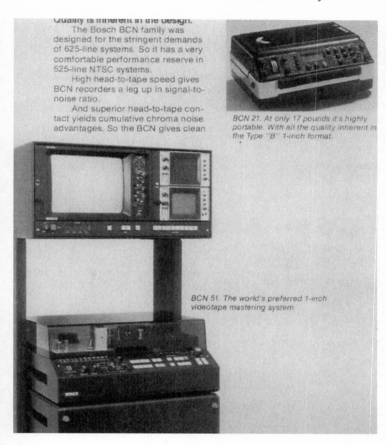

Quality is inherent in the design.
The Bosch BCN family was designed for the stringent demands of 625-line systems. So it has a very comfortable performance reserve in 525-line NTSC systems.

High head-to-tape speed gives BCN recorders a leg up in signal-to-noise ratio.

And superior head-to-tape contact yields cumulative chroma noise advantages. So the BCN gives clean

BCN 21. At only 17 pounds it's highly portable. With all the quality inherent in the Type "B" 1-inch format.

BCN 51. The world's preferred 1-inch videotape mastering system

1983. Bosch-Fernseh BCN-51 type "B" videotape recorder. (Bosch-Fernseh.)

transport of the IVC-9000 with Cezar's triband recording technique. Three components were recorded, with the Y band at 4.2MHz, I band at 1.5MHz, and Q at 600kHz providing full NTSC color playback. Sadly, the IVC couldn't give the television industry what it wanted, a compatible type C format, and the industry had rejected its expensive recorder (IVC 9000). It seemed at first that the IVC 9000 would have a large market overseas, but it never materialized, and the U.S. market was simply not interested in a machine with a different standard. The IVC-1 was to cost $29,500 and would be available in July.[68]

In June 1982, it was reported that NHK and CBS had sponsored a series of high definition demonstrations starting in January 1982. The system was developed by NHK with the cooperation of Panasonic, Sony and Ikegami. CBS's rationale for proposing a high-definition system for the USA was that "while our current system has served us well, continued dependence on that standard would mean that the United States would enter the 21st Century with the lowest technical-quality broadcasting system in existence." It added that "CBS supports the NKH proposal of 1125 lines, 60 fields, and a 5:3 aspect ratio."[69]

On June 22, 1982, Sony submitted its new half-inch Beta format to the SMPTE for standardization consider-

ation. Thomson-CSF had adopted this format and would manufacture and market its own half-inch camera-recorder. They also received a proposal from RCA, Matsushita and Ikegami to use their standard.[70]

On July 29, 1982, Vladimir Kosma Zworykin died at the Princeton Medical Center, one day before his 93rd birthday. He had often been referred to as the "father of television" because of his inventions of the iconoscope and kinescope which made today's electronic television possible. He was quick to disclaim that distinction, claiming that television had many fathers, and no one scientist out of the many whose inventions and developments had led to modern television could be the sole progenitor.[71]

From September 18 to 21, 1982, the International Broadcast Convention (IBC) was held in Brighton, England. It had several new items that usually were reserved for NAB. The first was an Ampex/Nagra type C VPR-5 one-inch portable VTR. It weighed less than 15 pounds including battery and tape. It could be converted to use one-hour reels. The main frame was made out of aircraft aluminum alloy 7075, had a special lightweight type C scanner, and all drives were by brushless dc drive motors. It had features such as full video and audio confidence on playback, Nagra-featured audio processing, and a more sophisticated camera-VTR-operator interface. It was probably the most well-designed videotape machine ever built. It was priced around $45,000.[72]

Ampex also showed its ARC-10 EJ combination camera that used a half-inch VHS videotape cassette. The complete system included an ARC-40 studio editing VTR and the ARC-30 editing control system. In addition, Ampex showed its new VPR-3 video recorder that had a vacuum capstan transport. This was a first in type C machines. It used advanced gas-film guiding technology for

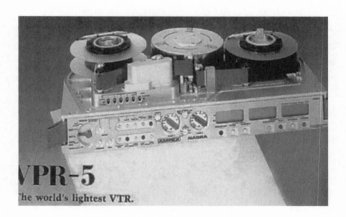

VPR-5
The world's lightest VTR.

1983. Ampex Nagra VPR-5 one-inch VTR with one-hour reels. (Ampex brochure.)

1983 Ampex ad for the new VPR-3 video recorder. (Ampex.)

optimum tape handling at all modes and had multitrack audio performance. Three independent channels were standard and there was an EBU channel optional. It had an SC/HI phase meter to avoid potential phasing problems. Any 30-second segment could be cued in 2.5 seconds. It had automatic scan tracking, video confidence, frame playback that effectively doubled the resolution, and shuttle speeds up to 450 ips. The VPR-3 was priced from $60,000 to $100,000 depending on accessories.[73]

The 124th SMPTE technical conference and equipment exhibit was held in New York City from November 6 to 12, 1982. It covered over 125 papers, tutorials, demonstrations and film and slide presentations. One of the highlights was the honors and awards luncheon. The Eastman Kodak Gold Medal went to Erik Barnouw, the noted television historian and educator. The Alexander M. Poniatoff Gold Medal for Technical Excellence went to Dr. Ray M. Dolby in recognition of his contributions to the advancement of magnetic sound recording. He was noted for his work in the design of the first Ampex videotape recorder and for the design and introduction of noise-reduction systems for use in sound and video recordings. The Progress Medal, the highest award the society can be-

stow, was given to Frank Davidoff for his outstanding technical contributions to the motion picture and television industries. The technical sessions had over 125 presentations and over 300 exhibitors. Eleven foreign countries were represented.[74]

In November 1982, Eastman Kodak reported on an experimental Triniscope for improved video-to-film recording. This device was designed to be used with Eastman color inter negative II film 7272. While slow, it had increased sharpness. It used five-inch-round high-resolution CRTs with electrostatic focus and magnetic deflection. In addition, it had new CRT geometry correction techniques and raster line compensation. Phosphors were P221 for red, P43 for green and P11 for blue. It used a Leitz/Noctilux 50mm f1 lens. Due to high levels of x-rays, the entire CRT area was shielded. The video input was from an Ampex VR2000B VTR.

In November 1982, it was reported that ABC Television had purchased 100 one-inch helical-scan machines from Ampex at a cost of $10 million. ABC also ordered Ampex VPR-3 recorder systems for its coverage of the 1984 winter and summer Olympic Games and political conventions.[75]

In December 1982, with the abundance of portable camera-recorders introduced in the year, it seems that the CBS engineering department had urged affiliates to hold off on half-inch purchases in the absence of a single format. Nonetheless, Art Biggs, VP of engineering of Corinthian Broadcasting, said that "the lack of a unified format posed no problem for Corinthian and that the group's serious investigation of half-inch began when SMPTE announced its inability to reach a compromise." Five of the Corinthian stations were CBS affiliates. Corinthian had bought 75 Betacam cameras and over 50 Betacam editing systems and accessories. It was a multimillion-dollar deal, with all equipment to be in place by July 1984. Another rebuke for the CBS engineering department.[76]

In December 1982, Sony announced that it was introducing dynamic tracking (AST) in its BVU-820 U-matic recorder. It meant that the U-matic machine could, for the first time, display freeze frame, and show slow motion in fast forward or reverse. This was not the first in the industry, as Philips and Grundig had introduced it in a home recorder in February 1980, with the Video 2000.[77]

In December 1982, the Panasonic Industrial Company introduced its new camera-recorder, the Panasonic Recam model AU-100. The AU-100 had its own standard for recording. It recorded frequency modulated luminance signal on a single track, and at the same time, I and Q signals were recorded on another parallel track. As a result, color noise, streaking and other two-phase color problems were eliminated. The scanner was very small, only 2.4 inches in diameter. Only the final product was NTSC encoded. It also recorded audio on two longitudinal tracks and time code on a third track. It used a VHS cassette with a tape speed of 8 ips offering 20 minutes from a T120 cassette. There was also an AU-300 playback-editing system that went with it.

In the camera portion either ⅔-inch diode-gun Plumbicons or ⅔-inch Saticon tubes could be used. Resolution was 600 lines with an S/N ratio of 50db. Dynamic focus and corner registration added to the quality and there was two-line vertical contouring. It was claimed that the Recam was actually superior to a ¾-inch master. This was because the AU-300 six-head scanner played and recorded separate Y and Q tracks so there was no loss of luminance or chroma information. The Recam system weighed only 24 pounds with f1.4 lens, microphone and battery.[78]

By the end of 1982, there were at least three incompatible tape formats. There was the VHS of Matsushita, RCA, Ampex, Ikegami and Hitachi, the Beta system of Sony, and the quarter-inch format of Bosch. The main difference was the frequency modulated signals of the M format versus the time-multiplexed components (R-Y and B-Y) of the Betacam.[79] As one editor stated, the proliferation of component analog half-inch formats wasn't really a bad thing. Since they were bringing up better quality, they were OK. In most cases, the result was not the interchange of tapes at all. Usually, the half-inch tape was "bumped" up to ¾-, one- or two-inch tape for editing or broadcast on the air.[80]

On February 5, 1983, the Ampex Corp. gave details of its new VPR-3. The first and most revolutionary change was in the area of tape handling. The VPR-3 included a combination of air and roller guides to virtually eliminate the friction buildup. Next was the elimination of the pinch roller and the use of a vacuum capstan that controlled tape speed in all modes of operation. This allows the tape to be accelerated to full shuttle speed from play speed without transfer of controlling elements. In addition, there was a high-resolution tachometer attached to the capstan assembly to sense precise tape speed and direction at all times. The machine could be up to 50 times play speed in less than one second. Thus the machine could cue back to the start of a 30-second segment and roll in less than two seconds. Driven by the tachometer, the Ampex AST allowed disturbance-free pictures. The video system was automatically optimized. The audio portion had been optimized too. The control system of this VTR was microprocessor-based.[81]

Thomson-CSF also showed a new Betacam EJ/EFG combination camera. Rank Cintel showed a new low-cost digital telecine, a second-generation telecine television

programming system that replaced "Topsy," and a slide file digital still-store machine. The new telecine, ADS-1, used CCDs to detect blemishes concealed by frame-store manipulation techniques. Topsy was replaced by "Amigo" in which dynamic events could be programmed in a cosinusoidal or linear mode. Sony demonstrated an HDTV system on a large-screen monitor. The display included 1125-line cameras, VTRs, and switching equipment. Sony claimed that it did not intend to set up a world standard, but just to demonstrate HDTV capability. All agreed that the results were equal to 35mm film quality.

There were two answers to high definition in Europe. First was the BBC's extended PAL system that stayed with analog techniques and maintained reverse compatibility with existing PAL receivers. The other was the IBA MAC system which switched to digital techniques and required a special decoder at the receiver. It was pointed out that this system worked equally well for SECAM. It differed from normal PAL in that the video signal was divided into luminance and chrominance components and compressed into sequential segments of the horizontal-line time. Following a 4milliseconds sync word, the next 20msecs. were color and the following 40m-secs. luminance. The MAC receiver restored the signal, usable by the video circuitry, to display a superior image. It was claimed that the IBA was trying to get EBU to accept MAC as the DBS (direct broadcast satellites) standard in Europe.[82] Julian Barnathon of ABC stated that TV technology was designed to fulfill future needs, not just to add dazzling hardware.[83]

In March 1983, Ampex advertised its new ARC system recorder-camera ensemble. Ampex had decided to use the M format of Matsushita. It used the popular VHS videocassettes. ARC included a portable VTR, a studio editing VTR, and an editing controller.[84] Also in March 1983, Ampex announced that they had sold over 7,000 VPR series recorders since 1976. They had just sold their 5000th VPR-2 to Reeves Teletape in New York City.[85] Another highlight of the exhibition was the appearance of the new Ampex/Nagra 15-pound recorder.[86]

1983. New Ampex ARC camera-recorder using "M" format. (Ampex.)

Again in March 1983, the new Ampex Museum of Magnetic Recording was opened. It was located at the Ampex Corporation headquarters at Redwood City, CA. The curator was Peter Hammar who was responsible for bringing together all the necessary artifacts—everything from a 1911 Telegraphone model C wire recorder to the Ampex VRX 1000 tape recorder. This VRX was the fourth produced and had been sold to CBS. CBS used it for 22 years and retired it in 1978 for a new machine. Hammar worked for two years at a cost of over $1 million to create this edifice. He worked closely with Harold Lindsey who had designed the Ampex model 200. The museum is arranged in a series of 28 stations each with its own TV monitor to augment each piece of historic hardware.[87]

In April 1983, Ampex introduced the ESS digital video still store. The basic system has one access station, a single disk drive, and a rack-mountable electronic chassis to provide a single video output. Designed to store and manipulate images, it could have up to 16 disk drives, several access stations, and provide five video outputs.[88]

In June 1983, the International Television Symposium was held at Montreux. The major topic seemed to be getting a worldwide standard for high-definition TV. There seemed to be two camps: one comprised the advocates of the 1125-line system of NHK, developed by Sony-Ikegami-Matsushita; the other included engineers who thought that it would be better to improve on the current PAL, NTSC and SECAM standards rather than accept another new standard. One thing they all agreed upon was that a worldwide standard now would be in everyone's interest.

Sony gave a demonstration of digital recording. RCA surprised all when it demonstrated a three-chip CCD color camera. It used three new half-inch CCD sensors in a frame transfer device in which the video was read out during the vertical interval. The camera, that was in the Hawkeye frame, had an S/N ratio of 65 db. Static and dynamic resolution were equal to those of the best ⅔-inch tubes when 18db gain was used, and sensitivity of 590 lux was achieved at f1.4 opening. The camera performed superbly. RCA stated that they would not license the CCD device and that extensive patents had been granted. RCA promised that a product would be developed from this new experimental camera, but stated that the low manufacturing yield of the CCD chips was holding progress up.[89]

In September 1983, NEC America displayed their new camera-recorder, model SPC-3. It was all solid state. It had three NEC-developed ⅔-inch CCDs. Two were used for the green channel and one for the combined red-blue. The camcorder boasted some 500-line resolution, and it also interfaced directly with half-inch Beta or M tape formats. The camera measured 3.9 × 9.1 × 15 inches. It weighed some 7.3 pounds.[90]

In October 1983, Matsushita Electric Company announced a new NV0800 VHS recorder that featured stereo sound quality to the standard of home hi-fi equipment. Matsushita mounted the audio head on the video head cylinder. The audio signal was superimposed by the video signal and since the azimuth patterns were different, no cancellation occurred. It also had a fixed audio head to maintain reverse compatibility.[91]

In October, it was announced that CBS had decided to suspend their Teletext experiment. The reason given was that there was no decoder available for its teletext standard. NBC followed suit and cut its service by 50 percent. Part of the problem was the high cost of the decoders, some $300 to $1,000.[92]

1983. *Above:* Interior shot of Ampex Museum of Magnetic Technology, Redwood City, CA. *Right:* Ampex Museum curator Peter Hammar. (Ampex.)

On October 30, 1983, it was revealed at the 125th SMPTE winter conference that for the first time Ampex was making RCA's newest VTRs. These included the Ampex VPR-80 being made as the TH-400 and the VPR-3 as the TH-900. The VPR-80 was shown as the TH-400 with an RCA paint job and new logo.[93] The TH-900 had all the features of the VPR-3. All servicing, warranty, installation assistance, training and spare parts would be provided by RCA's broadcast systems division. This was quite a switch. RCA had first used Sony's type C machine under the RCA label. Then they had come out with their own machine in 1980, the RCA TR-800. It had become obvious that the competition in type C machines was ferocious. Ampex and Sony were competing in a race that only their kinds of dedicated organizations could survive. At any rate, at least RCA had chosen an American company to team up with, even if it was Ampex, their long time rival.[94]

Also at the 83rd SMPTE Convention, Dr. Ray Dolby was awarded the Progress Medal of the SMPTE for contributions to noise reduction, to theater sound, and quality improvements in audio and video systems. The award was also in recognition of Ray Dolby as a prime inventor of the videotape recorder.[95]

At this same convention, Michael O. Felix, vice president of Ampex's advanced technical division, received the Alexander M. Poniatoff Gold Medal of Technical Excellence. This was for his pioneering efforts in high-band recording that resulted in a vastly improved quality of color recordings. The concepts he developed are used in most of the professional-quality video recorders in worldwide use today and his ongoing work is a major influence on analog video recorder designs.[96]

In October 1983, the 3M Company announced its new fourth-generation TT-8000 videotape recorder. It was a one-inch type C recorder offering considerable improved signal performance. 3M claimed that it had all the standard features of other C machines plus full audio-video confidence heads, sync channel, and so on. It also featured auto track following (the Ampex ATS system) as an option. The machine was made for them in Japan by Nippon Electric Company.[97]

In December 1983, Sony claimed that it had sold more than 1,000 Betacams all over the world. They claimed that it was the lightest, smallest, most compact half-inch system with picture quality rivaling one inch, and the least expensive.[98] Also in December 1983, RCA reported record sales and higher earnings in that year. Sales were over $2.12 billion.[99]

In England in 1983, it was reported that the BBC was using portable single-camera equipment. They were using an Ikegami camera and Sony high-band portable U-matic recording and editing machines. The BBC expected to have 13 crews in London and the regions operational in the near future. (Obviously they had never heard of electronic journalism.[100])

In February 1984 it was revealed that CBS was still struggling to make a success of its CBS/Sony editing system at CBS Studio Center. Although licensed to it, Sony had no plans to market this machine. (In November 1986, CBS claimed that they were using this system to edit the weekly "Twilight Zone" TV series. This was not true; it was edited at Post Sound Corp. in Hollywood, CA.[101]

By this time there were other machines that used touch screens such as Control Video's Lightfinger and Ampex's ACE editing system. Ampex had a choice of a standard ASCII keyboard, a dedicated keyboard, or the screen.[102] One of the complaints of touch screens was that they were slow when used. A new edit device — EditDroid by Lucas Film in conjunction with Convergence — had a very simple keyboard with five Motorola microprocessors. It used optical disks as a source medium. Designed for the feature film editor, the system concentrated more on the front end of the postproduction process by using an electronic log-in station. The editor decided up front which variation of the scene and take to edit. With editing choices completed, an industry standard EDL (edit decision list) was produced.[103] It was summed up that the keyboard remained the prime choice of editors and would probably remain so for a long while.[104]

In March 1984, Eastman Kodak announced that they were introducing a new series of Videotapes. They were offering tape with the quality, consistency and dependability that Kodak was known for. The tape was to be available in cassette size for both VHS and Beta. One-inch tape would be available in mid–1984. The tape was actually made by TDK in Japan for Eastman, as they wished to provide users with the best quality product for production and postproduction purposes. So even though most TV programs were being shot on film, Eastman knew that almost all films made for television would be distributed on tape.[105] (In February 1960, Eastman Kodak had announced that it was going into the production of videotape sometime in 1961; it decided not to after selling a few reels of tape made by another manufacturer.)

At this time, Kodak also announced the introduction of its new modular TV system 2000 called Kodavision. This camcorder combined a video camera and recorder in a single five-pound unit made by Matsushita. It used the new 8mm worldwide standard, with either evaporated metal or metal particle tape videocassettes made by TDK but to be marketed by Kodak, and a ⅓-inch Newvicon color tube camera. The camcorder had a cradle with optional tuner-timer which connected the camera to a TV receiver for transferring and editing the imaging. In other words, they were taking no chances of the future being an all-electronic medium. Kodak stated that they

1984. First ad for new Kodak videotape. (Kodak.)

were going to make significant contributions to electronic development.[106]

The annual NAB convention was held April 29–May 2, 1984, in Las Vegas. Here, RCA finally showed its CCD camera that had only been seen before in Montreux and Los Angeles. Its performance was spectacular. It was housed in a rather "boxy" enclosure that gave it an experimental look. It also featured enhancement of normal images, including higher resolution due to the half-element-offset principle in the green channel.

1984. Kodak brochure for the new Kodavision Series 2000 8mm video recorder. (Kodak.)

RCA stated that the chips used in the camera measured 0.325×0.415 inches. Each chip contains 403 horizontal picture elements (pixels) and 512 effective vertical pixels. It used the frame transfer method for its potential high sensitivity and low output capacitance. The frame transfer structure had an image area on top and a storage area with an output register at the bottom. The Angenieux Company had provided a special zoom lens with a shuttering mechanism that gave outstanding image sharpness of moving objects. RCA claimed that they were about eight months ahead of all competition on CCD cameras. They also showed their new Saticon camera tubes,[107] and their TK-47C with further software advances. Sony showed their advanced BVP-360 high-end studio/field cameras.

In cart machines, Asaca showed its 300 cassette system with four M format or Beta acting as backup. Sony also showed its cart system that supported 40 cassettes in a random-access vertical holder and four playback decks. An optical bar code generated by a printer identified each cassette with all information for its use.

In April 1984, NEC announced its newest three-chip CCD color camera. NEC had developed a total new interline CCD chip in which the contents of the multiple solid-stated data registers were read out during the vertical interval. It featured a vertical overflow drain (VOD) positioned under rather than beside the photodiode, thus increasing the cells area. Three of these interline VOD CCD image sensors were used: two for the green channels and one for the combined red-blue (R-B) channel. This dual green system provided much higher resolution and sensitivity. There was a vertical stripe filter in the R-B channel. The CCD chips were mounted directly on the optical assembly at the factory and no adjustment was ever needed. The camera was said to have over 500 lines of resolution, signal to noise ratio of 55db and a sensitivity of f5 at 2,000 lux. NEC stated that the camera offered complete freedom of interface with any videotape system.[108]

In April 1984, RCA announced a new solid-state Hawkeye II portable camera, lag free and with superb highlight handling, recorders and accessories, as well as a new TH400 one-inch VTR and the TKP-47C automatic studio camera.[109] RCA showed its M format multicassette cart system.

While RCA showed its TKP-47C automatic studio camera, Sony showed its DXC-1820 camera with the Sony Trinicon tube and a signal to noise ratio of 53db. The DXC interfaced with all portable VCRs. Thomson-CSF was showing its automatic version of the half-inch Betacam camcorder, model TGV-1623, and the new TTV-1525C studio camera. Sony was displaying Betacam multicassette player using the half-inch format. Microtime had added a TBC/frame synchronizer to its line, the S-230D, that could handle nonsynchronous signals from ¾- and ½-inch VTRs as well an internal/external signals such as satellite feeds, microwave and remote video feeds. Harris Video had the HVS 540 time-base corrector and the 635 frame synchronizer with component video output.[110]

In editing machines, the Montage Picture Processor was there with its 14 small monochrome monitors and 17 video playback machines. It could hold up to five hours of material. At no stage was a cut actually made, as each edit decision was held in the computer memory. A light pen and a digitizing pad for the editor to write notes on were superimposed on the small 3½-inch monitors. A separated VDU and keyboard for special functions completed the hardware.[111] CMX had a new model to replace the 3400+—this was EditDroid from Convergence and Lucas film that had a console that looked like something from *Star Wars*. As in film-style editing, there was a Moviola type of lever that shuttled the picture and a separate computer-style screen on the right that displayed editing information. In the center was a large projection sort of picture and on the left was a color monitor with an alternative image.[112]

In August 1984, RCA announced the TKS-100 telecine camera. It used three CCD sensors in place of tubes. A central electronics unit provided monitoring and control for up to three transports that could handle both 16mm or 35mm film.[113]

In September 1984, CBS TV and Sony Broadcast agreed to a major purchase of Betacam products worth $11 million. The deal included BVP-30 cameras with BVV-1 detachable recorders, BVW-20 field players, 32 BVW-40 recorders-editors, and four BVC-10 Betacart systems. CBS planned to use this equipment at New York and WCAU, Philadephia.[114] This, of course, was quite a blow to RCA and its new portable camera-recorder systems.

In September 1984, it was announced that the new RCA CCD-1 solid-state camera had first been used at the Democratic and Republican conventions (held in August). NBC had two cameras there, both on the convention floor and sending their signals back by microwave. The camera's high sensitivity, lack of smearing, and ability to handle a wide contrast ratio made them ideal for this application.[115]

On September 11, 1984, the Trustees Award of the National Academy of TV Arts and Sciences was given posthumously to Dr. Vladimir K. Zworykin for his pioneering work in television and electronics that spanned 70 years and included inventing the first practical tube for picture transmission. Robert R. Frederick, president of RCA Corp., accepted the Emmy at the academy's annual dinner in New York. The Trustees Award is the National Academy's highest distinction for contributions to the television industry.[116]

The tenth IBC convention was held from September 21 to 25, 1984, in Brighton, England. There were many items on display. Sony's HDTV looked better than last time, Ampex had a superior PAL type C recorder, and Philips E-MAC had more motion adaption. The BBC's stereo audio sounded superb. The IBA was still promoting C-MAC for DBS in Europe. All the major English manufacturers—Marconi, Rank, Thorn/EMI, British Aerospace, Vinten and Link—were on display. RCA showed a 625-line PAL version of the CCD EJ camera that had made such a hit at NAB '84 in Los Angeles. Sony had a high definition system using a one-inch VTR operating on the NHK proposed 1,125-line system. There were 1,000 delegates and over 130 exhibitors.[117]

1984. The author (right) with Manfred von Ardenne. August 1984, Dresden, Germany. (Collection of the author.)

1984. RCA portable solid-state color camera, with CCD-1. (RCA.)

In October 1984, Ampex announced its newest type C machine, the VPR-6. They claimed that all machine setups could be done at its highly efficient control panel. It had better, gentler tape handling and could approach speeds of 500 ips with automatic sensors for the end of the tape. Single-frame jog was included. It had a new TBC-6 time-base corrector and built-in editing facilities. It also had two high quality audio channels and a fourth channel for EBU systems.[118]

In October 1984, Hitachi announced its newest videotape recorder, the HR-230. The company had taken its retractable-guide innovations and extended them. The recorder had an air support system that cut down on tape wear and Hitachi said that its half-second lockup was the fastest of any VTR. It was one of the few machines that could handle three-hour reels.[119]

JVC introduced a VTR that was a VHS machine with hi-fi audio qualities. The quality was so good that it could be used to replace open-reel masters when recording a long program. This was the BR-7000U.[120]

1984. New Ampex VPR-6 videotape recorder. (Ampex brochure.)

TV pioneer Waldemar J. Poch died on October 13, 1984, at the age of 79. Poch was part of the RCA television project under the guidance of Elmer Engstrom. He went to the USSR in 1937 to supervise the installation of the RCA television system in Moscow and went back there with Dr. Zworykin in 1959 as part of the American television exhibition. After his retirement from RCA, he traveled extensively in Europe and the Soviet Union.[121]

The 12th SMPTE technical conference was held from October 29 to November 2, 1984, in New York. Very few new TV cameras were shown. RCA again showed its CCD-15 solid-state camera which now had a 1/500 second shutter which improved slow-motion and stop-action playback. It was called the Super Duper Slow Motion machine. It was claimed that this camera had been field-tested at the 1984 World Series. Video recordings showed that pitched fastballs were stopped in midair with the seams clearly visible on the balls' covers. (It was claimed that results were better than the Sony-ABC slow-motion camera.) Prices on the camera were $42,000 for the CCD-1S and $37,500 for the CCD-1. RCA had nine CCD-1 cameras at its booth and had a backlog of orders for more than 50 cameras.[122]

One of the highlights of the convention was a series of papers comparing video to film. The CBS Technology Center in Stamford claimed that normal theater projection usually achieved about 700/800 lines of effective resolution under average conditions. (This agreed with the findings of High-Definition Films, Ltd. in 1952.) Therefore, an HDTV system with 1,050 or 1,125 lines of 20 to 22MHz bandwidth would do as well or better. HDTV could easily compete with film. They had compared both 35mm film and an HDTV system under similar conditions.[123] Immediately the film people cried foul and claimed that CBS had tilted all the film parameters to worst-case conditions while putting video's best foot forward. One film aficionado was so upset by this paper that he wrote the board of editors of SMPTE urging "them not to publish this paper." This, of course, would have been censorship of the worst kind and the journal published anyway, as they should have.[124]

Film experts started counting pixels again, claiming that the total number of pixels in each 35 mm film frame was about equal to a 2,000-line to 4,000-line TV picture. Unfortunately this argument falls apart when it is realized the toll that is taken by film in normal photographic processing and ultimate projection on a large screen. It loses so much resolution as to barely rank with an equal HDTV projection.[125]

On October 30, 1984, Elmer W. Engstrom died at the age of 83 years. Dr. Engstrom joined General Electric in 1923. He transferred over to RCA in 1930, and in 1931 supervised the Zworykin Television Laboratory at Camden, New Jersey. This work created the RCA electronic television that was adopted worldwide. He later became head of the RCA Laboratories and in 1961 became chairman of the board and chief executive of RCA. He received honorary degrees from 14 colleges and universities and numerous prestigious awards.[126]

On November 2, 1984, Louis Pourciau delivered a paper to the SMPTE comparing film to television. Pourciau contended that a high-resolution TV system would produce 35mm film release prints equal in quality to those shown in theaters. He compared the two systems with respect to resolution, contrast range and gray scale, and sensitivity. He concluded that the resolution of the film system to be about 400 TV lines/picture height. He concluded that a TV system employing existing technology could provide the resolution capability necessary to match the 35mm film system.[127]

Finally, Allen Trost, principal engineer of Ampex, received the Alexander M. Poniatoff Gold Medal for Technical Excellence, John Baldwin of the IBA received the same honor for the best journal paper, and Dick O'Brien received the David Sarnoff Gold Medal for his long career in television.[128]

In November 1984, Paramount Pictures Corporation announced the completion of video production and postproduction facilities at Paramount Studios in Hollywood. The facility consisted of a master control area-tape machine area, a camera control room, and two identical video production-postproduction suites with two audio production suites.[129]

Also in November 1984, it was announced that the "B" PAL format of Robert Bosch had been adopted by the EBU as the standard for Europe.[130]

In December 1984, Ikegami Tsushinki celebrated its 20th anniversary. It had sold its first "Handy Looky" cameras to CBS in 1962 to record a space flight. Then in 1973, it had delivered its first color camera, the HL-33 to NHK and to CBS for its entry into electronic journalism. Ikegami claimed that they had sold the 5,000th HL-79 in 1984. (RCA had sold 3,000.) It was now selling the HL-95 Unicam recorder-camera.[131]

Around this time, it was reported that the BBC VHF 405-line service had ended after almost 50 years.[132]

Harley Iams, an early associate of Dr. Zworykin, died on December 3, 1984, at the age of 79. Iams had worked with Zworykin at Westinghouse in 1927 and transferred with him to RCA in 1931. He was part of the team that developed both the kinescope and iconoscope that made our modern television system possible. In 1933, Iams became manager of the RCA tube works at Harrison, NJ, where all the Iconoscope tubes were built for experimentation. Together with Dr. Albert Rose he invented the low-velocity tube, the orthicon, that led to the image orthicon. He left RCA in 1948 to join North American Aviation where he participated in various guided-missile projects. He retired in 1970.[133]

Chapter 12

The Death of RCA, or the G.E. Massacre (1985–1989)

In January 1985, NBC announced that it was dropping Teletext on network feeds. The reason given was the lack of reasonably priced decoders for the consumer. Local stations could continue to provide local service, but not from the network.[1]

George Lisle Beers died on January 30, 1985, at the age of 84. Dr. Beers was part of the Westinghouse team that transferred to RCA in 1930, and he became head of the radio receivers division. In 1935, he was placed in charge of television studio equipment design and development, which covered most of the design and manufacture of studio and terminal equipment for the NBC television stations. He received more than 60 patents during his years with RCA. He retired in 1965.[2]

The 19th annual TV conference of the SMPTE was held February 15, 1985, in San Francisco. It was mainly concerned with the many different standards used in component systems. Demonstrations were given of the S-Mac (Studio Multiplexed Analog Component) system. It used time compression techniques to multiplex luminance and color difference signals. In all cases in spite of impairments, filters and the obstacles, the decoded signals were virtually indistinguishable from the original signal. Also shown were component and NTSC encoded signals to demonstrate the advantages of picture manipulation in the component domain. However, it was finally admitted that the future of analog components, digital TV, and HDTV was far from clear.[3]

Also shown for the first time was a 35mm film, *An American Symphony* from Rock Solid Productions, that was projected onto a large screen. The quality was considered excellent even though it had been shot on half-

inch Betacam and then transferred to film by Image Transform. It was literally impossible to tell that it had not been originated on 35mm film. Also shown was the new M-2 format which was not compatible with the M format. It offered, for the first time, the use of standard half-inch cassettes to fill 60 minutes from a T-120 tape.[4]

In February 1985, Hitachi demonstrated a prototype HDTV Camera, DVTR and large-screen HD projector. The HDTV deck used a Hitachi type C analog recorder with one-inch tape and five recording heads each recording at 92 Mb/sec for a total bit rate of 460 Mb/sec. Error correction resulted in a signal to noise ratio of 50db. It operated on the NHK 1,125 line standard. The Hitachi HDTV camera used three one-inch diode-gun Saticon pickup tubes developed with NHK. There was also a 54-inch rear-projection system with high-contrast ratio and twice the brightness of other HDTV projectors. Hitachi stated that the system would probably be available in one or two years at a price of $400,000. The camera was to cost about $250,000 and the display $40,000 or less.[5]

The 63rd annual NAB convention was held in Las Vegas starting on April 14, 1985. RCA showed its new solid-state CCD-1S model which was a CCD-1 with a 1/500 second shutter that improved slow-motion and stop-action playback. NBC had field tested this camera during the 1984 World Series and used it at other sporting events. The CCD-1 cost $37,500 and the CCD-1S $42,500 without lenses. RCA said it had a backlog of orders for over 50 units and could guarantee delivery of the cameras at a rate of five a week.[6]

NEC also showed its solid-state SP-3A CCD EJ camera. It had 3db better S/N (58 db), better than 5f at 12db

1985. Hitachi shows off new one-inch digital prototype HDTV VTR Shown are Yoshizumi Eto (left) and Hishashi Makamura of Hitachi. (Hitachi.)

gain sensitivity, and had a higher-quality viewfinder. It was available for $17,900 for head and viewfinder and an NTSC adapter was $3,100. These were the only two solid-state cameras shown. However, Ampex showed two TV-quality frame-transfer CCDs: the NXA 1010 monochrome chip with 420 line resolution and the NXA 1020 color chip with over 300 lines of resolution.[7]

Sony showed its BVP-360 studio camera which used ⅔-inch Saticon tubes. Deliveries of a triax version would begin the following month. The company also offered an optional seven-inch color viewfinder which they predicted would be a boon to sports cameramen. It had new Sony developed ⅔-inch mixed field (electrostatic deflection, magnetic focus) Saticon tubes. It had a Sony developed FET that was built into the tube and yoke, and yielded an extraordinary signal to noise ratio. It featured a new f1.2 prism with increased sensitivity and depth of field. It had a microprocessor-based setup function. It could transmit its signals via triax or multicore, or function as a stand-alone camera.[8]

Other cameras were offered by Philips: a new generation LDK-54 recorder-camera, and its LDK-6 family including the LDK-26, a ⅔-inch studio field camera completely compatible with the LDK-6 line. Panasonic showed several new cameras. One, the Nighthawk, was designed for low-light operations. Sensitivity was 20 lux at +18db gain. It used three one-inch Newvicon tubes that resisted burning. Hori-

1985 RCA CCD-1 solid-state camera with variable shutter. (RCA.)

zontal resolution was over 600 lines and it had an S/N ratio of 57db. The Nighthawk weighed 12 pounds. Without lens, it cost $4,995.[9]

Hitachi showed its K-970 auto setup Compucam with ⅔-inch tubes, along with its portable companion the SK-97. Hitachi also featured the SR series of quarter-inch recorder-cameras. Thomson-CSF showed the new TTV-1525C studio camera that used one-inch diode-gun lead oxide tubes, and a TTV-1623 Betacam (Saticon version) and the new TTV-1624 Betacam (Plumbicon model). Harris showed the TC-90S with its TC EJ/EFP camera which laid down both SMPTE and VITC time codes during shooting.

Finally, JVC featured its KY-110 and KTY-210 professional video cameras. JVC also added a super compact BT-C100U VideoMovie recording-camera to its professional line. This nifty little camera sold for only $1595 and incorporated an integral VHS-C recorder with a 20-minute cassette. It used a single half-inch Saticon and only weighed 4.2 pounds. It was aimed at the business and educational market.[10]

The issue of videotape editing was taken up. The real problem, said Emory Cohen of Pacific Video, was that *true film editing was a process of re-editing*, a major weakness of most editing systems. However, he noted that many newer systems were beginning to address this problem. There were many editing systems there, with CMX introducing its new 3400 A along with its new 330XL and the "Edge," which was just below the 340 Editor, and the "Picture Cutter" system from Montage, the company that now had a controlling interest in Panavision. The Picture Cutter system started at around $125,000 and went up to $200,000 for a fully loaded version. Over 22 systems had been sold. EditDroid was now a separate company with Bob Doris of Lucasfilm, president and CEO of the Droid Works. The EditDroid technology was geared mainly toward postproduction of feature films, and was called the "Star Wars" editing system.[11]

Ampex showed its new ACEm system that was compatible with other Ace systems. The editor provided full-feature editing with up to four machines. Four general purpose interfaces and RS-232 printer port were standard components. It would work with VTRs of all formats.[12] The basic keyboard system sold for $29,500 and the ACE touchscreen was $37,000. Convergence Corp. introduced its new 205 that could be used with mixed formats: one-inch, ¾-inch M-format, Betacam, and VHS. Fully loaded, it sold for $40,000.[13]

In telecines, Rank Cintel showed a prototype of the Mark IIID high-definition flying-spot scanner operating on a 1,125-line, 60 field standard featuring 20MHz bandwidth and a digital RGB store. It also showed its anti-weave film gate. Bosch-Fernseh showed its FDL-60 CCD telecine with Varispeed, color correction and optional built-in digital gain reducer. Marconi showed its CCD telecine, and Ikegami its complete system, the TKC-990.[14]

In high-definition displays, the NHK standard HDTV camera was on view. Ikegami showed its 1,125-line NHK standard HDTV camera and monitors, and Hitachi introduced its new high-definition camera, the SK-1200.[15]

Sony also showed a digital VTR that used 19mm cassette tape. The tape transport was an overgrown BVU-800, while the signal processing unit was the size of an oversized TBC. It featured four channels of digital audio and showed slow motion, stop motion, and accelerated motion that made editing as simple as on an analog machine. The unit used the D-1 format, sure to be chosen by SMPTE and the EBU. It used 4:2:2 components and ultra thin (16 microns) tape to give longer playing time. The tape coating was cobalt-doped gamma ferric oxide with a coercivity of 850 oersteds.[16]

Panasonic privately showed its AU-600 new M-II VTR using half-inch tape with a new MII format. It was a two-channel analog component-recording system using an improved chrominance time-compression multiplexing (CTSM) technique. The luminance (Y) signal was FM recorded for the Y channel and the two color difference signals (R-Y and B-Y) were time-compressed into a single serial signal that was FM recorded for the chominance channel. A 2.25MHz burst was inserted in each of the video channels (C and Y) during recording to serve as a reference for phase alignment and jitter correction on playback. Luminance band width was 3.5MHz at -3db, the K factor was 2 percent, and the chominance S/N ratio was 50db. SMPTE time code was recorded using internal readers and generators. A set of deflectable video heads (AST) allowed the playback in still and nonstandard forward and reverse tape speeds.

The AU-600 had been developed by Matsushita for NHK who wanted to replace its 350 transverse machines, but not all with one inch, which it deemed would be obsolete in the next few years. It used a VHS style cassette with high coercivity iron particle tape of 1,500 oersteds. A demonstration showed that its quality was equal to one-inch machines. Its price was to be about $50,000 less than half of a fully equipped type C recorder. According to a spokesman (Sadashige), it was to be the last analog VTR to be used before the next generation of digital VTRs.[17]

After selling more than 1,200 RCA and Ampex cart machines during the previous six years, Sony and RCA were coming out with new more compact cart machines using Beta (Sony) for its Betacart machine and M (RCA) for its "Silverlake" recorder. (Silverlake, NJ, was where the RCA machines were made.) RCA's machine would hold 281 VHS M format cassettes—about 93 hours of programming. It had six VTR transports and seven columns

1985. Panasonic's MII VTR. (Panasonic.)

in an octagonal tower that held 43 bar-coded cassettes each. Ampex was supposed to be working on a cart machine but no details were forthcoming. Panasonic also showed an upgraded version of its machine.[18] In addition, RCA displayed its new TH-700 videotape recorder. Again, as in the past few years, Ampex was making RCA's newest VTRs. These included the Ampex VPR-80 as the TH-400, the VPR-3 as the TH-900, and the VPR-6 as the TH-700.[19]

There were the usual products in the field of time-base correction, multiple-image displays, high-definition switchers, still stores, and digital animation. Finally, there was a plethora of tape manufacturers exhibiting their production — Agfa-Gevaert, Maxell, Sony, Ampex, Fuji, 3M, and last but not least Eastman Kodak.[20] Kodak introduced a new term called "imaging technology" to designate the future of film in an electronic world.[21]

In May 1985, it was reported that the Ampex Corporation had sold 30 of its VPR-6 VTRs to a variety of broadcast and production houses in Japan. They were NHK, Pioneer, JVC, Matsushita, Nippon Columbia, Tel Tech and ABC, Eigasha and Toyo Recording. Toyo Recording had installed a complete Ampex postproduction system. It included five VPR-3 one-inch VTRs, a two-channel ADO system, an ACE computerized editing system, an AVC-33 production switcher and ATR-102/104, and MM 1200 audio recorders. This was really a plum for Ampex for the Japanese were not accustomed to buying American equipment if they could help it. It proved the superiority of Ampex over Sony at this time. The new VTRs were built at the Audio-Video Systems state-of-the-art manufacturing facility in Colorado Springs, Colorado.[22]

In May 1985, Barnathan of ABC announced a new super-slow-motion system developed by ABC and Sony. It had first been used at the 1984 Olympic Games in Los Angeles, and covered the track and field events using special Sony BVP-3000 cameras scanning at 90 frames/sec, three times normal NTSC speed. A special recorder, the BVH-2700, used three recording heads spaced 120 degrees apart. The tape moved at three times type C speed; thus, each signal recorded a perfect type C signal. By playing back at normal speed, the pictures were reproduced at one third of the speed with perfect resolution and detail. They were fed into a regular type C playback machine that could then vary the playback from normal to freeze frame.[23]

In May 1985, it was announced that George Spiro Dibie had been elected to the office of president of Local 695 of the International Photographers Guild in Hollywood, CA. He was starting a program, in cooperation with producers, to retrain skilled camera personnel to be equally skilled video camera operators.[24]

From June 6 to 12, 1985, the 14th International TV Symposium and Technical Exhibition was held in Montreux, Switzerland. It attracted some 35,000 attendees from 50 countries. Most of the convention was concerned with the future of television from the consumer's point of view. However, some technology was shown. Small-format recording systems included the SMPTE designated type L (Betacam) and type M (M format) half-inch system, as well as two quarter-inch formats. Eight millimeter was on the agenda, with a four-head scanner operating at 60rps or even 120rps being exhibited. CBS continued to back the Betacam format, although ABC was said to be staying with ¾-inch, especially with a highband U-matic in the offing. NBC wanted a smaller format than U-matic, something like the new M-II format of Matsushita.[25]

When it came to high definition, it was agreed that two major questions were unanswered. One was "when?" and the other "which method?" While 1,125/60 systems were shown, there was concern over the 50 field (Pal and SECAM) systems converting to 60 fields. Sony gave a demonstration of its high-definition system using a 200-inch screen. They showed a film-style production of RAI in Italy, "Oniricon," that was of such a high standard that it was hard to believe that it was not a high-quality film. A 1,249 line/50 field high-definition camera was also shown. The CBS engineering department gave the gloomy forecast that if none of the field rates were chosen, CATV, VCRs and the videodisc would become the only source of higher definition. (Wrong again!) At the time, DBS remained as the last source of high-definition programming. Finally, digital video recording appeared close to international standardization with EBU recommendation pending.[26]

Ampex announced the sale of its 500th Ampex ADO (Ampex Digital Optics) video effects system to ABC television. ADO was designed for on-air applications and had 30 on-line preprogrammed effects. A single keystroke could incorporate zooms, flips, tumbles, and other effects into live programming. It also included variable-aspect ratio, continuously variable compression, posterization, solarization, and soft key edges.[27]

Ampex also announced the Zeus I video processor, a fully digital system that expanded and compressed broadcast material with no visible image degradation. It was an advanced video processor-TBC capable of eliminating picture blurring during slow motion and picture compression, by removing interfield vertical motion. It also removed picture shifts caused by bad color frame edits. Compatible with all Ampex type C recorders, it included a full frame store, enhanced dropout replacement, and improved S/N ratio.[28]

In August 1985, Sony announced that the BVP-3 Betacam had been replaced by the BVP-30 and the BVP-3A Betacam cameras. The three-tube cameras offered major improvements, including a new high-resolution viewfinder and a channel one audio level indicator in the viewfinder.[29]

In September 1985, it was announced that Dr. Marvin Camras had been inducted into the National Inventors Hall of Fame. He was credited as being the inventor of the magnetic recorder, and the pioneers of magnetic sound tracking for motion picture stereo and video recording. There had been only 58 inventors who had had this honor bestowed upon them.[30]

The 127th technical conference of the SMPTE was held from October 27 to November 1, 1985, in Los Angeles. Sony showed its HDTV system developed for NHK. This system was demonstrated in wide screen (5'3" aspect ratio) on color monitors up to 40 inches diagonal and larger screens up to ten feet across. The images came from live cameras or from a Rank telecine operating at the 1,125 rate. Sony type C one-inch VTRs showed their images. There was also an Ultimatte system for chroma-keying HDTV signals. There were two projection theaters to show HDTV material, as well as 35mm film transfers.

At this convention, the world's first all-digital television production was described and shown. It was a four-minute, 20-second video entitled "Nous Deux" ("We Two") starring French rock singer Jess Garon. It was made by Société Française de Production of Paris, France. It included two cameras (TTV 1525), three digital VCRs provided by Bosch GmbH, one character generator, one digital slide scanner (TTV-2710) and a digital mixer (TTV-5640). The all-digital studio had three color correctors: two were connected to each VTR and the third to any source. Shooting was accomplished in two days in an SFP Studio in

Paris with a single camera delivering three wideband RBG signals to a digital encoder. This encoder fed a digital VTR in a truck behind the camera control unit. It was claimed that improved stage utilization resulted in fewer sets and faster shooting. The technical cost was lowered with reduced time and fewer cameras.[31]

Yves Faroudja and David Claybaugh of the Faroudja Laboratories showed an improved NTSC signal system. The intent of the exhibition was to show that the NTSC system could yield near RGB image quality if the full potential of its intrinsic capabilities were taken advantage of.

NBC demonstrated the S-MAC studio system. The technology now compressed both chrominance signals on each horizontal line, thus retaining full vertical color resolution. This meant that all video signals could be manipulated and still come out with pictures superior to those of NTSC.[32]

On January 31, 1986, the Ampex Corp. had a company wide celebration for Charles P. Ginsburg. This was in recognition of Ginsburg's retirement following 34 years with Ampex. Roy H. Ekrom, president and CEO of Ampex, said that Charles's contributions to television and Ampex were immeasurable. Ginsburg had been Ampex's vice president for advanced technology and planning at the time of his retirement.[33] He later joined AVP Communications, Westborough, MA, as a consultant specializing in technology planning.[34]

The 20th annual SMPTE television conference was held in Chicago on February 7 and 8, 1986. The theme was "Tools and Technologies for Tomorrow's Television." It was mainly concerned with the discussion of the new digital television tape recorder (DTTR) specifications agreed upon by SMPTE and EBU. The standards avoided dictating any particular recorder design, and allowed systems to function with equal ease in 525 and 625 lines. The decision of Ampex to introduce a composite digital signal for its ACR-25 was criticized. The conference was mostly concerned with the broadest possible acceptance of the D-1 standard. A paper by NHK described its role in the development of the Panasonic M-II format. Hitachi gave details of a new 8mm metal tape recorder for EJ use. Other papers were on the new stereo television sound.[35]

There was some opposition to the introduction of the Ampex nonstandard digital composite format cart machine. It came mainly from the EBU, the Canadian Broadcasting Corp., and CBS. CBS, hung up on standards (or the lack thereof), stated that the Ampex argument was a "rationalization." However, Ampex stated that its format would be more easily adapted to existing NTSC broadcast plants. Both NBC and ABC were generally supportive of the Ampex format because of a growing need for a composite digital unit to fit into existing broadcast facilities.[36]

Before the NAB convention, it was announced that Ampex (and Philips, Bosch, and Thomson) had signed an agreement with Sony to use its Betacam SP system. Ampex had made this choice convinced that Betacam SP was the best format. Ampex's prior use of the MI format had failed miserably. Sony's sales of Betacams had already reached 25,000 units with 5,000 to 6,000 sold in the USA alone. Ampex promised to have its first units out by early the following year, and Sony had agreed to accept the Ampex technology used in the ACR-225 cart machine. So here was a rare kind of cooperation between the two giants of VTR production in the world. This allied them against Matsushita which was coming out with its new half-inch MII format to replace the type C format.[37]

The 64th annual NAB convention was held in Dallas, Texas, from April 13 to 16, 1986. For the first time in NAB history, RCA was not a major exhibitor — no cameras, VTRs, no transmitters, antennas, or other major radio or television equipment. Despite RCA's upcoming demise, it was planned to display a limited line of camera pickup tubes and FM, VHF, and UHF power tubes.[38]

Sony and Toshiba showed new solid-state cameras. It seemed that the big news was that NBC had decided to buy over $50 million dollars worth of Matsushita's improved MII equipment. NBC decided to replace all of its present equipment (¾-, half-inch and two-inch) with a universal recorder format. NBC had turned down both Sony and Ampex as not having met their specifications for this new equipment. It was claimed that NHK had over 170 units working using the new MII recorders and had no problems with the technology.[39]

Sony showed an early version of the Betacam SP system. In addition to better performance, it provided up to 90 minutes of recording time on a cassette. It used a new metal particle tape developed by Sony. Sony also showed its new lightweight three CCD Betacam BVW-105 weighing 19½ pounds and costing $25,000. The Sony BVW-105 Betacam was a second-generation camcorder as a result of its three chip CCD (ICX018-K-L) camera. Rated at 2000 lux at f5.6, the camera put out full video levels with only 15 lux illumination (18db gain). Each sensor offered 510H and 492V pixels for high-quality imaging. Luminance was increased to 550 lines by offsetting the green pixels horizontally by one half-pixel in relation to the red and blue pixels. This gave almost 1,020 samples per lines for luminance. The camera boasted an S/N ratio of 58db. The BVW 105 camcorder was expected to be available in July at a list price of $24,500. Sony also showed a new three-CCD camera, the Sony DXC-3000 with a resolution of 520 lines of luminance and S/N ratio of 56db. The price was $6,700 without lens.[40]

Sony showed its new digital video recorder, the DVR-1000, as a studio recorder. It was claimed that Sony had

1986 Sony BVW-105 (ICX018-K-L) *Left:* 3CCD camera. *Right:* With camcorder. (Sony.)

sold 12 of the new recorders and had orders for 300 more. The DVR-1000 and the DVCP signal processor cost about $120,000. Sony also showed two new one-inch machines, the BVH-2000-10 and the BVH-2000-12 with less than top-of-the-line functions.

Ampex showed its new ACR-225 Digital Cart Spot Player, a digital composite cart system. While the machine did not conform to the CCIR and EBU recommendations, Ampex considered that it was really designed to air commercials and to replace the two-inch cart machines it and RCA had manufactured. Each cartridge could offer only 20 minutes of playback time. It did use the 19mm videotape cassette, and had one channel of digital composite video and four channels of digital audio. As many as 265 cassettes could be on-line, and a library database could identify over 100,000 cassettes. Fast access to the on-line cassettes was provided by transports with instant lock-on, thus enabling a sequence of ten-second spots to be played back to back. Ampex announced plans to license its Composite DVTR format used in the ACR-225 digital spot player. The company reiterated that it was still committed to the SMPTE/EBU Digital format.[41]

Ampex also showed it new ADO 1000 for under $40,000. It was designed for on-air as well as off-line production. It had 30 preset effects, including flips, tumbles, rolls, mosaics, mirror blur, posterization, solarization, luminance reversal, and A/B inputs. Effects could be run forward or backward. Up to four ADO channels could be integrated through a production switcher.[42]

Quantel showed prototypes of its new enhancements for its Mirage 3D effects box. It included real-time three dimensional shading and variable spectrum highlighting and positioning. A new device, Contour, allowed video to be shaped around almost any three-dimensional shape. All Quantel products were based on the CCIR 601 digital standard. The full capacity of a digital effects network was 14 Encore Mirage machines.[43]

Quantel's Harry system could operate independently of Paintbox with a choice of free-standing control stations. Harry was a real-time digital video recorder that could replay frames in random order in real time. Harry was shown digitally interfaced with the Quantel Encore effects system via CCIR.

Microtime introduced the T-300 series of TBCs designed for half-inch and ¾-inch nonsegmented heterodyne VTRs offering a wide correction window and genlock or stand-alone sync-generator operation.[44]

1985. Sony's digital VTR. (Sony.)

1986 Ampex prototype ACR-225 cart player with composite digital coding. (Ampex.)

In cameras, both Sony and Toshiba showed CCD units. Panasonic showed a broadcast camcorder, the AG-155, using half-inch CCDs. It featured a piezo focusing system. NEC also showed its new three-CCD camera, the SP-3AE-S, with an electronic shutter. It interfaced with any video recorder including the latest MII and 8mm formats.[45] Ikegami's popular HL-95 Unicam was shown, configured to connect with the new Panasonic MII metal particle tape recorder (the NBC choice). The HL-95 B boasted new ⅔-inch Plumbicon pickup tubes (with diode electron guns and electrostatic focus) for high sensitivity and high resolution.[46]

In telecines, Marconi showed its CCD telecine system which allowed the user to calculate the percentage of compression or expansion or to let the machine perform the calculation itself. It also featured function for a color correction during still frame. The Bosch FDL-60 CCD telecine included slow-motion playback, reversable speeds of 16 to 30 frames/sec, and full-format playback for Cinemasope films (Panscan). Rank showed its new M3 HDTV high-definition version for the 1,125/60 frame standard. Rank also showed its solid-state ADS1 multiplexed on-air telecine. Ikegami exhibited its 1,125/60 format high definition system using three one-inch low capacitance Saticon tubes featuring 1,200 lines of resolution and 30MHz bandwidth. It was pin-registered to eliminate vertical jitter.[47]

At this NAB on April 15, 1986, Dr. George H. Brown a former RCA engineering executive, received the 1986 Engineering Achievement Award. Brown had retired in 1974 after a long rewarding career with RCA. He had described his career in his book, *And Part of Which I Was: Recollections of a Research Engineer*. Dr. Brown had collected many awards during his distinguished career including the David Sarnoff Award for Outstanding Achievement in Radio and Television.[48]

On April 7, 1986, in an interview about his accomplishments, Brown had nothing but praise for both David Sarnoff and RCA. Of RCA, he stated "we were leaders; there was no question that we were innovators." The previous year's demise of RCA's broadcast systems division was clearly a disappointment to him. He noted that the coming NAB would be the first one without its presence. "What was at one time the company's highest profit maker was ruined by sheer stupidity." As far as the takeover of RCA was concerned, he had a dim view of General Electric's motives. He stated simply, "RCA will disappear."[49]

After losing $580 million, RCA had abandoned its Selectavision videodisc system on April 4, 1984, even though by the end of 1983 over 500,000 players had been sold. It had failed in the marketplace for two reasons. First was the booming video rental market, and second was that the public wanted a machine that would record as well as play back. It had cost RCA over $400 million to develop. RCA also cut back on its core business of microwave, cable television, mobile radio, avionics and broadcast radio products in which it had excelled. The 66-year-old broadcast systems division in Gibbsboro, NJ, was the hardest hit. On October 3, 1985, RCA had announced that the group was closing, affecting over 500 employees. However, in March 1986, RCA stated that RCA Broadcast Systems would continue to provide a variety of technical support programs for customers during the phase-out period.[50]

Despite its miserable end, there was the period between 1975 and 1985 that RCA was prospering. It divested itself of CIT (Commercial Credit and Investment Company) and made money on the deal. NBC was experiencing a turnaround and was showing profits for the first time in years. The 1985 RCA annual report showed that its earnings were the highest in a long time. This, of course, made the company a more tempting target for a takeover. After-tax profit was $369,500,000, and earnings per share were $3.79. As a result, there were rumors that MCA was going to make an offer for RCA, but that collapsed in final negotiating sessions.

General Electric saw in RCA a company that would provide them with a more domestic business (especially NBC) and a greater presence in the business sector. RCA president Thornton F. Bradshaw claimed "that the merger would give [RCA] the financial capacity to do what we have to do." But General Electric's president, John F. Welch, Jr., who had a reputation as a "nonpareil cost cutter and economizer," had other ideas in mind. Welch was known as "Neutron Jack," i.e., "when he went through a plant the buildings remained, but the people were gone." It was noted that General Electric's corporate culture was different from RCA's and perhaps G.E. would envelope it.

This is exactly what happened. General Electric was attracted by the now cash-rich RCA, and on November 6, 1985, Robert Welch met with Thornton F. Bradshaw to talk about a deal. On December 12, 1985, it was announced that G.E. would purchase RCA for $66.00 a share, for a total of $6.20 billion in cash. It was claimed that RCA stock worth was over $90 a share. This gain was in spite of a parade of RCA CEOs who kept changing company direction.

On February 12, 1986, G.E. asked the FCC to approve its acquisition of RCA. G.E. stated that it needed 18 months to break up NBC's grandfathered radio and TV stations, but that they would have to go. It stated that three RCA board members would be added to G.E.'s current board, with the individuals to be named later. This board would constitute the complete boards of G.E., RCA and NBC. G.E. said it intended to make a separate wholly owned subsidiary of NBC. It was presumed that RCA would also continue as a subsidiary of G.E.[51]

On June 9, 1986 (ahead of the FCC's final order), the subsumption of RCA by General Electric went through. The following month it was announced that the FCC had paved the official way for completion of the takeover, which carried a price tag of more than $6 billion. It authorized the transfer of all units including NBC to G.E. It also approved the transfer of NBC from RCA to a newly created division of General Electric that had promised to keep the network operation independent of the rest of the company. There was speculation that GE would sell the entire NBC radio network. Within six months, General Electric had eliminated the RCA entity for all time. All RCA manufacturing divisions were shut down.[52]

In February 1987, it was reported that General Electric had donated the RCA Laboratories to the Stanford Research Institute in Menlo Park, California getting a $75 million to $100 million tax deduction for the gesture. The Stanford Research Institute International (SRI) was a nonprofit research and consulting firm. General Electric said that it couldn't support two separate corporate research centers—it operated its own corporate research center in Schenectady, NY. General Electric promised that it would fund SRI to the tune of $250 million in contracts over the following five years. There was no contemplated move of the Sarnoff Center at that time, although its staff would have to be reduced by 25 percent.[53]

News of General Electric's donation of RCA Laboratories to the Stanford Research Institute broke on February 6, 1987, the opening day of the SMPTE winter TV conference. It appeared to draw mixed reactions from engineering attendees, many of whom had worked at or with the lab during the four decades it had dominated television research.

RCA Labs executives present at the conference spoke positively about the move, and seemed pleased that other G.E. options, such as closing the labs or merging them with G.E.'s central research facility in Schenectady and reducing staff, were not exercised.

Others were less sanguine about the decision, however, particularly with the 25 percent job cuts expected after SRI took over the 1,200-person facility the following April. SMPTE conference program chairman Joseph Roizen said the move had put the operation "on the road to oblivion," while Cap Cities/ABC's Robert Thomas, who had worked at RCA during the early days of color TV development, said he "felt a sense of loss" about the move.

Another former RCA executive, Robert Hopkins, executive director of the Advanced Television Systems Committee, said, "Many feel what G.E. is doing with RCA [Labs] isn't what they'd like to see happen, but they'd rather have it open." He also added that some were concerned

that the facility might have difficulty maintaining a high level of television research once General Electric's initial five-year, $250-million research contracts were complete.

James Tietjen, director of RCA Labs (more formally known as the David Sarnoff Research Center, after RCA's late leader), later said that General Electric's "decision was an outstanding solution" that would not only allow the continuance of the labs' work, but would allow General Electric to gain "cost-effective" research in color television. He said the lab expected to earn $85 million in revenues during its first year under SRI, approximately the same level it had earned under GE-RCA, with revenues remaining stable or slightly increasing over the ensuing five years.

General Electric's $250 million contract, the majority of which was for television and consumer electronics research, would grow progressively smaller over the five-year period, Tietjen explained, with the last year's commitments in the $25 million to $30 million range.

The anticipated job cuts, which the company said were required to insure a "competitive cost structure" for the labs, would be "reasonably uniform" across all areas of research, Tietjen said, as well as between administrative and research positions. SRI had had some television research in the past, but the facility — which employed 2,700, mainly in science, engineering research and management consulting — at that time conducted little TV research.[54]

This destruction of what was once the best radio laboratory in the world was a crime. Since 1942, the David Sarnoff Research laboratory had paved the way for most of the advances in television — 45 years. From the image orthicon, the Vidicon, to the tri-color kinescope, to the basic color system that led to the NTSC color system, liquid-crystal displays and CMS computer chip technology, and finally to the introduction of a color CCD camera, it was unsurpassed. Only the invention of the videotape recorder escaped the laboratory's record. The radio network was sold, as were the name and logo, to Thomson-CSF, the powerful French firm which intended to put out a line of video products using the RCA name. Only NBC was kept by G.E. It was alleged that General Electric went through the RCA Building in New York and carefully tore out any signs of the RCA logo.

Various authorities give different versions of what happened, but all agree on one point: RCA had lost the leadership and management capabilities to stay in business. General Electric sensed this and came in for the kill. There was no doubt that they had wanted to eliminate RCA from the start.[55]

All authorities agree that RCA, with the right leadership, could have survived alongside General Electric, but that was not to be. They all concur that the removal of Robert Sarnoff was the beginning of the decline of RCA (not that he had done such a worthy job). It went outside of its core industries into car rentals, food processing, carpets, financial institutions and finally head to head with IBM in computers.

RCA had a few bright spots that could have saved it. For instance, its portable TK-76 camera was the unquestioned standard of the world, selling over 3,000. Its TK-47 automatic studio camera was also highly successful, in spite of ferocious Japanese and European competition. Another breakthrough, the Hawkeye camera that led the trend to one-piece camera-recorders, failed to sell and was abandoned in only two years. (It was later reported that production of the Hawkeye camera stopped in April 1985, a victim of the Sony Betacam success.[56]) Then another RCA breakthrough, the first solid-state CCD camera, was shown in a cumbersome housing design that belied its performance. It was also a failure even though its performance was brilliant. At any rate, it too floundered along with the rest of RCA.[57] This shutting down of RCA now left the Ampex Corporation of Redwood City as the only major manufacturer of video equipment in the United States.

A more descriptive look at RCA's demise was given in September 1987 by Dr. Kerns H. Powers, formerly of the RCA Laboratories. In a lecture before the Royal Television Society he had nothing but praise for RCA and David Sarnoff. He spoke of a kind of kindred spirit among RCA people, especially in the television section. Part of RCA's success was due to Sarnoff, when a corporate commitment was made (as it was with color TV) by him, RCA had the leadership and financial strength to carry such a development through the dark periods of adversity. The failure of RCA's Selectavision videodisc could be attributed to the lack of corporate commitment and to a discontinuity of leadership during the investment phase of the business. It had been replaced by diversification, acquisition, agility and portfolio management philosophy with shorter-term goals.

The one bright spot of the demise (if one can call it that) of RCA was the announcement of the new compatible high-definition system called advanced compatible television (ACTV). Preliminary work on such a system had started in the late 1970s in Princeton. A demonstration would be given on October 1, 1987, in New York City by NBC-G.E.-RCA consumer electronics. It was followed by a demonstration through simulation in Ottawa, October 5–8, 1987. Powers concluded his speech by stating, "the Sarnoff spirit is alive and well and living in Princeton."[58]

In May 1986, it was reported that CCIR at its meeting in Dubrovnik, Yugoslavia, had postponed its HDTV standard action. While the 1,125/60 proposal was confirmed, thus making it an annex to the CCIR's only report on HDTV, experts were urged to complete HDTV studies before 1989. There was much opposition to this standard from countries using the 625/50 line standard. They feared that their consumer electronic industries would be hurt by the Japanese headstart in 1,125/60 TV. They intended to develop alternative systems to compete with the 1,125/60 standard developed by NHK. Just as had happened in May 1965, with the loss of the adoption of the American NTSC color system, the adoption of the Japanese/American 1,125/60 high-definition system was a victim of European politics and protectionist pressures.[59]

In June 1986, it was announced that the Advanced Televisions Systems Committee (ATSC) would continue to explore the potential improvements in the 525 line NTSC system. Noting the fact that their had been no agreement on the 1,125/60 system proposed by the CCIR, it was decided to continue with the work chaired by Dr. Kerns Powers of RCA Laboratories in Princeton. The work included using high definition cameras and TV receivers with comb filters and sequential scanning, as well as the NTSC encoding technique incorporating a precombing filter developed by Faroudja Labs that could help eliminate cross-color and cross-luminance artifacts.[60]

In May 1986, the CCIR put an end to the hopes for an HDTV standard for at least four years. It had been backed by the USA, Japan and Canada (60 cycle), but opposed by the majority of western European governments (50 cycle). The European nations had concern over using a 60Hz system while over half the world was on 50 cycles. It was decided to wait for 1990 to make a decision. With the existence of the 1,125/60 cycle system it was feared that a defacto standard would appear through broad user acceptance. This would be Sony's third defacto standard: first was the ¾-inch U-matic, then the Betacam system, and now a working high-definition system. Even with costs around $450,000, Sony had some 35 to 50 units in use throughout the world. Presumably, most users would shoot in high-definition and release their product on 35mm film.[61]

In June 1986, Ampex announced its new Computerized Editing System (ACE). It was a family of modular, computer-controlled editing systems handling video and audio recorders, video mixers and effects generators. It could be used with either a touch screen or a dedicated keyboard plus CRT. It was software-controlled which made its operation easier and more versatile. Each edit decision could be compiled automatically on a an edit decision list (EDL), and stored on a floppy disc for later modification or print out.[62]

The 11th IBC convention was held in Brighton, England from September 20 to 23, 1986. There were over 14,000 delegates and over 180 companies showing their wares. Ninety technical papers were scheduled. The main topic seemed to be high-definition TV. The European broadcasters wanted improved imaging but only with an orderly move from multiplex-analog component transmission (MAC) to HD-MAC. Compatibility with MAC and pre–MAC receivers was a requirement. DBS drew attention with MAC encoding and Philips, which was instrumental in its opposition to the 1,125/60 HDTV system, showed its 1,250/50 high-definition system which was somewhat disappointing but compatible with MAC. IBC '86 marked the introduction of both Sony and Ampex's digital component and composite video recorders.[63]

In September 1986, it was announced that *The Patriot* had become the first theatrical release to be completely edited on the videodisc-based EditDroid system. The 35mm negatives were brought to a postproduction house where they were developed and transferred to tape on a Rank Cintel unit. Copies were brought to Pacific Video and transferred onto videodiscs at FotoKem. Here the editor used the EditDroid machine, and once the edit was completed, a computer cut list was generated and a film work print was constructed. The editor stated that if he had his choice, "he would never edit a film conventially again."[64]

In September 1986, the first production DVTR was described, the Sony DVR-1000. In 1982, the basic parameters of the 4:2:2 (13.5MHz, 6.75MHz, 6.75 MHz) sampling standard were settled. The luminance component of the input signal was processed at 13.5MHz/sec, the "4" factor that derived from the historical discussions of introducing a four-times color subcarrier frequency digital sampling rate ($4f_{sc}$). The chrominance components, R-Y and B-Y, were sampled at 6.75MHz/sec, the "2" factors. For each line of video, 4:2:2 digital coding used 720 samples/line for luminance, plus 360 samples for R-Y and another 360 samples for B-Y for a total of 1,440 bytes in both 525/30 and 625/25 systems. In 1985, the broadcast quality format known as D-1 was approved by the SMPTE, and by the MAGNUM (MAGnétoscope NUMérique) digital videotape recorder group of the EBU and CCIR.

The Sony digital VTR used the DVR-2000 tape transport and DVPC-1000 digital signal processor. The tape format consisted of the 4:2:2-based video track, control

track, SMPTE time code, analog cue track and four digital audio channels. It could be used on both 525/60 and 625/50 standards. It accommodated both the M and L cassettes designed for the D-1 format, and held 34 to 76 minutes of programming. The first production machine would be delivered in 1987.[65]

The 128th convention of the SMPTE was held October 24–29, 1986, in New York City. Approximately 300 exhibitors were there. Keynote speaker was Mark L. Sanders, vice president of marketing and new technology for Ampex Corp. On October 27, addressing the Honors and Awards Luncheon, was Dr. George Brown of RCA (retired). He had served on the board of directors of RCA for many years. The luncheon was attended by 800 people.[66] President Reagan sent a letter to the convention congratulating the SMPTE for its work in the advancement of commutation technology. Charles E. Anderson, formerly of Ampex, was awarded the Alexander M. Poniatoff Gold Medal for Technical Excellence. Michael O. Felix, also formerly of Ampex, received the David Sarnoff Gold Medal Award.[67]

In October 1986, a description was given of the upcoming MUSE HDTV television system by NHK. The demonstration was not promoting use of the Japanese 1,125-line HDTV technology; rather, its goal was to help maintain the technical competitiveness of terrestrial TV services. According to project director Ben Crutchfield of NAB, with alternative and enhanced TV technologies under rapid development, broadcasters must try to persuade the FCC and Congress not to give away or allow the degradation of the UHF TV spectrum.

The demonstration began at the site of a WUSA (TV) broadcast tower in Washington where an HDTV videotape recorder would be fed program material in the 1,125-line, 5:3:3 aspect ratio HDTV format. The HDTV signal, at this point 25MHz wide, would be fed to an NHK-supplied encoder (dubbed MUSE for its use of multiple sub–Nyquist sampling encoding circuitry) which would reduce the signal by almost a third, to 8.1MHz.

The MUSE bandwidth-reduced HDTV signal would

1986 Sony DVR-1000 digital videotape recorder.

1986 meeting of SMPTE at Ampex Museum, celebrating 30th anniversary of the Ampex videotape machine. (L. to r.) Charles Anderson, Alex Maxey, Donna Foster-Roizen, Ray Dolby, Charles P. Ginsburg, and Peter Hammar. (Ampex.)

then be transmitted in two forms. The first, using standard TV's vestigial sideband AM transmission, would be sent via a special transmitter manufactured by ITS and a modified antenna from Micro Communications. The AM signal, transmitted at 1.5kw ERP, would be aired, given FCC authorization, over channels 58 and 59. The second signal would go out as a 1W FM transmission in the 13GHz direct-broadcast satellite band to demonstrate the capability of using the DBS band for terrestrial applications. A modified Harris antenna and transmitter would be used.

According to Crutchfield, three receiving points would be employed: one at NAB headquarters, another at the FCC, and a third at the U.S. Capitol. At each of the receive points, two special wideband receiver-demodulators would feed one or the other incoming signal to the MUSE decoder, which would then reconstitute the HDTV signal and pass it on for viewing either to HDTV video monitors or a large-screen HDTV projection unit. At the receive points, viewers would be able to switch between the AM and FM versions of the HDTV signal, and at least one site would also be able to see the 1,125-line signal down converted to standard 525-line NTSC for comparison purposes.

Among the viewing materials would be a 10- to 12-minute HDTV videotape of Washington scenes produced for the project by noncommercial WETA-TV Washington, DTV videotapes from the 1984 Olympics, an Italian HDTV music video, and other materials, including possibly a 35mm film transfer to HDTV.[68]

In November 1986, Ampex announced that it was using the Betacam recorder format with its portable TV cameras.[69] Also in November 1986, it was announced that CBS was closing its CBS Technology Center. CBS's Emil Torick and Tom Keller of NAB agreed "that it was a sad day for our industry." It was closed to help CBS's ailing financial situation. It had a long history of new advances including color TV, the first audio cassette, the long-playing record, and the first photos from the moon. Its latest project was an FM noise-reduction system (FMX).[70]

On November 12, 1986, television pioneer Raymond Davis Kell died. Kell had started in television with Dr. Alexanderson at G.E. in 1927. He transferred over to RCA in 1930 and became part of Dr. Zworykin's television group. He worked on TV cameras for guided missiles and fire control during WWII then led the RCA team in the development of the RCA color system after the war. Among his honors was the V. K. Zworykin Television Award of the IEEE in 1966.[71]

From December 15 to 16, 1986, a meeting sponsored by the Annenberg School of Communications was held. Its main topic was the status of international HDTV. The speakers included NAB president, Eddie Fritts, and FCC mass bureau chief, James McKinney. Fritts objected to

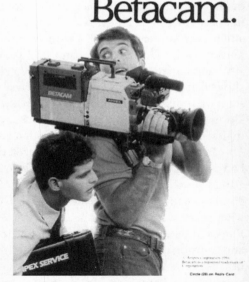

the pending FCCs proposal to increase sharing of UHF TV with land-mobile services. He said that HDTV was already a reality. McKinney acknowledged that HDTV was very real and was on the verge of delivery, but stated that perhaps other methods of bringing HDTV into the home, by means of cable, videotape or videodisc, might be desirable alternatives to terrestrial delivery.

1986. *Above:* Ampex Betacam camera-recorder. *Below:* Ampex Betacam CVR-40 studio recorder (1987). (Ampex.)

The next day, Ambassador Diana Lady Dougan, coordinator for the Bureau of International Communication and Information Policy of the U.S. State Department, stated that she believed that the 1,250/60 system would become such a de facto standard. She added, however, "That if de facto standards develop just because they come from the, 'biggest gorilla in town' they don't necessarily serve the customer." It was mentioned that advocates of a European 50Hz HDTV technology were doomed. One expert averred that the prospect of a 50 cycle HDTV system was "unacceptable, it doesn't work, the flicker is unbearable and finally it is useless."[72]

On December 15, 1986, it was reported that the Ampex Corp. (and six other electronic firms) were to be put on sale by Allied-Signal. The parent company wanted to help finance a share buy-back program to reduce company debt and allow for increased investments in aerospace, automotive and related industries. It expected to complete the sale by mid–1987. It was mentioned that three European and five Japanese firms were interested in the sale, but it would be difficult for any non–American firm to buy Ampex due to the amount of government military contracts for Ampex equipment. Jules Barnathan of Cap

Cities/ABC Broadcasting believed that the sale would not hurt Ampex, if a more aligned buyer were to purchase it. Remembering what had happened to RCA in 1986, he said, "They are a valuable asset and I am hopeful that it will survive. It is very important to have an American Company in this area."[73]

The first American demonstration of the so-called Hi-Vision (NHK's term for the MUSE system) was given on January 7, 1987, in Washington, DC. The 1,125 line HDTV signal was broadcast on channels 58 and 59 from a site across the capital. The picture, which showed several minutes of the 1984 Olympics, was clearly superior to the 525-line NTSC picture shown along side it. The receiving system was a wide-band demodulator that fed a 32-inch CRT and a 54-inch rear-projection system. There was also a consumer HDTV videodisc player and two MII HDTV VCRs. Key members of Congress were invited to a special presentation on January 21, 1987. It was claimed that the system performed well. The demonstration involved a computer simulation transmitted in 1050-line pictures inside the six MHz bandwidth of the existing NTSC system. It was claimed that observers were impressed by the simulated pictures as "pleasing to look at," but had questions about the feasibility of the system.[74]

JVC unveiled a new format Super VHS at the winter Consumer Electronics Show in Las Vegas in January 1987. Planned only for the consumer market, it had a new recording-head technology, a new tape formulation, and an upward shift in bandwidth for its luminance and color carrier. It was now claimed that it had better quality than Super Beta, and, of course, it had ¾-inch decks. (Sony was forced to shift Beta's color carrier from 800 to 1.2MHz in order to introduce its incompatible SuperBeta 1-5 mode.) JVC stressed that Super VHS decks could also play VHS tapes with no changes. JVC planned to license Hitachi, Matsushita and Sharp in the new format.[75]

In February 1987, it was reported that Turner Broadcasting System would equip its new CNN and Headline News crews with Betacam-format news and production equipment. It would buy more than 200 systems.[76]

In February 1987, it was also reported that NEC America had agreed to furnish NBC with large numbers of the SP-3A CCD cameras for use by NBC news crews. The cameras accepted both Beta and MII format VTRs, had built-in variable speed shutters to provide sharp images during slow-motion playback, and provided NTSC, component video and RGB outputs. They were for use with Panasonic's MII VTR system. Deliveries would begin immediately.[77]

The 21st annual SMPTE TV Conference was held in San Francisco, February 6–7, 1987. The program chairman was Joseph Roizen whose theme was "The 21st Conference Looks to the 21st Century." Among the topics to be reported were tape recording formats and video graphics. A major portion of the convention was to be devoted to the "Frontiers of Global Television Research." The limited number of equipment manufactures present were related to the papers delivered.[78]

In February 1987, both Ampex and Sony submitted Ampex's new composite digital video recording format to the SMPTE/ANSI standards committee. Based on a sampling frequency that was four times that of the subcarrier, ($4f_{sc}$), the format used the 19mm D-1 cassettes with metal particle tape and many of the mechanical parts of D-1 VTRs. A rare case of cooperation between Ampex and Sony![79]

The annual equipment convention of the NAB was held in Dallas, Texas, from March 28 to 31, 1987. JVC gave a demonstration of its MII line. It showed its new KRX-400L portable VCR weighing less than 14 pounds. JVC also offered the HR-800 U-matic SMPTE time-code generator, time-base corrector, noiseless slow motion and still mode. Sony showed its $33,000 studio Betacam BVW-75, a dynamic tracking version of the Beta BVW-49 capable of handling both 30- and 90-minute tape cassettes that was fully compatible with over 30,000 existing units in use worldwide. Other products included the BVV-5 portable SP recorder that offered Y and CTDM playback through the viewfinder. The BVW-505 CCD units and the BVW tube unit were the two camcorder models that incorporated the BVV-5. Sony also showed type 7 and type 9 U-matic equipment, and three D-1 digital recorders. Ampex continued to support the Betacam SP technology. They introduced three new recorders, for both studio and field use. BTS (Bosch-Philips) also supported the Betacam SP format, the BCB-35 Betacam and the BCB-75 studio unit.[80]

In CCD cameras, NEC had the SP3A with an electronic shutter — a high-end CCD camera with an S/N ratio of more than 60db and a horizontal resolution of 550 lines (it used a hybrid chip which had the transfer characteristics of both interline and frame transfer). Toshiba showed its PK-70 CCD (using the interline transfer chips) EJ camera with an S/N of 58db with sensitivity of 2000 lux at f/5.6. Philips (with Bosch) had a new LDK-90 camera that used a chip that transferred an entire frame (full frame) worth of information at once which reduced smear. Sensitivity was a good 1750 lux at f4 with an S/N of 58db. Ikegami introduced a new high-end CCD camera, the CCD-770 with a variable speed electronic shutter. It had 480 lines of resolution and an S/N of 53db or better. Panasonic planned to have a CCD camera, the AU400, ready by the end of the year. It had resolution of 580 lines and an S/N of 58db. JVC had a new CCD camera, the KY-20U, with 56db S/N and horizontal resolution of 530 lines. Sony had the company's DXC-3000, as well as a BVW-105 CCD camera (using interline transfer [IT] chips) designed to operate with the Betacam or Betacam/SP recorder. It offered 550 lines of resolution with an S/N of 58db. Ampex was using the same technology as Sony in its CVC-50 CCD camera, but for the first time the camera was built in Ampex's Colorado Springs factory. It featured frame interline transfer (FIT) CCD sensors and a switchable electronic shutter. It also includes automatic iris control, automatic black-white balance, linear matrix and color-bar generator.[81] Hitachi had abandoned its MOS technology in favor of CCD (using the Sony chips). Thomson offered frame transfer technology (FT) (also made by Sony) in its new CCD EJ camera, the TTV-1640.[82]

In cart machines, Panasonic showed its Marc I spot player and the 1,000 plus cassette Marc II library management system. Both units used the x-y robotic system built by Matsushita. Odetics Broadcast was now offering the machine, developed with RCA, with MII or Beta decks. NBC had already purchased two of these machines. Lake Systems also showed its first robotic-arm cart system. Its $300,000–$400,000 automatic library system could accommodate libraries of 500, 1,000, or 1,500 cassettes. Asaca showed its established ACL-6000C video cart system with 600-cassette capability for both Beta and Mark II decks. Ampex showed its prototype ACR-225 cart machine. It had software enhancement enabling the x-y robotic system to handle continuous seven-second spot playbacks using four transports. It featured the company's composite digital recording system. Sony claimed that it had sold 160 of its 40-cassette Betacart system, and it was coming out with a 1,200-cassette Beta SP library which it used four Beta SP decks. The Sony unit that used an x-y robotic cassette-handling system was still undergoing modifications. However, Sony expected to deliver the first units by mid 1988.

For the first time, NEC America showed its new SR-10 solid-state recorder that could be used for instant replay in place of a one-inch machine. It used 3,000 one-megabit computer chips in four separate memories, could record up to 34 seconds of video, and could be used for instant replays as well as producing video effects and animated graphics. More recording time (up to 136 seconds) could be added for extra money. The basic unit cost $150,000. BTS (Bosch-Philips) demonstrated a prototype of a digital disc storage system capable of storing 25 seconds of video in a CCIR 601 format. It was designed to interface with the BTS FGS-4000 and the FGS-4500 graphics systems. Asaca showed it magnetic-optical disk technology. Developed by NHK, it was capable of recording up to ten minutes of video (or 18,000 still frames). It was meant for playback of news clips and commercials because of its quick access and precise cuing capabilities.[83]

In March 1987, the *SMPTE Journal* featured an arti-

cle by Richard J. Stumph of Universal City Studios. The article compared HDTV with regular 35mm film technique. He found that there had been very little change in the amount of film shot each year. The introduction of the so-called 35mm video cameras (Ikegami EC-36 and the Panacam video camera) had had very little effect on production techniques. For the few pictures that used this equipment, the savings in cost were negligible. He summed up by stating, "The majority of the film making community is very happy with film as a creative medium. Its capacities are well understood by a large number of craftsmen who are ready [and] available to light, photograph, and create special effects." To make things plain, film was very convenient to use for production. Another reason film people resisted videotape was that many felt they would rather stick with what they knew rather than attempt to learn a new technology. He summed up the situation stating that unless HDTV got a worldwide standard, HDTV would just become another standard to service with yet another videotape format.[84]

Perhaps this is a good place in this history to discuss what it is that high-definition was going to replace. First of all, the film production process is probably the worst example of cost effectiveness in the world. It starts with the purchase of the raw stock. Enough film must be bought to insure that the emulsion comes from the same batch. It is well known that film varies from manufacturer to manufacturer, emulsion to emulsion and from batch to batch. One of the problems here is something called "'short ends." When used in a camera, a reel of film lasts about 20 minutes. So the number of takes is limited. If there is any chance of running out of film in the middle of a take, a new reel of film is inserted and shooting continues. This leaves about one quarter to one third of the original raw film unused in the production. It is usually sold at bargain prices. Next, is the actual shooting of the scene itself. Here for almost 100 years, the picture was at the mercy of the camera operator or DP. Only they "knew" what was being caught on film. Until the advent of video assist, there was a great guessing game in which the cinematographer was gambling that with their past experience, they were getting on film what they thought they were getting. (We are not talking about acting technique here, but such things as boom shadows, poor composition, unwanted objects in the picture, camera malfunction, and the like.) So this leads to the next wasteful practice, the use of "dailies" or "rushes." Until these are screened the same night or the next day, there is little chance to tear down the set or move on to the next scene. This entails a laboratory process in which the film is developed and a positive print made. The good takes are then printed and married to a soundtrack. Once all the rushes from all the days' shooting have been okayed they are sent to the editor who then prepares a work print (so as not to touch the original negative again). After a laborious process involving all kinds of special effects from plain old dissolves and fades to black to the most complicated optical effects that can be dreamed up, involving audio sweetening, including new dialogue, and, of course, involving the musical score, a complete print is made for approval of the powers that be. Now the real work begins. The negative is timed and color-corrected and cut by hand to conform with the editors' notes. All special effects and other additions must be inserted in their proper place. From the original negative a dupe negative is made from which the prints are to be made. Here through a printing process comes the task of turning out perhaps some 10,000 prints and shipping them to the theaters all across the country. Depending on the projection device, they are assembled on large platters for projection. After the movie has seen its run, it is then unassembled and put in shipping cans and sent back to the film distribution centers. Then comes the final part of the process, in which the thousands of prints are returned to registered dumps or landfills to be reclaimed or destroyed. There are many landfills that have been used for the last hundred years of film making for this purpose. (Kodak's big secret!) We didn't even mention the environmental pollution associated with the many chemical labs in the development and cleaning of film that must be done. The original negative and dupe negatives are preserved for further use when the picture is resurrected for rerelease or for showing on television. In a true high-definition process where no film is used, more than half of this costly process would be eliminated.[85]

On April 6, 1987, it was reported that Allied-Signal Inc. had sold its Ampex subsidiary to the Lanesborough Corp. for $479 million plus certain liabilities. Ampex sales were in excess of $500 million and it was one of seven electronic businesses that Allied-Signal was selling. At this time Ampex claimed that it had its biggest sale year ever with buyers coming from both international and U.S. markets. The year before it had profits of $53 million on revenues of $532 million. Lanesborough, a privately held chemical manufacturing concern, intended to finance the transaction through a leveraged loan of $479 million and the assumption of additional liabilities for a total of $515 in cash to Allied-Signal. Edward J. Bramson, president and CEO of Lanesborough, stated that Ampex would continue to operate with its present management and organizational structure intact. There had been other bidders including several Japanese firms, but a foreign investor was not eligible due to the many military contracts that Ampex had with U.S. government.[86]

The closing of the CBS Technology Center and the David Sarnoff Research Center was taken quite seriously by the NAB. During the last meeting in April 1987, chairman Eddie Fritz had made a suggestion to establish an NAB technology center. Fritz cited the fact that these closings deprived technicians of vital resources that had spurred some of the industry's technical breakthroughs. While most of the industry approved of the idea, there were many obstacles in the way, such as funding, the antitrust laws, and the question of which projects to fund.[87]

In May 1987, CapCities/ABC formalized its Betacam decision. It had decided to give both Sony and Ampex equal orders for about 1,000 Betacam studio and field recorders over a five-year period. It was claimed the orders were worth in the "tens of million" of dollars. The decision was made on the basis of over 35,000 Betacam units in operation. They had chosen Betacam over MII because it was incompatible. Ed Johnson, director of engineering for ABC, admitted that the decision was made 80 percent for business reasons and 20 percent for technical reasons. Sony had "featured a better network pricing deal than Panasonic." Sony was always ready to cut its price in order to make a deal. CBS on the other hand had just bought 22 portable VTRs, 13 camera-recorders, and three EJ cameras from Sony.[88]

By June 1987, NBC had increased its order of wide-band MII equipment by 245 units, bringing the total to 650 pieces to date. Cost savings of over $26 million were predicted during the five-year contract.[89]

The 15th biennial Montreux International Television Symposium was held for June 11 to 17, 1987. High-definition television (HDTV) digital video recording and direct satellite broadcasting (DBS) were the main focus of the convention. There were over 2,000 executives in attendance with over 340 companies with 220 exhibits. Also held during the convention was the first electronic cinema symposium by the American Film Institute. There were frequent showings of the RAI production of *Julia, Julia*. It didn't seem to be too popular, with sparse attendance. Much of the debate was whether HDTV should emulate the "film look" or take advantage of its own distinctive properties. It was generally agreed that no system of HDTV would get under way until a production system was standardized. Surprisingly, most of the participants didn't believe that HDTV gained any particular cost savings in feature or program production or that the consumer would be willing to pay more for higher-resolution wide-screen pictures. The biggest news of the convention seemed to be that Thames TV, the UK's largest independent station, had bought over $15 million dollars worth of the MII system of Matsushita. This would be over 120 machines over five years. Ampex announced that it did more business internationally than in the USA, and Sony stated that it had taken orders for 300 D-1 DVTR recorders with a price tag of over $200,000 each.

Ampex introduced its new composite digital VTR

D-2 videorecorder, claiming that it was more economical than D1 with three times the record-play times of a D1 machine and simpler processing to digital composite machines. It was another of the great innovations that Ampex had made since it had introduced its original recorder in 1956.[90] Its promise was so good that Sony was the first company to take out a license to use this format. One of the highlights of the convention was the presentation by Jimmy Moir of the BBC of a documentary of the first BBC television broadcasts from the Alexandra Palace in 1936.[91]

In June 1987, Ampex also announced a new improved ACE 200 computerized editing system that provided up to 6,000 lines of edit-decision-list (EDL) storage via a 20-MB hard disk. It could control up to 16 devices including Ampex VTRs, switchers and the company's ADO digital effects systems.[92]

In September 1987, it was reported that 80 percent to 85 percent of all prime-time programs were produced on 35mm film. Hollywood produced over 1,700 hours of prime-time programming for a cost of between $1.2 million and $1.5 million an episode. All the efforts of the CBS engineering department had been in vain to change this. In spite of rising costs, Hollywood had decided to stick with its tried and true methods of shooting on film. They were simply not about to change their habits. On the other hand, the trend to electronic production was apparent in the almost mandatory use of video assist on the sets, and in most postproduction.[93]

In addition, in October 1987, it was reported that while some of the major Hollywood studios were participating in HDTV experiments, none wanted to risk the heavy capital investment to make high-definition programs. First they were awaiting a world wide standard that was agreeable to broadcasters, producers and manufacturers. Around the world, there were fewer than a half-dozen producers experimenting with HDTV. The Canadian Broadcasting Corporation and Northernlight & Picture Corp. were producing a 14½-hour, $9 million miniseries called "Chasing Rainbows." (So apropos!) Also in Italy, RAI (Radio Televisione Italia) had completed a major motion picture starring Kathleen Turner and Sting called *Julia, Julia*. Sony, that had the most to gain, was offering large discounts to Hollywood producers in hopes of showing them the advantages of the new medium.

However, they knew that this acceptance was very far off. At the major studios, one was dealing with an environment where film had a long, long history. The people, the unions, the craftspeople and the artists were all well-entrenched in film technology. They absolutely saw no reason to try a new medium which might or might not produce a product that was acceptable to them and the public. Hollywood was steeped in tradition. (The changeover from silent to talking pictures was a perfect example

of this syndrome: at first, it was considered a novelty that really wasn't needed or wouldn't last!) Besides, HDTV *smacked* of television, and TV, even with all of its advantages (yet to be proven in practice), was considered to be a lesser medium. Everyone knew of the superiority of 35mm motion picture film. So what was to be gained?

It was noted that nobody was clamoring to use HDTV, although there was a lot of interest, said Richard Stumpt, vice president of engineering and development for Universal City Studios. He claimed that technically, high-definition tape was not as sensitive as film, the motion was uneven, and the equipment was not as portable as standard film cameras. Besides, rental of film cameras was very inexpensive (only the raw stock was costly) compared to buying or renting a whole high-definition system. He did agree, though, that the HDTV system produced a 35mm-quality picture. It also had advantages in shooting high-quality mattes (background shots). Other advantages were in the electronic editing and compositing processes. Stumpf finally agreed that, "It could be a superior production tool."

David Niles along with Barry Rebo hoped to expand to Hollywood in six to nine months. They claimed to have several deals with the studios as well as the networks. Marty Katz, senior vice president of motion picture and television production at Walt Disney Pictures, stated that the problems with HDTV were minor compared with its potential value. He attributed the lack of enthusiasm for HDTV to "a lot of vested interest and capital investment in keeping things that already exist."[94]

In October 1987, the Advanced Television Systems Committee T3 group voted to support a 1,125/60 voluntary HDTV standard. The reasons given were that there was much HDTV production equipment already being manufactured and marketed. They pointed out the many commercials, music videos and even some feature films already using 1,125/60 equipment. It was claimed that numerous businesses in the entertainment industry had staked their futures on this standard and by passing it, had proved that the American TV industry was organized and going ahead.[95]

Also in October 1987, a study group of the SMPTE delivered a report stating that there were more advantages than disadvantages in shooting of motion picture film at 30 frames/sec rather than 24 frames/sec. The report stated that the 30-frame rate reduced undesired film effects of flicker and strobing, and of granularity. The report concluded that film production would be enhanced by shooting at 30 frames/sec and that modern film cameras and projectors were capable of operating at the higher frame rate.[96]

On October 1, 1987, NBC announced that a single-channel NTSC-compatible "extended definition" broadcast system had been developed by NBC, the David Sarnoff Research laboratories and G.E./RCA Consumer Electronics. The system, called the Advanced Compatible TV (ACTV), produced a wide-screen enhanced-resolution picture within a single 6MHz channel. No demonstration was given at this meeting but a simulated demonstration from videotape was given the week of October 4–7 in Ottawa, Canada.

The ACTV system produced 1,050 lines at 29.97 frames per second with an aspect ratio of either 4:3 or 16:9. It had a luminance bandwidth of 12.4MHz, and a chrominance bandwidth of 3.75MHz for I and 1.25MHz for Q. It was claimed that existing sets would display a standard 4:3 NTSC picture.

In the ACTV system, the main NTSC signal contained the center panel from the original wide-screen images, as well as the side panel's low frequencies time-compressed into 1 m-sec on each side of the active picture. The time compressed side panels were hidden by the normal overscan in home receivers. In other words, the low frequency components from each side of the wider picture were squeezed together to form a narrow band on each side of the center picture. These narrow bands were in the side regions not visible on existing receivers.

In the advanced receiver, they were unsqueezed to assist recovery of the side panels of the original wide-screen picture. The second component was the time-expanded side panel high frequencies, while the third component was the extra horizontal detail. These three components were digitally processed and then combined into one NTSC-compatible base-band signal. The extra vertical detail was combined with the three base-band components on the RF carrier. The resulting NTSC-compatible signal could then be decoded by an old receiver as a standard NTSC 4 × 3 picture. That same signal could also be decoded by a new ACTV receiver into a wide-screen enhanced definition image.

The demonstration in Ottawa featured a wide-screen high-resolution monitor, flanked by two NTSC monitors as well as two projection devices. The resulting picture looked good, but one commentator stated, "in terms of quality, it is not Muse." Alfred Sikes, head of Commerce's National Telecommunications and Information Administration, stated that "if the Sarnoff/NBC approach makes it possible to offer viewers much higher technical quality, without commanding more channels or obsoleting existing equipment, this is a very positive step in just the right direction."[97]

The 129th SMPTE technical conference and equipment exhibit was held October 31 to November 4, 1987, in Los Angeles.[98] A total of 148 papers were presented. There were demonstrations of films produced on HDTV and then transferred to 35mm film that were impressive

in their technical and artistic quality. Honors and awards were given to Don McCroskey for Outstanding Service to the Society, and the 1987 Alexander M. Poniatoff Gold Medal for Technical Excellence was awarded to Alex A. Maxey.[99] The 1987 David Sarnoff Golf Medal Award went to Yves C. Faroudja for his contributions in optimizing NTSC signal performance by developing techniques presently used in video processing equipment.[100] John Frayne gave a short history of the SMPTE from its founding in 1916 by Charles Francis Jenkins.

Among the new fellows of the society were John L. E. Baldwin of the Independent Broadcasting Authority;[101] William C. Nicholls of CBS Engineering;[102] Mark Sanders of Ampex; and Lou F. Wolf, Jr., of Universal City Studios.

Some of the machines described in the HDTV and enhanced TV sessions were also shown. A new HDTV camera, the EC-1125, was introduced by Ikegami Electronics. The camera had more film camera-style capability, was easier to focus, and was more light-sensitive. The camera was meant for electronic movie makers who planned to transfer the tape to film. Ikegami was not yet delivering the camera which would sell for $500,000. Ikegami also introduced an enhanced NTSC large-screen projection system the TPP-700. It projected 800-line pictures on either 70- or 100-inch screens. Results showed little degradation compared to live shots. Excellent NTSC pictures were also shown by Faroudja Labs with improved resolution and color. The system was compatible with any tape machine with RGB outlets. The CTE-N cost $7,850, and the CFD-N $6,250.

Ampex showed its D-2 composite signal videotape recorder which was currently undergoing standardization by the SMPTE. The biggest advantage of the D-2 and the already accepted D-1 standards, according to Ampex, came in postproduction applications. Ampex claimed the recorder could produce 20 generations without noticeable degradation. The company added that it would abandon D-1 if the D-2 took off in the marketplace.[103] Ampex also showed a prototype of its ACR-225 D-2 commercial spot player. The prototype and its prices would be available at the next NAB, and deliveries were to begin in late 1988.

The Sony Corp. was showing its BVP-5 CCD camera with frame-interline transfer chips. It also had an electronic shutter. NEC showed its latest NEC SP-3A camera with an electronic shutter and 550 lines of resolution. Ampex introduced its CVC-50 CCD camera which was being made in Colorado Springs. It also had an electronic shutter, redesigned viewfinder, durability, was lightweight, and performed well under harsh conditions. Other CCD cameras were shown by Panasonic, Hitachi Denshi America, and Broadcast Television Systems (BTS) of Bosch-Philips.[104]

In the keynote address by Daniel E. Slusser of Universal City Studios, the main topic seemed to be the replacement of film on our sound stages by video cameras and tape recorders. He was quoted as saying, "We had been promised the significant below-the-line cost savings in an electronic production. The replacement of film on our sound stages by video cameras and tape recorders has been advocated several times in the past by well-meaning groups. Again, we are being told about the significant below-the-line cost savings inherent in electronic production, but with HDTV, we won't have to give up the quality performance of 35mm film. Now, several studios, ours among them, have seriously used videotape in production for TV network shows. Other studios have even tried videotape for features. Everyone who has worked with videotape for dramatic action shows demanding single-camera production values, have without exception reverted back to film. So, why all this interest in HDTV if filmmakers don't see it in widespread use as a prime production medium? Why spend the time and effort to understand and hopefully influence the standards which will define HDTV systems of the future?

"It is simply this— we see the future of our industry closely tied to the merging of electronic processes with filmmaking. More simply stated, it is a marriage that must occur! Some experts believe that the quality resulting on 35mm prints of HDTV electronic compositing exceeds that which would result from film methods using 35mm elements. This assertion requires verification, but the instantaneous results of the electronic method certainly out distances the days and weeks involved in equivalent film compositing techniques. We feel this example is just the beginning of a wide range of useful processes, which in all probability will be digital in nature and also available for manipulating and modifying images, and even creating images to serve the creative filmmaker.

"We do not want technology for technology's sake, but we seek better ways to do the creative job. Merging electronics with film images offers great promise, but there appears to be a great deal of work to be done before this goal can be achieved. In doing this, engineers must not lose sight of the absolute need for transparent conversion between film and the electronic media. Also, the rendition of motion in the final product must be smooth, even, and symmetrical."

However, he agreed that, "Another reason for the film community to get behind HDTV development is the promise that HDTV offers a single standard for electronic program interchange. The achievement of this goal would give us all electronic equivalent of 35mm film for high quality program distribution, a great value to filmmakers. It could wipe out costly, troublesome, and quality damaging conversion in providing material for today's television. It will avoid multiple standards, duplicate vaulting, and massive record-keeping requirements. We enthusiastically support this important objective of one worldwide HDTV standard."[105]

In November 1987, an article discussed the status of electronic postproduction. It stated that at that time, more than 80 percent of network prime-time shows were shot on film, and approximately 60 percent edited electronically. The editing was always done by film-trained editors but unfortunately, the film-style tape editing systems still required intensive training of the film editor. The final result was always an EDL (edit decision list). Electronic systems cut down the editing room hours by 30 to 40 percent resulting in genuine cost savings. It was claimed that using electronic editing could save as much as $12,000 to $15,000 per episode in postproduction. The article concluded by saying that the only reason producers didn't shoot electronically (HDTV) as well, is that they wanted to have a film master available for future use.[106]

In November 1987, the NAB announced the formation of the Broadcast Technology Center to bring HDTV to reality for terrestrial broadcasters. Thomas Keller, NAB vice president, would head the center. Ben Crutchfield, the HDTV project director, would work with Keller and other engineers. The funding would come from the $700,000 already allocated by the NAB for HDTV research. The new center would include a laboratory and the necessary electronic and computer equipment.[107]

Dr. George H Brown died at the age of 79 on December 11, 1987, in Princeton, New Jersey. Some of his many achievements have been chronicled in this history.[108]

In December 1987, it was reported that Merlin Engineering of Palo Alto had rebuilt an Ampex VR-1000 for the American Museum of the Moving Image at Astoria, New York. The machine had originally been delivered to the University of Missouri in Columbus in early 1959 and used until 1984. John Streets of Merlin Engineering stated that the machine had most of its original components and was furnished a new rotary head. It would be on display at the Museum which was scheduled to open in early 1988.[109]

In January 1988, the Ampex Corp. announced the CVC-50 CCD camera designed for sports, electronic journalism and electronic field production. It featured frame interline transfer CCD sensors and a selectable electronic shutter. Any of seven shutter speeds from 1/100 to 1/2000 NTSC, 1/60 to 1/1600 PAL, could be selected and displayed in the viewfinder. It included automatic iris control, automatic white-black balance, linear matrix, and a color-bar generator.

Ampex also announced a new TBC-7 time-base corrector that allowed broadcasters to expand or compress material without visible degradation. It included a fully

1988 Ampex CVC-50 3CCD camera. (Ampex.)

digital velocity compensator, a 28-line correction window, and edit-ready functions. It was compatible with all Ampex type C recorders.[110]

In January 1988, the Sony Corp. announced that it was entering into an agreement with Matsushita to build and sell VHS recorders. All of Sony's efforts to make Beta survive had failed. Even the introduction of a three-hour machine in 1978 did nothing to keep the format alive. This was one of Sony's rare failures in the marketplace.[111]

The 22nd TV conference of the SMPTE was held from January 29 to 30, 1988, in Nashville, TN. The theme was "Technology in Transition." There were 28 papers and 16 equipment manufactures. The focus was on digital recording, the D-1 (component digital) of Sony, and the D-2 (composite signal) of Ampex. The working group on HDTV production met on Sunday, January 31, the day after the close of the conference.[112] When it came to HDTV, Larry Thorpe of Sony stated that the SMPTE and ATSC had chosen the right time to begin making the 1,125/60 HDTV the standard. He said that in order for HDTV to flourish, production studios must be established to create enough demand for mass production to lower the cost of the equipment. The cost of HDTV equipment was three times that of non–HDTV (NTSC) equipment.

Cinema Products showed a 70mm camera that shot at 60 frame/sec. It was claimed that human physiological responses to various picture frame rates indicated that 60 frames/sec was substantially better than 24 frames/sec. The camera was designed to shoot film to be transferred to high-definition videotape for theatrical use.[113]

A discussion about D-1 threw some doubts on its use in postproduction. Ampex said that the component digital D-1 was a "no expense-spared perfection format and was expensive" and wondered whether it was "ideal for post production." However Richard Taylor, manager of Quantel, disagreed, stating that for postproduction "it releases us from the almost intractable problem of color film and color code/decode characteristics." Taylor criticized the use of the new Ampex D-2 for postproduction use. However, Ampex replied that the use of the new Ampex

D-2 would not result in the added expense of component color conversion at a typical TV studio and was quite suitable for postproduction. He stated that D-2 was supported by Sony, that there was an awful lot of interest, and that they would soon be taking orders for this machine.[114]

The 1988 NAB convention was held in Las Vegas from April 4 to 12, 1988. There were 725 exhibitors and attendance was 46,871. Even President Reagan showed up, he became the first president to be covered and recorded on HDTV while making a major speech. Among the main attractions were both Ampex's and Sony's D-2 composite digital recorders. Sony was selling its D-2 recorders at a "special" price of $72,5000 (not $75,000). They were not about to let Ampex dominate the D-2 market. It was felt that the D-2 would replace the 40,000 one-inch reel-to-reel recorders then used by the industry. Sony had sold 137 DVR-10s, and Ampex more than 300 VPR-300 digital recorders, with 70 being ordered by PAL networks in the UK (BBC), Austria (ORF), and elsewhere.

D-2 had been developed by Ampex (over protests that it usurped the D-1 format for digital recorders) as a less expensive alternate to the D-1 composite digital format adopted by the CCIR. Its attractions were the 20+ generations of copies it could produce with no quality deterioration, its compact size and cassette tape convenience, its economical tape consumption (one third of the of D-1), and its low price range. It

had been adapted by both Sony and Hitachi. The SMPTE was expected to standardize the D-2 format late that year. Ampex had its biggest year ever. It sold over $30 million of D-2 equipment. AME of Burbank (a postproduction house) bought 50 VPR-300s for $5 million. They were also the first production house on the West Coast

1990 Ampex VPR-200 Series D-2 studio VTRs. (Ampex.)

1981. The author (right) with Kenjiro Takayanagi at JVC in Tokyo, Japan.

1987. First actual Ampex (D-2) VPR-300 machine. (Ampex.)

Central and South America, and other selected worldwide markets. Steinberg had come from the Ampex Corp. where he had worked from 1958 to '63 as executive vice president, then president, and from 1963 to 1988 as chief executive officer. Steinberg appointed William G. Connolly to head the newly created advanced systems division for such emerging technologies as HDTV. Connolly had joined Sony in 1974 after 25 years with CBS.[118]

to receive a new Sony DVR-10 D-2.[115] The BBC bought 12 D-2 recorders: eight from Ampex and four from Sony.

Like D-1, D-2 could duplicate video images digitally up to 20 generations. However, because the circuitry for building composite rather than component color was less expensive, and because existing studios were equipped with composite gear, D-2 was considered to be more economical than D-1 for studios looking to replace their type C one-inch gear. There was no need for extensive wiring changes, new routing, distribution and signal processing systems, a new production switcher and other pieces of new equipment. Sony continued to sell its D-1 machines, and claimed that about 90 D-1 recorders had been sold the previous year and that 100 more were on order. Sony also had an advanced technology exhibit at the Tropicana Hotel where it showed a tapeless video recorder, high density optical disc storage, new 8mm devices and an array of new HDTV products.[116]

NBC was to present a demonstration of its Advanced Compatible TV system (ACTV) at the Riviera Hotel. ACTV was being developed for NBC by David Sarnoff Research Center and Thomson Consumer Electronics. A full prototype was expected by the end of the year.[117]

In July 1988, it was announced that Charles Steinberg had been named executive vice president of Sony Corp. of America. Steinberg was to be in charge of nonconsumer products as well as the Sony Information Systems Co. He would also be responsible for marketing Sony professional products in Mexico,

1988 Sony DVR-10 D-2 composite digital VTR. (Sony.)

The 130th SMPTE technical conference and equipment exhibit was held on October 15–19, 1988, in New York at the Jacob K. Javits Convention Center. Approximately 15,500 people attended. The theme, introduced in a paper given by William G. Connolly, was "Innovations in Imaging and Sound." There were 165 technical papers delivered in total. Television field-rate systems from 60 field/sec (HDTV) to 59.94 field/sec (NTSC) were demonstrated. Honorary membership was given to Kenjiro Takayanagi of the Victor Company of Japan. He was often called the "father of television" in Japan and held over 200 patents. He made his first television transmission in 1926 (see volume one of this *History*) and founded the Japanese television industry. Honorary membership was also given to Stefan Kudelski, Kudelski S.A., who developed the lightweight NAGRA recorder and crystal controlled camera driver which made possible high quality recording in remote locations. The Progress medal was awarded to Kerns H. Powers formerly of the David Sarnoff Research Center.[119]

Shown for the first time was Panasonic's (Matsushita's) new D-3 digital videotape recorder. Like Ampex's D-2 system, it had composite rather than component color of the D-1 world digital standard. Its tape transport was based on Matsushita's MII component analog half-inch tape format. It's biggest feature was the use of smaller (half-inch) rather than ¾-inch tape. The goal was to provide a universal format that could be used in every studio application. Therefore, D-3 could be used for portable camcorders and field recorders. Panasonic claimed that its success depended on its pricing. It offered lower tape consumption, smaller physical size, and a variety of applications.[120]

Sony was selling its D-2, DVR-10 for $75,000. It claimed to have sold more than 100 machines in the USA and more than 200 worldwide. More than 100 D-2 machines were sold in England alone. Its price was $75,000 — less than half the price of the D-1, which was $160,000. Hitachi

1988. Panasonic's new D3 digital video-tape recorder. (Panasonic.)

planned to market its own D-2, the VG-500 VTR, in the coming spring. Like Ampex, it would take all three D-2 cassette sizes. It would cost about $75,000, the same as Sony's and have nearly all the capabilities of Ampex's recorders.

Ampex had not yet begun delivering its VPR-300 D-2 recorders or its ACR-225 spot players, of which 70 had been sold at prices from $200,000 to $400,000, but was expected to do so before the end of 1988. Matsushita claimed that it had sold 41 of its Marc II cart systems; 15 had been delivered so far. Odetics claimed that it had sold 48 systems, more than any competitor in the field.[121]

Ampex introduced its new ALEX character generator that included animated characters and symbols, character color changes, "write-on" signatures rather than right to left, and all in 1,500 typefaces and more than 16,000,000 colors. Cost was some $15,000 to $50,000 depending on options such as additional keyboards, additional disc drives, and RGB color monitors. Deliveries were to begin in early 1989. The big news in cameras was that Ikegami had sold 55 of its HL-55 frame interline transfer CCD cameras to NBC News by the end of the year. The list price of the HL-55 was $28,000. NEC America showed a production model of the SP-30 CCD camera, a high-resolution, high-end EJ camera. It was priced at $25,000 for the camera head only. It used the interline frame transfer CCD chips incorporated in its EP-3 production-studio camera.[122]

In October 1988, NBC submitted its new 1,050/59.94 high-definition system to the SMPTE for approval. Michael Sherlock, NBC president, operations and technical services, stated that this system departed from other proposals and would be uniquely suited for any transmission system intended to be compatible with the existing U.S. system, NTSC. This proposal was endorsed by CAP/Cities/ABC, North American Philips Corp., Zenith Corp., Tribune Broadcasting Co., Faroudja Labs, Thomson Consumer Electronics and the David Sarnoff Research Institute. As usual, the CBS engineering department reacted to the NBC initiative more in sorrow than anger. It claimed that introducing a new standard at this time could only make the prospect more difficult and lead to further division worldwide.[123]

In December 1988, it was announced that the Pentagon's Defense Advanced Research Projects Agony (DARPA)

planned to solicit proposals from video display manufacturers and research labs for the twin purposes of development of low-cost, high-resolution displays for defense applications, and the perpetuation of the vital video display and semiconductor manufacturing facilities in the United States. Not much was revealed in the media about the use of high-definition in the military. It was known that television played a vital part in air defense, either in guided missiles or in visual displays, and a wide role in communications vital to the needs of the armed forces generally. However, little was published as to the actual systems used or the standards adopted. In addition to securing high-resolution screens and computer-generated graphics for the military, the Pentagon hoped to act as a sort of venture capitalist to insure a vital American electronics industry producing HDTV equipment in the future. Craig Fields, Pentagon deputy director for DARPA research, said, "We want to push the state of the art a little bit, but we don't want to make too much of a leap."[124]

In January 1989, it was confirmed that the DARPA would be accepting proposals from research labs. The deadline was February 13, 1989. Each proposal would have a 40- to 50-page summary of potential benefits and a two page summary of the organization's style, use of personnel, and so on.[125]

The 23rd SMPTE television conference was held in San Francisco, February 3–4, 1989. It was planned to spend half of the conference studying existing technology and half on the technology of tomorrow. NHK stated that it would have its NTSC-compatible MUSE-6 and MUSE-9 (with a 3MHz augmentation channel), Narrow Muse, and Muse E available for viewing. They were the fourth, fifth or perhaps sixth proposal for the FCC. Others were Faroudja's Super NTSC system, and the North American Philips' HDS-NA (for satellite transmission only).

Sony showed its new HDC-300 color camera with 240M colorimetry on 1,125/60. It used a new 25mm tube designed jointly by Sony, Hitachi and NHK that had longer life and better lag performance. Its camera control unit had been reduced to one box. The conversion from U-matic to half-inch was causing concern from station employees. One NBC station stated that employees felt their jobs threatened by the use of the new Marc automated playback system that contained the station's entire MII tape library. On the other hand, in postproduction studios, there was no reluctance to learn the new digital formats. However, it was concluded that at that moment, 35mm film was the most efficient medium for program production.[126]

On March 1, 1989, Joseph Roizen died of a heart attack while attending a conference of the International

Electrotechnical Commission in Paris. He was 65 years old. "Born in Romania and educated in Canada, Roizen made many contributions to television technology and held 22 patents. Following early work on color television with Paramount Pictures and KTLA-TV in Los Angeles, he joined Ampex as a project engineer shortly after the introduction of their first VTR in 1957. He later became manager, video products, and spent much time traveling the world arranging the installation of VTRs. He left Ampex in 1968 and formed Telegen, an independent consultancy for engineering work and technical writing, with his wife and business partner, Donna Foster Roizen. He was a fellow of the Royal Television Society, of BKTS, and of the SMPTE, serving two terms as governor of the last.

"A prolific writer and contributor to many journals, Joe averaged a quarter million miles a year visiting television facilities and attending conferences as well as covering every Olympic Games from 1960 to 1988.... His ability to simplify complex technical issues and to deliver a lecture with style and wit made him a most sought-after speaker. A lover of good food, but not alcohol, Joe had a fund of stories, some brilliant, some dreadful, but all told with great good humor.

"Joe was, and will remain, an institution in the world of television and film, and will be sorely missed. We extend our sympathy to his wife, his two sons, his daughter and their grandchildren." (This lovely obit was written by Charles Anderson et al.)[127]

On April 12, 1989, the first digital HDTV transmission was made between California and Japan. It was a co-operative effort of Intelsat, Comsat, AT&T and the Japanese carrier KKD (Kohasai Denshen Denwa). The signals came from Malibu by way of a satellite to a dish in Tokyo, and were the equivalent of high-quality, high-definition television signals.[128]

Konosuke Matsushita, founder of Japan's largest electronics firm, died on April 27, 1989, at the age of 94. He founded Matsushita Denki Kigu Seisakusho, the predecessor of Matsushita Electric Industrial, at the age of 23. His invention of the double light-bulb socket allowed the company to expand rapidly. Today, Matsushita employs 180,000 people around the word.[129]

In the United States, 1989 was celebrated as the 50th anniversary of the birth of television, which started with the official opening of the World's Fair in New York City on April 30, 1939. The opening was addressed by President Franklin Delano Roosevelt, and his was the first presidential address to be televised. Half a century later, the Smithsonian Institution was to present an exhibit in Washington, D.C., with the theme of "TV through the ages." It would be a year-long exhibit with artifacts from the museum's vast collection of old television sets. The NAB intended to have a special luncheon in Las Vegas on April 29, during its convention. The Museum of Broadcasting planned to produce a television special by David Wolper and Jack Haley.[130]

William Connolly, president and chief executive officer for Sony's advanced systems, was given the 1989 NAB Engineering Achievement Award. Connolly's award was mainly in recognition of his work in the 1970s when he was a leader in the research and development at CBS Labs that pioneered electronic news gathering techniques and electronic still-store systems. He shared credit with other engineers at the CBS Labs whose sole responsibility was to determine what products needed inventing.[131]

The 67th annual NAB convention and equipment exhibit was held in Las Vegas from April 29 to May 2, 1989. Sony introduced a portable D-2 recorder, the DVR-1. The 22-pound unit was designed for connection to Sony's BVP-70 field camera or similar cameras with 26 pin connectors. CBS made a deal worth $5 million dollars for Sony DVR-10 decks. Sony also introduced another D-2 deck the DVR-18 studio recorder that could accept the large-size D-2 tape cassettes with playing time of over 208 minutes. The DVR-18 could record up to three hours. It had two plug in options: one for serial digital transmission and one for time compression with built-in digital pitch-corrected audio. Plus, of course, it had 20 or more generations of transparent digital dubbing, four channels of PCM digital audio, and write-after-read editing. It would cost $81,000, about $6,000 more than the DVR-10. Again Sony reported that it had sold 100 D-2 recorders during the show. A new D-2 recorder was introduced by Hitachi Denshi, the VL-500. It was claimed that this machine was easier to operate than both Ampex's and Sony's. Ampex announced its M-GEN software for its D-2 machines in which errors in multigenerational recordings were corrected. It allowed 20 generations to be recorded before any possible degradation showed up.[132]

Ampex also announced a slow-motion controller, the SMC-200, which was compatible with all recording systems. Its programming allowed the user to review a multiple camera shoot by playing back cues from any number of recorders in normal, slow-motion or still-frame mode. Functions included gang roll, and multiple machine or synchronous slow-motion control with continuously variable forward and reverse speed adjustment and still-frame pause. Ampex also introduced a family of digital signal translators, the DST-300 series, that cost-effectively converted composite digital video signals to a 4:2:2 component digital signal and vice versa.[133] Ampex was not making D-1 digital recorders but was still selling type C machines. They even advertised that selling D-2 digital recorders was their first priority, but claimed that type C was the world's broadcast interchange and distribution standard that there were many advantages of type

C machines, and that much type C business was readily available.[134]

Sony also announced that it had sold over 50,000 three-chip cameras in the last six years. The company exhibited two prototype cameras: the BVP-370, using an advanced frame interline transfer (FIT) chip to capture 700 lines of resolution, and the BVP-270 with regular interline transfer for general studio use. Sony also showed its second one-piece camcorder, the BVW-300, weighing some 15 pounds and providing 670 lines of resolution, with 380,000 pixels. Broadcast Television Systems introduced two new cameras: the LDK-910 for studio and field production and the LDK-91 field unit. Both had a new concept in CCD frame-transfer chips developed by Philips of Holland. Panasonic showed the AQ-20 which was the first camera to have all-digital processing. It used three FIT chips resulting in 400,000 pixels. Ampex showed its CVR-300 (similar to Sony's BVW-300) one-piece camera for $35,000. It captured 670-line images and would accept 30-minute Betacam SP tapes. They also displayed the CVC-70 camera that showed 700 lines with 420,000 pixels. This unit sold for $34,900. There were two EJ cameras from Ampex. The SK-F1 produced 650 lines and operated in either triax or multicore. It weighed only some 6.8 pounds. The SK-F3 had auto setup operations and a high resolution 650-line viewfinder. Finally, Ampex showed the CK-2B which would dock with either Betacam, SP, MII or S-VHS recorders. It had a built-in six-speed electronic shutter. Ikegami displayed its 6.8-pound HL-55 with FIT CCDs which provided for 400,000 pixels and 700 lines of resolution. The HL-53 was less expensive and cost $25,000. For studio use, the company introduced a new version of the HK-323A tubed camera. It used new "SS" tubes (static focus and static deflection). Lastly, Ikegami introduced the HK-327 camera that used magnetic electrostatic Plumbicon tubes that captured over 800 lines of horizontal resolution.[135]

Sony had also moved into "systems" technology by introducing a new switcher, a graphics effects device, a still store, and a solid-state recorder. Sony showed its solid-state recorder, the DEM-1000, designed for live sports production, instant replay, "real-time" slow motion, and on-air frame-by-frame replay. It could also be used as an editing tool. Its 20-second record time could be extended to three minutes. Ampex admitted that this move by Sony was a cause for concern for they were a very strong company and a strong competitor. But they were not surprised by this move, as Sony had developed customized high-end equipment for the Japanese market and it was only a matter of time before they got the costs down and offered it as a mass product.[136] Sony stated that this move was part of its emphasis on the customer buying all equipment from one vendor. For some reason, in

their view, buying from different manufacturers didn't work quite right. In truth, some equipment just didn't work well with other brands. Two reasons were given for their philosophy: first, it was easier to call one number for maintenance and repair; and second, it "is easier to work out flexible discount rates when a customer is buying several different kinds of equipment at the same time."[137]

Sony claimed that it had sold 11 library management systems, most with D-2 configuration. The company also claimed that it had sold 35 systems worldwide: eight in the USA and three in Canada. CBS had bought two DVC-1000 LMS systems (with a capacity of 1,000 cassettes), and Sony said that this was the first purchase of composite digital D-2 recorders by one of the three major networks.[138]

Ampex claimed that it had shipped over 200 of its VPR-300s and 20 of its ACR-225 library systems. However, Odetics Broadcast maintained that it led the industry in sales with about 70 of its 280 cassette cart machines delivered. They showed PAL and D-2 versions of their cart machines. Hitachi Denshi showed a production model of a D-2 model VL-D500 that had simpler controls and improved diagnostics. It was claimed that it had been designed for ease of operation. It was noted that the broadcast industry was divided up, with NBC favoring the MII Matsushita recorder, CBS favoring the Sony DV-10, and ABC splitting the market between Sony and Ampex. ABC was still buying most of its studio equipment from Ampex, though, and using the Sony Betacam SP format.[139]

BTS (Broadcast Television Systems) GmbH introduced a one-inch HDTV component videotape recorder based on the Eureka working standard of 1,250 lines/50Hz field frequency. This VTR that combined the advantages of digital signal processing with proven analog recording, served as an experimental component for Eureka's new television systems.[140] They also introduced a new portable recorder for PAL, the DCR-2P. Based on the D-2 format, it provided recording with 6MHz video bandwidth and four digital audio channels. It had a replay section for quality control and direct broadcast.[141]

Sony had also developed Hi8 to be used in addition to the still thriving U-matic market. A one-piece one-CCD camera, the EVO-9100 camcorder, weighed only 4.9 pounds and produced 420,000 pixel RBG pictures. Panasonic was championing its S-VHS system. The company showed a portable VTR, the AG-7450, that could record 400 lines and deliver two-channel Dolby stereo. It would be available in September for $3,500.[142]

Part of the NAB convention was demonstrations by the HDTV Product Expo '89 group of 31 manufacturers and production companies. Eleven proposed systems were demonstrated, with five of those exhibiting hardware. The demonstrations were held at the Tropicana Hotel, which

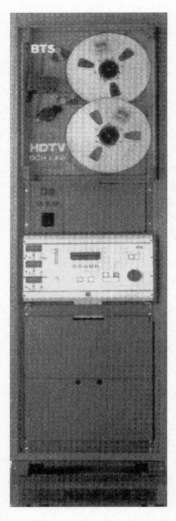

1990. BTS one-inch videotape recorder. (BTS.)

had six theaters including projection systems for two full cinema-sized screens using an Eidophor system. Sony's electron-beam tape-to-film technology was used to transfer these images. Rank Cintel showed its film-to-tape flying-spot Mark III HD telecine transferring a film print of *Gone with the Wind* to tape.

At the convention center, alternatives to the 1,125/60 system were shown by NBC and the David Sarnoff Research Center. They exhibited an ACTV system that was a conventional 525/59.94 modified to a 16:9 aspect ratio. They ran a tape of the first broadcast of its NBC's one-channel, receiver-compatible ACTV-1 that took place on April 20, 1989. Taking part in this demonstration was Ampex, which had previously remained neutral in the HDTV question. They had furnished four VPR-300 composite digital tape machines, an ADO digital effects system, an AVC Vista switcher, and an ACE 200 editor. In its coverage of this demonstration, the press noted that Ampex was the last major U.S. owned videotape equipment manufacturer.[143] Faroudja Labs' Super NTSC system was shown in an over-the-air broadcast from KBLR (TV) channel 39. It was demonstrated in 5:3 ratio with, for the first time, a two-channel encoding system developed by Dolby Labs.[144]

In May 1989, four major companies—Capcities/ABC, NBC, Westinghouse and Tribune Broadcasting said the process was to pre-empt the advanced TV market in the USA and put off the arrival of a true high-definition TV system for ten years or so, so that engineers could produce a digital 6MHz HDTV system. CBS as usual stated that they had no objection to Faroudja types of experiments, as long as they were properly tested. However, they felt that it would slow efforts to implement a true HDTV system. CBS still believed that the true HDTV system of the future would require 12MHz of spectrum. It

was felt that the FCC would find it difficult to warehouse very valuable UHF spectrum space while this happened.[145]

In May 1989, CBS announced the first CBS Movie of the Week, *The Littlest Victims*, was to be shot in high-definition television. With this chance to use its facilities at Studio Center, CBS shot this movie on location in Atlanta, Georgia, using outside facilities. The movie was shot using an HDTV camera, the Sony HDC-100 with a Nikon 7:1 zoom lens mounted on a film dolly. There were two cameras available that fed two analogue HDTV recorders. Sound was fed to a Nagra quarter-inch recorder along with SMPTE/EBU time and control code. All good takes were edited together in HDTV using a van supplied by 1125 Productions, New York City. This became a dailies reel and was made into a one-inch copy and two VHS copies through a Sony down-converter at 59.64 frame rate. The editing was then done on a Montage editing system by one editor and one assistant in Los Angeles.[146]

The first cut was turned over to the director to review and make changes. Two weeks later, the final cut, 95 minutes long, was sent out for music and effects. Then the tape was color-corrected in HDTV, which was RGB and which made that process simpler. After the sound track was added, the HDTV tape was down-converted to one-inch type C format. The result was claimed to "look better than 35mm film transferred to tape." The movie was broadcast on April 23, 1989, by CBS-TV. CBS bragged that the process "was similar to that of regular movies shot on 35mm film even though the director did not want to work in high definition, had a DP who was totally unfamiliar to video lighting requirements and a film crew who felt clearly threatened by the technology." How much better would it have been if the movie was shot under different circumstances?[147]

In May 1989, there was a progress report on improving the NTSC system. With the amount of revenue from videocassette rentals surpassing those of the movie box office, it was thought imperative to upgrade the images from VCRs. There were developments to upgrade the quality of the NTSC images by (1) JVC with Super VHS, (2) 8mm Hi Band by Sony and (3) Super NTSC by Faroudja Labs. It was claimed that better cameras such as HARP (high gain avalanche rushing amorphous photoconductive) Saticon configurations and broadcast quality CCDs as image sources, made for better NTSC encoding.[148] Super NTSC was the process by Faroudja Laboratories to produce superb NTSC pictures at cost-effective and affordable prices. Super NTSC had the visual characteristic of a 1,050-line picture, 59.94Hz, 15MHz RGB signal without NTSC artifacts. It included luminance detail processing, Y and C adaptive combing before NTSC decoding, Y/C multiplicative bandwidth expansions, and motion-compensated line doubling. Larger-sized LCD displays, with better resolution and brightness levels that could be watched in a well-lit room, coupled with line doublers, produced superb NTSC pictures. It was hoped that with these developments NTSC would have many years of greatly improved useful life left in it.[149]

In May 1989, the USA blocked the adoption of the European standard of 1,250/50 by suggesting that a world standard be put off until 1994. The USA was in a bad situation since there were 23 50Hz countries versus only six 60Hz countries. A common image report was to be prepared for CCIR in October.[150]

In June 1989, the Defense Department Advanced Research Projects (DARPA) agency stated that it would award five companies contracts to develop high-definition television displays. It selected Texas Instruments of Dallas, Newcom, Inc. of San Jose, Rachem Corp. of Menlo Park, Projectavison, Inc. of New York, and Photonics Technology of Northwood, Ohio. Zenith Corp. was to get funding for its flat-tension mask display. In total, $30 million in funding was involved. One government stipulation was that none of the companies be foreign owned. However, it was claimed that some non–U.S.-owned companies such as Sony Corp., Thomson, and Dutch Philips had submitted proposals.[151]

The 16th International Television Symposium and Technical Exhibition was held in Montreux, June 17–23, 1989. Over 40,000 people attended. One of the main topics was the use of fiber optics. The big advantage of fiber was that it carried high signal quality further with fewer amplifiers. European researchers were designing systems with up to 1.3 gigabits per second digital transmission capability. Most of the participants were unhappy with the proliferation of videotape formats. It seemed that they were faced with a choice of the expensive D-1 component color format or the less expensive composite digital D-2 format. The introduction of the D-3 by Matsushita further complicated the issue. It was agreed that it was important to reform the standardization process. However, both CBS and NBC said that it was beneficial to have a lot of choices, which prevented stagnation in the industry.[152]

Another controversial topic was HDTV, with the world split between 1,250/50 (Europe) and 1,125/60 (Japan and the United States). Both sides agreed on one thing— HDTV was not going to replace film; however, everyone said HDTV would be used for postproduction, especially where special effects were needed. They also thought that the probability of a world standard was not high. HDTV, they said, should be considered a new tool for filmmakers. Shown on the floor was Hitachi Denshi's new HF-5200 disc recorder. It could hold 30 HDTV pictures or, with an optical disc, 130 pictures. Sony also showed a digital 1,125/60 one-inch VTR. They claimed that it was very

much like D-1 in performance except that it was high definition. It was said that Eureka planned to have a digital VTR prototype of 1,250/50 in 1990. on the topic of HDTV, one dissenting voice was Ampex who stated that HDTV was not one of its major concerns. They complained that many in the U.S. government and in the business community did not know much about Ampex or the TV industry. One Ampex staffer said that, "I am glad I am not a broadcaster; imagine spending millions of dollars to upgrade a local plant for a mere handful of receivers. Its just an incredible nightmare."

The Second Electronic Cinema Festival was opened on June 18, 1989. Fifty-three HDTV programs were reviewed by a jury, and 32 were to compete for awards. The main criteria was the creative use of HDTV. It was noted that only one of the 53 entries was shot in 1,250/50. This was an 11-minute drama, "Un Bel Di'Vedremo," produced by RAI in Florence, Italy. It seems that RAI, Italy's state-run network, was anxious to be a leader in HDTV in both 1,125 and 1,250 formats. This was to make up for their delay in getting into color TV that nearly destroyed Italy's electronics industry.[153]

On September 26, 1989, the National Academy of Television Arts and Sciences gave out several engineering awards. Ray M. Dolby received an Emmy for audio noise-reduction systems in professional tape recorders. The Ampex Corp. received its 10th Emmy, in recognition of its developments and implementation of the D-2 composite digital videotape format. This Emmy was shared with the Sony Corp. for its efforts on behalf of D-2. Sony had three professional D-2 recorders in its line. It was also Sony's 10th Emmy award.[154]

In September 1989, Gretag of Switzerland announced its new HDTV high resolution Eidophor electronic projector. They claimed that with wide-angle anamorphic lenses it could project color pictures up to 40 feet wide. It was planned to be used for either front or back projection.[155]

The SMPTE's 131st annual convention was held in Los Angeles, October 21–25, 1989, at the Convention Center. Over 15,000 people attended. The conference's theme was "Technology and Tradition — Parties in Progress." One hundred seventy-nine papers in 23 concurrent sessions were presented. There were 258 displays from manufacturers of motion picture and television equipment.[156] It was becoming increasingly clear that as HDTV was introduced, program production with 35mm film would continue to be more common than video production. Awards were given to: Reville McMann (CBS retired)— the Progress Medal; Angelo D'Alessio, Ampex Italiana and Joseph Roizen (posthumously)— the Presidential Proclamation; Lawrence Thorpe and Yoshio Ozaki — SMPTE Journal Awards; Donald McCroskey — the Eastman Kodak

THE HDTV EIDOPHOR:
A REVOLUTION IN RESOLUTION

You have to see it to believe it. The startling clarity. The electrifying colors. The breathtaking, bigger-than-life images. With a high definition resolution that creates picture quality of 35mm caliber, it's the perfect large-screen projector for electronic cinemas, indoor sporting events, concerts, training purposes, closed circuit TV broadcasts and entertainment. Ideal for on-air studio use, too.

And the HDTV EIDOPHOR® can be used for front or rear projection. With the wide-angle anamorphic lenses producing color pictures up to 12 meters (40 ft.) wide! See this spectacle for yourself. For more information, call our representatives at (201) 567-2010.

GRETAG SWITZERLAND

EIDOPHOR®
Distributed by INFORMATION DISPLAY SYSTEMS, A Division of SAIC
100-C West Forest Avenue, Englewood, NJ 07631

1989. New HDTV Eidophor projector. (Eidophor.)

Gold Medal; and Terrence W. Mead, Rank Cintel — the Agfa-Gavaert Gold Medal.[157]

The battle between film and HDTV got heated up when Kodak claimed that film had made amazing advances in imaging capabilities. They claimed that new color negative stocks were capable of twice the resolution of HDTV and that high speed films could be used in almost total darkness. They also claimed that their high-resolution electronic intermediate system — whereby the original was shot on film and then all editing was done in the electronic domain, with the final result transferred by a laser film recorder back again to 35mm film — gave the best results. In addition to claiming that film had a contrast range of 1,000:1, versus 50:1 for HDTV, and that film had more flexibility, they also brought up the so-called "film look" which they admitted defied exact definition but had a powerful appeal.

Both Larry Thorpe of Sony and John Galt disagreed with this thesis and brought out many points to disprove it. A highlight of the show was the transmission of the HDTV "live" all-digital link between the Los Angeles Convention Center and the KKD (International Telecommunications Co. of Japan) building in Tokyo. The pictures were excellent and the sound better than the local

audio. This was the first transmission from Tokyo to the USA.[158]

Avid Technology showed its two-year-old editing machine, the Avid/1 (first shown at NAB the previous spring), and sold five. The company claimed that it now had 14 systems in operation. Avid's goal was to develop less sophisticated, low-cost editing systems that could be used from corporate production to high-end postproduction. The Avid was based on the Apple Macintosh personal computer. The company predicted that within two years it would introduce totally tapeless editing.

Eastman Kodak announced a CCD telecine that would be manufactured in a partnership with Rank-Cintel. Rank announced that it had sold one of its flying-spot scanners to Club Theater Network (CTN) which was establishing a 14-location chain of theaters that would present movies in high-definition video. CTN was waiting for an 1,125/60 version of the telecine to transfer first-run movies for showing at the theaters. The first screens would be small, some 12 by 6 feet, but would expand to 20 by 10 feet. Their plan called for the movies to be transferred to video and played back from a central location in Pompano Beach, Florida.

In cameras, Panasonic showed it AQ-20, the first camera to use all-digital processing. It incorporated frame-line transfer (FIT) CCD chips, captured a 400,000 pixel picture with 750 lines of resolution and 60db S/N and was priced at $32,500. BTS stated that the LDK-91 field camera would succeed the LDK-90, and the LDK-910 studio-field model would take over the LDK-900. Both cameras used frame-transfer chips and produced 800 pixels per line with 700 lines of resolution.

Ikegami showed a production model of the HK-355 CCD studio-field camera. It claimed over 800 horizontal lines and an S/N of 62db. It had a variable shutter speed ranging from 1/60th to 1/5,000th of a second. Ikegami also showed a 30mm tubed camera using the 30mm Mag-Sta Plumbicon tube. This high-end camera was planned to be used throughout the 1990s. Hitachi Denshi showed two interline (IT) CCD cameras. One was the SK-F2 3 CCD EJ camera, to replace the SK-F3, using FIT chips, which sold for $24,000. They also showed the Z-ONE, an IT field model with an electronic shutter. It was made to dock with either Betacam SP VTRs or to MII and S-VHS with an adapter. It was priced at $15,500.[159]

Sony announced that it had sold over $1 million worth of D-2 recorders to Viacom. They were to replaced type C and U-matic machines in Long Island. By February, all pay services would be digital. It was Sony's largest sale of equipment to date.

Ampex announced that it had sold 250 of its VPR-300 decks and delivered 200 of them. Sadly Ampex admitted that flaws had been found in the early machines and the company was forced to stop shipments of the deck. In September, a solution was found and a retrofit began. It had also sold 40 of its ACR-225 D-2 video library systems, with 11 on line.

BTS's (Bosch-Philips) new D-2 deck, the DCR-10 (built by Sony), was selling for $60,000. They claimed they were working on a machine to be built in Germany. With Sony, they were also building D-1 decks and a D-1 (component) for D-2 standards converters.

Panasonic showed the engineering model of its composite digital D-3 deck. They also showed a half-inch digital camcorder. It had a 400,000 pixel unit with 700 lines of resolution. The digital tape cassettes were slightly larger than the existing MII half-inch cassettes sold by Panasonic. Panasonic claimed that there was little chance for a camcorder based on the three-quarter D-2 format. Sony of course had the DVR-2 that was a 26-pound unit that connected with Betacam SP cameras. It could record up to 94 minutes.[160]

In October 1989, Ampex announced that it had sold its 4,000th type C VPR-80 recorder.[161] They also announced that by the end of the year they had sold their 500th ACE 25 editing system. The system was shipped to the International Education Association, Washington, DC. In addition they had sold an ADO 2000 digital effects system, two Betacam SP studio players, a VPR-6 videotape recorder and an AVC Vista 18 switcher. Ampex admitted, however, that softness in demand and manufacturing-related delays regarding such machines as the VPR-300 D-2 VTR and ALEX character generator, had led to layoffs at Redwood City and the Colorado Springs plant. Nonetheless, their other successes had led to a 5 percent increase in revenues in 1989 over the year before.[162]

By December 1989, Ampex admitted that all 200 VPR-300s had been fixed and new models were being shipped. But Ampex was in trouble. More than half of its sales were to foreign buyers and the strength of the American dollar made them more expensive than Japanese or European goods. Domestic sales had slowed down and sales in 1990 were expected to be about the same. There had been a change in management, with Ronald Ritchie being promoted to president and chief operating officer. He replaced Max Mitchell who was retiring. Finally, there were rumors of a takeover following these events. Ampex's future had never looked so gloomy.[163]

Chapter 13

The Grand Alliance
(1990–1994)

The 24th Television Conference of the SMPTE was held at Disney World, Florida, January 26–27, 1990. High-definition TV was the main topic. It was assumed that a common world standard had been lost. Three items of discussion were (1) whether to adopt progressive scanning or interlaced as an interim step, (2) the common number of active lines and (3) whether the shape of the pixels should be rectangular or square. The Sony Corp. argued mostly for interlaced scan as the Japanese industry had the most time and money invested in an interlaced 1,125/60 system. They were quick to point out that pickup tubes needed more sensitivity and that CCDs were even worse. But Merril Weiss, director of advanced systems at NBC, stated that if they built an infrastructure only around interlaced scan, then the move to progressive scan would be put off for some ten years.

There was also a discussion about the use of adopting a production TV standard of 24 frames/sec. It was argued that since most HDTV programming was going to be shot on film at 24fps, perhaps it should be adopted for TV as well. This was in contradiction of the recent SMPTE argument that film should be shot at 30fps to accommodate the TV system. There was little hope for this idea, though, as it meant changing all the projectors in theaters worldwide.[1]

In February 1990, Ampex announced that it was offering a retirement plan to 400 of its U.S. employees. This came after the company had already laid off 5 percent or 300 of its workforce in 1989. To be eligible, they must have served at least five years with Ampex and be 50 years or older. Ampex employed 6,000 people worldwide at that time.[2]

In March 1990, it was reported that Sony had sold more than 1,500 D-2 recorders and that it would pass 2,000 by the end of the year. But broadcasters were only buying 10 percent of them. Sales of digital tape had finally passed that of one-inch even though it cost $90 an hour versus the $60 for one-inch. Ampex claimed that while D-2 cassettes were growing, that it would be some time before D-2 consistently outsold the one-inch format. Sony was introducing a DVR-18 studio recorder, as well as a new DVR-2 for electronic field production. The DVR-2, which was the same as the old BVH-500 A, but with digital quality, sold for $37,500.

Ampex was not enjoying the same sales for its D-2 machines, however. Faults in its VPR-300 decks caused recalls and cut into its sales. As a result, Ampex was introducing three new D-2 recorders. The new VPR-200 was positioned for recording and on-air program playback. It could be integrated with Ampex's ACR-225 video library system, and played all three sizes of videocassettes. Below it was the VPR-250 that only accepted the small and medium-sized cassettes and was offered for broadcast production and postproduction. Finally, there was the VPR-350 with all the high-end post production features of the VPR-300 which was aimed at studio production and postproduction houses.[3]

Nonetheless, Ampex was not following Sony's lead into portable D-2 equipment any time soon. The company felt that it would take a lot of doing to unseat Betacam SP and would watch the market closely. Ampex conceded that the lower prices for the Sony D-2s allowed them to sell more of the earlier D-2 decks than Ampex. However, Ampex claimed that there was good reaction to the new VPR-200 D-2 machines.

Both Sony and Ampex were gearing up for competition from Matsushita and JVC with their new D-X half-inch format recorders. Matsushita would supply 400 D-X tape decks for the 1992 Olympic Games at Barcelona, Spain, in 1992. This was unusual as they had no orders from a major broadcaster. Meanwhile, NBC, who was Panasonic's biggest customer, had ordered another $2 million of MII equipment.

Ampex introduced a full digital component system for its low cost ADO 100 systems. They stated that more than 900 ADO units had been shipped since July 1990. The ADO-100 with 2-D software cost around $20,000 with a ceiling of about $30,000 for full 3-D effects and Infinity software interface, and the ADO 2000 sold for $60,000, and the ADO-3000 for about $100,000.

Sony introduced the BVW-400 one piece camera. It used FIT chips, and the hole accumulated diode (HAD) sensor which had 700 lines of horizontal resolution. It weighed slightly over 15 pounds, ran for 50 minutes on an NP-1A battery, and could work with nearly all Betacam SP external recorders. They also introduced the BVP-270 (for general studio use) and BVP-370 cameras (for mobile van applications) using HAD sensors with 700 lines of resolution. Both cameras featured high-sensitivity, 62db S/N with an electronic shutter with speed from 1/1,000 to 1/2,000 of a second.

Ampex introduced the CVR-400 Betacam SP integrated camcorder featuring an advanced high-resolution frame interline transfer (FIT) CCD sensor, which eliminated vertical smear. It was made under license at Colorado Springs, and was the exact equivalent of the Sony BVW-400. It was intended for electronic field production and high-end electronic journalism, had a 700-line TV resolution, and weighed fully loaded, just over 15 pounds.[4] Ampex claimed that it would introduce any new Sony cameras as part of the Ampex line.

Ikegami introduced its HK-355 three-chip unit and claimed that it had better sensitivity and superior colorimetry than the Sony BVW-400. It had three FIT CCDs for 700 lines of resolution and an S/N of 62db. It had a computer-controlled CPU and operated in either triax or multicore mode. It was priced at $50,000 without lens.

BTS (Bosch-Philips) Broadcast Systems introduced its LDK-391 camcorder. It used the same FT (frame transfer) CCDs used in the BTS LDK-91 camcorder. The camcorder featured a 1.5-inch viewfinder and an optional battery supply for up to 150 minutes of operation. It sold for $8,500.

Panasonic's all-digital processing camera, the AQ-11, was announced. It offered 700 lines of resolution, sensitivity of *f*5.6 at 2,000 lux, and weighed about seven pounds without the VTR. It would dock with any half-inch recorder without an adapter. Hitachi introduced the

only tube-based camera, the SK-H50. It used Harpicon tubes developed by Hitachi with NHK, and provided 700 lines of resolution with a sensitivity of *f*4 at 200 lux, three times greater than the sensitivity of conventional Saticon tubes. The camera's best application was at sporting events shooting at dusk. Not to be outdone, Ikegami offered a low-light camera, the HL87M ULTRA, designed to operate in almost no light. It was a three-FIT camera with 380 lines of resolution. The sensitivity was *f*5.6 at 150 lux. The company claimed that it could film interviews and the like with no additional lights. The camera docked to either Betacam SP or MII recorders.[5]

From March 30 to April 2, 1990, the annual NAB convention was held in Atlanta, Georgia. Over 50,443 people attended. The crowning achievement was the live HDTV telecast of President Bush at the Congress Center on April 2.[6]

BTS (Broadcast Televisions Systems) added the LDK-9 studio-quality frame transfer CCD camera system. It was to replace all BTS tubed cameras for studio and outside broadcasts. It had a high-resolution seven-inch viewfinder and component outputs for resolution of over 700 lines. It featured remote control of camera head parameters such as flare, gamma contours, and matrix, while shading was stored in the camera head memory.[7]

NHK and Hitachi showed a one-inch camera for HDTV studio use. It used three one-inch HDTV HARP camera tubes, its sensitivity was 32 times higher than that of the Saticon, and had a limiting resolution of over 2000 TVL as a result of the tube's incorporating of new static focus static deflection. They also announced an HDTV experimental camera incorporating half-inch CCDs (776 H by 980 V) pixels with an aspect ratio of 4:3. It had a limiting resolution of 900 TVL and an S/N ratio of 50db and a sensitivity of *f*2.8 at 200 lux. These excellent results came from the use of the dual green system.[8]

The Ampex Corp. introduced the AMC-225 optional external device controller. When used with the ACR-225 automated cassette system, up to ten devices could be operated directly from the products playlist. These could include variable format VCRs such as Betacam, type C, and D-2.

Sadly Ampex was having great difficulties with the new D-2 deck. Aimed at high-end production facilities, defects were discovered in the delivered machine which slowed D-2 sales and cut into the company's profits. Over 300 workers were laid off due to these problems. Ampex's new VPR-200 was positioned for recording and on-air program playback and was an ideal VTR to integrate into AMPEX 225-library system. Ampex was introducing a new VPR-3000 which could handle cassettes up to 90 minutes and was more gentle on tape apparatus than the older D-2s resulting in longer life. Rewind and fast forward were 60 times play speed. There was also a VPR-250, a lower-cost version that accepted only small and medium-sized cassettes and was also being offered for broadcast production and postproduction. A third new VTR was the VPR-350, the lower-cost version of the original VPR-300 with capability to record and play back small and medium cassettes. All three included all of the high-end postproduction features of the VPR-300.[9]

Warp effect capabilities called warp speed were added to the Ampex ADO 100 digital effects system. The company's ALEX character generator featured significant improvements in hardware and software. The system had 4:2:2 pipeline architecture that provided advanced real-time animation speed and quality. It had an effective character resolution of 4.6nsec and 256 levels of anti-aliasing and transparency for superior video quality.[10]

Ampex announced the ACE-10 edit controller that was an A/B roll-, three-machine system that operated on a standard computer platform. List outputs could be either CMX 340 or SMPTE format.[11] Ampex's CVR-85 Betacam SP Studio VTR and DAP-85PCM digital audio processors featured digital audio recording and playback while maintaining the Betacam SP format. These products were available in PAL only.[12]

Broadcast Television Systems GmbH (BTS) extended its range of video recorders using the D-2 format. The DCR-10 and DCR-18 had the same specs, except that the DCR-18 had an extended play time of 208 minutes and equipment for remote and automatic control. These products were available for NTSC and PAL. They also introduced a DCR-2P portable recorder for PAL, which stored audio and video signals in digital quality.[13]

Walter Bruch, one of the most creative geniuses of the television industry, died on May 5, 1990. He was 82 years of age. A professor and doctor of engineering, Bruch would be best remembered for the development of the PAL system, or phase alternation line system, where the color sub-carrier phase was shifted from one line to the next through the transmission of a line-switching signal and a color burst. Today, this is the standard for television transmission in more than 70 countries in Europe, South America, and Asia.[14]

On June 1, 1990, General Instrument (GI) Corp. of New York proposed an all-digital HDTV system. Called DigiCipher, GI's digital-encoding technique had been under design for cable TV and DBS transmission for two years and was now being put forward as a terrestrial broadcast system as well. Executives of GI went to Washington to meet with officials of the FCC advisory committee and the Advanced Television Test Center (ATTC) to submit their system, with the intention of it becoming an ATV (terrestrial) standard. They had just met the deadline for inclusion of the various proposed HDTV systems testing.

It was planned to show a simulation on July 9, 1990, in Nashville, and by November and December to send NTSC signals to the Video-Cipher labs in San Diego. As early as April 1991, they planned to give the first public demonstration at NAB in Las Vegas. The system had a 16:9 aspect ratio with a 1,050 line interlaced scan with 59.95 fields per second. It was operating within a 6MHz channel that was not compatible with NTSC receivers. An interesting comment on the system was made by NHK scientist Keiichi Kubota who was quoted as saying that, "it is very difficult to realize an all-digital HDTV broadcast system based on our experience."[15]

A fascinating aspect of the proposed new DigiCipher system was its ability to deliver multiple digital NTSC signals. General Instrument vice president and chief developer, Jerrold A. Heller, claimed that the system could transmit up to ten NTSC and two HDTV signals terrestrially over a 6MHz channel![16]

In July 1990, it was announced that Charles P. Ginsburg had been inducted into the National Inventors Hall of Fame. He led the six-member team that conceived and created the Ampex VRX-1000 during the 1950s. He shared patents with Charles E. Anderson, Ray M. Dolby, Shelby Henderson, Alex R. Maxey and R. Fred Pfost. The new videotape exhibit at the Inventors Hall of Fame in Akron, Ohio, included portraits of the Ginsburg team and the VTR machine and a sample strip of recording tape from 1959.[17]

On July 23, 1990, the noted Japanese television pioneer, Kenjiro Takayanagi, died of pneumonia in a hospital at Yokosuka, Japan. He was 91 years old. Takayanagi was known as the "Father of Japanese television," a well-deserved title, and his exploits were chronicled in many books.[18]

In August 1990, it was reported that CBS television stations had bought 14 SK-F750 CCD studio cameras from Hitachi Denshi, America. As each camera cost $75,000, the deal was worth over $1.05 million.[19]

At the same time, it was reported that Ampex had sold $6.5 million of equipment to a new satellite transmission facility in West Drayton, England. It included nine Betacam SP videotape recorders, four studio cameras, seven tape-editing systems, two computer-effects systems, five production switchers, four character generators, and one still stores and one paint system.[20]

In September 1990, it was revealed that D-2 recorders had a serious problem with audio editing. Due to the way the audio tracks were laid out, in the still mode, the audio chattered and was unusable. Ampex had solved the problem allowing a specific location to be accurately picked on all digital tracks. Ampex was shipping its Accu-Mark accessories for its line of D-2 recorders.[21]

IBC's 1990 convention was held September 21–25,

1990, at Brighton, England. It drew some 20,000 attendees and more than 280 exhibits. Britain's Satellite and Broadcasting (BSB) and the Independent Broadcasting Authority (IBA) demonstrated "live" and with videotape BSB's new wide–MAC 16:9 wide-screen system. It was claimed as the first wide-screen TV service ever displayed. Ferguson, Britain's leading maker of televisions and VTR, displayed a new 16:9 wide screen TV. (Ferguson was part of France's Thomson Group.) IBC claimed that it was developing an enhanced version of the European PAL TV system called PAL-plus with a 16:9 aspect ratio. They had adopted the so-called letterbox approach with viewers of 4:3 seeing black bars above and below the image. The question was whether British viewers would be comfortable with this approach as it was proven that American widescreen proponents had rejected it. The BBC was experimenting with digital TV techniques and had demonstrated an enhanced PAL system decoded for display on a European 1,250-line monitor. It produced just a fair picture.

DigiCipher by General Instrument was demonstrated (by computer simulation) for the first time in Europe at Brighton. While admitting that basic digital coding schemes or algorithms had been known for some time, GI noted that the key to DigiCipher was "very powerful error correction techniques." It was claimed that this was missing from European research. Veteran engineers impressed by General Instrument Corp.'s display were worried by the system's response in the terrestrial band. Japan's NHK were also reported working on digital transmission systems even though they had spent millions on the analog MUSE.[22]

In October 1990, it was reported that the British Broadcasting Corp. (BBC) had selected the new digital composite D-X format of Panasonic. They claimed that the use of a half inch cassette offered the greatest economy with the same performance and operation features. About 180 decks would replace aging type C one-inch decks. Meanwhile it was reported that Sony had sold its 3,000th D-2 VTR to London Weekend Television.[23]

The 132nd SMPTE technical conference was held October 13–17, 1990, in New York City. Approximately 12,000 people attended the conference. The theme was "Film and Television — One World?" Approximately 130 papers were presented. Highlights included a discussion of "Electronic Editing of Film Product — What is the Best Way?" More than 185 companies had displays.

John Galt of Sony Advanced Systems claimed that he "represented the lunatic fringe that believes that in the future post-production of motion pictures will be done electronically." He saw high-definition electronic imaging becoming more commonplace. "Four perf 35mm film will be post-produced electronically." Larry Thorpe, also

of Sony, stated. "No way was HDTV ever intended to replace film. It is intended to bring new tools to that community for them to use as they wish." It was noted that 65 percent of all prime-time TV shows were shot on 35mm film while 80 percent of these shows were finished electronically.[24]

The biggest digital news was the showing of the new digital format by Japan's Matsushita (with NHK). It was the long-awaited Model AJ-D350 studio recorder. This was similar to the D-2 format in video and audio recording parameters, except it used half-inch tape. Matsushita was offering three-hour and four-hour tapes, in three D-X cassette sizes. The company was also offering a digital-processing camcorder with a D-X VTR (AJ-D310). Physically, it was not dissimilar to the Matsushita MII half-inch system.[25]

Sony announced that D-2 machines were rapidly replacing type C. Sony stated that it took five years for other manufacturers to sell 2,000 to 3,000 machines, but in their case, they had sold about 3,000 machines in two years: 1,100 in the USA, a thousand in Japan, and perhaps 500 in Europe.[26]

At the SMPTE conference luncheon, Dr. Marvin Camras, research professor at Illinois Institute of Technology and a pioneer in early magnetic tape recording,

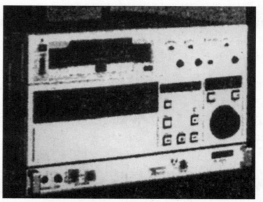

1991. Pansonic's half-inch (D3) composite digital recording system. (Panasonic.)

was the guest speaker. Camras demonstrated one of his inventions—an early wire tape recorder, with a recording of the voice of Marian Anderson that astonished the audience with its clarity. Camras was given the SMPTE's 1990 Honorary Membership Award.[27]

CBS chairman, William S. Paley, died of a heart attack on October 26, 1990, at his Fifth Avenue apartment in Manhattan. Aged 89, he had been in failing health for several weeks. More than 1,600 industry leaders, performers, friends and family paid tribute to him at New York's Temple Emanu-El on November 12, 1990. CBS president emeritus, Frank Stanton, praised him as a defender of broadcast freedoms and said that programming was his genius.[28]

In January 1991, it was reported that Ronald J. Ritchie, president and chief executive of Ampex Corp., had resigned. Ed Bramson, owner of Sherborne Corp. that owned Ampex, would divide Ritchie's duties between himself and other Ampex executives. They reported that Ampex would record about $700 million in revenue for 1990, which was the same as in 1988 and 1989. They predicted no growth for 1991—flat at $700 million.[29]

In January 1991, the Ampex Corp. announced that it had added several new devices to the Ampex line. They included a digital layering device, the AMPEX Digital/Analog Production Tool (ADAPT) used in conjunction with existing analog switchers. It provided flawless mixing of any two D-2 sources without degradation. It could accept up to four composite digital sources and up to six analog sources, and could layer any two such applications as a key-over background or mix between two backgrounds. The basic ADAPT unit sold for $16,000 and the price could go up to $30,000 with options such as digital chromakey, or serial digital input/output modules. Ampex was advising producers to keep their composite analog switchers for a three- to five-year transition phase until affordable, industry-standard component, digital serial-interface switchers were available.

Other products included open reels, reference tape, storage systems, open-reel components, labeling and protective packaging. Ampex claimed that the company was stronger than outward appearances might suggest.[30]

The 25th annual SMPTE television conference was held in Detroit, February 1–2, 1991. The theme was "A Television Continuum—1967–2017," and the chairman was Rudy Kryger. This was the first joint conference between the SMPTE and the Audio Engineering Society (AES). Fred Remley was awarded the society's 1990 Progress Medal, and he also gave the get-together luncheon address. He mainly addressed the efforts of Howard Town in Detroit to assemble an early videotape network using Ampex VR-1000 B machines to tie together educational TV stations in the early 1960s. He also mentioned the changing scene when it came to manufacturing of equipment. He stated that in 1991, Japan had a strong position in the professional video recording field, and also on camera pickup-tube design and CCD sensor design. He reminded the audience that old companies such as RCA and G.E. Broadcast had disappeared. The only old-timers left were Ampex, Grass Valley and Dynair.[31]

On the day before the opening, there was a demonstration of the three 525-line digital videotape formats: D-1 (three-quarter inch component color) by Sony, D-2 (three-quarter inch composite color) by Ampex Corp, and DX (half-inch composite color) by Panasonic Broadcast Systems. D-1 was lauded for its higher editing quality in which six D-1 decks were linked together. D-2 stood apart because of the stunt modes, such as slow motion, fast motion, freeze frame and others. Ampex claimed that the D-2 format was a balance between electrical, mechanical and economic factors. NHK stated that they had created D-3 because of an increasing need for multigeneration applications in the field.

NHK announced a prototype Super-HARP HDTV camera that was ten times more sensitive than the original HARP cameras. The new tube would allow for video production in dark theaters, art galleries and other places where lights could not be used.[32]

In February 1991, General Instrument Corp. and the Massachusetts Institute of Technology agreed to merge their efforts to develop all-digital, high-definition television transmission systems. The new project would be known as the American Television Alliance. They would submit two digital simulcast HDTV systems to the FCC for possible approval in 1993. Since General Instrument had proposed the first all-digital system the previous June, by February four out of the six systems under consideration to be the standard were to be all-digital. Another digital system had been developed by the Advanced Television Research Center (ATRC), a consortium comprising NBC, North American Philips, Thomson Consumer Electronics, and the David Sarnoff Research Center. NHK's Narrow-Muse was the only analog system under consideration.[33]

In March 1991, Edward Bramson, owner, president and chief operating officer of Ampex, gave a rare interview in which he declared that the company was financially sound and that the hundreds of layoffs had ended. He admitted that the perceptions surrounding Ampex in recent years had often been negative. He stated that new product development would receive greater attention in 1991, and that research and development would remain at 10 percent of sales into the future. The teams that developed D-2, he said, would now apply digital technology to other areas. One goal was the development of an affordable component switcher in the mid '90s.

In the "nontelevision" area, Ampex's aim was to find ways to use its digital TV technology expertise in other high-tech sectors. Bramson claimed that digital recording had a very high data rate, higher than was needed for computing, but as computers got faster, the need for high-speed storage would present a business opportunity. What was left unsaid was that Ampex's brilliant development of D-2 was one of the factors leading to its downfall. Not only had Sony taken over the sales of D-2, but the initial poor performance of Ampex's D-2 machines had hurt its reputation as a manufacturer and in the market place.[34]

In March 1991, NBC announced that it would use Panasonic's new composite digital videotape equipment for its coverage of the 1992 summer Olympics in Barcelona, Spain. The sale included half-inch digital camcorders, studio recorders and digital processing studio cameras. NBC claimed that it had bought over 2,000 pieces of equipment from Panasonic during the past five years.[35]

In April 1991, it was reported that television pioneer Dr. Albert Rose had died at the age of 80. Rose was responsible for three of television's most important developments: the Orthicon, the image orthicon, and Vidicon camera tubes. Born in New York City, he received his A.B. degree from Cornell University in 1931. From 1931 to 1934, he served as a teaching assistant at Cornell, and in 1935 received a Ph.D. degree in physics. Upon graduating, he joined the RCA Manufacturing Co., at Harrison, NJ, as a research engineer. While at RCA he became an associate of Harley Iams, a developer of the original iconoscope under Dr. Vladimir K. Zworykin. Iams and Rose joined forces and by 1937 had designed and built some of the first low-velocity scanning-beam camera tubes. This resulted in the Orthicon, the first successful low-velocity tube, in 1939.[36]

The NAB convention was held April 15–18, 1991, in Las Vegas, in conjunction with the HDTV World Conference and Exhibition at the same time. Ampex was expected to highlight its new ADAPT digital layering system which was a composite digital layering device capable of complex, multigenerational effects interfacing with current composite analog production switchers. It would also demonstrate a new two-channel version of its ADO 100 effects system, and show hardware and software advances to its ALEX character generator. Over 100 of the ALEX systems had been installed, the company claimed.[37]

Ampex was also concentrating on its Accu-Mark feature which greatly simplified D-2 audio editing. It would also offer the 4.0 D-2 software package with automatic tracking, scanner phase adjustment, head-end tape, and cue-point storage. The scanner phase featured a lateral and longitudinal adjustment, which was automatic with the push of a button.

As noted earlier, NBC and Panasonic had signed contracts for the 1992 Olympics for Barcelona, Spain, and CBS with Sony for the winter games in Albertville, France. (Nothing for Ampex.) Sony was to introduce eight new videotape recorders. Two were new D-2 recorders: the DVR-28 and the DVR-20. Both accepted the small and medium tape cassettes, and this facility made them a bit more cost-effective. Both included ten-bit video recording (compared to eight-bit) 20-bit audio recording (over 16-bit), three-line correlating comb filter in slow motion, and improved shuttle speed. The DVR-20 sold for $52,000 and the DVR-28 for $70,000. Sony was offering a control panel option BKDV-201 ($5,500) designed for broadcast operations. A simpler version, the BKDV-200 ($3,500), provided menus for the most basic VTR functions.

In addition Sony showed their new UNIHI half-inch analog high-definition format, HDV-10. It was priced at $85,000, much less than recorders built for full 1,125/60 quality. Sony hoped this machine would function as an efficient, inexpensive tape distribution format.

Both Hitachi and BTS demonstrated D-2 at the convention. Hitachi showed an updated version of the VL-D500 composite digital D-2 VTR. It was billed as the "smallest full-featured D-2 recorder on the market." It had a simplified control panel, new simplified menus, faster shuttle speed and variable play back from -1 to +3 times normal.

Hitachi's newest field camera, the SK-F3S, was fitted with the company's FIT Microlens Array CCD. Sensitivity was *f*8 at 2,000 lux. The CCD system was similar to Sony's Hyper-HAD chips in that it had improved sensitivity by activating microscopic lenses built into the CCD imager that focused light more efficiently on the camera's sensors. A new FP-C10, which docked to Hi-8 recorders, could also be used with the Microlens Array chip.

Ikegami also introduced the HC-V, an S-VHS-C (8mm) one-piece camcorder. The 14.3-pound camera imaged 750 lines with a sensitive of *f*5.6 at 2,000 lux. It was priced at $14,995.

1991. Sony HDV-10 high-definition UNIHI half-inch analog VTR. (Sony.)

Panasonic demonstrated studio recorders, one-piece camcorders and other related equipment in the new half-inch format. Now named D-X, it was expected to be called D-3 when formally accepted by SMPTE. Its main feature was the use of the smaller half-inch cassette which allowed it to be built into an all-digital camcorder. Panasonic also showed a three–CCD high-definition camcorder, based on the half-inch format. The camera imaged 1.3 million pixels and 1,000 horizontal lines at better than 50 db signal to noise ratio.

Sony claimed that D-2 was first and was the defacto composite digital standard to replace composite NTSC recording. They claimed that they had sold over 4,000 D-2s worldwide (nearly 1,500 in the USA), but admitted that they had never anticipated the demand and market acceptance for D-2 would be so great. Ampex, who had invented D-2, had sold only a little over a 1,000 machines, but they were going to put out a standards conversion kit in the D-2 format that converted NTSC to PAL (and vice versa) thus saving the price of a second D-2.

Sony stated that D-X was an attempt to provide an all-purpose digital format that replaced two different areas: D-2 and Betacam SP. Critics, however, felt that it did not do an adequate job in supplanting either. They stated, "The half inch digital EJ equipment is too heavy to replace Beta Cam SP in the field and not robust enough to replace D-2 in the studio." Panasonic still didn't offer serial interfaces for its new equipment. Sony of course was determined to keep its dominant position in the field of video recording at all costs. It was the traditional Sony versus Matsushita battle all over again, with Ampex nowhere to be seen.

Sony introduced the Sony BVW-D75 recorders that would be the first machines to bridge the divide between Betacam and digital. It would have embedded serial digital interfaces built in. Costing $32,000, it would be available the following fall. Sony also introduced its component digital VTR, the DVR-2100, with a sales price of $120,000 which was half of the cost of the original D-1.[38]

The 17th International Television Symposium and Technical Exhibition was held in Montreux, June 13–18, 1991. The focus was HDTV and digital video. The 1991 symposium included 17 sessions on broadcast television technology, 15 sessions on cable technology, and eight technical workshops. The fourth annual International Electronic Cinema Festival (IECF) for the best high-definition production was held concurrently. IECF was sponsored by the American Film Institute in cooperation with the Directors' Guild of America. There were 1,125/60 demonstrations by Thomson, Philips, BASF, Grundig and Rhodes & Schwarz, and 1,250/50 demonstrations sponsored by Sony, NEC, Tektronix and General Instrument Corp.[39]

For the first time, Ampex announced a new component digital videotape format at Montreux. Ampex planned to demonstrate prototypes of its new component digital videotape equipment and have it ready during calendar year 1992. No details were made public, but it would be compatible with CCIR 601 parameters and would have all the capability and quality of type C equipment. Ampex stated that there was tremendous need in Europe for a cost-effective digital component VTR, where most studios were built for component formats. They were hoping to change Ampex's prospects, especially overseas where they still had reasonable sales. Ampex stated that it was also continuing to develop enhancements to D-2.

Sony and Matsushita were to announce similar formats but not before 1993 and were surprised at Ampex's efforts to beat them to this market. Sony stated that its new component digital system would be a small-cassette format (half-inch) using approximately the same design as its Beta SP component analog format. But they promised that the new VTRs would play back the existing Betacam tapes as well as record digital video. Panasonic would only say that theirs would be a half-inch system.

General Instrument gave the first international transmission of a digital compression system for conventional and HDTV broadcasting. Four compressed signals were transmitted on Ku-band over Pan Am Sat-1 from GI's VideoCipher Division in San Diego to Montreux where they were displayed live for six days with no digital errors detected. A five-day International Electronic Cinema Festival was held with 38 competitors. Five of nine categories were won by Japanese producers using 1,125/60 while European producers using 1,250/50 were three of the winners.[40]

In June 1991, Ampex introduced a new Betacam SP studio VTR with component digital serial interface capabilities. The CVR-D75 accepted 4:2:2 input from various component digital systems. Using internal converters, the basic record-playback circuitry remained analog Betacam SP. D-1 serial input and output were provided with three switchable input and output audio channels. The VTR included TBC proc-amp control, external reference input and TBC genlock reference. Ampex also announced a CVR-50 Portable Betacam SP VTR, and new CVC-7A camera and CVRE-300A camcorder.[41]

In June 1991, it was reported that the Jameson Entertainment Group (JEG) in partnership with Ikegami Electronics and Azro Enterprises, had recently launched a joint project for sending HDTV satellite transmissions worldwide for chains of theater complexes. A demonstration of the system using the Ikegami TPP-1500 projection system with the EC-1125 Ikegami HDTV camera was given at the El Rey Theatre in Los Angeles. A laser disk presentation was later given. It was claimed that laser disk duplication and distribution would cost a fraction of the expense of 35mm film print distribution, which was about $1,500 per print. The biggest problem seemed to be the lack of a high brightness electronic projector suitable for theater use.[42]

In July 1991, Ampex announced that it had layed off some 250 people from its Recording Media Corp. All but 50 were from the tape manufacturing plant in Opelika, AL. In addition they announced that the company's research and development department would streamline development, and that new technologies would be introduced. The newly organized staff would concentrate on the completion of Ampex's new videotape format announced at Montreux in June.[43]

A survey in July 1991 showed that broadcasters expected D-2 digital and one-inch type C formats to share dominance in studio production and that D-2 would compete strongly with Betacam SP by 1994. Interestingly enough, more than 800 broadcast cable, video production, postproduction and institutional video users, stated that 52 percent of TV stations would use D-2 in their studio and 52 percent said they would also use one-inch. In the field, 57 percent expected to use Betacam, 47 percent D-2, and 15 percent high-definition (HDTV) cassettes.[44]

In October 1991, Ampex again announced that it had reorganized its Recording Media Corp. It had eliminated over 250 positions more worldwide and streamlined its operations. It was claimed that the rebalancing of resources would enable the company to absorb the economic pressures brought on by the prolonged U.S. recession, as well as the recent appreciation of the dollar against most of the international currencies. Both R&D and manufacturing-engineering were to be consolidated. Ampex also announced a new ADO-500 system that included 3-D page turns, variable warps, and image-processing effects.[45]

The 133rd SMPTE Technical Conference and Equipment Exhibit was held in Los Angeles, October 26–29, 1991. Gregory Peck was the featured speaker on October 26. For the very first time, Ampex chose not to exhibit there. They claimed that it was an indication "of our marketing strategy, not our financial welfare." They had decided to attend only two shows in 1991: NAB and the International Television Symposium and Technical Exhibition in Montreux. This was in keeping with the mood of many manufacturers that called for fewer shows, perhaps two a year. Even Sony agreed to cut appearances from 153 in 1990 to 58 in 1991.[46]

In November 1991, there were several manufacturers showing tapeless recording products capable of storing not just seconds-long animation or graphics segments, but longer full-resolution video for news, entertainment and even live sports programming. These included Grass Valley, Pioneer Communications of America, Broadcast

Television Systems, Optical Disc Corp and Symbolics. Pioneer was offering a recorder VDR-V1000 laser recorder with a magneto-optical disc priced at $39,950. Each disc held 32 minutes of time-compressed, analog component video and cost $1,295. Pioneer claimed Betacam-quality reproduction, SMPTE time codes, separate or simultaneous PCM stereo audio, and interface with VTRs, edit controllers and graphics and effects system. Ediflex demonstrated the automated Ediflex II using multidiscs. Grass Valley had a five-inch disc recorder holding 7½ minutes of ten-bit, noncompressed D-1 digital video on two channels. It was promised for 1992. Symbolics showed its Paint-Animation effects system, the VideoDISK-120 priced at $106,000. It stored six minutes of D-1 digital video, but came in models with up to 40 minutes of storage.[47]

In January 1992, it was announced that broadcasters could see the first real-time, over-the-air transmission of digital high-definition television ever seen anywhere. It would be shown during the NAB convention, April 12–16, 1992, in Las Vegas.[48]

In February 1992, it was announced that ADTV (Advanced Digital HDTV) had been given final certification to begin testing in April 1992. ATRC—comprising NBC, Philips Consumer Electronics, David Sarnoff Research Center, and Compression labs—stated that its system's picture, sound and coverage would match those of General Instrument/Massachusetts Institute of Technology and Zenith/AT&T. With the MPEG compression standard as its basis, ADTV would prove compatible with digital video, consumer electronics, telecommunications and computer industries around the world, and with the computer friendly square pixel-format. Other features would allow users to assign "packets" of digits to variable services carrying a header identifying it as video, audio, or data. The 24Mb/sec signal would also use forward and backward motion estimation.[49]

In March 1992, it was announced that Ampex planned to exhibit a near-production model of its new digital component technology (DCT) VTR. The company claimed that it was to be a high-end model to fit the needs of the high-quality component video user, especially in Europe where large-format D-1 had become standard among broadcasters as well as production houses. The European TV industry needed a practical and affordable digital component VTR. Ampex was going against the strategy of Sony and Panasonic who were expected to introduce new formats capable of playing back both the new component and the well-established composite digital videotapes as well. Ampex stated that they were not going to build in the extra overhead required to do such a thing. It was a bold move by Ampex to regain some of its past glory. The American broadcast market was gone; perhaps the company could be revitalized in Europe where it still had a good reputation. Ampex stated that wide-screen 16:9 could be an option, and emphasized the need for a complete studio system of established VTRs, cart machines, switchers and graphics systems.

Panasonic was planning a new D-5 (D-4 was passed over for a variety of reasons) half-inch digital component machine capable of processing either 4:3 or 16:9 digital component video. It was a ten-bit, CCIR digital recorder in order to provide the 4:2:2 level of quality. Panasonic claimed that the advantages of component digital were best realized when the least amount of compression was applied.[50]

Sony was planning to come out with a new version of the Betacam format to be called Digital Betacam, which used the Betacam's component nature and cassette form. The company claimed a breakthrough in technology called coefficient recording (CORE) technology. It was a new form of bit-rate reduction (data compression) using several new (proprietary) important information-handling schemes. It was claimed that the technology could also playback in analog component Betacam SP format.[51]

Charles P. Ginsburg, a pioneer of videotape technology, died of pneumonia on April 9, 1992. He was 71 years old. Ginsburg, who had suffered a series of strokes in recent years, had moved to Oregon two years before. A memorial service was held Monday, April 13, for the man whose research on the Ampex Videotape Recorder forever changed television production and broadcasting and set the stage for today's booming videotape market.[52]

The annual NAB convention was held, April 12–16, 1992, in Las Vegas. Over 50,000 were in attendance. General Instrument conducted the first public demonstration of digital HDTV on its own DigiCipher as part of an HDTV world exhibition. The live and taped signal was beamed via microwave transmitter over a quarter mile from the Las Vegas Hilton where a TTC 20-watt transmitter broadcast it over channel 15. HDTV sets at HDTV Center received the broadcast.[53]

Toshiba planned to show an advanced prototype ¾-inch digital HDTV cassette recorder that it claimed matched existing one-inch open-reel HDTV VTRs. The HV-D920 on the 1,125/60 standard used 16 drum-mounted integrated amplifier circuits to facilitate a 1.2 gigabits per second data rate (five times faster than NTSC rates). It also showed an 8mm prototype consumer cassette HDTV recorder developed with American Television Alliance (General Instrument Corp. and the Massachusetts Institute of Technology) whose DigiCipher HDTV system Toshiba endorsed. The demonstration was to prove that DigiCipher could use existing mechanisms such as 8mm VTR and camcorders. As part of the demonstration, pictures from the Toshiba CCD camera were sent via microwave radio STL to a 20-watt transmitter atop the Las

Vegas Convention Center some 1,000 feet away. The video returned to the HDTV world exhibition via a standard antenna, was taped and re-transmitted and displayed both on one-inch and the Toshiba 8mm VTR. Ampex showed working prototypes of its DCT (Digital Component Technology) system. It was due out in June, but without a 16:9 option — they agreed with Sony on that. They also showed a complete studio system including a full line of established format VTRs, cart machines, switchers and graphics systems.[54]

Sony showed a third-generation CCD-based HDTV camera, the HDC-500, with two million pixels per image. Sony also announced two second-generation D-2 compatible digital players, the DVR-P20 and the DVR-P28, both priced 20 percent under the original units.[55]

1986. Toshiba H-2 HDTV videotape recorder. (Toshiba.)

Panasonic Broadcast and Television Systems showed multiformat widescreen NTSC options VTRs. They debuted a wide-screen (16:9 aspect ratio) enhanced MII of analog, half-inch products, including a line-doubled 525-line source. They also showed a prototype of a half-inch component digital format for delivery in mid 1993, and created side by side 4:3 and 16:9 displays from the same machine. It offered an 18MHz scanning-rate option, likely to be controversial because of the 13.5MHz standard. The president of Matsushita, T. Murase, was there to celebrate the $5 million D-3 sale to NBC. They claimed they had delivered 3,000 D-3s by that summer. Panasonic also showed a new composite serial digital routing switcher, edit controller, composite-component converter and D-3 field VTR, as well as seven new MII VTR models. The new MII showed a wide-screen (16:9) output.

Sony stated that they had not yet made widescreen NTSC as a supplement to HDTV and that the company had only plans to offer a PAL version of its half-inch digital component format for "digital Betacam." Sony claimed that there was customer confusion in introducing three formats: NTSC 16:9, NTSC and HDTV. Yet the choice could be useful in the adoption of a terrestrial HDTV system, since broadcasters could send 16:9 NTSC until HDTV programs become widely available. At this time, Sony was celebrating the tenth anniversary of Betacam's introduction in the USA.[56]

Ampex promised to highlight its new digital component technology videotape format with a complete studio system approach including a full line of conforming VTRs, cart machines, switchers and graphics systems. The company said that it would exhibit "very close to a production model" for its DCT VTR and planned to begin shipping before the end of 1992. Ampex hoped to win the high-end market with a VTR that did not have extra overhead built in and which could play back other formats. "We're proposing to bring to market a line of products very specifically sculptured to meet the needs of the high-quality components video users, especially in Europe, where large format D-1 digital components ... have become the standard among broadcasters, as well as of the post-production houses."[57]

On May 7, 1992, an agreement was made by four major HDTV developers. A consortium of Zenith and AT&T, developers of the Spectrum-Compatible HDTV system, and a consortium of General Instrument Corp. and the Massachusetts Institute of Technology, developers of Digi-Cipher and Channel Compatible DigiCipher Systems, signed an agreement to share royalties and some development costs if one of their systems was chosen by the FCC.

The three all-digital systems were to be separately tested at the Advanced Television Test Center. Zenith/AT&T and GI/Massachusetts Institute of Technology continued to promote their own systems and the winner was expected to draw a large percentage of the royalties. There would be no technology sharing until after selection. Two other groups were also under consideration. One was Japan's NHK, with its analog narrow MUSE. The other was the Advanced Television Research Center (ATRC), which included NBC, the David Sarnoff Research Center, and the European owned Philips Electronics and Thomson Consumer Electronics, which had another all-digital HDTV system.[58]

In May 1992, Zenith and AT&T debuted digital spectrum compatible HDTV with a 6MHz broadcast from WMVT (TV) Milwaukee (channel 36) to a directional antenna atop Zenith's Glenview, IL, technical center, 75 miles away. FCC Commissioner Ervin Duggan, and NAB senior VP Michael Rau stated that the great pictures proved that digital provided coverage at a tenth of the power. The compressed 787.5-line progressively scanned signal —

including 1,125/60 HDTV images, multimedia and computer graphics, 60- and 24-frame film images and up-converted 525-line video— were decompressed and monitored in Glenview and by a Zenith mobile unit some 50 miles away. The transmission proved there was no sudden drop-off of signal. Zenith felt that as a result, their system would come out ahead in the competition for a compatible HDTV system.[59]

On May 21, 1992, the Japanese Ministry of Post and Telecommunications (MPT) told a Massachusetts Institute of Technology media lab symposium on digital television that they were going to establish a new R&D company, Digital Movies Laboratory (DML), to make recommendations concerning the "right directions of digital video by the end of 1992." Kazuhiko Nishi stated "the consumer demand for on-line or personalized television requires a *strategic retreat* from analog high definition. Japan is seeking the next digital TV system: it will not be called HDTV but UDTV."

They were planning a subcarrier, 2,000 line, 150Mb/sec system able to carry all forms of analog and digital media that should last for 50 years. Many experts in the USA stated that his address was an admission that Japan was scrapping its global ambition for the 20-year, $1 billion analog high-definition project (MUSE) developed by Japan Broadcasting Corp. or NHK. According to Nishi, UDTV would incorporate a universal video coding technology to handle NTSC and HDTV (digital and analog) computer video graphics, videotape, videodisc and movie making with a 150Mb ceiling. It would also use super high efficiency data compression to improve on and encompass the 24mbps ADTV system then being tested in the USA. One observer stated, "the Japanese have admitted defeat, and their strategy is to leapfrog the leapfrogger." It was a stunning victory for the struggling American television industry.[60]

In light of this Japanese defeat, Europe became less than optimistic about a world standard. While the EC stated that it would welcome cooperation among countries on technical standards, European HDTV policy remained in political deadlock. This was due mainly to different technical requirements. This despite the fact that the grand alliance included both Philips and Thomson who were both involved in Europe's original HDTV plans and the failed D2-MAC standard.[61]

In June 1992, Ampex stated that it was trying to expand beyond the U.S. television business. The sale of recorders still accounted for almost a quarter of the $526 million in total 1991 revenue. But VTR sales, at $130 million the previous year were only about half of what they had been two years before and were expected to decline further in 1992. Ampex's sales in the USA had been diminishing for years. CBS had stopped buying Ampex in

1977 when the first type C machines came out (15 years before); NBC in 1986 (6 years) when it ordered its first MII from Matsushita; and finally ABC in 1989 (three years before) when it stopped buying equal amounts of machines from Ampex and Sony. In 1992, the networks were replacing all their Ampex VPR-2s with Sony D-2 VTRs. So the company had no support from the American broadcast industry.[62]

Ampex claimed that three quarters of its revenues came from half-inch analog recorders that were Sony products with the Ampex name on them. The worse problem was with Ampex's new D-2 recorders which it had developed. They were not selling due to what Ampex claimed was "adverse economic conditions in the U.S. market." (Sony was selling five D-2 machines to Ampex's one.) The only bright spots were tape sales for the 35,000 Ampex machines sold worldwide, and the general market for library systems, switchers, digital special effects machines, editors and graphic devices. Another fairly good source of income was royalties from technology licensed to others (such as AST and D-2 for example) and finally an "after market for spare parts and the resale of products accepted as trade-ins." Little is known of Ampex's sales to the military, which in the past had been considerable.

So Ampex was in trouble financially. The changeover from analog to digital storage products had cost them $39 million in 1991. Even cutting the workforce in half in four years hadn't helped. Finally, its indirect parent, NH Holdings, Inc. (NHI), was in debt for about $485 million from its acquisition of Ampex, and Ampex itself carried $150 million in long-term debt at interest rates of 13 percent. Ampex was hoping to raise about $55 million for working capital and to repay previous working capital borrowings. To have recovered from all of this adversity would have taken a miracle and there were no miracles in sight. Ampex's slide into oblivion was preordained.[63]

In June 1992, Ampex introduced its new DCT (digital component technology) production system. It was the industry's first practical CCIR-601 digital component production system, providing the highest-quality multigeneration and digital layering capabilities for post production applications. The system consisted of a new format 19mm digital component tape drive (DCT-700d), companion tape cartridges (DCT-700t Series), post-production switcher (DCT-700s), edit controller (DCT-700e), digital effects system (DCT 500a), and interconnect products.[64]

The important features of the system were as follows. It used highly advanced mathematics that had been applied to the development of compression algorithms with multigenerational performance. Track parameters closely matched the D-2 format. The Ampex DCT 700d transport had many important features. Tape width was

1992. New Ampex DCT digital component production system. (Ampex.)

19mm. It could accelerate from stand still to 60x in one second, recue a 30-second spot in 1.5 seconds, and rewind a 30-minute spot tape in 30 seconds. It used the gas-film technology of the VPR-3 by feeding compressed air through laser drilled holes in the tape guides. Thus the tape rode on a layer of air, reducing friction. It used a direct-coupled pinch-rollerless capstan that functioned as a primary controller device. A two-function scanning assembly allowed the tape to disengage from the scanner when searching for time-code numbers and let make contact it for shuttle operation. It had 525/625 switchability and a 3.5 floppy disc drive that accommodated future software updates. Headroom in such a system allowed for advanced technology additions such as the proposed 16 × 9 13.5MHz system, although an interface with existing digital signal processing using the CCIR 601 international standard was provided. It weighed about 100 lbs and allowed cassette performance from 15 minutes to 3 hours.[65]

There were other features. All signal processing occurred in the component digital domain. The frame of the DCT 700d transport was an aluminum sandcast structure. The air filtration system lasted about 2,000 to 3,000 hours. Head life, because of the closed-loop system, was about 7,000 to 8,000 hours. A new design was provided for the AST heads. Because of the need to transverse three-track width (525) or four-track width (625), the AST system used a system like the design of hard-disk systems for computers. The head was driven by a voice coil motor (VCM) and operated the same way. This construction permitted change of heads in about ten minutes. Finally, due to design considerations, there were no flying erase heads needed for edit accuracy.[66]

In June 1992, in one of television's most perverse moments, it was revealed that a company called Filmlook had actually patented a process whereby anything shot on tape could be made to "look" like film! The process mimicked the motion and luminance characteristics of film, by simulating the "2-3 pull down" central to film-to-video transfer as well as the graininess of film. The inventor suggested the Filmlook process could be used for "artsy content, where you are not looking so much for details. In my opinion, it gains an exact film look." So for about $650 an hour, advertisers could make a 30-second national spot for less than $10,000. He admitted that for a large budget spot he would go for film in a second. He was proving a strange point, that to get the elusive "film look" one had to degrade the video process. The process was cited by the Television Academy "for achievements that exhibit a high level of engineering and are important to the progress of the industry."[67]

The 1992 International Broadcasting Convention took place July 4 through 7 in Amsterdam, the Netherlands. James McKinney, chairman of the Advanced Television Systems Committee, was prepared to tell the European Community (EC) that it was riding to ruin by advocating enhanced analog TV. His speech was titled, "Enhanced Widescreen–Why?" He stated that to withhold HDTV from the public simply to sell them first an enhanced TV receiver was a matter of unconscionable greed on the part of the equipment manufacturers. He charged that Europe's push for outdated analog technologies could only be for purely political reasons. It put the ATRC (including France's Thomson Consumer Electronics and the Netherlands Philips [NV]) out of the running and opened a commercial highway to the Japanese. Support for the pro–American position came from the French National Assembly deputy, Michel Pelchat, and Studio Hamburg president, Martin Willich. McKinney conceded that the Americans were more free to switch from analog to digital, "because we have *no* consumer industry left." Japan, he suggested, was selling receivers to the public at enormous prices, so "they don't dare to shift technologies at this late date." Sadly, he admitted that the American television industry did not want to invest in any new equipment at all. The bottom line was that "no analog television system can now succeed and an analog enhanced system is certain to fail. You still have time to do it right."[68]

The first public HDTV simulcast was provided on September 30, 1992, when the Advanced Television Research Consortium (ATRC) gave the first public simulcast of live programming over both standard analog and digital HDTV channels. ATRC showed HDTV, NTSC, down-converted HDTV, and up-converted NTSC on side-by-side wide-screen (16:9) and narrow-screen (4:3) monitors. The signals were received at sites around Washington. ATRC also used a van to test both the 5kw AD-HDTV signal and a 5kw NTSC signal from a low power mobile transmitter. It was claimed that clear pictures and sound were displayed from as far as 70 miles away. Meanwhile General Instrument had been privately testing Digi-Cipher HDTV in San Diego over a VHF channel squeezed between upper and lower adjacent channels and against a co-channel NTSC, said Robert Rast, vice president for HDTV development.[69]

On September 21, 1992, a working party of the Advisory Committee on Advanced TV Service completed picture quality and spectrum analysis of NHK's Narrow Muse system. They found that it would only accommodated 92.6 percent of the 1,699 TV stations marked for HDTV channel allocation — a figure that, several experts averred, would put the final nail in the coffin of MUSE, the only analog system left in the testing process. However, a senior scientist Keiichi Kubota of NHK, said that corrections made since testing had brought the accommodation figure up to 100 percent.[70]

The 134th Society of Motion Picture and Television Engineers technical conference and equipment exhibit was held, November 10–13, 1992, at the Metro Toronto Convention Center in Toronto, Ontario, Canada. The theme was "Images in Motion: The Second Century." Only 8,500 attended — fewer than the last show. Over 115 papers were presented. Grass Valley Group agreed to market Panasonic D-3 digital composite VTRs, editors, cameras and camcorders in the USA, and would also market D-3 as part of its CVG Model 3000 production switcher. It was claimed that D-3 sales had reached 3,000 units. As announced, AMPEX was not an exhibitor. There were all-day HDTV demonstrations, given by Vision 1250, a group of European broadcasters, manufactures, and independent video and film producers who were committed to the production of HDTV programs. The 1,125/60 group also gave demonstrations.[71]

Ray Dolby was named for honorary membership in the SMPTE for his role in consumer and professional audio and video recording and his role in the development of the Ampex VRX-1000. Charles Steinberg of Sony was nominated for the Presidential Proclamation in light of his contributions to the industry and support of SMPTE activities, and Fraser Morrison of Ampex received the SMPTE Progress Medal for his role in the design of digital magnetic recorders and experimental D-1 and D-2 technology.[72]

NHK and Matsushita had an HDTV hand-held camera that was used at the Barcelona Olympic Games. It was the world's first ⅔-inch CCD camera. NHK also showed a portable battery-operated HiVision VTR it had developed, which weighed half as much as the standard UNIHI VTR HDTV CCD camera.

BTS introduced the first full-bandwidth HDTV CCD broadcast camera. Using frame transfer technology sensors, the new LDK 900 was a commitment to the Eureka EU95 HDTV project. It had a sensitivity of *f*5.2 at 2,000 lux, a S/N ratio of 60db (PAL) and 62db (NTSC), plus low aliasing, high contrast range and complete freedom from smear. It offered both 4:3 and 16:9 formats, and included a variable-speed shutter.

The BBC announced that D-3 would be its standard for television operations. Sony introduced second-generation D-1 recorders, models DVR-2100 and DVR-2000, with DVR-2100 having dynamic tracking. Models DVR-P20 and DVR-P28 were second-generation D-2 playback-only models featuring ultrasonic guide, digital jog sound, dynamic tracking for clear slow motion, and (only on the DVR-P28) 208 minutes playback. Betacam SP BVW-D75 editing recorder with 4:2:2 component serial digital interface.[73]

In November 1992, Avid Technology augmented its Media Composer with two new compatible products. One was a digital audio-for-video, Macintosh-based Audio-Vision audio editor; the other was a 24-frames/sec version of the Media Composer allowing film editors to edit films in the digital realm without having to face artifact problems associated with film conversion.[74]

In December 1992, USA Networks made a $7.5 million purchase of Panasonic D-3 record-playback systems. They agreed to purchase four digital Marc-800 type III library management systems, each with ten external video-tape recorders and 800-cassette playback. An additional 30 D-3 VTRs would solve time-zone delays and serve in postproduction.[75]

In February 1993, NHK (Japan) announced that it had withdrawn its Narrow-Muse analog based system from high-definition contention. They claimed that it had done so because of a fatal flaw resulting from vastly inferior tests to those of the competing all-digital systems.[76]

In April 1993, the engineering department of the BBC claimed that it had transmitted HDTV in a single 8MHz channel, in cooperation with French Thomson-CSF/Laboratoires Electroniques de Rennes (TCSF/LER), using high-spectral efficiency modulation. The digital TV signal, broadcast from a low power transmitter at the Crystal Palace in London, was able to convey about 60Mbits/sec (split in two signals) in a single 8MHz TV channel. Each 30Mbits/sec signal compressed an orthogonal frequency division modulation (OFDM) ensemble of approximately 500 closed spaced carriers, all of which were digitally modulated using 64 QAM.[77]

The National Association of Broadcasters held its annual convention in the Las Vegas Convention Center from April 18 to 22, 1993. Attendance was over 64,000. It was claimed that the battle of VTR giants began on day one. Ampex, Panasonic and Sony each had a new technology. Ampex showed that its DCT concept really did work. According to the company, DCT tape drives had been sold to several production houses and were being well accepted.

Panasonic unveiled its long talked about and recently named D-5 format. This was based on the D-3 half-inch format composite digital format. The D-5 featured record and playback of the CCIR 601 format in its full ten-bit uncompressed form and full digital audio. It was suitable for both 4:3 and 16:9 aspect ratios and offered playback of D-3 composite digital recording in the component domain. The series of machines would record in three modes: ten-bit 4:2:2, eight-bit 13.5MHz, and 18MHz 16:9.[78]

Sony unveiled its Digital Betacam format at the National Association of Broadcasters' 1993 convention in Las Vegas. Sony claimed over 165,000 Betacam units were then in place around the world, including four machines, two record-players and two players. The DVW-500 recorded and played back digital Betacam cassettes and featured analog and digital inputs, as well as analog and digital component and composite outputs, and an optional NTSC decoder that allowed it to accept analog composite inputs. One unique feature was that two of the VTRs were capable of not only recording and playing digital signals, but also of playing back standard analog Betacam tapes. Both Ampex and Sony used some form of video signal compression. It was claimed that Betacam superiority over D3 was in the use of higher quality component color recording. Sony expected the Betacam DVW-500 digital recorder would be the workhorse format for broadcast and postproduction in the 1990s.[79]

Ampex was also featuring a DST 600 series tape drive. It was a single, stand-alone tape drive based on the robust 19mm helical-scan format. It was used for storing and retrieving large amounts of data, and moved data at a very high transfer rate.[80]

On May 3, 1993, the FCC HDTV advisory committee announced that the first system to be tested was General Instrument's CCDC, a progressive scan system. Next were two traditional interlaced scan systems, the Advanced Television Research Center's AD-HDTV and another General Instrument System called DigiCipher. The last one would be Zenith's progressive scan DSC-HDTV.[81]

On May 24, 1993, the FCC announced that the organ known as HDTV proponents— GI, Zenith, AT&T and ATRC— had agreed to merge their efforts and develop a single system using a progressive scanning. This was to appease

1993. Sony DVW-500 Series of component VTRs. (Sony.)

the computer people who had always used progressive scanning. It was agreed that the new sets could use both progressive or interlaced scan and must recognize an interlaced scan at say 787.5 resolution at 30 frames/sec or recognize a 1,050-line progressive scan at 24 frames/sec. The sets would do this all automatically. One of the items to be resolved was whether to use vestigial sideband or quadrature amplitude modulation. One complaint was that the computer industry had gotten more out of the system than broadcasters. However, it was agreed that the overall plan was solid.[82]

In June 1993, Ampex reported that it had sold a *second* DCT system to Film and Videotechnik B. Gurtier GmbH, Hamburg, Germany. Also Highlight Productions, San Francisco had installed a DCT 700s postproduction switcher and a DCT 700i analog interface. Ampex had also sold two DCT 700d tape drives to Omnicon Video and Apocalypse Video in Sydney, Australia. Broadway Video, New York, had incorporated a DCT 700d tape drive into a digital component suite scheduled to open in June.[83]

In June 1993, the FCC Advisory Committee on Advanced Television Service was approached to review a single digital HDTV system proposed by the "Grand Alliance" of entities that had sponsored the four remaining competitive HDTV systems. If the proposed system was recommended by the advisory committee and adopted by the FCC, it could place the United States in the forefront of high-definition video technology with an all-digital standard that would enable interpretability among broadcasting, cable, computer and telecommunication technologies worldwide.

Important aspects of the Grand Alliance technical proposal included the employment of progressive scan transmission (where entire picture frames were transmitted sequentially) and the use of so-called "square pixels" (where the dots on a TV screen were arranged in equally spaced rows and columns). These design aspects were important for the interoperability of HDTV with computers, telecommunications and other media and applications. Interlaced scan transmission also would be accommodated in the initial deployment.

The members of the Grand Alliance agreed that all large-screen HDTV receivers (34 inches in diagonal and above) would incorporate a 60 frame/sec, 787.5-line or higher progressive scan display mode. Progressive display would be optional for smaller screen receivers. The proponents also concurred that all transmission of film material would be in a progressive-scan format when HDTV service began.

The Grand Alliance endorsed the objective of migrating the standard to a high line number (i.e., thousand-line plus) progressive scan transmission, as soon as feasible, and pledged to work together to eliminate the interlaced-scanning format from the transmission path in the future.

To support multiple transmission formats, the merged system would feature source adaptive processing. To promote system flexibility and extensibility, the merged system would also feature a prioritized, packetized data transport structure. The Grand Alliance agreed to support the proposed HDTV compression system in the International Standards Organization as the MPEG-2 HDTV profile.[84]

The 18th International Television Symposium was held in Montreux, June 10–15, 1993. The festival attracted more than 220 registered guests from 72 countries. The major theme of the event was digital technology and digital compression. New features were a weekend forum where there were discussions on "HDTV in Cinema Production," "HDTV—New Panoramas in Creativity," "HDTV Strategies and Economics," and "A View from Three Continents."[85] One of the main topics was the possibility of a world digital HDTV standard. Richard Wiley of the FCC said he hoped that broadcasters from other nations would join U.S. manufactures to forge an international standard dubbed, "La très Grande Alliance" by French Parliamentarian Michel Pelchat. It was hoped that the next TV standard would be international. While many Europeans believed in the possibilities of a world standard, they needed a solution that would satisfy European needs. This related mainly to the old 50Hz versus 60Hz obstacle, which meant that there was no chance of having the same transmission scheme around the world.

Another issue that was brought up was whether the American public really wanted an HDTV system. One comment was that, "it was awfully hard to see a guy watching a football with a long neck beer in his hand wanting to pay extra for HDTV." One solution to the problem was for broadcaster to transmit HDTV programs a certain amount of time and other revenue-producing programs the rest of the time.[86]

At this point, it was reported that the European Community was cool to prospects of a worldwide HDTV standard based on the U.S. model. Their main objection now was the bandwidth that was 8MHz in Europe and 6MHz for North America and Japan. Other than that, it seemed that they were interested in creating a system that had as much in common as possible.[87]

In June 1993, Zenith demonstrated its 16-VSB (vestigial sideband transmission) system in San Francisco. It promised to pack two HDTV channels into a single cable channel. Zenith claimed that 16-VSB provided one third more data than 64 QAM (quadrature amplitude modulation) which also promised to put two HDTV signals into one channel.[88]

In July 1993, the plans of the Grand Alliance were

laid out for the FCC. The committee agreed to drop consideration of the four separate HDTV systems and to concentrate on a unified system proposed May 24, 1993, to develop a broadcast standard. This was to be a finished prototype ready for testing by mid May, 1994. They were to adopt the 1,080 active line screen. The committee also asked the alliance to use 1,920 pixels across. This would be compatible with the 1,080 by 1,920 screen size proposed in HDTV systems abroad, especially in Japan. This removed another obstacle to an international broadcast standard. The alliance planned to combine all these elements into a working prototype by March 1, 1994.[89]

In August 1993, it was announced that Ampex had been selected by Sunset Post, Los Angeles, to supply a DCT system which would serve as the foundation for the facilities transfer to all-digital editing and film-to-tape transfer. WTTW-TV Chicago had also purchased an entire DCT digital component postproduction system. Other buyers were Charles, New York, with three DCT 700d tape drives, Tele-Cine Ltd, London, with two DCT 700ds, and Picture Company, Dublin, Ireland, with a complete DCT edit suite.[90]

On August 16, 1993, Digital Imaging Systems (Texas Instruments) introduced a silicon chip measuring ⅓-inch square that had 400,000 tiny mirrors on its surface. The mirrors could be directed to reflect light onto a projection system. It was claimed that the quality of the images were superior in every category to that generated by a CRT or a liquid crystal light valve (LCD). Square and only 17 millionths of an inch on their side, the mirrors were attached by two tiny poles. The support bars could rock up and down to allow the mirrors to turn side to side. Each mirror was directed by charging the surface of the chip only two millionths of an inch beneath the mirror. This attracted the loose corner of the chip causing it to turn on its pivots. In operation, the white light was projected through a rotating wheel which in turn had red, green and blue filters. Thus each mirror corresponds to a picture pixel. The standard NTSC signal was run through a scanner and converted to a single 480-line progressive scan picture for 67 milliseconds of video. Each line of video was broken into component red, green and blue parts. The color wheel then scanned the mirrors stopping for each color for 5.55 milliseconds. Each pixel thus gave the right color at the right time to complete the scan.[91]

In September 1993, it was reported that CBS had spent at least $10 million for Sony D-2 equipment for its Ed Sullivan Theatre in New York City. The network had also bought Ikegami cameras, SSL audio, and Grass Valley switchers.[92]

In October 1993, BTS announced the first deliverable 16:9/4:3 switchable broadcast CCD camera, the LDK-91/69. It used a new FT-11 sensor which provided 600,000 elements in 16:9 and 450,000 in the 4:3 mode. The sensor used the same technology as the FT-55R then employed in the BTS LDK-9 and 9P cameras. Because of FT architecture, there was no vertical smear under any conditions.[93]

In October 1993, it was reported that "once-mighty Ampex" was de-emphasizing its television business. It was dropping its older lines of analog equipment and reducing the number of existing product lines. It would only offer a single line of high-end digital equipment known as DCT, to production houses rather than TV stations and to companies trying to meet the growing demand for storage capacity in the computer industry. This shift from being a full-service broadcast outlet ended almost a 50-year era in which Ampex had provided virtually every kind of superb broadcast product from cameras to tape. Things hadn't been the same since new owners took over in the 1980s. Between 1990 and 1992, sales of VTRs fell from $184 million to only $79.1 million. The one bright spot was in developing the DCT high-speed data-storage system in which sales doubled in two years to $37.5 million.

Financially, the company was in deep trouble. Ed Bramson, majority stockholder of Ampex, had just gone into bankruptcy and Ampex stock had dropped from $6 to $3 a share. In addition, Ampex had been losing too many key executives and veterans who left after Bramson took over. The loss of Charles Steinberg in July 1988 who went over to Sony certainly hurt Ampex deeply. Critics pointed to the fact that Ampex was going to sell its tape division as proof that it couldn't survive. It had been hoped that customer loyalty, built up over decades of manufacturing quality broadcast equipment, could carry the company through, but this hope had long since disappeared. Ampex couldn't even sell Sony equipment with the Ampex name on it.[94]

In October 1993, Ampex announced the sale of DCT 700d tape drives to Post Perfect, New York. They were to be used for an eight-hour miniseries.[95] Nonetheless, *Broadcast Engineering* in December 1993 showed some disturbing facts about how badly the new Ampex DCT system was going. Ampex stated, however, that they had installed two DCT tape drives at Turner Broadcasting Systems' Graphic Factory in Atlanta.

In October 1993, Ampex revealed its new DCRsi digital instrumentation system. This revolutionary new technology was based on Ampex's original transverse-scan recording system. Ampex claimed that DCRs had been used for more than six years in a wide range of successful commercial and military applications. Over 700 units had been installed in the field. It was employed in remote sensing, reconnaissance, testing and other ground-based laboratory applications across the USA and around the

1991. *Above:* BTS LDK91 CCD camera. *Below:* BTS LDK910 CCD camera. (BTS.)

world. It was extensively used (over 70 units) during Operation Desert Storm where it endured in heat and dust. The transverse scan it used, Ampex claimed, had none of the problems of helical scan. It was shockproof and the short azimuth track was vibrationproof. The cartridge held 48 gigabytes, up to four times the capacity of conventional 28-track longitudinal recording systems.[96]

During the week of November 8, 1993, it was announced by the Grand Alliance that a joint HD-TV system was to use the new Dolby AC-3 audio compression system. Only the form of chip to be incorporated was uncertain; the chip would either be stand alone or it would be coupled to a chip with a video compression system for TV sets or converters.[97]

In December 1993, Sony Broadcast International stated that it had more than 1,500 of its Digital Betacam VTRs installed. They had been sold to NRK, Norway; RTE, Dublin, Ireland; DirectTV, North America; and STAR-TV, Hong Kong.

In December 1993, BTS (Bosch-Philips) Simi Valley, CA, provided a central routing switcher, control system and eight D-1 digital tape machines to the Filmworkers Club, Chicago. They also furnished an LDK-491SR camcorder and 15 Betacam SP VTRs. They provided to United Video, New York, with two central routing switches, two digital mixer-keyers, and 25 Betacam SP recorders.[98]

All of the activity of the Grand Alliance had much impact worldwide, especially in Europe. In December 1993, it was reported that in Britain, both the British Broadcasting Corporation (BBC) and National Transcommunications Ltd. (NTL), in some cases working on their own, in others as partners with European collaborators, were active in many HDTV research projects.

The Europeans seemed to be concentrating most of their new efforts on terrestrial broadcasting of digital TV. It was thought to be easier to derive further compatible systems on cable and on satellite from the terrestrial solution than the opposite. This approach was shown by the emergence of a number of national and local projects, all having the same rough objectives, which are described below.[99]

In the UK, ITC and NTL had developed the SPECTRE (special purpose extra channels for terrestrial radio-communications enhancements) prototype that was begun in 1988, using an OFDM (orthogonal frequency modulation mutiplexing) based system with 16-QAM modulation for terrestrial broadcasting of digital HDTV or EDTV. ITC had already used this equipment to make field tests. A digital transmitter was operated at a power level 30db lower than a PAL transmitter occupying an adjacent channel. Both were found to have comparable coverage areas with acceptably low mutual disturbances.

In Germany, a project called HDTV-T (T for "terrestrial"), launched in June 1991, was at the end of a definition phase leading to some general service orientations and general technical guidelines. These guidelines were strongly oriented towards HDTV, considering the role of public broadcasters who had a de facto monopoly on programs having nationwide coverage, together with the existence of free channels.

In the Nordic countries, the source codec of a project called HD-DIVINE (HD digital video narrow band emission) was demonstrated in June 1992. The channel coder — based on the OFDM system with 16-QAM modulation on 512 carriers for 24Mbit/sec total output — was expected to be completed soon.

In France, Thomson LER started a project called

DIAMOND (digital scalable modulation for new broadcasting), also based on OFDM techniques using a 64-QAM modulation on a carrier with dual polarization. Thus, it offered a total rate of X35=70Mbits/sec for fixed receivers. This was used with a codec based on HIVITS (high-quality videotelephone and high-definition television system) demonstrations of HDTV, in cooperation with the German branch of Thomson.

CCETT, Rennes, France, was also following the same OFDM line in the STERNE (système de télévision en radiodiffusion numérique) project. CCETT had considerable experience in television contribution coding and associated standardization matters. It had a leading and innovative role in the Eureka 147 digital audio broadcasting (DAB) project, where the principles of COFDM were successfully defined and defended. On these bases, the STERNE project aimed at specifying and developing prototype equipment for digital television broadcasting. It combined digital image coding with an adaptation of the COFDM coding system to television. Unlike the other local projects mentioned, it was not just one more digital HDTV experiment; instead, it attempted to define an introduction strategy based on a hierarchy of services, including a feature unique and specific to terrestrial broadcasting: portability. Three modes of reception (also developed from experience gained with DAB) were therefore taken into account: DAB's mobile reception, portable (also called "plug-free") reception, and traditional fixed rooftop antenna reception. STERNE was to be demonstrated by the fourth quarter of 1992 and finalized by the end of 1993.[100]

In February 1994, the Sony Corporation announced that it was rapidly expanding its digital editing market. It unveiled an upgrade of its year old Destiny system that would allow disc-based random-access editing. This was supposed to be competition to AVID-Matrox, ImMix and Lightworks editing devices. Avid was the market leader in editing devices with sales of $112 million in 1993. Sony also showed the first all-digital Betacam camcorder, the DVW-700, to be available in October for $66,000. The company also showed a slightly expensive camera ($62,000) that tied the digital camera to an analog Betacam recorder. They were also introducing a lower price UWV-100 camcorder with a three-chip CCD imager coupled to an analog UV Betacam SP recorder, selling for about $14,000 without lens. Sony continued pushing their Digital Betacam claiming sales of 30,000 recorders and players since its debut the previous year. Sony claimed that its backward compatibility had led to several large orders from industry. Tapes recorded on analog Betacam SP machines could be played back on Digital Betacam, so it bridged the analog world of the past and the digital world of the future.[101]

In February 1994, the FCC cleared the way for testing the so-called Grand Alliance system featuring a Zenith transmission subsystem. The Grand Alliance system combined elements of systems proposed by AT&T/Zenith Electronics, General Instrument/MIT and Philips Consumer Electronics/David Sarnoff Research/Thomson Consumer Electronics. The technical subgroup adopted the Zenith VSB transmission subsystem after it beat out GI's QAM subsystem in side-by-side tests in January and February.[102]

In March 1994, it was announced that Japan was planning to abandon its MUSE analog HDTV system. The victory of digital HDTV over MUSE was a double victory for Frenchman Michel Pelchat, a leading proponent of terrestrial and digital high definition for Europe. He was proposing La Très Grande Alliance, a world digital HDTV broadcast standard. He believed that now that Europe had effectively abandoned its plans for analog HDTV (the D2MAC and the HDMAC System) and the USA had its Grand Alliance system, that it was an opportune time to agree on and pursue a world digital transmission standard. He proposed an immense alliance with the USA, Europe and, of course, Japan.[103]

The NAB was held in Las Vegas, March 20-24, 1994. It attracted 71,082 attendees. The count was up from the previous year's 64,510. The big news at NAB was tapeless recording.

At NAB, Panasonic announced several new products. At the top of the list was the D-5 digital videocassette recorder for postproduction. The company claimed that D-5 exceeded the D-1 VCR in quality and transparency and was fully compatible with the D-3 machine. The D-5, AJ-D580 cost $65,000 and could handle two hours on a single cassette. It was suitable for the 4:3 and 16:9 aspect ratios and offered playback of D-3 recording in the component domain with an internal digital decoder for electronic news gathering. Panasonic also introduced Supercam, a one-piece camcorder composed of a camera with three CCDs and a S-VHS recorder. According to the company, for less than $10,000 broadcasters would get a camera with features they were used to getting in costlier camcorders. In addition to the frame interline transfer CCDs, it featured an electronic shutter and a digital processing unit. It was to be available in April. Panasonic also introduced in the S-VHS series, a WV-E550 for $5,000, as well as an S-VHS editing videocassette recorder, the AGDS-850, with slow-motion capabilities and digital signal processing, which cost less than $10,000. It also pushed its sixth generation of W series of MII half-inch component videocassette recorders and players. The AU-W35H recorder ($10,400) and the AU-W32H studio player ($8,800) featured time-base correctors, built-in time-code generators and readers, and noiseless freeze frame. The AU-W33H

1993. Panasonic D-5 component digital VTR. (Panasonic.)

($10,400) also included auto tracking for full control of noiseless slow-motion and still playback. Finally, the company announced that it was to introduce a 6mm (quarter-inch) digital tape format for professional use based on a consumer standard that a Japanese consortium had been developing.

In March 1994, there was much discussion on the possibility of replacing videotape with digital disk. It was admitted, though, that VTR makers were not ready to abandon tape quite yet. As a result, Panasonic unveiled its D5 format in the form of the AJ-D580 VTR. It was claimed that the D5 machine would play D3 material and allow two hours of recorded material on a cassette. It was claimed that Panasonic had sold 5,000 machines since their introduction two and a half years ago. Sony claimed that it had sold 3,000 Digital Betacam machines in the past year. JVC claimed that analog tape machines maintained the advantage in recording times, maintenance and cost, and, in addition, they were established in the marketplace. Sadly it was announced that Ampex was looking to get out of the tape business and had been seeking a buyer for its recording media division since early 1993.[104]

In April 1994, it was announced that Avid, Ikegami and BTS Broadcast System were planning to get into the disk-based image computer technology which would make disk drives practical for cameras. At that moment, disk drives only stored 20 minutes of Betacam quality video. BTS was participating in the development effort and hoped to have a camera ready the following year. But not all authorities were in favor of disk-based systems. Sony's Larry Thorpe noted that broadcasters would be unwilling to sacrifice features they enjoyed with tape cameras, or pay more money to plug a disk system into their digital systems. Other objections were about camera robustness. There were many problems that disks would have relating to jarring and abuse. Spinning disks and heads just did not work well in portable devices. Some maintained that the end for tape may never come.[105]

In June 1994, it was reported that Ampex had sold a series of its DCT machines to a group of Los Angeles post-production houses. Encore Video had bought three DCT tape drives for its facility and Varitel Video had bought four more tape drives. A total of 11 DST tape drives have been sold to post-production houses in the area.[106]

1997. Philips D-6 digital recorder. (Philips Labs.)

It was reported in July 1994 that Sony had sold three Digital Betacams VTRs to Hollywood Digital, Hollywood, and to Hughes DirecTV Service. They had bought over 200 Digital Betacam VTRs and 60 Flexicart automated playback systems.[107]

In July 1994, BTS announced its new Media Pool "tapeless recorder." It was claimed that it could store as many as 100 hours of compressed video. The previous week, they had demonstrated the completed working version of the hardware. The machine carried an expandable memory to store from ten minutes to 100 hours of uncompressed video. The machine could compress video at ratios up to 20:1. Applications were anywhere from promo spots to high-end editing facility. The price was about $128,000 and orders were being accepted for late 1994 delivery.[108]

Also in July 1994, Sony disclosed that it had sold a series of digital Betacam VTRs to USA and Canadian broadcasters. They had sold 42 Digital Betacam VTRs to Turner Broadcasting and another 110 to Canadian Broadcasting Corp. Sony also sold more machines to WFAA-TV, Dallas and WHIO-TV in Dayton, Ohio.[109]

In August 1994, the Ampex Corp. agreed to supply tape drives to Korea's new cable TV system through Hyundai Electronic Industries Co. Ampex would supply the new system with its DCT 1700d tape drives. The Korean company had ordered 26 of the DCT 1700d drives with related equipment, including DCT 700 switchers, DCT 500 special-effects systems, DCT 700e editors, and DCT 700i and 710i interface units.[110]

In August 1994, CBS announced that it was going to install a Hewlett-Packard tapeless video server at its Miami-owned and -operated station. It was part of a plan of incremental moves to tapeless program and editing. The HP broadcast server could store between six and 51 hours of video and audio. It used MPEG compression to store video at data rates ranging from 1.5Mb and 1.5mbps. Options included incremental storage capacities of 17, 24, and 51 hours at the 15mbps rate. Prices started at $210,000 for the basic servers that came with six hours of storage capacity at 15mbps. WCIX hoped to have the machine installed and running by January.[111]

In August 1994, ABC News announced that it was going to go to digital technology, and replace Beta tape machines with 12 D2 recorders. They were to be used for on-line editing and were to be the core of a planned all-digital post production room in Washington. ABC planned to use Grass Valley editors. The Grass Valley machines could change the in points of an edit without changing the duration of the edit. This could not be done with the original Sony software.[112]

In September 1994, it was announced that Media General Production had bought a series of D-3 half-inch composite digital equipment from Panasonic Broadcast & Television Systems Co. They had also purchased an AQ-20D digital signal-processing camera, an AJ-D320 digital portable recorder-player, an AJD-350 digital studio recorder-player, and an AS-D700 composite digital switcher. Media General stated that it was using the gear to offer compete digital production to its clients.[113]

The IBC convention was held in Amsterdam from September 16 to 20, 1994. It was claimed that digital TV was the hit of the IBC. Philips transmitted digital video broadcasting (DVB) MPEG 2 signals from France, received them in Amsterdam via the Telecom IC satellite, and displayed them through consumer decoders. For the previous 24 months, DVB had been the focus of attention of over 130 partners in the project. Satellite broadcasting of the DVB standard would start the following year via the Astra and other satellite programs. As for terrestrial broadcasting, the complex standard was expected to be finished by the end of 1995. According to Dr. Theo Peek of Philips Business Electronics, among the drawbacks of terrestrial digital TV were the hostile transmission environment and the lack of free channels in most countries. Nonetheless, terrestrial broadcasters still had an alternative PAL Plus, designed for compatibility with existing 4:3 PAL sets and also for providing full resolution pictures on new 16:9 sets. The PAL Plus system operated by transmitting a letter-box image to 4:3 sets. Digital helper information was included in the black bands and was used to recreate a full resolution 16:9 image. The image quality on a non–PAL Plus set was improved. A half dozen

broadcasters already were transmitting PAL Plus signals and 18 broadcasters in nine countries planned to start transmission in the following 12 months.[114]

The 136th SMPTE was held in Los Angeles, October 12–15, 1994. The theme was "Digital Era Ready or Not." A collection of cable and broadcast operations affirmed that they were ready. Both Harris Allied and Avid Technology arrived in Los Angeles with contracts to design all-digital facilities for new cable channels. Intel along with CNN was launching a new effort to pipe digital pictures to desktops for use by news producers. Northwest Cable News said that it would employ disk-based tools such as the Avid Media Recorders, AirPlay and the NewsCutter units, but would not use tape machines. CNN announced plans to enhance its EJ operation with a new system for providing its Newsource feeds directly to desktops. The system would take incoming satellite news feeds from Newsource and use an Intel compression scheme to distribute the video over local area networks within TV stations. The idea was for staff to review the news sources from their desks as the video feeds came in, rather than reviewing the tapes in editing suites.[115]

In October 1994, the Ampex Corp. announced that it was closing its Betacam production facility in Hong Kong. The company would no longer sell Betacam recorders and systems. Ampex planned to place more emphasis on Ampex-designed products such as its DCT system. Ampex plans to work with Sony to assure continuing service and parts supply for Ampex Betacam products. The company would stop taking orders for Betacam recorders, cameras and camcorders as soon as existing inventories were gone.[116]

In November 1994, JVC Professional Products announced that it had sold $500,000 worth of cameras, camcorders and editing gear to Morning Studios, a division of Fox Circle Production, for its new fX cable network. The purchase included 12 JVC KY-27B low-light cameras, 2A/B roll-editing suites, and 30 JVC decks.[117]

In November 1994, the Advanced Television Systems Committee (ATSC) documented Dolby's AC-3 digital audio technology a part of the advanced TV standard being developed by the seven-company Grand Alliance. ATSC was documenting various parts of the advanced television standard, including compression and transports subsystems. The committee said it documented the audio system after conducting a six-week letter ballot in which 40 participants voted in favor of AC-3 and only one against.[118]

On December 12, 1994, Reuters Television announced that it was pulling out its old newsreel footage from the vault for transfer to digital tape. Reuters was using the Ampex DCT 700d tape machine. It was claimed that Fox was also using this Ampex machine to archive filmed program material and NFL footage. It provided disk-drive-like technology for fixing flaws in the digital video data. It was claimed that DCT units carried coding technology that allowed them to calculate missing pixel information when gaps in the digital picture date appeared on a tape. Such gaps could occur on blemished areas of a tape. Ampex used an error correction that required an actual calculation of the missing data; it did not use error concealment as that required the exact information. It was claimed that DCT drives could digitally record material for eight hours without having to rely on error concealment. The drives used metal particle tape — such tape had a longer shelf life than other videotapes. Reuters agreed that the importance of error correction was a big factor in the company's choice of the Ampex DCT format. They planned to initially start with 1,000 hours of footage taken from a library of tens of thousands of hours, consisting mainly of highlight-reel material. It was claimed that the original digitization cost less than $500,000. Future digitization would take place once they could gauge marketplace demand for the footage.

This was a real plus for Ampex, but barely enough to keep it alive.[119]

Chapter 14

"E-Cinema" and the 1080p24 Format (1995–2000)

In January 1995, Panasonic Broadcast & Television Systems Co. was supplying its MII half-inch component analog video gear to the news departments of the Scripps Howard Group for their news operations. The purchase included 63 MII VTRs and players along with 18 AU-410 MII dockable VTRs. Panasonic was also supplying MII gear for the edit suites supporting the America's Talking Network. The network had also purchased 32 AU-66 MII enhanced series studio recorders and players as well as 11 AU-55H portable recorder-players.[1]

In January 1995, Sony Broadcast announced that four PBS stations had adopted the Digital Betacam format for recording production and playback. Also KUON-TV Lincoln, NE, had bought seven of the Digital Betacam decks. In addition, Twin Cities Public Television had bought seven of the machines for KTCA-TV and KTCI-TV.[2]

In February 1995, the JVC Professional Products Co. introduced a professional HDTV VTR. The company's SR-W32OU could record component signals with 1,125 lines for up to three hours. A standard definition mode allowed the unit to record NTSC or other signals in component format. It carried a list price of $9,850.[3]

In February 1995, the Ampex Corp. ran an ad in the various media announcing that "The Ampex DCT 1700d is possibly the best video recorder ever built." Now, of course, this was quite a statement to make, especially from an Ampex that was fighting for its very existence. Ampex finally had a very saleable product in its DCT line for storage and archival purposes, but it posed no threat to any of the major Japanese companies in television equipment who were selling their machines in the thousands. From all reports, the Ampex DCT recording ma-chines were being used by many companies for storage and archival purposes. It seemed that Ampex had finally produced a product that was unique and filled a need. Although it was no longer a major company and posed no threat to anyone either foreign or domestic, only two weeks later the Matsushita Electric Corp. of America, using its Panasonic label, took great exception to the Ampex claims. (Neither Sony nor JVC joined in the battle.) Panasonic claimed that its D-5 format was a superior product, and it claimed so for two reasons: one, it was a ten-bit machine, and second, it did not use compression. Ampex was quite shocked by this response and suggested that perhaps Panasonic should be reminded of the great contributions that Ampex had made to the video recorder. They particularly mentioned the use of slow motion, which Panasonic was using under Ampex license, and the excellent relations that had been maintained between them in Japan. Nothing was mentioned about the fierce (government-subsidized) competition that had been driving Ampex out of business. (Nor was there mention of the poor management and conditions that had led to Ampex's destruction. However, it should be stated here that neither the American broadcast industry nor the U.S. government did anything to support Ampex in its hour of need.)

Of course this was poor taste on the part of Matsushita. If they were angry they should have just put it aside and forgotten it. After all, Ampex was not hurting any part of Matsushita's market. If their ego was hurt, why make such an issue out of it? If their machine was the better machine, so be it. (It was certain that other Japanese companies such as Sony and JVC had machines comparable to the D5 and declined to join the fray.) To challenge them in the press was to show no compassion for a brother company that was suffering hard times. At any rate, Ampex answered their challenge by inviting Panasonic to a public test demonstration to be made with five machines from each company, dubbing for 100 generations apiece. Ampex's terms were simple: "Either send us a written apology, or we plan to see you at the test." As far is known, Panasonic declined the test.[4]

In April 1995, it was announced that Avid had sold worldwide more than 7,000 products since its introduction in 1987. It had sold its first Media Composer editing systems in 1989 and had some $200 million in sales the previous year. For fiscal 1994, its net profit was $13 million. It had sold its products to more than 600 broadcasters worldwide with half the revenue coming from the USA.[5]

In April 1995, Avid Technology announced that it was preparing to introduce a disk-based camera in conjunction with Ikegami. According to Avid president Curt Rawkey "videotape will die within five years. They planned to unveil this camera at that month's NAB convention.[6]

The annual National Association of Broadcasters conference was held in Las Vegas from April 19 to 23, 1995. Panasonic rolled out a digital line at NAB including a re-recordable digital optical VideoDisk recorder-player (LQD5500) that provided broadcast quality recording and playback of digital and analog video. The unit recorded up to 45 minutes of digitally compressed video with two channels of PCM audio and instant access to any random individual frame on the disk. It would be available that summer. They also showed an enhanced version of the Panasonic composite digital VTR, the AJ-D351, that featured improved tape and provided faster response to edit. It would be available that same month.[7]

Dr. Marvin Camras died Friday, June 23, 1995, in his 80th year (he was born January 1, 1916). It was said that we had lost one of the grandest old men of audio. Dr. Camras of the Illinois Institute of Technology (ITT), invented the application of high-frequency ac bias to magnetic recording which revolutionized the medium. (USA Patent 2,351,004 was one of over 500 he was awarded.)[8]

In September 1995, it was reported that the green light had been given to the Grand Alliance system. The FCC planned to wrap up its work by November 28, 1995, by recommending the Grand Alliance Advanced TV system as the broadcast industry's next transmission standard. There was some objection to the decision by the Advanced Television Systems Committee (ATSC) to approve the document before describing the system's results. One complaint came from the American Society of Cinematographers (ASC) who wanted a 2:1 aspect ratio

rather than the 16:9. But they were too late: in spite of the fact that the ASC had had over three years to lodge any protests, they had waited till the last moment. Also Apple Computer had complained of the decision to use interlaced scanning which they claimed would impede interoperability of computers.[9]

In October 1995, Ampex announced the role that DST products played in the area of image storage for film and television. Near on-line storage was more massive storage from which error-free data in either compressed or uncompressed form, could be transferred to the on-line server without the use of an operator. They displayed the DST 410 with a 1.1 megabyte capacity and two interface drivers.[10]

Also in October 1995, the Sony Corp. announced the sale of its 10,000th Digital Betacam recorder. It was sold to CNN which was presented with a special "10,000" logo on the videotape recorder. It also announced that it had sold more than $2 million worth of its digital equipment to Post-Newsweek station KPRC-TV. It included 11 DVW-A500s, five DVW-A510s and one DVW-A501 Digital Betacam VTR, and an LMS and a Flexicart System to go along with 13 BVW-300A portable Betacam SP camcorders.[11]

In December 1995, it was announced that the Ampex Corp. had completed the sale of its magnetic-tape subsidiary, Ampex Media Group, to a new group of shareholders that included Equitable Life Assurance Society. The new company, now called Quantegy, Inc. would market its media products under the Ampex brand name.[12]

In January 1996, it was announced that the Fox affiliate, KCPO (TV) Seattle, had purchased more than 20 Panasonic D-5 digital component VTRs and a dozen all-digital broadcast monitors. The purchase was valued at $1.5 million and represented the largest domestic sale of D-5 equipment.[13]

In January 1996, it was announced that NBC had signed a $21 million deal with Panasonic for the network's coverage of the 1996 Summer Olympic Games. NBC claimed that it had already purchased 80 D-3 recorders and was leasing another 140 on top of that. For editing and recording, NBC would use 223 D-3 digital composite VTRs (140 would be the newer, smaller AJ-D360 units), 31 AJ-D580 D-5 digital component VTRs, and 16 LQ-D5500 rerecordable digital optical-disc recorders and a handful of MII and S-VHS VTRs. The D-5 machines would be used primarily for high-end graphics, The digital optical-disk recorders would provide rapid access and playback for graphic stills and moving clips. NBC will also employ 19 AJ-300 D-3 camcorders to supplement coverage from point-of-view (POV) cameras mounted in fixed locations. Finally, eight AQ-23W 16:9/4:3 switchable cameras would make their debut in the International Broadcast Center.[14]

In March 1996, it was announced that Empire Video had added Ampex DCT 1700D tape drives to its new digital component editing room. It was claimed that the drives were fast and had all the editing features Empire had been accustomed to with D2. All archiving would be done to DCT tape.[15]

In April 1996, Philips (BTS) with Eastman Kodak introduced the new Spirit DataCine film scanner that combined a 525-line/625-line telecine and a film scanner capable of producing high-resolution digital files virtually in real time. The scanner could scan film at 24 frames/sec, but was limited to ten frames/sec by existing computer interfaces. However, this was still faster than the 30 seconds-per-frame transfer time for most digital film scanners.[16]

In May 1996, Sony became the latest member of the Advanced TV Technology Center—a nonprofit consortium of TV broadcast and manufacturing companies formed to solve the technical problems facing broadcasters in implementing the Grand Alliance HDTV standard.[17]

In July 1996, Panasonic announced that it had sold 38 AJ-D750 DVCPRO VTRs, 22 AJ-DVCPRO camcorders, and 20 hand-held AG-EZ1U DV camcorders to Time Warner all-news cable station. Also in July 1996, BTS Broadcast Television Systems Company became Philips Broadcast Television Systems Company.[18]

In July 1996, it was announced that the White House had called for a digital TV standard. Lionel Johns of the Science and Technology Policy told the FCC that "a single transmission standard would ignite investments in digital TV technology." He continued that it took just "a look at the experience with AM stereo to realize that the acceptance and likelihood of new broadcast technologies are greatly enhanced when a standard is adopted." Nevertheless, the FCC questioned the government's need to mandate a digital broadcasting standard, citing several concerns including potential barriers to innovations. The FCC claimed that it was "always open to reviewing new alternative standards ... when technological freeze ... [is] occasioned ... [by] the failure to adopt a standard."[19]

In August 1996, HD Vision of Irving, Texas, was providing high-definition TV facilities to Japanese broadcaster NHK as part of NHK's complete high definition coverage of the Atlanta Olympics. HD Vision, one of three high-definition production companies in North America, was the only U.S. company joining NHK's production; it helped to provide both live and tape-delayed broadcast to Japan.[20]

In August 1996, Philips Broadcast Television Systems sold three LDK cameras to Denver PBS affiliate KRMA-TV and three to Denver ABC affiliate KMGH-TV. They would use the LDK-10P cameras for both studio and field applications.[21]

In October 1996, Sony announced the sale of 29 Betacam SX DNW-A50 hybrid recorders to CNN's Sports Illustrated channel. They also announced the sale of $1 million of Beta-cam SX equipment by WCYB-TV for the station's all digital newsroom.[22]

In November 1996, Tribune Broadcasting had decided to test Sony's Betacam SX component digital tape format at its stations in New York, Chicago, and Atlanta in hopes of supplementing SX gear throughout its 16 stations. Sony said that the purchase was worth more than $1 million. However, Ira Goldstone stated that while Panasonic's existing 4:1:1 version of DVCPRO was fine for Tribune's cable news operation, he believed that Tribune would probably choose either Sony's Betacam SX or Panasonic's upcoming DVCPRO-50 format for its broadest stations. DVCPRO used 4:2:2 compression which gave it the potential for upconversion. Nonetheless, Tribune had a large investment in Betacam SX with its backward compatibility with Betacam SP.[23]

In November 1996, Ethnic-American Broadcasting Corp., a satellite distributor for foreign language programming, chose JVC's Digital-S as the house videotape format for its new 24-hour Russian broadcast service. The price was $124,000 for nine Digital-S digital tape decks. The new decks would be integrated with Ethnic-American's 20 Betacam SP VTRs. The main reason for the company's decision was costs. Digital-S tapes were in the $30 range while Betas were in the $50 range. They plan to unload some of its Betacam SP VTRs and use others for in-house production.[24]

In December 1996, the FCC commissioners adopted the digital TV compromise, which required that broadcasters delivering digital TV use the remaining elements of the Grand Alliance standard, which included specs for compressing video, delivering sound and sending the signals over the airwaves. The FCC killed the idea that DTV broadcasts would only be sent to DTV receivers. The commissioners still needed to resolve the issue of how long the broadcasters would be able to hang onto their analog channels and whether they needed to deliver any high-definition programming.[25]

In January 1997, it was announced that Radio Canada's French language network had purchased over $1 million of DVCPRO equipment from Panasonic Canada. The component digital DVCPRO equipment would replace existing analog equipment at Radio-Canada's bureaus nationwide and would be used to produced both regional and national news reports. The order was for 63 units. It was claimed that CBC was facing extensive budget and staff cutbacks—DVCPRO would definitely allow them to meet budget objectives while operating more efficiently.[26]

In January 1997, it was announced that Panasonic

had been chosen as the official broadcast supplier and prime systems contractor by the Nagano Olympic Committee. The games were scheduled to be held in Nagano, Japan, in February 1998. The equipment comprised several systems, including DVCPRO, D3 and D5 VTRs, and digital cameras to acquire, record, edit and archive the TV broadcasts of the games. Matsushita had performed the same job in Barcelona in 1992 and in Atlanta in 1996.[27]

On February 2, 1997, it was claimed that NBC had made television history by broadcasting the first live network show in digital high definition. It was "Meet The Press." According to reports this was the first time that a high-definition program had not been transmitted off a tape machine. Sadly, because of the lack of HDTV receivers, the program had to be received off air by WHD's Zenith 8-VSB demodulator and viewed on a wide screen Sony monitor. The show was also recorded on a Panasonic D-3 deck and a Sony full-bandwidth high-definition VTR. It was claimed that "seeing the actual broadcast was astounding."[28]

In February 1997, Panasonic announced that it had delivered more than 10,000 DVCPRO units worldwide. The latest sale was to the Ackerly Group in Seattle that had bought 13 DVCPRO camcorders and 32 studio editing VTRs for news acquisitions and production.[29]

In February 1997, Hitachi introduced the SK-3000 HDTV camera, a multistandard camera that supported simultaneous HDTV and NTSC (16:9 or 4:3) outputs. The digitally processed camera head uses two million-pixel CCDs and operated in a 16:9 format at all times. The 1.5gbps digital output was digitally converted to NTSC serial digital component outputs in addition to the standard HDTV output. The camera could produce 1,200 lines of HDTV resolution.[30]

In March 1997, Hewlett-Packard announced that it had developed an MPEG-2 digital disk recorder that could function either as a stand-alone on-air unit or as a cache device in conjunction with HP's existing broadcast video servers. It incorporated the redundant RAID storage architecture in a unit the size of a standard Betacam SP tape deck. The HP Mediastream disk recorder had a base price of $65,000 for a unit with five hours of storage (at an encoding rate of 8mbs) and two channels (input/output) and could be scaled up to a $115,000 configuration with nine hours of storage. It had four major applications, two using both the disk recorder and the HP server over a fiber channel network, and two using the disk recorders as a stand-alone unit.[31]

In March 1997, it was announced that the CamCutter, a disk based camcorder developed by Avid and Ikegami, had been redeveloped. They claimed that the picture quality had been brought up to the level of competing digital news tape formats. It was now made in two ver-

sions: the Editcam DNS-101, which had an IT sensor and sold for $40,000; and the DNS-11, which had an FIT sensor and sold for $55,000. It was claimed that the recorders were ready to be shipped. Several units had been tested and Avid and Ikegami were trying to integrate the machine with the present Avid equipment.[32]

The noted German television pioneer, Prof. Dr. Manfred von Ardenne died on May 26, 1997. (He was born in Hamburg, Germany, on January 20, 1907.) Von Ardenne was among the earliest television pioneers furnishing cathode ray tubes for experimental early work on radar in England. This dependence on a foreign supplier (especially a German source) gave the British impetus to start producing cathode ray tubes in England. In 1930, von Ardenne continued to work on television until the German television industry was put under the control of the German Air Ministry in August 1935. He then turned to work on the electron microscope and was about five years ahead of every one else in this field. He, like Zworykin, turned to medical electronics in 1964 and operated a clinic for cancer research at his home laboratory.[33]

In April 1997, it was reported that CBS had bought $24 million worth of DVCPRO gear. CBS Television stations were replacing their analog Betacam field equipment. More than 1,400 DVCPRO units including camcorders, laptop editors, studio editing VTRs and DV format camcorders were to go to 13 CBS-TV stations. Robert Ross, VP of engineering and operations, CBS TV stations, had been looking for a new acquisition format for CBS-owned and -operated stations as their Betacam gear bought in 1988 was getting old. He admitted that Sony's Betacam SX was a nice format, but that Sony did not have all the pieces necessary to convert to a news operation. Ross also admitted that DVCPRO's price was also an advantage.[34]

However, also in April 1997, it was announced that Sony would supply CBS with all-digital broadcast facilities for its coverage of the 1998 winter Olympics at Nagano, Japan. The contract marked the third winter Olympics that Sony would be outfitting CBS with production and playback gear. CBS would use all-serial-digital video with embedded digital audio. The facility would have two production studios, nine edit bays, and more than 60 Digital Betacam VTRs with an extensive LAN tying together and collecting data from venue sites. CBS claimed that lots of the gear would be brought back to CBS's New York broadcast center and used for network news.[35]

Also in April 1997, the smaller Benedek Broadcasting Co., which owned 22 TV stations in small or midsized markets, bought $2 million worth of DVCPRO gear to upgrade news operations at ten of its network-affiliated stations. The 192-unit order included 40 DVCPRO camcorders and assorted accessories. It was claimed that they were impressed with DVCPRO's ease of operation and high picture quality.[36]

In May 1997, it was announced that KCTS-TV had purchased a Sony HDC-750 high-definition camera, making it the first North American owner of Sony's new HDTV production gear. It was to replace a Sony HDC-500 that was damaged in a helicopter accident in 1994. It supported the 1,035-line interlace Japanese developed chips, although Sony was hoping to develop its own 1080i ATSC sensor chips by late 1998. The HDC listed for $190,000.[37]

In May 1997 Phillips announced the D-6 TV recorder. It was a cassette-based VTR using 19mm (¾ inch) metal particle tape. It offered uncompressed high-definition recordings on a D-1 sized cassette. It included multiple standard HD recording, 1,125/60 and 1,250/50 (Europe) and the ability to handle 1,080 active lines.[38]

In June 1997, it was reported that ABC affiliate KGTV San Diego had made a $430,000 purchase of Panasonic DVCPRO gear. It included 30 AJ-D700 camcorders, three AJ-LT-175 lap editors, and 13 AJ-D750 studio editing VTRs, all to be delivered in June. This order was to replace aging Betacam SP cameras. KGTV bought DCVPRO because the Betacam SX digital format was a little costly and they didn't like Sony's spin on MPEG 4:2:2.[39]

In June 1997, JVC introduced a new Digital-S camcorder at the Infocomm show in Los Angeles, bringing its 4:2:2 component digital format into the field acquisition market. The new DY-700U three-chip camera had a base price of $11,999 including lens and viewfinders. It used Digital-S half-inch metal particle tape in lengths of 10, 34, 64 and 104 minutes. It was hoped that the new 17-pound camera would allow Digital-S to compete with the EJ market where Panasonic's DVCPRO digital format had been so successful. Its price was said to be unbeatable, and its quality was compared to that of Betacam SP.[40]

In June 1997, it was reported that Sony had sold more than 200 Betacam SX units, including VTRs, hybrid VTRs, camcorders and DNW-220 portable field editors to France 2, part of the French network, France Television Group. France 2 was adopting Betacam SX for its new tape format for news production as part of its move to a new location the following year.[41]

Also in June 1997, ITN, the UK's commercial TV news organization, selected Panasonic's DVCPRO as its next-generation field operation format to replace its Betacam SP equipment. ITN had ordered 50 DVCPRO VTRs, 32 cameras, and 12 laptop editors.[42] Also Panasonic had sold 20 DVCPRO VTRs to German pay-TV operator Premiere, and 15 VTRs, five camcorders and a Smart-Cart automation system to Canal+ Spain.[43]

In August 1997, it was discussed that HDTV was falling out of favor. It appears that many stations decided to use their new-found digital standards to create multiple standard definition channels. For instance, ABC had announced plans to offer a multiplex of wide-screen, standard-definition pictures, some on a subscription basis. CBS still maintained that it would offer a single channel of HDTV as much as possible, although it was still considering multiplexing as a potential revenue source. The network insisted that it would definitely offer HDTV in prime time. Fox was still considering a multichannel SDTV service such as six to eight compressed 480p streams into the 6MHz TV channel. NBC stated that it would offer HDTV in prime time and might offer multiple channels of SDTV during the day.[44]

In September 1997, more Panasonic DVCPROs were sold in Europe to Universal Studios, BSkyB and German broadcaster MDR. DVCPRO-50 was Panasonic's next-generation DVCPRO format. It used 4:2:2 compression at a data rate of 50Mb/sec giving it picture quality suitable for contribution and studio use.[45]

In September 1997, Hewlett-Packard released its HP MediaStream AirDirect. A low-cost system that used HP MediaStream disk recorders, it was designed to provide broadcasters with basic spot insertion and playback capabilities. AirDirect ran via a simple PC interface and offered VTR-source dubbing, playlist editing, and AsRun logs. The price for a single PC system with two-channel playback, five-hour disk recorders was $79,000. A two PCAir Directs system with a four-channel, 18-hour disk recorder was $147,000.

In October 1997, CBS announced that it had taken delivery of 143 pieces of Panasonic DVCPRO equipment to upgrade its station and news in the field. Included in the order is 25 AJ-D700 camcorders, 18 AJ-D750 studio editing VTRs, 44 AJ-D230 desktop VTRs, nine A850 edit controllers, and an AJ-LT75 laptop editing system. Also in October 1997, the BBC outside broadcast unit purchased from Thomson Broadcast, France, the world's largest production switcher and installed it in a new 20 camera DMCCR remote truck. It provided direct access to 48 production sources, with an additional 16 on an upstream router as secondary signals.[46]

In October 1997, Panasonic Broadcast announced the AG-EZ20 DV format minicam. The ultracompact digital camcorder weighted less than 1.5 pounds and could record up to 90 minutes of component digital video and digital audio on quarter-inch cassettes that could be played back on Panasonic DVCPRO VTRs (with an optional adapter). The minicam came with a four-pin Firewire (IEEE 1394) digital interface and an adjustable 3.8 inch LCD monitor and a built-in EBU time-code generator. It was equipped with 10X and 25X digital zoom that moved from wide-angle to full zoom in less than a second. List price was $2,895.[47]

In October 1997, the Advanced Television System

Committee took its HDTV roadshow to Sydney, Australia, transmitting HDTV pictures from the TCN Channel 9 tower in Willloughby and receiving and displaying them at the Observatory Hotel. The tests were organized by the Federation of Australian Commercial Stations (FACTS) which was evaluating American DVB ATSC and European DVB digital systems for implementation in Australia's 7MHz broadcast band.[48]

In November 1997, it was announced that NBC affiliate, KHQ-TV Spokane, had purchased $740,000 worth of Panasonic digital gear to replace aging MII for its news department. The order included 13 AJ-D700 DVCPRO camcorders, 14 AJ-D650 studio editing VTRs, and seven AG-850 edit controllers. This equipment was bought because old MII decks badly needed replacement. It was decided to buy DVCPRO for both editing and acquisition. KHJ would continue to use MII machines (which were still performing well) in master control for commercial playback, program record and delay. They expected to replace the master control decks with video servers.[49]

In November 1997, it was announced that Fox had purchased 11 digital camera systems from Philips BTS for its new all-digital Network Center in Los Angeles. The order included six LDK 20S "HiRes" digital cameras and five LDK 20PS cameras. They would be installed in Fox's Stage A in January 1998. Fox had been a longtime user of Philips cameras and used them at Fox News Channel in New York and at its News Bureau in Washington.[50]

In December 1997, Panasonic introduced its next generation DVC-PRO 50 line at the SMPTE conference in New York City. Panasonic claimed that it had delivered more than 25,000 of its DVCPRO component digital tape format machines, including 11,000 in the USA. The company announced new sales to Sinclair Communications, LIN Television and Ziff-Davis totaling $2.5 million. The DVCPRO 50 line included a switchable 16:9/4:3 525-line progressive camcorder and a VTR switchable between 50 and 25mbs making it backwards compatible with DVCPRO-25 gear. Panasonic was also selling a $95,000 AJ-HD2000 recorder that incorporated an D-5 VTR with a HDTV processor to allow high definition recording. Warner Bros. had bought two AJ-HD2000's for its film mastering facility in Hollywood and planned to buy several more in the coming 18 months.[51]

In December 1997, the ABC-owned and -operated KFSN-TV Fresno, purchased four Hitachi SK-2600 PW digital studio cameras for its studio production of local newscasts and community service programs. The portable 16:9/4:3 switchable units would replace the station's Philips LDK-6 cameras. Hitachi machines were picked for their image quality and ultrawide-band RGB triax system."[52]

In January 1998, it was announced that Charles Steinberg, president of Sony Electronics Broadcast and Professional Company, was preparing for retirement. Steinberg had been an advisor to Sony's president and CEO, Dr. Teruaki Aoki, since 1988. Steinberg's duties as head of Sony BPC were to be taken over by BPC executive vice president Michael Vittelli.[53]

Also in January 1998, HDTV pioneer REBO Studio was providing CBS and PBS with an HDTV programming feed to the Consumer Electronics Show in Las Vegas. The feed drew from REBOs extensive HDTV library. While PBS and CBS were used to broadcast terrestrial TV stations in Las Vegas (KLVX and KLAS-TV) to the convention floor, REBO's feed was from cable.[54]

In February 1998, Sony announced the $3 million sale of Betacam SX equipment to WHCH-TV, the NBC affiliate in Boston which purchased seven DNW-GWS camcorders, 12 DNW-A100 hybrid recorders, six DNW-A45/50 hybrid recorders, one DNE-700 news editing system, 26 DNW-A22 players, and nine DNW-A220 portable field editors.[55]

Also in February 1998, Sony announced that it was developing a line of 480p progressive-scan equipment that it would demonstrate at NAB. Sony stated that its customers had asked for 480 and they believe it to be complementary to 1080i. Larry Kaplan, Sony senior VP, said that Sony planned to support 480p and would add a 480p output to its HDC-700 and 750 cameras. Sony would also introduce a 1080p production format under the ATSC standard within five years. In addition, the company demonstrated a 1080p24-frame telecine for film-to-tape mastering at NAB.[56]

In February 1998, it was claimed that both ABC and NBC were taking a hard look at the 720p format (to replace the 1080i). ABC told affiliates that it favored the 720p format as it allowed the network to simultaneously broadcast a second 480-SDTV service at the same time. NBC was also considering 720p but was concerned about the availability of equipment to support the format. CBS was still committed to 1080i but was studying other formats to see if they made sense. However, Fox stated that it was not going to either 1080i or 720p but was looking at the 480p standard, as it would meet the needs of viewers for years to come.[57]

In June 1998, Hitachi introduced a three-CCD color camera, the HVD-15, with a single chip digital VLSI that provided video processing and decoding. The camera used 13-bit digital signal processing with all signal processing accomplished within the single chip VLSI. The HVD-15 used three half-inch 410,000 double-sampled Y-channel digital processing to provide 800 lines of resolution. The suggested list price was $5,270.[58]

In June 1998, Avid Technology won its third Emmy for its digital editing technology. By grouping its Media

Composer and Film composer it allowed for real-time camera grouping. The Avid gave editors the capacity to group and edit from an unlimited number of camera sources. It was claimed that the technology was used to edit more than 40 TV shows in the 1997 prime-time season.[59]

In July 1998, WCNC-TV, Charlotte, NC, the Belo station and NBC affiliate, invested more than $1 million in Sony's Betacam DX gear. The station bought 14 DNW-9 switchable 4:3/16:9 cameras, 14 DNW- \A75 VTRs, five DNW-225 portable editors, and four DNW A-22 players. This equipment was bought to replace aging Betacam SP equipment because of SX's backwards-compatibility with SP tapes. Belo stated that while Panasonic had a good format, he preferred to stay with Sony as the price Sony offered was "very competitive." He said that the station used the Avid NewsCutter to perform its daily news edits and that it would continue to implement SX.[60]

However, in August 1998, the NBC News channel in Charlotte, NC, converted its operations from analog Sony Betacams to Panasonic's DVCPRO digital tape format. The deal included 63 DVC PRO units to be used by the EJ staff to cover sports, news and pre-planned features.[61]

In August 1998, CBS announced that it had purchased Pluto Technologies HyperSpace high-definition digital video recorders to perform commercial insertion for three of its stations: KYW-TV, Philadelphia, WCBS-TV, Los Angeles, and KPIX-TV, San Francisco. They were to be used as HDTV spot servers operating under the Louth automation protocol.[62]

In September 1998, it was announced that the pioneering HDTV production firm of REBO was suspending operations. This just as the long-awaited HDTV movement was getting started in the USA. REBO, founded in 1986, had been expected to cash in now that U.S. broadcasters were going digital, but founder Barry Rebo stated that the HDTV market was developing much slower than expected and his production firm was just too expensive to maintain.[63]

In October 1998, it was announced that the SMPTE had wisely included an initial documentation of the 24-frame progressive variant of the 1920 × 1080 format within the SMPTE 274 standard. It was claimed that in July 1997, Sony announced the development of the E-Cinema system, a 24-frame progressive digital system that would be developed in concert with the moviemaking industry.[64]

In January 1999, it was announced that Charles Steinberg, president of Sony's Broadcast and Professional Company (BPC), was "transitioning" to a new strategic assignment within Sony in preparation for his mid–1999 retirement. Steinberg's duties as head of Sony BPC were to be taken over by BPC executive vice president, Michael Vitelli.[65]

In February 1999, it was announced that Dolby Laboratories had developed an audio technology intended for professional use by digital TV program producers and DTV broadcasters. The system, called "Dolby E," was designed to serve as an economical in-plant digital format for DTV broadcasters transmitting 5.1 channel Dolby digital (AC-3 audio) as a part of their digital broadcasts. Dolby E allowed up to eight discrete digital audio channels to be distributed through an existing AES/EBU audio pair recorded on two tracks of a digital VTR.[66]

In April 1999, an article entitled "The 24p 1920–1080 approach," stated that "the Laser Pacific Media Corp. of Los Angeles had unveiled a 24 frame progressive (24p) High Definition System in February 1999." It claimed that Sony and other manufacturers had been leaning toward a 24p solution for "DTV, DVD, the internet and all other electronic and digital distribution mediums." Sony claimed that this was the first format ever created specifically to fill this need. The 24p approach permitted a single postproduction facility to switch between 1080p24 and 1080/50i, which allowed for 60 field interlaced recording (60i) for high-definition video and in 25 frames progressive for international distribution (25p). Sony claimed that it would provide a full family of products: telecine, VTR, editor, production switcher, digital effects monitors and peripheral products.

Panasonic also promised a full line of 24p products at that year's NAB. This was to include a master 1080p/24 frame D-5 HD based VTR.[67] It was anticipated that this system would be introduced before the end of 2001.[68]

This concept was the essential object of the long search for a single worldwide HDTV format for studio origination and international program exchange. All HDTV studios around the world would produce programs to a single video format. This key point was the original driving force for the standardization of the 1,125/60 format by SMPTE and other organizations. MPEG-2 was rapidly becoming the de facto standard for professional video, and related signal parameters tended to fall in line with it. Program exchange was one of the reasons MPEG-2 was chosen by the Grand Alliance DTV system and the European DVB project. The 24 frames video mastering concept took electronic imaging to a lighter level of standardization and exchange capabilities.[69]

On April 26, 1999, NBC launched the first nightly television show in both digital and 16:9, 1080i high-definition video. This was Jay Leno's "Tonight Show" on NBC. The program originated from NBC's Burbank Studio 3. The finished HD show was taped in the new HD edit suite and fed directly to affiliates via SBS-4. The NTSC feed went to New York via AT&T fiber and was uplinked by New York to its affiliates. The audio was not 5:1, but two channel stereo. Ten Sony HD cameras, including four

HDC-700As, three HDC-750As, and three DXCH10-POVs were used. The control room had a Sony HDS7000 switcher with an HDME-7000 multieffects system and an HD SDI video router. It was claimed that for 49 years, the "Tonight Show" had been the mainstay of late-night viewing on NBC. It began taping in black-and-white on May 29, 1950, and shifted to color in 1956. In 1980, it moved to Burbank.[70]

During April 1999, the Fox Network Center claimed that it was operating the first fully tapeless master control operation. It was based on a fiber channel and file server–based networked, and digital topology supported by Ampex DST recorders. It was claimed that this system eliminated reliance on videotape and its associated multiple quality-control checks. The system comprised of 16 PDR200s, two Ampex DST library systems, and four Ampex 312 stand-alone recorders. Ampex digital tape DSTs provided near-line archives of what previously had been warehouses of videotape. For example, prime shows were now moved around on networks and copied on digital data tape (which provided for speed and compactness). The combination of servers and DST eliminated the need to move material around on tape or baseband video. Additionally, the technology increased quality and reduced generation losses at the Fox Center. Fox could now store approximately 20 program episodes in a single cassette the size of a laptop computer and transfer that programming in one third the time it would take in real time. For example, an entire season of "The Simpsons" could be stored on a single 330GB Ampex digital tape. At KCET, there was a similar video file service setup incorporating Ampex 712 data-tape libraries using RAID (a redundant array of independent drivers), an assembly of multiple-disk techniques using Tektronix Profile PDR 200s and Ampex DST data-tape libraries.

A digital video server was just a large storage system using computer hard drives under the control of one or more computer processors to access stored video, time code and associated audio program elements according to a number of predetermined rules.[71]

Ampex was on display at the 1999 NAB convention. It demonstrated its complete line of DST digital tape drives and automated cartridge libraries for video, image and data archives in broadcast facilities, postproduction houses, and so on. Ampex's newest product was the DST library extension that connected to a DST 712 library, providing a storage capacity of up to 23.2 terabytes of data.[72]

In May 1999, it was announced that Avid shares had fallen 27 percent, in spite of the fact that Avid had announced that it would release its unity shared-storage product and 24-frame progressive format editing systems later that year. Avid explained that they were inundated with orders and weren't able to process all of them.[73]

Also in May 1999, CBS announced that it had purchased Faroudja Digital Format Translator (DFT) up-converters for its second wave of DTV stations, WBBM, Chicago, WBZ-TV, Boston, and WWJ-Detroit, which were scheduled to roll out their digital services on May 1, 1999.

In June 1999, ABC-TV announced that it planned to produce the traditional "Monday Night Football" games in high definition. This was to celebrate the 30th anniversary of the sports show. Panasonic was to furnish the AJ-HD2700 tape machines (which were D5 format, ten-bit, CCIR 601 digital recorders) to provide a 4:2:2 level of quality that was selectable between 720p and 1080i. In addition, the games would be broadcast on the regular NTSC networks. The ABC season was to start on September 13 with Miami at Denver.[74]

Video and audio tape pioneer, John (Jack) Mullin, died in Camarillo, CA., on June 24, 1999, of heart failure. He was 85. He was born in San Francisco on October 5, 1913. As related in these pages, Mullin was instrumental in bringing high-fidelity audio recording to the USA. He also built the first operational video recorder prototype in the world. His efforts helped bring the Ampex company to prominence which led to the first practical videotape recorder, which in turn led to the revolution in television. Nonetheless, Jack Mullin died virtually unknown.[75]

In July 1999 appeared one of the first articles describing the use of television for projecting motion pictures. It was more than plain old large-theater television, the article was talking about. Entitled, "Electronic Cinema — Digital delivery for the big screen," the piece spoke of the many advantages of using electronic techniques for exhibiting motion pictures— "E Cinema" as the method was called. The article told of the many advantages electronic projection had over film projection, and discussed the stages of transferring, transporting or storing, and projecting digital images. First, it raised the tremendous cost of shipping finished filmprints to and from the millions of theaters. (Nothing was mentioned of the cost of the mass destruction of the millions of prints after they had been shown.) Next, the story talked about the traditional method of shooting 35mm film and making copies from a master negative or duplicate negatives with each stage of transference degrading picture quality. (It was assumed that the normal theater print was the equivalent of a fourth-generation print of the original recorded image.) It also covered the major problem of transferring the 35mm film master to electronic media. (Actually this was the simplest problem as videotape readily accepts the colorimetry of motion picture film.) Finally, the article mentioned that "film is likely to remain the medium of choice even after the rest of the system is all electronic." The piece went on to cover the various means of electronic projection giving great emphasis on the Texas Instruments (MEM) mirror instrument projector. It also discussed solid-state liquid-crystal (LC) devices, the Direct Drive Image Light Amplifier (D-ILA) made by Hughes-JVC, plasma technology, lasers, and finally the absolute dearth of hope for cathode ray tubes (CRTs).[76] It was claimed that the Hughes-JVC-12K had been installed at the Estudio Gigante nightclub in Santiago, Chile, and also at two Disney regional parks in Orlando, Florida and Chicago.[77]

During the week of July 4, 1999, a digital film experimentation was held in four Los Angeles theaters: two in Westwood and two in Burbank. Using both the JVC/Hughes-JVC ILA 12K large-screen electronic projector[78] and the Texas Instruments' mirror system, special copies of the *Star Wars — The Phantom Menace* were projected before large audiences.

The first report of this screening was not too promising. According to the *Los Angeles Times,* "The showings drew capacity crowds and were the talk of Hollywood today. Even if they failed to prove that Electronic cinema is ready for prime time, the images on the screen were as free of jiggles and blurs as a music CD is free of pops and warps and impressed many observers with their clarity. But others were disappointed by their color and resolution, especially when compared to film prints of the same pictures. In any event, the exhibitions were overseen by squadrons of professional engineers and backed up by regular analog movie prints running in sync." The article ended up with the quote, "Unless the result is picture quality vastly superior to today's [so] that audiences will go out of their way to sit in a digital theatre, exhibitors will refuse to pay the freight. What is missing of course at the present time is an affordable large-screen projector. Very few multi-screens could afford the $150,000 per screen to retrofit their theatres."[79]

In September 1999, it was reported that Panasonic had used its D-5 HD equipment in the postproduction and playback of Lucasfilm's recent *The Phantom Menace.* In the production of the digital master of the film, Panasonic's AJ-HDP500 HD processor was teamed with Pluto Technologies' hard-disk-based HD digital video recorder for playback of the HD images at the four *Star Wars* test cinemas. Panasonic claimed that the advantages of component digital were best realized when the least amount of compression is applied. Yet compression adapters were developed to allow HDTV and other formats to be recorded on standard D-5 VTR. One adapter compresses the 1.2Gbs, 1125/60 signal by a ratio of about 4:1. Other adapters have been developed to allow progressively scanned 525 and 720 line images to be recorded on a D-5 using a "bit bucket" approach. The 525p and with 720-line were being developed for use in Japan.[80]

1999. Hughes-JVC ILA-12K electronic large-screen projector. (Hughes-JVC.)

Also in September 1999, the interest in E-Cinema was reported in *Cinema Technology.* It seems that the interest was worldwide. A survey of the various companies involved in E-Cinema showed Texas Instruments to be the front runner at that moment. TI claimed to have delivered 150,000 DLP subsystems to customers and to be supplying more than 25 projector manufacturers worldwide. Their goal seemed to be to furnish their technology exclusively to manufacturers. Hughes-JVC was next on the list with its ILA-12K projectors which it claimed to be the most sophisticated and highest-quality electronic cinema technology available in the marketplace. Other manufacturers were Ampro, which used TI technology as well as HDTV panels from IBM and in-house patents for light valve technology. Barco used both CRT and LCD technology for its range of projectors. Electrohome used both the TI DLP engines as well as some CRT based projectors. The Sony Corp. utilized the full spectrum of technology including CRT, DLP and LCD for its line of projectors. It was claimed that Sony had yet to make a significant impact on the market at that time. Of interest was the Principia Optics company that was trying to create a commercial application for its laser cathode ray tube (LCRT) technology. It was allied with the P. N. Lebedev Physical Institute in Moscow. The tube was to be ready by the autumn of

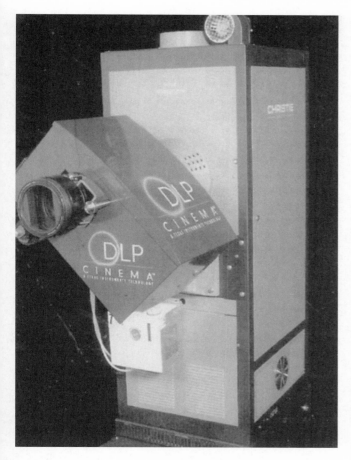

1999. Texas Instruments DLP digital projector. (Texas Instruments.)

2000. The article concluded with a survey of the various attempts for a worldwide system.[81]

In July 1999, yet another HD production format was described, spurred on perhaps by the postproduction industry. 1080p24, as the format is sometimes known, used the ITU common image format (CIF) of 1920 × 1080 (WxH) pixels, but at a nominally 24Hz frame rate.

This signal could be recorded on a new version of the D5 (made by Panasonic, it was a ten-bit, CCIR digital recorder) to provide the 4:2:2 level of quality.[82] Tentatively called the HD-3000, 1080p24 could be expressed in the format 1080p24sf, which means segmented frame. In this process, the 24-frame signal was split (i.e., segmented) into two parts which could be recorded on a modified recorder originally intended for interlace-scanned signals. The signal appeared as if it was an interlaced signal, but both fields came from the same 24Hz (film) frame.

The 1080p24 format was greeted with tremendous acceptance by the postproduction community. They saw it as a format that they could use to edit and perform most operations on film-based material in its original acquisition format (and frame rate) regardless of its ulti-mate distribution format (and frame rate). This preserved their options for different format video releases later on.

This 24Hz video could be frame doubled to 48Hz, or tripled to 72Hz for display on computer monitors. It could also be converted to 60Hz for viewing on conventional video monitors by adding the 3:2 pulldown process.

The single 24Hz master recording could be converted to all of the popular video release formats, and even some of the not-so-popular ones. SD and HD versions of the same film material could be derived from the 24Hz master in a variety of ways. Repeating every frame twice and running the VTR at 25Hz instead of 24Hz could produce a 50Hz version. While this may be considered heresy by some sections of the industry, it is an established and accepted practice in 50Hz countries.

It is important to realize that the development of these VTR formats was not necessarily dependent on a tape-based recording media. Increasingly, the compression schemes used in these recorders were being broken out into technologies that could be applied to hard disk, optical and RAM-based recorders. Perhaps, as they say, advances in digital recording technology, including compression, were just as applicable to other recording technologies as they were to tape. Each medium's strengths must be individually evaluated.[83]

In July 1999, Avid (noted for its editing devices) announced that it had released a 24P universal editing and mastering version of its Avid Symphony editing machine.

1986. The author (left) with Charles P. Ginsburg at Ampex in Redwood City, CA, September, 1986. (Collection of the author.)

Its universal mastering enabled editors to edit 24-frame progressive content at the push of a button, and deliver NTSC, PAL, 4:3, 16:9 and letterbox formats. It could also output a list format, such as film cut lists and 24 frames/EDL for HD conforming. The machine was said to result in greater speed and efficiency.[84]

In August 1999, it was announced that Charles Steinberg had been given the Academy of Television Arts and Sciences Lifetime Achievement Award. He had retired as president of Sony's Broadcast and Professional Company on June 30, 1999. Steinberg had been president of the Ampex Corp. where he had worked from 1958 to 1963 as executive vice president, then president, then chief executive officer from 1963 to 1988. It was during this period that Sony continued its phenomenal growth and Ampex went into its fatal decline.[85]

In September 1999, it was announced that Seattle/Portland ABC affiliates had selected Ampex DST's 312 digital tape drives to archive commercial material and free up space on video servers.[86]

Nineteen ninety-nine ended on a sad note. On October 2, Akio Morita, founder and great entrepreneur of the Sony Corporation, died at the age of 78. Morita had suffered a stroke in 1994 that left him in a wheelchair. He died in a Tokyo hospital from pneumonia. One could not praise him more for his efforts to advance television.[87]

Postmortem: I initially was determined not to make any predictions about the future of television. As tricky as it would be, however, I decided against my own better judgment to go ahead anyway. As comic Mort Sahl often stated, "The future lies ahead." Enough said. As the year 2000 started, the future of television was never so murky. One thing is certain, television as we know it today will be vastly changed. The one single act that changed TV's future forever was the failure of the FCC to set a single high-definition standard. Instead, it allowed each broadcaster to pick from a myr-

1987. The author (right) with Ray Dolby in San Francisco, CA, September 1987. (Collection of the author.)

1999. Akio Morita, founder of Sony, died October 2, 1999. (Sony Corp.)

iad (18) of standards the one (or ones) that would allow them to transmit several programs within their allotted channel. This (reminiscent of the AM stereo fiasco) left both the broadcasters and the public in a quandary. As a result, the amount of HDTV broadcasting is minimal and the public today only has the choice of buying an $8,000 to $10,000 set (plus a decoder) that may or may not receive this programming. So they are sitting by waiting for the smoke to clear. Television as we know it will make a last-gasp effort to maintain both terrestrial networks and cable companies. The competition will be ferocious.

The emergence of the worldwide Internet has changed everything. It is almost certain that every Internet user will ultimately have their own camera and sound system. They will communicate with anyone (who is connected) anywhere in the world. There may come the day when every neighborhood will have its own transmitting station. Surely every store and business will have the same. Advertising, as we know, will be rampant.

Publishing both books and magazines will change drastically. There will be no need to print millions of magazines when they can be sent electronically to the home without paper. (We will save the forests!) Instead each home will have a reading device connected to its computer and every week, *Time* or *Newsweek* will transmit (download) to its subscribers the latest issue. Even daily newspapers will be affected. Every day one's "paper" will come into the home (in a slightly larger form), complete with all of the news, sports and other news of the day. The latest book (upon subscription) will come into the home entirely digitally, to be read in an electronic book-shaped device. The contents can be saved in some type of memory device for future reading or simply thrown away (erased).

There will be no more TV rental stores for pictures or music. These will be downloaded right into the home (for a price) and played on a beautiful 40- or 50-inch color flat screen in dazzling high-definition with multidimensional sound.

People will still like to go the movies. However, all "films" will be projected electronically (E-Cinema) by means of microwave, videodisc or cassette. No more thousands of film prints to be shipped or destroyed when their play is over. All movies will be shot on 24-frame *videotape* (not film); they will be edited, and the special effects added, on tape. This should cut the costs of making movies, and the hope is that the savings will be put into better pictures. (I doubt this, knowing how the industry operates.) However, will the studios help pay theater owners for the costly changeover to E-Projection? This is the major problem area. Why should the theater owners pay these enormous sums to change their theaters? Actually, they will be getting no advantage at all. The public is quite satisfied with normal 35mm film projection and couldn't care less how the film is presented. E-Projection offers them nothing they don't have at the moment. There is talk of using E-Projection for "live" events such as football games, special events and the like. (This brings back memories of the fifties when large-screen theatre TV promised the same thing.) There may be some subsidies from the major TV manufacturers who might see a worldwide market for large-screen projectors in a variety of non-television venues such as school auditoriums, corporate conference rooms, and defense installations. However, it is doubtful that the major film studios will do anything unless dragged by their hair. The road ahead is dim, rocky and filled with traps.[88]

Notes

Chapter 1
Television and World War II (1942–1945)

1. Robert Sobel, *RCA*, Stein and Day, New York, 1986, pp. 137–139. Eugene Lyons, *David Sarnoff*, Harper & Row, New York, 1966, pp. 232–235. Kenneth Bilby, *The General: David Sarnoff*, Harper & Row, New York, 1986, pp. 156–157.

2. Joseph C. Boyce, editor, *New Weapons for Air Warfare*, Little, Brown, Boston, 1947, p. 228.

3. V. K. Zworykin, "Flying Torpedo with an Electric Eye," *RCA Review*, 7 Sept. 1946, pp. 293–302. See also Bilby, op. cit., pp. 156–157.

4. "RCA and NBC Telecast Program from Plane in NYC," *New York Times*, March 17, 1940, p. 25:5.

5. Lyons, op. cit., pp. 224–225. See also Albert Abramson, *Zworykin, Pioneer of Television*, University of Illinois Press, Urbana and Chicago, 1995, p. 171.

6. Abramson, op. cit., p. 173.

7. Hugh Dryden, *Aerodynamics of Aircraft Bombs, 1927*.

8. Boyce, op. cit., pp. 228–229.

9. J. McQuay, "TV Takes to the Air," *Radio News*, Feb. 1947. "TV Reconnaissance," *Electronic Industries*, May 1946, p. 96.

10. *New York Times*, Mar 22, 1946, p. 16.

11. McQuay, op. cit.

12. R. E. Shelby, F. J. Somers, and L. B. Moffett, "TV Reconnaissance," *Electronic Industries*, May 1946, p. 96.

13. "Naval Airborne Television Reconnaissance System," *Television*, vol. 4, *RCA Review* (1942–1946), p. 370.

14. E. Redpath, et al., "Television Development and Application in Germany," Office of Technical Services, Washington, DC, BIOS Final Report no. 867, 1946.

15. Gerhart Goebel, "Das Fernsehen in Deutschland bis zum Jahre 1945," *Archiv für das Post- und Fernmeldewesen*, Frankfurt, August 1953, no 5. p. 379. I had the honor of visiting Herr Goebel and his lovely wife in 1979 in Darmstadt. He related his long experiences in German television before and during the war that resulted in this magnificent paper. Sadly he was badly crippled from a leg operation that gave him constant pain. But he was the perfect host, plying me and my wife with loads of wine and food. He gave me an autographed copy which has been a great source of information about television in general which I cherish. We corresponded for many years until his untimely death.

16. W. A. Atherton, "Pioneers, Walter Bruch," *Electronics & Wireless World*, November 1988, pp. 1101–1102.

17. Walter Bruch, *Die Fernsehe Geschichte*, Telekosmos-Verlag Stuttgart, 1969, pp. 138–139.

18. Frithjoh Rudert, "50 Years of Fernsehen 1929–1979" (Bosch publication), 1979.

19. See article by William Uricchio. It is from an unnamed journal p. 194. See Combined Intelligence Objectives Subcommittee (CIOS) Report no. 28–41, no. 31–1, no 31–8; British Intelligence Objectives Subcommittee (BIOS) Report no. 867; Public Records Office (London) AIR MIN files 40/1650, 40/2000. The supposed cooperation between Telefunken and RCA was not possible. David Sarnoff would not have permitted RCA to give any aid to any German company during this period.

20. Goebel, op. cit., p. 380.

21. C. J. Marshall and L. Katz, "Television Equipment for Guided Missiles," *Proc. Inst. Radio Engrs.*, June 1946, vol. 34 no 6, pp. 375–401.

22. "Tele-Guided Missiles," *Electronic Industries*, May 1946, vol. 5, pp. 62–65, 118.

23. "Remington-Rand Shows Video Camera Used in Project," *Broadcasting*, Nov. 5, 1945, pp. 44. "Tele-Guided Missiles," *Electronic Industries*, May 1946, vol. 5, pp. 62–65, 118. See also "A question of Law," by H. Newcomb Morse, *EDN*, March 20, 1980, pp. 113–115, 118.

24. Boyce, op. cit., p. 241.

25. A. Rose, P. K. Weimer, and H. B Law, "The Image Orthicon — A Sensitive Television Pick-up Tube," *Proc I. R. E.*, vol. 34, July 1946, pp. 424–432.

26. P. K. Weimer, H. B. Law, and S. V. Forgue, "Mimo-Miniature Image Orthicon," *RCA Review*, vol. VII no 3, Sept 1946, pp. 358–366.

27. Boyce, op. cit., pp. 249–265.

28. Boyce, op. cit., p. 244.

29. Robert M. Fraser, "Motion picture photography of television images," *RCA Review*, vol. 9, June 1948, pp. 202–217.

30. This was first reported in 1946 in *Television* by Baker who wrote, "Within this country, military television equipment played its part in the Manhattan Project and in other wartime manufacturing processes which required constant surveillance of operations too dangerous to be approached by men themselves." G. M. K. Baker, "Military Television," *Television* vol. IV (1942–1946), January 1947, p. 354.

31. More information has come from the FOIA through the Dept. of Energy. At the moment, I can also report the following information from Carl A. Holloman, CID agent, to Officer in Charge, Clinton Engineer Works, Oak Ridge, TN, memorandum, Nov. 21, 1944 — I received this document from the Department of Army Intelligence on Nov. 18, 1993. Oak Ridge was the home of K25, Y12 and X10, where atomic bomb materials were being processed.

32. V. K. Zworykin, E.G. Ramberg, and L. E. Flory, *Television in Science and Industry*, John Wiley & Sons, Inc., New York, 1958, pp. 22–23.

33. Richard Rhodes, *"The Making of the Atomic Bomb,"* Simon and Schuster, New York, 1986, p. 604. (According to Rhodes there were three of them operating at Hanford [p. 602].)

34. Rachel Fermi and Esther Samra, *Picturing the Bomb: Photographs from the Secret World of the Manhattan Project*, Harry N. Abrams, New York, 1995, p. 74.

35. From Hanford Engineer Works technical manual, document number HW-10475, Section C dated May 1, 1944, pp. 1011–1012. Received October 23, 1988.

36. *The New World*, p. 220–221. Baker in "Military Television" also stated (page 354), that television had been used by the military to avoid placing personnel at dangerous observation sites (see note 30 above). This was reiterated by A. G. Jensen in "The Evolution of Modern Television (1930–1954)," *Jour. SMPTE*, 63, Nov 1954, pp. 174–188. In May 1991, he stated that "image dissectors were used in industrial applications such as reading of instruments in inaccessible or dangerous locations." Unfortunately I have not been able to get a picture of this equipment. But see note 37 for details of the installation at Hanford.

37. Gene Weisskopf, Hanford message by Internet dated 18 November 1999. Also the following document sent by mail: *"DESIGN AND PROCUREMENT HISTORY OF HANFORD ENGINEER WORKS* U.S Contract W-7412-Eng-1 DuPont Project 9536 and Clinton Semi-Works U.S. Contract W-7412-Eng-23 Du Pont Project 9733 From the Engineering Department E. I. Du Pont De Nemours and Company (Inc) Wilmington, Delaware, December 1945," pp. 189–191.

38. P. Hæmardinquer, "Television in France," *Electronic Engineering*, 17 Sept. 1945, pp. 692–693.

39. Paul Mandel, "1015-Line Television Apparatus of the Compagnie des Compteurs, Montrouge," *L'Onde Elec.*, Jan. 1946, vol. 26, no 226, pp. 26–37.

40. Paul Mandel, "L'Appareillage de Télévision à 1015 lignes de la Compagnie des Compteurs, à Montrouge," *Société française des Electriciens*, 7 July 1945, pp. 31–33.

41. René Barthelemy, "The Isoscope: A Slow-Electron Image Analyser," *L'Onde Elec.*, Nov. 1945, vol. 20–25, pp. 103–115.

42. Goebel, op. cit., pp. 380–382. See also P. Hæmardinquer, "Television in France," *Electronic Engineering*, 17 Sept. 1945, pp. 692–693; "Television in France," *Jour. TV Society*, vol. 4, 1944–46, pp. 96, 224–225.

43. Charles Fabry, "Fernand Holweck (1890–1941)," *Cahiers de Physique*, 8 June 1942, pp. 1–16.

44. "Television in France," *Jour. TV Society*, vol. 4, no 9, 1945, pp. 224–225.

45. IRE for 1945 in records.

46. *New York Times*, 1945.

47. *Ibid.*, or probably IRE records.

48. M. G. Scroggie, "The Genius of A. D. Blumlein," *Wireless World*, vol. 66, Sept. 1960, 451–456. "A. D. Blumlein — an Electronic Genius," *Electronics and Power*, vol. 13, June 1967, pp. 218–224.

49. "Browder J. Thompson, 1903–1944," *Proc. of the IRE*, vol. 33, Feb 1945, p. 71.

50. Michael Hallett, *John Logie Baird and Television*, Priory Press Ltd., East Sussex, 1978, p. 78.

51. The (London) *Times*, Dec. 19, 1941; "Baird High Def Colour TV," *Jour. TV Society*, May 1942, p. 19.

52. G. Parr, "Review of Progress in Colour Television," *Jour. TV Society*, Dec. 1942.

53. "J. L. Baird 'Telechrome,'" *Jour. Royal Television Society*, 1944/1947, pp. 58–59. "Electronic Color Television," *Electronic Industries*, November 1944, p. 101. "Telechrome," *Radio-Craft*, December 1944, p. 149.

54. T. C. M. Lance, "Swiss Television Large Screen Projector," *Elec. Eng.*, Dec. 1944, pp. 294–296.

55. Peter C. Goldmark, *Maverick Inventor*, Saturday Review Press/E. P. Dutton & Co., New York, 1973, pp. 66–83. See the Chapter entitled "The Fake Navy."

56. Sally Bedell Smith, *In All His Glory*, Simon and Schuster, New York, 1990, pp. 207–227. William S. Paley, *As It Happened: A Memoir*, Doubleday & Company, Garden City, New York, 1979, pp. 154–171.

57. *Radio News*, op. cit., October 1944.

58. *Wireless World*, May 1945, TV Committee Report, pp. 130–132. This report was published in March 1945. Briggs, op. cit., vol. IV, p. 187.

59. Briggs, op. cit., p. 187.

60. *Broadcasting*, op. cit., Oct. 29, 1945, p. 94.

61. *New York Times*, Dec. 2, 1945.

62. *New York Times*, Dec. 14, 1945, 20:01.

63. *Broadcasting*, Dec. 17, 1945, p. 99.

64. René Barthélemy, "The Isoscope: A Slow Electron Image Analyser," *L'Onde Electrique*, vol. 25, November 1945, 103–115. Paul Mandel, "L'Appareillage de Télévision à 1015 lignes de la Compagnie des Compteurs, à Montrouge, *Société française des Electriciens*, 7 July 1945, pp. 31–33.

65. "French Continued Video Work Despite War, Observer Reports," *Broadcasting * Telecasting*, Dec. 10, 1945, p. 42. René Barthélemy, "The Isoscope: A Slow Electron Image Analyser," *L'Onde Electrique*, vol. 25, November 1945, 103–115. Paul Mandel, "L'Appareillage de Télévision à 1015 lignes de la Compagnie des Compteurs, à Montrouge, *Société française des Electriciens*, 7 July 1945, pp. 31–33. H. Delaby, "The Paris Television Transmitting Centre," *Jour. TV Society*, 1945, pp. 307–313.

Chapter 2
The Postwar Era (1946–1949)

1. Bilby, op. cit., p. 138.

2. Sobel, op. cit., p. 150.

3. "RCA Color TV Status," *Electronic Industries*, March 1946, pp. 102, 135–138.

4. W. R. Fraser and G. J. Badgley, "Motion Picture Color Photography of Color Television Images," *Jour. SMPTE*, June 1950, p. 736.

5. *New York Times*, March 22, 16:1.

6. J. McQuay, "TV Takes to the Air" *Radio News*, Feb 1947. "TV Reconnaissance," *Electronic Industries*, May 1946, p. 96.

7. *New York Times*, Mar. 27, 12:6.

8. Don Drenner, "Engineer Finds Magnetophon Superior," *Broadcasting*, November 19, 1945, pp. 36–84. "German Tape-recording Equipment," *Electronic Industries*, Nov. 1945.

9. *AUDIO*, August 1984, p. 96.

10. John T. Mullin, "Creating the Craft of Tape Recording," *High Fidelity Magazine*, April 1976, pp. 62–67.

11. Mullin's obituary noted, "Mullin's love of classical music and his support of public radio led to his work as a volunteer engineer and on-air talent at KCPB-FM in Thousand Oaks, California,

and at KZYX-FM in Philo, California. His tenor voice was well known to local public radio audiences as he played his favorite classical music and offered his views on the art of performance and the history of recording.

"He was a Fellow and Honorary Member of the Audio Engineering Society, a recipient of the Emile Berliner Award, and was an elected member of the 3M Carlton Society."

According to Snell, the specifications for the original machine were (1) tape speed roughly 40"/sec (2) frequency range almost straight from 50 to 5000 cycles; (3) noise level — 35db; and (4) pre-magnetisation and erasure by DC current (18).

12. For the full story, see Harold Lindsay, "Magnetic Recording Part 1," *db Magazine*, Dec. 1977, pp. 38–44.

13. *AUDIO*, op. cit., August 1984, p. 97.

14. Briggs, op. cit., p. 199.

15. *Elect. Eng.*, Jan. 1947, p. 31, with picture.

16. B. Clapp, "John L. Baird — Television Pioneer," *Electronic Engineering*, August 1946, pp. 236–237. Sydney Mosely, "John Baird," *Wireless World*, July 1946, p. 246.

17. "TV Today," *Electronic Industries*, August 1946, p. 86.

18. Goldmark, op. cit., see p. 24.

19. *Electronic Industries*, January 1946, p. 178.

20. Bilby, op. cit., p. 181.

21. Peter C. Goldmark, *Maverick Inventor*, pp. 66–83, 182.

22. Kenneth Bilby, *The General*, Harper & Row, New York, 1986, pp. 181–182.

23. William Paley, *As It Happened*, Doubleday & Co., New York, 1979, p. 223. For a total cost of $20 million.

24. Paley, op. cit., p. 280.

25. *Ibid.*, p. 222.

26. Briggs, op. cit., pp. 10–11, 208–209, vol. IV.

27. Gordon Ross, *Television Jubilee*, W. H. Allen, London, 1961, pp. 68–72.

28. R. D. Kell, "An Experimental Simultaneous Color Television System, Part I — Introduction," *Proc. IRE*, Sept. 1947, pp. 861–862; and G. Z. Sziklai, R. C. Ballard and A. C. Schroeder, "Part II — Pickup Equipment," *Proc. IRE*, Sept. 1947, pp. 862–870.

29. *Broadcasting*, Nov. 4, 1946.

30. Bruce Robertson, "RCA Shows Electronic Color Video," *Broadcasting*, May 5, 1947.

31. J. L. Boon, W. I. Feldman, and J. Stoiber, "Television Recording Camera," August 1948, *Jour. SMPTE*, pp. 117–126.

32. Thomas T. Goldsmith and Harry Milholland, "Television Transcriptions," paper presented before *SMPTE*, October 1947. Date is from *Broadcasting*, p. 16, December 15, 1947.

33. "Development and Performance of TV Camera Tubes," *RCA Review*, June 1949, p. 191.

34. "90% Cut in Studio Light Needs Claimed for RCA's New Image Orthicon Camera," *Broadcasting*Telecasting*, June 23, 1947, p. 19.

35. Zworykin, op. cit., p. 194.

36. "TV Export Possibilities," *Tele-Tech*, March 1948, p. 90.

37. Bilby, op. cit., p. 173.

38. *Electronics*, July 1947, p. 190.

39. Albert Abramson, *Electronic Motion Pictures*, University of California Press, Berkeley, 1955, p. 117.

40. *Ibid.*, p. 116.

41. "Ross TV Jubilee," op. cit., p. 74.

42. Arthur B. Bronwell, "The Chromoscope," *Electronic Engineering*, June 1948, pp. 190–191.

43. R. B. Janes, R. E. Johnson, and R. R. Handel, "A New Image Orthicon," *RCA Review*, Dec. 1949, pp. 586–592.

44. *Wireless World*, op. cit., Feb. 1948.

45. *Ibid.*, Feb. 1948.

46. Amos, D. C. Birkenshaw and J. L. Bliss, "TV Engineering," 1953, p. 94, 100–101.

47. "The New Television Camera," *Electronic Eng.*, Feb. 1948, p. 59.

48. T. H. Pratt, "The Infra-Red Image Converter Tube," *Elec. Engineering*, Sept. 1948, p. 277.

49. Abramson, *Electronic Motion Pictures*, pp. 117–118.

50. Byron H. Spiers, "ABC Used Magnetic Tape for Delayed Broadcasts," *Radio and Television News*, April 1950, pp. 41, 42.

51. Goldsmith, *TV*, Vol. VI.

52. Goldsmith, *RCA Review*, 1946.

53. Goldsmith, *RCA Review*, *1946*.

54. Goldsmith, *RCA Review*, Vol. VI, p. 346.

55. Fraser, op. cit., *RCA Review*, June 1948.

56. *Sobel*, op. cit., pp. 92–93.

57. Goldmark, op. cit., p. 142.

58. *New York Times*, July 1, 1948.

59. "Transistor May Replace Vacuum Tubes," *Tele-Tech*, August 1948, pp. 17–20.

60. *New York Times*, June 13, 1948.

61. Abramson, *Electronic Motion Pictures*, op. cit., pp. 128–129.

62. *Ibid.*, p. 128.

63. L. C. Jesty, "Review of Television Recording 1946–1956," *British Kinematography*, October 1957, vol. 31, no 4, pp. 87–103.

64. E. Aisberg, "Cinema Television," *Radio-Electronics*, April 1949, p. 31.

65. Abramson, *Electronic Motion Pictures*, p. 157. I am indebted to an article in the July 1951 issue of *Jour. SMPTE*, by E. A. Hungerford, Jr., entitled "Techniques for the Production of Electronic Motion Pictures," pp. 18–22. It was the first article that I found that gave the advantages of the making of motion pictures by electronic means. Hungerford worked for General Precision Laboratories who were making television recorders as well as television cameras at the time.

Reaction to *Electronic Motion Pictures* (published in 1955) was quick at first. There were several mentions in the trades (without mentioning the book by name) referring to the demise of all film-making. This soon died down and it wasn't until May 1969 that Dr Wilton R. Holm, Executive director, Motion Picture and Television Research Center, took exception to that part of my book (Wilton Holm, "Communications Technology of the Future," in the *American Cinematographer*, May 1969, p. 467) where I predicted that "the film camera had been replaced by the electronic television camera, motion picture film is being superseded by magnetic tape and even the motion picture projector is giving way to the large screen electronic reproducer." He thought that I had been caught up in the wave of enthusiasm for an outstanding technological innovation, namely videotape recording. He was right of course. At the time, 1955, to me the advent of videotape recording was the greatest event of the 20th century. He pointed out, "Today, almost fifteen years later, there is more film used than ever before. Videotape recording has also flourished, and most probably will continue to do so, as far as we can see at the time." He was, of course, correct. My *crystal ball* had told me such a revolution would take about 25 to 30 years, or take place about the years 1980 or 1985 at the latest. Yet today film is still dominant in both ends of film production. Most major motion pictures are still shot on 35mm motion picture film and no Electronic Cinema has occurred. Thirty-five millimeter film is still distributed and shown in theaters all over the world. Of course, the rest of the production process is in the electronic domain with everything from viewfinding (video assist), special effects done with computers, and editing all done electronically. The revolution will still take place, but at this time I would not venture a guess as to the time frame. (My crystal ball needs a new microchip!) The May 1979 *Jour. SMPTE*, ("Progress Committee Report for 1978," p. 285) also took me to task. They stated that the imminent death of film had been predicted regularly. "But film laboratories show an increase in footage processed, box office revenue is up 15%, and in TV 81% of the prime time network programming was on film, a 4% gain over last year." I never wanted the demise of the film industry; all that I wanted was a more efficient and less costly means of production and distribution. By the year 2000 it has finally begun to come to fruition. Instead of being called large screen theater television (which it is), it is called E-Cinema.

66. Abramson, *Electronic Motion Pictures*, p. 157.

67. *Ibid.*, pp. 157–158.

68. *Ibid.*, p. 165. *New York Times*, June 13, 1948.

69. Ross, *TV Jubilee*, p. 75.

70. Briggs, op. cit., p. 273.

71. Ross, *TV Jubilee* pp. 75–76.

72. R. W. Hallows, "Why the 405 standard is the best," *Wireless World*, Dec. 1948.

73. *Elec. Engineering*, Nov 1948.

74. "The Video Freeze," *New York Times*, October 3, 1948. Also *New York Times*, October 1, 1948.

75. "Radio and Television," *New York Times*, November 18, 1948, p. 54.

76. "The 1949 NAB Broadcasting Engineering Conference," *Communications*, May 1949, p. 8.

77. R. B. Janes, R. E. Johnson and R. R. Handel. "A New Image Orthicon," *RCA Review*, Dec. 1949.

78. H. B. Fancher, "TV 16-mm Pulsed-light projector," *Communications*, July 1949, pp. 14-16.

79. E. I. Aisberg, "French High Definition," by *Radio-Electronics*, March 1949, pp. 58–59.

80. *Electronic Eng.*, Mar 1949, *p. 74.*

81. See USA Pat. no. 2,622,220, filed March 22, 1949; issued Dec. 16, 1952.

82. "New Directions in Color Television," *Electronics*, Dec. 1949, pp 71.

83. John H. Battison, "Color Television Transmission Systems," *Tele-Tech*, Oct. 1949, pp. 18–20, 52.

84. Roger D. Thompson, "A Cathode-Ray Tube Scanner," *Communications*, Sept. 1949, pp. 24–25, 33.

85. R. B. Janes, R. E. Johnson, and R. R. Handel, "A New Image Orthicon," *RCA Review*, Dec. 1949, pp. 586–592.

86. Zworykin and Morton, op. cit., V. K. Zworykin and G. A. Morton, *Television*, 2nd edition, John Wiley & Sons, New York, 1954, p. 373.

87. "Tube Engineering News (5820 Image Orthicon)" *RCA Review*, Dec. 1949 p. 500. *Communications*, Sept. 1949, p. 28–29.

88. P. K. Weimer, "The Image Isocon, An Experimental TV Pickup Tube Based on the Scattering of Low Velocity Electrons," *RCA Review*, vol. 10, Sept. 1949, pp. 366–386. See USA Pat. no. 2,579,351, applied Aug 30, 1949; issued Dec. 17, 1951.

Chapter 3
The Second NTSC and Color (1950–1953)

1. "Videotape," *Electronics*, Feb. 1950, p. 65.

2. *New York Times*, Jan 22, 1950, III: 1,2

3. *Radio News*, April 1950.

4. Issue of *Radio and TV News*, March 1950, p. 18.

5. Fink, *Electronics*, August 1951, pp. 90–93. Fink, 1952, p. 26.

6. *New York Times*, Feb. 9, 1950, 34:4.

7. Franklin Loomis, "Interim Report on Color TV Hearings," *Tele-Tech*, January 1950, pp. 36–50.

8. "BBC Television Progress," *Electronic Engineering*, March 1950, p. 110.

9. Ross, *TV Jubilee*, pp. 75–76.

10. "The European Broadcast Union," *Jour. SMPTE*, April 1990, p. 335.

11. Briggs, op. cit., p. 278; "Boat Race," *Briggs*, op. cit., pp. 273.

12. *New York Times*, Mar 8, 1950, 52:1

13. *Tele-Tech*, April 1950.

14. Albert Rose, *Vision: Human and Electronic*, Plenum Press, New York–London, 1974, p. 72.

15. Weimer et al., *Electronics* or *RCA Review*, 1950

16. Zworykin TV, *Science and Industry*, p. 55.

17. Zworykin and Morton, p. 376. See also P. K. Weimer, S. V. Forgue, and R. R. Goodrich, "The Vidicon Photoconductive Camera Tube," *Electronics*, vol. 23, pp. 70–73, May 1950 or *RCA Review*, vol. 12, pp. 306–313.

18. Zworykin and Morton, p. 376. (See USA Pat. no. 2,810,257, S. V. Forgue, applied Nov. 29, 1950; issued Oct. 15, 1957.)

19. *Wireless World*, May 1950, pp. 162–163.

20. George H. Brown, *And Part of Which I Was*, Angus Cupar Publishers, Princeton, New Jersey, 1982, p. 198.

21. *Ibid.*

22. Dr. Ed Herold, *RCA Engineer*, June/July 1974. Harold B. Law, "The Shadow Mask Color Picture Tube: How it Began," *Jour. SMPTE*, April 1977, pp. 214–221. "Color Television Issue," *Proc. IRE*, October 1951.

23. Brown, op. cit., p. 199.

24. *New York Times*, April 7, 1950, 44:5.

25. *Ibid.*

26. *Tele-Tech*, May 1950, p. 20

27. Bilby, op. cit., p. 185.

28. *Ibid.*

29. Paley, op. cit., p. 222.

30. *New York Times* ? 29, 1950, 73:3.

31. *Electronic Engineering*, June 1950, p. 214.

32. P. Mandel, "Reversible Process for Recording on and Electronic Reproduction from Cinematograph Film," *Engineering*, London, 22 August 1952, vol. 174, no. 4517, pp. 206–213.

33. *New York Times*, July 9, 1950, 18:4.

34. See Douglas Gomery, "Theatre Television: A History," *Jour. SMPTE*, February 1989, pp. 120–123.

35. Sydney Head, "Broadcasting in America," 1972, p. 227.

36. *Ibid.*, pp. 228–229.

37. Vidicam System from *Engineering*, July 1950, p. 27. It was announced by William Van Praag, VP of Television Features Inc.

38. Dr. Werner Fleschig, DRP Pat. no. 736,575, filed July 12, 1938; issued May 13, 1943.

39. W. R. Fraser and G. J. Badgley, "Video Recording in Color," *Tele-Tech*, August 1950.

40. Brown, op. cit., p. 211

41. Goldmark, op. cit., pp. 108–109.

42. *Radio and TV News*, September 1950, p. 106.

43. Bilby, op. cit., p184.

44. From Goldmark, p. 109.

45. Goldmark, p. 108.

46. An unidentifiable newspaper clipping.

47. Brown, op. cit., p. 206.

48. *Tele-Tech*, October 1950, p. 26.

49. Coy.

50. *New York Times*, Sept. 16, 1950, 32:7.

51. "The FCC Color-TV Decision," *Tele-Tech*, Oct. 1950, pp. 26–27.

52. *New York Times*, Nov 21 and Oct 12, 1:6. Brown, op. cit., p. 213.

53. *New York Times*, Dec 6, 1:2.

54. *New York Times*, 24 June 1951, "Color TV Is Here," p. X9. (Fink, 1955 p.10)

55. Fink, 1955, p. 10.

56. *New York Times*, Oct. 20, 1951.

57. Paley, op. cit., p. 210.

58. "New Color Tube for TV Created," *New York Times*, Oct. 6, 1953.

59. *New York Times*, Mar. 23, 1951.

60. *New York Times*, June 20, 1951. Also in *Tele-Tech*, August 1951, p. 57.

61. E. A. Hungerford, "Techniques for the Production of Electronic Motion Pictures," *Jour. SMPTE*, July 1951, pp. 18–22. This of course was the first time I had heard this term. I was intrigued by it and started the research that led to my first book entitled, *Electronic Motion Pictures* (University of California Press, Berkeley, CA, 1955).

62. See *Tele-Tech*, August 1951, p. 57.

63. "NTSC Panels Reorganized for Color-TV," *Tele-Tech*, August 1951, p. 57.

64. "NTSC Color Field Test Specifications," *Tele-Tech*, Jan. 1952, pp. 61, 102–103. Also Brown, op. cit., pp. 221–222.

65. *Wireless World*, November 1951, p. 461.

66. "Simplified Operating Keynoted In New TV Equipment," *Tele-Tech*, October 1951, pp. 94–49, 68.

67. "Paris Television Show — Domestic Receivers for Two Standards," by A. V. J. Martin, *Wireless World*, Nov. 1951, p. 459.

68. "New Lawrence Tricolor Tube Shown," *Electronics*, November 1951, pp. 146–147.

69. "Analysis of Lawrence Color-TV Tube" by J. H. Battison, *Tele-Tech*, November 1951, pp. 38–39.

70. "Television Broadcasting in Holland," *Jour. TV Society*, Oct./Dec. 1951, vol. 6, no. 8, p. 299.

71. *New York Times*, May 27, 1951.

72. From Abramson, *Jour. SMPTE*, Mar. 1973.

73. Michael McClay, "I Love Lucy," *Warner Books*, 1995, p. 32.

74. *New York Times*, October 15, 1951, 11:1; October 20, 1951, 1:2.

75. *New York Times*, Nov 12, 1951.

76. "Videotape Recording," *Tele-Tech & Electronic Industries*, May 1952, p. 64.

77. Jack Mullin, "Videotape Recording — Need for a Magnetic Video Recorder," presented Thursday, April 30, 1953. (See USA Patent applied for on November 14, 1950; Mullin; 2,794,066; issued May 28, 1957.)

78. In "Forum," *IEE Spectrum*, August 1996, p. 6, Dr. Camras's sons, Michael and Robert, stated "that their father had actually given a demonstration of his contemplated video recorder to Ampex engineers." There has never been any proof of such a demonstration. The logistics were against him. For Camras to have built such a complicated device and to record and play back pictures would have been a Herculean task. There was more involved than just dragging a piece of tape across rotating heads. He certainly would have taken pictures of such a device to prove his priority. All that exists is the mockup that he showed me. But the idea certainly was his, for which we give him great credit.

79. See letter, dated 23 November 1951, from Myron J. Stoloroff to Mr. Long, Poniatoff, Selsted. (In Ginsburg file.)

80. Stewart Wolpin, "The Race to Video," *Invention & Technology*, Fall 1994, pp. 52–62. This is an interesting article on the Ampex project. He makes a few errors in it. For instance on page 54 he asserts that Dr. Camras "used two inch tape." There is absolutely no proof that Camras ever demonstrated anything but a mockup. He repeated this mistake on page 55 when he said that they "saw a casual demonstration of his rotating-head recorder." This never happened. On page 58 Wolpin stated, "Ginsburg would play dumb whenever Mullin asked about his video experiments." This is not true. Mullin knew about the video project and he told me so in 1953, but he didn't think it would work. As a result, I left out the name of Ampex in my first book *Electronic Motion Pictures*, a scoop that I regretted failing to make ever since. On page 60 he gives

Maxey credit for turning the head drum around. This was actually the idea of Walter Selsted, according to a letter he wrote me on June 10, 1998. Also the use of the term "Quad" is in error. Ampex never used such a term. This was invented by RCA to differentiate between the Ampex transverse machine and their clone.

81. Charles P. Ginsburg, *The Birth of Videotape Recording*, Publication of AMPEX, March 1981. "According to Conversation with Charles Ginsburg," *Videography*, April 1983, pp. 66. The date was January 21, 1952 (p. 61).

82. See Paul D. Flehr, "Charles P. Ginsburg, Videotape Recorder," *Inventors and Their Inventions*, Pacific Books, Palo Alto, 1990, p. 68.

83. See "Conversation with Charles Ginsburg," *Videography*, April 1983, p. 64.

84. Ray Dolby, "30th VTR Anniversary — Some Personal Recollections," presented at 128th Technical Conference of SMPTE, October 24, 1986, p. 6. Ginsburg says October 1952. See "Conversation with Charles Ginsburg," *Videography*, April 1983, p. 64.

85. Charles Ginsburg, "The Horse or the Cowboy: Getting Television on Tape?" *Jour. Royal Television Society*, Nov./Dec. 1981, p. 12. See also "Conversation with Charles Ginsburg," *Videography*, April 1983, pp. 64–66. The first time I heard this story was on one of my many trips to Redwood City to interview him. During one interview he told me the story with a wonderful Russian accent. We both got a great laugh out of it. Then he told me that he had been invited to give the Shoenberg Lecture for the Royal Television Society which was a great honor. But being rather shy and unassuming he was rather reluctant to do so. So I of course emphasized to him what a great honor it would be. I had no idea that he would give the lecture the title he did. But he did have a very wry sense of humor. I was honored to know him.

86. "Conversation with Charles Ginsburg," *Videography*, April 1983, p. 64. Ray Dolby, "30th VTR Anniversary — Some Personal Recollections," presented at 128th Technical Conference of SMPTE, October 24, 1986, p. 14.

87. Charles P. Ginsburg, *The Birth of Videotape Recording*," publication of AMPEX, March 1981, p. 1.

88. Ray Dolby, "30th VTR Anniversary — Some Personal Recollections," presented at 128th Technical Conference of SMPTE, October 24, 1986, p.14.

89. Personal Interview with Ginsburg, April 1981, at Redwood City.

90. "Conversation with Charles Ginsburg," *Videography*, April 1983, p. 68.

91. *Ibid.*, p. 66.

92. Charles Ginsburg, "The Horse or the Cowboy: Getting Television on Tape?" *Jour. Royal Television Society*, Nov./Dec. 1981, p. 12. See also "On IEEE People," *The Institute*, vol. 10, #6, August 1986, p. 12. "Conversation with Charles Ginsburg," *Videography*, April 1983, p. 66.

93. Eduard Schüller, DRP Pat. no. 927,999, applied for July 13, 1953; published Sept. 23, 1954; and granted April 28, 1955.

94. Personal conversation with Mullin in April 1953. Mullin told me of the Ampex project using a rotating head. "AMPEX scanning across tape using rotating scanner." He had such little faith in it that I did not include Ampex in my 1955 book, *Electronic Motion Pictures*. I have regretted this ever since!

95. Marvin Camras, USA Pat. no. 2,900,444. Applied for January 12, 1953; issued August 18, 1959.

96. From "Broadband Recording Equipment." *Final report for Period 1 March 1953 to 20 May 54.* Prepared by Shoup Engineering Co., 1516 S. Wabash Ave, Chicago, Illinois, 5.

97. From "Interim Engineering Report No. 11. Wide Band Magnetic Recording System," G.E. Electronics Division, Syracuse, N.Y., 11 February 1955.

98. Brown, op. cit., p. 271.

99. Lyons, *David Sarnoff*, pp. 301–302. See also *New York Times*, Nov. 4, 1951.

100. This was confirmed by Brown, op. cit., p. 271.

101. Earl Masterson, USA Patent no. 2,773,120; issued Dec. 4, 1956.

102. Brown, op. cit., p. 271. See Masterson patent.

103. H. F. Olson, W. D. Houghton, A. R. Morgan, Joseph Zenel, Maurice Artzt, J. G. Woodward and J. T. Fischer, "A system for Recording and Reproducing Television Signals," *RCA Review*, March 1954, vol. XV, pp. 3–17.

104. Norman Collins and T. C. Macnamara, "High Definition Films," *British Kinematography*, August 1952, pp. 32–38.

105. Peter Wayne, "Making Films on Television for the Cinema," *Jour. Royal Television Society*, March/April 1953, p. 178.

106. "Transistor Device in First Test," *New York Times*, Mar. 4, 1952.

107. "TV Freeze lifted: 2,053 new stations to Blanket the Nation," *New York Times*, April 14, 1952, p. 1.

108. "Commons Gives B.B.C. Ten Year Extension," *New York Times*, June 24, 1952.

109. *New York Times*, August 9, 1952.

110. *Jour. TV Society* from *Wireless World*, August 1952.

111. "Eidophor Color TV System," *Radio-Electronics*, Sept. 1952, p. 10.

112. "Color TV status," *Radio-Electronic Engineering*, Jan. 1952, p. 2.

113. "The Eidophor Projector" by Aaron Nadall, *Radio-Electronics*, October 1952, pp. 33–35.

114. "Back-Pack Camera — TV's Roving Eye," *Tele-Tech*, Sept. 1952, p. 65. See also A. E. Ohler, "The "Walkie Lookie," a Miniaturized TV Camera, Custom Built for use by NBC at the National Conventions," *Broadcast News*, vol. 71, pp. 8–15, Sept./Oct. 1952.

115. "Mullin Speech on Videotape Recording," April 30, 1953, from *EMP*, p. 198.

116. "Tape-Recorded TV Nears Perfection," *New York Times*, Dec. 31, 1951.

117. "Bing's Mirror to Reflect in December," *Electronics*, Feb. 1953, p.8.

118. From *Daily Variety*, May 25, 1954, p. 8.

119. See Abramson, *History of Television, 1880 to 1941* (Jefferson, NC: McFarland, 1987), p. 168.

120. "Hand TV May Help Mother Eye Baby," *New York Times*, Mar. 27, 1953.

121. "Televising the Coronation," *Jour. TV Society*, 1953m pp.46–47.

122. "Net of Paramount Expected to Rise" *New York Times*, June 3, 1953, p. 52.

123. *New York Times*, June 3, 1953, 17:3.

124. *New York Times*, April 28, 55:1.

125. Jack Gould, "Television in Review: A Color Show," *New York Times*, October 9, 1953, p. 24.

126. Donald Fink, *Color Television Standards*, McGraw-Hill Book Company, Inc., New York, 1955, pp. 37–40.

127. *Ibid*.

128. "Coast to Coast TV is Shown in Color," *New York Times*, Nov. 4, 1953.

129. "Movies Put on Tape for TV 'Live' Color Show Replayed," *New York Times*, Dec. 2, 1953, p. 1? From *Daily Variety* May 25, 1954, p. 8. "Pictures on Tape," *Radio & TV News*, Feb. 1954, p. 56. "Recording TV on Magnetic Tape," by B. Osbahr, *Tele-Tech & Electronic Industries*, Jan. 1954, p. 81.

130. "Recording TV on Magnetic Tape," by B. Osbahr, *Tele-Tech & Electronic Industries*, January 1954. See also Harry F. Olson, W. D. Houghton, A. R. Morgan, M. Artzt, J. A. Zenal, and J. G. Woodward, "A Magnetic Tape System for Recording and Repro-ducing Standard FCC Color Television Signals," *RCA Review*, Sept. 1956, vol. XVII, pp. 330–392.

131. Jack Gould, "Radio and TV: Catching Up," *New York Times*, Dec. 13, 1953.

132. Brown, op. cit., p. 228.

133. *Ibid.*, pp. 228–229.

Chapter 4
The Ampex Revolution (1954–1956)

1. "Television In Review," *New York Times*, January 1, 1954, p. 19.

2. "TV Film Vidicon," *Radio-Electronic Engineering*, Jan. 1954, p. 20.

3. W. L. Hurford and R. J. Marian, "Monochrome Vidicon Film Camera," *RCA Review*, Sept. 1954, pp. 372–388.

4. A.C., French article, "Hommage A René Barthélemy, Member of the Institute," 1954.

5. "The Marconi Flying-Spot Telecine Equipment," *Jour. TV Society*, April-June 1954, p. 262.

6. "Video Magnetic Tape Recorder," *Tele-Tech & Electronic Industries*, May 1954, pp. 77, 127–129.

7. *Radio & Television News*, June 1954, p. 129.

8. *New York Times*, Sept. 20, 20:6.

9. T. C. Macnamara, "Electronic Film Making," *British Kinematography*, vol. 25, no. 4, October 1954, pp. 104–106.

10. T. C. Macnamara, "High Definition Films," *Jour. TV Society*, January-March 1955, vol. 7, no. 9, pp. 363–367. See also T. C. Macnamara, W. D. Kemp, A. M. Spooner. B. R. Greenhead, and N. Q. Lawrence, "New Studio Techniques at Highbury," *British Kinemagraphy*, vol. 25, no. 6, Dec. 1954, pp. 109–123.

11. *New York Times*, September 19, 1954.

12. Richard Pack (London), "English Experiment in Video Films," *New York Times*, Sept. 19, 1954.

13. L. Heijne, P. Schagen, and H. Bruining, "An Experimental Photoconductive Camera Tube for Television," *Philips Technical Review*, vol. 16, 1954/55, pp. 23–25. (See USA Pat. no. 2,890,359, convention date, June 13, 1953; L Heijne, J. Dorrestein, H. Bruining and Peter Shagen, applied June 15, 1954; issued June 15, 1954.)

14. *BBC Engineering Monograph*, no. 39, October 1961.

15. John Dickson, "Modern Optics," *International TV Technical Review*, September 1961, p. 13.

16. D. G. Smee, "Brief History of the 4 1/2 inch Image Orthicon," *Int. TV Tech. Review*, May 1962, p. 274.

17. "CBS Demonstrated 19-inch Color Tube" *Broadcasting Telecasting*, July 12, 1954, p. 76.

18. "CBS Color Patents Licensed to RCA," *Broadcasting Telecasting*, Dec. 20, 1954, p. 80.

19. Albert Abramson, *Zworykin, Pioneer of Television*, University of Illinois Press, Champagne, IL, 1995, pp. 198–199.

20. "Magnetic Recording — State of the Art," *Tele-Tech & Electronic Industries*, August 1954, pp. 94–95, 173.

21. Personal note from Selsted to author, June 10, 1998. According to Ginsburg it was for 160 man-hours. "Conversation with Charles Ginsburg," *Videography*, April 1983, p. 68. The Ampex patent for turning the head around was USA no. 2,866,0123, filed May 6, 1955; issued December 23, 1958 to C. P. Ginsburg and Shelby F. Henderson, Jr.

22. Charles P. Ginsburg, "The Horse or the Cowboy — Getting Television on Tape," *Jour. Royal Television Society*, Nov./Dec. 1981, p. 16. See A. R. Maxey, USA Patent no. 2,912,518, filed January 24, 1956; issued November 10, 1959. A similar British patent was filed on Jan. 11, 1950, by Richard Theile, British no. 686,009, issued January 14, 1953.

23. Joe Roizen, "A History of Videotape Recording" (Shoenberg Memorial Lecture), *Jour. TV Society*, vol. 16, no. 1, Jan./Feb. 1978, p. 20. Charles P. Ginsburg, "The Horse or the Cowboy — Getting Television on Tape," *Jour. Royal Television Society*, Nov./Dec. 1981, p. 12.

24. Ray Dolby, "30th VTR Anniversary — Some Personal Recollections," presented at 128th Technical Conference of SMPTE, October 24, 1986, p. 17.

25. *Ibid.*, p. 16.

26. *Ibid.*

27. Charles P. Ginsburg, "The Horse or the Cowboy — Getting Television on Tape," *Jour. Royal Television Society*, Nov./Dec. 1981, p. 13.

28. *Ibid.*

29. Charles P. Ginsburg, "The Birth of Videotape Recording," Ampex Brochure, March 1981, p. 3.

30. *Broadcasting Telecasting*, Jan. 17, 1955, p. 99. *Electronics*, Feb., March and Nov. 1955. Willys was compared with the three-color flat tube of Gabor in England. All from Jesty, *Jour. TV Society*, Oct./Dec. 1955 (paper read April 21, 1955).

31. George H. Brown, *And Part of Which I Was*, Angus Cupar Publishers, Princeton, New Jersey, 1982, pp. 274–275.

32. "Tape Used For Color TV on Network," *Electronics*, June 1955, p. 8. See also H. F. Olson, W. D. Houghton, A. R. Morgan, M. Artzt, J. A. Zenel, and J. G. Woodward, "A Magnetic Tape System for Recording and Reproducing Standard FCC Color Television Signals," *RCA Review*, Sept. 1956, pp. 330–392.

33. "Tape TV Color Success 'Beyond Dreams,' Says Mullin," *Broadcasting*Telecasting*, May 16, 1955, p. 7.

34. "Airborne Recorders," *Tele-Tech & Electronic Industries*, August 1955, p. 108.

35. *Broadcasting*, Aug. 15, 1955, p. 104.

36. Al Simon, "The Video-Film Camera," by *American Cinematographer*, March 1955, pp. 140, 164.

37. J. Caddigan and T. T. Goldsmith, Jr., "An Electronic-Film Combination Apparatus for Motion-Picture and Television Production," by *Jour. SMPTE*, January 1956, vol. 65.

38. "DuMs Live and Film Camera Focuses Industry Attention on Its Projected No-Cable Network Set for Fall Bow," *Variety*, Wednesday, April 20, 1955, p. 26.

39. "TV Webs to Film," *Variety*, April 20, 1955, p. 42.

40. "Moviemakers Use More Electronics," *Electronics*, October 1956, p. 30.

41. NBC Triniscope color system.

42. "Crosby Goal for Color Tape Commercial Use — 12–18 Mos," *Broadcasting*Telecasting*, Nov. 14, 1955, pp. 70,72–73. "The Video-Film Camera by Al Simon," *American Cinematographer*, March 1955, pp. 140, 164.

43. "Ampex TV Tape System in Experimental Stage," *Telecasting-Broadcasting*, Feb. 13, 1956, p. 109.

44. "*FINAL REPORT.* Research and Development. Wide Band Magnetic Recorder," to Rand Corp. from Ampex Corp., October 1957.

45. Mark Sanders, "The Ampex Development of the AST systems," *Video Systems*, April 1980, p. 47. See Figure 3 on p. 47. See also P. Hammar, "The Birth of Helical Scan Recording," *Broadcast Engineering*, May 1985, pp. 86–94. He states that a monochrome-only helical using two-inch tape and signal processing similar to the VR-1000 was produced in 1956 (p. 86). He shows a picture of Maxey with a helical scan prototype "circa 1957." The 1956 date is also repeated by Ginsburg in an interview, "Conversation with Charles Ginsburg," *Videography*, April 1983, p. 72, where he stated, "Helical machines made their appearance internally in 1956." Ginsburg also stated, "toward the end of 1956, Maxey came up with another proposal for a one-headed recorder, this time a helical wrap machine using two inch wide tape, an eight inch drum, a tape

speed of 15ips, a video head velocity of 1500ips and writing or reading a complete television field with each head pass." This last quote was from Charles P. Ginsburg, "The Horse or the Cowboy — Getting Television on Tape," *Jour. Royal Television Society*, Nov./Dec. 1981, p. 16.

46. Mark Sanders, "The Ampex Development of the AST systems," *Video Systems*, April 1980, p. 47. (Maxey filed for the first Ampex helical recorder on March 26, 1958; granted August 29, 1961.) See also J. Roizen, "Videotape Recorders" by *Broadcast Engineering*, April 1976 pp. 26–30.

47. "Spectacular Gains in TV Reported at IRE Meeting" *Broadcasting*Telecasting*, March 26, 1956, p. 96. See also H. R. L. Lamont, "Color TV on Tape," by *Wireless World*, April 1957, pp. 183–187.

48. "Color TV Industry Host to European Study Group," *Tele-Tech & Electronic Industries*, April 1956, p. 22.

49. "British Demonstrate Color Television," *Electronics*, May 1956, pp. 14–15.

50. "British Colour Television," *Wireless World*, April 1956, p. 181.

51. Ray Dolby, "30th VTR Anniversary — Some Personal Recollections," presented at 128th Technical Conference of SMPTE, October 24, 1986, p. 20.

52. Charles P. Ginsburg, "The Horse or the Cowboy — Getting Television on Tape," *Jour. Royal Television Society*, Nov./Dec. 1981, p. 13.

53. *Ibid.*

54. Ray Dolby, "30th VTR Anniversary — Some Personal Recollections," presented at 128th Technical Conference of SMPTE, October 24, 1986, p. 23.

55. Interview by author with Walter Selsted, May 5, 1982, Redwood City.

56. "The First VTR," *Audio-Visual Communications*, vol. 15, no. 3, March 1981, p. 26. It seems that Ampex had not used 3M tape before as 3M was involved in the other (RCA and Crosby) videotape recording projects. This story is confirmed in *Broadcast Engineering* (April 1981) "The 25th anniversary of the videotape," p. 88, where it is related that after a hurry-up call to 3M in St. Paul an "untested 2-inch wide magnetic tape that theoretically worked for video was developed without 3M researchers ever seeing the first Ampex videotape recorder." Oddly the same article mentions that they were working on an experimental helical videotape for RCA. I have never come across such a helical project from RCA anywhere in the literature. Nor does RCA acknowledge the existence of such a project.

57. Charles P. Ginsburg, "The Horse or the Cowboy — Getting Television on Tape," *Jour. Royal Television Society*, Nov./Dec. 1981, p. 14.

58. "The 25th anniversary of the VTR," *Broadcast Engineering*, April 1981, pp. 88–89.

59. Charles P. Ginsburg, "The Birth of Videotape Recording," Ampex Brochure, March 1981, p. 5. "Ampex Has 82 Commercial VTR Orders," *Broadcasting*Telecasting*, April 30, 1956, pp. 95–96. V. Adams, "TV is Put On Tape by New Recorder," *New York Times*, April 15, 1956, p. 1. "TV Tape Recording Process," *Electronics*, May 1956, p. 7. "TV Programs on Magnetic Tape," *Radio & Television News*, July 1956, p. 92.

60. Ray Dolby, "30th VTR Anniversary — Some Personal Recollections," presented at 128th Technical Conference of SMPTE, October 24, 1986, pp. 23, 24.

61. *Ibid.*, p. 24.

62. *Ampex Playback*, May 1956.

63. George H. Brown, *And Part of Which I Was*, Angus Cupar Publishers, Princeton, New Jersey, 1982, p. 275.

64. George H. Brown, *And Part of Which I Was*, Angus Cupar Publishers, Princeton, New Jersey, 1982, p. 273.

65. George H. Brown, *And Part of Which I Was*, Angus Cupar Publishers, Princeton, New Jersey, 1982, p. 277.

66. Brown, op. cit., pp. 279–280.

67. Charles P. Ginsburg, "The Birth of Videotape Recording," an Ampex publication, March 1981. (This paper was reproduced in slightly different form in *Jour. SMPTE*, October 5, 1957, p. 5. Paul D. Flehr, "Charles P. Ginsburg: Videotape Recorder" *Inventors and Their Inventions*," Pacific Books, Palo Alto, CA, 1990, p. 74.

68. "Ampex Had 82 Commercial VTR Orders," *Broadcasting*Telecasting*, April 30, 1956, p. 95–96.

69. *New York Times*, July 23, 41:4.

70. *New York Times*, July 24, 1956, 53:3. Arnold E. Look, "New Portable TV camera-Transmitters," *Electronic Industries & Tele-Tech*, September 1956, pp. 52–53.

71. *New York Times*, Aug. 4, 1956, 33:5.

72. "Transistorized TV Pickup," *Radio-Electronics*, Oct. 1956, p. 12.

73. "Tiny TV Cameras Come into Vogue," *Broadcasting*Telecasting*, July 30, 1956, p. 64.

74. *Broadcasting *Telecasting*, Sept. 1956, p. 52.

75. "Ampex VTR," *Broadcast Engineering*, April 1976, pp. 26–30. Joe Roizen, "The Videotape Recorder Revolution," *Broadcast Engineering*, May 1976, pp. 50–53. See also Joe Roizen "Shoenberg Memorial Lecture," (delivered Dec. 11, 1975) *Jour. TV Society*, 1976, vol. 16, no. 1, pp. 15–21.

76. "Ampex VTR Prototypes Set for CBS, NBC," *Broadcasting*Telecasting*, October 1, 1956, p. 9.

77. Source *New York Times*, Sept. 13, 1956, 71:1. "NBC TV Shows Its Color Kinescope Film," *Broadcasting*Telecasting*, September 17, 1956, p. 78.

78. "Color TV Now Ready for Next Stage," *Broadcasting*Telecasting*, June 17, 1957, p. 62. Thomas Pryon, "TV Show Halted by Labor Dispute," *New York Times*, Sept. 13, 1956. See also "Lenticular Film for Color Kines," *Electronics*, April 1956, pp. 190–191.

79. "Lenticular Film for Color Kines," *Electronics*, April 1956, pp. 190–191. J. M. Brumbaugh, E. D. Goodale, and R. D. Kell, "Color TV Recording on Black-and-white Lenticular Film," *IRE Transactions*, October 1957, pp. 71–75.

80. *New York Times*, Sept 30, II, 13:1.

81. *New York Times*, Sept. 1956, 49:1.

82. "DuMont to Produce Chromatic Color Tube," *Electronic Industries & Tele-Tech*, Nov. 1956, p. 5.

83. "Healey Heads West Coast Mincom Division of 3–M," *Broadcasting*Telecasting*, Oct. 1, 1956, p. 9.

84. "Tape Maker Takes Over Video Recording," *Electronics*, October 1956, p. 10.

85. "Sarnoff 'Gifts' Are Presented by RCA," *Broadcasting* Telecasting*, October 8, 1956, p. 94. No more was seen of this machine.

86. D. Gabor, "A New Flat Picture Tube," by *Jour. TV Society*, vol. 8, no. 4, October–December 1956, pp. 142–147. "Flat Tube for Colour TV," *Wireless World*, December 1956, pp. 570–572. "New Flat Color CRT Uses Folded Beams," *Electronic Industries & Tele-Tech*, January 1957, pp. 80–118.

87. "Videotape Goes to Work," *Electronics*, February 1, 1957, p. 20.

88. *Broadcasting*Telecasting*, Dec. 3, 1956.

89. A. D. Cope, "A Miniature Vidicon of High Sensitivity," *RCA Review*, Dec. 1956, pp. 460–467.

90. L. E. Flory, G. W. Gray, J. M. Morgan, and W. S. Pike, "Transistorized Television Cameras Using the Miniature Vidicon," *RCA Review*, December 1956, pp. 469–502.

91. "Inspecting NBC-TV's First Ampex," *Broadcasting*Telecasting*, Dec. 24 1956, p. 60.

92. "CBS Shows off Tape-Recorded TV," *New York Times*, Dec. 21, 1956. p. 43:1.

93. "Videotape Recorder Aim for Color," *Electronics*, Dec. 1956, p. 16.

94. "Conversation with Charles Ginsburg," *Videography*, April 1983, pp. 72.

Chapter 5
Europe Turns Down NTSC (1957–1960)

1. George H. Brown, *And Part of Which I Was*, Angus Cupar Publishers, Princeton, New Jersey, 1982, p. 280.

2. *35 Years of World TV*, 1957, p. 37.

3. "Colour Television," *Electronic & Radio Engineer*, March 1957, p. 79.

4. "Closed circuit," *Broadcasting*, Jan. 28, 1957, p. 5.

5. "Five Week Day Series on Tape," *Broadcasting*, Jan. 28, 1957, p. 72.

6. J. E. Attew, "Television Camera Channel Design," *Electronic & Radio Engineer*, March 1957, pp. 80–89.

7. TV Advertisement for March 1957.

8. "VTR: Out of the Lab, onto the Firing Line," *Broadcasting*Telecasting*, April 1, 1957, pp. 120–123.

9. "Ampex Expects Color Tape to Be Ready in 18 Months," *Broadcasting*Telecasting*, April 8, 1957, p. 9.

10. "RCA Alone in Color TV Field," *Broadcasting*Telecasting*, June 17, 1957, p. 62.

11. *Electronics*, August 1, 1957.

12. "Ginsburg bio" (in Ginsburg file). (See also "On IEEE People," the *Institute*, vol. 10, no. 6, August 1986, p. 12.

13. "Charles P. Ginsburg," *Jour. SMPTE*, Nov. 1969, p. 1022.

14. "Videotape Recorders," *Electronics*, August 1, 1957, p. 141.

15. Paul Flehr, "Charles P. Ginsburg," *Inventors and Their Inventions*, Pacific Books, Palo Alto, CA, 1990, p. 76.

16. Brown, op. cit., pp. 279–281. This was not true. Actually, Ampex got the worst part of the deal. It allowed RCA to copy and use all of the Ampex improvements that came out in the following ten years. Everything from Intersync, Amtec, Colortec, Electronic Editing, Velocity Error Compensator, and of course the high-band system that Ampex had developed. In return RCA contributed nothing. (Note: the term Quadraplex did not exist at this time.) What Ampex did not know was that the RCA patent department had *previously* applied for two patents covering the Ampex machine on October 1, 1957 (A. C. Schroeder USA no. 2,979,557; and E. M. Leyton, USA no. 2,979,558, filed October 2, 1957), which were both issued April 11, 1961. Both reflected complete imitations of the Ampex transverse recorder. How this got through the U.S. Patent Office is beyond my comprehension.

17. Marge Costello, "Conversation with Charles Ginsburg," *Videography*, April 1983, p. 61. I was surprised that Ampex had not complained at the demonstration about RCA using the Ampex system before any licensing agreement had been reached. This demonstration of power on RCA's behalf was strong-arm tactics at their worst. Up to this time, however, Ampex was in awe of RCA and "scared to death that RCA would come out with the videotape recorder before we did." (Direct quote from "Conversation with Charles Ginsburg," p. 61.) As history has proven, without the FM patent RCA could not have built any type of videotape recorder even with a rotating head that would have worked well enough to market, and they knew it. On October 1, 1957, RCA filed for two patents based on the Ampex machine. They were (1) A. C. Schroeder, USA Pat. no. 2,979,557, issued April 11, 1961; and (2) E. M. Leyton, USA Pat. no. 2,979,558, issued April 11, 1961.

18. "Sequential Colour Again," *Wireless World*, September 1957, pp. 426–429.

19. P. Cassagne and M Sauvenet, "FM Sequential Signals Kill Multi-Colored Ghosts," *Electronics*, May 1962, p. 50. See "Variations in Internal Color Transmission," *Broadcast Engineering*, February 1978, p. 52.

20. "Sequential Colour Again," *Wireless World*, September 1957, pp. 426–429.

21. Ray M. Dolby, from "30th VTR Anniversary — Some Personal Recollections," *Jour. SMPTE*, presented October 24, 1986, p. 30.

22. "First Ampex VR1000 Expected in November," *Broadcasting*, October 14, 1957, p. 82.

23. "BBC Colour Tests," *Wireless World*, Dec. 1957, p. 567.

24. "RCA Shows Color VTR Model," *Broadcasting*, 25 October 1957, p. 88.

25. "Color Videotape Recorder," *Broadcast News*, Dec. 1957, pp. 6–11.

26. "RCA Plans to Start Delivery of TV Recorder at end of 1958," *Broadcasting*, Nov. 25, 1957, p. 94.

27. "New Color Camera Announced by GE," *Broadcasting*, November 25, 1957, p. 92.

28. "BBC Colour Test," *Wireless World*, Dec. 1957, p. 567.

29. J. Polonsky, "A French Portable TV Camera," *Jour. TV Society*, April-June 1958, pp. 423–431.

30. "Delivery This Year," *Broadcasting*, Jan. 20, 1958, p. 96.

31. *Ibid.*

32. A. H. Lind, "Color Processing in RCA Videotape Recorders," *Broadcast News*, 6–7 Feb. 1958, p. 99.

33. Charles E. Anderson, "The Progression of Videotape Recording," *Broadcast Engineering*, May 1979, pp. 62–64. Anderson mentions that perhaps it had something to do with the fact that the quadrature of the four heads could be spaced precisely apart to cure the geometric problem.

34. "RCA Production Model TV Tape Recorder Highlights Latest Advancement," *Broadcast News*, 1958, pp. 52–58.

35. A. H. Lind, "Engineering Color Videotape Recording," *RCA Engineer*, March 1958, vol. 3, no. 4, pp. 22–26.

36. "TV Tapes Top 100 Mark," *Electronics*, March 21, 1958, p. 54.

37. "VTR," *Jour. TV Society*, vol. 9, no. 11, 1961.

38. "NBC Tape Central Goes into Action," *Broadcasting*, May 5, 1958.

39. "RCA Videotape Recorders in Operation at NBC Central, Burbank, Calf," *Broadcast News*, April 1959, pp. 8–11.

40. C. Anderson and J. Roizen, "A Color Videotape Recorder," *Jour. SMPTE*, October 1959, pp. 667–671. Also *Broadcasting*, April 24, 1958.

41. Joseph Roizen, "How the Videotape Recorder Works," *Radio & TV News*, September 1985, pp. 48–50. (RCA was laying down single 30-cycle edit pulses.) *Broadcast News*, April 1958, p. 13. See also Joe Roizen, "974 VTR Review," *Broadcast Engineering*, July 1974, pp. 40–44, 61.

42. "Videotape Gets New Trick, New Fans," *Broadcasting*, Sept. 8, 1958.

43. "Storm Warnings Are Up," *Electronic Industries & Tele-Tech*, Sept. 1956, p. 50. "VTR: Prodigy Poses Some Problems," *Broadcasting*, May 12, 1958, pp. 31–32.

44. "Progress Report," *Jour. SMPTE*, May 1958, p. 321.

45. "BBC Perfects Video Recorder," *Electronics*, May 23, 1948, p. 14.

46. "Three Track TV Tape System," *Electronics*, July 25, 1958, p. 24. "VERA: The BBC Vision Recording Apparatus," *Jour. TV Society*, April-June 1958, vol. 8, no. 10, pp. 398–400. "Magnetic Recording of Television Programs," *Jour. Brit IRE*, May 1984, pp. 273–276. Joe Roizen, "Video Recording," *Broadcast Engineering*, April 1976, p. 30. J Roizen, "The Videotape Recorder Revolution," *Broadcast Engineering*, May 1976, pp. 50–53.

47. "Videotape Recording," *Wireless World*, August 1958, pp. 362–363.

48. "Progress Report," *Jour. SMPTE*, May 1959, p. 317.

49. *Jour. SMPTE*, Aug. 1958, p. 556.

50. "Magnettrommelspeicher statt Röntgenfilmbild," Heft 16, *Funkschau*, 1959, p. 372. (See also J. H. Wessels, "A Magnetic Wheel Store gor Recording Television Signals," *Philips Technical Review*, 4 November 1960, pp. 1–10.

51. It lasted until January 1960. *New York Times*, Jan. 22, 1957, pp. 49, 60.

52. Flaherty claims that CBS did "The Red Mill" in 1957 with 168 edits in the 90-minute program.

53. "Eight papers on Videotape and Recording," *Jour. SMPTE*, November 1958, pp. 721–745. They were (1) Charles E. Anderson, "Signal Translation Through the Ampex Videotape Recorder," pp. 721–725; (2) Ray N. Dolby "The Video Processing Amplifier in the Ampex Videotape Recorder," pp. 726–729; (3) Kurt R. Machein "Factors Affecting the Splicing of Videotape," pp. 730–731, in Los Angeles, (4) Joseph Roizen, "Electronic Marking and Control for Rapid Location of Vertical Blanking Area for Editing Videotape Recordings" pp. 732–733; and Charles P. Ginsburg, "Interchangeability of Videotape Recorders," pp. 739–743 on April 24, 1958.

54. "Eidophor Color Projector Unveiled at Science Meeting," *Broadcasting*, Dec. 29, 1958, p. 9.

55. "The Eidophor Colour Projection System," *Jour. TV Society*, vol. 9, no. 4, 1959, pp. 127–131.

56. I. J. P. James, "A Vidicon Camera for Industrial Colour Television," *Jour. Brit IRE*, March 1959, pp. 165–180.

57. "Battle of the Tape Titans," *Broadcasting*, March 23, 1959, p. 70.

58. *Broadcasting*, March 23, 1959, p. 71.

59. "New Ampex," *Broadcasting*, May 11, 1959, p. 71.

60. "Taping the Globe," *Broadcasting*, April 20, 1959, pp. 95–96.

61. *Jour. TV Society*, 109/61/62 1959, p. 439

62. "Technical Topics," *Broadcasting*, April 16, 1959, p. 98.

63. "Super-Sensitive TV Camera Tube," *Electronics World*, August 1959, p. 94.

64. N. Sawazaki, "Helical Scan VTR System," Toshiba Research and Development Lab.

65. N. Sawazaki, M. Yagi, M. Iwasaki, G. Inada, and T. Tamaoki, "A New Videotape Recording System," *Jour. SMPTE*, Dec. 1960, pp. 868–871. "Domestic, Foreign Gear Shine," *Broadcasting* May 8, 1960 pp. 88–89. I was given a paper entitled "Helical Scan VTR System" by Norikazu Sawasaki from the Toshiba Research and Development Lab during my visit to Toshiba in 1981. I had the honor of meeting with Sawazaki and was treated royally by his company.

66. Pete Hammar in May 1985 gives a date of 1956. Hammar had the full resources of the Ampex library when he built his museum in 1984. Pete Hammar, "The Birth of Helical Scan Videotape Recording," *Broadcast Engineering*, May 1985, p. 86.

67. "Sharp Clash Between VP Nixon and Premier Khrushchev Recorded by TV Cameras," *New York Times*, July 25, 1959, 1:8.

68. "SECAM/60, an Approach to Color Educational Television," *Educational Television*, March 1970, p. 2.

69. C. E. Anderson and J. Roizen, "A Color Videotape Recorder," *Jour. SMPTE*, 68, October 1959, pp. 667–671.

70. "Ampex Offers New Camera," *New York Times*, Oct 1, 1959, 71:5. "British to Market TV Camera Here," *Electronic Industries*, November 1959, p. 8.

71. "Big Boost for Color TV," *Broadcasting*, Dec. 7, 1959, p. 78. "Less Light Needed," *Broadcasting*, December 23, 1959, p. 60.

72. "New Orthicon Tube," *Broadcasting*, December 29, 1959, p. 60.

73. "Japan Begins Mass Output of Color TV Sets Under RCA Licenses," *New York Times*, March 24, 47:2. Bilby, *The General*, p. 222. "Japan Launches Color TV," *Electronics*, January 22, 1960, p. 27.

74. "Thermoplastic Recording," *New York Times*, Dec. 24, 39:2. "Thermoplastic Recording Shown," *Broadcasting*, Jan. 18, 1960, p. 110.

75. "Thermoplastic Recording," *Electronics World*, March 1960, p. 47. " 'TPR' Recording," *Electronic Industries*, vol. 19, no. 2, February 1960, pp. 75–79. W. E. Glenn, "Thermoplastic Recording," *Jour. SMPTE*, Sept. 1960, pp. 577–580.

76. *Broadcasting*, Feb. 20, 1960, p. 140.

77. "Long-Play Tape Machine Shown by C.B.S. inventor of LP Disk," *New York Times*, March 24, 1960, p. 1.

78. Peter C. Goldmark, *Maverick Inventor*, Saturday Review Press, E. P. Dutton & Co., New York, 1973, pp. 158–162.

79. See also Robert Angus, "75 Years of Magnetic Recording," *High Fidelity Magazine*, March 1973, pp. 42–50. Angus claims that the Philips cassette was similar to the earlier RCA device and that it was a dictating machine and nothing more. Philips did not charge a royalty for the use of its license.

80. C. H. Coleman, "A New Technique for Time Base Stabilization of Video Recorders," *IEEE Trans on Broadcasting*, vol. 17, March 1971, pp. 29–36. (See USA Pat no. 3,202,769, filed Aug 2, 1960; issued Aug. 23, 1965.)

81. K. B. Benson, "Video-Tape Recording Interchangeability Requirements," *Jour. SMPTE*, 70, Dec. 1960, pp. 861–867. *Broadcasting*, May 15, 1961, p. 83.

82. "Pixlock System for TV Recorders," *Int. TV Tech. Review*, November 1962, p. 534–35.

83. "Domestic: Foreign Gear Shine," *Broadcasting*, May 9, 1960, pp. 88–90. "New Products," *Jour. SMPTE*, June 1960, p. 458.

84. C. P. Ginsburg, "The Horse or the Cowboy: Getting Television on Tape," *Jour. Royal Television Society*, Nov./Dec. 1981, p. 17.

85. A paper by Bendell and Kozanowski described the new camera.

86. John H. Roe, "All New Monochrome Studio Camera TYPE TK-12," *Broadcast News*, March 1960, pp. 57–58.

87. "Colour Television from Paris," *Wireless World*, June 1960, p. 287.

88. "French 625 Service," *Int. TV Tech. Review*, June 1962, p. 319.

89. *Jour. SMPTE*, May 1960, p. 342 with picture.

90. "The Future of Television," *Electronic Technology*, July 1960, vol. 37, no. 7, July 1960, p. 251.

91. "Synchronizer Forms Composite TV Pictures," *Electronics*, Sept. 30, 1960, p. 104.

92. Ampex ad in *Broadcasting*, September 9, 1960.

93. *Broadcasting Telecasting*, May 1961, p. 79.

94. "Portable Color TV Tape Recorder, $60,000," *Broadcasting*, May 29, 1961, p. 79.

95. "New Products," *Jour. SMPTE*, October 1960, p. 780.

Chapter 6
From Helicals to High Band (1961–1964)

1. "Two-Head Color VTR," *Japan Electronics*, January 1961, p. 21.

2. "Advantages of the Two Head Videotape System," *Int. TV Tech. Review*, July 1961, pp. 19–21.

3. "NAB Convention," *Broadcasting*, May 15, 1961, p. 84. According to Sadashige, the color-under technique was considered one of the significant technical developments of VTR technology in recent times. See his article in 1976, "Color-Under System — Overview of Time Base Correction Techniques and Their Application," by Koichi Sadashige, *Jour. SMPTE*, Oct. 1976, pp. 787–791.

4. "Japan Develops Color TV Tape Recorder," *Electronics*, Feb. 10, 1961, p. 34. "Japanese Pushing TV and Computers," *Electronics*, May 26, 1961, p. 32.

5. "Ampex, RCA Reveal Economy Priced VTR," *Broadcasting*, March 20, 1961, p. 64. "Ampex Introduces Single-Head Recorder for Closed Circuit," *International TV Techn. Review*, April 1961, p. 23.

6. "NAB Convention," *Broadcasting*, May 15, 1961, p. 84.

7. *Jour. SMPTE*, Nov 1961, p. 955.

8. From Nick Lyons, *The Sony Vision*, Crown Publishers, Inc., New York, 1975, pp. 202–205.

9. James Lardner, *Fast Forward*, W.W. Norton, New York, 1987, p. 66.

10. "Japanese Company to Make Ampex Gear," *Broadcasting*, Sept. 28, 1964, p. 105.

11. Shigeo Shima, "The Evolution of Consumers VTR's — Technological Milestones," Sony Publication *IEEE Trans on Consumer Electronics*, vol. CE, May 1984, p. 72. This article also claims that the first full transistor Quad/VTR, the VR1100, was a joint development of Ampex-Sony.

12. Lardner, op. cit., pp. 65–71.

13. *Broadcasting*, Nov. 18, 1968, p. 72.

14. Sony biographer Lyons (op. cit.), 1975, p. 66.

15. Ginsburg, *Jour. Royal Television Society*, Nov./Dec. 1981, p. 17.

16. "Non Broadcast VTR," *Broadcasting*, March 13, 1961, p. x. "Billiges Ampex-Videobandgerät für Industrielles Fernsehen." *Funkschau*, Heft 8, 1961, p. 184.

17. "Television and Film Techniques," *Wireless World*, June 1961, p. 312.

18. "New Products," *Jour. SMPTE*, 70, p. 575, July 1961. "New Videotape Units Unveiled," *Broadcasting*, May 15, 1961, p. 83. Joe Roizen, "The Technical Aspects of Recording NTSC Color" *Int. TV Tech. Review*, vol. 2, Dec. 1961, pp. 31, 32–34.

19. "NAB Convention," *Broadcasting*, May 15, 1961, p. 84. See also RCA ad in *International TV Technical Review*, September 1961, p. 29. I have not been able to find out who built this machine. The ad states that one of the five machines was *not* built by RCA. It was obviously one of the Japanese manufacturers which built them.

20. "NAB Preview," *Broadcasting*, May 1, 1961, p. 92.

21. Norman Bounsall, "Electronic Editing of Videotape," *Wireless World*, September 1962, 405.

22. "Single-Frame Storage Device by Siemens & Halske," *Jour. SMPTE*, May 1962, p. 351.

23. "Der Erste Video-Bandaufzeichnungerät aus Deutscher Entwicklung," *Funkschau*, Heft 17, 1961, p. 873.

24. "Progress Report," *Jour. SMPTE*, September 1961, p. 760.

25. "The German Television Society Annual Convention," *Jour. TV Society*, Oct./Dec. 1961, p. 505.

26. "Videotape Goes Slow Motion at ABC-TV," *Broadcasting*, Nov. 20, 1961, p. 73. This was done with the new Mach-Tronics helical scan machine.

27. English Electric ad in *International Technical Review*, November 1961, p. 30.

28. "Color Television," *Wireless World*, July 1962, p. 307.

29. "RCA Unveils New Four Color TV Camera," *Broadcasting*, March 19, 1962, p. 81.

30. "RCA Colour Camera," *Broadcasting*, April 9, 1962, p. 56.

31. G.E. ad in *Broadcasting*, March 26, 1962, pp. 80–81.

32. *Broadcasting*, May 28, 1962, p. 63.

33. *Jour. SMPTE*, October 1962, pp. 765–768.

34. "Live Images Transmitted Across Ocean First Time," *New York Times*, July 11, 1962. "Progress Report," *Jour. SMPTE*, May 1963, pp. 378–9.

35. "Portable Videotape Rig Uses One Inch Tape," *Broadcasting*, June 4, 1962, p. 64. "One Inch Portable TV Recorder," *Int. TV Tech. Review*, August 1962, p. 385 with picture.

36. "MVR-10 Displayed," *Broadcasting*, June 18, 1962, pp. 86–87. In a personal interview I had with Mr. Machein, he confirmed that he had asked Ampex many times to produce such a lightweight one-inch machine and they did not seem to be interested at the moment. Interview with Machein, 1981, Mountain View.

37. Peter Hammar, "The Birth of Helical Scan Videotape Recording," *Broadcast Engineering*, May 1965, pp. 86–94.

38. "Mach-Tronics Counter-Sues Ampex," *Broadcasting*, August 12, 1962, p. 56.

39. "Mach-Tronics denies theft of Ampex secrets," *Broadcasting*, September 3, 1962, p. 70.

40. Ginsburg, *Jour. Royal Television Society*, p. 15.

41. "RCA Now Turning Out Transistor Recorders," *Broadcasting*, Oct. 29, 1962, p. 68.

42. "TK-60 Cameras Arriving in TV Studios," *Broadcast News*, November 1962, p. 8.

43. *Jour. TV Society*, vol. 10, no. 3, 1962, p. 92.

44. "Progress Report," *Jour. SMPTE*, May 1962, p. 399.

45. "Ampex Unveils Portable Videotape Recorder" *Broadcasting*, Dec 12. 1962 p. 116.

46. Douglas Birkenshaw, "Shoenberg: Faith in Electronic Television," *Jour. Royal Television Society*, Sept./Oct. 1980, pp. 56–57.

47. "Kinescope Eliminated in Tape-to-Film Move," *Broadcasting*, January 12, 1963, p. 58.

48. W. R. Smith and R. B. Ferber, "A Simultaneous Videotape and Direct 16mm Film Recording System," *Jour. SMPTE*, June 1963, pp. 386–588.

49. *Broadcasting*, July 8, 1963, p80.

50. "Closed Circuit Television Tape Recorder," *Wireless World*, October 1963, p. 488. See also "New Products," *Jour. SMPTE*, April 1963, p. 354; and C. R. Webster, "Television Tape Recording — history and trends," *Int. TV Techn. Review*, December 1963, pp. 432–435.

51. "Telcan," by E. P. L. Fisher, *Int. TV Tech. Review*, July 1963, pp. 238–239, 262.

52. "New TV Tape Recorder for Less Than $200?" *Radio-Electronics*, Oct. 1963, p. 6.

53. "British Home TV Recorder Not Due Until '64," *Broadcasting*, August 4, 1963, p. 10.

54. "Rosy Promise," *Broadcasting*, July 1, 1963.

55. "Mobility Becomes Reality with the MVR," *Broadcasting*, July 22, 1963, p. 66.

56. "European Color TV Developments," *Electronics World*, July 1963, pp. 66–67.

57. "Cinerama Gets Rights to Telcan Distribution," *Broadcasting*, Sept 9, 1963, p. 54.

58. "Ampex Introduces Now Portable VTR," *Broadcasting*, Sept. 9, 1963. Also "New Products," *Jour. SMPTE*, October 1963, p. 838.

59. C. Taylor, "The Plumbicon, a Completely New TV Breakthrough," *Int. TV Rev.* vol. 4, June 1963, pp. 202–203, 226–228. "CBS Is Helping Out," *Broadcasting*, September 30, 1963, p. 63.

60. "New Line Converter Perfected by BBC," *Broadcasting*, September 2, 1963, p. 69. "Electronic Standard Conversions," *Wireless World*, October 1963, p. 494.

61. Brown, op. cit., p. 239. M. Cox, "PAL," *Wireless World*, December 1963, pp. 584–586. J. Rogers, "The PAL Colour TV System," *Jour. Inst. Elec. & Radio Engineers*, March 1967, pp. 147–160. See "Variations in Internal color transmission," *Broadcast Engineering*, February 1978, p. 52.

62. D. Loughlin, "The Revolution and Evolution from Dot Sequential to NTSC," *IEEE Trans on Consumer Electronics*, vol. CE-30, May 1984, pp. 18–23.

63. "BBC Favors U.S. Color System," *Broadcasting*, Oct 28, 1963.

64. "Ampex's Editec Allows Tape Color Animation," *Broadcasting*, January 20, 1964.

65. "Portable Tape Recorder," *Electronics World*, March 1964,

p. 31. It was the same as the JVC machine DV220. "New Products," *Jour. SMPTE*, June 1964, p. 522.

66. "Two World's Fairs Are Scenes of TV History in the Making," *Broadcast News*, June 1964, p. 4.

67. "A Home TV Tape Recorder for the Consumer," *Broadcasting*, April 13, 1964, pp. 106–107.

68. "New Products," *Jour. SMPTE*, June 1964, p. 524.

69. "New Products," *Jour. SMPTE*, vol. 75, June 1964, p. 524.

70. Joseph Roizen, "High Band Videotape Recording," *BM/E*, March 1965, see also M. O. Felix, "F. M. Systems of Exceptional Bandwidth," *Electronics Record Proceedings IEE* 112, Sept. 1965, pp. 1659–1668.

71. Ginsburg, *Jour. Royal Television Society*, op. cit., p. 16. "Quality Tape Portables Seen," *Broadcasting*, April 20, 1964. See also Joe Roizen, "High Band Videotape Recording," *Broadcast/Management*, March 1965, pp. 57–59. H. D. Felix, C. H. Coleman, and P. W. Jensen, "The Theory and Design of FM Systems for Use in Color Television Tape Recording," International Conference on Magnetic Recording, London 1964. "Colour TV Recorders," *Int. TV Tech. Review*, September 5, 1964, p. 327.

72. *Broadcasting*, April 20, 1964, p. 93–94. "Color TV Recorders," *Int. TV Tech. Review*, Sept. 1964, pp. 325–327.

73. *Int. TV Tech. Review*, July 1964.

74. "Quality Tape Portables Seen," *Broadcasting*, April 20, 1964.

75. *Broadcast News*, August 1964, pp. 26–29.

76. "Electronic Accessories for TV Tape Systems," *Broadcast News*, Dec. 1965, p. 43.

77. *Broadcast News*, May 1964, pp. 46–51.

78. "General Electronics to Make Color Tube," *Broadcasting*, May 4, 1964, p. 56.

79. "Successful Telstar II Used for Two Transmissions," *Broadcasting*, May 23, 1964, p. 84.

80. "CBS-TV to Use New Camera at GOP," *Broadcasting*, June 29, 1964.

81. *Jour. SMPTE*, May 1965, p. 412.

82. "Smile Man in the Moon, You're on Camera," *Broadcasting*, August 10, 1964, p. 72.

83. *Ibid.*

84. "*Hamlet* on Broadway Stage Filmed by TV System Using Only Available Light," *Broadcast News*, vol. 123, October 1964, p. 3.

85. E. F. de Hann, A. van der Drift, and P. P. M Schampers, "The 'Plumbicon,' a New Television Camera Tube," *Philips Technical Review*, 7 July 1964, pp. 133–151. E. F. DeHaan and A. G. Van Doorn, "The Plumbicon, a Camera Tube with a Photoconductive Lead Oxide Layer," *Jour. SMPTE*, vol. 73, June 1964, pp. 473–476. C. Taylor, "The Plumbicon, a Completely New TV Breakthrough," *Int. TV Review*, vol. 4, June 1964, pp. 202–203.

86. "New Circuitry May Lower Recorder Price," *Broadcasting*, August 31, 1964, p. 75.

87. "Sony Import Due Here Next Year," *Broadcasting*, December 21, 1964, p. 52.

88. *Int. TV Tech. Review*, July 1964, p. 259. See also "Ein Relativbilleges Video-Aufzeichnungsgert," *Funkschau*, Heft 18, 1964, p. 483.

89. "One-Gun Picture Tube," *Electronics*, Sept. 21, 1964, p. 38.

90. Nick Lyons, *The Sony Vision*, Crown Publishers, Inc., New York, 1976, pp. 133–134.

91. "Weaver Has Interest in $3,000 Home TV Tape Recorder," *Broadcasting*, October 8, 1964, p. 74.

92. "Sony Import Due Here Next Year," *Broadcasting*, Dec. 21, 1964, p. 52.

93. Ampex ad in *Int. TV Tech. Review*, December 1964, p. 120 including a picture. Two-inch tape was used as it had twice the resistance to longitudinal tension and three times better transverse rigidity. See also Joe Roizen, "1974 VTR Review," *Broadcast Engineering*, July 1974, pp. 40–44, 61.

Chapter 7
Solid-State Cameras (1965–1967)

1. George H. Brown, *And Part of Which I Was*, Angus Cupar Publishers, Princeton, New Jersey, 1982, p. 264. See also "The Colour Situation," *Wireless World*, March 1965, p. 130.

2. *Jour. SMPTE*, March 1965, p. 294.

3. *Broadcasting*, Feb. 15, 1965, p. 64. See also *Broadcasting*, Feb 22, 1965, p. 110.

4. See *Broadcasting*, Feb. 22, 1965, p. 100.

5. "Plumbicon Cameras Ready," *Broadcasting*, Feb. 22, 1965, p. 110.

6. "Using 4 TV Cameras, Electronovision Hope to Shoot 'Harlow' in 5 Days," *Daily Variety*, Mar. 30, 1965, p. 3.

7. "Videotape Recorder for Home Use," *Japanese E. E.* March 1965, vol. series 2, p. 35.

8. *Broadcasting*, April 5, 1965, p. 52. *Broadcasting Management/Engineering*, April 1965, p. 26.

9. *Broadcasting*, January 3, 1966, p. 40.

10. *Broadcasting*, April 1965, p. 51.

11. *Broadcasting*, April 1965, p. 65.

12. *Broadcasting*, April 1965, p. 61 with picture.

13. *Ibid*.

14. *Broadcasting*, April 5, 1964, p. 62.

15. *Broadcasting* April 11, 1965, p. 66. *Broadcast Management/Engineering*, 1965, p. 26.

16. *Broadcasting*, April 5, 1965, p. 62.

17. "Videotape Is an Improved Item," *Broadcasting*, April 5, 1965, p. 62. Also *Broadcasting*, April 11, 1965, p. 88.

18. *Jour. SMPTE*, Nov. 65, p. 1060. (See USA Patent no. 3,450,832, D. B. Mcleod et al., filed January 3, 1966; issued June 17, 1969.)

19. *Jour. SMPTE*, April 1965, p. 366.

20. E. Di Giulio, "A 35mm Reflex Camera System Incorporating Video Monitoring and Recording," *Jour. SMPTE*, July 1965, pp. 600–611. See also *Broadcast Eng.*, July 1965, p. 486.

21. "Color Television Deadlock," *Wireless World*, May 1965, p. 239. "Colour TV for Europe," *Electronics World*, May 1965, p. 65.

22. *Broadcasting*, May 10, 1965, p. 73.

23. *Jour. SMPTE*, June 1965, pp. 571–72.

24. *Electronics*, May 17, 1965, p. 25.

25. "Tubeless TV Camera," *Electronics*, March 1967, p. 26.

26. Brother Dowd, letter.

27. Wescon Technical Papers, vol. 77, part 7, session 13, August 1967. K. Sadashige, "An Overview of Solid State Sensor Techniques," *Jour. SMPTE*, February 1987, pp. 180–185.

28. *Broadcasting*, July 1965, p. 76.

29. *Jour. SMPTE*, Sept. 1965, p.782.

30. Brown, op. cit., p. 265.

31. "Montreux Television Symposium," *Wireless World*, July 1965, pp. 349, 350.

32. *Broadcast Management/Engineering*, July 1965.

33. "Broadcast Industry News," *Broadcast Management*, July 1965, p. 6.

34. A. Ettlinger and P. Fish, *Jour. SMPTE*, October 1965, p. 954. "A Stop-Action Magnetic Videodisc Recorder," *Jour. SMPTE*, November 1966, pp. 1086–1088.

35. "The Videodisc," *Jour. SMPTE*, October 1966, p. 1058.

36. R. Streeter and R. L. Cobler, "CBS Experiences with Plumbicon Color Cameras," *Jour. SMPTE*, August 1966, p. 749.

37. "Eastman Kodak Co. Testing Videotape," *Jour. SMPTE*, Sept. 1965, pp. 884–886.

38. Ampex Loses in Antitrust Suit," *Broadcasting*, Sept. 27, 1965, p. 53

39. "New Products," *Jour. SMPTE*, July 1965, p. 642. "Sony Home Video Recorder," *Electronics World*, May 1966, pp. 42–44. See also F. Cinnamon, "Home Video Recorder: They're coming in the windows," *Radio-Electronics*, May 1966, pp. 35–36.

40. "Hope Dims for U.S. Color System Abroad," *Broadcasting*, October 4, 1965, p. 83.

41. "Ampex Final Plea in December for New Trial Denied," *Broadcasting*, October 18, 1965. "Color TV for Europe," *Electronics World*, May 1965, p. 65.

42. *Jour. SMPTE*, 1965, p. 986.

43. "A Portable (90-lb) Television Tape Recorder," "New Products," *Jour. SMPTE*, October 1965, p. 986. 1965 SABA ad in *Funkschau*, February 1965.

44. *Jour. SMPTE*, March 1966, pp. 195–197.

45. "Ampex, Precision Settle Suits," *Broadcasting*, December 6, 1965, p. 58.

46. Joseph Roizen, "Television Ready to Take Forward Step in Eastern European-bloc Countries," *Electronics*, January 10, 1966, p. 168.

47. See *Electronics*, Feb. 7, 1966, p. 168.

48. Tubeless TV Camera," *Electronics*, March 1967, p. 26.

49. *Broadcasting*, Feb. 21, 1966, p. 99.

50. "Four Plumbicon Color Camera," *Wireless World*, February 1966, p. 58–59.

51. "Light Weight Tape Camera a Hit at NAB," *Broadcasting*, April 4, 1966, p. 98.

52. "One Man Crew," *Electronics*, April 4, 1966, pp. 40–41. *Broadcasting*, April 11, 1996, p. 66. "New Products," *Jour. SMPTE*, April 1966, p. 430. *Broadcast Management/Engineering*, June 1966, p. 46.

53. *Broadcasting*, April 4, 1966, p. 98. *Broadcasting*, April 11, 1996, p. 65.

54. *Broadcasting*, March 21, 1966, p. 134.

55. *Broadcasting*, March 7, 1966, p. 70.

56. *Broadcasting*, March 28, 1966, p. 104.

57. *Broadcasting*, March 14, 1966, p. 166.

58. "New Products," *Jour. SMPTE*, vol. 75, April 1966, p. 441.

59. *Jour. TV Society*, Winter 1966/67, p. 188.

60. "Sony May Bring Chromatron Tube to US," *Broadcasting*, April 18, 1966, p. 61.

61. *Broadcasting*, May 2, 1966, p. 56. *Jour. SMPTE*, June 1966 p. 632.

62. Hayden, "TV Aids to Motion Picture Film Making — The Livingston ADD-a-Vision and E.F.S. system," *Brit. Kine.*, vol. 48, May 1966, pp. 140–151.

63. *Broadcast Television*, June 6, 1966, p. 88. "Portable VTR," *Broadcast Management/Engineering*, November 1966, p. 48.

64. "Ampex and MVR Bury the Hatchet," *Broadcasting*, June 13, 1966, p. 75.

65. *Jour. SMPTE*, 1966, p. 622.

66. *Jour. SMPTE*, May 1967, p. 447.

67. New Products," *Jour. SMPTE*, June 1966, p. 632.

68. "Under $500 Home-Videotape Recorder Developed," *Broadcasting*, July 11, 1966, p. 74. "Home Tape Recorder," *Jour. SMPTE*, April 1966, p. 412.

69. "New Products," *Jour. SMPTE*, July 1966, p. 723. "New Equipment," *Broadcast Management/Engineering*, August 1966, p. 42.

70. *Broadcasting*, July 11, 1966, p. 72.

71. *Broadcasting*, July 18, 1966, p. 56.

72. *Broadcasting*, Aug. 1, 1966, p. 85.

73. T. R. Haskett, "What Happened at Oslo?" *Radio-Electronics*, pp. 41–43. See also Brown, op. cit., p. 264.

74. "Acme Claims Breakthrough in Tape-to-Film Transfer," *Broadcasting*, August 15, 1966, p. 9.

75. "Portable TV Recorder," *Broadcast Management/Engineering*, August 1966, p. 44.

76. "Eine Deutsche Videoaufzeichnungsanlage," *Funkschau*, Heft 12, 1966, p. 418.

77. "Bosch Fifty Years of Television," 1966, p. 54.

78. *Broadcast Television*, Sept. 12, p. 82. *Jour. SMPTE*, Nov. 1966, pp. 1144–1145.

79. "A New Film System to Replace Kinescope?" *Broadcasting*, September 1966, p. 82.

80. *Technician-Engineer*, January 1970, pp. 8–9. See also "New Products" *Jour. SMPTE*, January 1970.

81. "Live TV Set for First Apollo's Shot," *Broadcasting*, October 16, 1966, p. 80.

82. *Broadcasting*, July 11, 1966, p. 72. "Cameras Get Smaller and Smaller," *Broadcasting*, Aug. 1, 1966, p. 80.

83. "New Products," *Jour. SMPTE*, Oct. 1966, p. 1058. "MVR Corp," *Broadcast Management/Engineering*, Nov. 1966.

84. "Some New Goodies from RCA's Labs," *Broadcasting*, October 10, 1966, p. 77. "A New Module for High-Band Color TV," *Jour. SMPTE*, Nov. 1966, p. 1146. See also *Broadcast News*, 1966–67, p. 45.

85. *Broadcasting*, November 28, 1966, p. 73. "New Products," *Jour. SMPTE*, January 1967, p. 75. *Wireless World*, Jan. 1967, p. 12. *Electronics World*, March 1967, p. 26.

86. *Jour. SMPTE*, Nov. 1966, p. 445.

87. *Jour. SMPTE*, 1967, p. 445.

88. *Electronics World*, November 1966, p. 36.

89. "TV D Disc Recorder," *Broadcast Management/Engineering*, Dec. 1966, p. 52.

90. *Jour. SMPTE*, Jan. 1967, p. 75.

91. *Broadcasting*, Jan. 1967, p. 58.

92. See "1966 Progress Report," *Jour. SMPTE*, Jan 1967.

93. "New Products," *Jour. SMPTE*, January 1967, p. 517.

94. *Broadcasting*, Feb. 6, 1967, p. 5.

95. *Jour. SMPTE*, Feb. 1967, p. 6.

96. *Broadcasting*, Feb. 27, p. 95.

97. *Jour. SMPTE*, April 6, 1967, p. 404.

98. *Broadcasting*, Feb. 27, 1967, p. 95.

99. *Jour. SMPTE*, Feb. 1967.

100. *Broadcast Television*, March 20, p. 83.

101. *Broadcasting*, March 20, p. 83.

102. *Broadcast Management/Engineering*, March 1967, p. 106.

103. J. P. Kane, *Broadcast Television*, March 27, 1967, p. 84. "Instant Replay," *Electronics World*, November 1968, pp. 38–39.

104. From *Broadcast Television*, April 3, 1967, p. 90, and *Jour. SMPTE*, July 1967 p. 726.

105. "Engineers in a Can Do Mood," *Broadcasting*, March 1967, p. 82.

106. Nick Lyons, op. cit., pp. 136–143. "U.S. to See New Sony Tube in May," *Broadcasting*, April 22, 1968, p. 58.

107. "New One-Gun Color CRT," *Electronics World*, July 1968, p. 6.

108. "Sony's New Single-Gun Color Tube," *Electronics World*, August 1968, p. 34. S. Miyaoka, "The Trinitron Colour TV Tube," *Wireless World*, Dec. 1971, pp. 589–592.

109. From *Broadcasting*, April 3, 1967, p. 90. *Broadcasting*, April 17, 1967, p. 78. *Broadcasting*, April 7, 1969, p. 55. "VTR Equipment," *Broadcast Management/Engineering*, May 1969, p. 40.

110. "VTR Equipment," *Broadcast Management/Engineering*, May 1969, p. 40.

111. "Ampex to Show Back Pack Camera VTR," *Broadcasting*, April 3, 1967, p. 90.

112. *Broadcasting*, April 3, 1967, p. 90.

113. "Instant Replay," *Electronics World*, November 1968, pp. 38–39.

114. "Newell Shows Recorder for Home Color-TV," *Broadcasting*, May 22, 1967, p. 54. "High Speed Tape Transport," *Wireless World*, Dec. 1967, p. 600.

115. *Broadcast Television*, April 13, 1967, p. 144, and *Broadcast Television*, July 10, 1967, p. 64.

116. Color TV in Europe—the Latest Situation," *Wireless World*, July 1967, p. 324.

117. "CBS Unveils Plans for Cableless Color Camera," *Broadcasting*, July 17, 1967, p. 62.

118. "One-Man TV Station," *Radio-Electronics*, August 1967, p. 6.

119. *Broadcasting*, July 17, 1967, p. 62.

120. *Wireless World*, July 1967, p. 323.

121. *Broadcasting*, Aug. 21, 1967.

122. "Pickup Tube Progress," *Broadcast Management/Engineering*, Sept. 1968, p. 7.

123. *Wireless World*, Nov. 1967, p. 540.

124. Peter C. Goldmark, *Maverick Inventor*, Saturday Review Press/E. P. Dutton & Co. Inc., New York, 1973, p. 172.

125. *Ibid.*, p. 161. In 1960, CBS and 3M and Revere (Wollensak) came out with an audio cartridge device in which the cartridge was inserted into the machine and the tape was pulled out to be played. After play, the tape was reeled back into the cartridge.

126. *Ibid.*, pp. 180–192. Date is from *Broadcast Television*, Dec. 16, 1968, p. 76.

127. "Breakthrough in Home TV Gear?" *Broadcasting*, August 28, 1967, pp. 67–68. "Dead End Ahead for Film, Tape?" *Broadcasting*, October 23, 1967, pp. 23–25. *Jour. SMPTE*, Nov. 1967, pp. 1165. "CBS TV Film Device," *Radio News*, Sept. 1967, pp. 18–19.

128. *Broadcasting*, August 28, 1967, pp. 67–68.

129. *Jour. SMPTE*, Aug. 1967, p. 850.

130. Source probably *Broadcasting*, April 1968.

131. The source is me as I worked with Mr. Hill. In fact, I had the honor of recording the first time code on a two-inch tape after hours at TV City. This of course was done without management's knowing about it at the time.

132. "Colour Minicamera Developed by Philips," *Broadcasting*, October 23, 1967, p. 47.

133. *Jour. SMPTE*, Nov. 1967, p. 1167. See also E. R. P. Leman and D. F. Eldridge, "The IVC One-Inch Helical Scan VTR Format," *Broadcast Management/Engineering*, March 1968, pp. 56–60.

134. *Jour. SMPTE*, May 1968 p. 499.

135. *Jour. SMPTE*, May 1968, p. 499.

136. "The Ampex Portable Two Plumbicon Color Spells Lots of Gadgetry," *Broadcast Management/Engineering*, June 1968, pp. 40–43.

137. "Compact Studio Camera Simplifies Colorization," *Broadcast Management/Engineering*, January 1969, pp. 37–40.

138. *Broadcast Television*, Nov. 13, 1967, p. 70.

139. *Broadcast Television*, Nov. 1967, p. 66.

140. *Broadcast Television*, Dec. 4, 1967, pp. 38–39.

141. "ABC Using New Ampex Hand-Held Color Cameras," *Broadcasting*, Nov. 6, 1967, p. 9.

142. *Jour. SMPTE*, May 1968, p. 511.

Chapter 8
Television's Finest Hour: Apollo 11 (1968–1971)

1. "Home Color," *Electronics Review*, Feb. 1968, pp. 47–48. *Broadcast Television*, Feb. 19, 1968, pp. 9–10.

2. *Broadcast Television*, Feb. 1968, p. 59. *Broadcast Management/Engineering*, May 1968.

3. *Electronics*, May 13, 1968, p. 136.

4. *Broadcast Management/Engineering* April 1968, p. 89.

5. *Jour. SMPTE*, June 1968, p. 680.

6. "Developments in Color Tape," *Broadcasting*, April 15, 1968, p. 80. *Jour. SMPTE*, June 68, p. 682.

7. "A Convention of Vision IBC 1968," *Wireless World*, November 1968, p. 420.

8. *Broadcast Television*, April 15, 1968, p. 80.

9. *Jour. SMPTE*, July 1968, p. 786. Also *Jour. SMPTE*, May 1969, p. 324.

10. *Broadcast Television*, April 1, 1968, pp. 100–101. Also *Broadcast Management/Engineering* August 1968, p. 28.

11. *Broadcast Television*, April 1, 1968, p. 102.

12. "CBS Labs Device Enhances TV Images," *Broadcasting*, April 1, 1968, p. 104.

13. *Broadcast Television*, April 15, 1968, p. 60.

14. May 9, 1968, *Jour. SMPTE*, Dec. 1968, pp. 300, 302. C. Boise, "New Videodisc Slows and Stops the Action," *Broadcast Management/Engineering*, June 1968, pp. 48–49.

15. *Broadcast Management/Engineering*, May 1968.

16. *Broadcast Management/Engineering*, June 1968, p. 42. "New Cameras Color Them Plentiful," *Broadcast Management/Engineering*, July 1969, pp. 22–29.

17. *Broadcast Television*, April 15, 1968, p. 74.

18. "PAL-SECAM Rapprochement," *Wireless World*, May 1968, p. 110.

19. F. Haines, "Shortcuts in TV Camera Design Make for Big Cuts in Price," *Electronics*, Nov. 11, 1968, pp. 134, 140.

20. "NCTA Gets Look at Latest CATV Gear," *Broadcasting*, July 8, 1968, p. 54.

21. J. D. Drummond, "Waiting for Home VTR? Don't Hold Your Breath," *Electronics*, Sept. 30, 1968, p. 102.

22. "One Tube Color Camera Shown," *Broadcasting*, Nov. 25, 1968, p. 74.

23. "One-Tube Color Camera," *Electronics*, Dec. 9, 1968, pp. 47–48. "New Cameras Color Them Plentiful," *Broadcast Management/Engineering*, July 1969, pp. 22–29.

24. "New Products," *Jour. SMPTE*, October 1968. "One-Tube Color Camera Shown," *Broadcasting*, Nov. 25, 1968, p. 74. "Visual Introduces Low-Light Camera Tubes," *Broadcast Management/Engineering*, December 1968, p. 6. They were the P880 (three-inch) and the P850 (4½-inch). English Electric ad in *Wireless World*, Dec. 1968, p. 3.

25. "Good-bye Kine, Hello EBR-1000," *Broadcast Management/Engineering*, November 1968, p. 15.

26. "CBS at Last Shows EVR in Public," *Broadcasting*, Dec. 16, 1968, pp. 76B, 76C. "Electronic Video Recording Demonstrated in London," *Jour. Royal Television Society*, vol. 2, no. 5, Spring 1969, pp. 116–117.

27. RCA ad *Broadcasting*, Dec. 30, 1968.

28. "IVC VTRs for PAL, SECAM, NTSC," *Broadcast Management/Engineering*, Dec. 1968, p. 55.

29. "IVC Display Recorders and EMI Color Cameras," *Broadcasting*, Feb. 24, 1969, p. 70.

30. "Latest Design Three Tube Color Camera," *Broadcast News*, June 1969.

31. "Data Memory Acquires MVR for $2 Million," *Broadcasting*, Feb. 3, 1969, p. 63.

32. "Focusing in," *Electronics*, Feb. 17, 1969, pp. 54–57. See also this same article, *Electronics*, Feb. 7, 1966.

33. "All Wound Up," *Electronics*, March 31, 1969, pp. 181–182. "New Duplication Process Found by Matsushita," *Broadcasting*, April 14, 1969, p. 65.

34. "Sony VTRs at Bargain Basement Prices," *Broadcast Management/Engineering*, March 1979, p. 6. To my knowledge, G.E. hadn't made a video recorder since 1957 to sell to the government.

35. *Broadcast Television*, April 7, 1969, p. 55.

36. "Industrial News," *The Royal Television Society*, vol. 12, no. 5, Spring 1969, p. 114.

37. "Technicolor Devising Vidtape System for Feature Film Use," *Daily Variety*, November 20, 1969, pp. 1, 8.

38. "Color by Cassette," *Electronics*, May 12, 1969, p. 239.

39. "New Duplication Process Found by Matsushita," *Broadcasting*, April 14, 1969.

40. "VTR Equipment," *Broadcast Management/Engineering*, May 1969, p. 40.

41. *Broadcast News*, June 1969, p. 36.

42. "Cartridge-Type VTR to Be Marketed by Vistro of Japan," *Electronics*, June 23, 1969, p. 213.

43. "New Hand Camera Readied for Apollo 9 Mission," *Broadcasting*, Feb. 17, 1969, p. 87.

44. "Colorful Look at Luna Planned for Apollo 10," *Broadcasting*, April 28, 1969, p. 73.

45. *Technician Engineering*, January 1970, pp. 8–9.

46. "Videotape Recorder," *Broadcast Management/Engineering*, Aug. 1969, p. 48.

47. *Broadcasting*, Sept. 1969, p. 64.

48. "Chromium Dioxide Tape Revisited," *Broadcast Management/Engineering*, September 1969, p. 8.

49. Lardner, op. cit., p. 80.

50. George H. Brown, *And Part of Which I Was*, Angus Cupar Publishers, Princeton, New Jersey, 1982, pp. 282–283. See also Lardner, op. cit., p. 79.

51. W. J. Hannan, "RCA Color–TV Tape Player by 1972," *Broadcasting*, October 6, 1969, pp. 57–59. "Holotape: A Low Cost Prerecorded Television System Using Holographic Storage," *Jour. SMPTE*, November 1973, pp. 905–915.

52. "'Selectavision' Willing, Able But Not Ready," *Electronics*, October 13, 1969, pp. 43–44.

53. "What Is It?" *Broadcast Management/Engineering*, November 1969, p. 53.

54. Brown, op. cit., p. 79.

55. L. Briel, "A Single Vidicon Television Camera System," *Jour. SMPTE*, April 1970, pp. 326–330.

56. "Towards Compatible VTRs," *Electronics*, November 13, 1969, pp. 236–238.

57. "And Another VTR from Sony," *Electronics*, Nov. 10, 1969, p. 236.

58. "Sony Will Enter TV Player Market," *Broadcasting*, Nov. 24, 1969, p. 82.

59. "World's First Video Cartridge Tape System," *Broadcast News*, Dec. 1969, pp. 8–9, 31–35.

60. "Easy Load VCRs Add to Market Muddle," *Broadcast Management/Engineering*, January 1970, pp. 28–29.

61. *Ibid.*

62. "Ampex Makes Copying Quicker," *Broadcasting*, Feb. 2, 1970, p. 63.

63. "SMPTE Winter Conference," *Broadcast Management/Engineering*, April 1970, pp. 18–21.

64. "TV Camera for Low-Light Levels," *Wireless World*, January 1970, p. 9.

65. "David Sarnoff Retires," *Broadcast Management/Engineering*, Feb. 1970.

66. "The Highly Personal Corporate Style of David Sarnoff," *Electronics*, March 2, 1970, p. 102.

67. "CBS Makes Color Device for Final TV Adjustment," *Broadcasting*, Feb. 9, 1970, p. 65.

68. *Broadcast Management/Engineering*, August 1970, p. 22.

69. "Zworykin Recipient Named," *Broadcasting*, March 9, 1970, p. 57. *Broadcast Management/Engineering*, April 1970, p. 64.

70. "First Helical VTR Standard," *Broadcast Management/Engineering*, April 1970, p. 48.

71. "Firms Set Standards for Video Players," *Broadcasting*, March 30, 1970.

72. Lardner, op. cit., p. 73.

73. "Soon the Home Video Will Record in Color," *Broadcasting*, March 30, 1970, p. 50.

74. "IVC Recorder," *Broadcast Management/Engineering*, April 1970, p. 32.

75. *Broadcasting*, April 20, 1970, p. 61.

76. "Color TV with Available Light," *Broadcast Management/Engineering*, April 1970, pp. 34–35.

77. "New Concepts in VTR's" *Broadcast Management/Engineering*, May 1970, p. 26.

78. *Broadcasting*, April 20, 1970, pp. 59–60. Howard Town, "Design Features of the Ampex Videocassette Recorder," *Broadcast Management/Engineering*, September 1970, pp. 31–34.

79. Ampex ad in *Broadcast Management/Engineering*, April 1970.

80. *Broadcast Management/Engineering*, August 1970, p. 22.

81. "See EVR Cost Dropping," *Broadcasting*, May 4, 1970, p. 10.

82. "Videotape Player Updated," *Broadcast Management/Engineering*, May 1970, p. 8.

83. *Electronics*, Sept. 28, 1970, p. 90.

84. "Avco Joins Race for Home-TV Dollar," *Broadcasting*, June 1, 1970, p. 45. "Now It's Cartridge Color from Avco," *Broadcast Management/Engineering*, September 1970, p. 6.

85. "The Poniatoff Award," *Broadcasting*, June 15, 1970, p. 56. I don't want to create any controversy here, but Ray Dolby was not given the award for his herculean efforts to help design and build the first Ampex recorder until 1982 or 1983. In my opinion, with all due respect to Charles Ginsburg, it is possible that the project would have foundered or even failed if it were not for the efforts of Ray Dolby.

86. "Industrial News," *Wireless World*, vol. 13, no. 5, Sept./Oct. 1970, p. 125. A. Harris, "The Teldec Television Disc," *Electronics World*, Feb. 1971, pp. 36–37, 80.

87. "Videodisc Looks Good for Playback," *Electronics*, August 8, 1970, pp. 127–128.

88. "Domestic Video Records," *Wireless World*, July 1970, p. 340.

89. *Tape Recording Magazine*, June 1970, p. 383.

90. "Video Recorders First Use Taping for Feature Film," *Hollywood Reporter*, July 14, 1970, p. 3.

91. J. A. Flaherty, "Trends in Television Recording," *Jour. SMPTE*, July 1970, p. 582. 18 years later at the SMPTE conference in Nashville (Feb. 1988), he admitted that he had confessed, in his first article for the *Journal SMPTE*, that videotape could never compete with the quality of 16mm film. "Engineers Come to Terms with Transition in Nashville," *Broadcasting*, Feb. 8, 1988, p. 106.

92. "An American View on Film and Tape," *Jour. Royal Television Society*, Nov./Dec. 1970, p. 148.

93. "Portable VTR Reproduces Color," *Electronics*, Sept. 14, 1970, pp. 155–158. "Instavision Cartridge VTR System," *Jour. Royal Television Society*, Jan./Feb. 1971, p. 165.

94. M. Offenheiser, "Cartridge TV Rush Loses Momentum," *Electronics*, October 25, 1971, p. 106.

95. "Newest Video Player Unveiled," *Broadcast Management/Engineering*, October 1970, p. 6.

96. "Name Change," *Broadcasting*, March 29, 1971, p. 107.

97. "EVR in Production," *Jour. Royal Television Society*, vol. 13, no. 5, Nov./Dec. 1970, p. 139. "Domestic Video Records," *Wireless World*, July 1970, p. 340.

98. J. C. G Gilbert, "The Video Disc," "*Wireless World*, August 1970, pp. 377–378. Also "Video on a Disc," *Broadcast Management/Engineering*, January 1971, p. 8.

99. "Another Firm Unveils Video Playback System," *Broadcasting*, Oct. 25, 1970, p. 54.

100. "EVR Manufacturing Pact," *Broadcasting*, Nov. 30, 1970, p. 49.

101. "Sony Reveals $1000 Color TV Camera," *Broadcast Management/Engineering*, March 1971.

102. "One Tube Color Camera," *Technician-Engineer*, Feb. 1971, p. 12.

103. "'Convention,' SMPTE Winter Conference," *Broadcast Management/Engineering*, March 1971, pp. 16–17.

104. J. Flaherty, Jr. and K. Taylor, "New Television Production Techniques," *Jour. SMPTE*, August 1971, pp. 605–611.

105. "CMX," *Broadcast Management/Engineering*, May 1971, p. 46.

106. "CMX," *Broadcasting*, March 22, 1971, p. 126.

107. J. Flaherty and W. H. Butler, "Why Use Film?" *American Cinematographer*, August 1971, pp. 828–829.

108. "CBS-Memorex Venture Hits Pay Dirt," *Broadcasting*, March 22, 1971, p. 125. "CMX-600 Edits Film or Tape by Mini-computer," *Daily Variety*, March 19, 1971, p. 30.

109. Albert Abramson, "Pioneers of Television — Philo Taylor Farnsworth," *Jour. SMPTE*, November 1992, pp. 770–784.

110. "Cassettes: Special Report," *Broadcasting*, April 26, 1971, p. 61.

111. "Cartridge TV Rush Loses Momentum," *Electronics*, October 25, 1971, p. 106.

112. M. Offenheiser, "Videotape on the Spot — from AKAI," *Broadcast Management/Engineering*, April 1971, p. 6.

113. "Magnetic Videotape Recording Glossary," *Jour. SMPTE*, May 1971, p. 414. I wrote a bitter letter to Charles Anderson of Ampex, who was in charge of the committee, stating that the term "quadruplex" had no basis in fact. There was never a simplex, duplex or triplex recorder mentioned anywhere in any RCA report that I could find; it was merely a device by RCA to make it seem that they had invented the Ampex machine. I also complained about using the terms "headwheel" instead of drum and Anderson said that the word "drum" was confusing (*Jour. SMPTE*, Dec. 1970, p. 1104). The word "headwheel" never came up until after RCA came up with its version of the Ampex transverse recorder. The same was true of "vacuum guide" instead of female guide, and so on. I received no answer from Anderson. By November 1988, it seemed that headwheel had been replaced by drum after all. The term headwheel was "limited to small rotatable wheels used in transverse recorders. Larger wheels are usually referred to as drums or head drums." In regard to transverse recording it was stated that "Quadruplex recording is a *specific* standardized example of this method." What nonsense! Then to add to the confusion a *scanner* was defined "as a mechanical assembly containing a drum, rotating pole tips and tape guiding elements used to record and reproduce videotape recordings." So what happened to headwheel? "TV Tape Recording Nomenclature," *Jour. SMPTE*, November 1988, pp. 928–935.

114. "The Alexander M. Poniatoff Award," *Jour. SMPTE*, May 1971, p. 420.

115. "Quadraphony and Home Video Steal the Berlin Show," *Wireless World*, October 1971, p. 488. *Broadcasting*, Oct. 25, 1971, p. 58, says the date was June 24, 1971.

116. "Other Stars of Apollo: The Cameras," *Broadcasting*, August 9, 1971, p. 27. "Color TV Cameras Shines in Spectacular Apollo Mission," *Broadcasting*, August 16, 1971, p. 37–38.

117. "200 Motels, a Rock 'n' Roll Tour on Film," *Los Angeles Times*, October 30, 1971.

118. "Tape to Film Revolution," *Variety*, Nov. 17, 1971, p. 9.

119. "3M, Sony in Videocassette Pact," *Technician-Engineer*, Oct. 1971, p. 3. "3M and Sony in Cross-License Agreement," *Int. Broadcast Engineer*, Jan. 1972, p. 25. The Sony U-matic recorded color by a heterodyned carrier (color under) with a limited bandwidth (approximately 2.5MHz) but not good enough for broadcast purposes. Then FM modulated a carrier with the video sync tip setting at 3.8MHz. Color, separated by a comb filter, was mixed from 3.8 MHz to around 688kHz, then both signals were expanded back to their original 63.5 u/sec length and modulated onto the 3.58MHz subcarrier for encoded composite video. C. Bentz, "½

inch — No Passing Fad," *Broadcast Engineering*, November 1984, p. 130.

120. *Broadcast Management/Engineering*, November 1971, p. 7.

121. "Super 8 Sound-Film Videoplayer Developed," *Broadcasting*, Oct. 25, 1971, p. 56. "Kodak Readies Video System," *Broadcasting*, Nov. 15, 1971, p. 48.

122. "Super 8 TV," *Radio-Electronics*, February 1972, p. 4.

123. "Low Cost Color TV Camera," October 1971, *Broadcast Management/Engineering*, p. 36.

124. Photo caption, *Broadcast Management/Engineering*, Nov. 1971, p. 7.

125. 'Last Tributes to David Sarnoff,' *Broadcasting*, Dec. 20, 1971, p. 28.

126. E. W. Engstrom, "David Sarnoff 1891–1971," *RCA Review*, 1971. I chose Mr. Engstrom's remarks as he was best qualified to speak for David Sarnoff. Engstrom had been in television since 1932 and coordinated the Zworykin group at Camden in their production of a practical television system that is still with us today.

127. "CMX Out Commercially," *Broadcasting*, Dec. 20, 1971, p. 51.

128. Paley, *Glory*, p. 470.

129. "A Miracle Turns Sour for CBS," *Broadcasting*, Dec. 27, 1971, pp. 16–17.

130. Goldmark, op. cit., p. 198.

131. Paley, *As It Happened*, op. cit. p. 227.

132. "The Goldmark Era to End at CBS Labs," *Broadcasting*, Aug. 21, 1971, p. 28.

133. Joe Roizen, "Videocassettes Exhibition, VIDCA, Cannes, March 1972," *Broadcast Management/Engineering*, November 1972, p. 42.

Chapter 9
The Rise of Electronic Journalism (1972–76)

1. "JVC Videocassette System Is Compatible with Sony's," *Broadcast Management/Engineering*, January 1972, p. 8.

2. *Broadcasting*, January 10, 1972. *Broadcast Engineering*, March 1971, p. 97.

3. D. M. Amagill, "Color Cameras See Red," *Broadcast Management/Engineering*, April 1972, p. 39–41. "Mass Production of Silicon Vidicons Holds Key to Picturephone's Future," *Electronics*, January 19, 1970, pp. 81, 131. See also: E. I. Gordon and M. H. Crowell, "A Charge Storage Target for Electron Image Sensing," *Bell System Tech. Jour.* November 1968, pp. 1855–1873; M. H. Crowell' and E. F. Labuda, "The Silicon Diode Array Camera Tube," *Bell System Technical Journal*, May-June 1969, pp. 1481–1528; P. K. Weimer, "Multi-Element Self Scanned Mosaic Sensors," *IEEE Spectrum*, vol. 6, pp. 52–66, Jan. 1969; W. S. Boyle, and G. E. Smith, "Charge Coupled Semiconducting Devices," *Bell Systems Tech. Jour.* 49, pp. 587–593, April 1970; A. J. Woolgar and C. J. Bennett, "Silicon Diode-Array Tubes and Targets," *Jour. Royal Television Society*, vol. 13, no. 3m, May-June 1970; "Tivicon Image Tubes from Texas Instruments," *Bulletin CO-142*, Texas Instruments Inc., Dallas, Texas; and R. K. Johnson, "Application of RCA Silicon diodes Array Target Vidicons," *Camera Tube Application*, Note AN-4623, RCA Corp., Lancaster, Pa. 17604.

References from Weimer paper, "A Historical Review of the Development of Television Pickup Devices (1930–1976)" by Paul K. Weimer, *IEEE Transactions on Electron Devices*, July 1976, pp. 739–752:

P. K. Weimer, "Systems and Technologies for Solid-State Image Sensors," *RCA Review*, vol. 32, 1971, p. 251; G. Strull et al., "Solid State Array Cameras," *Applied Optics*, vol. 11, p. 1032; R. H. Dyck and G. P. Weckler, "Integrated Arrays of Silicon Photo-Detectors for Image Sensing," *IEEE Transactions Electron Devices*, vol. ED-15, 1968, p. 196; T. P. Brody et al., "A 6 × 6 Inch 20-lpi Electroluminescent Display Panel," *IEEE Transactions Electron Devices*, vol. ED-22, 1975, p. 739; F. L. J. Sangster and K. Teer, "Bucket-Brigade Electronics — New Possibilities for Delay, Time Axis Conversion and Scanning," IEEE *Journal Solid-State Circuits*, vol. SC-4, 1969, p. 131; W. S. Boyle and G. E. Smith, "Charge-Coupled Semiconductor Devices," *Bell System Technical* Journal, vol. 49, 1970, p. 587; F. L. J. Sangster, "Integrated MOS and Bipolar Analog Delay Lines Using Bucket Brigade Capacitor Storage," in *1970 IEEE International Conference Digest of Technical Papers*, (Philadelphia, Feb. 18–20, 1970), p. 74; P. K. Weimer, "Self-Scanned Image Sensors Based on Charge Transfer by the Bucket-Brigade Method," *IEEE Transactions Electron Devices*, vol. ED-18, 1971, p. 996; M. G. Kovac et al., "Solid State Imaging Emerges from Charge Transport," *Electronics*, vol. 45, 1972, p. 72; C. H. Séquin et al., "A Charge-Coupled Area Image Sensor and Frame Store," *IEEE Transactions Electron Devices*, vol. ED-20, 1973, p. 244; L. Walsh and R. H. Dyck, "A New Charge-Coupled Area Imaging Device," in *CCD Applied Conference Proceedings* (Naval Electronics Laboratory, San Diego, CA, TD-274), 1973, p. 21; News Item, *Electronics*, July 10, 1975, p. 38; and R. L. Rodgers, III, "Charge-Coupled Imager for 525-line Television Presented at the 1974 IEEE Intercon Meeting in New York."

4. L. M. Biberman "IDA's Biberman Sees SEC Tube as a Work Horse," *Electronics*, September 1, 1969, pp. 66–73.

5. From "Color Cameras See Red," *Broadcast Management/Engineering*, April 1972, p. 39–41.

6. "New Products," *Jour. SMPTE*, May 1971, p. 371.

7. L.M. Biberman, "IDA's Biberman Sees SEC Tube as a Work Horse," *Electronics*, September 1, 1969, pp. 66–73. "New Products," *Jour. SMPTE*, November 1970.

8. W. S. Pike, M. G. Kovac, F. V. Shallcross and P. K. Weimer, "An Experimental Solid State Camera Using a 32 × 44 Element Charge-Transfer Bucket-Brigade Sensor," *RCA Review*, vol. 33, September 1972, pp. 483–501.

9. "A Very Mini Camera in the Testing Stage," *Broadcasting*, March 20, 1972, p. 47.

10. "Old Technique Spawns Hybrid Vidicon Imager," *Electronics*, November 6, 1972.

11. Ad in *Broadcast Engineering*, March 1972, p. 58.

12. "Color TV Cassette Uses 8-mm Film," *Electronics*, March 27, 1972, p. 56.

13. F. J Haines, "Color Cameras See Red," *Broadcast Management/Engineering*, April 1972, pp. 39–41, 80. "Color Camera," *Broadcast Management/Engineering*, May 1971, p. 28.

14. "Will Ampex Rise from Almost the Ashes?" *Broadcasting*, April 10, 1972, pp. 102–103.

15. "Videocassette Machine," *Broadcasting Engineering*, June 1972, p. 43.

16. "The VCR Is on the Way," *Broadcasting*, May 29, 1972, p. 46.

17. "NAB Convention," *Broadcast Management/Engineering*, June 1972, p. 44.

18. "Hardware Sales Take Off in Chicago," *Broadcasting*, April 17, 1972, p. 74–75.

19. It was described in the March issue of *Wireless World*, 1972, p. 138.

20. "I. E. E. E. Show in New York," *Wireless World*, May 1972, p. 243.

21. "Live Instant Replay," *Radio-Electronics*, May 1972, p. 4. "World's Biggest TV Screens in New Orleans Superdome," *Radio-Electronics*, July 1972, p. 4.

22. "Three Nations' EVR Combine," *Broadcasting*, May 22, 1971, p. 56.

23. "American Boost for European EVR," *Wireless World*, May 1972.

24. Videotape Editing Equipment Plentiful," *Broadcast Management/Engineering*, July 1972, p. 16.

25. G. Swetland, "Editing Videotape Easy with SMPTE Code," *Broadcast Management/Engineering*, July 1972, pp. 23, 37.

26. "Video Cartridge Advance," *Broadcasting*, June 26, 1972, p. 53.

27. "Looking Ahead," *Radio Electronics*, July 1972.

28. "New RCA Color Tube," *Radio-Electronics*, Sept. 1972, p. 4. For further details, see "New and Timely," *Radio Electronics*, Sept. 1972, p. 6.

29. "New RCA Color Tube," *Radio-Electronics*, September 1972, p. 4.

30. "RCA Redoes the Color Tube," *Broadcasting*, June 19, 1972, p. 52

31. "Super 8 Is at a KDUB-TV," *Broadcasting*, Aug. 21, 1972, p. 38.

32. "Ampex Recorder Is Here," *Broadcasting*, July 10, 1972, p. 45.

33. "RCA's Home TVR," *Radio-Electronics*, July 1972, p. 4.

34. "Videotape Editing Equipment Plentiful," *Broadcast Management/Engineering*, July 1972, pp. 16–17. The last CMX 600 was still in use at One Pass Video in San Francisco in 1984. See Art Schneider, *Broadcast Engineering*, April 1984, p. 282

35. H. A. Shepard, "Videotape Editing with Computer Control," *Broadcast Management/Engineering*, July 1972, pp. 24–26, 40.

36. "Army Testing Sony Cartridge Television," *Electronics*, July 1972, p. 30.

37. "Conversation with Charles Ginsburg," *Videography*, April 1983, p. 72.

38. James Lardner, "*Fast Forward*," W. W. Norton & Company, New York, 1987, p. 70.

39. "The Videocassette Is Beginning to Roll," *Broadcast Management/Engineering*, October 1972, pp. 40–41.

40. "Catching up," *db Magazine*, March 1973, p. 20.

41. "CCDs Spawn All-Solid State Color TV Camera," *Electronics*, August 14, 1972, pp. 39–40.

42. "New VTR's," *Broadcasting*, Sept. 11, 1972.

43. Ampex ad in *Broadcast Management/Engineering*, September 1972, p. 2.

44. "Ampex Decided to Scrap Its Instavideo System," *Broadcasting*, Oct. 16, 1971, p. 60.

45. *Variety*, Aug. 7, 1972, p. 2.

46. Art Schneider, "The Videodisc Revolution," *Broadcast Engineering*, April 1984, p. 282.

47. At this time CBS and the IBEW had been in contract negotiations for some three months. Two weeks after the *Sandcastles* shooting, the Union voted to go out on strike against CBS. When this happened, CBS moved the CMX-600 to TV City where, with the help of management, New York engineers hoped to get some of the snags out of the machine. But even here they could not do much with it. It was just too cumbersome and useless. When the strike was over and they had not got the right to shoot tape at Studio Center, the machine was sent back to Studio Center where it languished for a while and was then sold for a fraction of its cost. I was there at the time. It was claimed that the picture was edited on the CMX-600 and the first cut of the movie was ready to be reviewed the day after shooting was completed. See "On Videotape Haste Doesn't Make Waste," *Broadcasting*, October 16, 1972, p. 59.

48. J. Beigel, "Videotape Revolution — or Is It Evolution? Grows in Film World," *Los Angeles Times*, Nov. 4, 1972, p. 16.

49. "Sandcastles," *Variety*, Oct. 17, 1972, p. 9.

50. Delmer Daves, "You've Come a Long Way, Baby," *Action* (Journal of the Screen Directors Guild), Sept.-Oct. 1972, pp. 28–32.

51. "Video Long Playing Records," *Wireless World*, October 1972, p. 474.

52. "Sony, IVC Upstage Exhibitors at NAEB," *Broadcasting*,

Nov. 6, 1972, p. 53. The first picture of the new IVC one-inch videocassette recorder was shown in June 1973. It was being distributed in England by Bell & Howell Video Systems Divisions, Middlesex. It had actually been introduced in November 1972.

53. "Sony, IVC Upstage Exhibitors at NAEB," *Broadcasting*, Nov. 6, 1972, p. 53.

54. F. H. J. Van De Poel and H. Foerster, "Television Studio Color Recording with Helical Scan," *Jour. Royal Television Society*, pp. 147–150.

55. "An LP Videodisc," *Radio Electronics*, Nov. 1972, p. 4.

56. "Disco-Vision Premiered," *Broadcast Management/Engineering*, February 1973. "MCA Enters Disk in Marketing Race for TV Playback," *Broadcasting*, Dec. 18, 1972, p. 49.

57. "Is Videotape Taking Over — Can Film Hang in There?" *Broadcast Management/Engineering*, January 1973, pp. 24–31.

58. "The Newest Believer in CBS's Minicam; NBC News's Dick Wald," *Broadcasting*, May 14, 1973, p. 52.

59. "Portability and High Performance in New VTR from Echo Science," *Broadcast Management/Engineering*, March 1973, p. 32.

60. "Catching Up," *db*, March 1973, p. 20.

61. "Largest-Ever NAB Convention Witnesses Turning Point in Technology and Regulations," *Broadcast Management/Engineering*, May 1973, p. 26.

62. "NAB," *Broadcasting*, April 2, 1973, pp. 84–85.

63. *Ibid*.

64. "A Vote for Videotape," *Broadcasting*, April 2, 1973, p. 89.

65. "Montreux Television Symposium," *Wireless World*, July 1973, p. 333.

66. "Four New Tape Standards Promoted," *Broadcast Management/Engineering*, September 1973, pp. 39, 40, 62–68. B. E. Guisinger, "A New Segmented-Scan Helical Broadcast Video Recorder," *Jour. SMPTE*, Feb. 1974, pp. 94–99.

67. "New Tape Standards," *Broadcast Management/Engineering*, September 1973, p. 67. An article about Quad II by J. L. Grever, "An Analysis of Quadruples and Helical Scan Video Recording," *Jour. SMPTE*, February 1974, pp. 109–113, was quite different. Here a Quad 1A for 525 line standards was mentioned.

68. "Four New Tape 'Standards' Promoted," *Broadcast Management/Engineering*, December 1973, pp. 39–40, 68.

69. "Has Tape, Will Travel," *Broadcasting*, July 4, 1973, p. 65.

70. "Sterling-Manhattan Cable TV Combines Time Base Corrector with U-matic Cassette," *Broadcast Management/Engineering*, July 1943, p. 7.

71. "Home TV readout," *Radio Electronics*, October 1973, p. 4.

72. "Miniature Solid-State TV Camera," *Wireless World*, October 1973, p. 478.

73. "New Super 8 Sound Camera and Ultra-Fast Processor Announced by Eastman-Kodak," *Broadcast Management/Engineering*, December 1973, p. 6.

74. "Ampex, IVC Locked in Tape-Patent Suit," *Broadcasting*, Nov. 19, 1973, p. 53.

75. "Conversation with Nick Nishi," *Videography*, April 1985, pp. 85–86.

76. "Smaller Is Better for CBS–News," *Broadcasting*, Nov. 12, 1973, pp. 54–55.

77. "Ampex Debuts Miniature VTR," *Broadcast Management/Engineering*, November 1973, p. 6.

78. "Midget," *Broadcasting*, Sept. 17, 1973, p. 49.

79. "Videoplayer Census," *Radio-Electronics*, July 1974, p. 4.

80. "Tape and Film: The Fight Goes On," *Broadcast Management/Engineering*, January 1974, pp. 28–33.

81. "Electronic News Gathering," *Jour. SMPTE*, May 1974, p. 376.

82. Lardner, op. cit., p. 73.

83. "Signal Cleaner," *Broadcasting*, Feb. 11, 1974, p. 57.

84. "Price Cut," *Broadcasting*, Feb. 4, 1974, p. 42.

85. "Picture This," *Broadcasting*, Mar. 18, 1974, p. 83.

86. "All the Comforts of Home Base," *Broadcasting*, March 25, 1974, p. 66.

87. "CCD Imager Achieves Full TV Resolution for the First Time," *Electronics*, March 21, 1974, p. 229–39. R. L. Rogers II, "Charge-Coupled Imager for 525 Line Television," paper presented at the 1974 IEEE Intercon Meeting in New York.

88. *Broadcast News*, July 1974, p. 13.

89. RCA ad in *Broadcast Management/Engineering*, December 1975, p. 22.

90. "New TV Recorder Hardware Unveiled in Houston," *Broadcasting*, Mar. 25, 1974, p. 65.

91. "NAB Show in Print-74," *Broadcast Management/Engineering*, May 1974, p. 26.

92. "NEW TV Recorder," *Broadcasting*, March 25, 1974, p. 65.

93. "Nab Convention Highlights— A Modular Quad," *Broadcast Management/Engineering*, May 1964, p. 6.

94. RCA ad in *Broadcast Management/Engineering*, December 1975, p. 22.

95. *Broadcasting*, March 25, 1974, p. 65.

96. "Recent Advances in Videotape Recorders," *Broadcast Management/Engineering*, Feb. 1975, p. 45.

97. *Broadcast Management/Engineering*, May 1974, p. 26.

98. *Ibid.*, p. 28.

99. "NAB Show in Print-74," *Broadcast Management/Engineering*, May 1974, p. 30.

100. H. Lind, "A Portable Camera Control Unit for the TKP-45 Color Television Camera," *Jour. SMPTE*, Feb. 1976, pp. 65–69.

101. "NAB Show in Print-74," *Broadcast Management/Engineering*, May 1974, p. 35.

102. "Roizen Given Award," *Broadcast Engineering*, May 1974, p. 11.

103. Ken Winslow, "Television Techniques," *Photo Methods for Industry*, June 1974, pp. 49–50.

104. "Experimental Digital Recorder," *Wireless World*, June 1974, p. 185. There were several articles on digital recording, starting in 1973 (from *Jour. SMPTE*, July 1975, p. 555): (1) J. P. Chambers, "The Use of Coding Techniques to Reduce the Tape Consumption of Digital Television Recording," a paper presented on 17 Oct. 1973 at the Society's 114th Technical Conference in New York. (2) V.G. Devereux, "Bit-Rate Reduction of Digital Video Signals Using Differential PCM Techniques," International Broadcast Conference, London, Sept. 1974. (3) Charles F. Spitzer, "Digital Recording of Video Signals up to 50 MHz," presented at the SPIE Conference on Military Airborne Video Recording, 3-5 Apr. 1973, Dayton, Ohio. (4) J. S. Griffin, "Ultra High Data Rate Digital Recording," a paper presented at the SPIE Conference on Military Airborne Video Recording, 3–5 Apr. 1973, Dayton, Ohio. (5) J. P. Chambers and A. H. Jones, "Digital Magnetic Recording: Conventional Saturation Techniques," BBC Research Dept., Report No. 1972 /9. (6) A. H. Jones and F. A. Bellis, "An Experimental Approach to Digital Television Recording," International Broadcast Conference, London, Sept. 1973. (7) A. H. Jones and F. A. Bellis, "An Experimental Approach to Digital Television Recording: A Review of Current Development," BBC Research Dept., Report No. 1973/29.

105. CVS ad in *Broadcast Engineering*, July 1974, p. 1. It is strange that Television Microtime Inc. doesn't even get a mention in the development of the digital time-base corrector. In a history of the time-base corrector, the author goes right from the Ampex Amtec analog system to the 1973 NAB Convention in Washington when CVS introduced a digital time-base corrector with a window of +1.5 horizontal lines, two magnitudes better than any other. H. Blakeslee, "Time Base Correctors Arrive Just in Time," *Broadcast Engineering*, January 1975, pp. 28–31.

106. "NBC Leaning to Fernseh as Minicam Entry in $25 Million Deal Prospect," *Broadcasting*, Sept. 30, 1974, p. 37.

107. "CMX Systems" ad in *Broadcast Management/Engineering*, October 1974, p. 57.

108. "New ⅔ Inch Plumbicon," *Broadcast Management/Engineering*, November 1974, p. 69.

109. "New from Ampex," *Broadcasting*, Dec. 9, 1974, p. 58.

110. "Tubeless CCD TV Camera Shown by RCA," *Broadcast Management/Engineering*, March 1975, p. 6.

111. Casey Davidson, "Electronic News Gathering," part 1 "The Lightweight Revolution," *Jour. Royal Television Society*, October 1977, p. iv. (Of course, this does not agree with Flaherty's statement that *he* was responsible for the start of ENG at CBS News.) "CBS," *Broadcast Management/Engineering*, January 1975, p. 48.

112. "CBS," *Broadcast Management/Engineering*, January 1975, p. 48.

113. *Ibid.*, p. 48.

114. *Ibid.*, p. 49.

115. "Today's 16mm Film Cameras Are Designed for Television News Gathering," *Broadcast Management/Engineering*, April 1975, pp. 32–34.

116. "Miniature Solid State TV Camera," *Wireless World*, Feb. 1975, pp. 59–60.

117. "The Sony MV-1000 Helical Scan VTR," *Broadcast Management/Engineering*, Feb. 1975, p. 48.

118. "NAB 1975," *Broadcast Management/Engineering*, March 1975, p. 46. (From Asaca ad on p. 126.)

119. "1 INCH QUADRUPLEX PORTABLE HIGH BAND VTR MODEL ASACA AVS 3200," *Asaca Products Guide*, 1975.

120. "Number 200," *Broadcasting*, March 24, 1975, p. 47.

121. J. Roizen, "SMPTE Provides a Forum for Electronic Journalism," *Broadcast Engineering*, March 1975, pp. 48–52, 53.

122. CVS ad in *Broadcast Management/Engineering*, May 1975, p. 13.

123. "Mastering U-matic VTR Adds Edit Capability to Cassette Convenience," *Broadcast Management/Engineering*, February 1975, p. 77.

124. "Broadcaster-Orientated Features on the U-matic Product Line at NAB," *Broadcast Management/Engineering*, March 1975, p. 96.

125. "Separate Record and Playback Deck from Sony," *Broadcast Management/Engineering*, March 1976, p. 6.

126. "Second Generation," *Broadcasting*, Feb. 23, 1976, p. 86.

127. Lardner, op. cit., p. 96.

128. Lardner, op. cit., p. 96.

129. "Progress Report," *Jour. SMPTE*, May 1976, pp. 312–313.

130. Lardner, op. cit., pp. 87–96.

131. "An Experimental 'Tubeless' Camera," *Jour. SMPTE*, May 1975, p. 430.

132. "Final Chapter May Be Written on CBS Labs," *Broadcasting*, April 7, 1975, p. 92.

133. "Coming Soon Home Video Players," *Radio-Electronics*, June 1975, pp. 33–34.

134. "Cartrivision," *Radio-Electronics*, June 1975, p. 34.

135. "V-Cord," *Radio-Electronics*, June 1975, p. 34.

136. "For July Delivery," *Broadcasting*, June 30, 1975, p. 56.

137. "Creative Teleproduction Boosted by New Editing Systems," *Broadcast Management/Engineering*, June 1975, p. 39.

138. "The TK-76," "New Products," *Jour. SMPTE*, July 1975. "TK-76 — A New Portable Video Color Camera," *Broadcast News*, December 1975, p. 28.

139. "Portable Camera," *Broadcast Engineering*, March 1975, p 38.

140. "The TR-1000," "New Products," *Jour. SMPTE*, July 1975, p. 582.

141. Bilby, *RCA*, p. 295.

142. Bilby, op. cit., pp. 295–296.

143. "More from the Berlin Show," *Wireless World*, November 1975, p. 599.

144. "Growth Rate of ENG is High," *Broadcast Management/ Engineering*, December 1975, pp. 8–9.

145. "Cinemascope-like Color TV Is Now Possible with New System," *Radio-Electronics*, 1975, p. 6.

146. "RCA VTR Postponed," *Radio-Electronics*, 1975, p. 4.

147. "The MB-201 TV Camera," "New Products," *Jour. SMPTE*, January 1976, p. 50.

148. R. Ouodomine, "Total Changeover to ENG Improves Product, Raises Efficiency, Saves Money at WOR," *Broadcast Management/Engineering*, January 1976, pp. 58–60. I can attest to this personally. At CBS it was always brought to our attention that we were not creative but only technicians. Management was always trying to put us down. Why, I'll never know, for CBS television technicians in Hollywood were the finest in the industry. Proof of this was the fact that independent producers would pay extra money to do their production at TV City knowing that, even though the technical equipment was the same, the crews would give them a perfect show. Somehow New York engineering was down on us and never let up.

149. Casey Davidson, "Electronic News Gathering, Part 1: The Lightweight Revolution," *Jour. Royal Television Society*, October 1977, p. iv. This was not true in Hollywood. Here CBS summarily fired all of its news film crews and news film editors, without giving them a chance to be retrained in the new technology.

150. "Ampex Corp," *Broadcast Management/Engineering*, January 1976, p. 20.

151. "The Cinevid-16," "New Products," *Jour. SMPTE*, August 1975, p. 686. See also "CINEVID-16" ad from Cinema Products in *Broadcast Management/Engineering*, January 1976, p. 75. "Cameras and Their Accessories, Progress Report," *Jour. SMPTE*, May 1976, p. 271.

152. Ikegami ad in *Broadcast Management/Engineering*, Feb. 1976, p. 16. In April 1985, they claimed that they had sold more than 5,000 Hl-79s by 1984. "Conversation with Nick Nishi," *Videography*, April 1985, pp. 84–90.

153. "TMM Group Orders Ten IVC-9000's," *Broadcast Management/Engineering*, Feb. 1976, p. 20.

154. Ad in *Broadcast Management/Engineering*, Feb. 1976, p. 29. "Live Journalism Joins Weight Watchers," *Broadcast Engineering*, June 1976, p. 30. "Microcam I: A New Concept in the Design of a Portable Color Camera for Broadcast Applications," by R. H. McMann and C. W. Smith, *Jour. SMPTE*, Sept. 1976, pp. 724–728.

155. "Ampex, IVC Call Off Eight-Year Court Fight," *Broadcasting*, Feb. 16, 1976, p. 72.

156. "The Electronic Still Store System," *Jour. SMPTE*, February 1976, p. 104. "Digital Still Store System," *Broadcast Engineering*, Dec. 1976, pp. 79–80. W. G. Connolly, "The Electronic Still Store," *Jour. SMPTE*, August 1976, pp. 609–613.

157. J. Roizen, "The Videotape Recorder Revolution," *Broadcast Engineering*, May 1976, pp. 50–53.

158. "NAB Video Review," *Broadcasting Engineering*, May 1976, p. 20. "NAB Celebrates 20th Anniversary of the VTR," *Broadcast Engineering*, May 1976, p. 50.

159. "The VPR-1," "New Products," *Jour. SMPTE*, April 1976, p. 250. "NAB Video Review," *Broadcasting Engineering*, May 1976, p. 21.

160. "Correction on 1 Inch VTR Standard," *Broadcast Management/Engineering*, October 1977, p. 105.

161. Mark Sanders, "The Development of the Ampex AST System," *Video Systems*, April 1980, pp. 46–53. See also R. A. Hathaway and Ray Ravazza, "Report of 121st Technical Conference — Development and Design of the Ampex Auto-Scan Tracking System (AST)," *Jour. SMPTE*, January 1980, p. 7.

162. "NAB Video Review," *Broadcasting Engineering*, May 1976, p. 25.

163. "NAB Show in Print," May 1976, *Broadcast Management/Engineering*, p. 42.

164. *Ibid.*

165. "AVR-3," "New Products," *Jour. SMPTE*, April 1976, p. 248. "NAB Show in Print," *Broadcast Management/Engineering*, May 1976, p. 44.

166. "The IVC-9000-4" "New Products," *Jour. SMPTE*, April 1976, p. 252.

167. "NAB Show in Print," May 1976, *Broadcast Management/Engineering*, p. 62.

168. "NAB Convention," *Broadcast Management/Engineering*, February 1977, p. 80.

169. "Portable Color Camera," *Broadcast Engineering*, September 1976, p. 164.

170. D. M. Rody, "A 22 lb, ¼ Inch Portable Color Video Camera/Recorder System," *Jour. SMPTE*, August 1975, pp. 607–609.

171. "NAB Show in Print," *Broadcast Management/Engineering*, May 1976, p. 42.

172. "A New Slow Motion Color Videodisc Recorder," "New Products," *Jour. SMPTE*, April 1976, p. 250.

173. "NAB Show in Print," *Broadcast Management/Engineering*, May 1976, p. 58.

174. *Ibid.*, pp. 58, 174.

175. "Live Journalism Joins Weight Watchers," *Broadcast Engineering*, June 1976, p. 34. Sony ad in *Broadcast Engineering*, October 1976, p. 17.

176. "NAB Show in Print," *Broadcast Management/Engineering*, May 1976, pp. 33–68.

177. "Union of Soviet Socialist Republics: Cinematography," *Jour. SMPTE*, August 1976, p. 627.

178. From Hitachi ad in *Broadcast Management/Engineering*, July 1976, p. 65.

179. "George Schlatter," *Jour. SMPTE*, August 1976, p. 655.

180. *Ibid.*

181. *Ibid.*

182. *Ibid.*

183. Rowland Gould, *The Matsushita Phenomena*, Diamond Sha Pub. Co., Tokyo, 1970, p. 101. It is interesting that the Victor Company of Japan had been working on television in the early '30s due to their connection with RCA in the USA. Most of their research was done by the Japanese television pioneer Kenjiro Takayangi who gave his first TV demonstration in 1928. This is also related in *The Matsushita Phenomena* on p. 64. After the War he worked for the Victor Company as the head of the television research department.

184. For early details of Takayangi's career, see Abramson *The History of Television*, vol. 1, pp. 112–114.

185. "Profile of Mr. Kenjiro Takayangi," *JVC press release*, 1981, p. 1.

186. This came from Lardner, *Fast Forward*, pp. 89–98. The information on the V-Cord and VX-2000 came from "Videotape Recorders for 1978," *Radio-Electronics*, February 1978, pp. 52–55.

187. "TMI Will Make and Sell Faroudja Image Enhancer," *Broadcast Management/Engineering*, Sept. 1976, p. 13.

188. "NBC Marks Its Golden Anniversary," *Broadcast Management/Engineering*, Sept. 1976, p. 18.

189. RCA ad in *Broadcast Management/Engineering*, Sept. 1976, pp. 54–55.

190. JVC ad in *Broadcast Management/Engineering*, Sept. 1976.

191. "Progress Committee Report for 1976," *Jour. SMPTE*, May 1977, p. 332.

192. Ed DiGiulio, "The ENG 'Emperor' Has No Clothes!" Cinema Products ad in *Broadcast Management/Engineering*, October 1976, p. 23.

193. "Interest in ENG Exceeded Arrangements at IBC 76," *Broadcast Management/Engineering*, November 1976, pp. 72–76.

194. Muller, "Videotape Post Production: A Survey of Methods and Equipment," *Jour. SMPTE*, April 1977, p. 210. In 1984, only one CMX-600 was in use.

195. R. Merrill, "What's Ahead for Broadcasters?" *Broadcast Engineering*, December 1976, pp. 28–32.

Chapter 10
Television Enters the Studios (1977–1979)

1. "ENG Extends the Reporter's Day," *Broadcast Management/Engineering*, January 1977, pp. 40–65.

2. "Home Screen Competition Heats Up with RCA Entry," *Broadcast Management/Engineering*, October 1977, p. 6.

3. Sobel, *RCA*, p. 231.

4. "New One-Inch VTR Formats Go into Action," *Broadcast Management/Engineering*, April 1977, pp. 33–42.

5. "Digital Developments, Production Trends, Satellite Progress Highlight 10th International Television Symposium," *Broadcast Management/Engineering*, August 1977, pp. 52–56. J.L. Baldwin, "Some Aspects of Digital Video Magnetic Recording," 10th International Television Symposium, Montreux, 1977. See also John Baldwin, "Digital Television Recording with Low Tape Consumption," *Jour. SMPTE*, July 1979, pp. 490–492.

6. "CBS Mounts Assault on 35mm Film Use," *Broadcast Management/Engineering*, August 1977, p. 6.

7. W. G. Connolly, "Videotape Production at CBS Studio Center," *Jour. SMPTE*, November 1987, pp. 761–763.

8. G. A. Robinson, "The Silicon Intensifier Target Tube, *Seeing in the Dark*," *Jour. SMPTE*, June 1977, pp. 414–418.

9. "BVH-500," *Jour. SMPTE*, July 1977, p. 522.

10. "Progress Report," *Jour. SMPTE*, May 1978, p. 309.

11. Sir Charles Curran, "The Competition between Videotape and Film: Some Observations," *Jour. SMPTE*, Nov. 1977, pp. 809–811.

12. "1 Inch VTR Standard OK'd," *Broadcast Management/Engineering*, August 1977, pp. 6–8.

13. "V. K. Zworykin," *Jour. SMPTE*, August 1977, p. 578. See also Albert Abramson, *Zworykin: Pioneer of Television*, University of Illinois Press, Urbana, IL, 1995. I had the privilege of meeting Dr. Zworykin and at his request wrote his biography. His efforts at RCA led to the system of television that is now worldwide.

14. "The Saticon Color Television Camera Tube," by Robert G Neuhauser, *Jour. SMPTE*, March 1978, pp. 147–152. Neuhauser gives an excellent history of the Vidicon in this article.

15. "Hollywood Editors Guild Looks at Tomorrow," *Jour. SMPTE*, December 1977, pp. 894–895.

16. D. Horowitz, "CBS' New-Technology Station, WBBM-TV," *Jour. SMPTE*, March 1978, pp. 141–146.

17. "Further Details on 1 Inch Video Format Released," *Broadcast Management/Engineering*, November 1977, p. 6.

18. J. Roizen, "1 Inch VTRs," *Broadcast Engineering*, Feb. 1978, p. 34.

19. "The Reliable ENG Camera," ad by Cinema Products, *Jour. SMPTE*, December 1977, p. 951.

20. "Despite Gains by Video Technology Film Will Be the Medium for Prime Time Programming for the Foreseeable Future," *Broadcast Management/Engineering*, December 1977, pp. 29–33.

21. "New Products Developments," *Jour. SMPTE*, April 1978, p. 263. "Camera and the Accessories," *Jour. SMPTE*, May 1978, p. 280.

22. J. Jurgens, "Steadicam as a Design Problem," *Jour. SMPTE*, September 1978, pp. 578–591.

23. "RCA to Market One Inch Videotape Recorders Produced by Sony Corp," *Broadcast Management/Engineering*, Feb. 1978, p. 8. "A 1 Inch Type C Helical Scan Recorder," *Jour. SMPTE*, September 1978, p. 658. "1-Inch Helical VTR," *Broadcast Communications*, Nov. 1978, p. 67.

24. "Progress Committee Report for 1977," *Jour. SMPTE*, May 1978, p. 310.

25. Lardner, op. cit., pp. 164–167.

26. *Ibid.*, pp. 165–167.

27. "CBS's VTR Facilities Unused by Producers," *Broadcasting*, May 29, 1978, p. 44.

28. W.I.C. Nicholls, "A New Edit Room Using One-Inch Continuous Field Helical VTRs," *Jour. SMPTE*, November 1978, pp. 764–766.

29. "Peter Carl Goldmark," *Jour. SMPTE*, February 1978, p. 95.

30. "United Kingdom Progress Committee Report for 1977," *Jour. SMPTE*, May 1978, p. 317.

31. "Progress Committee Report," *Jour. SMPTE, Jour.* May 1978, p. 276. (I don't know whose edit machine is used but it looks like a CMX3.)

32. "New Products," *Jour. SMPTE*, May 1978, p. 362.

33. "A Small Size Prototype Color Video Camera," *Jour. SMPTE*, June 1978, p. 408.

34. "Ampex Corp. and N. V. Philips," *Jour. SMPTE*, June 1978, p. 408.

35. John Baldwin, "Digital Television Recording with Low Tape Consumption," *Jour. SMPTE*, July 1979, pp. 490–492.

36. "Progress Committee Report for 1977," *Jour. SMPTE*, May 1978, p. 322.

37. "Slant-Track VTR," *Broadcast Communications*, October 1978, p. 84. "The VPR-2 Helical Videotape Recorder," *Jour. SMPTE*, October 1978, p. 732.

38. R. Whittaker, "Film Techniques and Videotape Co-Star in Return Engagement," *Broadcast Communications*, October 1978, pp. 32–36. The term "film look" was quickly picked up by Eastman Kodak in their advertising. Somehow it meant "superiority" to the television image that was produced by electronic cameras.

39. "International Broadcast Standards," *Broadcast Communications*, October 1978, p. 42.

40. D. K. Fibush, "SMPTE Type C Helical Scan Recording Format," *Jour. SMPTE*, November 1978, pp. 755–760.

41. B. Pauchon, "Film Techniques Improved Video Production Costs," *Broadcast Communications*, February 1979, pp. 32–37.

42. Joe Roizen, "Ampex Unveils Digital VTR at Winter SMPTE Meeting," *Broadcast Communications*, March 1979, pp. 124–129. This is one of Roizen's finest articles. He covered every aspect of the new digital video recording process. "Digital Technology, One Inch VTRs Dominate 13th Annual SMPTE Winter Television Conference," *Broadcast Management/Engineering*, March 1979, pp. 203–204. "The 13th Annual SMPTE Television Conference," *Broadcast Engineering*, March 1979, pp. 72–73. Maurice Lemoine, a principal engineer in Ampex Corporation's audio-video systems division, received the 1980 David Sarnoff Gold Medal from the Society of Motion Picture and Television Engineers. Lemoine received the award for his leadership in and technical contributions to digital equipment design that led to the introduction of digital time base correctors for several videotape recorders as well as to advances in quality for videotape recording. Lemoine's name has long been associated with the continuous pursuit of higher performance in digital videotape recording.

43. "Broadcasters Descend on Montreux," *Broadcast Engineering*, July 1969, p. 36.

44. "Digital Technology, One Inch VTRs Dominate 13th Annual SMPTE Winter Television Conference," *Broadcast Management/Engineering*, March 1979, pp. 203–204. "The 13th Annual SMPTE Television Conference," *Broadcast Engineering*, March 1979, pp. 72–80. Joe Roizen, "Ampex Unveils Digital VTR at Winter SMPTE Meeting," *Broadcast Communications*, March 1979, pp. 124–129.

45. "Digital Video Recording," *Jour. SMPTE*, March 1979, p. 184.

46. "NAB Show in Print-79," *Broadcast Management/Engineering*, May 1979, p. 38.

47. "VTR and TBC," *Broadcast Engineering*, March 1979, p. 184D. "NAB Show in Print-79" *Broadcast Management/Engineering*, May 1979, p. 41. "1 Inch VTR," *Broadcast Engineering*, July 1979, p. 65 "Sony," *Broadcast Communications*, May 1980, p. 131.

48. "Ampex," *Broadcast Engineering*, March 1979, p. 54.

49. "NAB Show in Print-79," *Broadcast Management/Engineering*, May 1979, p. 44.

50. "New Products, Two New 1 Inch Helical Broadcast Format 'D' Videotape Recorders," *Jour. SMPTE*, March 1979, p. 212. "NAB Show in Print-79," *Broadcast Management/Engineering*, May 1979, p. 44.

51. "NAB Show in Print-79," *Broadcast Management/Engineering*, May 1979, p. 44.

52. *Ibid.*, p. 49.

53. *Ibid.*, p. 56.

54. *Ibid.*, p. 92

55. *Ibid.*, p. 105.

56. *Ibid.*, pp. 114, 120. Could one imagine a situation where a film camera and its processors were available but not an electronic camera and microwave transmitter? "Transfer System," *Broadcast Engineering*, July 1979, p. 65.

57. "Eidophor Wows Audiences," *Broadcast Engineering*, March 1979, p. 198.

58. Albert Abramson, *The History of Television, 1880 to 1941*," McFarland & Co., Jefferson, NC, 1987, p. 134.

59. "Digital Technology and Satellite Broadcasting Capture International Symposium in Montreux," *Broadcast Management/Engineering*, August 1979, pp. 81–91.

60. "Broadcasters Descend on Montreux," *Broadcast Engineering*, July 1979, p. 36.

61. "Digital Television," *Broadcast Engineering*, July 1979, p. 68.

62. "Digital Telecine," *Broadcast Management/Engineering*, September 1979, p. 205.

63. K. Yokoyama, S. Nakagawa, and H. Katayama, "An Experimental Digital Videotape Recorder," *Jour. SMPTE*, March 1980, pp. 173–180.

64. "Sony, Ampex Share Emmy for Type C Development," *Broadcast Management/Engineering*, November 1979, p. 8.

65. "CBS-EIA Issue Teletext Results," *Broadcast Management/Engineering*, November 1979, pp. 97–98.

66. Joe Roizen, "Speaking of Technology, an Interview with Jules Barnathan," *Broadcast Communications*, February 1981, pp. 85–86.

67. "SMPTE Conference Sets High Mark for this Decade," *Broadcast Management/Engineering*, December 1979.

68. Michael London, "CBS Previews Computerized Editing for TV," *Los Angeles Times*, October 30, 1979.

69. "Edit Controllers at NAB 80/Las Vegas," *Broadcast Engineering*, June 1980, pp. 52–54.

70. "Formula for the Future," *Broadcast Management/Engineering*, July 1980, pp. 26–28. All of this to break a union contract! "SMPTE Conference Sets High Mark for this Decade," *Broadcast Management/Engineering*, December 1979.

71. "Progress Committee Report for 1979," *Jour. SMPTE*, May 1980, p. 358.

Chapter 11
Introduction of the Camcorder (1980–1984)

1. "Videocassette-Dual Tracks Gives 8 Hour Play," *Popular Science*, February 1980, p. 64. Barry Fox, "From Two-Inch Quad to Quarter-Inch Cassettes in Twenty-Five Years," *Jour. Royal Television Society*, 1980, p. 19.

2. "NAB Show in Print," *Broadcast Management/Engineering*, June 1980, pp. 18–35.

3. "RCA Broadcast System," *Broadcast Engineering*, June 1980, p. 111. Also see RCA ad in *Broadcast Management/Engineering*, June 1980, p. 85.

4. "NAB Show in Print," *Broadcast Management/Engineering*, June 1980, pp. 18–35.

5. 3M ad for their new one-inch TT-7000 Type "C" recorder, *Broadcast Engineering*, June 1980, p. 47. "NAB Show in Print," *Broadcast Management/Engineering*, June 1980, p. 21.

6. "NAB Show in Print," *Broadcast Management/Engineering*, June 1980, p. 22.

7. "New Graphics System Could Find Election Reporting Applications," *Broadcast Management/Engineering*, May 1980, p. 44. "Ampex," *Broadcasting Engineering*, June 1980, p. 74. "NAB Show in Print," *Broadcast Management/Engineering*, June 1980, p. 140.

8. "Business Brief," *Broadcast Management/Engineering*, April 1980, p. 18.

9. "NAB Show in Print," *Broadcast Management/Engineering*, June 1980, p. 22.

10. *Ibid.*, p. 24.

11. *Ibid.*

12. *Ibid.*, p. 27.

13. *Ibid.*

14. "NAB Show in Print," *Broadcast Management/Engineering*, June 1980, p. 28–29 "EC-35" *Broadcast Engineering* June 1980 p. 102.

15. "NAB Show in Print," *Broadcast Management/Engineering*, June 1980, p. 29.

16. *Ibid.*, p. 30.

17. "A CCD Color TV Camera," *Jour. SMPTE*, October 1980, p. 774.

18. "NAB Show in Print," *Broadcast Management/Engineering*, June 1980, p. 30–52.

19. Faroudja ad in *Broadcast Management/Engineering*, May 1980, p. 88. "NAB Show in Print," *Broadcast Management/Engineering*, June 1980, p. 60.

20. "NAB Show in Print," *Broadcast Management/Engineering*, June 1980, p. 73.

21. *Ibid.*, p. 144.

22. "The Signal Companies," *Jour. SMPTE*, May 1980, p. 414.

23. "Ampex Corp," *Jour. SMPTE*, August 1980, p. 611.

24. "Ampex/Signal Merger Finalized," *Broadcast Management/Engineering*, January 1981, p. 8. "Ampex, Signal Complete Merger," *Broadcasting Engineering*, March 1981, p. 252.

25. "Sony Unveils First Camera/Recorder Unit," *Educational & Industrial Television*, July 1980, p. 6. Linda Grant, "Sony Unveiled New 4 Pound, Videotape Home Movie Camera," *Los Angeles Times*, July 2, 1980, p. 2. "CCD Camera from Sony," *Millimeter*, December 1980, p. 181. "Sony Pulls a Surprise," *Education & Industrial TV*, July 1980, p. 20. "Sony Aims for 'Video Movie Standard," *Jour. TV Society* Sept./Oct. 1980, p. 18.

26. Dr. V. Stone, "RTNDA Equipment Survey: Looking at ENG Gear," *Broadcast Communications*, July 1980, pp. 20–28.

27. "Technicolor Enters VCR Ring with 1/4" Recorder." *Educational & Industrial TV*, September 1980, p. 14. "LVR's and More," *Popular Science*, November 1980, p. 95.

28. M. Heiss, "Video Grabs the CES Spotlight," *Videography*, September 1980, pp. 40–50.

29. Jane Wollman, "Consumer Beat: Pre-recorded Tape: A Booming Business," *Videography*, Sept. 1980, pp. 74–76.

30. "Video Technology and Social Responsibility," *Jour. Royal Television Society*, May/June 1981, p. 51.

31. David Fisher, "Programs Over the Counter," *Jour. Royal Television Society*, July/August 1981, p. 11.

32. M. Heiss, "Video Grabs the CES Spotlight," *Videography*, September 1980, pp. 40–50.

33. "Hitachi Offers Peek at One-Piece Camera/VCR," *Educational & Industrial Television*, October 1980, p. 6. "Hitachi Develops Color Video Camera to Set Standard," *Hollywood Reporter*, Sept. 23, 1980, p. 15.

34. "Tape Industry Moved Because Bing Crosby Did," *Los Angeles Times*, October 27, 1980, p. 24. "Poniatoff dead at age 88," *Broadcast Engineering*, December 1980, p. 10. From his boyhood in Kazan, Russia, where he was born on March 25, 1892, Poniatoff was fascinated with mechanical principles and technology. His university studies (University of Kazan, the Imperial College in Moscow, and the Technical College of Karlsruhe, Germany) earned him degrees in mechanical and electrical engineering. Following military service in World War I (as a pilot in the Imperial Russian Navy) he fought with the White Russian forces in the Russian Revolution. After the Bolshevik victory he escaped in 1920 to Shanghai, China, where he worked as an assistant engineer for the Shanghai Power Company. In 1927 he immigrated to the United States, becoming an American citizen five years later.

In 1944 he founded Ampex (the name was created from his initials, AMP, plus "ex" for excellence). Three years later the company experienced its first breakthrough, despite a postwar recession that had whittled the roster to a mere eight employees. This 1947 milestone was the introduction of the first practical audio recorder in the United States. In 1956 Ampex once again set the pace for the multibillion dollar industry it had helped to launch, this time by introducing the first practical videotape recorder, an invention with revolutionary implications for the television broadcast industry.

Poniatoff died on October 24, 1980, at the age of 88.

35. Teletext for October 1980.

36. John Purvis, "The Great Debate," *On Location*, November 1980, p. 16.

37. Most of this information came from a letter I wrote to the *American Cinematographer* on 26 September 1991. Having been in electronic production for 35 years, I predict that within a generation, we will look back on the "*film look*" and wonder how we put up with it for so long.

38. Joe Roizen, "SMPTE moves on to S.F.," *Broadcast Communications*, January 1981, pp. 10–14. Bill Rhodes, "122nd SMPTE Technical Conference Highlights," *Broadcast Engineering*, February 1981, p. 69.

39. "SMPTE Exhibits: Mid Season Changes," *Broadcast Management/Engineering*, January 1981, p. 101.

40. Gerland C. Engbretson, "Production and Post Production in the Eighties: The 15th Annual SMPTE Television Conference," *Jour. SMPTE*, April 1981, pp. 296–316, 320–324.

41. "Videotape Recording Marks 25th Year," *Broadcast Communications*, March 1981, p. 70. Ampex ad in *Broadcast Engineering*, March 1981, pp. 8–9.

42. Joe Roizen "Eyeball Euphoria — A New Twist for the NAB," *Broadcast Communications*, May 1981.

43. "Matsushita and RCA Show Single ENG Unit," *Jour. Royal Television Society*, May/June 1981, p. 10.

44. "Self-contained Camera-VTR System," *Jour. SMPTE*, May 1982, p. 458. "New Products," "The Hawkeye color TV," *Jour. SMPTE*, June 1981, p. 566.

45. J. Cleave, "The Hawkeye System," *Jour. Royal Television Society*, March/April 1983, pp. 48–50. See *Broadcast Management/Engineering*, March 1982, p. 191. All this from "*SMPTE 1982*," *Broadcast Management/Engineering*, January 1983, p. 73. It was reported that production of the Hawkeye camera stopped in April 1985, a victim of the Sony Betacam success. John Rice, "The Big Story on Small Format," *Videography*, April 1985, p. 55.

46. "RCA," *Broadcast Communications*, May 1981, pp. 165–66.

47. "Sony," *Broadcast Communications*, May 1981, pp. 170–171. Sony ad in *Jour. SMPTE*, December 1982, pp. 1238–1239. M. Takano and I. Segawa, "Betacam — A VTR in Camera," presented at 123rd SMPTE Conference in October 1981.

48. *Broadcast Communications*, May 1981, p. 163.

49. Phillip Keirstea, "ENG Camera/Recorder Leads New Technology Parade," *Broadcast Communications*, May 1981, pp. 92, 94.

50. "Update on VCRs," *Broadcast Engineering*, January 1982, p. 54.

51. "Another Video Camera with Built-in Recorder," *Jour. TV Society*, March/April 1981, p. 10.

52. "Matsushita Produces 2 Million VTRs," *Broadcast Engineering*, March 1981, p. 250.

53. "Videodisc Hit and Misses," *Jour. Royal Television Society*, May/June 1981, p. 11. Sobel, *RCA*, pp. 254–255.

54. Blair Benson, "SMPTE Panel Examines HDTV," *Broadcast Engineering*, November 1981, p. 70.

55. Golda Savage, "Coppola's Electronic Cinema Process," *Millimeter*, October 1981, pp. 52–70. See also "New Video Formats for Small and Large Screen," *Jour. TV Society*, July/August 1981, pp. 27–29.

56. "News Feature," *Broadcast Management/Engineering*, November 1981, pp. 105–106.

57. "RCA Broadcast Systems," *Educational & Industrial Television*, December 1981, p. 38.

58. "CCIR Agrees On Inter'l Standard for Digital Video," *Educational & Industrial Television*, December 1981, pp. 4–5. "The parameters agreed to include: A basic sampling frequency of 13.5 MHz for luminance and 6.75MHz (or half the luminance) for R and B chrominance. This is one of the few frequencies common to both the 525- and 625-line picture specification. Digitization is of signal components rather than of the composite signal. The sampling for chrominance will be on the basis of the luminance signal (Y) minus the chrominance elements (Y-R and Y-B). Agreed to tentatively are: sampling frequency of 720 per line for luminance, and half that for chrominance. A sample rate of 8 bits. A quantisizing rate of 4:2:2 for minimum quality. There was also discussion of a 4:4:4 rate for high-quality picture generation, but no agreement on the possible acceptance of some lower-quality picture standard, e.g., 2: 1: 1. An orthogonal pattern with chrominance co-sites that are field/frame repetitive. This provides for the picture elements in the second TV line to fall directly under those in the first line. (There had been some discussion of using a stepped pattern à la bricks in a wall.) The co-site parameter permits the two chrominance samples to lie on top of each other, and both to lie on top of every other luminance signal (the 4:2:2 rate provides twice as much luminance as chrominance). A bandwidth of 5.8MHz for luminance, 2.75MHz for chrominance."

59. Sasano, E. Maruyama, K. Tada, and T. Aoki, "A High Resolution Tri-electrode Pickup Tube Employing an Se-As-Te Amorphous Photoconductor," *Jour. SMPTE*, December 1982, pp. 1148–1152. Of course, this was the tube that Paul Weimer of RCA had built in March 1955 with very little success.

60. Hitachi ad in *Industrial and Educational Television*, December 1981, p. 7.

61. Larry See and Dave Edmonds, "New Single Tube ENG Camera Enters the Market Place," *Broadcast Communications*, December 1981, pp. 66–70.

62. Ampex ad in *Broadcast Management/Engineering*, February 1982, p. 8.

63. "Polonsky Dies," *Broadcast Engineering*, March 1982, p. 8. Joseph Roizen, "Joseph Polonsky," *Jour. SMPTE*, April 1982, p. 424.

64. "Harry F. Olson," *Jour. SMPTE*, June 1982, p. 592.

65. Sony ad in *Jour. SMPTE*, June 1982, pp. 606–608. M. Takano and I. Segawa, "The Betacam System," *Broadcasting Management/Engineering*, presented at NAB in April 1982.

66. M. Takano and I. Segawa, "Betacam: Integrated ENG," *Jour. Royal Television Society*, March/April 1983, pp. 74–78. "SMPTE: 1982" *Broadcast Management Engineering*, January 1983, p. 73.

67. "SMPTE: 1982," *Broadcast Management/Engineering*, January 1983, p. 72.

68. "1982 NAB Show-in-Print," *Broadcast Management/Engineering*, June 1982, pp. 71–83.

69. "CBS and NHK Present High Definition and Electronic Cinema Demonstrations," *Jour. SMPTE*, June 1992, p. 585.

70. "Sony Corporation and Thomson-CSF," *Jour. SMPTE*, December 1982, p. 1212.

71. "Obituary, Vladimir Kosma Zworykin," *Jour. SMPTE*, November 1982, p. 1116. I, of course, had the honor of writing Dr. Zworykin's biography in 1995. See Albert Abramson, *Zworykin, Pioneer of Television*, University of Illinois Press, Urbana and Chicago, IL, 1995. I also wrote a history of Dr. Zworykin that appeared in the *Journal of SMPTE* in July 1981. See Albert Abramson, "Pioneers of Television — Vladimir Kosma Zworykin," *Jour. SMPTE*, July 1981, pp. 579–589. "Dr. Vladimir K. Zworykin" 1889–1982," *Broadcast Engineering*, September 1982, pp. 36–42. "Television Pioneer dies," *Jour. TV Society*, Sept./Oct. 1982, p. 12. There was very little publicity about his passing. A whole generation who grew up with television were unaware that this pioneer was still living. There were scattered reports of his death all across the nation's newspapers, too many to be inserted here. It is generally accepted that the three foundations of modern television are Zworykin's Kinescope (1929), Zworykin's Iconoscope (1931), and Randall Ballard's interlaced scanning patent (1932).

72. C. T. Hasty, "Development of the VPR-5," *Broadcast Management/Engineering*, March 1983, pp. 203–208. Also "World Update," *Broadcast Communications*, November 1982, p. 26. "A Portable 1 Inch Helical Scan Videotape Recorder," *Jour. SMPTE*, January 1983, p. 146.

73. "The Ampex VPR-3 One Inch Recorder," *Jour. SMPTE*, February 1983, pp. 232–234.

74. "The 124th SMPTE Technical Conference and Equipment Exhibit," *Jour. SMPTE*, January 1983, pp. 4–103.

75. "World Update," *Broadcast Communications*, November 1982, p. 26.

76. "RCA, Sony Score with Half-Inch Sales," *Broadcast Management/Engineering*, December 1982. "Sony Broadcast Products," *Broadcast Communications*, December 1982, pp. 20–21.

77. Sony ad in *Broadcast Engineering*, September 1982, pp. 72–73. Sony ad in *Jour. SMPTE*, December 1982, p. 1215.

78. Panasonic ad for its new RECAM portable camera/recorder, *Broadcasting Management/Engineering*, December 1982, pp. 8–9. K. Renwanz, "Panasonic RECAM Camera/Recorder System," *Broadcast Engineering*, March 1983, pp. 276–285.

79. "The Sony format using the high tape speed allows the recording of the newly developed compressed time division multiplex component format. Luminance is recorded on one track while R-Y and B-Y color difference signals are compressed 2:1 in time and alternately recorded on a second track. In the playback process, R-Y and B-Y signals are restored to their original form and delayed 2H. The time difference is compensated by a digital retiming built into the BVW-10 player unit." "*SMPTE 1982*," *Broadcasting Management Engineering*, p.74.

"The Bosch format quarter inch LinePlex system takes advantage of the fact that the density of the chrominance recorded signals in NTSC is three times less than that of luminance. Bosch elected to use a signal expansion and compression technique to record equal densities by expanding luminance by a factor of 1.5 and compressing chrominance by two. Two tracks are to record odd and even tracks of multiplexed luminance and chrominance. By displacing heads, two horizontal line intervals are located in parallel in correspondence with appropriate picture elements. The RCA approach which is to record the Y FM signal and the I and Q FM signals on separate tracks delivers the full NTSC bandwidth." See *Broadcast Management/Engineering*, 1982, p. 191. *Broadcast Management/Engineering*, January 1983, pp. 73–73.

80. Glen Pensinger, *Broadcast Communications*, July 1983, p. 42.

81. W. F. Carpenter, "The Type-C Format — A Moving Target," *Jour. SMPTE*, September 1983, pp. 923–926. J. Mahedy, "Ampex VPR-3," *Broadcast Engineering*, Sept. 1984, pp. 204–213.

82. Joseph Roizen, "Report on IBC, 82," *Jour. SMPTE*, December 1982, pp. 1203–1208.

83. "IBC Is Site of Major Improvements," *Broadcast Communications*, November 1982, pp. 10–14.

84. "The ARC System," Ampex ad in *Broadcast Management/Engineering*, March 1983, p. 51.

85. "Ampex Bulletin," *Jour. Royal Television Society*, March 1983, p. 10.

86. Robert Rivlin, "Montreux Symposium Reveals Europeans Hungry for Technology," *Broadcast Management/Engineering*, September 1983, pp. 95–100.

87. Bill Rhodes, "The Ampex Museum of Magnetic Recording," *Broadcast Engineering*, March 1983, pp. 310–316. "Ampex's Museum of Magnetic Recording," *E-ITV*, March 1983, pp. 104–106. See also Jerry Whitaker, "Preserving Technology," *Broadcast Engineering*, June 1984, pp. 144–152. I too was part of the creation of this magnificent museum. I was consulted many times by Pete Hammar for my knowledge of the early video recorders. At this time (April 2002) I am pleased to state that the Ampex Museum is safe and sound in Colorado Springs, Colorado, in a building at 600 Wooten Road. It has been kept as an *open secret* in order to keep it from being legally separated from the rest of the company. Other museums that are still in existence are the Broadcast Pioneers Museum, Washington, DC, the National Broadcast Museum, Dallas, Texas, and the Forest Hills Wireless Museum, New York.

88. "Television," *Jour. SMPTE*, April 1984, p. 331.

89. Robert Rivlin, "Montreux Symposium reveals Europeans Hungry for Technology," *Broadcast Management/Engineering*, September 1983, pp. 95–100. "Trials and Tribulations of Trying to Do Business at Montreux," *Jour. TV Society*, July/August 1983, pp. 189–190. "RCA, NEC Show CCD Camera Developments," *Broadcast Management/Engineering*, January 1984, p. 83. "Cameras, Recorders and Related Equipment," *Jour. SMPTE*, April 1984, p. 331. Barry Detwiler, "The Montreux International Symposium," *Jour. SMPTE*, October 1983, pp. 1094+.

90. "New Products, the SPC-3 Color Camera," *Jour. SMPTE*, September 1983, p. 1004.

91. "Stereo Home Video," *Television/Broadcast/Communications*, October 1983, p. 28.

92. Terry Connelly, "Teletext Enhances WKRC's Local New Image," *Television Broadcast Communications*, October 1983, p. 52.

93. Joe Roizen, "SMPTE," *Television/Broadcast/Communications*, January 1984, p. 56.

94. "RCA and Ampex," *Broadcast Engineering*, April 1984, p. 336. See also Ron Merrell, "Special Report: VTRs," *Television/Broadcast/Communications*, October 1984, p. 96.

95. "Ray M. Dolby," *Broadcast Engineering*, January 1984, p. 92; "Ray M. Dolby," *Jour. SMPTE*, January 1984, p. 83. Ray Dolby is the man behind the DOLBY name that one finds these days on every film, sound system, tape and video recorder worldwide. His greatest achievements have been in the field of noise reduction units for film, tape, radio and television.

Dolby holds many patents. He has won a number of awards including the Silver Medal Award from the Audio Engineering Society, the Samuel L. Warner Memorial Award (1978) from the SMPTE, and the Alexander Poniatoff Gold Medal for Technical Excellence (1982). He is a fellow of the British Kinematograph, Sound and Television Society (BKSTS), the SMPTE, and the Audio Engineering Society (of which he is also past president). Subjects on which he has published papers include videotape recording, long-wavelength x-ray analysis, and noise reduction.

Dolby was born in Portland, Oregon, in 1933. By 1949, at the age of 16, he was working on projects for Ampex, whose videotape recording system was among his special projects. Working on the system from 1952 to 1957, he was largely responsible for developing its electronic aspects. In 1957 he received a B.S. in electrical engineering from Stanford, and upon receipt of a Marshall Scholarship, he left Ampex that same year to study at Cambridge. There he received his Ph.D. in physics in 1961. In his last year at Cambridge he was also a consultant to the United Kingdom Atomic Energy Authority.

From 1963 to 1965, Dolby served as a United Nations adviser in India; he then returned to London, where he established Dolby Laboratories. He later returned to the United States, settling his home and his company in San Francisco, where they remain today.

I have found Ray Dolby to be a warm and gentle soul whose modesty belies the scope of his achievements. All Dolby units are used in the original recordings of sound tracks including records, disks, television and motion pictures. In addition Dolby units are used in stereo recordings that may be from 2 to 5 channels wide, especially motion pictures and television. His products are sold worldwide and he has licensed every major manufacturer, including Philips, Sony, Paramount and Warner Bros., to use his equipment. He has very little competition from anyone in the world including Japan.

96. "Michael O. Felix," *Broadcasting Engineering*, January 1984, p. 94; *Jour. SMPTE*, January 1984, p. 82. Following his studies at City and Guilds College, London (BS in telecommunications, 1942), and World War II service in the Royal Air Force, Michael Felix joined British Telecommunications Research. There he helped to develop the first 160MHz battery-operated transmitter-receivers. His next achievement was at Canadian Westinghouse, where he was involved in the development of the first 4GHz wideband tropospheric scatter system. In 1960 he joined Ampex, eventually becoming vice-president and general manager of the advanced technology division. While at Ampex he developed the theory of FM video recording. Other projects with which he was involved included the transverse recorder auto scan tracking, digital TV recording based on a computer disk system, and the first TV graphics system (AVA). By 1984 he had been granted eight patents for his work at Ampex and received the company's highest award for technical excellence, the Gold Poniatoff award.

97. "A Fourth Generation Videotape Recorder," *Jour. SMPTE*, October 1983, p. 1148.

98. Sony ad in *Broadcast Engineering*, December 1983, pp. 66–67.

99. "Business Briefs," *Broadcast Management/Engineering*, April 1984, p. 292.

100. "Studio Systems and Equipment," *Jour. SMPTE*, April 1984, p. 392.

101. "TV Innovators Receive Emmys," *Broadcast Engineering*, November 1986, p. 154. This was not true. According to editor Phillip J. Seretti, the "Twilight Zone" series was edited at Post Sound Corp. in Hollywood, "Corrections/Clarifications," *Broadcasting Management/Engineering*, April 1986, p. 19.

102. Robert van der Leeden, "Ace — The Ampex Computerized Editing System," *BKTS Jour.* June 1986, pp. 286–289.

103. "Hardware for Random Access," *Broadcast Engineering*, July 1986, p. 83.

104. Eva Blinder, "Improving the Editor Interface," *Broadcast Management/Engineering*, Feb. 1984, pp. 53–62.

105. Kodak ad in *Broadcast Management/Engineering*, March 1984, p. 42.

106. "Kodak Enters Broadcast, Amateur Video Markets," *Broadcast Management/Engineering*, February 1984, p. 12. "Kodak's New Vision," *International Television*, March 1984, p. 80. "Conversation with William Koch," *Broadcast Engineering*, July 1984, pp. 122–126. "New Products," *Jour. SMPTE*, May 1984, p. 520.

107. J. Roizen and B. Detwiler, "A Report on NAB 84," *Jour. SMPTE*, Sept. 1984, pp. 852–856. "The CCD-1," *Jour. SMPTE*, July 1984, p. 680.

108. M. Mitsui, "NEC's New 3-Chip CCD Color Camera," *Broadcast Engineering*, April 1984, pp. 286–294.

109. "RCA Broadcast Systems," *Broadcast Management/Engineering*, April 1984, pp. 152–153.

110. "NAB '84 Equipment Exhibition," *International Television*, May 1984, pp. 52–61.

111. "Montage," *BKTS Journal*, June 1986, p. 110. It was claimed that Montage had 40 systems in the USA with six at 20th Century-Fox and three at Disney Studios. The technology had been used on two major features, *Power* and *Sweet Liberty*. It was claimed that *Full Metal Jacket* was edited on a Montage machine in England in 1987. A good description of the Montage editing system was given in Tom Mann, "Non-linear Off-line Editing for HDTV and Film," *Image Technology*, December 1989, pp. 541–546

112. J. Roizen and B. Detwiler, "A Report on NAB 84," *Jour. SMPTE*, Sept. 1984, pp. 852–856.

113. "New Products," *Jour. SMPTE*, August 1984, p. 772.

114. Carl Bentz, "½-Inch — No Passing Fad," *Broadcast Engineering*, November 1984, p. 130. "Sony Broadcast Products," *Jour. SMPTE*, January 1985, p. 56.

115. "RCA CCD Cameras See Convention Use," *Broadcast Management/Engineering*, September 1984, p. 12.

116. "News," "Zworykin Receives Emmy Posthumously," *Broadcast Engineering*, November 1984, p. 4. "National Academy of TV Arts and Sciences Present Six Awards for Engineering Excellence," *Jour. SMPTE*, Dec. 1984, p. 1163.

117. Joseph Roizen, "Report on IBC '84," *Jour. SMPTE*, December 1984, pp. 1164–1166.

118. Ampex ad in *Television/Broadcast/Communications*, October 1984, p. 27. "New Products," *Jour. SMPTE*, November 1984, p. 1082.

119. Ron Merrell, "Special Report: VTRs," *Television/Broadcast/Communications*, October 1984, p. 96.

120. *Ibid.*

121. "Waldemar J. Poch," *Jour. SMPTE*, January 1985, p. 60.

122. "New York SMPTE," *Television/Broadcast/Communications*, January 1985, p. 84. Joe Roizen, "Equipment Update and Issues Dominate," *Television Broadcast Communications*, January 1985, pp. 82–84. "SMPTE Show in Print," *Broadcast Management/Engineering*, January 1985, p. 81.

123. Arthur Kaiser, Henry W. Mahler, and Renville H. McMann, "Resolution Requirements for HDTV Based Upon the Performance of 35mm Motion Picture Film for Theatre Viewing," *Jour. SMPTE*, June 1985, pp. 654–659.

124. "Letters to the Editor," *Jour. SMPTE*, June 1985, p. 685.

125. J. A. Mendrala, "Electronic Cinematography for Motion Picture Film," *Jour. SMPTE*, November 1987, pp. 1090–1094. For a definitive work on film versus HDTV see Larry Thorpe, "The HDTV Papers," *Millimeter*, August 1987, pp. 103–111. See also: Otto Schade, Sr., "Image Gradation, Graininess and Sharpness in Television and Motion Picture Systems," Part I: "Image Structure and Transfer Characteristics," *J. SMPTE*, 56:137–177, February 1951; Part II: "The Grain Structure of Motion Picture Images — An Analysis of Deviations and Fluctuations of the Sample Number,"

58:181–222, March 1952; Part III: "The Grain Structure of Television Images," 61:97–164, August 1953; Part IV A&B: "Image Analysis in Photographic and Television Systems," 64:593-618, November 1955. See also my paper, Albert Abramson, "Picture Quality; Film versus Television" *Jour. SMPTE*, June 1986, pp. 613-621.

126. "Elmer W. Engstrom," *Jour. SMPTE*, January 1985, p. 60. For more details of Engstrom's work, see Abramson, *History of Television, 1880 to 1941*.

127. Louis Pourciau, "High-Resolution TV For the Production of Motion Pictures," *Jour. SMPTE*, December 1984, pp. 1112-1120. This article caused a stream of protest from the advocates of film. By the way, my 1986, paper, "Picture Quality; Film versus Television," *Jour. SMPTE*, June 1986, pp. 613–621, was in the bibliography.

128. "New York SMPTE," *Television/Broadcast/Communications*, January 1985, p. 84. Carl Bentz, "Focusing on the Future: SMPTE '84," *Broadcast Engineering*, January 1985, p. 94.

129. "Paramount Pictures Corp," *Broadcast Engineering*, November 1984, p. 128.

130. "Robert Bosch," *Broadcast Engineering*, November 1984, p. 128.

131. "Ikegami Celebrated Twentieth Anniversary," *Broadcast Management/Engineering*, April 1985, p. 15. "Ikegami Celebrates 20 Years in the United States," *E-ITV*, March 1985, pp. 4–5. "Conversation with Nick Nishi," *Videography*, April 1985, pp. 84–96.

132. *Jour. SMPTE*, April 1984, p. 381.

133. "Harley Iams," *Jour. SMPTE*, May 1985, p. 804. "Harley Iams," *Jour. Royal Television Society*, April 1985, p. 100. I had the great honor of meeting Harley Iams several times. He was the perfect gentlemen and host. His wife Margaret treated me and my wife Arlene like family. From him I learned the true story of how Zworykin invented both the Kinescope and iconoscope. For details see Abramson, *History of Television, 1880 to 1941*. When he was ill he left me a cardboard box containing many priceless artifacts including the original movement from the Westinghouse film projector used in tests between April and August 1929. I wrote this obituary, which appeared in the *Journal* even though he was not a member of SMPTE.

Chapter 12
The Death of RCA, or the G.E. Massacre (1985–1989)

1. "NBC," *Broadcast Engineering*, January 1985, p. 16.

2. "George Lisle Beers," *Jour. SMPTE*, May 1985, p. 604.

3. Glen Pensiger, "Setting the Standards for Component Video," *Television/Broadcast/Communication*, April 1985, pp. 54–60.

4. "SMPTE TV Conference Defines Components of the Future," *Broadcast Management/Engineering*, April 1985, p. 18.

5. "Hitachi Demos Prototype Camera, DVTR," *Broadcast Management/Engineering*, February 1985, p. 13. "A High Definition TV System," *Jour. SMPTE*, May 1985, p. 804.

6. "Cameras," *Jour. SMPTE*, July 1985, p. 765.

7. "SMPTE Show in Print," *Broadcast Management/Engineering*, January 1985, p. 42.

8. Sony ad *Broadcast Engineering*, March 1985, p. 35. "Less Glitter but Lots More Substance in NAB Camera Market," *Broadcast Management/Engineering*, June 1985, pp. 36–37.

9. "The Nighthawk," *Jour. SMPTE*, August 1985, p. 860.

10. "Less Glitter but Lots More Substance in NAB Camera Market," *Broadcast Management/Engineering*, June 1985, pp. 36–37.

11. "Post Production," *Broadcast Management/Engineering*, January 1985, p. 85. "SMPTE Show in Print," *Broadcasting Management/Engineering* 1985, pp. 86+.

12. Ampex ACEm Editor, *Broadcast Engineering*, June 1985, p. 54. Ampex ad in *E-ITV*, March 1985, p. 6.

13. "SMPTE Show in Print," *Broadcast Management/Engineering*, January 1985, p. 66.

14. *Ibid.*, p. 70.

15. *Ibid.*

16. "The MII Format," *Television/Broadcast/Communications*, June 1985, p. 60.

17. Philip Livingston, "The MII Format," *Broadcast Engineering*, April 1986, pp. 96–104. See K. Sadashige, "Developmental Trends for Future Consumer VCR's," *Jour. SMPTE*, Dec. 1984, pp. 1138–46.

18. "SMPTE Show in Print," *Broadcast Management/Engineering*, January 1985, p. 60.

19. "The Type-C TH700 Videotape Recorder," *Jour. SMPTE*, June 1985, p. 696.

20. "SMPTE Show in Print," *Broadcast Management/Engineering*, January 1985, p. 870.

21. F. J. Watson, "Quality Control Techniques Vital for Tape Performance," *Broadcast Management/Engineering*, July 1985, p. 72.

22. "Japanese Firms Buy VTRs," *Broadcasting Engineering*, May 1985, p. 136. "Toyo Recording Co Ltd." *Jour. SMPTE*, April 1984, p. 448.

23. J Barnathan, "Super Motion," *Broadcast Management/Engineering*, May 1985, pp. 65–70. L. J. Thorpe, T. Nakamura, and K. Ninomiya "Super Slow Motion," *Jour. SMPTE*, September 1985, pp. 896–903.

24. "Georg Spiro Dibie," *Jour. SMPTE*, May 1985, p. 600. Dibie was a director of photography who had seen quite early that the future of motion picture photography was in electronics.

25. Carl Bentz, "Montreux Offers a Look at the Future," *Broadcast Engineering*, August 1985, p. 82.

26. Carl Bentz, "Montreux Offers a Look at the Future," *Broadcast Engineering*, August 1985, p. 82. "Montreux 85 — A Brief Report," *BKTS Jour.* September 1895, p. 531.

27. "Ampex," *Broadcast Management/Engineering*, July 1985, p. 93. "Special Effects," *Jour. SMPTE*, April 1986, p. 426. "Ampex Announced the Sale of Its 900th ADO in November 1986," *Broadcast Management/Engineering*, November 1986, p. 113.

28. "Zeus," *Jour. SMPTE*, April 1986, p. 429. "Ampex," *E-ITV*, January 1987, p. 26.

29. "The BVP-30 and BVP-3S Betacams," *Jour. SMPTE*, August 1985, p. 860.

30. "Marvin Camras," *Jour. SMPTE*, September 1985, p. 954.

31. Michel Oudin, "The World's First All-Digital Television Production," *Jour. SMPTE*, January 1987, pp. 11–15.

32. Joseph Roizen, "The Technology Display at the 127th SMPTE Technical Conference," *Jour. SMPTE*, January 1986, pp. 140–142.

33. "Charles P. Ginsburg Honored by Ampex," *Jour. SMPTE*, May 1986, p. 576.

34. *Broadcast Engineering*, August 1986, p. 124.

35. Eva Blinder, "Winter SMPTE Eyes Digital Directions," *Broadcast Management/Engineering*, April 1986, pp. 73–80. "The 20th Annual SMPTE Television Conference, February 7–8, 1986, Chicago," *Jour. SMPTE*, April 1986, pp. 476–500. "Component Digital TV Recorder Tops SMPTE Show," *Broadcasting*, Feb. 3, 1986, p. 58–59.

36. "Departing from the Standard," *Broadcasting*, January 20, 1986, p. 210. "Component Digital TV Recorder Tops SMPTE Show," *Broadcasting*, Feb. 3, 1986, pp. 58–59. "Ampex's Composite Cart Machine the Talk of SMPTE," *Broadcasting* February 17, 1986, pp. 36–44.

37. "Ampex, Sony Join Forces on Video Recording Front," *Broadcasting*, April 7, 1986, p. 41.

38. "RCA New Products," *Broadcast Engineering*, March 1986, p. 266. "NAB's Technological Cornucopia," *Broadcasting*, April 14, 1986, pp. 78–79.

39. "VTRs: NAB's Biggest Player," *Broadcast Management/Engineering*, June 1986, p. 21.

40. "VTRs: NAB Biggest Player," *Broadcast Management/Engineering*, June 1986, p. 46. L. Thorpe and E. Tamura, "A New 510 Element CCD Camcorder for ENG," *Jour. SMPTE*, June 1986, pp. 518–526.

41. "Whats Hot?" *Broadcast Management/Engineering*, March 1986,.p 44 "Ampex Will License Composite DVTR Format," *Broadcast Management/Engineering*, April 1986, p. 12.

42. "VTRs: NABs Biggest Player," *Broadcast Management/Engineering*, June 1986, p. 36.

43. *Ibid.*

44. *Ibid.*, p. 44.

45. *Ibid.*, p. 49.

46. *Ibid.*, p. 51.

47. *Ibid.*, pp. 19–78.

48. "Engineering Award," *Broadcast Engineering*, March 1986, p. 24. George H. Brown, *And Part of Which I Was, Recollections of a Research Engineer,* Angus Cupar Publishers, Princeton, NJ, 1979; *Jour. SMPTE*, May 1988, p. 418. Born in 1908 in Portage, Wisconsin, George H. Brown came to RCA in 1933 following studies at the University of Wisconsin that had earned him a BS, MS and PhD in electrical engineering. Brown began his RCA career as a research assistant and rose steadily through the company's ranks, becoming director of the Systems Research Laboratory in 1952; chief engineer, Commercial Electronic Products Division, 1957; president, engineering, 1959; vice president, research and engineering, 1961; and executive vice president, patents and licensing, 1968. Among the R&D projects with which he was involved were the NTSC's color TV system and the design of the batwing antenna used by most early TV stations.

Brown retired from RCA in 1972 and died on December 11, 1987, in Princeton, NJ. Over his lifetime he had received more than 80 U.S. patents, written more than 100 technical papers, and co-authored a text on radio-frequency heating. Much lauded by his industry peers, he received an honorary degree of doctor of engineering from the University of Rhode Island as well as many other honors and awards, including the DeForest Audion Award of the Veteran Wireless Operators Association, the Edison Medal, and the David Sarnoff Award for Outstanding Achievement in Radio and Television.

49. "RCA's George Brown: Technology Trailblazer," *Broadcasting*, April 7, 1986, p. 191.

50. "RCA Broadcast Systems," *Jour. SMPTE*, March 1986, p. 334.

51. "GE/RCA to Go for It at FCC," *Broadcasting*, Feb. 17, 1986, p. 29.

52. *Broadcast Management/Engineering*, July 1986, p. 20.

53. "RCA Think Tank to SRI," *Broadcast Management/Engineering*, March 1987, p. 16. "Industry Begins Scrutinizing NAB Plan for Technology Center," *Broadcasting*, April 20, 1987, pp. 75–76.

54. "Shutdown Reaction," *Broadcasting*, February 16, 1987, p. 74.

55. Abramson, *History of Television*, pp. 191–192. There had been no love lost between G.E. and RCA ever since RCA got its independence from G.E. and Westinghouse in 1932, because of an antitrust suit by the Department of Justice. Both G.E. and Westinghouse felt that David Sarnoff and RCA had gotten the best of the separation deal. This resulted in a smoldering relationship that lasted for years. G.E.'s action in killing off RCA was not unexpected.

56. John Rice, "The Big Story on Small Format," *Videography*, April 1985, p. 55.

57. Andrew M. Hilliard "RCA Revisited," *Broadcast Management/Engineering*, October 1986, pp. 121–128. Robert Sobel, *RCA*, Stein & Day, New York, 1986, pp. 255–260. Kenneth Bilby, *The General*, Harper and Row Publishers, New York, 1986, pp. 303–316.

58. "Reaction to NBC's ACTV," *Broadcasting*, October 26, 1987, p. 72. Kerns H. Powers, "The Treacherous Road to High Definition Television," *Jour. Royal Television Society*, November/December 1987, pp. 313–317.

59. "CCIR Puts an End to Hope for HDTV Standard," *Broadcasting*, May 19, 1986, p. 70. "CCIR Postpones HDTVsstandard Action," *Broadcast Engineering*, July 1986, pp. 4–121.

60. "ATSC Brings 525 Line NTSC Subgroup Off Back Burner," *Broadcasting*, June 16, 1986, p. 17. Yves Faroudja and Joseph Roizen, "Improving NTSC to Achieve Near RGB Performance," *Jour. SMPTE*, August 1987, p. 750–761.

61. "CCIR Puts End to Hope for HDTV Standard," *Broadcasting*, May 19, 1986, p. 70.

62. Robert van der Leeden, "ACE — The Ampex Computerized Editing System," *BKTS Journal*, June 1986, pp. 286–289.

63. "Hot Topics at IBC: HDTV, Digital Recording," *Broadcasting*, September 15, 1986, pp. 92–94. "IBC Provides Forum for Technical Growth Areas," *Broadcasting*, September 29, 1986, pp. 42–47. John Battison, "HDTV Highlights 11th IBC," *Broadcast Engineering*, December 1986, pp. 115–119.

64. "EditDroid Cuts Major Release," *Broadcast Management/Engineering*, September 1986, p. 22.

65. Curtis Chan, "Designing for Digital: The DVR-1," *Broadcast Management/Engineering*, September 1986, pp. 71–77.

66. Carl Bentz, "Show Preview," *Broadcast Engineering*, September 1986, pp. 122–128. Dr. Brown's part in the production of the RCA videotape recorder is covered in this volume, see Chapter 3. See also "SMPTE Probes Technology," *E-ITV Magazine*, October 1986, pp. 27–28.

67. "SMPTE '86: Almost but Not Quite," *Broadcasting*, November 3, 1986, pp. 71–73. "The 128th SMPTE Technical Conference," *Jour. SMPTE*, January 1987, pp. 75–161.

68. "HDTV Goes to Washington," *Broadcasting*, October 27, 1986, p. 90.

69. Ampex ad in *Broadcast Engineering*, November 1986, p. 46.

70. "CBS Tech Center Closing Spells Uncertainty for FMX," *Broadcast Management/Engineering*, November 1986, pp. 14–16.

71. "Ray D. Kell," *Jour. SMPTE*, April 1987, p. 431. I wrote this obituary for Kell. I had the great honor of meeting with him twice at his home in Princeton in 1976. As a member of the great Zworykin team, he made many advances in television technology. It is not well known that Kell was responsible for the first RCA efforts to create a compatible color system. His name lives on in the so-called "Kell Factor" in which he first examined vertical resolution of a television system. His work is well chronicled in Abramson, *History of Television, 1880–1941.*

72. "HDTV Lines Drawn at Washington Meeting," *Broadcasting*, Dec. 22, 1986, pp. 90–93.

73. "'For-Sale' Sign Out at Ampex," *Broadcasting*, December 15, 1986, p. 102.

74. "Terrestrial HDTV Broadcasting Debuts in Washington," *Broadcasting*, January 5, 1987, p. 214. "HDTV: Efforts to Redefine TV on Display in Washington," *Broadcasting* January 12, 1987, pp. 134–135. "HDTV Premiere Attended by Industry Leaders," *Broadcasting*, Jan. 19, 1987, p. 263. "Hi-Vision Comes to America," *Broadcast/Engineering*, February 1987, pp. 81–84. (The system was first described in October 1986.)

75. "New Analysis Super VHS: Just How Good? And Just How Cheap?" *Educational and Industrial Television*, April 1987, p. 7.

76. "TBS Converts Worldwide ENG to Betacam," *Broadcast Engineering*, February 1987, p. 134.

77. "NBC and NEC Enter in Agreement," *Broadcast Engineering*, February 1987, p. 136.

78. "The 21st Annual SMPTE Television Conference," *Jour. SMPTE*, January 1987, p. 40. (Sadly I never did find a report on the convention after it was held.)

79. "Ampex Submits Digital Format," *Broadcast Engineering*, Feb. 1987, pp. 4–11.

80. "NAB 87," *E-ITV*, June 1987, pp. 37–38.

81. "The CVC-50 CCD Camera," *Jour. SMPTE*, January 1988, p. 56.

82. "Finding a Camera," *E-ITV*, June 1987, pp. 38–39. According to *Broadcasting*, April 13, 1992, p. 9, the oldest CCD is interline transfer (IT) which suffers from smear and lag. Frame interline transfer (FIT) CCDs have less smear due to an added component, microlenses. The frame transfer (FT) CCD created by Philips has no lag and smear and pattern noise is low.

83. "Something for Everyone at NAB's Equipment Exhibition" *Broadcasting* March 23, 1987, pp. 63–74. "NAB 87: Taking Stock of the Tools of the Trade," *Broadcasting*, April 13, 1987, pp. 46–66.

84. Richard J. Stumph, "A Film Studio Looks at HDTV," *Jour. SMPTE*, March 1987, pp. 247–252.

85. Albert Abramson written on December 9, 1998, in Las Vegas.

86. "New Owner for Ampex," *Broadcast Management/Engineering*, May 1987, p. 12. "Ampex Is Newest Piece in Diverse Lanesborough Pie," *Broadcasting*, April 13, 1987, p. 38.

87. "Industry Begins Scrutinizing NAB Plan for Technology Center," *Broadcasting*, April 20, 1987, pp. 75–76.

88. "ABC Formalizes Betacam Decision," *Broadcasting*, May 11, 1987, p. 36. "ABC Deal Boosts Beta Format," *TV Technology*, July 1987, p. 6.

89. "ABC Commits to Betacam Format; NBC Increases MII Order," *E-ITV*, June 1987, p. 8.

90. Edwin Engberg, "The Composite Digital Format and Its Applications," *Jour. SMPTE*, October 1987, pp. 934–942. Richard Brush, "Design Consideration for the D-2 NTSC Composite DVTR," *Jour. SMPTE*, March 1988, pp. 182–193.

91. "Looking Toward Television's Future at Montreux," *Broadcasting*, June 8, 1987, p. 65–66. "Montreux's Swiss Miss: HDTV," *Broadcasting*, June 22, 1987, pp. 35–38. Joe Roizen, "Many Issues—Few Answers," *Jour. Royal Television Society*, July/August 1987, pp. 178–183.

92. "An Editing System and a Switcher," *Jour. SMPTE*, June 1987, p. 546.

93. Joe Flaherty, "Television: The Challenge of the Future," *Jour. SMPTE*, September 1987, p. 847.

94. "Hollywood on HDTV: Enthusiastic but Cautious," *Broadcasting*, October 26, 1987, pp. 76–78.

95. "ATSC Group Endorses HDTV Production Standard," *Broadcasting* October 12, 1987, pp. 89–90.

96. "In Favor of 30 fps," *Broadcasting*, October 12, 1987, p. 90. "SMPTE Releases Study on Film Rate," *Broadcast Engineering*, November 1987, pp. 4–140. "SMPTE Study Group on 30 Frame Film Rate," *Jour. SMPTE*, May 1988, pp. 404–408.

97. "NBC Debuts Advanced TV," *TV Technology*, November 1987, pp. 1–6.

98. This will be found in "The 129th SMPTE Technical Conference and Exhibit," *Jour. SMPTE*, December 1987, p. 1199; January 1988, pp. 75–114.

99. Engineer Alex R. Maxey was on the Ampex team that developed the first rotary-head videotape recorder, introduced in 1956. He was also a pioneer in developing the omega-wrap helical scan recording method. In 1964 he cofounded Westel Company (later Echo Science or Precision Echo), where his work in research and development led to many innovations. In 1977 he rejoined Ampex, where he focused on rotary data recorders. In 1986 he left Ampex for Datatape Corp., where he became the lead mechanical engineer for development of DTTR technology.

With more than 30 patented devices to his credit as designer or co-inventor, Maxey produced a body of work that has clearly been vital to both video and instrumentation recording. A member of the Video Hall of Fame, he has received numerous awards including the Weston Industrial Design Award of Merit, the Industrial Design Magazine Review Award, a Certificate of Appreciation from the National Association of Broadcasters, the Alexander M. Poniatoff Award for Technical Excellence, and an SMPTE recognition award.

100. Founder and president of Faroudja Laboratories, Inc., Yves C. Faroudja holds patents for a number of techniques that improved color television images. He holds one MS in electrical engineering from the Ecole Supérieure d'Electricité, Paris. In Europe, where he worked at ITT Research Laboratories in France and at NATO in Italy as a research engineer, Faroudja was a part of three engineering "firsts": the development and implementation of the first tide-power plant in the Rance estuary, the first transistorized Doppler radar, and the first laser activated on the European continent.

In 1965 Faroudja moved to the United States, working in color television. He founded Farjoudja Laboratories in 1981, and the company enjoyed success in such fields as the improvement of noise reduction and enhancement technologies, as well as in developing NTSC encoders and decoders. Faroujda himself has especially focused on optimizing NTSC signal performance to approach the quality of high-definition TV without a change in standard or bandwidth.

Farjoudja is a member of many technical societies in his field, including the SMPTE, the Institute of Electrical and Electronics Engineers, the Association des Anciens Elèves, the National Association of Broadcasters, and the Advanced Television Systems Committee. In 1987 he won the Monitor Award for excellence in engineering. He serves as a technical consultant to companies in the United States and elsewhere.

101. John L. E. Baldwin, a native of Hampshire, England, is internationally recognized (by such groups as the European Broadcasting Union, among others) for his technical achievements in television. At the time of his acceptance as a fellow of the SMPTE he was staff engineer, development, for the Independent Broadcasting Authority in England. With some 75 patents to his credit, he is in demand as a consultant on technical advances in the television industry.

After receiving a BS in physics from London University, in 1950 he joined Rank-Cintel, where he worked in R&D until moving to the Philips company in 1964. In 1967 he joined the Independent Broadcasting Authority.

Among Baldwin's honors are the Geoffrey Parr and PYE Color Television Awards of the Royal Television Society (1972), the David Sarnoff Gold Medal Award (1975), the Achievement Gold Medal (Montreux, 1977), and two *SMPTE Journal* awards for outstanding technical papers.

102. William C. Nicholls was affiliated with CBS as well as the European Broadcasting Union. A 1959 graduate of Purdue University (BS electrical engineering), Nicholls was employed in the engineering departments of two television stations (WCCO-TV in Minneapolis and WREX-TV in Rockford, Illinois) before coming to work at CBS. While at CBS he was involved with significant projects such as the development of slow-motion video disc recording, computer-controlled videotape editing, the teletext service, and CBS's single-camera edit system. His associations with professional societies included service on the SMPTE Television Recording and Reproduction Technology Committee.

103. Richard Brush, "Design Consideration for the D-2 NTSC Composite DVTR," *Jour. SMPTE*, March 1988, pp. 182–193.

104. "HDTV Provides Film-Broadcast Nexus at SMPTE," *Broadcasting*, Nov. 9, 1987, pp. 46–56.

105. "The 129th SMPTE Technical Conference," *Jour. SMPTE*, January 1988, p. 88.

106. Emory M. Cohen, "The Electronic Laboratory — a Working Reality," *Jour. SMPTE*, November 1988, pp. 915–924.

107. "NAB Forms HDTV Technology Center," *Broadcast Engineering*, November 1987, p. 4.

108. "George H. Brown," *Jour. SMPTE*, May 1988, p. 418. See reference no. 48.

109. "Vintage VTR Donated to Video Museum," *Broadcast Management/Engineering*, December 1987, p. 14.

110. "The CVC-50 CCD Camera and TBC-7," *Jour. SMPTE*, January 1988, p. 56.

111. "Beta No Longer Sony's One and Only," *Broadcasting*, January 18, 1988, p. 101.

112. "SMPTE Conference: Technological Transition," *Broadcasting*, January 25, 1988, pp. 82–83.

113. "Discussion," *Jour. SMPTE*, March 1988, p. 218.

114. "Engineers Come to Terms with Transition in Nashville," *Broadcasting*, Feb. 8, 1988, p. 106.

115. "AME Received First New D-2 DVR-10," *Broadcast Management/Engineering*, September 1988, p. 120.

116. "NAB Offers a Groaning Board of Technological Favorites," *Broadcasting*, April 25, 1988, pp. 45. "Joe Roizen's NAB Report," *Jour. Royal Television Society*, May/June 1988, pp. 117. Also "BBC," *Jour. SMPTE*, April 1989, p. 278.

117. "Broadcasting & Democracy" *Broadcasting*, April 4, 1988, pp. 45–64.

118. "Charles A. Steinberg," *Jour. SMPTE*, July 1988, p. 582. This, of course, put Sony in the position whereby Steinberg brought with him all of Ampex's plans for future developments.

119. "The 130th SMPTE Technical Conference and Equipment Exhibit," *Jour. SMPTE*, December 1988, pp. 995–999.

120. Philip Livingston and Johann Safar, "The D-3 Composite Digital VTR Format," *Jour. SMPTE*, Sept. 1992, pp. 602–605.

121. "The Next Step in Digital: D-3," *Broadcasting*, October 17, 1988, pp. 39–45.

122. "SMPTE HDTV," *Broadcasting*, October 24, 1988, pp. 64–68. "Wrapping up SMPTE," *Broadcasting*, October 31, 1988, pp. 47–49.

123. "NBC Unveils New HDTV Standard," *Broadcasting*, October 17, 1988, p. 31.

124. "Defense Department Wants in the HDTV Picture," *Broadcasting*, December 26, 1988, p. 54. "High Definition," *Broadcasting*, March 27, 1989, p. 14.

125. "Pentagon Takes First Step in HDTV Effort," *Broadcasting*, January 9, 1989, p. 54.

126. "SMPTE Tackles HDTV," *Broadcasting*, February 13, 1989, pp. 82–84.

127. "Joe Roizen, Hon FBKS," *Image Technology*, May 1989, p. 176. I had the honor and privilege of knowing Joe Roizen well, and I admired him. He was the author of many articles that I have used in researching this book, as well as many other papers. I was fortunate to have spent a night with him and his lovely wife, Donna Foster. They gave my wife and me an evening to remember.

The following obituary from the *Jour. SMPTE* (April 1989, p. 315) tells more about Roizen's life:

"Joseph Roizen, an SMPTE Fellow, died March 1, 1989, while attending a meeting of the International Electromechanical Commission in Paris. The 65-year-old Roizen suffered a heart attack. His wife, Donna Foster, was attending the IEC conference with him.

"Joe Roizen gave generously to the society for the 20 years he was a member. Most recently he served as a panel discussion moderator at the 3rd Annual SMPTE Television conference and sat on the current board of editors for the *SMPTE Journal*. He was Program Chairman of the 21st Television Conference, completed two terms as Governor of the Society, served as National Publicity Chairman and Secretary for the San Francisco Section, and was SMPTE Liaison Member to the EIA teletext Committee. Roizen was also frequent speaker at SMPTE national and regional functions.

"Joe Roizen was a prolific writer whose articles— more than 400— have been published in many trade publications, including the *SMPTE Journal*. He also contributed chapters to technical books such as the *McGraw-Hill Television Engineer Handbook* and the *Grolier Encyclopedia Americana*.

"In 1971, he founded Telegen, a consulting firm that provides technical market research on international revision to clients around the world. Telegen's president, he visited revision facilities in 90 countries and provided services to most of the major television networks.

"Before establishing Telegen, Roizen spent 12 years with Ampex Corp. While there, he made significant contributions to the development of broadcast videotape recorders for monochrome and color applications. In 1957, he conceived and developed the first VTR editing system to use electronic edit pulses recorded on the edge of the tape. A year later, he was project leader for the first commercially successful color VTR Ampex made. Both of these accomplishments led to patents in his name. In '59, Roizen supervised an Ampex or television installation at the first U.S. trade fair in the Soviet Union. The videotape recording made there of the Nixon/Khrushchev Kitchen Debate earned an Emmy citation in which Roizen was named. He was invited to participate in the 25th anniversary reunion of the debate, which was attended by Nixon and other U.S. government officials.

"Roizen began his career in the television division of Paramount Pictures, where he designed and supervised the construction of some of the first NTSC studio equipment.

"Beginning with the Summer Olympics in Rome in 1960, Roizen served as the technical consultant for most of the Olympics, plus the Asian Olympic Games in Tehran in 1974 and at the Pan American Games in Mexico City in 1975.

"Most recently, Roizen was involved with the emerging fields of Teletext and Viewdata. He studied systems around the world and wrote extensively about them.

"Throughout his career, Roizen received many awards and honors. In 1984 he was named the International Tape Association/Time magazine "Man-of-the-Year" for his contributions to the engineering and design of television broadcast systems. In 1975, Roizen presented the Royal Television Society's Shoenberg Memorial Lecture on the history of videotape recording. In 1976, he was elected a fellow of the Royal Television Society for his contributions to videotape editing and color television recording. He was the third American to be so honored. The RTS also awarded Roizen the Wireless World Premium (1961) and the EMI Premium (1974) for technical papers delivered to RTS conferences. The British Kinematograph, Sound and Television Society awarded Roizen honorary fellowship in 1985 for his commitment to education and the imparting of knowledge to others. Finally in October 1989 he was awarded the Presidential Proclamation of the SMPTE posthumously.

"Joseph Roizen was born September 9, 1923, in Romania. He received an Associate Degree in Science from Sir George Williams College in Montreal and took extension courses at McGill University and UCLA. He is survived by his wife and business partner, Donna Foster, of Portola Valley; sons Ron of Berkeley and Peter of Los Gatos; daughter Heidi Roizen of Mountain View; grandchildren Zoe, Ezra, Alexis, and Alexandra Roizen, and Sebastian Rupley, all of the San Francisco area; and sister Molly Tiss of Tucson, Ariz."

128. "Setting Records with HDTV," *Broadcasting* April 17, 1989, p. 32.

129. "Konosuke Matsushita," *Jour. SMPTE*, October 1989, p. 791.

130. "Television turns 50," *Broadcasting*, April 10, 1989, p. 34. Actually it was a premature opening that did not last long. Both General Electric and Westinghouse also had exhibits there. However, only RCA was happy with the results even though very few sets were sold. The rest of the television industry resented RCA's dominant position and during 1940, a series of events forced the FCC to create a National Television Systems Committee to come up with a set of standards agreed to by the members of the television community. The official opening of the American television system was July 1, 1941. See Albert Abramson, *History of Television, 1880–1941*, McFarland & Co., Jefferson, NC, 1987, pp. 269–272.

131. "Connolly Wins NAB Engineering Award," *Broadcasting*, May 8, 1989, p. 74.

132. "On the Road to NAB," *Broadcasting*, April 17, 1989, p. 67.

133. "Control Systems," *Jour. SMPTE*, April 1990, pp. 278–279. "Processing," *Jour. SMPTE*, April 1990, p. 283.

134. Ampex ad in *Broadcasting*, June 1989.

135. "NAB 1989," *Broadcasting*, May 15, 1989, p. 42.

136. *Ibid.*, pp. 42–43.

137. "Sony Will Introduce Switchers at NAB," *Broadcasting*, April 3, 1989, p. 56.

138. "Broadcasters Pick from Technological Buffet," *Broadcasting*, May 8, 1989, p. 66.

139. "On the Road to NAB," *Broadcasting*, April 17, 1989, pp. 67–68.

140. "Video Recording Devices," *Jour. SMPTE*, April 1990, p. 291.

141. "Recording Equipment," *Jour. SMPTE*, April 1991, p. 251.

142. "On the Road to NAB," *Broadcasting*, April 17, 1989, pp. 67–68. "NAB 1989," *Broadcasting*, May 15, 1989, pp. 38–39.

143. "NAB 1989," *Broadcasting*, May 15, 1989, pp. 38–39.

144. "High Definition's High Visibility in Las Vegas," *Broadcasting*, May 8, 1989, pp. 32–33.

145. "Broadcasters Joining TCI in Testing Faroudja," *Broadcasting*, May 29, 1989, pp. 32–33.

146. Tom Mann, "Non-linear Off-line Editing for HDTV and Film," *Image Technology*, December 1989, pp. 541–546.

147. William C. Nicholls and Cosmo Bolger, "The Littlest Victims," *Jour. TV Society*, May/June 1989, pp. 125–128. Strangely enough it was reported in March 1988, (*Broadcasting*, March 14, 1988, pp. 64–65) that CBS was to shoot an HDTV picture called the *Innocent Victims* for CBS Entertainment Division. It claimed that shooting started on Tuesday, March 8, 1988, in Atlanta, Georgia. The director was Peter Levin. Most of the postproduction was to be done at the Montage Studio in Los Angeles. There is even a photo of Levin and crew putting an HDTV camera through its paces. So something is wrong. It is presumed that the finished picture was so bad that it was never released, and was redone a year later. Also in "CBS-U.S.," *Jour. SMPTE*, April 1989, pp. 279–280.

148. K. Kurasoge et al., "Super-Sensitive HDTV Camera Tube with the Newly Developed HARP Target," *Jour. SMPTE*, July 1988, pp. 538–545.

149. Yves C. Faroudja and Joseph Roizen, "A Progress Report on Improved NTSC," *Jour. Royal Television Society*, May/June 1989, pp. 116–122. "Processing," *Jour. SMPTE*, April 1989, p. 254. Mitsuhiro Kurashige, "Super-Sensitive HDTV Camera Tube with the Newly Developed HARP Target," *Jour. SMPTE*, July 1988, pp. 538–545.

150. "U.S. Gets Its Way on HDTV at CCIR," *Broadcasting*, May 29, 1989, pp. 55–56.

151. "Five U.S. Companies Picked to Receive Defense Funds for HDTV Displays," *Broadcasting*, June 19, 1989, p. 42.

152. "Fiber, Component/Composite Mark Montreux's Close," *Broadcasting*, July 3, 1989, pp. 46–47.

153. "High Definition Dominates Montreux," *Broadcasting*, June 26, 1989, pp. 47–51.

154. "National Academy of TV Arts and Sciences Presents Engineering Emmys," *Jour. SMPTE*, December 1989, pp. 913–914.

155. "HDTV Eidophor," ad in *Jour. SMPTE*, September 1989, p. 703.

156. "The 131st SMPTE Technical Conference," *Jour. SMPTE*, April 1990, p. 318.

157. "SMPTE to Focus on Shifting Attitudes on HDTV," *Broadcasting*, Oct. 16, 1989, p. 64.

158. "SMPTE '89: HDTV and Beyond," *Broadcasting*, October 30, 1989, pp. 49–58.

159. "The New and Improved at SMPTE," *Broadcasting*, Nov. 16, 1989, pp. 74–77.

160. "SMPTE '89: HDTV and Beyond," *Broadcasting*, October 30, 1989, pp. 49–58.

161. "State of the Art Technology," *Broadcasting*, Oct. 23, 1989, p. 48.

162. "All Aces," *Broadcasting*, Jan. 1, 1990, p. 86.

163. "Ampex Lays Off Personnel, Cuts Inventory," *Broadcasting*, Dec. 11, 1989, pp. 65–66.

Chapter 13
The Grand Alliance (1990–1994)

1. "High Definition Gets High Visibility at SMPTE," *Broadcasting*, Feb. 5, 1990, pp. 62–64.

2. "Ampex retirement," *Broadcasting*, Feb. 26, 1990, p. 46.

3. "Sony and Ampex Hope This Is the Year for Digital VTR's," *Broadcasting*, Mar. 19, 1990, pp. 59–60.

4. "Progress Report 1990," *Jour. SMPTE*, April 1991, p. 235.

5. "Focusing on Cameras: CCD's Making Tubes Obsolete," *Broadcasting*, Feb. 26, 1990, pp. 41–42. "NAB: Focus On Technology, Tale of the Tape," *Broadcasting*, April 23, 1990, pp. 52–56.

6. "High Definition Gets High NAB Profile," *Broadcasting*, April 16, 1990, pp. 43–46.

7. "Progress Report 1990," *Jour. SMPTE*, April 1991, p. 235.

8. Fumio Okano, Junji Kumada, and Kenkichi Tanioka, "The HARP High Sensitivity Handheld HDTV Camera," *Jour. SMPTE*, August 1990, pp. 612–619. "Progress Report 1990," *Jour. SMPTE*, April 1991, pp. 235–236.

9. "FCC to Take Simulcast Route to HDTV," *Broadcasting*, March 16, 1990, p. 38

10. Progress Report 1990," *Jour. SMPTE*, April 1991, p. 242.

11. *Ibid.*, p. 248.

12. *Ibid.*, p. 251.

13. *Ibid.*

14. "Walter Bruch," *Jour SMPTE*, August 1990, p. 685. The following biography is from W. A. Atherton, "Pioneers: Walter Bruch," *Electronics & Wireless World*, November 1988, vol. 94, pp. 1101–1102.

"Born on March 2, 1908, Walter Bruch became fascinated with television early in his life. He was a radio hobbyist at 14 years of age, and at 17 he became mesmerized by the early electromechanical television apparatus be had the opportunity to admire at the Communications Exposition in Munich in 1925. From then on, his life was dedicated to the medium that in those days seemed no more than an unrealizable dream, much less ever thinkable in color. In total, he was granted some 200 patents.

"In 1925 he started his career as a simple mechanic. Later he worked as assistant installer for an electrical power station, where he had to maintain and replace overhead lines in the countryside, balancing himself precariously atop poles and roofs of buildings. He then attended the Engineering School in the town of Mittweida, and he visited the 5th Great Radio Exposition of 1929 in Berlin, an unforgettable event in this writer's own memory.

"In 1935 Bruch joined Telefunken, where he worked with one of the first of Zworykin's iconoscopes. He designed and built almost the entire television system for the transmission of the Olympic Games in Berlin in 1936, manning the cameras himself. He continued working with Telefunken, and during the war he was active in the development of television equipment for military uses. The aftermath of the war brought with it hard times for him, but in 1950 Telefunken called him back, and from then on he played an important role in the development and establishment of systems and equipment for the two existing German broadcasting systems. Under his guidance, in 1952 Telefunken's first postwar TV receiver, the FE8, was presented to the public. In 1959, AEG-Telefunken established a laboratory for his own use in basic research and development, where was created the highly original PAL system. Color television was inaugurated in the German Federal Republic in 1967 and was first shown at the 25th German Broadcast Exhibition of that year in Berlin.

"Bruch worked afterwards on numerous other things that today we take for granted: the nonprofessional video recorder, digital color television transmission, satellite transmission systems, analog-to-digital conversion, pulse-code modulation, and many, many more. In 1976 he retired, but he remained active for the rest of his years adding to the many publications he produced during his working years, working as a consultant and being of service to the many organizations in his chosen field.

"Many were the honors that came his way. He was an Honorary Member of the Fernseh-und-Kinotechnischce Gesellschaft (FKTG), which distinguished him with the Richard Theile Gold Medal. In 1989 the Society of Motion Picture and Television Engineers (SMPTE) presented him with its Honorary Membership Award. In 1971 he had already received the David Sarnoff Gold Medal from the SMPTE. He was made a Fellow of the Royal Television Society (England), and was awarded Honorary Membership by the Institution of Electronic and Radio Engineers (IERE, England) and other distinctions in Brazil, Australia, and Switzerland. In 1976 Bruch was the recipient of the Werner von Siemens Ring, and in 1985 he was the recipient of the Eduard Rhein Prize, both from the FKTG. He received the Great Cross of Merit with Star from the German Federal Republic. In 1964 the University of Hannover bestowed on him the title of Doctor in Engineering *Honoris Causa*, and the Minister-President of the Saarland awarded him the title of Professor in 1968. Numerous other awards and honors came his way — too many to list. His personality and achievements will always be commemorated, cherished, and admired worldwide by the television industry."

15. "Will It Revolutionize HDTV?" *Broadcasting*, June 4, 1990, pp. 33–34.

16. "GI Gives Full Story on DigiCipher," *Broadcasting*, July 2, 1990, p. 56.

17. "Charles P. Ginsburg," *Jour. SMPTE*, July 1990, p. 578.

18. *New York Times*, July 25, 1990, p. B11. See also Abramson, *History of Television 1880–1941*, p. 308, for his important role in the development of Japanese television.

19. "CBS Buys CCD," *Broadcasting*, August 13, 1990, p. 72.

20. "Britain Buys Ampex," *Broadcasting*, August 13, 1990, p. 72.

21. "Ampex Makes Audio Editing Easier," *Broadcasting*, Sept. 10, 1990, p. 90. "Recording Equipment," *Jour. SMPTE*, April 1991, p. 251. It was assumed that Sony's D-2s had the same problem.

22. "Wide Screen, Narrow Signals Are Talk of Brighton," *Broadcasting*, Oct. 1, 1990, pp. 64–67.

23. "BBC Picks Panasonic D-X," *Broadcasting*, Oct. 1, 1990, p. 67.

24. "New York, New York, It's a Digital Town," *Broadcasting*, Oct. 22, 1990, pp. 69–73.

25. "Digital: Choice of a New Generation," *Broadcasting*, Oct. 15, 1990, p. 48.

26. "Digital Dominates Less Crowded Stage in Atlanta (this should read New York City)," *Broadcasting*, Oct. 29, 1990, pp. 49–50.

27. "The 132nd SMPTE Technical Conference and Equipment Exhibit," *Jour. SMPTE*, April 1991, p. 292. See also "Get-Together Luncheon Address," *Jour. SMPTE*, April 1991, pp. 304–306.

28. "Requiem," *Broadcasting*, Nov. 19, 1990, p. 37. "Farewell to the Man in the CBS Eye," *Broadcasting*, Nov. 5, 1990, pp. 35–39.

"William Samuel Paley was born September 28, 1901, in Chicago, IL. He was the son of an immigrant Russian Jew who conducted a thriving cigar business in Chicago. The family moved to Philadelphia when he was ready for college, and he entered Wharton School of Finance at the University of Pennsylvania. There he earned a bachelor's degree and entered the new cigar business the family had set up in Philadelphia. He became vice president, and he signed an early radio advertising contract for the firm's products. He became convinced that radio advertising had an important future, and when the opportunity appeared he bought a small radio network, which in 1929 he renamed the Columbia Broadcasting System. He promptly began to build it into one of the world's leading radio and television networks. Paley retained or hired such entertainment stars as Bing Crosby, Kate Smith, the Mills Brothers, Will Rogers, Eddie Cantor, and Bob Hope, luring some of them from rival networks.

"News coverage was born at CBS in 1933 when it developed its own news gathering organization. He hired such outstanding reporters as Ed Murrow, Eric Severeid, William Shirer and Howard K. Smith.

"During World War II Paley served the US government as supervisor of the Office of War Information (OWI) in the Mediterranean, and later as chief of radio in the OWI's Psychological Warfare Division (1944–45), finally becoming deputy chief of the Psychological Warfare Division.

"Back at CBS after the war, Paley supported and encouraged Edward R. Murrow in building an outstanding news staff. He decided that ad agencies and producers had too much control in radio and decided to produce his own shows. Although initially skeptical about the new medium of television, he knew that it was just around the corner and gathered up many radio stars to give CBS a good start in tv. Paley had several bad moments in his career including the premature venture into UHF CBS color after the war, the acquisition of Hytron Radio and Electronic Corp., the ill-fated venture into Electronic Video Recording (EVR) with Goldmark that cost him millions, and finally with CBS cable which did not survive. He also owned the New York Yankees, Steinway Pianos, Creative Playthings, all of which turned out poorly. In 1966, Paley waived the CBS mandatory retirement rule so that he could stay as chairman of the board. He remained as chairman until 1983. In his final years, Paley saw his beloved CBS fall from eminence with an unfriendly takeover which just about ruined the company. He won many honours, including the US Order of Merit, the French Croix de Guerre, and the Italian Order of the Crown. See also: Sally Bedell Smith, *In All His Glory*, Simon and Schuster, New York, 1990, pp. 207–227; and William S. Paley, *As It Happened: A Memoir*, Doubleday & Company, Garden City, New York, 1979, pp. 154–171.

"See also "Sad Day At Black Rock," *Broadcasting*, Nov. 5, 1990, p. 90, that said, "Working for CBS was a status symbol, like graduating from Harvard or driving a Hispano Suiza (as Paley did in the 1920's). It meant working for the best. It meant working for Bill Paley." I had the good fortune to work for CBS-TV from 1952 to 1987 and agree totally. While he was in charge, CBS was a real family and going to work each day was pure pleasure. As a result, everyone was working at 110 percent. Our shows sparkled with an inner light that only comes from real craftsmanship, the love of the art, the feeling of accomplishment, and only comes so rarely. Our unofficial motto was, 'The difficult is done right now; the impossible takes a little longer.'"

29. "Ritchie Leaves Presidency of Ampex," *Broadcasting*, January 21, 1991, p. 57.

30. "Ampex Proposes Evolutionary Path to All-Digital Production," *Broadcasting*, Jan. 28, 1991, p. 51. "New Products," *Jour. SMPTE*, May 1991, p. 380.

31. "The 25th Annual SMPTE Television Conference," *Jour. SMPTE*, April 1991, pp. 298–306.

32. "Broadcasting Readying for All-Digital Future," *Broadcasting*, Feb. 11, 1991, pp. 73–75.

33. "GI and MIT Form HDTV Alliance," *Broadcasting*, Feb. 4, 1991, p. 42.

34. "Ampex Head Says Company Is Back on Track," *Broadcasting*, Mar. 4, 1991, p. 66.

35. "NBC to Use Half-Inch Tape for Olympics Coverage," *Broadcasting*, March 18, 1991, p. 55.

36. "Albert Rose," *Jour. SMPTE*, April 1991, p. 314. This was Rose's obituary, which continued:

"In 1942 Rose moved to the RCA Laboratories in Princeton, NJ, where he engaged in important war work. One of his most successful projects was the development of the image orthicon camera tube in 1944. It was designed and built for a series of airborne missiles and reconnaissance aircraft. It was Rose's invention of the two-sided glass target that made this tube possible. The first model image orthicon (2P3) was available at the war's end and with many improvements it made post-war television possible. The product became the workhorse of the entire television industry until 1964. During that time Rose also did the preliminary research for the first photoconductive camera tube, the Vidicon. From 1955 to 1957 he directed research at the Laboratories RCA, Ltd., in Zurich, Switzerland. His interest in light sensitive film, television pickup tubes, and the human eye resulted in a paper and a subsequent definitive book on the subject, entitled 'Vision: Human and Electronic.' A noted speaker, Rose lectured at the University of Illinois, California Institute of Technology, Massachusetts Institute of Technology, Polytechnic Institute of Mexico City, and Hebrew University in Jerusalem, Israel. He also served as visiting lecturer at Princeton University and visiting professor at Cornell, and was awarded an honorary degree by the Rochester Institute of Technology. He retired from RCA in 1975 and became a fellow of the technical staff. During his lifetime Rose held over 40 patents and published over 50 technical papers and articles. Awards presented to him include the Television Broadcasters Association Award, the Morris Liebman Award, the David Sarnoff Outstanding Achievement Awards in Engineering and Science, and the SMPTE David Sarnoff and Journal Awards. He also received the Edison Medal of the IEEE for his basic contributions in television camera tubes. In 1986 the Institute for Graphic Communications created the Albert Rose Electronic Imager of the Year Award in his honor.

"He was a member of both Phi Beta Kappa and the Société de Physique. In 1975 he was elected to the National Academy of Engineering. He was also a fellow of the American Physical Society and a life fellow of the IEEE."

37. "Graphic, Video Effects Color New TV World," *Broadcasting*, March 11, 1991, pp. 61–64.

38. "NAB Plans Larger HDTV Exhibit," *Broadcasting*, March 25, 1991, pp. 84–87. "Seeking Digital Video Recording Evolution," *Broadcasting*, April 1, 1991, pp. 66–68. "The Road Revisited: Sights and Sounds of NAB 91," *Broadcasting*, May 20, 1991, pp. 63–65.

39. "Montreux to Focus on HDTV, Digital Video," *Broadcasting*, Dec. 1990, p. 52.

40. "Digital Developments Dominate in Montreux," *Broadcasting*, June 24, 1991, pp. 20–21.

41. "A Betacam SP Studio VTR," *Jour. SMPTE*, June 1991, p. 444.

42. "HDTV Cinema for the World," *Broadcasting*, June 14, 1991, p. 122.

43. "Ampex Lays off 250 from Recording Media," *Broadcasting*, July 22, 1991, p. 44.

44. "Survey Projects D-2 and Type C Parity," *Broadcasting*, July 22, 1991, p. 45.

45. "Ampex Recording Media Corp.," *Jour. SMPTE*, Oct. 1991, p. 832. Also "New Products," *Jour. SMPTE*, Oct. 1991, p. 840.

46. "Manufacturers Call for Fewer Shows," *Broadcasting*, Nov. 18, 1991, p. 66.

47. "Closing in on a Videotape Replacement," *Broadcasting*, Nov. 4, 1991, p. 29.

48. "HDTV Debut," *Broadcasting*, January 27, 1992, p. 42.

49. "ATRC Says Its Digital HDTV Could Lead to a Single Video, Computer Standard," *Broadcasting*, Feb. 10, 1992, p. 55.

50. "Format of Which Year?" *Broadcasting*, Mar. 23, 1992, p. 64. Ampex knew that it could no longer compete with Sony and Panasonic for the broadcast market. Perhaps it would have success with the film-to-tape and postproduction markets where producers required a cost-effective high-quality, digital component format.

51. "Sony Digital Betacam," *Broadcast Engineering*, March 1993, pp. 160–164.

52. W. Saxon, "Charles P. Ginsburg, 71, Leader in Developing Video Recording," *San Jose Mercury News*, April 19, 1992, p. 7B. This obituary of Gibson continued:

"The son of a Russian-Jewish émigré and his American wife, Mr. Ginsburg was born and raised in San Francisco, where he graduated from Lowell High School. When he was four he was diagnosed with diabetes and would take daily insulin shots for the rest of his life. When he entered the University of California, Berkeley, Mr. Ginsburg majored in premed, then transferred to UC–Davis to study animal husbandry two years later. His daughters said he was "broke" by 1940 and dropped out of school, supporting himself through a succession of jobs in electronics. He enrolled at San Jose State in 1942 and graduated six years later with a BA in engineering and math. Meanwhile, Mr. Ginsburg married Louise Hammer, daughter of a well-known San Jose family and older sister of Philip Hammer, husband of San Jose mayor Susan Hammer.

"The couple had five daughters and moved to Los Altos in 1952. They divorced in the early 1960s. Mr. Ginsburg, who took a job in college with radio station KQW, forerunner of KCBS, heard of the newly formed Ampex Corp. and was hired early on to develop videotape technology. Mr. Ginsburg and his second wife Edna Perkins Ginsburg lived in Menlo Park from 1962 until they moved to Oregon two years ago. He had two passions, photography and golf. It was golf that helped his recovery when he lost a leg due to complications of diabetes in 1968. In 1960, Mr. Ginsburg was named a vice president of Ampex. He retired in 1986 as vice-president of advanced development."

See also Albert Abramson, "Charles Ginsburg, Video Recording Pioneer," *New York Times* April 17, 1992, p. B1; and "Charles P. Ginsburg," *Jour. SMPTE*, July 1992, pp. 505–506. It is perhaps ironic that the same *SMPTE* issue that reported Ginsburg's death also announced the new Ampex DCT system.

There was an article, "Report on the Memorial Ceremony for Charles P. Ginsburg," in *Jour. SMPTE*, October 1992, pp. 733–734. According to Pete Hammar, "Charlie was the glue that held the Ampex videotape recorder R & D team together for more than four years, from 1952 to 1956, a disparate group of talented individualists." But Charles Anderson saw it differently. He said, "Ginsburg's gift was that he was able to take this group of very different and probably fairly *ordinary* engineers and put them together and get the best out of them. The sum was greater than the parts." I dispute that last statement; surely neither Anderson nor Dolby was an ordinary engineer. It was a matter of the right people together at the right time and in the right place. Ginsburg may not have been the greatest engineer in the world, but he knew how to get the best out of each man. In this he was similar to V. K. Zworykin who inspired his team to just go out and do the job.

53. "1992: The Year of HDTV?" *Broadcasting*, March 23, 1992, p. 62.

54. "NAB 1992," *Broadcasting*, March 23, 1992, p. 74.

55. "HDTV: Hardware Begins to Replace Theory," *Broadcasting*, April 20, 1992, pp. 22–24.

56. "All-New HDTV at NAB," *Broadcasting*, April 13, 1992, p. 43.

57. "NAB '92: Geared for Changing Times," *Broadcasting*, April 27, 1992, pp. 46–47.

58. "1992: The Year of HDTV?" *Broadcasting*, March 23, 1992, p. 64.

59. "HDTV Competitors Reach Royalty-Sharing Accord," *Broadcasting*, May 11, 1992, p. 14.

60. "Zenith/AT&T: Long Distance Digital HDTV," *Broadcasting*, June 1, 1992, p. 11.

61. Peter Lambert, "Japan: Land of the Rising Digits?" *Broadcasting*, June 1, 1992, pp. 32–33.

62. "HDTV," *Broadcasting & Cable*, June 7, 1992, p. 98.

63. "Progress Report," *Jour. SMPTE*, April 1993, p. 315.

64. "Ampex Terms U.S. Television Market 'Mature,'" *Broadcasting*, June 15, 1992, pp. 22–23.

65. *Jour. SMPTE*, June 1992, p. 430.

66. Michael Arbuthnot, "The Ampex DCT 700d Transport," *Broadcast Engineering*, Sept. 1992, p. 20. Specifications from excerpt from M. Arbuthnot, *Jour. SMPTE*, August 1992, p. 583.

67. Michael Arbuthnot, "Ampex DCT 700d Tape Drive," *Broadcast Engineering*, February 1933, pp. 68–73.

68. "Faux Film Is Emmy Winner, Budget Saver," *Broadcasting*, June 29, 1992, p. 23.

69. "McKinney Decries EC Emphasis on Analog," *Broadcasting*, July 6, 1992, pp. 48–49. "Report on SMPTE Participation in the International Broadcasting Convention," *Jour. SMPTE*, October 1992, p. 720.

70. "NBC, Sarnoff Group Provide First Public HDTV Simulcast," *Broadcasting*, October 5, 1992, p. 15.

71. "Early Muse Returns," *Broadcasting*, September 28, 1992, p. 39.

72. "134th SMPTE Technical Conference and Equipment Exhibit Metro Toronto Convention Centre, Canada," *Jour. SMPTE*, January 1993, pp. 41–63. "The New and Improved on View at SMPTE," *Broadcasting*, Nov 16, 1992, pp. 57–58.

73. "SMPTE Announces Award Recipients," *Broadcast Engineering*, October 1992, p. 4.

74. "Progress Report 1992," *Jour. SMPTE*, April 1993, pp. 298, 312, 319.

75. "Avid Technology," *Broadcasting*, Nov. 16, 1992, p. 58.

76. "USA Networks Buy Panasonic D-3," *Broadcasting*, Dec. 21, 1992, p. 47.

77. Randy Suskow, "Now There Are Four," *Broadcasting*, Feb. 15, 1993, pp. 6–11.

78. "Progress Toward Terrestrial Digital HDTV," *Broadcast Engineering*, April 1993, pp. 4–17.

79. "New Products," *Jour. SMPTE*, August 1993, p. 732.

80. "New Products," *Jour. SMPTE*, August 1993, p. 734. Brad Dick, "From the Show Floor," *Broadcast Engineering*, June 1993, pp. 22–30. Steve McClellan, "Sony Unveiling Small Format Digital Gear," *Broadcasting and Cable*, March 18, 1993, p. 50.

81. "Ampex Corp," *Broadcast Engineering*, June 1993, p. 58.

82. "HDTV Testing Rescheduled," *Broadcasting & Cable*, May 3, 1993, p. 59.

83. "The 'Grand Alliance' Becomes Reality," *Broadcasting & Cable*, May 31, 1998, pp. 59–60.

84. "Ampex Systems Corp.," *Broadcast Engineering*, June 1993, p. 124.

85. "FCC Considers HDTV Grand Alliance Proposal," *Broadcast Engineering*, June 1993, p. 4.

86. "SMPTE Participate in 18th International Television Symposium and Technical Exhibition," *Jour. SMPTE*, September 1993, pp. 828–829.

87. "Très Grande Alliance: World Standard?" *Broadcasting & Cable*, June 21, 1993, pp. 54–56.

88. "HDTV," *Broadcasting & Cable*, June 28, 1993, p. 43.

89. "Zenith Demonstrates Its 16-VSB," *Broadcasting & Cable*, June 14, 1993.

90. "Grand Alliance Lays Out Its Battle Plan," *Broadcasting & Cable*, July 12, 1993, p. 69.

91. "Industry Briefs." *Broadcast Engineering*, Aug. 1993, p. 79.

92. "Mirror in the TV Set," *Broadcasting & Cable*, August 16, 1993, p. 44. See also V. Markandey and Robert J. Gove, "Digital Display Systems Based on the Digital Micromirror Device," *Jour. SMPTE*, Oct. 1995, pp. 680–685.

93. "Really Big Job," *Broadcast & Cable*, September 1993, p. 61.

94. "16:9 Cameras Have Arrived," *Broadcast Engineering*, October 1993, p. 58.

95. "Once-Mighty Ampex Cuts TV Product Lines," *Broadcasting & Cable*, October 4, 1993, p. 65. What remained unsaid was that Ampex was the last major American company left. All the others (except RCA perhaps) were driven out of business by the ferocious Japanese competition promoted by the Japanese government. The fact that Ampex had not only withstood this competition, but had the Japanese on the run at times was a monument to American ingenuity. It is a shame that both the American industry (broadcasters particularly) and the U.S. government did nothing to prevent the Japanese takeover from happening. But that would have been un-American!

Oddly enough at this very same moment, the American television industry had broken the back of the Japanese government's (NHK's) plan when it came to the a high-definition terrestrial standard. However, this would not prevent both Sony and Matsushita from dominating the television equipment industry worldwide as they usually did.

96. "Industry Briefs," *Broadcast Engineering*, October 1993, p. 92.

97. "DCRsi Technology Overview," *Ampex Data Systems*, October 1993.

98. Sean Scully, "Cutting Edge," Nov. 8, 1993, *Broadcasting & Cable*, p. 34.

99. "Industry Briefs," *Broadcast Engineering*, December 1993, p. 76.

100. H. A. Cole, "HD in the United Kingdom," *Broadcast Engineering*, December 1993, p. 72.

101. B. Marti, D Nasse, P. Bernard, and B. Le Flock, "Problems and Perspectives of Digital Terrestrial Television in Europe," *Jour. SMPTE*, August 1993, pp. 703–711.

102. Harry A Jessell, "Sony Remaking Its Destiny," *Broadcasting & Cable*, Feb. 21, 1994, pp. 66–76.

103. "Green Light to Testing of HDTV Prototype," *Broadcasting & Cable*, Feb. 28, 1994.

104. "Towards HDTV Immense Alliance," *Broadcasting & Cable*, Mar. 7, 1994, p. 51.

105. "VTRs: Not Dead Yet," *Broadcasting & Cable*, Mar. 28, 1994, p. 38.

106. "Disk Camera Bandwagon Picks Up Speed," *Broadcasting & Cable*, April 18, 1994, p. 40.

107. "Ampex Corp.," *Broadcasting & Cable*, June 13, 1994, p. 47. Also *Broadcast Engineering*, July 1994, p. 76.

108. "Industry Briefs," *Broadcast Engineering*, July 1994, p. 76.

109. "Media Pool Test the Tapeless Waters," *Broadcasting & Cable*, July 18, 1994, p. 60.

110. "Sony Closes a Series of Digital Betacam VTR Sales," *Broadcasting & Cable*, July 18, 1994, p. 62.

111. "Ampex Corp," *Broadcasting &Cable*, Aug. 22, 1994. p. 30.

112. "CBS Picks H-P for Its Tapeless Debut," *Broadcasting & Cable*, Aug. 15, 1994, p. 43. The term "video server" comes from the computer industry. It is a system that provides mass storage of data or application programs to be used by one or more of the clients connected to the network. It involves more than video storage; it also includes file management. Phillip J. Hejtmanek, "Video Servers," *Broadcast Engineering*, Feb. 1996, pp. 27–30.

113. "ABC News Going Digital in DC," *Broadcasting & Cable*, Aug. 22, 1994, p. 36.

114. "Panasonic Broadcast and Television Systems," *Broadcasting & Cable*, Sept. 12, 1994, p. 56.

115. Steve Homer, "Digital TV Is the Hit of IBC," *Broadcasting & Cable*, Sept. 26, 1994, pp. 58–59.

116. Chris McConnell, "Delivering on Digital Promises," *Broadcasting & Cable*, Oct. 17, 1994, p. 10.

117. "The Ampex Corp," *Broadcasting & Cable*, October 24, 1994, p. 46.

118. "JVC Pro Products," *Broadcasting & Cable*, Nov. 7, 1994, p. 67.

119. "The Cutting Edge," *Broadcasting & Cable*, Nov. 28, 1994, p. 82.

120. "Reuters Digitizing Newsreels," *Broadcasting & Cable*, Dec. 12, 1994, pp. 86–87. See *Broadcast Engineering*, July 1999, p. 38, for an article on DCT compression.

Chapter 14
E-Cinema and the 1080p24 Format
(1995–2000)

1. "Cutting Edge," *Broadcasting & Cable*, January 9, 1995, p. 70.

2. "Cutting Edge," *Broadcasting & Cable*, January 30, 1995, p. 43.

3. "Cutting Edge," *Broadcasting & Cable*, Feb. 27, 1995, p. 43.

4. Ampex ads in *Broadcast & Cable*, Feb. 1995 and March 1995.

5. "Avid for Broadcasters," *Broadcasting & Cable*, April 3, 1995, p. 65.

6. Curt Rawley, "Avid Advocate for a Disk-Based Future," *Broadcasting & Cable*, April 3, 1995, p. 63.

7. "Panasonic to Roll Digital Line at NAB," *Broadcasting & Cable*, Mar. 13, 1995, p. 70.

8. Camras was a great innovator whose interest in recording technology began early: Among his first successes was a magnetic wire recorder he built in high school to help a cousin practice his singing. Later he was involved with wire recorders for the military in World War II. Associated all his life with the Armour Research Foundation — which later became the Illinois Institute of Technology — Camras continually moved the recording and broadcasting industries forward with his inventions. AC bias, which dramatically reduced noise and distortion in magnetic recording, was probably his best known invention.

Camras introduced both high-coercivity magnetic oxide for tape and, in 1946, pre-sprocketed 35mm magnetic film. The one-inch track down the middle of the magnetic film may have seemed, at first glance, a wasteful use of space, but actually it vastly improved the efficiency of editing. The magnetic track meant that the film and picture could be easily edited in sync, using existing editing equipment with only the addition of a magnetic playback head. Hence there was no longer any need to record and edit the cumbersome optical track. Only two years after Camras introduced his pre-sprocketed film, optical equipment that weighed eight tons was being replaced by magnetic packages weighing only 270 pounds. Producers today still use Camras's system for shooting "dailies," i.e., film that is viewed at the end of each production day.

Camras continued to work with Armour Research on such projects as binaural and three-channel stereo recording (1947); video recording (Armour demonstrated a prototype rotating-head recorder in 1950); and memory drums and disks for computers (1951). In 1962, the Institute of Electrical and Electronic Engineers asked Camras and others to describe the technologies they thought would exist in 2012. Among Camras's predictions were that tape recorders would evolve into "memory elements" about the size of a pack of playing cards, with no moving parts, holding vast amounts of information. He envisioned several applications for these "memory packs," including use by consumers (in shopping and in the use of home entertainment systems) and physicians (in diagnosis and treatment). Camras also imagined a paperless, cashless society in 2012, which would include direct deductions of taxes from all transactions "so that the government is always up to date on collections."

Dr. Camras received many awards in his lifetime, including the National Medal of Technology (1990) and the Coors American Ingenuity Award (1992). Yet the satisfactions of research and discovery seemed always the greatest reward for this old-fashioned, hands-on scientist. Camras died at age 79.

For another obituary, see *Spectrum IEEE*, August 1995.

9. Chris McConnell, "Green Light Given to Grand Alliance System," *Broadcasting & Cable*, September 18, 1995, p. 55.

10. "Section Meetings," *Jour. SMPTE*, Oct. 1995, p. 695.

11. "Industry Briefs," *Broadcast Engineering*, October 1995, p. 110.

12. "Cutting Edge," *Broadcasting & Cable*, Dec. 4, 1995, p. 79.

13. "Fox Digital Buy," *Broadcasting & Cable*, January 1, 1996, p. 47.

14. Glen Dickson, "NBC Signs Olympian Deal with Panasonic," *Broadcast & Cable*, January 29, 1996, pp. 44.

15. "Cutting Edge," *Broadcasting & Cable*, March 11, 1996, p. 80.

16. Glen Dickson, "Philips BTS Introduces New Film Scanner," *Broadcasting & Cable*, April 17, 1996, p. 12.

17. "Cutting Edge," *Broadcasting & Cable*, May 6, 1996, p. 58.

18. "Industry Briefs," *Broadcast Engineering*, July 1996, p. 96.

19. C. McConnell, "White House Calls for Digital TV Standard," *Broadcasting & Cable*, July 22, 1996, p. 19.

20. "Cutting Edge," August 5, 1996, *Broadcasting & Cable*, p. 78.

21. "Cutting Edge," *Broadcasting & Cable*, August 12, 1996, p. 86.

22. "Industry Briefs," *Broadcast Engineering*, October 1996, p. 110.

23. "Tribune Invests in Sony's SX," *Broadcast & Cable*, December 3, 1996.

24. G. Dickson, "Another Digital-S Deal for JVC," *Broadcasting & Cable*, November 25, 1996, p. 66.

25. "DTV Standard: It's Official," *Broadcasting & Cable*, December 30, 1996, p. 4.

26. "CBC Makes $1 Million DVCPRO Buy," *Broadcasting & Cable*, January 20, 1997, p. 58.

27. Glen Dickson, "Cutting Edge," *Broadcasting & Cable*, January 20, 1997, p. 61.

28. Glen Dickson, "Meet the Press Goes Hi-Def," *Broadcasting & Cable*, Feb. 10, 1997.

29. Glen Dickson, "Panasonic Restructures into Six Units; Unveils Plans for NAB Show," *Broadcasting & Cable*, Feb. 10, 1997, p. 54.

30. "*NAB 97* Product News," *Broadcasting & Cable*, February 24, 1997, p. 68.

31. Glen Dickson, "HP Debuts Disk Recorder," *Broadcasting & Cable*, March 3, 1997, p. 67.

32. "Camcorder Still Kicking," *Broadcasting & Cable*, March 17, 1997, p. 8.

33. Further details were given me in a personal interview at his home on the Elbe in Dresden on August 3, 1984. Von Ardenne was considered a "wunderkind" who more than once set fire to his parents house with his early experiments. He graduated from the "gymnasium" at 16 and attended the University of Berlin for only two years, 1925–1926. By 1928, he had established a laboratory in the basement of his home in Lichterfelde, and had already received several patents and published his first book. His experiments with cathode ray tubes led him to his all-electric cathode ray system that he demonstrated in 1931. Von Ardenne worked on television until 1935, when all research was taken over by the Luftwaffe. He then experimented with image tubes and was one of the earliest inventors of the electron microscope, including the scanning electron microscope and the x-ray projection microscope. During World War II, he made significant contributions to the German atomic bomb project, which had little success. In 1945, he *voluntarily* went to the USSR to work on their atomic bomb project. He returned to Dresden in 1955. Here he set up a lavish castle on the Elbe in 1964, with a medical laboratory for cancer research.

34. "CBS Makes 24 Million DVCPRO Buy," *Broadcasting & Cable*, April 7, 1997, p. 102.

35. Glen Dickson, "Sony Joins CBS in Nagano," *Broadcasting & Cable*, April 9, 1997, p. 16.

36. "Benedek Tape DVCPRO," *Broadcasting & Cable*, April 7, 1999, p. 102.

37. "KCTS-TV Buys New Sony HDTV Camera," *Broadcasting & Cable*, May 5, 1997, p. 69. Kenneth Hunold, *Broadcast Engineering*, May 1997, pp. 100–102, 128.

38. G. Dickson, "KGTV Goes DVCPRO in San Diego," *Broadcasting & Cable*, June 16, 1997, p. 63.

39. G. Dickson, "JVC Unveils Digital-S Camcorder," *Broadcasting & Cable*, June 9, 1997, p. 50.

40. "Cutting Edge," *Broadcasting & Cable*, June 30, 1997, p. 76.

41. *Ibid.*

42. *Ibid.*

43. J. M. Highness, "SDTV Falling Out of Favor," *Broadcasting & Cable*, August 18, 1997, p. 4.

44. "DVCPRO Continues Its European Invasion," *Broadcasting & Cable*, September 22, 1997, p. 66.

45. "Industry Briefs," *Broadcast Engineering*, October 1997, p. 129.

46. "Technology," *Broadcasting & Cable*, October 6, 1997, p. 67.

47. "Advanced TV Systems Committee," *Broadcasting & Cable*, October 6, 1997, p. 66.

48. "KHJ-TV Going to DVCPRO," *Broadcasting & Cable*, November 17, 1997, p. 72.

49. "Cutting Edge," *Broadcast & Cable*, November 3, 1997, p. 60.

50. "Panasonic Debuts DVCPRO50 Line," *Broadcasting & Cable*, December 1, 1997, p. 76.

51. "Cutting Edge," *Broadcasting & Cable*, December 22, 1997, p. 31.

52. "Sony's Steinberg Shifts Roles," *Broadcasting & Cable*, January 4, 1998.

53. "Cutting Edge," *Broadcasting & Cable*, January 5, 1998.

54. "Cutting Edge," *Broadcasting & Cable*, February 9, 1998, p. 92.

55. "Sony Touts 'Digital Reality,'" *Broadcasting & Cable*, February 9, 1998, p. 50.

56. "Cutting Edge," *Broadcasting & Cable*, January 9, 1998, p. 52.

57. "Industry Briefs," *Broadcasting & Cable*, June 8, 1998, p. 80.

58. "Cutting Edge," *Broadcasting & Cable*, June 15, 1998, p. 64.

59. "WCNC Chooses Sony SX," *Broadcasting & Cable*, July 8, 1998, p. 44.

60. "NBC News Channel Goes with DVCPRO," *Broadcasting & Cable*, August 24, 1998, p. 64.

61. "Cutting Edge," *Broadcasting & Cable*, August 24, 1998, p. 64.

62. Glen Dickson, "Rebo Group Closes Shop," *Broadcasting & Cable*, September 27, 1998.

63. L. J. Thorpe, "Contemporary DTV Acquisition — Some Perspectives on the Related Standard, the Technologies, and the Creative [Aspects]," *Jour. SMPTE*, August 1999, pp. 551–562.

64. "Cutting Edge," *Broadcasting & Cable*, January 4, 1999, p. 74.

65. Glen Dickson, "Dolby Unveils Audio for DTV," *Broadcasting & Cable*, Feb. 15, 1999, p. 71.

66. "Panasonic Announced a 1080/P24 Frame Film Production System," *Jour. SMPTE*, August 1999, p. 589.

67. "Panasonic Announces 1080/P24 Frame Film Production System," *Jour. SMPTE*, August 1999, p. 589.

68. "The 24P Approach," *Broadcast Engineering*, April 1999, p. 28. See also Jerry Whitaker, "HDTV: The Marriage of Film and Video," *Broadcast Engineering*, April 1999.

69. Larry Bloomfield, "'Tonight Show' Becomes First HD Network Program," *Broadcast Engineering*, June 1999, pp. 14–16.

70. Hal Reynolds and Geordie Douglas, "Fox Digital Tape Center," *Broadcast Engineering*, April 1999, pp. 66–82. Darrell Wehhardt, "KCET," *Broadcast Engineering*, July 1999, pp. 46–50. "Digital Servers," *Broadcasting & Cable*, April 3, 1995, p. 3.

71. "Exhibits," "NAB 1999, Exhibit Guide," April 1999, p. 44.

72. "Cutting Edge," *Broadcasting & Cable*, May 3, 1999, p. 42.

73. "ABC's Monday Night Football Goes HD," *Broadcast Engineering*, June 1999, p. 18. "Cutting Edge," *Broadcasting & Cable*, May 3, 1999. p. 42.

74. "John T. Mullin, the Man Who Put Bing Crosby on Tape," obituary from Pete Hammar, 19 July 1999.

I had the honor of knowing Jack Mullin when he was showing his first video recorder. I attended many demonstrations and was amazed at what he had done. (Actually the pictures were very bad, but they were pictures.) One downhearted note: I was writing my first book, *Electronic Motion Pictures*, at the time and asked him who was also working on an experimental video recorder. He mentioned the Ampex Company but said that since they were working with a rotating head, the machine would never work. So I left Ampex out of the list on page 172. I had blown the scoop of a lifetime. (I still have my notes showing this!)

75. "Electronic Cinema — Digital Delivery for the Big Screen," *Cinema Technology*, July 1999, pp. 8–11. Sadly, the author has had a high brightness line-scan CRT U.S. patent available for over ten years now. It will, nonetheless, be the projector of the future! His cathode ray tube should have high brightness, no moving parts and a lower cost than existing machines. So far, all attempts to get the industry to build a working model have been unsuccessful. But the author still has hope that soon one of the major manufactures will realize the worth of his scheme and build a prototype.

76. *Ibid.*, p. 12.

77. "Digital Cinema Moves Coser," *Cinema Technology*, April 1999, pp. 12–16.

78. A. Hiltzik, "Hollywood 2010," *Los Angeles Times Magazine*, Nov. 7, 1999, pp. 14–15.

79. "Screen Shot," *Broadcast Engineering*, September 1999, p. 168. See "Industry Briefs," *Broadcast Engineering*, May 1997, p. 128.

80. "Electronic Cinema," *Cinema Technology*, September 1999, pp. 6–7.

81. From *Broadcasting & Cable*, Feb. 28, 1999, p. S10.

82. Kenneth Hunold, "Digital Videotape Formats," *Broadcast Engineering*, July 1999, p. 106.

83. "Avid 24P Universal Editing and Mastering," *Broadcast Engineering*, July 1999.

84. "Business Wire," *Broadcast Engineering*, August 1999, p. 120. See also "People," *Broadcast Engineering*, September 1999, p. 168.

85. "Business Wire," *Broadcast Engineering*, September 1999, p. 162.

86. "Business Giant Morita of Sony Dies at 78," *New York Times*, October 3, 1999, p. A4. "Sony Co-founder Akio Morita Dies," *Broadcast Engineering*, November 1999, p. 29.

87. Peter D. Lubell, "A Coming Attraction: D-Cinema," *Spectrum*, March 2000, pp. 72–78. Also "Cost of Digital Cinema is Debated," *Las Vegas Sun*, March 10, 2000, p. 5A.

Selected Bibliography

Abramson, Albert. *Electronic Motion Pictures*. Berkeley: University of California Press, 1955. Reprint, New York: Arno, 1974.

_____. *The History of Television, 1880 to 1941*. Jefferson, NC: McFarland, 1987.

_____. *Zworykin: Pioneer of Television*. Chicago: University of Illinois Press, 1995.

Barnouw, Erik. *A History of Broadcasting in the United States, 1933–1953*. 2 vols. New York: Oxford University Press, 1966–68.

_____. *Tube of Plenty: The Evolution of American Television*. New York: Oxford University Press, 1975; 3rd ed., 1990.

BBC Eng Monograph No. 39. October 1961. See Combined Intelligence Objectives Subcommittee (CIOS) Report no. 28-41, no. 31-1, no 31-8. British Intelligence Objectives Subcommittee (BIOS) Report no. 867; Public Records Office (London) AIR MIN files 40/1650, 40/2000.

Bilby, Kenneth. *The General: David Sarnoff and the Rise of the Communications Industry*. New York: Harper & Row, 1986

Binns, Joseph. *Vladimir Kosma Zworykin Those Inventive Americans,* Washington, DC: National Geographic Society, 1971.

Boyce, Joseph C.(ed) *New Weapons for Air Warfare*. Boston; Little, Brown and Company, 1947.

Briggs, Asa, ed. *A History of Broadcasting in the United Kingdom*. 4 vols. London: Oxford University Press, 1961, 1965, 1970, 1979.

_____. *The BBC: The First Fifty Years,* London: Oxford University Press, 1986.

Brown, George H. *And Part of Which I Was*. Princeton, NJ: Angus Cupar, 1982.

Bruch, Walter. *Kleine Geschichte des deutschen Fernsehens*. Berlin: Haude & Spenersche Verlaghandlung, 1967.

_____."*Die Fernseh Story.*" Stuttgart: Telekosmos-Verlag 1969.

Burns, R. W. *British Television: The Formative Years*. London: Peter Peregrinus/Science Museum, 1986.

_____. *Television: An International History of the Formative Years*. London: IEEE/Science Museum (History of Technology Series 22), 1998.

Cahill, John T. , Roger L. Werner, Ray S. Houston, and Eugene E. Beyer, Jr. *Before the FCC: Petition of Radio Corporation of America and National Broadcasting System for Approval of Color Standards for the RCA Color Television System*. Washington, DC: 1953.

Chinn, Howard. *Television Broadcasting*. New York: McGraw-Hill, 1953.

Dreher, Carl. *Sarnoff: An American Success*. New York: Quadrangle, 1977.

Dunlap, Orrin E., Jr. *The Future of Television*. New York: Harper and Brothers, 1942.

Everson, George. *The Story of Television: The Life of Philo T. Farnsworth*. New York: W. W. Norton, 1949.

Farnsworth, Elma G. *Distant Vision: Romance and Discovery on an Invisible Frontier*. Salt Lake City: Pemberly Kent, 1989.

Fermi, Rachel, Esther Samra, and Richard Rhodes. *Picturing the Bomb: Photographs from the Secret World of the Manhattan Project*. New York: Harry N. Abrams, 1995.

Fink, Donald G. *Color Television Standards*. New York: McGraw-Hill, 1955.

_____. *Principles of Television Engineering*. New York: McGraw-Hill, 1940.

_____. *Television Standards and Practice*. New York: McGraw-Hill, 1943.

Flehr, Paul D. *Inventors and Their Inventions*. Palo Alto: Pacific, 1990.

Frithjoh, Rudert. *50 Years of Fernseh 1929–1979*. Stuttgart: Bosch Technische Berichte, 1979.

Ginsburg, Charles P. "The Birth of Videotape Recording," Ampex Brochure, March 1981. (This paper was delivered in slightly different form in *Jour. SMPTE*, October 5, 1957, p. 5.)

Godfrey, Donald G. *Philo T. Farnsworth: The Father of Television*. Salt Lake City: University of Utah Press, 2001.

Goebel, Gerhart. *Das Fernsehen in Deutschland bis zum 1945*. Frankfurt: Archiv für das Post und Fernmeldewesen 5, Aug. 1953.

Goldmark, Peter C. *Maverick Inventor: My Turbulent Years at CBS*. New York: Saturday Review Press/E. P. Dutton, 1973.

Gorham, Maurice. *Television: Medium of the Future*. London: 1949.

Gutterman, Leon, ed. *The Wisdom of Sarnoff and the World of RCA*. Beverly Hills: Wisdom Society, 1967.

Hanford Engineer Works Technical Manual. Document number HW-10475, Section C, dated May 1, 1944, pp. 1011–1012. Received October 23, 1988.

Head, Sydney W. *Broadcasting in America*. Boston: Houghton Mifflin, 1956; 2nd ed., 1972.

Head, Sydney W., and Christopher H. Sterling. *Broadcasting in America: A Survey of Electronic Media*. 4th ed. Boston: Houghton Mifflin, 1990.

Heijne, L., P. Schagen, and H. Bruining. "An Experimental Photoconductive Camera Tube for Television." *Philips Technical Review,* vol. 16, 1954/55.

Holloman, Carl A., CID agent, to Officer in Charge, Clinton Engineer Works, Oak Ridge, TN, memorandum, Nov. 21, 1944.

Inglis, Andrew F. *Behind the Tube: A History of Broadcasting Technology and Business.* Boston: Focal, 1990.

Keller, Wilhelm. *Hundert Jahre (1883–1983) Fernsehen.* Berlin: VDE-Verlag GmbH, 1983.

Lardner, James. *Fast Forward.* New York: W. W. Norton, 1987.

Lewis, Tom. *Empire of the Air.* New York: HarperCollins, 1991.

Lyons, Eugene. *David Sarnoff.* New York: Harper & Row, 1960.

Lyons, Nick. *The Sony Vision.* New York: Crown, 1976.

Maclaurin, William R., and R. Joyce Harmon. *Invention and Innovation in the Radio Industry.* New York: Macmillan, 1949. Reprint, New York: Arno, 1971.

McLean, Donald F. *Restoring Baird's Image.* London: IEE/Science Museum (History of Technology Series 28), 2000.

Norman, Bruce. *Here's Looking at You: The Story of British Television 1908–39.* London: British Broadcasting Corporation, 1984.

Paley, William S., *As It Happened.* Garden City, NY: Doubleday, 1979.

Rhodes, Richard. *The Making of the Atomic Bomb.* New York: Simon and Schuster, 1986.

Rose, Albert. *Vision: Human and Electronic.* New York: Plenum, 1974.

Ross, Gordon. *Television Jubilee: 25 Years of BBC Television.* London: W. H. Allen, 1961.

Sarnoff, David. *Looking Ahead.* New York: McGraw-Hill, 1968.

Shiers, George, ed. *Technical Development of Television.* New York: Arno, 1977.

_____, with May Shiers. *Bibliography of the History of Electronics.* Metuchen, NJ: Scarecrow, 1972.

Sinclair, Ian. *Birth of the Box.* London: Sigma, 1993.

Smith, Sally Bedell. *In All His Glory: William Paley and His Brilliant Circle.* New York: Simon and Schuster, 1990.

Sobel, Robert. *RCA.* New York: Stein & Day, 1986.

Sterling, Christopher, and John Kitross. *Stay Tuned: A Concise History of American Broadcasting.* Belmont, CA: Wadsworth, 1978.

Swift, John. *Adventure in Vision: The First Twenty-Five Years of Television.* London: John Lehmann, 1950.

Takayanagi, Kenjiro. *Pioneering Television: The Autography of Kenjiro Takayangi.* Trans. Mayumi Yoshida. San Francisco: San Francisco Press, 1993.

Tebbel, John. *David Sarnoff.* Chicago: Encyclopaedia Britannica Press, 1963.

Television. 6 vols. New York: RCA Institutes Tech Press, 1936, 1937, 1946, 1947, 1950.

Von Sychowski, Patrick. *Electronic Cinema: The Big Screen Goes Digital.* London: Screen Digest, 2000.

Weisskopf, Gene. Hanford message by Internet dated 18 November 1999. Also the following document sent by mail: *DESIGN AND PROCUREMENT HISTORY OF HANFORD ENGINEER WORKS* U.S Contract W-7412-Eng-1 DuPont Project 9536 and Clinton Semi-Works U.S. Contract W-7412-Eng-23 Du Pont Project 9733 From the Engineering Department E. I. Du Pont De Nemours and Company (Inc), Wilmington, Delaware, December 1945, pp. 189–191.

Zworykin, V. K., "The Early Days: Some Recollections." *Television Quarterly* 1:4 (Nov), 1962.

_____, and G. A. Morton. *The Electronics of Image Transmission.* New York: John Wiley, 1940.

_____, and _____. *Television: The Electronics of Image Transmission in Color and Monochrome.* 2nd ed. New York: John Wiley, 1954.

_____, _____, E. G. Ramberg, J. Hillier, and A. W. Vance. *Electron Optics and the Electron Microscope.* New York: John Wiley, 1945.

Zworykin, V. K., and E. G. Ramberg. *Photoelectricity and Its Applications.* New York: John Wiley, 1949.

_____, _____, and L. E. Flory. *Television in Science and Industry.* New York: John Wiley, 1958.

Zworykin, V. K., and E. D. Wilson. *Photocells and Their Applications.* New York: John Wiley, 1930.

Index

303